Community Practice

Community Practice
Theories and Skills for Social Workers

Second Edition

David A. Hardcastle

Patricia R. Powers

with Stanley Wenocur

OXFORD
UNIVERSITY PRESS
2004

OXFORD

Oxford New York
Auckland Bangkok Buenos Aires Cape Town Chennai
Dar es Salaam Delhi Hong Kong Istanbul Karachi Kolkata
Kuala Lumpur Madrid Melbourne Mexico City Mumbai Nairobi
São Paulo Shanghai Singapore Taipei Tokyo Toronto

Copyright © 2004 by Oxford University Press, Inc.

Published by Oxford University Press, Inc.
198 Madison Avenue, New York, New York 10016

www.oup.org

Library of Congress Cataloging-in-Publication Data
Hardcastle, David A.
Community practice : theories and skills for social workers / David A.
Hardcastle, Patricia R. Powers, Stanley Wenocur—2nd ed.
p. cm.
Includes bibliographical references and index.
ISBN 0-19-514161-X (pbk.)
1. Social service. 2. Social workers. I. Powers, Patricia R.
II. Wenocur, Stanley, 1938–. III. Title.
HV40 .H289 2003
361.3'2—dc21   2003006312

1 3 5 7 9 8 6 4 2

Printed in the United States of America
on acid-free paper

Preface

The *social* in social work is that part of our practice that helps individuals and families, as well as groups, organizations, and communities, address the social conditions that shape their behavior and opportunities. Attention to the interplay between the individual and the social environment is social work's great strength as a profession, and a feature that distinguishes it from other kindred helping professions. An expanded view of helping—beyond therapy—invites affirmation of social work's historic commitment to social justice: to serve and advocate for the victims of modern industrial global society and to contribute to developing supporting communities. In our view, social work's continuing legitimacy as a profession rests on its commitment to social justice and community welfare. This commitment is especially important during this age of rampart individualism, economic globalization, and slavish obedience to a market economy ideology with its concentration of income, wealth, and social power at the top. We see a mission for the profession to address the diminishing middle class, demonization of the poor, social retrenchment and welfare state devolution, restriction of civil rights and liberties in the name of patriotism, and pathologizing of diverse human behavior as reflected in an expanding *Diagnostic and Statistical Manual of Mental Disorders*. We continue to argue that revitalization of communities and our social connectedness are critical requisites for a socially and economically healthy United States. Social work must renew its commitment to social justice and community residents. Our drift away from social justice and community has not resulted in great status, income, or well-being for social work, its clients, and the community.

Others in social service and community work hold similar sentiments. At a recent national gathering of the United Neighborhood Center Association (UNCA), board president Tony Wagner passionately shared his concerns. He stated,

> [In the past,] ideals such as grassroots democracy, fairness, justice, respect and dignity for all, especially the poor and outcast, and the belief that people from a variety of cultural and economic backgrounds could work together to better themselves, their families and their neighborhoods, kept us firmly rooted in the quest for bringing about a "nation of neighbors". . . . [But then, seeking funds,] we "over-professionalized" our work, we learned to speak the language of corporate management, we categorized and specialized, and worst of all, we relegated the people we serve to the status of "client". . . . We need to gear up, to articulate a clearer vision and move to new heights. Today's settlement houses and their national organization need to get a lot more edgy, a lot harder and leaner. We need to tolerate less bullshit, confront more often, and speak out with more pride and confidence. The movement needs to pay more attention to public policy and mobi-

lization of our neighbors. We've got to advance our agenda and move our values closer to the core of what we do. To remain stuck in old patterns and ideas that devalue the prominence of the people we serve trivializes our work, our mission, and our lives. Our communities call out for professionals who are committed, accessible, and street-wise. (UNCA National Summit, September 21, 2002)[1]

The bottom line is that we must commit to on-the-ground social work rather than hooking our star to trendy notions or abstract outcome schemes.

In our first edition's preface, we observed the growing number of students coming to schools of social work wanting to be therapists rather than social workers. Their desire is perhaps understandable as they observe the devolution of the welfare state, growth of contingent and contract employees in social agencies, and the increasing privatization and commodification of social services. (These trends are occurring without much vocal protest from the social work profession, whether in practice or academia.) Usually, the student's vision of therapy involves some sort of psychosocial counseling of dysfunctional individuals and families in individual or group therapy groups on a more or less regular schedule of hourly visits in an office or clinic over some specified time period. Not much reflection is given in this dream to funding sources for client services, practice management, and social justice. It is an incomplete vision of helping because it leaves out the *social* in social work.

Prospective and current students need to understand how community comes into play emotionally, in the hearts and minds of their clients, as well as practically in the opportunities and blocks it may present. They need to know that what unifies social work practice that builds on community is a philosophy of being there for people that goes beyond psychological support. A commitment to community means being available to any group in the community, hearing what all citizens want, and providing for those most in need. It means choosing locations, hours, and staff that will make service users experience us as being there for them, available to them. It means providing the political support needed for programs to start, survive, thrive, and protect the vulnerable and marginalized. Fortunately, once students are enrolled in school and attending classes, some of their professors will stress that social workers can strengthen the capacity of community members to solve community problems and to reform the institutions that affect their lives. We assert that, despite discouraging social forces at work in the world, many constructive changes are taking place at the local level, and our text includes exemplars and best practices. Thus, both demoralizing and encouraging factors are discussed in the text.

In the 1930s, it was hard to ignore the impact of a malfunctioning social system. Some social workers became politically active while staying in the casework trenches. Both caseworkers and community practitioners recognized the obvious relationship between private trouble and public issues that blurred the distinction between community work and casework. Social workers clearly had to attend to both. Many did. The knowledge and skills of each played a part in the creation of a new system of basic social protections and services. The same is true in our current struggles. The script is written. It entails struggle, but struggle, of course, with the tools, technologies, and opportunities this era affords to construct a different and more humane social order. To the extent that this book contributes to social workers strengthening their community-building skills and allegiance to the contest for social justice, we will have positively contributed to the struggle.

As we look at the current field of social work, its future resembles past struggles. Poverty is escalating. Ethnic, racial, and social divisiveness is increasing. Reactionary forces under the guise of conservatism and patriotism are abandoning and outright destroying the social safety net that undergirded the community from the New Deal of the 1930s to 2000. As with the previous "Red" scares, diminished civil liberties, civil rights, and an increase in the police powers of the state are justified and secured as patriotic actions necessary for *homeland security*. The U.S. design for the market economy helps large corporations and the top 1% prosper while socially and economically relegating working and middle-class people to economic insecurity. The new millennium's first decade has seen a recession, with record unemployment, a decline of workers' real wages and stock prices, an increase in poverty, and a loss of middle-class retirement security with the *Enron* summer. It has also witnessed a continuing growth of per capita income and continuing tax cuts for the superrich. Our political leaders tout this as progress and reform. As during the twentieth century's Great Depression, social workers now are doubly injured. Our lives and livelihoods as well as our clients are directly and harshly affected. What should we do? There are no easy answers, but there are answers.

Our goal for this edition remains the provision of a comprehensive and integrated text covering community theory and skills necessary for all social work practitioners and students. It contains topics that build a foundation for those interested in either social administration or community organization, and it covers materials of general interest to all would-be macropractitioners as well. Special care has been taken to create a text that is relevant and useful to frontline social workers. This second edition is intended to assist anyone who desires to contribute to better communities and a better world and wants to galvanize the reticent into action. The text does not assume that all students or practitioners are community organizers, but it does presume that community skills and a commitment to social justice are necessary as a true and effective foundation for direct service practice, community organization, and social services management. It is a foundation textbook for social work practice. The book addresses requisite theories and practice skills related to communities, organizations, interorganizational practice, small groups, and individual cases. Such skills are required to be effective direct service practitioners, case workers, case managers, clinicians, and private practice social workers.

We assume that a direct service practitioner needs a commitment to social justice. The chapter on community social casework, a reformulation of case management, reflects this commitment. We concentrate on the skills, knowledge, personal fortitude, and ethical commitments required of today's social workers to help their service users address the social environment. We call these helping activities and skills *community practice*. The concept of *community* captures the humanness, the passion, and the interconnectedness among people in a way that sterile labels such as social environment, social ecology, social systems, task environment, and other borrowed physical science metaphors seem to miss. However, we do use these theories and concepts and others from marketing and from other professions in developing our model of community practice. As social work practice is broad, eclectic, and intersects with many other fields, we deliberately use diverse practice theories and examples to illuminate our points. We feature the difficulties people face individually and collectively in their daily lives, as well as ways that social workers can be of assistance beyond the psychological domain.

The textbook has two sections. The first part covers the ideological, ethical, emotional, and programmatic foundation necessary for community practice. We believe professional social work practice requires this ethical, ideological, and emotional grounding as well as theoretical knowledge as foundations for the practice skills. Our ideology is clear. People and their communities are fundamental. The text also reflects our belief that personal fortitude, integrity, and dedication must accompany the application of any practice knowledge and skills. The second section is devoted to community practice skills, such as entering communities safely and unobtrusively, and with sensitivity to culture. Social workers need to be able to go into communities where clients live and work in order to provide services effectively. The skills chapters follow what we believe is a logical order; however, instructors, students, and readers can arrange them to fit their preferences. We have updated and revised all chapters, some appreciably, taking into account suggestions from students and instructors. More attention is devoted to community and community practice theories and the skills of community assessment and analysis, asset utilization, networking, bargaining, and negotiation. There is new material on multiple topics such as computers, and there are many additional references. New chapters on community organizing have been added at the request of text users. In the broadest sense, both Chapter 5 and Chapter 14 delve into community organizations. Chapter 5 introduces the concept of community building and examines the current scene of civic activity and associations—how diverse citizens are banding together. Chapter 14 features community organization tools, methods, skills, and role models. It covers imaginative ways to connect people in communities.

Although we sometimes use terms such as *clients*, our philosophy is to view individuals and families as collaborators and to view citizens as partners, whether the level of activity is case work, group work, or community work. We have struggled to find neutral terms to describe those whom social workers wish to assist. At the microlevel, *client* has much negative baggage, yet *service user* is more awkward. At the macrolevel, *citizen* or *community resident* seemed appropriate until issues were raised about immigrants who are not official residents. We have used a mixture of labels, knowing that terminology will continue to evolve as people strive for dignity and inclusion. The accompanying *Instructor's Manual* contains student practice exercises (supplemental to those in the text) to develop, simulate, and apply the community practice knowledge and skills. The most recent curriculum accreditation requirements of the Council on Social Work Education were reviewed in developing the text.

At various points throughout the book, we have used the specific words of community practitioners to describe their helping practice. Many of these quotes were taken from interviews conducted by graduate students at the University of Maryland School of Social Work for a project on the experiences, views, and perspectives of social advocates directed by one of the authors. These interviews have been compiled in two monographs, *Stirring People Up* (1994) and *Challenging* (1993).

Our foundation social work practice course on communities, social networks, and community practice skills provides the contours for this textbook. We found that there was a dearth of resources on the development and application of community practice skills by direct service practitioners.

We have, of course, drawn upon our own and our colleagues' practice experience and theoretical and methodological knowledge. The authors' combined community and social work practice exceeds a century. Our experience includes community organization and development, social group work, administration, child welfare, aging, disabilities, consumer self-help, mental health, hunger and homelessness, fundraising, labor organizing, lobbying, antipoverty work, AIDS programs, and more. Many of our case examples come our professional experiences or are composites of our professional experience. We also have drawn upon the experiences and contributions of others in the professional community and the larger advocacy field.

Note

1. Wagner, A. R. (2002, Aug–Oct.). Where are UNCA and the Settlement Movement today. *UNCA Newsletter.* Speech given by R. A. Wagner, President of United Neighborhood Centers Association, at UNCA National Summit, Cleveland, OH. September 21, 2002.

Acknowledgments

The authors are grateful for solid, insightful suggestions from Fred Brooks of Georgia State University; Mayling M. Chu of California State University, Stanislaus; and Thomas Packard of San Diego State University. Of course, we take responsibility for the final product. We thank Dean Jesse Harris of the School of Social Work, the University of Maryland at Baltimore, and our colleagues, especially those in the School's Management, Administration, and Community Organization Concentration, for their encouragement, suggestions, and criticisms of the first edition and subsequent revision and their confidence that the project would be completed. We have incorporated their work into some of the exercises and examples. We expressly thank the students in the community practice classes over the past 35 years for their critiques of our theories. We are especially appreciative to the students over the past decade for their use and critiques of the book's material and ideas for revisions. It was their stimulation, needs, and demands for coherence in community practice as a basic skill for all social workers that inspired the book. Furthermore, we gratefully acknowledge the communities, clients, and practitioners with whom we gained our community practice experience and refined our theories, understanding, and skills. We appreciate the community practitioners, lay and professional, who shared with us their experience in services facilitation and advocacy for people and their communities. Their service and commitment to better neighborhoods and communities as places for people to live informed our discussion of skill building with clients, linkages with systems, and utilization of pressure points in forging change. We hope the book will continue their contribution to enhancing community practice and humane communities.

The relationship and contributions of Dr. Stan Wenocur to this project are enduring. He was a major contributor to the first edition. Subsequent to that edition, Stan has retired from most formal social work practice and education, although he is still keeping involved in community. He is now a professional artist with palette and devoted to his painting.

Individually, we wish to thank our families for their patience, empathy, reassurance, and periodic critiques. Without them, there would be no completed work. David Hardcastle particularly thanks his wife and colleague, Dr. Cynthia Bisman of the Graduate School of Social Work and Social Research of Bryn Mawr College, who helped to define and elaborate community practice for direct practice applications. She is a persistent and consistent helpmate, colleague, supporter, and an enduring inspiration. Patricia Powers thanks her spouse, Tom Harvey, who has contributed in countless ways to both editions of this book, to nonprofit organizations, and to social causes. His daily experiences as a manufacturer have given Pat much-appreciated insight into the lives and challenges of working people, including former prisoners, immigrants, the developmentally disabled, and the many who are overextended financially. Pat also appreciates the support of Joe Volk and colleagues at the Friends Committee on National Legislation and particularly the loving support of her sons Brendan McTaggart and Duncan McTaggart and family (Lisa, Brendan & Andrea). Additionally, the authors wish to thank associate editor Maura Roessner and managing editor Jessica A. Ryan of Oxford University Press.

We continue to salute the work of the pioneer community theorists and reformers. The profession needs more heroes now. Two such heroes were Arthur Dunham and Harry Specht. The late Arthur Dunham was concerned with peace and the global village. Arthur was a role model in his personal and professional life. The late Dr. Harry Specht made fundamental constant contributions to community and social justice as central facets of social work practice. His steadfast and clarion call for maintaining community and social justice as social work practice's living central tenets, while sometimes discomforting to many in our profession, has guided our thinking, practice and instruction. The book reflects our efforts to help Harry keep the profession faithful and bring community and social justice back into all social work practice.

D.A.H. and P.R.P.

Contents

Community Practice

1

Community Practice: An Introduction

Community practice is the core of social work and necessary for all social workers, whether generalists, specialists, therapists, or activists. Although usually associated with community organization, social action, social planning (Rothman & Tropman, 1987; Wells & Gamble, 1995), and other macropractice activities, direct service and clinical social workers engage in community practice when they make client referrals, assess community resources, develop client social support systems, and advocate to policymakers for programs to meet clients' needs. Social work claims an ecological perspective. Social ecology is about community. Whittaker, Garbarino, and associates (1983) persuasively argue that "the ecological-systems perspective . . . will compel us to do several things: (1) view the client *and* the situation—the 'ecological unit'—as the proper focus for assessment and intervention, (2) see the teaching of environmental coping skills as the primary purpose of helping, and (3) place environmental modification and the provision of concrete services on an equal plane with direct, face-to-face interventions with clients" (p. 59). Indeed, as this text illustrates, social work practice is about using the community and using naturally occurring and socially constructed networks within the social environment to provide social support.

This chapter presents an overview of community practice, explores our conception of community practice as social work practice, reviews the importance of community practice knowl-edge and skill for all social workers, describes the generic social work community problem-solving strategy and its use in community practice by clinical and community development social workers, and examines the ethical constraints of community practice.

COMMUNITY PRACTICE

Community practice is the application of practice skills to alter the behavioral patterns of community groups, organizations, and institutions or people's relationships and interactions with these entities. Netting, Kettner, and McMurtry (1993) conceive of community practice as part of macropractice. They define macropractice as the "professional directed intervention designed to bring about planned change in organizations and communities" (p. 3). Community practice as macropractice includes the skills associated with community organization and development, social planning and social action, and social administration.

Community organization and the related strategy of community development is the practice of helping a community or part of a community, such as a neighborhood or a group of people with a common interest, to be a more effective, efficient, and supportive social environment for nurturing people and their social relationships. Ross (1967), an early sponsor of bringing community organization into the social

3

work profession, conceived of community organization as "a process by which a community identifies its needs or objectives, orders (or ranks) these needs or objectives, develops the confidence and will to work at these needs or objectives, finds the resources (internal and/or external) to deal with these needs or objectives, takes action in respect to them, and in so doing extends and develops cooperative and collaborative attitudes and practices in the community" (p. 28).

Social planning, a subset of community organization, addresses the development and coordination of community agencies and services to meet community functions and responsibilities and to provide for its members. Social action, another subset of community organization, is the development, redistribution, and control of community statuses and resources, including social power, and the alteration of community relations and behavior patterns to promote the development or redistribution of community resources.

Well and Gamble (1995) elaborate this basic tripartite community practice prototype into an eight-component model that combines practice acts or the *doing* with the purposes of the practice. The unifying features of their inventory are purpose and objectives. Community practice's purpose is "empowerment-based interventions to strengthen participation in democratic processes, assist groups and communities in advocating for their basic needs and organizing for social justice, and improve the effectiveness and responsiveness of human services systems" (p. 577). Community practice's objectives are to

- develop the organizing skills and abilities of individuals and groups,
- make social planning more accessible and inclusive in a community,
- connect social and economic involvement to grassroots community groups,
- advocate for broad coalitions in solving community problems, and
- infuse the social planning process with a concern for social justice. (Well & Gamble, p. 577)

The model's eight practice domains are (a) neighborhood and community organizing, (b) organizing functional communities, (c) community social and economic development, (d) social planning, (e) program development and community liaison, (f) political and social action, (g) coalitions building and maintenance, and (h) so-

cial movements (Well & Gamble, 1995, pp. 580–589). While the domains are not mutually exclusive, the schema does expand the scope of community practice. More important, it specifies a range of social work roles or skills necessary to fulfill the domains: organizer, teacher, coach, facilitator, advocate, negotiator, broker, manager, researcher, communicator, facilitator. These are roles and skills that cut across all social work practice domains.

We advocate further expansion of crosscutting social work community practice skills and assert that they are or should be shared by social workers regardless of the client systems: individuals, families, primary groups, organizations, and geographic and functional community groups. These skills are necessary to fill social work micro- or macrodomains. The additional skills or *acts of doing* encompass campaigning, staging, marketing and social marketing, and acting as network consultant and facilitator.

When a social worker engages in developing, locating, linking with, and managing community resources to help people improve their social functioning and lives, the social worker is engaging in community practice. When a social worker helps clients make better use of the social environment's resources, the social worker is involved in community practice. Advocacy is a community practice task common to all social work practice (Ezell, 2001; Schneider & Lester, 2001). All social workers should, under the profession's ethical code, advocate in social and political arenas to achieve an equitable distribution of the community's resources and for social justice (National Association of Social Workers, 2003). Social workers seeking licensure protection for the profession or stronger laws against child abuse from the state legislature are participating in social action.

The macro social worker (the community organizer, planner, and social activist) and the direct service or clinical social worker may differ in perspective. The community organizer assumes that if the community, with its organizations and institutions and behavior patterns, can function more effectively and be more responsive to its members, the members of the community will be healthier and happier. In direct service practice, the community is viewed as a supportive or potentially supportive resource for a specific client or a class of clients, and the community change efforts are designed to improve the community for these clients. In attempting to improve the quality of life for individual clients, the social worker may operate from the perspective that if enough individuals can be made healthy, the community will be better for everyone. Both sets of practitioners require knowledge of community structures and behavior and the skills to effect behavior changes in some part of the community. Both sets of social workers generally use a similar problem-solving strategy that is described later in this chapter. Additionally, social workers often engage in both sets of practices, either simultaneously or sequentially. They work directly with clients and, at the same time, develop community resources. Social work supervisors, administrators, and social activists often begin their professional careers as direct service social workers.

THE COMMUNITY IN SOCIAL WORK PRACTICE

Communities are always the context, if not always the content, of social work practice. Communities and community practice have been central to social work's history and development. Understanding, intervening in, and using the client's social environment as part of the helping process are skills consonant with the profession's ecological foundation. Social systems, especially communities, strongly influence the ways people think and act. Communities can be nurturing environments and provide basic social, economic, and emotional supports to individuals and families. Conversely, communities can be hostile places when there are inequities that contribute significantly to individual and family malfunctioning (Anderson & Carter, 1984). One's self-concept, at least in part, is developed through involvement in and identification with social and community groups (Miller & Prentice, 1994).

Community theories explain what communities are and how communities function. Often the theories offer propositions delineating how communities should function to serve their members most effectively. Community theories tend to be complex because the concept of community, like many social science concepts, is a slippery, intricate, ideological, and multifaceted summary concept covering a range of social phenomena. Cohen (1985) has cataloged more than 90 different definitions of community used in the social sciences literature.

Communities are nonetheless real for most people, although, as discussed in Chapter 4, the concept of community means different things to different people. Community can mean a geographic space, a geopolitical or civic entity, and a place of emotional identity. It is the emotional identity of community that gives it meaning for most people (Bellah, Madsen, Sullivan, Swidler, & Tipton, 1985, 1991; Cohen, 1985; Lasch, 1994).

Cohen (1985) emphasizes the emotional charging, personal identification, and symbolic construction of community by people. He conceives of community as "a system of values, norms, and moral codes which provoke a sense of identity within a bounded whole to its members. . . . Structures do not, in themselves, create meaning for people. . . . [Without meaning] many of the organizations designed to create 'community' as palliative to anomie and alienation are doomed to failure" (p. 9). The community, Cohen continues, is "the arena in which people acquire their most fundamental and most substantial experience of social life outside the confines of the home. . . . Community, therefore, is where one learns and continues to practice how to 'be social'" (p. 15).

If we accept community's central importance to people, it follows that community knowledge and community practice skills are necessary for all social work practitioners. Community practice calls on social workers to employ a range of skills and theories to help clients use and contribute to the resources and strengths of their communities. Indeed, postmodernist social work theorists such as Pardeck, Murphy, and Choi (1994) assert that "Social work practice, simply stated, should be community based. . . . [Community] is not defined in racial, ethnic, demographic, or geographic terms, as is often done. Instead a community is a domain where certain assumptions about reality are acknowledged to have validity" (p. 345).

Communities and Clients

1. Community forces shape and limit client behaviors.
2. Community provides opportunities for and limits to client empowerment.
3. Client empowerment requires that clients have a capacity to access, manage, and alter community resources and forces.
4. Clients need a capacity to contribute to, reciprocate, and affect the welfare of their communities.
5. Community involvement provides clients with a capacity to affect their communities.

COMMUNITY PRACTICE SKILLS REQUIRED FOR ALL SOCIAL WORKERS

Community practice as a shared foundation skill of all social workers is rooted in the profession's purpose and mission, its history, the policies of the two major professional social work associations, and the changing environment of social work practice.

Social Work's Purpose and Mission

Gordon (1969), a leading social work theorist until his death in the early 1990s, stated that improvement of the client's social functioning is the cardinal mission of contemporary social work practice. The profession's attention is focused on the transactions between people and their social environment and the management of these transactions. "Transaction is *exchanges in the context of action or activity* [italics added] (Gordon, p. 7).

Polsky (1969) concurred and advocated even more strongly for community knowledge and skills by the practitioner and participation by the client in community change. "Changes in dysfunctioning individuals cannot be effectuated [or] sustained unless the system in which they function also undergoes modification through client efforts" (Polsky, p. 20).

The importance of the client's community is reflected in social work's dual perspectives of *person in environment, person and environment,* and the *ecological approach* to social casework practice promoted by Bisman (1994), Ewalt (1980), and Germain (1983). Bisman (1994) clarifies the dual perspective and the community's role in social work practice with the following conception: "What has been called the dual perspective of person and environment actually has three components. Person and environment means the consideration of individuals within the context of the community and its resources, societal policies and regulations and the service delivery of organizations" (p. 27).

Specht and Courtney (1994), in their critique of the contemporary profession, *Unfaithful Angels: How Social Work Has Abandoned Its Mission,* emphatically insist that

> The objective of social work is to help people make use of social resources—family members, friends, neighbors, community organizations and social service agencies, and so forth—to solve their problems. . . . They (i.e., social workers) deal with social problems, which concern the community, rather than personality problems of individuals. Helping individuals to make use of their social resources is one of the major functions of social work practice. And just as important is the social worker's function of developing and strengthening these resources by bringing people together in groups and organizations, by community education, and by organizational development. (p. 23)

Specht & Courtney (1994), like Gordon (1969), further contend that social workers should examine and facilitate the transaction between clients—indeed, between all people—in the community and inveigh against the social isolation of psychotherapy: "Social work's mission should be to build a meaning, a purpose, and a sense of obligation for the community. It is only by creating a community that we establish a basis for commitment, obligation, and social support. We must build communities that are excited about their child care systems, that find it exhilarating to care for the mentally ill and frail aged, that make demands upon people to behave, to contribute, and to care for one another. Psychotherapy will not enable us to do that. . . . to give purpose and meaning to people's lives, and enable us to care about and love one another" (Specht & Courtney, p. 27).

Emphasizing the centrality of community theory and community practice skills in all social work practice is not *antipractice* or *anti–clinical practice.* It is *pro–social work practice.* It is critical of social work practice (done with blinders) that does not recognize social obligations of clients and the social context of the client and the client's well-being. Community knowledge and community practice skills have been distinguishing attributes separating the complete social worker from the wanna-be psychiatrist, a social worker who is only marginally professionally competent. Without community knowledge and skill, the social worker is limited in the capacity to understand and assist clients in shaping and managing the major forces that affect their lives and the capacity to help clients empower themselves to develop and manage personal and social resources. It assumes that the client as an individual is unaffected, whether in Decca or Des Moines.

Social Work's History

Community practice skills are and have been an indispensable component of social work's repertoire since the inception of the profession. The recognition of and attention to the community and its influences, the *social* in social work, is one of the properties that has historically distinguished the social work profession and effective social work practice from the profusion of other counseling and therapeutic professions (Doherty, 1995, p. 47).

From its formation as a profession at the beginning of the twentieth century, social work's central concern has been to improve individual and collective social functioning. Mary Richmond, a pioneer in American social casework, indicated the importance of community theory, the social environment, and community practice skills for social casework in her two books *Social Diagnosis* (1917) and *What Is Social Casework?* (1922/1992). Social casework was concerned with the case in the community rather than being limited to an insular therapy.

The methodology and techniques of social casework proposed by the 1929 Milford Conference on Social Work followed Mary Richmond and went beyond counseling, advice giving, and modeling and demonstration of behavior, to include the community practice skills of information gathering and referrals to other community resources (American Association of Social Workers, 1929). The conference's purpose was to specify social work's professional content and boundaries.

The social casework that Richmond and the Milford Conference championed was not desk bound or introspective counseling; rather, it involved confronting the client's problems in the community where the client lived and the problems existed. The Charity Organization Society (for a time, Mary Richmond's principal agency and the leading casework agency of the era in Great Britain and the United States), held community work fundamental to casework. Bosanquet, an early leader of the British Charity Organization Society movement, is quoted by Timms (1966) as stating that "Case work which is not handled as an engine of social improvement is not . . . Charity Organization Society work at all" (p. 41).

The profession's often-reviewed cause and function strain between social action, social change, and reform, on one hand, and individual treatment and change, on the other, poses a spurious dilemma. It is a dilemma only when wrongly framed as an either/or choice between two mutually exclusive activities rather than as two interrelated and complementary social work components. Porter Lee, in his 1929 presidential address to the National Conference on Social Welfare, recognized the necessity of both cause and function for the profession (Bruno, 1948).

Lee is often credited with conceptualizing the strain in this "cause and function" address. But the speech's title and emphasis were cause *and* function, not cause *or* function (Spano, 1982, p. 7). Lee saw no dichotomy or dilemma, nor is there one. Social work has emphasized and does emphasize individual help, use of the social environment in providing assistance, and social action and reform (Pumphrey, 1980).

National Association of Social Workers and the Council on Social Work Education Policy

Social work's largest professional association, the National Association of Social Workers (NASW), and social work education's accrediting body, the Council on Social Work Education (CSWE), recognize the importance of community theory and skills for all social work practitioners. NASW (2003) states that the

> primary mission of the social work profession is to enhance human well-being and help meet the basic human needs of all people, with particular attention to the needs and empowerment of people who are vulnerable, oppressed, and living in poverty. *A historic and defining feature of social work is the profession's focus on individual well-being in a social context* and the well-being of society. *Fundamental to social work is attention to the environmental forces that create, contribute to, and address problems in living* [italics added].
>
> Social workers also seek to promote the responsiveness of organizations, communities, and other social institutions to individuals' needs and social problems. ("Preamble," paras. 1–2)

The professional code does not limit these obligations to community practitioners. It holds all in the profession responsible. NASW's *Code of Ethics* (2003) also has set forth a set of ethical principles to which all social workers should aspire. First among the principles is that "Social workers' primary goal is to help people in need and to address social problems (Ethical Principle 4, NASW, 2003)." Additionally, "social workers recognize the central importance of human relationships (Ethical Principle 4, NASW, 2003)." This principle holds that social workers "seek to strengthen relationships among people in a purposeful effort to promote, restore, maintain, and enhance the well-being of individuals, families, social groups, organizations, and communities" (NASW, 2003).

NASW developed and advocates that social caseworkers and social work clinicians use a person-in-environment (P-I-E) diagnostic and classification system. Social environment in the P-I-E schema is defined as "systemic relationships that people have by virtue of being in the same location" (Karls & Wandrei, 1994, p. 3). The social environment in the P-I-E classification system is essentially the same as the conception of community just presented.

NASW's formulation of the practice methodology claimed by a majority of NASW members—clinical social work—reinforces the importance of community theory and skills. "The perspective of person-in-situation is central to clinical social work practice. Clinical social work includes intervention directed to interpersonal interactions, intrapsychic dynamics, and life-support and management issues" (NASW, n.d., p. 4). Standard 4 of the policy's 11 standards guiding clinical practice requires that "Clinical social workers shall be knowledgeable about the services available in the community and make appropriate referrals for their clients" (NASW, n.d., p. 8).

The Council on Social Work Education's Commission on Accreditation, the national accrediting organization for graduate and undergraduate professional social work education, charges that all social work students acquire knowledge and skill in social relations and the range of social systems (including organizations, social institutions, and communities) as part of their professional foundation. Indeed, the Commission recognizes that a basic purpose of social work is the "promotion, restoration, maintenance, and enhancement of the social function of individuals, families, groups, organizations, and communities" (1. Purposes of the Social Work Profession, 2003).

Changing Nature of the Social Work Practice Environment

The last quarter of the twentieth century saw profound changes in the social work practice environment. After the 1960s and 1970s, with their emphasis on federal government involvement and services coordination, since the 1980s we have seen federal, state, and local human services policies move toward reduction, competition, divestiture, and privatization of public programs. These changes are accompanied by the rhetoric, if not always the reality, of returning power, responsibility, and control to state and local governments and the private sector for welfare and social services, and an increase in personal and family responsibility. The federal government's role and responsibilities for welfare and human services probably are undergoing their greatest transformation since the New Deal era of the 1930s. Reforms first instigated by conservative governments have subsequently been embraced and expanded by the traditionally liberal political parties (Deacon, 1997; Gillespie & Schellhas, 1994: Gingrich, Armey, & the House Republicans, 1994; Mishra, 1999; Morgan, 1995; Mullard & Spicker, 1995; Room, 1990, pp. 106–111; Wagner, 1997).

The national political landscape is conservative. The 1995 Congressional elections saw Republicans gain control of both houses of Congress for the first time since 1958, a majority of the governorships up for election, and significant Republican gains in state legislatures (Connelly, 2000). Republicans recaptured the presidency in the 2000 election after an arduous, contested, and contentious process involving disputed recounts and a dubious U.S. Supreme Court ruling. They also retained control of the House of Representatives. After Vermont's Senator James Jeffords dropped his Republican Party membership for Independent status and voted with the Democrats, the Democrats controlled the Senate. The 2002 elections were a dis-

---

Our Position on Community Practice

Our position, theory, and set of propositions, briefly stated, on the requirement for community practice is that people exist in social ecologies or communities. Behavior is biopsychosocial and not exclusively biopsychological. It is shaped by interactions, engagements, and exchanges with the social ecology. Personal empowerment requires the capacity to develop and manage the interactions and exchanges with the social ecology. All people, including social work clients, have the capacity to develop and improve their social management skills and functioning. If all people have this capacity and if empowerment is a goal of social work, then all social workers will need to develop knowledge and skills to enable them to better assist people in developing and managing supportive social ecologies or communities.

aster for the Democrats, no matter what the spin. The Republicans, after a vigorous campaign by President Bush, increased their margin of control in the House and regained control of the Senate. Both parties have moved to the political right. The Democrats have become more conservative in their welfare policies and in general, since the September 11, 2001, terrorist attacks on the World Trade Center and the Pentagon. Ideological identification, regardless of party, tends to support the thesis that American voters are more conservative than liberal, with 43% of the voters identifying themselves as conservative, 25% as liberal, with 32% in between, as far back as 1988 (Ladd, 1989, p. 17). Coupled with the increasing conservatism of the voters is the declining voting rate. Voting is lowest among the young, minorities, and lower income citizens (Connelly, 2000; Doherty & Etzioni, 1994–1995; Ladd, 1989, p. 11; U.S. Bureau of the Census, 1995, pp. 226–292). If these voting and electoral patterns continue, support for a welfare state and public social services will steadily degenerate (Dowd, 1994; Shapiro & Young, 1989, pp. 61–62).

The world's economies are moving toward globalization. The United States, although it is the sole superpower, has dramatically increased military spending since September 11, 2001, and is engaging in more global military adventurism. With increased military spending and dominance, there is a devolving welfare state. Devolution of the welfare state involves decreasing federal responsibility for welfare and returning greater authority and responsibility to states, localities, and the private sector. With devolution and increased local authority, control, and responsibility for social welfare, all social workers need community practice knowledge and skills. Social workers will need to assess local communities for needed resources; to develop resource networks and support systems for themselves and their clients; to advocate for their clients and to broker services; and to engage in social marketing of their services, social ideals, and themselves.

Community practice competence is vital as the social work profession moves out from under the protective umbrellas of public and voluntary, not-for-profit social service agencies into an often harsh, competitive marketplace of proprietary and private practice with its contracts for service, managed care, and the privatization of social services. Increasingly, social work practitioners will be responsible for developing, managing, and marketing their practices. Agencies will not be providing clients, other needed resources, and an employment safety net (Sherraden, 1990; Williams & Hopps, 1990). As social workers have to develop their own resources in an increasingly competitive world, clinical skills alone are insufficient for professional maintenance. With privatization, private practice, and managed care, social workers will not survive unless they are able to market themselves and their services, to get themselves included on managed-care vendor lists, and to access and manage networks. These trends toward privatization, contract services, managed care, and proprietary practice by social workers will continue. The proprietary practice of social work, either solo, group, or employment by for-profit corporations, either full or part time, has become pervasive (Gibelman & Schervish, 1993; Hardcastle, 1987; O'Neill, 2003).

Advocacy skills are particularly imperative for clinical social workers as mental health services under managed care grow; as efficiency becomes the deciding criterion; and where, in the absence of convincing evidence in the movement to evidenced-based practice, proprietaries seek to cut costs (Asch & Abelson, 1993). Direct service practitioners, if they are to help their clients, will have to engage in social action in the increasingly fragmented community to develop or protect resources and rights for both clients and social workers. Consider the 1994 Pennsylvania Supreme Court decision that held that an individual cannot be convicted of rape unless the victim struggles and physically resists the attacker. Simply saying no, regardless of how often and how forcefully, apparently is not enough. Physical resistance must be made. It does not matter that physical resistance may place the rape victim in jeopardy of harm beyond the physical and emotional trauma of the rape itself or that other victims of physical assault do not have to resist. The Pennsylvania Supreme Court argued that its interpretation is compelled by Pennsylvania's rape statutes, which require physical resistance if rape is to be legally considered. Clinicians in rape counseling centers and members of the public, if they wish to reduce the risk to women, will need to engage in social action—lobbying—to change the law so that a clear "no" will suffice as a refusal, and life-threatening physical resistance will not be required. Social action to change the law probably will be more effective than after-the-fact rape counseling in sparing women the emotional and physical traumas of rape. With growing cutbacks in financial support for social programs, social action is required more than counseling to meet the needs of women.

THE NEED FOR REVITALIZATION OF
THE COMMUNITY AND THE SOCIAL
IN SOCIAL WORK

Although social work has a rich history of community practice, many critics inside and outside the profession hold that the importance of community practice in social work is declining. With this decline, social work's unique professional contribution is also dwindling. In *Unfaithful Angels,* Specht and Courtney (1994) allege that social work has abandoned its historic mission of service, especially service to the poor, in the pursuit of psychotherapies, private practice and autonomy from social agencies, and increased income and status. The therapies used often lack any scientific basis; instead, some social workers even embrace faddish interventions resting on spiritualism and mysticism. The problem is not so much that individual social workers have abandoned the traditional mission of the profession and, in a sense, the profession, but rather that the profession itself has abandoned its historic service mission, the community, and the community's most needy and vulnerable citizens.[1]

The profession's movement away from community and social concerns is illustrated by NASW's social action and legislative agenda. NASW's major legislative efforts and successes, nationally and by state chapters, over the past decades have been toward obtaining licensure and the legally mandated capacity to receive third-party vendor payments for therapies (Hardcastle, 1990). The major social work professional associations were largely silent in the legislative battles on welfare reform and health care. Salcido and Seek's (1992) conclusions, after a survey of the political activity of 52 NASW state chapters, still generally holds true. The chapters "seemed to act on behalf of goals related to promoting the profession and to a lesser extent on those promoting social services legislation. . . . These findings imply that the thrust of future chapter political activities may be associated with professionalization and to a lesser degree with political activism on behalf of disadvantaged groups" (Salcido & Seek, p. 564).

Forsaking a mission goes beyond social work's employment auspices and venue. Social workers can pursue the profession's mission or they can renounce it, whether they are employed by social agencies or engaged in entrepreneurial practice. Social workers can and often have abandoned the historic mission and service calling even when practicing under the auspices of public and not-for-profit agencies. When the profession allows the payer to call all the plays—that is, when funding sources and employing agencies unilaterally determine professional functioning and mission—social work forsakes its claim to professionalism. The mission is determined by the strength of the profession's and each professional's service commitment rather than by employment auspices. It is the service commitment that separates professions from occupations (Gustafson, 1982; Lubove, 1977). Without a strong understanding of the impact of the community on individual behavior and opportunities, and the skills necessary for developing and using community resources to enhance the individual's functioning, social work will indeed abandon its mission of service in the pursuit of status.

The importance of the social—the community—is emphasized in the profession's name, *social work.* But far too little attention is directed to developing the community practice skills of all social workers, compared with the attention given to development of the more circumscribed clinical skills. Specht and Courtney (1994), Bellah et al. (1985), and Doherty (1994–1995) maintain that psychotherapy as therapeutic individualism can be socially amoral, isolating, and at odds with the mandate to strengthen the community and social commitments. Participating in and looking to primary social structures and groups such as the family, church, and neighborhood for guidance has often been replaced by therapy and the therapist. The therapist becomes teacher, spiritual guide, and moral arbiter without a moral base. Therapy is nonjudgmental; it emphasizes looking out for number one and teaches that if it feels right, it is right. While this message may appear liberating, it hardly allows the building of mutual support, a sense of the common good, and a feeling for community.

Social work as a profession exists in and reflects the larger society. The decay of social work's social skills and commitment has accompanied the erosion of community spirit and social commitment in the United States. It is reflective of the "me-ism," the libertarian, self-centered philosophy presently rampant, and the social isolation and fragmentation of contemporary America (Bellah et al., 1985; Etzioni, 1993; Lasch, 1994).

Communities as unifying social institutions are declining. This decline does not bode well for the future of the individual or the country as a whole. Strong communities enhance individual rights and individual well-being. The 1980s and 1990s—the Generation X decades—were an age of anomie and breakdown of social standards with a focus on the self—self-gratification and immediate rewards—with an increase in illegitimacy, public violence, and public and private crime often excused solely on the basis that the opportunity was present or the perpetrator was victimized earlier in life. Our high homicide, violence, and incarceration rates are unrivaled in any other industrialized nation (Gray, 1995). Fewer Americans are involved in active civic participation, as reflected by the decline in voting rates, volunteer services, and church participation (Putnam, 2002). Community service has become a penalty imposed by the courts for criminal offenses or an educational requirement in many states (Bellah et al., 1985, 1991; Doherty & Etzioni, 1994–1995; Etzioni, 1993; Specht & Courtney, 1994).

Community as a basis of identification is becoming exclusionary rather than inclusionary, socially fragmenting rather than integrating, and now rests on a negative rather than a positive base. Support groups focus on negative attributes and separateness rather than on positive traits and ways to integrate their participants more fully into the community. The community has become a means for division rather than integration. In negative communities, the individual is socially isolated and the sense the "person makes of his or her life and the social relationships on which it is based is essentially an individual task" (Specht & Courtney, 1994, p. 41). Too often the reasons for community participation are individualistic, fragmented, and therapeutic.

Social workers need to integrate clients and constituencies into positive communities. Positive communities are nonutopian, cohesive communities where personal relations are captured by agreed-on communal purposes. The positive community offers the individual a shared structure of meaning, explanation, purpose, and support in both good times and bad (*The Responsive Communitarian Platform*, 1992).

Democratic communities and societies thrive not on the individualistic isolation of their members but on the robust functioning of their intermediate structures such as families, neighborhoods, voluntary associations, and community schools (Berry & Hallett, 1998; van Deth, 1997). These are Berger and Neuhaus's (1977) *mediating structures*. Mediating structures serve to counterbalance the impact of both individual and state excesses.

The Catholic theologian Hollenbach (1994–1995) asserts that both democracy and freedom require dynamic community involvement by its members: "Solitary individuals, especially those motivated solely by self-interest and the protection of their rights to privacy, will be incapable of democratic self-government because democracy requires more. It requires the virtues of mutual cooperation, mutual responsibility, and what Aristotle called friendship, concord, and amity" (p. 20).

THE SOCIAL WORK PROBLEM-SOLVING STRATEGY

The social work general problem-solving strategy is a planned change process that begins with the identification of a problem—a condition that someone wants changed—and terminates with the evaluation of the change effort (Compton & Galaway, 1979, pp. 232–450; Epstein, 1980, pp. 2–5; Hepworth & Larsen, 1986, pp. 25–44; Lippitt, Watson, & Westley, 1958; Netting et al., 1993, pp. 203–220; Pincus & Minahan, 1973, pp. 90–91). The strategy, not limited to social work, is a comprehensive and rational approach to problem analysis, resource analysis and aggregation, and intervention. Its social work application is constrained by the profession's values and ethics and usually by the preferences of the client and the client system. The client or client system can be individuals, families and other primary groups, communities, community organizations, and community groups such as neighborhoods or interest groups.

Phase 1: Recognition of a Problem and Establishment of the Need for Change

Problem-solving and change efforts begin with the recognition by an individual or a group, the initiator of the change effort, of a condition perceived as a problem that requires change. The initiator may be the client, a parent, a couple experiencing marital discord, or others such as an

---

The Social Work Problem-Solving Strategy

1. Recognition of a problem and establishment of the need for change
2. Information gathering
3. Assessment and the development of a case theory and plan for change
4. Intervention and the change effort
5. Evaluation and termination of the change effort

individual who fears child abuse or neglect by another person and refers the situation to a protective services agency. A community group may also pinpoint problems of employment, crime, or poor treatment received from public or other social organizations. Implicit, if not explicit, in the identification of the problem and the recognition of the need for change are the goals and objectives sought. Without a statement of desired outcomes, data gathering and assessment, especially resources assessment, is hindered. This phase will be discussed more fully in Chapters 3 and 4.

Although the labels *goals* and *objectives* are often used interchangeably, goals will be used here as the broader, more final objective of a case plan. *Objectives* are more specific outcome events that, when accomplished, lead to the next event and eventually to the goals. Sub-objectives are the events that lead to the next level of objectives. Operational goals and objectives are set forth in a SMARRT format (adapted from *Administrative Systems for Church Management*, n.d.; Reddin, 1971). The SMARRT format criteria indicated in Box 1.1, require goals and objectives that are *specific, measurable, acceptable, realistic, results oriented,* and *time specific.* SMARRT formatted objectives guide case planning, case theory, and the intervention and problem-solving strategy. At the conclusion of the assessment phase, a case theory and a SMARRT case plan specifying goals, objectives and responsibilities should be completed.

Phase 2: Information Gathering

Phase 2 in the problem-solving process is to gather information on the problem and on possible resources for intervention to achieve the SMARRT objectives. During this phase, the social worker gathers information on the problem in order to develop an intervention plan. The information-gathering phase is guided and limited by the theoretical perspective of those working for the change, on the causes of the problem and the potentially available interventions. This phase includes accumulating information on the problem itself; the client system, including strengths and potential resources useful for intervention; the strengths and limitations of support and potential support systems; and any potential constraints and limitations of any change effort by the target system. Community-based practice models devote more attention to the social ecology, the environment, and the social systems in gathering information on the condition and the potential resources than do psychologically centered problem-solving strategies.

Phase 3: Assessment and the Development of a Case Theory and Plan for Change

The third phase is assessment and the development of the case theory and plan for change to accomplish a SMARRT objective. The case can be an individual, a group, a community, or part of a community. However, the change effort extends beyond the individual unit to include its ecology and situation. Case theory, like all theory, involves an explanation of phenomena and situation. Case theory (Bisman, 1994; Bisman & Hardcastle, 1999) is the theory or coherent explanation of a case's problem, a specification of desired outcomes, selection of intervention strategies and methods of changing a condition and producing the desired outcomes, and an explanation of why and how the selected interventions will work. To refine and specify SMARRT outcomes clearly during this phase, it may be necessary to collect additional information on the availability of potential resources. Case theory is developed from the data collected in Phase 2. The data are assessed and organized according to the change agent's, the social worker's, social and behavioral theories of choice. Examples of social and behavioral theories include systems theory, exchange theory, operant and social learning theory, and psychodynamic theories. The case theory is the social worker's construction of the problem and the model for the proposed change effort. As a case situation is both unique and complex, a case theory should avoid an overly reductionist view of cause and effect. The causes of any problems lie in a range of phenomena. Solutions also require a complex intervention strategy and resources appropriately coordinated and managed (Chazdon, 1991, p. x).

In community practice, the concept of assessment is generally preferred over the more limited concept of diagnosis. Gambrill (1983) provides a useful discussion of the distinction between diagnosis and assessment and insight into why assessment is preferred in community practice:

> The term *diagnosis* was borrowed from medicine. . . . Observed behavior is used as a sign of more important underlying processes, typically of a pathological nature. Methodological and

BOX 1.1	SMARRT OBJECTIVES EVALUATION CHECK SHEET

SMARRT objectives are the desired accomplishment and results of an intervention with a client system, the change sought. Objectives are stated in empirical and behavioral language and specify changes in the client system, target system, or ecology.

1. *Specific.* Goals and objectives, as well as the words, ideas, and concepts used to describe them, are precise and not stated in vague generic language such as "to improve the condition of" unless operational meanings are given for *improve* and *condition.* Specific goals and objectives need to be developed with and understood by the client and action systems.

2. *Measurable.* Goals and objectives need to contain operational and measurement criteria used to indicate their achievement. A case plan states how the goals and objectives are measured or judged. Client and action systems need to understand both the goals and the measurements used. Measurements can be quantitative and qualitative or, more often, both.

3. *Acceptable.* Goals and objectives must be acceptable to the client system and, ultimately, to the action system and other resource providers that cooperate with the problem-solving strategy. If the goals and objectives are unacceptable, participation is probably coerced. Acceptability implies informed consent by clients to the plan, its goals and objectives, and the intervention. The goals and objectives acceptability will be constrained by the mission and eligibility criteria of the social worker's agency and funding sources.

4. *Realistic.* Goals and objectives are potentially accomplishable within the complexities of the case, time frame, resources, and inter-

vention methodologies available. They are not so trivial as to be not worth accomplishing. Goals and objectives are realistic if they are achievable in the best judgment of the social worker, change agent and action system, and a client or client system, within the potential costs and resources available, the readiness for change of the target, and the knowledge and skills of the action system.

5. *Results oriented.* Final goals and all objectives are expressed as outcomes, events, and accomplishments by the client and action system or changes in a target rather than as a service event or a process. The provision of service or an intervention does not constitute an objective or meet this SMARRT criterion. The criterion requires that the results of the service and how it will benefit the client be specified. If an intervention or service provides skills training, the results are not the provision of skills training or a client's attending training classes. A result is a specified increase in the client's skills, brought about by the training.

6. *Time specific.* A specific time frame or target for accomplishing the goals and objectives is projected. Time limits are inherent in determining realism, and they are necessary for results. Time limits are based on an intervention's power, the resources available and conditions favorable to change, and the barriers blocking change and objective accomplishment. Without a time limit criterion, it is not possible to measure accomplishments or to have accountability. Without a time limit, achievement always can occur in the distant and indeterminate future. The condition can remain socially dysfunctional or a client can remain in trauma indeterminately while an ineffectual intervention is continued.

conceptual problems connected with the use of diagnosis include frequent low degree of agreement between people in their use of a given diagnosis, and the low degree of association between a diagnosis and indications of what intervention will be most effective. . . .

Assessment differs in a number of ways from diagnosis. Observable behaviors are not used as signs of something more significant but as im-

portant in their own right as *samples of* relevant behaviors. Behavior is considered to be a response to identifiable environmental or personal events. . . . Rather than using behavior as a sign of underlying intrapsychic causes, assessment includes an exploration of how current thoughts, feelings, and environmental events relate to these samples of behavior. (pp. 33–34)

Assessment is a more inclusive and generic concept than *diagnosis,* with a greater emphasis on social and environmental factors. Agreements on an assessment, SMARRT goals and objectives, and problem-solving strategies between social worker, client, and other relevant case participants working toward change are critical for cooperative efforts.

Phase 4: Intervention and the Change Effort

The intervention is the change efforts based on the theory of the case to achieve the desired outcome. While interventions in social work practice can be categorized under casework strategies, clinical approaches, community organization, or environmental and social change, each intervention plan involves a variety of skills, techniques, and tactics; a range of people or systems, either directly or indirectly; and the use of resources. The selection of the specific interventive methodologies and technologies is directed by the theory of the case.

Phase 5: Evaluation and Termination of the Change Effort

The last phase of the social work problem-solving strategy is the evaluation of its effectiveness in achieving the stated goals and objectives. Depending on the level of achievement and the stability of the change, the case may be terminated, the process repeated to enhance its effectiveness or to achieve additional objectives, or the case referred to additional service resources. While evaluation is generally presented in the models together with the termination phase, it is a continuous effort and a part of all the phases.

Pincus and Minahan (1973) rightly assert that the intent of the problem-solving process, whether targeted to individual or community change, is to help people, to change people, "not [deal in] vague abstraction such as the 'community,' 'the organization' or the 'system'" (p. 63). What is changed are the behaviors and interactions of the people who constitute the groups, organizations, communities, and systems.

Problem-Solving Systems

The people involved in a social work problem-solving and planned change strategy can be examined, using the system's metaphors, according to what they contribute and how the change process affects them (Netting et al., 1993, pp. 224–231; Pincus & Minahan, 1973, pp. 53–64). The system's metaphors, as demonstrated by Box 1.2, represent functions that people fulfill in the change effort. The same people can fulfill more than one function and hence can belong to more than one system in the change process.

Although some systems and people generally are involved throughout the problem-solving strategy's change process, such as the change agent and client systems, not all systems need to be involved. Table 1.1 illustrates that the same people at the same or difference phases in the process may be involved in multiple systems, and their involvement may shift as their contributions and their relationships to a change process evolve.

The change agent (that is, the social worker) must anticipate and identify the people who will comprise the various systems involved and perform the change functions in the problem-solving processes. The social worker should recognize that the people or the systems are not static. The membership and importance of a particular system's contributions vary with the phase of the change strategy.

Case Illustration of the Problem-Solving Strategy in Direct Practice: Ms. S.[2]

Phase 1: Recognition of a Problem and Establishment of the Need for Change

A working single mother, Ms. S., with two preschool-age children, ages 3 and 4, has difficulty finding a suitable baby sitter. She also recognizes that she is becoming more short-tempered with her children because of the fatigue and stress of working full time and raising the children alone, she worries about money, and she is distressed about the baby-sitting arrangements. It is becoming more difficult for Ms. S. to maintain her composure when disciplining her children, and she recognizes that if she loses control, she might physically abuse the children.

Ms. S. is not sure what to do, as she is very tired at the end of the day after getting up at 5:30 A.M.; fixing breakfast for herself and the children; getting the children up, dressed, and fed; taking them to whatever baby-sitter is available; and getting to work by 9:00 A.M. After the work day ends, she must first pick up the children, then fix dinner and put them to bed. She has no time to play with the children or to think of herself. Ms. S. recognizes that she is starting to resent the

---

BOX 1.2   **PROBLEM-SOLVING SYSTEMS IN SOCIAL WORK**

1. *Initiator system:* The person or persons who first recognize the problem and bring attention to the need for change.
2. *Support system:* The people who have an interest in and will support the proposed change and who may receive secondary benefits from it.
3. *Client system:* The people who sanction, ask for, or expect to benefit from the change agent's services and who have a working agreement or contract, whether formal or informal, with the change agent.
4. *Change agent system:* The people who will work directly to produce the change, including the social worker, any social action organizations and groups, clients, and the people who belong to the social worker's agency and the organization working to produce the change.
5. *Action system:* The change agent system and the other people the change agent works with

and through to achieve the goals and affect the target system. The action system generally includes the client as an essential component of the change process. Not all elements of an action system are part of a change agent system or need to favor the change.

6. *Controlling system:* The people with the formal authority and capacity to approve and order implementation of a proposed change strategy.
7. *Implementing system:* A subset of the host system composed of the people with day-to-day responsibility for implementing the change.
8. *Target system:* The people who are the targets of the change effort; the people who need to be changed to accomplish the goals of the change strategy and to produce the benefits for the client system. The target system can be people other than a client.

---

children and that at times she feels she would be better off without them.

Ms. S. saw a poster on a bus advertising the child guidance clinic's parent effectiveness training. She now goes to the child guidance clinic to obtain help in maintaining her composure when disciplining her children, and training to develop effective parenting skills. The social worker assigned by the agency to work with Ms. S. recognizes that she is under a lot of stress and needs assistance with more than her parenting skills.

Ms. S. is the initiator system, as she recognized a problem, perceived a need for change, and is

seeking to make a change. She and her children are the client system, as the beneficiaries of the change effort. The social worker is the change agent and part of the initiator system in recognizing the problem and helping Ms. S. define the need for change.

PHASE 2: INFORMATION GATHERING

The social worker obtains information about Ms. S., the children, and the children's father, who is regularly employed but pays no support and only occasionally visits the children. The social worker also obtains information on possible resources in Ms. S.'s neighborhood and other

---

Table 1.1 Systems Typically Involved in Phases of Problem-Solving Strategy

Problem-Solving Phase	Systems Involved
1. Recognition of problem and establishing need for change	Initiator, client, and change agent
2. Information gathering	Initiator, client, support, and change agent
3. Assessment and development of case theory and plan for change	Client, support, controlling, and change agent
4. Intervention and change effort	Client, support, controlling, change agent, action, and target
5. Evaluation and termination of change effort	Client, support, change agent, controlling, and action

possible social and community supports. She discovers the existence of a public 12-hour day care center.

Systems most involved in information gathering are the client and the change agent systems. The information is accumulated to define and build the other necessary systems. The necessary information goes beyond describing the client, her problems, and their etiology. It includes information about potential supports for the client and her children; for example, from the absent father, the day care center, and other potential community resources for the client that might be constructed into a support system. These potential resources make up a target system, the people who need to be changed to accomplish the goals of the change strategy and bring about benefits for the client, until they are formed into a support system for the client. The composition of the systems is dynamic over time.

PHASE 3: ASSESSMENT AND THE DEVELOPMENT OF A CASE THEORY AND PLAN FOR CHANGE

The social worker and Ms. S. review the information to explain why Ms. S. is stressed and fatigued and to decide what might be done to change the situation, including greater involvement of and responsibility by the father. The father has stated that he will not pay support until he has regular visitation with the children. Ms. S. will not allow visitation until he pays support, thus creating a standoff.

Both the theory and goals are straightforward and direct. Ms. S. is exhausted and stressed because she maintains a full-time work schedule in addition to the demands of being a single parent living financially on the edge. She has no social life because of the demands of work and caring for her children, which contributes to her resentment of the children. Her fatigue and resentment place the children at risk. She doesn't know if she can spare the time for parent effectiveness training, although she wants the training and would enjoy the social interaction and support provided by the sessions. The goals are to achieve stable child care, financial and social assistance from the children's father, and the use of any time gained by Ms. S. from a stable child-care arrangement and the father's increased responsibility for the children for parent effectiveness training and her own needs.

The client and change agent systems, the social worker and Ms. S., develop a case theory and plan with SMARRT objectives to resolve the problem. The plan specifies other needed systems. The father and Ms. S. are the target system clients, since the behavior of both must changed.

The day care center is also a target system because Ms. S.'s children need to be enrolled in the center. If the intervention called for by the plan is successful, the father will ultimately become part of Ms. S.'s support system. As an agent of the child guidance clinic, the social worker needs approval of the plan by the controlling system, the agency. The court, which must order the support payment, also is part of the controlling system. The agency is the host system, and the social worker is the implementing system. Ms. S., the social worker, and the parent effectiveness trainer are the implementing system, as they are the people "who will have the day-to-day responsibility for carrying out the change" (Netting et al., 1993, p. 228).

PHASE 4: INTERVENTION AND THE CHANGE EFFORT

The intervention plan resulting from the theory of the case is a social intervention. Ms. S. is to allow the children's father to have the children for one weekend a month and two evenings a week if he pays child support. A court-ordered support judgment will be obtained for the support and visitation. This should ease Ms. S.'s financial worries and provide help with parenting responsibilities and some time for herself. The social worker assisted Ms. S. in obtaining stable day care from the public neighborhood day care center. Ms. S. will attend the child guidance clinic's parent effectiveness training classes on one of the evenings that the father has the children.

Ms. S., the social worker, the court, and the parent effectiveness trainer form the action system to change the target systems: Ms. S., the father, and the day care center. As indicated above, if the change effort with the father and the day care center is successful, they become part of Ms. S.'s support system for subsequent changes and development.

PHASE 5: EVALUATION AND TERMINATION OF THE CHANGE EFFORT

At the conclusion of the parent effectiveness training classes, Ms. S., the social worker, and the father, now a part of the problem-solving process, will evaluate the current arrangements.

Although evaluation is the final phase, it is also a continuous part of the monitoring of the problem-solving process. The monitoring involves Ms. S., the social worker, and often the support, controlling, host, and implementing systems. The evaluation of a problem-solving strategy before its termination can involve all of these systems, including Ms. S., the social worker, the parent effectiveness trainer, the father, and possibly the child guidance clinic supervisors.

Case Illustration of the Problem-Solving Strategy in Rural Community Development and Action[3]

PHASE 1: RECOGNITION OF A PROBLEM AND ESTABLISHMENT OF THE NEED FOR CHANGE

California's San Joaquin Valley's natural climate is hot and arid for about 8 months of the year. It is very fertile. It naturally is a semidesert, with rainfall between 4 and 12 inches annually, depending on the location. With the expenditure of millions of federal and state dollars since the 1930s to bring water to the valley's communities and agriculture, the San Joaquin Valley is now the food basket of the nation. However, in the 1960s, there were small rural communities populated by Chicanos, black, and poor white agricultural laborers still without a public water supply. La Colonia was one of these rural communities.

La Colonia was a small Chicano rural farm labor village of about 100 families adjacent to a larger agriculturally based community, the Town, with about 5,000 people. La Colonia was a stable unincorporated area with a 90-year history. Its homes were generally owned by its residents. There was no formal government other than a local public utilities district (PUD) with a commission elected by La Colonia's property owners. The PUD provided no utility services because, after its formation and incorporation, it discovered that La Colonia was too small and poor to afford the startup costs of providing public services. Individual La Colonia homes received electric and gas services from the regional gas and electric utility company. The families provided their own sewage service in individual septic tanks or cesspools. Garbage and trash disposal was an individual household responsibility. The PUD and its commission basically serve as a forum to discuss community problems, mediate community disputes, and plan and conduct community events such as the celebrations of Cinco de Mayo and other traditional holidays. The families obtained their water from individual wells, a significant capital investment for a farm laboring family, by individual agreements with neighbors who had wells, by hauling water from the Town's public water tank taps, or from the irrigation ditches that surrounded La Colonia. Water from the wells was often polluted by septic tank and cesspool seepage. The irrigation canal water contained agricultural field runoff with fertilizer, herbicide, and pesticide contaminants.

The Town's water system was built largely by state and federal community development grants. It delivered abundant potable water to the Town's residents. The water system's mains were located less than a quarter of a mile from La Colonia. A water system connecting each home to the Town's water system could be constructed at a relatively low cost to La Colonia and the Town, as most of the cost would be paid with state and federal funds. However, the Town Council did not want to provide water to communities not incorporated into the Town, regardless of the cost. The Town Council did not want to establish a precedent and risk a possible demand from other rural communities more distant from the Town. The Town Council's policy was to restrict its provision of water to areas incorporated within its boundaries. La Colonia's PUD Commission, La Colonia's nominal leadership, did not want to be annexed to the Town, as they feared La Colonia would lose its identity, would be unable to remain a defined community with its own traditions, would simply become another Town barrio or ethnic neighborhood, and would perhaps incur a Town property tax increase. The Commission simply wanted good, affordable water.

The Commission approached the county's community action agency (CAA), a not-for-profit community development and social action organization, for help with their water problem. After a meeting of the CAA's director and the PUD Commission, the director assigned a Chicano community development worker (CDW) from the Town to work with La Colonia and the commission to obtain a potable water system.

La Colonia's PUD Commission was the initiator system and the client system. The contract was between the CAA and the commission. La Colonia was also part of the client system, as the commission was acting on the community's behalf. The change agents were the CAA director and the CDW. During this phase, the controlling system was the CAA and the commission. The CAA and the commission constituted the host system, with the CDW and volunteers from La Colonia composing the implementing system. The client system and the change agent system saw the Town Council as the target system.

PHASE 2: INFORMATION GATHERING

This phase involved the action system—the CDW, La Colonia volunteers, and CAA staff—gathering information on (a) the ability and willingness of La Colonia's residents to pay their share of the water system development costs, hookup cost, and monthly water bills; (b) grant requirements for state and federal community development funds; (c) the direct costs to the Town beyond La Colonia's costs and the state and federal grants for expanding the water system to serve La Colonia; (d) potential support systems in the Town and county; and (e) procedures for placing the item on the Town Council's agenda.

PHASE 3: ASSESSMENT AND DEVELOPMENT OF A THEORY FOR CHANGE

The initial SMARRT objective for the planned change strategy was to obtain a stable, cost-effective potable water supply and system for La Colonia. The CAA also had an empowerment goal endemic to community development: to develop La Colonia's capacity as a community to work together to solve its problems and achieve greater cohesion in the process.

The theory for change, the case theory, based on an assessment of the information obtained in Phase 2, was rather simple and direct. The problem—the lack of a stable potable water system—was a result of La Colonia's lack of resources and an unwillingness of the Town to connect La Colonia to its water system under mutually tolerable conditions. La Colonia could develop the infrastructure for the water system within its boundaries if a connection with the Town's water system was made. The Town was unwilling to connect the water system for political and economic reasons. Although the Town was ethnically diverse, its Council consisted of the white establishment that largely represented the agricultural interests. There were the fiscal costs of expanding the water system (though minor to serve La Colonia) and the fear of a precedent that would require expansion of the water system to all surrounding rural areas, with ever-increasing, though incremental, costs, accompanying each expansion. Eventually, the council reasoned, the incremental costs would necessitate a politically unpopular property tax increase, an equally disliked water use fee increase, or both.

The case theory explaining the lack of a stable water system for La Colonia rested on the intransigence of the Town Council and La Colonia's PUD. La Colonia could petition for a property owner's incorporation vote and, if it passed, obtain water as an incorporated area of the Town. The Town could alter its policy against providing water to areas not incorporated into the Town. As La Colonia was the client system, its preferences directed the change strategy to alter the Town's policy.

The information gathered in the assessment phase indicated that (a) one Town Council member had ambitions for higher office as a county commissioner, (b) several local churches were supporting civil rights efforts in other communities and were eager to do something locally, and (3) farm labor unionizing activity was occurring in the eastern part of the county. The Town and its growers were located in the western part of the county and, as yet, were unaffected by the union organizing activity.

4. PHASE 4: INTERVENTION AND THE CHANGE EFFORT

The intervention and change effort based on the case theory called for a combination of technical assistance to the Town, social action, and political persuasion and support. Its basic strategy was to target certain individuals and groups in the Town—ministers, church leaders, and a politically ambitious council member—to bring them into either the support or action system. The ministers and leaders were to be brought in by casting the problem as a civil rights issue. La Colonia was a Chicano community. The ministers and church leaders were first a target system, with an intent of making them part of a support system. This strategy called for expanding the action and support systems to induce the politically ambitious council member to become a sponsor of a proposal to expand the Town's water system to serve La Colonia. In return for this sponsorship, the support system would support her county commission bid. Additionally, the CAA would assist the Town and La Colonia in developing the proposals for federal and state community development funds. La Colonia leaders would also let it be known that if the proposal did not receive favorable consideration from the Town Council, La Colonia would approach the farm labor union for assistance in developing a water system for La Colonia. This would introduce the farm labor union to the west side and provide it with a local sponsor and sanction. When the support and action systems were expanded, the Town Council (the target system) would be addressed. If the proposal to expand the water system was accepted by the Town Council, it would become the controlling system, part of the action system, the host system, and—with the Town's city manager, water department, and CAA—the implementing system to take the final step in La Colonia's water system development.

PHASE 5: EVALUATION AND TERMINATION OF THE CHANGE EFFORT

Evaluation of the change effort by the client system and the CAA (as part of the action system) of the SMARRT objective of obtaining a potable water system was direct: The system was obtained. However, evaluation of the community development goals is more complex. Has the community increased its ability to continue its development?

The problem-solving approach for planned change, with its community practice skills of systems identification, community assessment, and developing and linking resources, is important whether the problem-solving strategy is used with a delimited client system such as Ms. S. and her family or a larger client system such as La Colonia.

ETHICS, ADVOCACY, AND COMMUNITY PRACTICE

No discussion of professional practice is complete without attention to a profession's ethics, the values that form the basis for the ethics, and the ethical standards of practice.

Profession as Calling

A profession is more than an occupation. A profession is a vocation, an avocation, and a calling. A profession's values constituting its service calling, not the profession's technology, distinguish it from occupations. Professions are given public protection and sanction to benefit the community, the public, clients, and the common good. Professions require a vision of and commitment to ends to be served and not just the techniques practiced (Howe, 1980; Lubove, 1977). Service is not only to the individual clients, but also to "a larger whole, to a larger good . . . of the community" (Gustafson, 1982, p. 512). It is the outward service to others that provides the basic requirements of ethical conduct and the inner rewards to the professional. The historical foundation of the profession, its service mission, and its ethical standards was the nineteenth-century social gospel movement in the United States (Gustafson, 1982; Lubove, 1977). This service mission and calling is reflected in a declaration by Brother Cyprian Rowe (a Marist brother and emeritus faculty member of the School of Social Work, the University of Maryland, Baltimore), a declaration that "I have an awe-filled notion of the meaning of social work. We are, in a sense, the hands of society; conscience. We really minister. . . . The people [the social workers] . . . on the line [should be well] prepared to do right and do well by the people they meet" ("Living a Life of Giving," 1994, p. 6).

The service mission to the community supersedes the accrual of personal wealth, the production of particular products or services, or the application of specific sophisticated techniques. Many occupations allow the accumulation of personal wealth, the production of products or services, the use of complex techniques, and they may even contribute to the public's welfare. But their prime motivation is not service. Although service as a pristine motive of profession has been tainted and is often ignored by contemporary professionals, it is embedded in most conceptions of profession. Adherence to the outward service orientation provides professions and professionals with the community's mandate and authority to be self-regulating (Hardcastle, 1977, 1990; Howe, 1980; Vollmer & Mills, 1966).

The service calling is both outward to the community and inward to the professional. Gustafson (1982) clarified the relationship of the outward and inward dimensions of professions:

> The outward is the larger context within which any person's contributions can be seen to have significance. It contributes to the meeting of human needs; it is an element, no matter how small, in the 'common good' of the human community. It serves a purpose that is not simply self-referential in the object of its interests. The inward significance is twofold: There is a dignity to one's work that can be affirmed, and thus a dignity to the worker; and there is a sense of fulfillment and meaning that can come from being of service to others and to the common good. (p. 504)

Social Work Ethics

Social work ethics, derived from more abstract values, are rules to guide the social worker's conduct and behavior. *Values* are "generalized, emotionally charged conceptions of what is desirable, historically created and derived from experience, shared by a population or group within it, and they provide the means for organizing and structuring patterns of behavior" (Reamer, 1995, p. 11). Values motivate ethics and behavior. Values direct the nature of social work's mission; the relationships, obligations, and duties social workers have for clients, colleagues, and the broader community. Social work's basic value configuration is the result of the many forces and orientations that the profession has been subjected to and embraced over the years. The orientations and forces buffeting the profession and forging its values range from its social justice orientation, political ideologies, religious base, and scientism. These represent some internal conflict. Scientism is an amoral orientation and a growing force in social work that rejects a strong value base of normative concepts. Instead, it places an emphasis on technical, *scientific* knowledge as the exclusive guide to *evidence-based* interventions (Reamer, 1993; Webb, 2000).

Ethics are prescriptions and proscriptions for professional behavior. Ethics deal with the right, the good, the correct, and the rules of behavior. They address the *whats* of behavior more than *whys* to behave. Ethics provide a basis for defining professional good guys and bad guys. The profession's and professional's values and ethics, along with technical and empirical research-based knowledge, provide the criteria for selecting actions and making judgments, choices, and decisions regarding interventive methods and practice behavior. *Interventions are not totally a matter of empirical science, nor is the profession merely an amalgamation of technologies and evidenced-based interventions. The profession and its interventions should reflect a set of coherent values capturing its service orientation and reflecting its ethical standards.*

The *Code of Ethics*[4] of the National Association of Social Workers provides ethical guidelines for social workers. Many states have adopted the NASW's code of ethics as part of their legal regulations for social work (Hardcastle, 1990). NASW's code is predicated on six core values. These core values, embraced by social workers throughout the profession's history, are the foundation of "social work's unique purpose and perspective" (NASW, 2003, "Preamble," para. 3). The values are *service, social justice, dignity and worth of the person, importance of human relationships, integrity,* and *competence.* The values lead to the ethical principles. For example, the value of *service* leads to the ethical principle that "Social workers' primary goal is to help people in need and to address social problems" (NASW, 2003, "Ethical Principles," para. 3).

Social workers elevate service to others above self-interest. Social workers draw on their knowledge, values, and skills to help people in need and to address social problems. Social workers are encouraged to volunteer some portion of their professional skills with no expectation of significant financial return (pro bono service) (NASW, 2003, "Ethical Principles, para. 4).

The value of *social justice* requires that all social workers "challenge social injustice" (NASW, 2003, "Ethical Principles," para. 5)."

Social workers pursue social change, particularly with and on behalf of vulnerable and oppressed individuals and groups of people. Social workers' social change efforts are focused primarily on issues of poverty, unemployment, discrimination, and other forms of social injustice. These activities seek to promote sensitivity to and knowledge about oppression and cultural and ethnic diversity. Social workers strive to ensure access to needed information, services, and resources; equality of opportunity; and meaningful participation in decision making for all people (NASW, 2003, "Ethical Principles," para 6).

ETHICS AND SOCIAL WORK'S FIDUCIARY RESPONSIBILITY

The *fiduciary responsibility* of a profession is embedded in its service calling and is the underpinning of all professional relationships (Kutchins, 1991). Clients have a right to expect professional competence: for professionals to be current in the valid knowledge and skills necessary to intervene in the problems of clients whose cases they accept, for professionals to know their limitations, and for professionals to adhere to *primum non nocere*—"Above all, not knowingly to do harm." Peter Drucker (1974), the management and social theorist, states the following:

> Men and women do not acquire exemption from ordinary rules of personal behavior because of their work or job. . . . The first responsibility of a professional was spelled out clearly 2,500 years ago, in the Hippocratic oath . . . *primum non nocere*—"Above all, not knowingly to do harm." No professional . . . can promise that he will indeed do good for his client. All he can do is try. But he can promise he will not knowingly do harm. And the client, in turn, must be able to trust the professional not knowingly to do him harm. Otherwise he cannot trust him at all. And *primum non nocere,* "not knowingly to do harm," is the basic rule of professional ethics, the basic rule of ethics of public responsibility. (pp. 366–369)

The client has the right to expect that the professional will make an effort to know. And any potential risks the client faces as a result of the social worker's intervention are the client's choice under informed consent.

The fiduciary responsibility inherent in the professional mission of service and shared with all professions is reflected in the values of *integrity* and *competence*. These values challenge social workers to "behave in a trustworthy manner" (NASW, 2003, "Ethical Principles," para. 11) and limit their practice to "their areas of competence," (NASW, 2003, "Ethical Principles," para. 13) also challenging them to "develop and enhance their professional expertise" (NASW, 2003, "Ethical Principles" para. 13).

"Social workers are continually aware of the profession's mission, values, ethical principles, and ethical standards and practice in a manner consistent with them. Social workers act honestly and responsibly and promote ethical practices on the part of the organizations with which they are affiliated" (NASW, 2003, "Ethical Principles," para. 12).

COMMUNITY PRACTICE AND THE FIDUCIARY RESPONSIBILITY

Community practice in all its forms, and the use of community practice skills by direct service practitioners, require adherence to the same high ethical standards of conduct as those required of any professional social work practice. Community practice does not represent a higher form of practice exempted from ethical constraints and fiduciary responsibility. Whether a client is an individual, a group or organization, or a community with the goal of fundamental structural change, the ethical constraints remain. Indeed, community practice may require greater adherence to ethical standards, as both the scope of an intervention and change's potential for good or harm often are greater. Community practice interventions can't rest on the teleological claim that moral and equitable ends can be justified by unethical means (Schmidtz, 1991, p. 3). Ethics govern means or practices as much as ends. Not only must the ends be ethical and just, but also the tactics and behavior used in the pursuit of the ends must meet ethical and moral criteria. No matter how well-meaning the social worker is in the search of noble ends for the client or community, the ethical constraints of informed consent and the rights of clients inherent in ethical codes remain operative, even if these ethical standards interfere with the processes of change.

Advocacy

Gilbert and Specht (1976) reinforce the need to guard against the seduction of the teleological position of ends justifying means in client and social advocacy. Advocacy is a professional responsibility (NASW, 2003, Standard 6). The advocacy responsibilities ethically mandated by Ethical Standard 6 extend beyond a particular client, group, or cause to social and political advocacy to achieve an equitable distribution of social resources and for social justice. Advocacy, simply defined, is representing and supporting a client, group, organization or cause to others. The ethical codes of most U.S. and international professional social work associations (Hardina, 1993; International Federation of Social Workers, 1994; NASW, 2003) do not proscribe advocacy and community action ethical obligations for direct service social workers. Case and client advocacy are inherent in the ethical standards addressing the social worker's responsibility to protect client self-determination. Otherwise, the standards are hollow rhetoric.

Informed Consent

A social worker's first responsibility to a client is not to risk the client for a greater good unless the client makes the decision to be at risk in the quest for greater good. An individual client should not be placed in harm's way to produce a subsequently greater social, collective, and institutional good without the client's *informed consent*. Informed consent requires that the consent be informed. Informed consent requires that a client has valid information on risks, the probability level that the risks will produce greater good, an appreciation of any personal gains and losses, and any organizational and employment constraints placed on the worker in the advocacy and change effort. The social worker has a duty to warn others of the risk that a client's behavior may pose to them, and a duty to warn a client of the risks faced in any personal or social change effort. Conflict situations, the social worker's ideological commitments, or employer interests do not remove ethical imperatives. Informed consent is necessary for worker accountability and client self-determination and empowerment.

Individuals, groups, and community organizations have the right to decide their risks (e.g., jeopardizing jobs, risking jail time, losing a home). They have a right not to be unilaterally placed in harm's way by a community practitioner pursuing a social, collective, or institutional good. Clients and action systems deserve the opportunity to participate or not to participate, on the basis of appraisal of the gains and risks to them. They need to be advised of the extent to which the social worker or sponsoring agency will go to protect them or to share the risks with them. Clients have a right to provide or refuse informed consent.

Dilemmas in Ethical Behavior

While consistently ethical conduct often is difficult for social workers, the difficulty generally lies in conflicts between a social worker's pursuit of pragmatic self-interest or meeting ethical obligations. True ethical dilemmas are rare. Pragmatic dilemmas are frequent. An ethical dilemma exists when two ethical imperatives appear to require equal but opposite behaviors and the ethical guidelines do not give clear directions or set a clear priority as to the ethical imperatives to follow. Typically, the competing ethical imperatives do not actually require different and opposite behaviors. Pragmatic considerations frequently make ethical behavior arduous and professionally or personally risky, but the pragmatic considerations and hazards are not ethical dilemmas. The dilemmas are between ethical behavior on one hand and pragmatic consequences on the other hand. There are substantial pragmatic self-interests dangers and possible conflicts between ethical behavior and pragmatic interests involved in both ethical examples discussed in the following sections.

Ethical Example 1: Advocating Client Interests Over Agency Interests

My agency has a rule that restricts long-term agency services to clients since its funding sources limit service reimbursement and provide capitation resources based on the numbers of clients. The funding limits don't prevent services but they limit the amount of reimbursement. This rule encourages workers to provide clients with the least number of service sessions necessary to justify reimbursement, rather than with the number of sessions required for effective intervention. All clients tend to get the same number of service sessions, regardless of assessment. Often, the services are superficial and do not allow clients to adequately address their problems. I have a client who wants to appeal this rule and practice to state regulators, as well as make it more publicly known. If I help my client to appeal and publicize this unfair agency rule and funding practice that denies client services, it will embarrass my agency and my colleagues, isolate me in the agency, limit my chances for promotion and salary raises, and may cost me my job and place my family and me at economic risk. However, if I don't help my client appeal and make the practice public, my client as well as many other clients will continue to suffer.

The preceding example is not an ethical dilemma or conflict. The strain is not between two equally compelling and opposed ethical imperatives. The strain is between ethical standards and pragmatic self-interests. These pragmatic interests are not trivial. The dilemma is the choice between the ethical imperative of primacy of the client's interest (Ethical Standards 1.01: Commitment to Clients and 1.02: Self-determination) and the social worker's self-interest imperatives of maintaining a job and economic viability for family and self, collegial work relations, and retaining the benefits of the employer's good will. The strain and the dilemma are real and important, but this is not an *ethical* dilemma. In helping the client protest the rules, the social worker adheres to the ethical standards and the ethical principle of social justice and the related social action ethical standards (6.01 and 6.04), although the social worker does risk his or her livelihood in so doing.

Ethical Example 2: Civil Disobedience to Maintain Ethical Behavior

Public law and policy have been amended to limit services provided to illegal immigrants.[5] The public law requires that service professionals report illegal immigrants to the Immigration and Naturalization Service. Should I as a social worker participate in and adhere to public policies and laws that restrict public services to illegal immigrants, a consideration of national origin, and report any clients who are illegal immigrants to law enforcement officials? Not reporting the illegal immigrant, if I'm discovered, can result in loss of my employment, my license, and in my being subjected to other civil and criminal penalties.

This second example does present an ethical dilemma to a social worker because the ethical code presents an apparent internal inconsistency. The dilemma is between the profession's values and its ethics. The conflict is between the profession's values of *social justice*, as reflected in Ethical Standards 4:4.02 and 6:6.04(d), and the ethical limitations Ethical Standard 1.01 places on a social workers' ethical responsibilities to clients:

1.01 Commitment to Clients

Social workers' primary responsibility is to promote the well-being of clients. In general, clients' interests are primary. However, social workers' responsibility to the larger society or *specific legal obligations may on limited occasions supersede the loyalty owed clients*, and clients should be so advised. (Examples include when a social worker is required by law to report that a client has abused a child or has threatened to harm self or others.) (NASW, 2003, Ethical Standards, 1.01)

4. Social Workers' Ethical Responsibilities as Professionals

4.02 Discrimination

Social workers should not practice, condone, facilitate, or collaborate with any form of discrimination on the basis of race, ethnicity, national origin, color, sex, sexual orientation, age, marital status, political belief, religion, or mental or physical disability. (NASW, 2003, Ethical Standards, 4.02).

6. Social Workers' Ethical Responsibilities to the Broader Society

6.04 Social and Political Action

(d) Social workers should act to prevent and eliminate domination of, exploitation of, and discrimination against any person, group, or class on the basis of race, ethnicity, national origin, color, sex, sexual orientation, age, marital status, political belief, religion, or mental or physical disability. (NASW, 2003, Ethical Standards, 6).

Ethical Standard 1.01 presents social workers with the challenge of reconciling specific *legal obligations* that may supersede the loyalty owed clients and to social justice that require engaging in civil disobedience by providing service to the client and ignoring national origin. The informed consent, or at least informing clients of risks, is an effort to ameliorate any ethical conflicts. Slavish adherence to public law in itself is not always moral, although here it is ethical. It negates civil disobedience, and historically this ethical requirement would have precluded social workers' participation in the civil disobedience of the civil rights movement or sheltering Jews and other persecuted peoples in Nazi Germany.

Whistle-Blowing and Ethics

A pragmatic dilemma for an agency-based social worker, or third-party financially dependent social worker, is *whistle-blowing*. Whistle-blowing calls public attention to social and legal wrongdoings by an agency's or funding source's personnel, usually persons in authority. A whistle-blower usually does not face ethical dilemmas, although whistle-blowing does carry with it very real personal costs, risks, and pragmatic dilemmas. No one appears to respect a snitch, even when snitching in the public good. Potential future employers become wary. Whistle-

blowing should be done prudently. Reisch and Lowe (2000) provide some guidance for potential whistle-blowers. After satisfactorily determining *who is being accused* and *whether or not the accusations are fair*, the whistle-blower must address the questions in the following section.

Guideline Questions for Whistle-Blowing

1. Am I acting in the public interest and good or for personal interests and motives?
2. Do the facts warrant this action? Have all internal alternatives been explored?
3. Does the obligation to serve the public interest outweigh my responsibility to colleagues and the agency?
4. Can the harm to colleagues and the agency be minimized? What are the least harmful methods available?

Whistle-blowing, under Ethical Standard 3.09: Commitment to Employers, should be done only after all other avenues for change within the agency are exhausted. The use of alternative avenues for change ethically can be rejected after consideration, according to Reisch and Lowe (2000), for three reasons: (a) when no alternatives exist for the situation at hand, (b) when there is insufficient time to use alternative channels and the damage of no change or exposure outweighs the damage of premature whistle-blowing before alternatives are exhausted, and (c) when the organization is so corrupt that there is an imminent danger of being silenced or falsely refuted.

MACROPRACTICE AND COMMUNITY PRACTICE'S FIDUCIARY CHALLENGES

As discussed above, community practitioners are not relieved of ethical principles or standards, although sometimes it's difficult to determine the *who*s and *what*s that the ethical standards serve and protect in community practice. NASW's *Code Of Ethics* is more reflective of Howe's (1980) *private model of profession*, one with members who "are primarily responsible to individual clients" (p. 179). Private professions in the main are concerned with the private good of individual clients. Reisch and Lowe (2000, p. 24) contend that NASW's ethical code assumes that the ethical issues it addresses arise primarily within the context of a clinical relationship and the administrative and supervisory environment of that relationship. They claim that social work's code of ethics does not provide sufficient ethical guidance to community practice and that the social work literature gives little attention to the ethics of community practice.

The Client in Community Practice

The *client* often is not clearly defined in macro- and community practice by traditional notions of a client relationship. Community practice shares with much of social work practice third-party employment, unwilling clients, and people not seeking the practitioner's service. The social worker is employed by and accountable to an agency. This clouds and often preempts any social worker's accountability to a client, target, or beneficiary of the professional action. In practice, care must be taken not to stretch the conception of client and a client relationship beyond recognition. Most conceptions of a *client* in a professional relationship indicate that a client is the person who in some way engages the professional service of another. Community practice, as pointed out by Gilbert and Specht (1976), emphasizes the importance of being clear about the responsibilities to client and to employing agency. But who is the client? The social worker in social advocacy, social action, community development, and much of macro- and community practice is employed and engaged by a social agency or organization to produce social change. The practitioner may have no formal or even implied or informal contract with a client group, let alone the client system. Community groups are used in the action system to pursue change. The social worker is not employed by the community. The funding may come from sources outside any target or beneficiary community. The problem-solving systems discussed earlier in this chapter require careful professional attention.

Social workers, community psychologists, and similar professionals must decide and be clear to whom they are accountable, as there are bound to be conflicting loyalties and vague mandates. O'Neill (1989, p. 234), a community psychologist, notes that we often intervene on behalf of groups who are "only vaguely aware that a professional is working to advance their presumed interests" and "who gave no consent at all." The conception and subsequent construction of a client system in situations where the practitioner is employed by a social organization other than client systems must be approached carefully. Client systems generally are the people who ask for and sanction the proposed change *and* who have a working agreement or contract, whether formal or informal, with the change agent as well as being the expected beneficiaries of the change agent's services. A meaningful conception of *client* goes beyond being a target of change, the agent of social change, or beneficiary of change to the inclusion of agreeing to the change.

As Reisch and Lowe point out (2000, p. 25), other challenges confronting community organizers include issues involving truth telling and competing interests and goals, paternalism and the limits on an organizer's interventions when there are divided professional loyalties, allocation of scarce resources between competing interests, and resolving differences between public and private interests.

Code of Ethics Challenges in Community Practice

1. Social Workers' Ethical Responsibilities to Clients
   1.01 Commitment to Clients—Who is the client and does primary commitment lie with client or with cause?
   1.02 Self-Determination—Who is the client, and how are self-determination decisions made for the community?
   1.03 Informed Consent—Who provides the informed consent for the community? Do all the problem-solving systems have the right to privacy and informed consent or is it limited to the client system only? What about the action system?
   1.09 Sexual Relationships—Sexual relations are proscribed with current and former clients and basically with the client's primary social networks. But how does this apply to the client systems in community practice?

What's a social worker in community practice seeking ethical guidance to do? The standards do not always provide behavior guidance for a community practitioner. They sometimes confuse it for all practitioners and conflict with values and principles. We suggest that practitioners look to the profession's values and ethical principles, and that practitioners, above all, should not knowingly do harm.

THE ORGANIZATION OF THIS BOOK

The book is divided into two parts. Part I explores the context, dynamics, and primary theories underlying community practice. This part contains four chapters that were not included in the first edition: Chapter 2, "Theories on Community Practice by Direct Service Practitioners"; Chapter 3, "The Nature of Social and Com-

BOX 1.3	SOCIAL WORK'S ETHICAL PRINCIPLES

Value: Service
Ethical Principle: Social workers' primary goal is to help people in need and to address social problems.

Value: Social Justice
Ethical Principle: Social workers challenge social injustice.

Value: Dignity and Worth of the Person
Ethical Principle: Social workers respect the inherent dignity and worth of the person.

Value: Importance of Human Relationships
Ethical Principle: Social workers recognize the central importance of human relationships.

Value: Integrity
Ethical Principle: Social workers behave in a trustworthy manner.

Value: Competence
Ethical Principle: Social workers practice within their areas of competence and develop and enhance their professional expertise.

Source: From "Ethical Principles," *Code of Ethics of the National Association of Social Workers* (retrieved May 25, 2003, from http://www.naswdc.org/pubs/code/code.asp). Copyright 2003 by the National Association of Social Workers.

munity Problems"; Chapter 4, "The Concept of Community in Social Work Practice"; and Chapter 5, "Community Intervention and Programs: Let's Extend the Clan." Part II, which addresses essential community practice skills for all social workers in the twenty-first century, is divided into 10 chapters. Chapter 6: Discovering and Documenting the Life of the Community, Chapter 7: Using Assessment in Community Practice, Chapter 8: Using Self in Community Practice: Assertiveness, Chapter 9: Using Your Agency, Chapter 10: Using Work Groups: Committees, Teams, and Boards, Chapter 11: Using Networks and Networking, Chapter 12: Using Social Marketing, Chapter 13: Using the Advocacy Spectrum, and Chapter 14: Using Organizing: Acting in Concert, Chapter 15: Community Social Casework.

Discussion Exercises

1. Could theories of human behavior and social work intervention be developed and used without a consideration of community influence? If so, would the theories be equally applicable to anyone in the world, without consideration of culture or community?

2. How are interventions and post intervention successes of clients affected by the community? Do the social relations, environment, and networks of a drug user affect drug use? Will drug use be influenced by a "clean" community and a social support network of nonusers?

3. Are there values that are shared by most communities? If so, what are they?

4. What are the social worker's ethical responsibilities to a client and the limits of the social worker's capacity to engage in client advocacy when employed by a social agency? Which ethical codes limit advocacy?

5. Are there limits to client advocacy because of resource scarcity?

6. Are there differences between the legal requirements and ethical obligations in duty to warn, client self-determination, and informed consent?

7. Do the simultaneous obligations to clients, the community, and the employing agency and advocacy of the primacy of the client's interests present practice dilemmas? What are they?

8. In social cause advocacy, does the social work advocate owe primary loyalty to the employing organization, the social cause, or the participants? Is there a client or a client system in social cause advocacy?

9. Can there be a profession sanctioned by the community for social reform and social reconstruction? Can reform and social change be pro-

fessionalized? Can a profession or occupation dependent on and employed by the public sector, either directly or under contract, become a radical change-oriented profession?

10. If the first ethical rule of all professional behavior should be *primum non nocere*—"first of all, do no harm"—what is your position on the question, "Should the social worker risk harming an individual client in order to produce social, collective, and institutional change that might result in good for a large number of people?" Defend the position based on the social work profession's code of ethics and values.

11. Can affirmative action be defended as ethical by the code of ethics? How is affirmative action compatible with the code of ethics?

12. Are there ethical canons that allow law and public policy to supersede the code of ethics?

Notes

1. For a somewhat different view of social work's need for a common base, see Wakefield (1988). Wakefield distinguishes between *clinical counseling* as social work and *psychotherapy* as lying outside of social work. Wakefield argues for unifying principles derived from John Rawl's conception of minimal distributive justice.

2. The case was provided by a clinical practice colleague.

3. The community development case is based on one of the author's practice experience. Similar *colonias* to the one described here currently dot the southwestern United States. A *colonia* is a "rural, unincorporated community . . . in which one or more of the following conditions exist: lack

of portable water supply or no water system, lack of adequate waste water facilities, lack of decent, safe, and sanitary housing, inadequate roads and/or inadequate drainage control structures" (Henkel, 1998, p. 18).

4. The complete and current *Code of Ethics* is available at http://www.naswdc.org/pubs/code/code.asp on the Web. All references to and excerpts from the NASW *Code of Ethics* were obtained from this source.

5. California voters had passed an initiative curtailing the provision of public health, education, and welfare services to illegal immigrants. The U.S. Congress was, and is, considering similar restrictions. California's law subsequently was declared unconstitutional by the federal courts.

References

Administration Systems for Church Management. (n.d.), Colorado Springs. Systemation, Inc.

American Association of Social Workers. (1929). *Social case work: Generic and specific, a report of the Milford Conference.* New York: Author.

Anderson, R. E., & Carter, I. (1984). *Human behavior in the social environment: A social systems approach* (3rd ed.). New York: Aldine.

Asch, A., & Abelson, P. (1993). Serving workers through managed mental health care: The social work role. In P. A. Kurzman & S. H. Akabas (Eds.), *Work and well-being: The occupational social work advantage* (pp. 123–137). Washington, DC: National Association of Social Workers.

Bellah, R. N., Madsen, R., Sullivan, W. M., Swidler, A., & Tipton, S. M. (1985). *Habits of the heart: Individualism and commitment in American life.* New York: Harper & Row.

Bellah, R. N., Madsen, R., Sullivan, W. M.,

Swidler, A., & Tipton, S. M. (1991). *The good society.* New York: Vintage Books.

Berger, P. L., & Neuhaus, R. J. (1977). *To empower people: The role of mediating structures in public policy.* Washington, DC: American Enterprise Institute.

Berry, M., & Hallett, C. (Eds.). (1998). *Social exclusion and social work: Issues of theory, policy, and practice.* Dorset, UK: Russell House Publishing.

Bisman, C. D. (1994). *Social work practices: Cases and principles.* Pacific Grove, CA: Brooks/Cole.

Bisman, C., & Hardcastle, D. (1999). *Integrating research into practice: A model for effective social work.* Pacific Grove, CA: Brooks/Cole, Wadsworth.

Bruno, F. J. (1948). *Trends in social work: As reflected in the proceedings of the National Conference of Social Work, 1874–1946.* New York: Columbia University Press.

Crazdun, S. (1991) *Responding to human needs:*

Community-based social services. Denver, CO: National Conference of State Legislatures.

Cohen, A. P. (1985). *The symbolic construction of community.* New York: Tavistock Publication and Ellis Horwood Limited.

Commission on Accreditation. (2003). Education Policy and Accreditation Standards. Retrieved July 8, 2003, from http://www.cswe.org/.

Compton, B. R., & Galaway, B. (1979). *Social work processes* (Rev. ed.). Homewood, IL: Dorsey Press.

Connelly, M. (2000, November 12). The election, who voted: A portrait of American politics, 1976–2000. *The New York Times,* p. wk 4.

Deacon, B. (with Hulse, M., & Stubbs, P.). (1997). *Global social policy: International organizations and the future of welfare.* Thousand Oaks, CA: Sage Publications.

Doherty, W. (1994–1995, Winter). Bridging psychotherapy and moral responsibility. *The Responsive Community: Rights and Responsibilities, 5*(1), 41–52.

Doherty, W. (1995, Spring). Community considerations in psychotherapy. *The Responsive Community: Rights and Responsibilities, 5*(2), 45–53.

Doherty, W., & Etzioni, A. (1994/1995, Winter). The commitment gap. *The Responsive Community, 5*(1), 75–77.

Dowd, M. (1994, December 15). Americans like G.O.P. agenda but split on how to reach goals. *The New York Times,* pp. A1, A24.

Drucker, P. F. (1974). *Management: Tasks, responsibilities and practices.* New York: Harper & Row.

Epstein, L. (1980). *Helping people: The task-centered approach* (2nd ed.). Columbus, OH: Merrill.

Etzioni, A. (1993). *The spirit of community: Rights, responsibility and the communitarian agenda.* New York: Crown.

Ewalt, P. L. (1980). *Toward a definition of clinical social work.* Washington, DC: National Association of Social Workers.

Ezell, M. (2001). *Advocacy in the human services.* Belmont, CA: Brooks/Cole.

Gambrill, E. (1983). *Casework: A competency-based approach.* Englewood Cliffs, NJ: Prentice Hall.

Germain, C. B. (1983). Using physical and social environments. In A. Rosenblatt & D. Waldfogel (Eds.), *Handbook of clinical social work* (pp. 110–133). New York: Jossey-Bass.

Gibelman, M., & Schervish, P. H. (Eds.). (1993). *Who we are: The social work labor force as reflected in the NASW membership.* Washington, DC: National Association of Social Workers Press.

Gilbert, N., & Specht, H. (1976). Advocacy and professional ethics. *Social Work, 21*(4), 288–293.

Gillespie, E., & Schellhas, B. (Eds.). (1994). *Contract with America: The bold plan by Rep. Newt Gingrich, Rep. Dick Armey and the House Republicans to change the nation.* New York: Times Books.

Gingrich, N., Armey, D., & the House Republicans. (1994). *Contract with America.* New York: Times Books/Random House.

Gordon, W. E. (1969). Basic construction for an in-ergative conception of social work. In G. Hearn (Ed.), *The general systems approach: Contributions toward an holistic conception of social work* (pp. 5–11). New York: Council on Social Work Education.

Gray, J. (1995, January 22). Does democracy have a future? *The New York Times Book Review,* pp. 1, 24–25.

Gustafson, J. A. (1982). Profession as callings. *Social Service Review, 56*(4), 501–505.

Hardcastle, D. A. (1977). Public regulation of social work. *Social Work, 22*(1), 14–20.

Hardcastle, D. A. (1987). *The social work labor force* (Social Work Education Monograph Series, No. 7). Austin: University of Texas at Austin, School of Social Work.

Hardcastle, D. A. (1990). Public regulation of social work. In L. Ginsberg, S. Khinduka, J. A. Hall, F. Ross-Sheriff, & A. Hartman (Eds.), *Encyclopedia of social work* (18th ed., 1990 suppl., pp. 203–217). Silver Spring, MD: National Association of Social Workers.

Hardina, D. (1993). *Professional Ethics and Advocacy Practice* New York: Annual Program Meeting of Community Organization and Social Administration Symposium Paper.

Henkel, D. (1998, November/December). Self-help planning in the colonias: Collaboration and innovation in southern New Mexico unincorporated areas. *Small Towns,* pp. 16–21.

Hepworth, D. H., & Larsen, J. A. (1986). *Direct social work practice: Theory and skills* (2nd ed.). Chicago: Dorsey Press.

Hollenbach, D. (1994/1995). Civic society: Beyond the public-private dichotomy. *The Responsive Community, 5*(1), 15–23.

Howe, E. (1980, May). Public professions and the private model of professionalism, Social Work, 25(3), 179–191.

International Federation of Social Workers. (1994). *The ethics of social work: Principles and standards.* Retrieved July 9, 2003, from http://www.ifsw.org/info/l.info//htm#anchor-ethics-33865.

Karls, J. M., & Wandrei, K. E. (Eds.). (1994). *Person-in-environment system: The P-I-E classification system for social functioning problems.* Washington, DC: National Association of Social Workers.

Kutchins, H. (1991). The fiduciary relationship: The legal basis for social workers' responsibility to clients. *Social Work, 36*(2), 97–102.

Ladd, E. C. (1989). The 1988 elections: Continuation of the post–New Deal system. *Political Science Quarterly, 704*(1), 1–18.

Lasch, C. (1994). *The revolt of the elites and the*

betrayal of democracy. New York: W. W. Norton.

Lippitt, R., Watson, J., & Westley, B. (1958). *The dynamics of planned change.* New York: Harcourt, Brace and World.

Living a life of giving. (1994, February 21–March 7). *The Voice,* University of Maryland at Baltimore, p. 6.

Lubove, R. (1977). *The professional altruist: The emergence of social work as a career, 1880–1938.* New York: Atheneum.

Miller, D. T., & Prentice, D. A. (1994). The self and the collective. *Society for Personality and Social Psychology, 20*(5), 451–453.

Mishra, R. (1999). *Globalization and the welfare state.* Northampton, MA: Edward Elgar.

Morgan, P. (Ed.). (1995). *Privatization and the welfare state: Implications for consumers and the workforce.* Aldershot, UK: Dartmouth.

Mullard, M. & Spicker, P. (1995). *Social policy in a changing society.* London: Routledge.

National Association of Social Workers. (2003). *Code of ethics of the National Association of Social Workers* [as approved by the 1996 NASW Delegate Assembly and revised by the 1999 NASW Delegate Assembly]. Retrieved May 25, 2003, from http://www.naswdc.org/pubs/code/code.asp

National Association of Social Workers. (n.d.). NASW policy statement 11, *NASW standards for the practice of clinical social work.* Silver Spring, MD: Author.

Netting, F. E., Kettner, P. M., & McMurtry, S. L. (1993). *Social work macro practice.* New York: Longman.

O'Neill, J. (2003). Private sector employs most members. NASW News, 48(2), 8.

O'Neill, P. (1998). Responsible to whom? Responsible for what? Ethical issues in community intervention. *American Journal of Psychology, 17*(3), 323–340.

Pardeck, J. T., Murphy, J. W., & Choi, J. M. (1994). Some implications of postmodernism for social work practice. *Social Work, 39*(4), 343–346.

Pincus, A., & Minahan, A. (1973). *Social work practice: Models and methods.* Itasca, IL: F. E. Peacock.

Polsky, H. (1969). System as patient: Client needs and system functions. In G. Hearn (Ed.), *The general systems approach: Contributions toward an holistic conception of social work* (pp. 12–25). New York: Council on Social Work Education.

Pumphrey, R. E. (1980). Compassion and protection: Dual motivations of social welfare. In F. R. Breul & S. J. Diner (Eds.), *Compassion and responsibility: Readings in the history of social welfare policy in the United States* (pp. 5–13). Chicago: University of Chicago Press.

Putnam, R. D. (2000). *Bowling alone: The collapse and revival of American community.* New York: Simon & Schuster.

Reamer, F. G. (1993). *The philosophical foundations of social work.* New York: Columbia University Press.

Reamer, F. G. (1995). *Social work values and ethics.* New York: Columbia University Press.

Reisch, M., & Lowe, J. I. (2000). "Of means and ends" revisited: Teaching ethical community organizing in an unethical society. *Journal of Community Practice, 7*(1), 19–38.

The responsive communitarian platform: Rights and responsibilities. (1992). Washington, DC: *Communitarian Network.*

Reddin, B. A. (1971). *Effective Management by objectives: The 3-d method of mba.* New York: McGraw-Hill.

Richmond, M. E. (1917). *Social diagnosis.* New York: Russell Sage Foundation.

Richmond, M. E. (1992). *What is social casework?* New York: Russell Sage Foundation. (Original work published 1922)

Room, G. (1990). *'New poverty' in the European community.* London: Macmillan.

Ross, M. (with Lappin, B. W.). (1967). *Community organization: Theory, principles, and practice.* New York: Harper & Row.

Rothman, J., & Tropman, J. (1987). Models of community organization and macro practice perspectives: Their mixing and phasing. In F. Cox, J. Erlich, J. Rothman, & J. Tropman (Eds.), *Strategies of community organization* (4th ed., pp. 3–26). Itasca, IL: P. E. Peacock.

Salcido, R. M., & Seek, E. T. (1992). Political participation among social work chapters. *Social Work, 37*(6), 563–564.

Schmidtz, D. (1991). *The limits of government: An essay on the public good argument.* Boulder, CO: Westview Press.

Schneider, R. L., & Lester, L. (2001). *Social work advocacy: A new framework for action.* Belmont, CA: Brooks/Cole.

Shapiro, R., & Young, J. T. (1989). Public opinion and the welfare state: The United States in comparative perspective. *Political Science Quarterly, 104*(1), 59–89.

Sherraden, M. (1990). The business of social work. In L. Ginsberg, S. Khinduka, A. Hall, F. Ross-Sheriff, & A. Hartman (Eds.), *Encyclopedia of social work* (18th ed., 1990 suppl., pp. 51–59). Silver Spring, MD: National Association of Social Workers.

Spano, R. (1982). *The rank and file movement in social work.* Washington, DC: University Press of America.

Specht, H., & Courtney, M. (1994). *Unfaithful angels: How social work has abandoned its mission.* New York: Free Press.

Timms, N. (1966). *Social casework: Principles and practice.* London: Latimer, Trend.

U.S. Bureau of the Census. (1995). Statistical abstract of the United States; 1994 (114th ed.). Washington, DC: U.S. Government Printing Office.

van Deth, J. W. (Ed.). (1997). *Private groups and public life: Social participation, voluntary associations, and political involvement in representative democracies.* London: Routledge.

Vollmer, H. W., & Mills, D. L. (Eds.). (1966). *Professionalization.* Englewood Cliffs, NJ: Prentice Hall.

Wagner, A. (1997). Social work and the global economy: Opportunities and challenges. In M. C. Hokenstad & J. Midgley (Eds.), *Issues in international social work: Global challenges for a new century* (pp. 45–56). Washington, DC: NASW Press.

Wakefield, J. C. (1988). Psychotherapy, distributive justice, and social work. Part I: Distributive justice as a conceptual framework for social work. *Social Service Review, 62*(2), 187–210.

Webb, S.A. (2000). Some considerations of the validity of empirical-based practice in social work. *The British Journal of Social Work.* 31(1), 57–79.

Well, M. O., & Gamble, D. N. (1995). Community practice models. In R. L. Edwards (Ed.-in-Chief), *Encyclopedia of social work,* Vol. 1 (19th ed., pp. 577–694), Silver Spring, MD: NASW Press.

Whittaker, J. K., Garbarino, J., & Associates (Eds.). (1983). *Social support networks: Informal helping in the human services.* New York: Aldine.

Williams, L. F., & Hopps, J. G. (1990). The social work labor force: Current perspectives and future trends. In L. Ginsberg, S. Khinduka, J. A. Hall, F. Ross-Sheriff, & A. Hartman (Eds.), *Encyclopedia of social work* (18th ed., 1990 suppl., pp. 289–306). Silver Spring, MD: National Association of Social Workers.

I

UNDERSTANDING THE SOCIAL ENVIRONMENT AND SOCIAL INTERACTION

2

Theory-Based, Model-Based Community Practice

I came to theory desperate, wanting to comprehend—to grasp what was happening around and within me. . . . Theory is not inherently healing, liberatory, or revolutionary. It fulfills this function only when we ask that it do so and direct our theorizing towards this end.

B. HOOKS (1991, PP. 1–2)

A CONCEPTUAL FRAMEWORK FOR PRACTICE

One way in which professional social work practice differs from nonprofessional practice is that social science theories, as well as a body of professional values, guide professional practice. With theory-based practice, social workers will presumably use similar interventions in similar situations to produce similar results. Under the clearest circumstances, the propositions of practice theory would thus take the form "If X occurs, or under X conditions, do Y," and professional training would primarily involve mastering the theories and their applications. So, for example, a proposition might be: "If you encounter group resistance to a new idea, then identify an opinion leader and try to persuade him or her, outside of the group context, to adopt your idea."

In social work practice, however, situation X is seldom the same as situation Y, and the complexity of human beings and human relationships is such that behavioral science theories cannot be applied quite so neatly. Nor is there a

single, unified master theory of human behavior. So, in the above example, group resistance is not a simple concept; resistance can take many forms and can be explained in many different ways. A Freudian would talk about unconscious conflicts; a Skinnerian would consider rewards and punishments. Similarly, persuasion can take many different forms. Therefore, interventions to overcome resistance will vary. Discovering the kind of persuasion that works best for overcoming particular forms of resistance represents a further elaboration of theory, indeed an improvement, but one that still will not yield a simple rule.

In fact, the enormous complexity of social work practice means that often we cannot find a direct correspondence between theory and practice. Social science theory seldom tells us directly exactly what to do, nor could it entirely, since ethical principles also inform professional practice.

Should we therefore abandon theory as useless? Not really. Instead, as professional practitioners, we need to develop a conceptual framework for ourselves, namely, a body of related concepts that help us understand and think about the phenomena we are encountering and help us make decisions about how to intervene. Since there is no unified grand theory of human behavior (for which we are thankful) or of social work practice, our conceptual framework will draw on a number of different theories, which will be refined through practice experience. The process of reflecting on our practice experiences in the light of social science theory (and vice versa), and making appropriate modifications in theory and practice as a result (sometimes referred to as *praxis*), helps us to make sense out of our practice world. Therefore, in this chapter, we will briefly outline the theories we believe are most pertinent to community practice. At the same time, as helpful as theory is, we should not overemphasize its importance either, for creative practice draws from many sources. In the words of Renato Rosaldo (as cited in Saleebey, 1994): "Rather than work downward from abstract principles, social critics work outward from an in-depth knowledge of a specific form of life. Informed by such conceptions as social justice, human dignity, and equality, they use their moral imagination to move from the world as it actually is to a locally persuasive version of how it ought to be" (p. 355).

In the sections that follow, we will identify several streams of theory and a number of the concepts and propositions embedded in them in order to suggest useful components of a conceptual framework for community practice (also see Martinez-Brawley, 2000; Rogge, 1995). Readers will still have the task of integrating these ideas and organizing their own frameworks.

THEORIES FOR UNDERSTANDING MACROPRACTICE

Entire books have been written about each of the theories discussed in this section. Our abbreviated presentation here includes ideas, concepts, and propositions that we view as especially pertinent for community-based practice.

Systems Theory and Organizations

A system can be viewed as a whole and its interrelated parts. Its guiding principle is organization. The main assumption underlying systems theory is that a well-integrated, smoothly functioning system is both possible and desirable. Examples of systems are mechanical systems such as computers and automobiles; human or social systems such as the Baltimore Orioles, the Department of Social Services, the AIDS Outreach Service of the health clinic, and Family Services of America; or, for that matter, any individual human being. To the extent that a system can remain closed—free of outside influences—the assumption that it is well integrated is tenable. But since systems are seldom entirely closed, and since human or social systems are inherently open, it is more reasonable to suggest that every social system is also inherently messy and that no human system can ever be perfectly integrated.

For a social system to exist, it must be separable from other systems and from its surroundings. It must have boundaries. At the same time, no human system can exist without relating to its environment, a proposition that defines the essence of an open system. Therefore, we could say that every human system is an open system striving for closure. Some degree of closure is necessary for a human system to function and remain intact or coherent. At the same time, every human system must exchange information and resources with other systems and act on that information, to maintain itself and flourish. In fact, the uniqueness of human systems is that they can process, create, and act on information; they can learn.

Thus we can say that every human system must negotiate its environment. Consequently, it must remain open to some degree, and it must manage some degree of uncertainty from external sources. If a human system cannot negotiate its environment, if it cannot process information well enough, then it must either exist in a protected milieu or die (Juba, 1997).

Social service agencies, like all organizations, can be viewed as open systems striving for closure. They were formed to carry out a particular mission; they are goal oriented. They also attempt to arrange their operations and decision-making rules so as to attain those goals. In short, they attempt to operate rationally. A bureaucracy, in the nonpejorative meaning of the term, represents an attempt to rationalize organizational decision making by locating expertise at the top of the decision-making structure and laying out clear rules and regulations for coordination and decision making by successively lower members in the hierarchy. The organizational chart, depicting the formal structure of authority in the organization, probably best symbolizes the organization as a rational system. This pure form of rational organization works well when the degree of uncertainty that must be managed is fairly low. So, when there is time to make decisions, when information is clear, and when resources are readily available to do the work, it is easier to operate rationally.

A bureaucracy, in the pejorative sense of the term, can be viewed as a nonrational, defensive organization. Our large public social service, health, and educational organizations tend to fall into this category. Required by law to serve or remain open to all who fit within their legislated service categories, yet with insufficient revenues to provide services adequately due to political struggles over the allocation of scarce resources, these public agencies develop red tape (that is, lengthy procedures for decision making and other defensive features) to stem the tide of unrelenting demand. They try to operate rationally but are overwhelmed by the demands of their environment.

Social service organizations, even nonprofit and proprietary agencies, exist in an increasingly complex, demanding, dynamic, external milieu that poses a great deal of *uncertainty* for them. (It goes without saying that the same is true for social workers and for individual clients.) Due to such factors as the exponential growth of communication and information-processing technologies, previously unrelated elements in the environment may link up and bring about unpredictable reactions with far-reaching consequences (Emery & Trist, 1965). Consider, for example, the complexity of the current health care debate and the difficulty of predicting the eventual effects on organizational resources and services, especially for health and mental health agencies (Morrison & Wolfe, 2001). How do new computers and other information system technologies affect an organization's ability to compete for clients, referral sources, and revenue? How will welfare reform affect the demand for services and the availability of funds?

Modern organizations also generate a good deal of internal system uncertainty from a variety of sources, that is, uncertainty that is built into the human differences among the members of the system and the nature of their relationships. Such sources of uncertainty include multiple and conflicting member goals and varying passions, values, interests, needs, and skills, as well as the dynamics of members' interpersonal relationships. So organizations have *informal systems* for making decisions based on the previously noted sorts of nonrational factors, as well as *formal systems* for decision making governed by written rules, job descriptions, and lines of authority.

In this complex and constantly changing environment, organizational decision making can be very difficult. An organizational manager stands at the nexus of political, social, and economic streams of information and relationships, requiring new kinds of management skills (e.g., networking and coalition building), new forms of organizational structures (e.g., problem-solving teams with members from all levels of the organization), and much more familiarity with information-processing technologies than ever before. Both organizational managers and community practitioners need to learn who the relevant group and organizational decision makers are for projects they are concerned about, as well as how those systems operate.

Social Learning Theory

Behavioral approaches to social work practice are usually identified with various forms of individual and group therapy. They are based on the work of a number of important learning theorists such as I. P. Pavlov, B. F. Skinner, Joseph Wolpe, and Albert Bandura. Social learning ideas are also useful in community-based practice, especially in understanding and influencing the behavior of individuals and groups. For example, the process of developing effective organization leaders, satisfied staff members, and influential social action strategies can benefit from understanding and using social learning concepts and principles.

The basic assumption of social learning theory is that human behavior is learned during interactions with other persons and with the social environment. This is not to deny the presence of biological or psychological processes that produce emotions and thoughts. However, little credence is given to the idea that some sort of internal personality governs behavior. Thus learning theorists are much more interested in observable behaviors and in the factors that produce and modify these behaviors.

A shorthand way of thinking about the factors that produce or modify behavior—that is, the *contingencies* of social learning—is as *cues, cognitions, consequences* (Silver, 1980). In Silver's words, "To understand social action, social learning looks to cues that occur prior in time, mental processes (cognitions) that mediate them, and rewarding or punishing consequences that follow. There is also feedback from consequences to cuing and thinking for future behavior. All together, these are the social learning *contingencies*" (p. 13).

One major form of learned behavior is called *respondent learning*, sometimes referred to as *clas-*

sical or *Pavlovian conditioning*. Examples of respondent behaviors include autonomic nervous system responses such as perspiring, salivating, and fight-or-flight reactions, as well as many fears, anxieties, and phobias. Respondent behavior is essentially learned through prior *cues* that produce an innate or unlearned response, such as the response to the smell of food when one is hungry, or to a strong reprimand. When an unconditioned stimulus (one that elicits an innate response) is paired with a neutral stimulus or event, that is, one that evokes little or no response, the neutral stimulus may acquire a similar ability to arouse a pleasurable or painful response. Thus the citizen who speaks at a legislative hearing, which was originally a neutral event, and is strongly attacked by a powerful opponent may be fearful of speaking at or even attending a legislative hearing in the future. This new response is considered a conditioned response, a behavior learned through pairing of a conditioned stimulus with an unconditioned stimulus that elicited a painful reaction.

Operant behavior, the other major form of learned behavior, refers to activities that can be consciously controlled, such as talking or studying; it is influenced primarily by the positive or negative *consequences* that follow it in time. These consequences are commonly referred to as *rewards* or *punishments*. Behavior that is rewarded, or positively reinforced, usually is maintained or increased, whereas behavior that is punished or not reinforced has a lower probability of being repeated. Praise and attention are common examples of positive reinforcers; disapproval or a physical slap are examples of negative reinforcers or aversive stimuli. The supply of positive and negative reinforcers is endless, although which is which depends a great deal on how the individual thinks or feels about it. That is to say, one's behavior is mediated by one's *cognitions*.

Social learning theory recognizes the importance of cognition in understanding and modifying human behavior. The human capacity to think and feel and to reflect on thoughts and perceptions, to believe, to remember the past and anticipate the future, and to develop goals—all of these affect how we behave. Social cognitive theory posits a model of reciprocal causation in which "behavior, cognition and other personal factors, and environmental influences all operate as interacting determinants that influence each other bidirectionally" (Bandura, 1989, p. 2). Thus, if I am a community worker, the manner in which I go about recruiting a prospect to join an AIDS education coalition may be influenced by how competent I think I am as a recruiter

(cognition). My success may also be affected by the prospect's prior positive or negative experiences with coalitions (consequences), as well as his or her strong belief in or skepticism about the value of coalitions for addressing a particular problem (cognition). If I succeed in forming the coalition, I will have modified the environment for addressing the AIDS problem, and this, in turn, may influence skeptics to join the effort, which may alter my perceptions of my personal competence or self-efficacy, and so on, in a continuous interactive causal chain involving behavior, cognition, and the environment.

The concepts of *perceived individual self-efficacy* and *collective efficacy* are particularly useful for community practitioners. Perceived individual self-efficacy may be viewed as self-appraisal of one's ability to determine and successfully carry out a goal-oriented course of action (Bandura, 1986). This perception stands between one's actual skills and knowledge and what one does in a given situation. So, for example, while a practitioner's skills may be quite good, his or her self-appraisal of the adequacy of these skills will affect how that worker performs. A practitioner whose perceived self-efficacy is low may often avoid challenges; the worker whose self-appraisal of efficacy is high may take them on.

When individuals give up trying to accomplish a goal because they judge their skills to be inadequate, we can say that they have *low efficacy expectations*. When they feel confident but give up trying because they are up against unyielding obstacles or unresponsive environments, we can say that they have *low outcome expectations* (Bandura, 1982). In the latter case, this inaction is akin to the concept of *learned helplessness* (Seligman, 1975), a state of mind that comes about after repeated failure to exert influence over the decisions that affect one's life. Still, some people keep on trying even after repeated failure. How can this apparent anomaly be explained?

Abramson, Seligman, and Teasdale's (1978) reformulation of learned helplessness takes a step in this direction by positing the concepts of *personal and universal helplessness*. When individuals believe they cannot work out problems that they should be able to solve—others do solve them—they feel personally helpless. They themselves are at fault. But when they judge that nobody can solve the problem—it is beyond anyone's control—they experience universal helplessness. Putting the various concepts together (Pecukonis & Wenocur, 1994), if we consider the idea of high perceived self-efficacy and low or high outcome expectancy (the degree of responsiveness of the environment), we can imagine several different states of mind and accompanying action-oriented or political kinds of behavior. Persons whose self-appraisal of efficacy is high and who have been successful in influencing decisions that affect their lives or their external environments develop a sense of *universal hopefulness*. They believe that they can succeed and that others can as well, and so they are willing to take action on behalf of change when needed. Persons with high perceived self-efficacy and low outcome expectations because of an unrewarding or unresponsive environment may develop a sense of *personal hopefulness* if they believe they are not personally responsible for their failures but see that the system is deficient. Such individuals are likely to mistrust the political system and, under certain conditions, will engage in militant protest to change it (Bandura, 1982). Being personally hopeful, they believe they can succeed even if the system tries to stop them. Persons who are angry at political and social injustice and who have a hopeful frame of mind often make excellent leaders in community planning and social advocacy efforts.

Applying the concept of efficacy to group life, *collective efficacy* can be defined as a shared perception (conscious or unconscious) that the members of a group hold about the group's ability to achieve its objectives (Pecukonis & Wenocur, 1994). Collective efficacy includes, but is more than the sum of, the individual members' perceptions of their own efficacy, because it is a property that pertains to the group as a whole, like the notion of group solidarity. A positive sense of collective efficacy is shaped by the experiences of the members in the group and by the group's interactions, as a group, with its external environment. At the same time, these experiences may also contribute greatly to the feeling of personal self-efficacy that each member comes to hold. When the collectivity is a social action group, successful experiences will greatly enhance feelings of personal worth and empowerment. Experiential learning (connecting experiences with knowing about oneself and the world) also create opportunities for political consciousness raising (Gowdy, 1994), an important ingredient in overcoming oppression, which will be discussed later.

Reality Construction

Helping clients gain a greater degree of power over the organizations and institutions that shape their lives is an important goal of social work practice. In the previous section, we proposed that both clients and social workers are more likely to take a step in that direction if they see the world as potentially changeable rather than fixed. To a large extent, this view of the world depends on the meanings that individuals attach to objects and events. In the words of Saleebey (1994), "Practice is an intersection where the meanings of the worker (theories), the client (stories and narratives), and culture (myths, rituals, and themes) meet. Social workers must open themselves up to clients' constructions of their individual and collective worlds" (p. 351).

But how do we develop our understanding of events and objects that make up everyday life? The theory of reality construction advanced by Peter Berger and Thomas Luckmann in *The Social Construction of Reality* (1967) suggests that those understandings come about through social processes. Objective facts do not exist apart from the subjective meanings that people attach to them as they are being perceived. "Men *together* produce a human environment, with the totality of its socio-cultural and psychological formations" (Berger & Luckmann, p. 51). Therefore, as the book title suggests, the everyday reality that people experience is not simply a confrontation of facts and objects; it is socially constructed. So, for example, in any society, people hold different kinds and amounts of riches, but the meaning of *rich*—who is rich and who is poor, what constitutes wealth and poverty—is subjectively experienced, socially defined, incorporated into individual consciousness or internalized through a process of socialization, and eventually taken as truth or reality. This latter process, "the process by which the externalized products of human activity attain the character of objectivity is [called] *objectivation* [italics added]" (Berger & Luckmann, p. 60).

The source of the objectivation process is that human beings are by biological necessity social animals. Humans must interact with other humans and with the various elements in their external environments in order to survive and grow, and to do this they need a certain degree of stability or order. This process of ongoing interaction with the external world is called *externalization* (Berger & Luckmann, 1967, p. 56). Social order and interpretations of reality are created through this process as people talk with each other about their experiences and validate their understanding of them, and as they develop established ways of doing things to accomplish their goals. Established behavior patterns and expectations, embodied in the ideas of roles and role behavior, lead, in turn, to the development of institutions, which strongly influence the meanings that the members of society take as truth (Greene & Blundo, 1999).

For example, the family is an institution whose meaning is very much in flux in U.S. society. Different segments of society are contending for acceptance of their definitions of family and, in fact, for a more inclusive definition of family, based on new and different roles for men and women and changing social and economic conditions. The traditional nuclear family in which Mom stays home with the kids and Dad is the breadwinner, if there ever was such a family, has given way to many different kinds of families— families in which both parents work, where one parent is absent, where divorce and remarriage have resulted in blended families, where same-sex parents and children constitute a family unit, and so on. And just as the meaning of family is changing, so is the meaning of home and marriage.

The relationship between human beings as the creators of reality and the reality that is the product of the process is a dialectical one. Thus the constructions that human beings produce—for example, the language they use, the meanings they derive, the roles they develop, and the organizations they form—all influence future constructions in a continuous back-and-forth process. "Externalization and objectivation are moments in a continuing dialectical process" (Berger & Luckmann, 1967, p. 61). So, the social order that human existence requires and creates is an order that is constantly being recreated as we negotiate our daily lives together. For community workers who must frequently help their clients as well as themselves in negotiating complicated bureaucratic systems to get resources to survive and perform valued social roles, reality is neither predetermined nor fixed for all time. Moreover, it is incumbent on practitioners to validate the experiences of the individuals and groups with whom they work—their realities.

Symbols, especially language, represent the major currency of social interaction through a body of conventionalized signs and shared rules for their usage. People give meaning and structure to their experiences through language and other symbols, and language, in turn, structures our thinking and beliefs. Feminists, for example, have argued that language is a major source of categorical thinking and helps to sustain the patriarchal order. In this view, *male* is a dominant category and "whatever is *not male* is female" (Sands & Nuccio, 1992, p. 491). Similarly, ethno-

centric thinking expressed in census reports has, until recently, treated *whites* as a dominant category, while African-Americans have been defined as *nonwhites*. Thus, language does not merely convey information "but is believed to thoroughly mediate everything that is known" (Pardeck, Murphy, & Choi, 1994, p. 343). Because language can be detached from the here and now, people can use it to record and pass on the past as well as to imagine the future. Language thereby helps to translate individual subjective experiences into objective reality and collective experiences into cultural knowledge. We live in a symbolic universe. Think about the meanings attached to, say, the flag of the United States versus the flag of the Confederacy. Think about the struggle of the United Farm Workers and the role of the Aztec blue eagle in that struggle. Think about the meaning of the historical "truth" so many of us learned in elementary school, that Columbus discovered America, despite the obvious fact that a people already lived on this continent when Columbus arrived.

Human organizations and institutions develop their own cultures and ideologies reflecting the composition of their membership and their most powerful stakeholders. And sometimes institutions become *reified*; that is, they seem to take on a life of their own or to exist as entities apart from their human origins and makeup. "Reification implies that man is capable of forgetting his own authorship of the human world, and further, that the dialectic between man, the producer, and his products is lost to consciousness" (Berger & Luckmann, 1967, p. 89). The expression, "You can't fight City Hall," for example, implies that City Hall exists apart from the politicians and workers who make it up, and that it is something not subject to human influence. Social work's traditional low-income constituents, along with many social workers, often hold this version of reality. Another common example of reification occurs when an organization becomes well established and then begins to lose its vitality because its members assume that the organization can continue to function effectively without their fresh energy, ideas, and leadership. Thus, not only do organizations need to continue bringing new members on board, but the newcomers need to be socialized in a manner that values their vigor and creativity.

The third moment in the process of reality construction, *internalization*, refers to the incorporation of socially defined meanings into one's own consciousness though a process of socialization. Socialization itself may be defined as "the comprehensive and consistent induction of an individual into the objective world of a society or a segment of it" (Berger & Luckmann, 1967, p. 130). Primary socialization occurs early in childhood when the significant persons in a child's life basically teach the child what the world is about and how to behave in it. During this process, the significant others necessarily filter objective reality for the child through the lenses of their own selective definitions and personal idiosyncracies. As the child bonds emotionally with these significant persons, she or he begins to establish an identity that is partially a reflection of the socializing agents. As a child continues to grow and relate to an expanding and ever more complex universe, secondary socialization into many new subworlds proceeds, mainly though the acquisition of role-related knowledge and skills.

The socially constructed realities produced through internalization are stabilized or altered on the microlevel as individuals test their plausibility against the new information and alternative definitions they are constantly receiving. At the macrolevel, as new generations arise, the institutional order itself requires explanation and justification, that is, legitimation, as it is tested against changing external conditions and challenged by ideologies that run counter to established beliefs. For example, as medical knowledge and the capacity to sustain premature infants expanded, the belief that life begins at birth was strongly challenged in the 1980s by the counterideology that life begins at conception. Thus will each successive generation have to construct its own complex reality.

Constructionist theory has implications for social work practice. Social phenomena such as health, crime, and normalcy cannot be defined simply in terms of empirical, objective facts. They are embedded in a "web of meanings, created and sustained linguistically" (Pardeck et al., 1994, p. 345), that make up our own and our clients' worlds. Effective social work practice requires skill in communications to understand and enter the assumptive worlds of our clients. The practitioner with such skill will be better able to make informed, sensitive assessments of client system problems, unhindered by potentially stereotypical and inappropriate diagnostic taxonomies (Pozatek, 1994; Saleebey, 1994). Thus "clients are not merely consulted through the use of individualized treatment plans . . . but supply the interpretive context that is required for determining the nature of a presenting problem, a proper intervention, or a successful treatment outcome. This is true client-centered intervention" (Pardeck et al., 1994, p. 345). From a macroperspective, a constructionist approach also suggests that social workers help clients understand "the oppressive effects of dominant power institutions" (Saleebey, 1994, p. 358) and tune in to the countervailing knowledge available in their own communities (Reisch, Sherman, & Wenocur, 1981).

Social Exchange Theory and Power

In that people act in their own interests, whether economic, social, or psychological, exchange is the act of obtaining a desired commodity from someone by offering something valued by the other party. Commodities exchanged can include adoration and praise for job security, information for status, sexual favors for protection, and influence for political donations. Whether exchange actually takes place depends on whether the two parties can arrive at terms that will leave each of them better off or at least not worse off, in their own estimation, after the exchange, compared with alternative exchanges possible and available to them. (See rivalry and cooperation in game theory, Nasar, 2001, Chapter 49.)

Social exchange theory, associated with theorists such as George C. Homans (1974), Peter M. Blau (1964), and Richard Emerson (1962), forms another conceptual building block for community practice. Built on the operant conditioning aspects of social learning theory and an economic view of human relationships as concerned with maximization of rewards or profits and minimization of punishments or costs, exchange theory underlies such skills as bargaining, negotiating, advocating, networking, and marketing. The part of exchange theory that deals with power and dependency is especially pertinent to community practice.

Community practice takes place in an action or exchange field. In terms of exchange theory, the exchange field represents a market consisting of two or more parties who interact with each other, at different times and in various combinations, to exchange desired resources or products. These resources can be tangible or intangible. They can include counseling and community organization services, money (a proxy for other products), information, ideas, political influence, goodwill, compliant behavior, meanings, and energy. For transactions to occur, the involved parties require information about the products to be exchanged and a desire for the exchange product(s). Given relevant information and desire, exchange theory holds that parties in a transaction select from all possible exchanges those that have the greatest ratio of benefits or rewards to costs. In social exchanges, this calculus is seldom as precise as in economic exchanges. For example, in a contribution to a United Way campaign, the donor is giving dollars (an easily measurable unit), but the products received in return—say, social status, community improvement, and assistance to people in need—are not easily measurable or readily comparable with alternative products for the donor's money.

All of the parties in an exchange field do not necessarily have relationships with each other at any given point in time. Two agencies, for example, might not have any transactions, but both might transact business with the same third organization. When Party A in an exchange field (be it an individual, a group, or an organization) can accomplish its goals without relating to Party B, and vice versa, these parties can be said to be *independent* of each other. However, as soon as either party cannot achieve its ends without obtaining some needed product or resource from the other and exchanges begin to occur, they can be considered *interdependent*. Usually, interdependent relationships are not perfectly balanced; that is, Party A may need the resources that Party B controls much more than B needs what A has to offer. In fact, B may not need what A can offer at all. In this extremely imbalanced situation, A may be said to be *dependent* on B. This imbalance in exchange relationships sets the stage for relations of power or influence among the members of an exchange field.

Stated most simply, in an exchange relationship, *power is a function of the ability to control the resources that another party needs.* To the extent that Party B has control over the resources that Party A must have in order to accomplish its goals, B has power over A. In that relationship, B's position is one of independence. B can, if it chooses, exercise its power over A by making its exchange of resources with A contingent on A's compliance with certain requirements. A is in a *power-dependent* position with respect to B in their exchange relationship. Consider the relationship between the social worker and the client through this lens (Cowger, 1994). Hearkening back to the contingencies of social learning, favorable exchange is a contingency of A's compliant behavior. If B also wants some of the resources that A controls—and remember that those resources may be tangible or intangible (e.g., money, services, goodwill)—then the relationship is interdependent, although weighted more in favor of one party than the other. These

parties have mutual dependencies, albeit in different degrees.

Suppose, for example, that the local health clinic would like financial support from the United Way for its AIDS Outreach Project, and right now that is the clinic's only hope for funding. In that exchange relationship, the United Way has power with respect to the clinic because it controls the resources that the clinic needs. Theoretically, if the United Way chose, it could establish preconditions (contingencies) for obtaining those funds, such as requiring the clinic to coordinate its services with an existing United Way–affiliated agency like the Family Services Society. More typical United Way preconditions usually include reporting requirements, a financial audit, and an agreement not to raise funds during the United Way campaign. Now, to the extent, say, that the United Way has been under pressure in the media to become more responsive to community needs, it might view the AIDS Outreach Project as a highly desirable prospect for funding. Therefore the United Way might be willing to relax its reporting or audit requirements to make it easier for the clinic to affiliate.

Parties who need resources that others control can engage in various *power-balancing strategies* in order to bring about more favorable exchanges. For the sake of discussion, let us consider Party A an as *action organization*, a community group that is trying to get resources from Party B, a *target organization*, say, a large private university in the area that has resources that A needs. Since A, the community group, is in a dependent position in this situation, B, the university, holds power with respect to A. In order to reduce B's power, A can adopt one of two approaches. Either A can find some way to decrease its dependency on B or A can find some way to increase B's dependency on A. These approaches lend themselves to the following power-balancing strategies: competition, revaluation, reciprocity, coalition, and coercion. Each of these strategies will now be described.

COMPETITION

This strategy requires Party A to find other ways to meet its goals than making exchanges with Party B. So long as B has a monopoly on the resources that A needs, A will be dependent and B will have power. If A can get needed resources from Parties F and G, then B's power will be reduced.

Suppose that A (the community group) would like B (the university) to donate, or sell at a low price, a parcel of land for a community recreation center. So long as A's goal is to build the recreation center and it needs this land, and there is no other place to get it except from B, B has power in relation to A. As a consequence, if both parties are willing to make an exchange, B could potentially force A, for example, to support a piece of controversial legislation before the city council. If there are other land-holding institutions in the community—say, a couple of churches (F and G) to which A might turn for inexpensive land, then B's power over A will be reduced.

REEVALUATION

In this strategy, because of either value or ideological changes, A becomes less interested in the resources that B controls, and B accordingly loses power over A. In situations such as this, the target organization, B, may try to maintain A's dependency on it by offering A inducements or new advantages to sustain the exchange relationship.

For example, A (the community group) may lose interest in its goal of building a recreation center because the level of community violence has increased, causing A to put its energy into a different issue: developing a community policing effort. B, the university, no longer has a resource that A needs, and it cannot use its relationship to get B's support on the controversial legislation it seeks to have enacted. Because B believes it might need A's support in the future, B may offer to contribute money or training to A's community policing effort or to lower the price of the land that A originally wanted for its recreation center.

RECIPROCITY

Here A seeks to find a resource that it controls that Party B would like. If A can thus make itself more attractive to B as a potential trading partner, then the dependent relationship could be transformed into an interdependent one, and A could achieve a more equitable balance of power.

Continuing the above illustration, if A (the community group) can gain control over a parcel of land that B (the university) would like for expanded student parking, then A owns a desirable resource. A might be able to use this resource to negotiate a favorable exchange with B, thereby achieving some balance of power in the relationship.

COALITION

A by itself may not be able to exert much influence over B. The same may also be true of C and D in their exchange relationships with B. But if A can coalesce with C and D, together each

may control some portion of what the target organization, B, needs. A and the other parties may thereby reduce their dependency by working out a more evenhanded relationship with B.

Let's say that A, C, and D are all community groups that are trying to influence the university's (B's) parking policy in the community. Although individually none of these organizations may be able to exert much influence over B, together they may be able to control enough votes on the city zoning commission to get B to adopt a more favorable parking policy for the community. These votes may even be important enough to the university to get it to lower the price of the land that A, the coalition leader, wants for the recreation center.

COERCION

Coercion is often defined as the use of physical force or intimidation (economic, reputational, etc.) to compel one party to do what the other party wants. Since threats, blackmail, or actual harm to persons and property are normally illegal and immoral, this strategy falls outside the bounds of professional acceptability. We would distinguish physical coercion from political coercion and from the use of disruptive tactics that are normally legal, such as sit-ins, rallies, strikes, or media blitzes. Social change authors Bobo, Kendall, and Max observe that a tactic available to social action groups is depriving "the other side of something it wants" (2001, p. 13).

In the above illustration, if A were to threaten to do harm to B's personnel or property in an effort to get B to sell its property cheaply, this would constitute an illegal form of coercion. However, if A organized a large demonstration of students and community residents outside the university president's office as a means of pressuring B to change its decision about selling the property by creating unfavorable public opinion, this could be an acceptable strategy. We would consider this a form of reciprocity, namely, gaining control over a resource needed by A— favorable public opinion—rather than inappropriate coercion. (Bobo, Kendall, and Max would regard it as conventional straight-up power politics.)

Although the dynamics of power and exchange are important, many transactions in an exchange field do not carry heavy overtones of power. People are constantly relating to one another, exchanging information, and sharing resources without trying to extract advantages from the transaction. In fact, the more people exchange resources with each other, the greater the likelihood that reciprocal obligations will develop and that these will be governed by norms of fairness. As positive relationships develop, exchange partners who each obtain a desirable resource may be attracted to one another and may form cohesive associations such as support groups, networks, new organizations, coalitions, and the like.

In general, within the framework of social exchange theory, it is important to note that exchanges involving power require building relationships among people, making connections where none may have existed previously, and creating interdependencies. Since the potential for building relationships with other people is limitless, the implication is that power is neither limited as a resource nor confined to a set group of people. Rather, power can be viewed as a dynamic resource that is ever expandable. In the words of Lappé and Du Bois (1994), "Power as it is being lived and learned, is neither fixed nor one-way. It is fluid. Based on relationships, it is dynamic. It changes as the attitudes and behavior of any party change. This understanding of power offers enormous possibilities: it suggests that by conscious attention to the importance of one's own actions, one can change others—even those who, under the old view of power, appear immovable. All this allows us to discover new sources of power within our reach" (p. 54).

Note also that the coalitional power-balancing strategy, in particular, underlies all community organization practice. It suggests that if individuals or groups by themselves do not have sufficient power to influence the decisions that affect their lives, they need to join forces with other people—friends, confederates, others who have power—so that together they can create new sources of influence that alone they did not possess.

Interorganizational Theory

Much community practice involves establishing and managing relationships with other groups and organizations. The selection of theoretical material thus far presented provides the groundwork for many of the ideas that help us understand these interorganizational relations. In this section, we try to understand the behavior of groups and organizations rather than individuals, so conceptually, in interorganizational relationships, the unit of analysis is the organization or organizational subunit rather than the individual.

The fundamental (by now obvious) idea in interorganizational theory is that every organization is embedded in a larger network of groups and organizations that it must relate to in order to survive and prosper. Within this interorganizational network or exchange field, each organization must carve out a specific *domain*, or sphere of operation. Levine and White (1961, 1963) did the seminal work on domain theory. An agency's *domain* is the claim for resources the agency stakes out for itself based on its purpose and objectives. The organizational domain usually involves some combination of (a) human problem or need, (b) population or clientele, (c) technology or treatment methods, (d) geographic or catchment area, and (e) sources of fiscal and nonfiscal resources. While some of the domain may be shared and other parts may be in dispute, all parts cannot be shared or be in dispute if the agency is to maintain itself as a separate entity. For example, although there may be overlap, no two organizations serving the homeless will have identical domains. One may serve only men and the other, families. One may refuse substance abusers; another may accept all who come but require attendance at religious meetings. Geographic boundaries may vary. Some organizations may include an advocacy function and others, only service.

The domain of an organization identifies the points at which it must relate to and rely on other organizations to fulfill its mission. Mother's Kitchen, which provides hot meals to the needy in South Bostimore, will need serving, eating, and storage facilities, a supply of volunteers, a supply of food, health department approval, and so on. Joe's Van, which supplies coffee and sandwiches on winter weekends to homeless persons in South Bostimore, will need different kinds of volunteers, facilities, and supplies. Depending on an organization's domain, then, we can readily see that the structure and dynamics of its external environment will have a lot to do with the organization's ability to achieve its objectives. In some environments, resources are scarce; in others, plentiful. So, volunteers may be relatively easy or hard to find. There may or may not be a food bank to draw on for inexpensive staples. Some environments have many competitors or regulations, others few. Complex organizations in dynamic environments may also have specialized positions or even whole departments to assist them in handling environmental transactions—for example, a director of volunteers, a public relations department, and a lobbyist or governmental affairs division.

It is useful to conceptualize the set of external organizations and organizational subunits that a focal organization must deal with to accomplish its goals as a *task environment* (Thompson, 1967). The task environment is the specific set of organizations, agencies, groups, and individuals with which the agency may exchange resources and services and with which it establishes specific modes of interaction, either competitive or cooperative, to achieve its goals and fulfill its mission. It is the part of the environment that can positively or negatively affect the agency's functioning and survival (Wernet, 1994; Zald, 1970). The task environment is influenced by the general environment's level of resources, the competition for resources by all alternative demands, the social ideology and philosophy of need meeting, and the socioeconomic demographics of the population (age distribution, family composition, income distribution, economic base, and so forth). To give but one example, the voluntary sector in a particular locale can be rich or poor (Mulroy & Shay, 1997, p. 517). Thus, families have many or few choices and helpers; this in turn affects a given agency. The resources in the task environment do not constitute a system; they are merely a set of things until they are organized into a system to support the agency and its mission and objectives (Evan, 1963). While the concept of *external environment* is somewhat abstract and amorphous, the task environment concept can be delineated quite specifically. The task environment consists of six categories of components (Hasenfeld, 1983, pp. 61–63; Thompson, 1967), which will now be described. For any given organization, some environmental units may fit into more than one category.

1. *Providers of fiscal resources, labor, materials, equipment, and work space.* These may include providers of grants, contributions, fees for products or services, bequests, and so on. Organizations often have multiple sources of funds. Mother's Kitchen may receive federal funds channeled through the local mayor's office of homelessness services, as well as contributions from a sponsoring church. At the same time, Mother's Kitchen may receive space from a local church, office supplies from a local stationer, and maintenance supplies from a janitorial products company. The school of social work may be an important source of labor via fieldwork interns.

2. *Providers of legitimation and authority.* These may include regulatory bodies, accrediting groups, and individuals or organizations that lend their prestige, support, or authority to the organization. The Council on Social Work Education (CSWE) accredits schools of social work. A school of social work may lend its support to a local agency's continuing education program. The dean of the school may serve on the board of directors of an agency serving the homeless, along with client representatives from the homeless union.

3. *Providers of clients or consumers.* These include those very important individuals and groups who make referrals to the agency, as well as the individuals and families who seek out the organization's services directly. The department of public welfare may be a major referral source of clients for Mother's Kitchen. Other clients may come on their own as word of mouth passes around on the streets. The South Bostimore Community Association may be a major source of referrals for a new health maintenance organization started by the local university hospital.

4. *Providers of complementary services.* These include other organizations whose products or services are needed by an organization in order to successfully do its job. Mother's Kitchen may use the university medical school for psychiatric consultations and a drug treatment center for substance abuse counseling services. The welfare department provides income maintenance for homeless families who use Mother's Kitchen.

5. *Consumers and recipients of an organization's products or services.* Social service agencies cannot operate without clients, a community organization cannot operate without members, and a school of social work must have students. Clients and consumers are critical to justifying an organization's legitimacy and claims for resources. So the consumers of an agency's services are the clients themselves, voluntarily or involuntarily, together with their social networks. Other organizations may also be consumers of an agency's products. For example, employers need to be available and willing to hire the graduates of the welfare department's employment training programs.

6. *Competitors.* Few organizations operate with a monopoly on consumers or clients and other resources necessary for them to function. With human service organizations, other such agencies are frequently competing for the same clients or for fiscal resources from similar sources. Several schools of social work in the same city may compete for students and will try to carve out unique domains to reach into different markets to ensure a flow of ap-

plicants. Similarly, private family agencies are competing for clients with social work private practitioners and psychotherapists. Since resources for social services are invariably scarce, the ability to compete successfully is almost always a fact of life for organization managers.

The power and exchange relations discussed in the previous section govern a good deal of interorganizational behavior. This is because the member units of an organization's task environment represent interdependencies that the organization must establish and manage successfully to operate in its domain. Clearly, to the extent that an environmental unit has some of the resources that your organization needs to carry out its business, that unit has power with respect to your organization. Furthermore, if your organization cannot establish the requisite interdependencies—and competitors could make that difficult—it will not be able to carve out a workable domain. Thus, Mother's Kitchen cannot operate as a soup kitchen without passing a state health department sanitation inspection and a city fire department safety inspection. Nor will your church be able to establish its homeless shelter without the approval of its neighbors. And a grant agency such as a state department of mental health or a private foundation is usually in a good position to dictate the terms of compliance for the dollars it awards.

Interorganizational relations become truly interesting when we think about the concepts of domain and task environment as dynamic rather than static entities. Imagine an exchange field with multiple individuals, groups, and organizations, each of which has its own domains and task environments but all of which are at least loosely connected, directly and indirectly, as would be the case, for example, in the city of Bostimore's homelessness sector." Since Bostimore is a city of 650,000 people and since homelessness is a complicated problem, hundreds of organizations provide different kinds of services to, and advocate for, homeless individuals and families. While enough order or consensus exists for these organizations to be able to get the resources they need to function (i.e., there is some level of *domain consensus* among the organizational players), thousands of exchanges are taking place. New organizational relationships are being formed and old ones altered, new needs and new information are emerging, new ideas are being created, available resources are shifting with political and economic developments, new players are entering the scene and

old ones exiting, new domains are being carved out in response to new opportunities and constraints, and so on. No organizational domain is static. Modern organizational life, in short, is really interorganizational life, and it involves a continuous process of negotiation in a complex, constantly changing, and highly unpredictable environment (Aldrich, 1979; Emery & Trist, 1965).

Conflict Theory

There is perhaps a natural tendency among human beings to search for social order and organization in their lives. Hence the processes of socialization and social control that support order seem very acceptable, while processes involving social conflict often make us uncomfortable. Yet, as we said earlier, disorder is also a natural and inevitable aspect of human life. Thus the dialectical conflict perspective in sociology, as propounded by theoreticians such as Karl Marx and Ralf Dahrendorf, can further inform social work practice.

Although their images of society differ, Marx and Dahrendorf share some basic assumptions about the nature of society (Turner, 1978) that help us to see social systems as dynamic entities. Both believe that (a) social systems systematically generate conflict, and therefore conflict is a pervasive feature of society; (b) conflict is generated by the opposed interests that are inevitably part of the social structure of society; (c) opposed interests derive from an unequal distribution of scarce resources and power among dominant and subordinate groups, and hence every society rests on the constraint of some of its members by others; (d) different interests tend to polarize into two conflict groups; (e) conflict is dialectical, that is, the resolution of one conflict creates a new set of opposed interests, which, under certain conditions, spawn further conflict; and (f) as a result of the ongoing conflict, social change is a pervasive feature of society.

For Marx, conflict is rooted in the economic organization of society, especially the ownership of property and the subsequent class structure that evolves. Production (the means by which men and women create their daily subsistence) is a central aspect of Marxist thought. It influences cultural values and beliefs, religion, other systems of ideas, social relations, and the formation of a class structure. Under capitalism, the means of production (factories, corporations) are owned by capitalists rather than by the workers.

Because workers must now depend on capitalists to be able to earn a living, they are rendered powerless and exploitable. Labor becomes a commodity to be bought and sold, moved and shaped, as the needs of capital dictate. In the modern world, Marx would argue that the movement of corporations to different parts of the United States or to foreign countries to gain tax advantages and find cheap labor is a manifestation of the commoditization process. But capitalism also contains the seeds of its own destruction (dialectical materialism). Therefore, as alienation sets in among the workers, a revolutionary class consciousness begins to develop. The workers begin to challenge the decisions of the ruling class, ultimately seeking to overthrow the system and replace capitalism with socialism.

For Dahrendorf (1959), writing a century after Marx, industrial strife in modern capitalist society represents only one important sphere of conflict. Still, conflict is pervasive, having a structural origin in the relations of dominance and submission that accompany social roles in any organized social system from a small group or formal organization to a community or even an entire society. If an authority structure exists, that is, a structure of roles containing power differentials, Dahrendorf calls these social systems *imperatively coordinated associations* (ICAs). The differing roles in ICAs lead to the differentiation of two quasi-groups with opposing latent interests. These quasi-groups are not yet organized, but when they become conscious of their mutual positions, they do organize into manifest interest groups that conflict over power and resources. This conflict eventually leads to change in the structure of social relationships. The nature, rapidity, and depth of the resultant change depend on empirically variable conditions, such as the degree of social mobility in the society and the sanctions that the dominant group can impose.

The transformation of an aggregate of individuals who share a set of common, oppressive conditions into an interest group that will engage in conflict to change the situation is critical for conflict theorists and has relevance for social work advocates and community practitioners. A main ingredient of that transformation seems to be the development of an awareness or consciousness of one's relative state of deprivation and the illegitimate positions of those in power. In a manual on consciousness-raising (CR) groups, for example, the National Organization for Women (NOW) wrote that "Feminist CR has one basic purpose: it raises the woman's consciousness, increases her complete awareness, of

her oppression in a sexist society" (NOW, 1982, p. 3). Thus, *political CR* may be defined as the method by which an oppressed group comes to understand its condition and becomes activated politically to change it (Berger, 1976, p. 122). But developing this awareness is not so easy. Marx argued that human beings are victims of a false consciousness born of the exploitive power of the capitalist system. For Gramsci, a neo-Marxist, an alliance of ruling-class factions maintains hegemony over the subordinate classes by means of *ideology* spread by the state, the media, and other powerful cultural institutions (Hall, 1977):

> This means that the "definitions of reality," favorable to the dominant class fractions, and institutionalized in the spheres of civil life and the state, come to constitute the primary "lived reality" as such for the subordinate classes. . . . This operates, not because the dominant classes can prescribe and proscribe, in detail, the mental content of the lives of subordinate classes (they too "live" in their own ideologies), but because they strive and to a degree succeed in *framing* all competing definitions of reality *within their range*, bringing all alternatives within their horizon of thought. They set the limits—mental and structural—within which subordinate classes "live" and make sense of their subordination in such a way as to sustain the dominance of those ruling over them. (pp. 332–333)

A capitalist system thus finds myriad ways to induce people to believe that happiness lies in the pursuit and achievement of material ends.

Just how and why the transformation into a conflict group takes place is not entirely clear, for many latent interest groups exist under cruel conditions without organizing for change. Both Marx and Dahrendorf, however, do stress the importance of leadership in this process. "For an organized interest group to emerge from a quasi-group, there have to be certain persons who make this organization their business, who carry it out practically and take the lead" (Dahrendorf, 1959, p. 185). In addition, it seems clear that the prospective members of this interest group have to be able to communicate their grievances to each other, that physical proximity helps, and that freedom of association may aid the process, although conflict groups have certainly emerged in totalitarian regimes (Dahrendorf, 1959; Turner, 1978).

Marxist and neo-Marxist theory applied to the role of the state in capitalist society also has special relevance for social workers because many social workers either work directly for government agencies or work in nonprofit organizations in programs funded with state dollars. Unlike conservative political economists, who want to greatly reduce the role of the state in regulating market system activities and its human costs, and unlike liberals, who view the state as a potential leveling force for reducing income disparities and alleviating distress, Marxist analysts view the state in a more complicated fashion. In the long term, they see it as serving the interests of the ruling class by maintaining social harmony (Piven & Cloward, 1971) and preparing a low-wage work force. On an ongoing basis, they argue that the state mirrors the contradictions in the capitalist system, hence it is an arena for ideological and practical struggles over the distribution of income, benefits, and rights (Corrigan & Leonard, 1979). In the words of Fabricant and Burghardt (1992), "To them, class struggle is not a simplistic 'war' between workers and owners, but an ongoing, complex, and contentious relationship among actors in the state, in the economy, and in other social groups struggling over the direction and extent of state intervention. Ultimately, this struggle will either enhance the legitimacy of social services through a combination of expansion and restructuring . . . or encourage greater accumulation and unfettered private investment—with the resultant industrialization of social services" (p. 52).

If social workers and managers of social service agencies can become conscious of themselves as actors in this struggle, they can share their awareness and analysis with their clients, and they can resist treating the problems of individual clients only as private troubles rather than as systemic dysfunctions.

ADDITIONAL FRAMEWORKS

Explanatory frameworks based on concepts of motivation, ecology, critique, difference, and complexity can also be applied to community practice. Key ideas will be sketched here. Several of these frameworks relate to the *postmodern* school, a hard-to-define, multidisciplinary, intellectual movement—highly influential since the 1980s—that challenges prior modern theories and assumptions (Irving & Young, 2002; McCormack, 2001; Robbins, Chatterjee, & Canda, 1998; Vodde & Gallant, 2000; Walker, 2001). A significant component of many forms of postmodernism theories is their more explicit recognition of the political in social science theory.

Motivational Theory

Motivational theory, which examines why, when, and how people act or decline to act, is linked conceptually with emotions and notions of human nature (Oliner & Oliner, 1995). When investigating causes of human behavior, motivation theorists often elect an inner orientation, focusing on individual rather than collective behavior. Nonetheless, motivation theory draws from political science, sociology, economics, business, and advertising (the technology of motivation), in addition to psychology and philosophy, and has macro-applications.[1]

Numerous explanations regarding individual motives have been suggested, including hedonism, unconscious urges, instinct, drive, optimal arousal, self-actualization, multiple and inconsistent wants (Apter, 1999). In line with these, motivation theorists discuss culture or conscience variables and reinforcement or incentive factors. However, as practitioners discover, success in discerning motives does not confer the ability to predict or even to persuade. Moreover, an individual's own explanation may be untrustworthy. And yet, human agency (volition, proactivity) and individual decision making are affirmed in this tradition in contrast with views of the empty self.

In terms of individual involvement in communities, motives include egoism, altruism, collectivism, and principlism (Batson, Ahmad, & Tsang, 2002, pp. 434–440). Thus, the debate about *self-interest* (individual and group) versus *social responsibility* (Leiby, 1997; Olson, 1971; Wuthnow, 1991) is a dimension of motivation and the concepts of empathy, altruism, and humanitarianism are part of this literature (Davis, 1996; Monroe, 1994; Schwartz, 1993; Wuthnow, 1993). What explains why certain people care so much about or identify with others? Some writing addresses motivations of citizens who are galvanized to get involved and mobilize others. Reform motives can include moral indignation; duty and shame; a desire for affiliation, visibility, or immortality; or an enjoyment of being contrary or rebellious. In community practice, understanding our own motives leads to effective use of self, while understanding the motives of others spells the difference between project success and failure. Inevitably, when we organize, opponents and potential allies (Gitterman, 1994, p. x) question the motives of change leaders and their followers or the modes of motivation utilized, and we have to respond to charges of manipulation.

Community practitioners will be particularly interested in collective motivations that contribute to a sense of heightened mutuality and meaningful action at the macrolevel, in a civic culture (Gottsegen, 1994) or community context. Popular thinkers such as Bellah and Putnam are concerned about motivation and the civic culture, but so are traditional theorists such as Habermas. He writes about the "problem of motivation" that creates "civil privatism" or lack of participation in the public or civic realm (as cited in Wuthnow, Hunter, Bergesen, & Kurzweil, 1984, pp. 202–203). In the community context, collective motivation is written about largely in the social change literature (Mansbridge and Morris, 2001). Motivational theory underlies a hearts-and-minds-of-people community organizing approach rather than resource mobilization and other approaches.[2]

Ecological Theory

Ecological theory draws on environmental, biological, and anthropological precepts to highlight interconnections between the social surround and geographic and other factors. Numerous illustrations make the point. Rainforests are destroyed and humans are hurt as an incidental repercussion. Diseases are exchanged between England and France, and between Africa and the United States. U.S. movies and music influence cultures around the globe. Spicy foods from Third-World countries replace more bland food in Western diets. An ecological framework underscores such transactions, adaptations, and shaping (Kuper & Kuper, 1999[3]).

This theory reminds us that human beings have ever-changing physical and cultural environments. Suppose that within 50 years, as some have predicted, a third of the earth's people live in areas of earthquake and volcanic activity. How might this change in physical environment affect our grandchildren and the relationships between nations? Cultural environments also shape things as they change. For instance, a statue of President Franklin Roosevelt, seated in a wheelchair, was recently erected. It took group advocacy to create a new cultural perspective on a bygone leader who—because of the mores of his era—never let the public know how dependent he was on a wheelchair.

Ideas about ecology and ecosystems of human groups have influenced helping professions (Germain & Gittelman, 1995; Pardeck, 1996). Factors that affect social functioning and a new orientation for intervention include the following:

- Viewing context to be as important as the immediate situation
- Seeing how mutuality and interdependence suggest values and obligations beyond family, neighborhood or nation
- Examining ways communities organize to maintain themselves in given areas
- Looking for ecological, natural, and impersonal influences in addition to personal causes of human problems

To date, social work has highlighted primarily the immediate environment rather than community groups or societal forces; for a critique of this emphasis, see Beckett and Johnson, 1995; Elizur, 1995; and Gardella, 2000. What is certain is that the community environment comes into focus as we work to protect children. Ecological theory stresses interdependence between elements in an environment (Scherch, 2000). Here is a distressing example: The vitality or inaction of public health systems directly affects the number of children who are brain damaged due to lead poisoning each year. In fact, the physical environment (extent of lead paint), social environment (many low-income landlords), and regulatory environment (funding levels for city inspection) all have effects. In some cities, 9% of children have been affected. The macrolevel ecosystem includes more than the community level. Federal political appointments may have local repercussions. According to newspaper accounts, the Secretary of the Interior Norton (of the 2001 Bush administration) previously lobbied for a lead paint company. Fortunately, the number of lead poisoning cases has diminished due to local vigilance and lawsuits.

Critical Theory

Critical theorists have a macro-orientation, an interest in the social totality and the social production of meaning, and a "focus on criticizing and changing contemporary society" (Ritzer, 1992, p. 149). Developed in Frankfurt in the 1920s, critical theory continues to influence many disciplines and professions, in part because of the work of Jurgen Habermas on communication and discourse. Critical theory focuses on dominating institutions and how the system works, on large-scale capitalistic structures and how they intersect with local environments. It prompts compelling questions such as this one: "How is it possible that penal systems could have expanded so rapidly and that corporate interests could have become so ensconced in punishment practices without a significant critical discourse developing?" (Washington, 1999, p. 1).

In our information and technology age, critical theory's concerns with the culture and knowledge industries seem even more relevant than earlier concerns with the industrial means of production and work. In an era of expanding rights and global influences, its concern with ideology, domination, and consciousness is of interest. One critical legal studies scholar said of Habermas, "He seems to explain the feeling that American corporate capitalism is burning up cultural meaning the way a Cadillac burns up gasoline" (Boyle, 1985, p. 23).

Critical theorists are aware of the loss of community and the need for meaningful discourse about fundamental values. They see the need for interrogation of knowledge and the received— all that comes to us as rules or givens (Swenson, 1998). Thus, rather than studying prejudice in an individual or group or legislative context, analysts may instead study the role of MTV, the music cable television show watched by young people; for example, what are the cumulative effects of pro-violence, homophobic, sexist lyrics of rap musicians aired regularly? Or, analysts might examine manipulations underlying programming formats used by public television or by Univision and Telemundo. What does specialized television reveal about underlying patterns of culture? In social work application, professionals can seek to unmask forces in the community that perpetuate inequity and injustice or hate. These forces may be radio talk shows, rigid bureaucracies, or abstract legal or religious doctrines. Should we not challenge passivity? Here are some compelling facts: U.S. vital statistics reveal that between 1990 and 1997, there were approximately 294,000 firearm deaths including unintentional shootings, suicides and homicides (Violence Policy Center, n.d.). Gun deaths are not natural and inevitable, and these statistics suggest that the National Association of Social Workers should vigorously oppose the National Rifle Association.

In line with critical theory, it is vital to consider more than the advocacy content as it could be written or stated. A picture can be a powerful way to communicate (Huff, 1998). In the international aid field, a news photograph of a vulture staring at a prone, starving, naked Sudanese child was used to generate money for refugee services.[4] At the most basic level, critical theory can help social workers grasp the connections between individual insight and societal change (Dean & Fenby, 1989).

Feminist Social Theory

The differentiation of people, at home and abroad, that sometimes leads to "honor killings" of women and girls and increased use of date-rape drugs has traditionally been discussed in terms of biology, customs, and atrocities. Like many theories, feminist theory explains "why things are the way they are, how they got that way and what needs to be done to change them" (Ryan, 1992, p. 60). Growing out of a social movement, feminist theory remains critical and activist, seeking world betterment, and may be the only theory in which those who developed it benefit so directly from the insights it provokes (Tong, 1992). Yet, it shares much with other multidisciplinary, contemporary theories because it asks us to

- relinquish conventional wisdom, thought categories, and dichotomies or binaries;
- interrogate traditional beliefs about roles, behavior, socialization, work, conception; and
- discern absences.

"Where are the women?" While Marxism encourages us to see the world from the perspective of workers rather than bosses, feminism asks us to consider the vantage point of what traditionally was the invisible half of humanity.[5] For instance, "feminist scholars reveal how gendered assumptions help to determine whose voices are privileged in ethnographic accounts" (Naples, 2000, p. 196). Among others, Nancy Hartsock (1998) introduced the idea of standpoint theory and feminist epistemology (ways of knowing). Feminist theory suggests that we question formal knowledge and core assumptions (Hyde, 1996; Kemp, 2001), since so much emanates from male-dominated scholarship.

For decades, the woman-focused perspective was considered more ideological than theoretical. Then, scholars began to realize how much had been missing from their usual scope of inquiry because women were seldom the objects of study, and their day-and-night experiences were so often ignored (Smith, 1999). Many fields have changed since addressing the question: "And what about the women?" (Lengermann & Niebrugge-Brantley, 1990). "The struggle against misogyny and for equality led to a broad array of social concerns: Social hierarchy, racism, warfare, violence [sports, domestic violence, pornography, and rape] and environmental destruction were seen to be the effects of men's psychological need for domination and the social organization of patriarchy" (Abercrombie, Hill, & Turner, 1994, pp. 162–163).

Insights about the role of gender have led social work to take a closer look at identity, difference, domination, and oppression. Concepts from feminist theory also have furthered an interest in experiential knowledge, personal narrative (telling your story), the actualities of people's living, and bodily being (Harris, Bridger, Sachs, & Tallichet, 1995; Tangenberg, 2000).

Feminist theory is sometimes subsumed under the heading of empowerment, justice, liberation, emancipation, and Queer theory. Such theory has the goal of recognition, an emphasis on how categories shape the way we see the world, insights regarding privilege, and an affirmation of resiliency. All of these features are common to new frameworks about race, ethnicity, disability, and sexual orientation as well as gender (Weed & Shor, 1997). Academics have begun to join activists in naming what contributes to marginalization. Empowerment theories may motivate social workers to take a critical look at processes of paternalism, silencing, and societal denial (Lamb, 1991; Profit, 2000). In community practice, we aspire to give voice in societal discourse to previously silenced persons.

Chaos Theory

Chaos theory and systems theory, which emerged from the physical sciences, both stress interrelationships. Systems theory assumes order, integration, logic, whereas chaos or complexity theory examines that which is less easily diagrammed. Newton's mechanical, determined universe is being replaced by one that is less predictable and more lifelike (Elsberg & Powers, 1992). Social work practice involves many components, changeable conditions, and endless occurrences. With its complexity of social environments, our profession can certainly relate to a dynamic view of reality in which random events and behavior can change the whole picture. For instance, the 2000 U.S. election made a mockery of academic models predicting who would be elected president; the predictors view the result as an outlier or random shock. Chaos scientists say, hypothetically, that a butterfly in

Tokyo creating lilliputian turbulence might contribute—in combination with other events—to a storm in New York (Grobman, 1999; Ward, 1995). This notion of amplifying effects is suggested in the title of an article by Edward Lorenz: "Can the flap of a butterfly's wing stir a tornado in Texas?" By curious coincidence, the "butterfly ballots" in one Florida county helped determine the outcome of a presidential election in favor of a Texan (whose brother was governor of Florida).

The postmodern scientific mind views the universe as constituted of forces of "disorder, diversity, instability, and non-linearity" (Best, 1991, p. 194). Unlike a *linear* analysis that might diagram regularity, parts, and progressions, a nonlinear analysis may sketch irregularity and what interferes, cooperates, or competes. Despite its name, chaos theory is not about total disorder because "even apparently random disorder may sometimes be patterned and to some extent accessible to probabilistic prediction" (Mattaini, 1990, p. 238), especially in short-term or nearby situations. Chaos theorists are intrigued by how tiny changes in initial conditions can have major consequences (Gleick, 1987). To use the election example: ironically, if Gore (usually the better debater) had accommodated Bush's fervent desire *not* to debate, Gore might have won the election, because as it turned out the media excoriated Gore on his debate style. Paradoxically, complexity theory also relates to the concept of self-organization or spontaneous emergence of order (Kauffman, 1995). Mattaini (1990) notes the relevance to social work: "This theory offers promise for practice within a contextual perspective, while suggesting the need for ongoing monitoring of results of intervention that may not be entirely predictable" (p. 237).

Complex phenomena tend to be counterintuitive and to require information not yielded by simple models. Forrester (1968) states that complex systems are counterintuitive in that "they give indications that suggest corrective action which will often be ineffective or even adverse in results" (p. 9). Such ideas help us think about cause and effect in a more analytical way, show us how to acquire new understandings, and allow us to view chaos as a beneficial force (Bolland & Atherton, 1999; Warren, Franklin, & Streeter, 1998; Wheatley, 2001).

There can be value in new science that renders older views more complex. Think of cognitive theorists such as Howard Gardner on intelligence; what if intelligence(s) were viewed more universally as *multidimensional* mental processes? Thus, for positive as well as negative reasons, in community practice we must face complexity, "not keep it at a distance with a passing nod of recognition" (Henderson & Thomas, 1987, p. 8).

THE FIELD OF ACTION IN COMMUNITY PRACTICE

For direct service practitioners, practice in the community will often start with understanding cultural and community influences on themselves and their clients as mutual participants in the larger system (Pardeck, 1996). Practice interventions may then move to a social system focus either to address and resolve system malfunctions (e.g., to replace a local school which has become physically unsafe) or to create development opportunities. To do that, we need theories that will help us to understand the behavior of individuals; the behavior of groups and organizations; relationships of power and exchange among individuals, groups, and organizations; and individual and group ideologies (Silver, 1980).

A useful way of conceptualizing community practice, then, is as a series of interventions that take place in a field of action or exchange. The important components of the field include

- individuals, groups, and organizations or organizational subunits;
- the main elements that these members exchange, namely, resources and information; and
- influential aspects of the relationships among the members, namely, power balances and rules of exchange, as well as individual and group ideologies, including values, beliefs, and feelings.

For our purposes, keep in mind that resources and information seldom exist apart from the individuals and organizations that control them. See Box 2.1 for components of a real-life field of community action.

Imagine a community practitioner trying to address the problem of the spread of acquired immunodeficiency syndrome (AIDS) among adolescents in a particular community by building a coalition that will mount an AIDS education project. What would this social worker need to consider in order to carry out this task effectively? Seeing the potential elements of the arena in which the interventions will take place,

namely, the action field, helps the worker assess the scope of the project. Since the problem is complex, the composition of the action field will also be complicated. Elements in the field will also vary in their importance at different points in the intervention process. Some of the main components of an action field in this case might be the following:

1. Adolescents (by no means a monolithic group)
2. Parents (also not a monolithic body)
3. Groups and organizations serving adolescents, such as high schools, recreation centers, clubs, informal cliques or friendship networks, and so on
4. Public health and social service organizations (nonprofit, for-profit, and governmental), such as the health department and the organization you work for, the AIDS outreach service of the health clinic, Planned Parenthood, and the department of health and mental hygiene of your state
5. Civic and community associations, such as PTAs, sororities and fraternities, neighborhood associations, and the Knights of Columbus
6. Churches and religious organizations
7. Elected officials and governmental bodies such as legislative finance committees
8. The media
9. Ideologies of these individuals and groups, including the way they view AIDS and the problem among adolescents, as well as their political, social, professional, and religious beliefs or philosophies
10. Relationships of exchange and power differentials that may exist among the members of the field, and the information and resources that the various members may control

Obviously, just knowing the potential components of the action field does not tell the worker how to go about building an effective coalition. The professional needs some theories about how this community operates to decide what to do to accomplish the task. The worker also needs to know something about how the members of the field relate to each other and how they might react to the proposed project. As a bare beginning, there are traditional models of practice with which the community social worker ought to be familiar. Such models try to put flesh on the bones of theories of justice (Nagel, 1999).

BOX 2.1	PHYSICIANS SHOULD . . . !

A SHIFT TO SYSTEMS THINKING: A SERIES OF COMMUNITY INTERVENTIONS

Physicians are asked to assume many roles. We counsel the troubled, heal the ill, deliver babies, set broken bones and remove tumours. We also immunize, advise, diagnose and comfort. But we could do more.

We think physicians should assume another role, in which the community becomes our patient. An apocryphal example will help support our case. When cholera epidemics ravaged London in the mid-19th century doctors were powerless because they could offer no effective treatment and did not know what had caused the outbreak. Dr. John Snow stepped in as community advocate. Rather than trying to treat individual patients in his surgery, he sought out the source of the epidemic. He determined that the area's water supply was the disease source and, so the story goes, removed the handle on the Broad Street pump. With its source eliminated, the water-borne epidemic died out.

By taking community action, Snow had an impact much greater than he could have had by remaining in his surgery and caring for patients one at a time. We suggest that Canadian physicians could have a similar impact on important health problems if they were to use their expertise and stature to act as community advocates . . .

Community advocacy can have an impact. In the 1960s it was recognized that accidental poisonings in Ontario's Essex County were an important cause of illness and death in children. Suggestions made to parents and creation of a poison-control centre did not reduce the number of cases, so a local pediatrician decided it was time to take community action.

In 1967, with the help of local pharmacists, the Essex County Medical Society launched a widely publicized campaign to promote the use of child-resistant containers. During the next 5 years poisonings caused by prescription drugs fell by 86%. This intervention has since become standard practice across the country.

Another example is found where we live. A major multilane highway was built north of Barrie, but no median barrier was provided and there were numerous collisions as cars tried to dart from service stations on one side to the lane of traffic on the other. A local orthopedic surgeon, appalled by the carnage, first approached, then hounded, his local member of the provincial parliament. He appeared before an Ontario legislature committee and pointed out the enormous cost of hospital admissions, nursing care and all other aspects of caring for the accident victims. His action led to construction of a barrier that, more than anything else, has reduced the traffic-accident toll in our area.

This surgeon's skill in repairing broken limbs had been very important in treating the accident victims but his role as community advocate was more effective because he helped eliminate the accidents.

Another example, again from our community, illustrates that physicians can have an impact outside their areas of specialization. A detoxification centre for alcoholics was needed to supplement existing services and one of our radiologists took it on as *his* challenge. He chaired the planning committee, wrote grant requests and went to the media—repeatedly. This physician played an important role in seeing the centre completed successfully. The fact that radiologists are seldom involved in treating alcoholism was immaterial . . .

There is a long list of areas in which doctors can have an impact on community health. It includes family violence, industrial safety, drunk-driving legislation, needle exchanges for drug addicts, water safety, environmental issues, health education in schools and water fluoridation. In all these areas physicians' specific knowledge, stature in the community and organizational and communications skills can have a major impact. However, doctors must be willing to go into the community and participate with others working in these areas. They cannot succeed by remaining in their offices . . .

Go to the community. Work with public health officials. Approach the media. Enlist the help of a local service club in promoting a project. Above all, stand up and stand out.

Source: From "Community Advocacy and the MD: Physicians Should Stand Up and Stand Out," by B. A. P. Morris and D. Butler-Jones, 1991, *Canadian Medical Association Journal, 144,* p. 1316–1317. Copyright 1993 by the *Canadian Medical Association Journal.* Used with permission.

TRADITIONAL MODELS OF COMMUNITY ORGANIZATION

Classic Conceptual Scheme

Like numerous formulations of community practice and social change, organizing has been categorized in a variety of ways (Fisher, 1995; Mondros & Wilson, 1990). Respected social work educator Marie Weil views models of social intervention as holding an intermediate place between theory and practice skills, since they "embody theory and illustrate the actions that put theory into practice." Weil (1996) goes on to say, "A conceptual model or framework is a way of putting together concepts or ideas. It provides a design for how to think about or illustrate the structure and interworkings of related concepts—a structure, a design or a system. A conceptual model is intended to illustrate the operation of a theoretical approach, and to build or demonstrate knowledge. . . . Conceptual models of community practice illustrate the diverse ways that community practice is conceived" (pp. 1–2).

Most social workers are familiar with Jack Rothman's highly referenced conceptual model of community practice. In 1968, Rothman devised a three-pronged model, a community practice framework that social work students everywhere have studied ever since. As mentioned in Chapter 1, the prongs are locality development, social planning, and social action. In Rothman's (1996) own words, his three approaches include the following:

1. the community-building emphasis of locality development, with its attention to community competency and social integration

2. the data-based problem-solving orientation of social planning/social policy, with its reliance on expertise

3. the advocacy thrust of social action, with its commitment to fundamental change and social justice (p. 71)

The Rothman model is easy to apply in real life. For example, remote Peapatch in Virginia coal country needs public water, because mines have destroyed its wells. The locality developer might recruit Peapatch residents to supervise the daily work and recruit volunteer laborers to run a water line up the mountain to service the 50 homes. The social planner might identify appropriate funding resources, such as Community Development Block Grants and the Appalachian Regional Commission, and development resources such as the Small Towns

Environment Program. The action organizer might demand that mining companies be held accountable under state law for damage to water sources (Timberg, 2001). In such real cases, intervention modes may overlap, as we will discuss after painting a fuller picture of each approach. No single approach to organizing is superior, as use depends on how the situation unfolds and often all three are used to varying degrees on the same issue.

Locality or Community Development

Locality development seeks to pull together diverse elements of an area by directing individual and organizational strengths toward improving social and economic conditions. This is an enabling style of organizing similar to those of Volunteers in Service to America (VISTA), Americorps, and the Peace Corps. Rothman (1987) turns to pioneer Arthur Dunham for development *themes*—"democratic procedures, voluntary cooperation, self-help, development of indigenous leadership, and educational objectives" (p. 5)—still relevant today. Urban parks—that draw together solitary individuals both during development and afterwards—are one of many community projects that fall under this rubric.[6] New voices should be heard. Difficult people also must be heard and involved. The locality developer role calls for self-discipline, suggests Rothman (2000): "The role is complicated and in some respects runs against certain human propensities, calling on practitioners to stay in the background and neutralize their contribution; to give credit to local participants rather than to themselves; to maintain positive working relationships with opponents and vexatious elements in the community; and to refrain from proposing solutions, even when practitioners possess requisite knowledge, so that solutions will emerge from local residents themselves" (p. 103).

Despite its challenges, locality development has never gone out of fashion as an approach to community practice.

It is a cool breezy spring evening and the gardeners have on sweaters to do their planting. As they dig, they exchange a few words about the benefits of daylight saving time. Only a dozen individuals had plots in the lot before it was cleaned up. Now thirty families are involved, and Jorge, who keeps records on which family has signed up for which plot, is triumphant. The public garden area is be-

tween a Latino neighborhood and an African-American one. Organized groups from each area fought hard with city officials to use this formerly idle land. It was their first joint project. Since then, Lou, the area's paid organizer, and the activists have been discussing other locality development projects—elementary school involvement and better fire protection.

Social Planning

Planning looks objectively at past, present, and future scenarios, using available data or collecting new data, to consolidate and meet service and civic needs and to address social conditions efficiently and systematically. This is a task-oriented style of organizing, similar to those of the United Way and housing authorities, that requires mastering bureaucratic complexity. The behind-the-scenes planner handles information technology, writes position or option papers, provides technical expertise, and works to fill service gaps. The part of planning that seems more like organizing involves public participation in decision making and human service plans. To ensure the involvement of a cross section of the population, the advocate planner should hold meetings and hearings and secure representatives from different sectors. Thus, the out-front planner plays the roles of community liaison, facilitator, outreach worker, interpreter of regulations and policies, translator between groups with different knowledge bases, and consciousness raiser for groups not initially interested in the needs of the target population.

A huge fan blows the technical papers around the table. The agency lawyer mutters about proceeding without a consensus, but Madison—the organizer—wants the citizen-advisors to the planning board to make the decision. Tasha, a single mother, shifts in her chair, feeling that she ought to get home for the sitter; she has decided to demand that child care be provided in the future. Twenty tired but determined heads bend over the reports again. Everyone has been reading and rereading the regulations, trying to figure out an angle that would give citizens more rights than the corporations. Then Kenny yells, "I figured it out!" and has their instant attention. Ba reopens his notebook ready to take notes and Nuit rushes back to the laptop. "We're ready, go ahead," smiles Madison.

Social Action

Activists on the right and left have used tactics associated with this model. The social action approach can involve either radical, fundamental change goals or reformist, incremental goals. Fundamental change has been embraced by Green Peace, the American Indian Movement, AIDS Coalition To Unleash Power (ACT UP), Students for a Democratic Society (SDS), Democratic Socialists of America (Rothman, 1996, p. 91), and the Ruckus Society (http://ruckus.org/), which trains antiglobalization protest participants. (For an overview, see Fisher, 1995.) Social action confronts—in different degrees and with a variety of tactics—hierarchical power relationships within a community in order to benefit powerless people, socially vulnerable populations, or others that feel locked out of decision processes. This adversarial style is used by citizen coalitions throughout the world. Just as U.S. farmers have brought their tractors to Washington to disrupt traffic, tens of thousands of pullers in India have used their rickshaws to physically block government centers. In July 2002, unarmed women took over four Chevron Texaco facilities in Nigeria to protest poverty, costing the company $2.9 million daily (for additional examples of citizen action in Africa, see All Africa Global Media's informative web site at http://allAfrica.com). The aim can be to make basic changes in major institutions or community practices (Rothman, 1987, p. 6) or in the policies of formal organizations (p. 18) or to redistribute power, resources, and decision making. There will be resistance, since social action involves a struggle for power. A critical mass is a long-term necessity; broad participation can launch initial changes.

On the day that the bus drivers pleaded with their bosses for relief, the action group knew that victory was near. It started when a teenage waitress was robbed and a developmentally challenged man was beaten two days later; both incidents took place in dark bus stops where there were no streetlights. Bus riders became uneasy and unhappy, grumbling that since only working people rode buses at night, no higher-up would do anything. An organizer overheard and amassed a group to write the bus company and the mayor, demanding installation of lights. To gain publicity, the group decided to carry unwieldy items on the buses—filling up space and disrupting the routine. Following media coverage about the two victims and the goal, ever more riders arrived with lamps, bunches of balloons, huge baskets, or suitcases.

Composites

As Rothman recognized, in actual organizations and ongoing projects the three organizing approaches often get combined in various forms. Cheryl Hyde (1996) has put forward pertinent organizational examples of single modes (such as when the staff of the Institute for Women's Policy Research intervenes as planners) and combined modes (such as when the staff of the State Commissions on the Status of Women combine planning with action; Hyde, p. 133). In actual practice, clinical and community work overlap, case management and advocacy overlap, so naturally the three organizing modes can as well. For instance, in Montreal, an organization called Dans la Rue (On the Street) creatively *combined locality development with social action*. Initially, street kids were asked what they needed from a mobile van designed to serve them in their territory, and eventually a shelter was created that the street kids staffed and named the Bunker. Such locality development service projects led to advocacy and then to "the organization of a demonstration against the increased number of police harassment and brutality cases reported" by homeless residents of the city.

Another project funded by the Bunker—and initiated by four street youths—was Punk, Not Junk. This initiative included sensitizing the public as to the punk culture and demystifying views of this subculture as consisting totally of individuals who are drug addicted and racist.

The project's primary goal was to raise awareness of the dangers of heroin ("junk"), yet it soon became a forum in which youths could discuss issues of alienation and stigmatization in mainstream society. The project continues to work out of the Bunker, and shelter workers act as guides who can provide advice when needed. Punk, Not Junk has become very popular among street youth and gained some media attention (Karabanow, 1999, p. 323).[7]

Related Community Intervention Model

Based on assessment, Rothman wanted community practitioners to fit their mode of action to the situation at hand. According to Ann Jeffries (1996) from the United Kingdom, "Rothman's identification of three models of community organization practice has permeated the community work literature on both sides of the Atlantic" (p. 102). Reworking Rothman, Jeffries proposes a four-square model of community practice. To oversimplify, Jeffries's approach renames Rothman's first two modes and divides social action into "nonviolent direct action" and "coalition building and campaigns" (see Figure 2.1).

Jeffries (1996) renames locality development *capacity and awareness promotion* because she believes "the ability is there, it just needs to be given a chance to blossom" (p. 115). This approach or mode of organizing starts with the personal concerns of neighborhood residents and moves on to "developing or giving scope for and recognition to the skills, or capacities of community groups" (p. 114). Community workers in this mode may call upon their own "interpersonal, educational and group work skills" (p. 115). She renames social planning *partnership promotion* because, rather than facilitating service

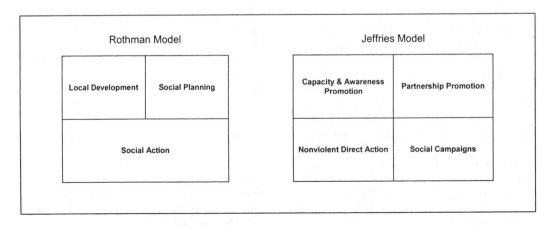

Figure 2.1   Models of community organizing.

delivery, the current emphasis is on collaborative planning with the community "to enable the community to act for itself" (p. 114). Ultimately, there could be "community management of services or community economic development" (p. 114) through this mode of organizing. In the third approach, having developed confidence and conviction—often from capacity and awareness promotion activities—community members can be ready to "get the attention of those in authority . . . and an unsympathetic power structure" (p. 116) using the *nonviolent direct action* mode of organizing. Community workers in this mode will strive to "coalesce interests into action groups" (p. 115). Such change-oriented protest work, often local or legislative in nature, can be contrasted with *social campaigns*:

> Clearly social campaigns have long been a key feature not only of single issue organizing but also of radical, change-oriented social movements. While the former often have a more specific objective and may align themselves with organizational elites, the latter are more comprehensive in scope. They may be seeking social justice or be promoting an ecological consciousness in society. . . . These days campaign organizers can take advantage of information technology to build country-wide and international campaign coalitions. Yet to generate the mass mobilization that may be necessary to take on multi-nationals or an unsympathetic government, it is important also to have strong community level organization. (Jeffries, 1996, p. 117)

Thus, Jeffries formulates four up-to-date, relevant, and serviceable characterizations of organizing. We suggest an example for each mode (our examples are in brackets):

- Capacity and awareness promotion [tribal gaming as economic development]
- Partnership promotion [local anticrime efforts]
- Nonviolent direct action [confronting U.S. Food and Drug Administration officials regarding AIDS medications]
- Social campaigns [preventing oil drilling in Alaska]

In summary, theories and models guide community practitioners. However, abstractions alone are insufficient. As stated earlier, in social work practice, such frameworks are melded with the political and the ideological. In fact, Jeffries (1996) herself says she is ultimately less interested in differentiation between ideal types and more interested in "ways to engage with whatever are the pressing issues of concern and to do so in a way that promotes the chances of both long-term and fundamental improvements in the community's quality of and approach to communal life, building a more just and empowering society and thus contributing to the feminist vision of a transformed society" (p. 105).

A NOTE ON THE USES AND LIMITATIONS OF THEORIES AND MODELS

This chapter has featured an array of theories and models of which community practitioners should be aware. We leave the reader with several cautions. Some caveats are in order regarding social science, theories, and models. Firstly, ideology is inherent in the social sciences and in their resultant theories and constructions of reality (Coates, 1992; Robbins, Chatterjee, & Canda, 1999). Theories are developed not only from our observations of nature but also from the paradigms used to guide the observations. Paradigms and their ways of finding out about nature, according to Kuhn (1970), not only have strong value and ideological components; they are ideology. Paradigms organize and order our perceptions of nature according to their rules. Some of the theories and models are descriptive; others are prescriptive. Some of the theories simply describe certain aspects of nature, of human behavior and interaction. Other theories and models prescribe what should be and what should be done by the social workers. The models are not empirical reality. Community practitioners should take care not to reify the models—not to make the models reality (McKee, 2003). Rather, they should use the models to guide, construct, and understand the complexities of reality.

Our view and construction of reality strongly reflect symbolic interactionism. Blumer (1969), a leading symbolic interactionist theorist, held that symbolic interactionism "does not regard meaning as emanating from the intrinsic makeup of the thing that has meaning, nor does it see meaning as arising through a coalescence of psychological elements in the person. Instead, it sees meaning as arising in the process of interaction between people. . . . Thus, symbolic interactionism sees meaning as social products, as creations that are formed in and through the defining activities of people as they interact" (pp. 4–5).

Wexler Vigilante (1993) elaborates on the relevance of symbolic interactionism or constructionism in social work practice. She asks us to "assume that systematic data gathering cannot accurately reflect the complexities of human functioning. The . . . strategy consists of the client and worker successfully framing and reframing the client's story until coherent and shared meanings are achieved" (p. 184).

Symbolic interactionism's emphasis, similar to that of assessment in practice, is on meaning. People tend to define, construct, and give meaning to their world partly as a result of their interactions with others, as we discuss more fully in Chapter 3. A practitioner needs to understand the meaning of the interactions and the social environment to the client, the client's system, and the other systems of the change process if the

practitioner is ever to understand the client's behavior. The client's constructions and meanings of reality, and hence the client's world and opportunities, can be improved with changes in the client's social interactions. A community practice task is to help the client establish new community interactions and hence to construct new realities with new meanings (Pozatek, 1994). Theory gives us a start on grasping what is happening around and within us, and practice models stimulate our imagination so we can make an effective beginning.

Discussion Exercises

1. "The law, in its majestic equality, forbids the rich as well as the poor to sleep under bridges, to beg in the streets, and to steal bread" (Anatole France, *Le Lys Rouge*, 1894, p. 89). Read the preceding quote. Analyze and explain the statement from each theoretical perspective. Do conclusions differ?

2. Right out of our communities:

   • A group of affluent high school athletes takes a neighbor girl with an IQ of 64 into a basement to sexually abuse her.

   • A city council—citing tradition—refuses to move their town to higher ground, even with federal help. So once a decade the low-lying section, where poorer residents live, floods and the rest of the community pitches in to clean up.

   Society often discusses complex motives in actual situations like those above. But aren't the following positive stories, pulled from newspapers, equally relevant to social work?

   • A political dissident gives up his career and easy life because of his democratic principles but, after years, emerges from disgrace as a powerful national leader.

   • A teenager forgoes the offer of a car and instead gives the money to a cause.

   • A 7-year-old collects 1,000 suitcases for foster children, so they no longer have to carry their belongings around in garbage bags.

   • A student spends three years in high school creating a course (for credit) in peace studies.

   • A man sells his business and shares $130 million of the proceeds with his employees (who

   keep their jobs under the new management), to recognize their hard work.

   What motivates people? Do motivation theories suggest that motivations can be shaped? What can community practitioners glean from theory to understand, encourage, or stop any of the above actions?

   Divide into two teams. Pick two theories from the chapter. Then debate whether the 7-year-old's efforts are useless; that is, by collecting the suitcases for children in foster care, was the 7-year-old just treating the symptoms? Just making the haves feel better? Or is a need for dignity met by this act, so that the effort should be appreciated?

3. Look at Box 2.1, the article about doctors and their communities. What three components were in their action field? What system malfunctions did the advocates address and resolve? What development opportunity was created by one doctor's action?

4. What is the difference between feminist theory and feminism, in your view? Why does a conservative such as Rush Limbaugh focus on Feminazis?

5. Do you know a professional whose work involves locality development, social planning, or social action? How does that person's work differ from Jack Rothman's models?

6. Does your fieldwork involve any interventions described by Jeffries (capacity & awareness promotion, partnership promotion, nonviolent direct action, social campaigns)?

7. Analyze antiglobalization street protests, first in theoretical terms and then as models of organizing.

Notes

1. As a macrolevel example, consider bargaining and game theory from economics and mathematics; see *A Beautiful Mind* (Nasar, 2001).

2. Joseph Davis (2002) argues that the new prominence of narrative (see Chapter 14, this volume), in at least nine academic disciplines, relates to renewed emphasis on "human agency and its efficacy" (Davis, 2002, p. 3). He goes on to note that earlier social movement theorists seemed stuck on "structural and interest-oriented explanations, to the near exclusion of ideational factors" (p. 4).

3. In Kuper and Kuper (1999), see especially the chapters on "Ecology" (by R. F. Ellen) and "Environmental Economics" (by D. W. Pearce).

4. The photo also won a Pulitzer Prize. Notwithstanding its impact, critical analysts questioned why the photographer waited for the perfect picture before scaring away the bird to protect the child (Kleinman & Kleinman, 1997). Within this framework, the critic will be critiqued, too.

5. In Western countries, women were invisible even though they outnumbered men. Worldwide, Amartya Sen (winner of the Nobel Prize in economics) calculates that as many as 60 to 100 million females are "missing" due to infanticide, sex-selective abortions, and nutritional and medical neglect based on gender. Such factors contribute to "excess mortality and artificially lower survival rates" for women in countries such as China and India (Sen, 1999, pp. 104–107).

6. Locality developers who emphasize community building assume a common good that people of many backgrounds working together can realize (see Project for Public Spaces, Inc., 1997).

7. A philosophical interview with a punk rock activist from Washington, D.C., named Mark Anderson, whose work also combines service and social action with youth, appears in Powers (1994).

References

Abercrombie, N., Hill, S., & Turner, B. S. (1994). *Dictionary of sociology.* New York: Penguin.

Abramson, L. V., Seligman, M., & Teasdale, J. D. (1978). Learned helplessness in humans: Critique and reformulation. *Journal of Abnormal Psychology, 87,* 49–74.

Aldrich, H. E. (1979). *Organizations and environments.* Englewood Cliffs, NJ: Prentice Hall.

Apter, M. J. (1999). Motivation. In A. Kuper & J. Kuper (Eds.), *The social science encyclopedia* (2nd ed., pp. 557–559). London: Routledge.

Bandura, A. (1982, February). Self-efficacy mechanism in human agency. *American Psychologist, 37,* 122–147.

Bandura, A. (1986). *Social foundations of thought and action.* Englewood Cliffs, NJ: Prentice Hall.

Bandura, A. (1989). Social cognitive theory. *Annals of Child Development, 6,* 1–60.

Batson, C. D., Ahmad, N., & Tsang, J. (2002). Four motives for community involvement. *Journal of Social Issues, 58*(3), 429–445.

Beckett, J. O., & Johnson, H. C. (1995). Human development. In R. L. Edwards (Ed.-in-Chief), *Encyclopedia of social work* (19th ed., pp. 1381–1405). Washington, DC: National Association of Social Workers Press.

Berger, P. L. (1976). *Pyramids of sacrifice: Political ethics and social change.* Garden City, NY: Anchor Books.

Berger, P. L., & Luckmann, T. (1967). *The social construction of reality.* Garden City, NY: Anchor Books.

Best, S. (1991). Chaos and entropy: Metaphors in postmodern science and social theory. *Culture as Science, 11,* 188–226.

Blau, P. M. (1964). *Exchange and power in social life.* New York: Wiley.

Blumer, H. (1969). *Symbolic interactionism: Perspective and method.* Englewood Cliffs, NJ: Prentice Hall.

Bolland, K. A., & Atherton, C. R. (1999). Chaos theory: An alternative approach to social work practice and research. *Families in Society, 80*(4), 367–373.

Bobo, K., Kendall, J., & Max, S. (2001). *Organizing for social change* (3rd ed.). Santa Ana, CA: Seven Locks Press.

Boyle, J. (1985). *Critical legal studies: A young person's guide.* Critical legal studies conference materials, Washington, DC. [Prof. James Boyle is now at Duke University Law School]

Coates, J. (1992). Ideology and education for social work practice. *Journal of Progressive Human Services, 3*(2), 15–30.

Corrigan, P., & Leonard, P. (1979). *Social work practice under capitalism: A Marxist approach.* London: Macmillan.

Cowger, C. D. (1994). Assessing client strengths: Clinical assessment for client empowerment. *Social Work, 39*(3), 262–267.

Dahrendorf, R. (1959). *Class and class conflict in industrial society.* Stanford, CA: Stanford University Press.

Davis, J. E. (2002). *Stories of change: Narrative and Social movements.* Albany: State University of New York Press.

Davis, M. H. (1996). *Empathy: A social psychological approach.* Boulder, CO: Westview Press.

Dean, R. G., & Fenby, B. L. (1989). Exploring epistemologies: Social work action as a reflection of philosophical assumptions. *Journal of Social Work Education, 25*(1), 46–54.

Elizur, Y. (1995). Ecosystemic consultation in the kibbutz: Social process and narrative in two cases of community "epidemic." *Contemporary Family Therapy, 17*(4), 483–501.

Elsberg, C., & Powers, P. R. (1992, November). *Focusing, channeling, and re-creating: Energy in contemporary American settings.* Presented at the Society for the Scientific Study of Religion, Washington, DC.

Emerson, R. (1962). Power-dependence relations. *American Sociological Review, 17*(27), 31–41.

Emery, F. E., & Trist, E. L. (1965). The causal texture of organizational environments. *Human Relations, 18,* 21–32.

Evan, W. (1963). The organizational set: Toward a theory of inter-organizational relations. In J. D. Thompson (Ed.), *Organizational design and research: Approaches to organizational design* (pp. 173–191). Pittsburgh, PA: University of Pittsburgh Press.

Fabricant, M. B., & Burghardt, S. (1992). *The welfare state crisis and the transformation of social service work.* Armonk, NY: M. E. Sharpe.

Fisher, R. (1995). Social action community organization: Proliferation, persistence, roots, and prospects. In J. Rothman, J. L. Erlich, & J. E. Tropman, with F. M. Cox (Eds.), *Strategies of community intervention* (5th ed., pp. 327–340). Itasca, IL: F. E. Peacock.

Forrester, J. W. (1969). *Urban dynamics.* Cambridge: MIT Press.

France, A. (1894). *The Red Lily.* Doylestown, PA: Wildside Press.

Gardella, L. G. (2000). The group-centered BSW curriculum for community practice: An essay. *Journal of Community Practice, 8*(2), 53–69.

Germain, C. B., & Gitterman, A. (1995). Ecological perspective. In R. L. Edwards (Ed.-in-Chief), *Encyclopedia of social work* (19th ed., pp. 816–824). Washington, DC: National Association of Social Workers Press.

Gitterman, A. (1994). Editor's note. In J. B. Mondros & S. M. Wilson (Eds.), *Organizing for power and empowerment* (pp. ix–x). New York: Columbia University Press.

Gleick, J. (1987) *Chaos.* New York: Viking Penguin.

Gottsegen, M. G. (1994). *The political thought of Hannah Arendt.* Albany: State University of New York Press.

Gowdy, E. A. (1994). From technical rationality to participating consciousness. *Social Work, 39*(4), 362–370.

Greene, R. R., & Blundo, R. G. (1999). Postmodern critique of systems theory in social work with the aged and their families. *Journal of Gerontological Social Work, 3*(3/4), 87–100.

Grobman, G. M. (1999). *Improving quality and performance in your non-profit organization.* Harrisburg, PA: White Hat Communications.

Hall, S. (1977). Culture, the media, and the ideological effect. In J. Curran, M. Gurevitch, & J. Woollacott (Eds.), *Mass communication and society.* London: Edward Arnold.

Harris, R. P., Bridger, J. C., Sachs, C. E., & Tallichet, S. E. (1995). Empowering rural sociology: Exploring and linking alternative paradigms in theory and methodology. *Rural Sociology, 60*(4), 585–606.

Hartsock, N. (1998). *The feminist standpoint revisited and other essays.* Boulder, CO: Westview Press.

Hasenfeld, Y. (1983). *Human service organizations.* Englewood Cliffs, NJ: Prentice Hall.

Henderson, P., & Thomas, D. N. (1987). *Skills in neighbourhood.* London: Allen & Unwin.

Homans, G. C. (1974). *Social behavior: Its elementary forms.* New York: Harcourt Brace Jovanovich.

hooks, b. (1991). Theory as liberatory practice. *Yale Journal of Law and Feminism, 4*(1), 1–12.

Huff, D. D. (1998). Every picture tells a story. *Social Work, 43*(6), 576–583.

Hyde, C. (1996). A feminist response to Rothman's "The interweaving of community intervention approaches." *Journal of Community Practice, 3*(3/4), 127–145.

Irving, A., & Young, T. (2002). Paradigm for pluralism: Mikhail Bakhtin and social work practice. *Social Work, 47*(1), 19–29.

Jeffries, A. (1996). Modelling community work: An analytic framework for practice. *Journal of Community Practice, 3*(3/4), 101–125.

Juba, D. S. (1997). A systems perspective on the introduction of narrative practice in human services organizations in the era of managed care. *Contemporary Family Therapy, 19*(2), 177–193.

Karabanow, J. (1999). Creating community: A case study of a Montreal street kid agency. *Community Development Journal, 34*(4), 318–327.

Kauffman, S. (1995). *At home in the universe: The search for the laws of self-organization and complexity.* New York: Oxford University Press.

Kemp, S. P. (2001). Environment through a gendered lens: From person-in-environment to woman-in-environment. *Affilia, 16*(1), 7–30.

Kleinman, A., & Kleinman, J. (1997). The appeal of experience; the dismay of images: Cultural appropriations of suffering in our times. In A. Kleinman, V. Das, & M. Lock (Eds.), *Social Suf-*

fering (pp. 1–23). Berkeley: University of California Press.

Kuhn, T. S. (1970). *The structure of scientific revolutions* (2nd ed., enlarged). New York: New American Library.

Kuper, A., & Kuper, J. (Eds.). (1999). *The social science encyclopedia* (2nd ed.). London: Routledge.

Lamb, S. (1991). An analysis of linguistic avoidance in journal articles on men who batter women. *American Journal of Orthopsychiatry, 61*(2), 250–257.

Lappé, F. M., & Du Bois, P. M. (1994). *The quickening of America: Rebuilding our nation, remaking our lives.* San Francisco: Jossey-Bass.

Leiby, J. (1997). Social work and social responsibility. In M. Reisch & E. Gambrill (Eds.), *Social work in the 21st century* (pp. 359–367). Thousand Oaks, CA: Pine Forge Press.

Lengermann, P. M., & Niebrugge-Brantley, J. (1990). Feminist sociological theory: The near-future prospects. In G. Ritzer (Ed.), *Frontiers of social theory* (pp. 316–344). New York: Columbia University Press.

Levine, S., & White, P. E. (1961). Exchange as a conceptual framework for the study of interorganizational relations. *Administrative Science Quarterly, 5*, 583–610.

Levine, S., & White, P. E. (1963). The community of health organizations. In H. E. Freeman, S. Levine, & L. G. Reader (Eds.), *Handbook of medical sociology* (pp. 321–347). Englewood Cliffs, NJ: Prentice Hall.

Mansbridge, J, & Morris, A. (2001). *Oppositional consciousness: The subjective roots of social protest.* Chicago: University of Chicago Press.

Martinez-Brawley, E. E. (2000). *Close to home: Human services and the small community.* Washington, DC: National Association of Social Workers Press.

Mattaini, M. A. (1990). Contextual behavior analysis in the assessment process. *Families in Society, 71*(4), 236–245.

McCormack, W. (2001, March 26). Deconstructing the election: Foucault, Derrida and the GOP strategy. *The Nation, 272*(12), 25–34.

McKee, M. (2003). Excavating our frames of mind: The key to dialogue and collaboration. *Social Work, 48*(3), 401–408.

Mondros, J. B., & Wilson, S. M. (1990). Staying alive: Career selection and sustenance of community organizers. *Administration in Social Work, 14*(2), 95–109.

Monroe, K. R. (1994). A fat lady in a corset: Altruism and social theory. *American Journal of Political Science, 38*(4), 861–893.

Morris, B. A. P., & Butler-Jones, D. (1991). Community advocacy and the MD: Physicians should stand up and stand out. *Canadian Medical Association Journal, 144*(10), 1316–1317.

Morrison, A. B., & Wolfe, S. M. (2001, January 7). None of our business and none of theirs, either. *The Washington Post*, pp. B1, B4.

Mulroy, E. A., & Shay, S. (1997). Nonprofit organizations and innovation: A model of neighborhood-based collaboration to prevent child maltreatment. *Social Work, 42*(5), 515–524.

Nagel, T. (1999, October 25). Justice, justice, shalt thou pursue: The rigorous compassion of John Rawls. *The New Republic, 4*(423), 36–41.

Naples, N. A. (with Sachs, C.). (2000). Standpoint epistemology and the use of self-reflection in feminist ethnography: Lessons for rural sociology. *Rural Sociology, 65*(2), 194–214.

Nasar, S. (2001). *A beautiful mind: The life of mathematical genius and Nobel Laureate John Nash.* New York: Simon & Schuster.

National Organization for Women. (1982). *Guidelines to feminist consciousness-raising.* Washington, DC: Author.

Oliner, P. M., & Oliner, S. P. (1995). *Toward a caring society: Ideas into action.* Westport, CT: Praeger.

Olson, M. (1971). *The logic of collective action: Public goods and the theory of groups.* Cambridge, MA: Harvard University Press.

Pardeck, J. T. (1996). An ecological approach for social work intervention. *Family Therapy, 23*(3), 189–198.

Pardeck, J. T., Murphy, J. W., & Choi, J. M. (1994). Some implications of postmodernism for social work practice. *Social Work, 39*(4), 343–346.

Pecukonis, E., & Wenocur, S. (1994). Perceptions of self and collective efficacy in community organization theory and practice. *Journal of Community Practice, 1*(2), 5–21.

Piven, F. F., & Cloward, R. A. (1971). *Regulating the poor: The functions of public welfare.* New York: Random/Vintage Books.

Powers, P. (Ed.). (1994). *Challenging: Interviews With Advocates and Activists* [Monograph]. Baltimore: University of Maryland at Baltimore, School of Social Work.

Pozatek, E. (1994). The problem of certainty: Clinical social work in the postmodern era. *Social Work, 39*(4), 396–404.

Profit, N. J. (2000). Survivors of woman abuse: Compassionate fires inspire collective action for social change. *Journal of Progressive Human Services, 11*(2), 77–102.

Project for Public Spaces, Inc. (1997, Spring). Crossing Delancey, Conservancy Brings Diverse Groups Together. *Urban Parks Online.* Retrieved May 29, 2003, from http://www.pps.org/topics/community/thecommunity/success_newyorkroosevelt

Reisch, M., Sherman, W. R., & Wenocur, S. (1981). Empowerment, conscientization, and animation as core social work skills. *Social Development Issues, 5*(2/3), 106–120.

Ritzer, G. (1992). *Contemporary sociological theory* (3rd ed.). New York: McGraw-Hill.

Robbins, S. P., Chatterjee, P., & Canda, E. R. (1998). *Contemporary human behavior theory: A critical perspective for social work.* Boston: Allyn & Bacon.

Robbins, S. P., Chatterjee, P., & Canda, E. R. (1999). Ideology, scientific theory, and social work practice. *Families in Society, 80*(4), 374–384.

Rogge, M. E. (1995). Coordinating theory, evidence, and practice: Toxic waste exposure in communities. *Journal of Community Practice, 2*(2), 55–76.

Rothman, J. (1996). The interweaving of community intervention approaches. *Journal of Community Practice, 3*(3/4), 69–99.

Rothman, J. (2000). Collaborative self-help community development: When is the strategy warranted? *Journal of Community Practice, 7*(2), 89–105.

Rothman, J. (with J. E. Tropman). (1987). Models of community organization and macro practice: Their mixing and phasing. In F. M. Cox, J. L. Erlich, & J. E. Tropman (Eds.), *Strategies of community intervention* (4th ed., pp. 3–25). Itasca, IL: F. E. Peacock.

Ryan, B. (1992). *Feminism and the women's movement: Dynamics of change in social movement ideology and activism.* New York: Routledge.

Saleebey, D. (1994). Culture, theory, and narrative: The intersection of meanings in practice. *Social Work, 39*(4), 351–361.

Sands, R. G., & Nuccio, K. (1992). Postmodern feminist theory and social work. *Social Work, 37*(6), 489–494.

Scherch, J. (2000). Riverton: Envisioning a sustainable community. In D. P. Fauri, S. P. Wernet, & F. E. Netting (Eds.), *Cases in macro social work practice* (pp. 157–171). Needham Heights, MA: Allyn & Bacon.

Seligman, M. E. P. (1975). *Helplessness: On depression, development, and death.* San Francisco: Freeman.

Sen, A. (1999). *Development as freedom.* New York: Anchor Books.

Silver, M. (1980). *Social infrastructure organizing technology.* Unpublished doctoral dissertation, University of California, Berkeley.

Smith, D. E. (1999). From women's standpoint to a sociology for people. In Abu-Lughod, J. L. (Ed.), *Sociology for the twenty-first century* (pp. 65–82). Chicago: University of Chicago Press.

Schwartz, B. (1993). Why altruism is impossible . . . and ubiquitous. *Social Service Review, 67*(3), 314–343.

Swenson, C. R. (1998). Clinical social work's contribution to a social justice perspective. *Social Work, 43*(6), 527–37.

Tangenberg, K. (2000). Marginalized epistemologies: A feminist approach to understanding the experiences of mothers with HIV. *Affilia, 15*(1), 31–48.

Thompson, J. D. (1967). *Organizations in action.* New York: McGraw-Hill.

Timberg, C. (2001, June 23). In Va., an uphill battle for water: Volunteers help lay pipes to their mountain homes in rare venture with government. *The Washington Post,* pp. B1, B5.

Tong, R. (1992). Feminine and feminist thinking: A critical and creative explosion of ideas. *Anima: The Journal for Human Experience, 18*(2), 30–77.

Turner, J. H. (1978). *The structure of sociological theory* (Rev. ed.). Homewood, IL: Dorsey Press.

Vigilante, F. W. (1993). Work: Its use in assessment and intervention with clients in the workplace. In P. A. Kurzman & S. H. Akabas (Eds.), *Work and well-being: The occupation social work advantage* (pp. 179–199). Washington, DC: National Association of Social Workers.

Violence Policy Center. (n.d.). Handgun ban backgrounder. Retrieved July 9, 2003 from http://www.vpc.org/fact_sht/hgbanfs.htm

Vodde, R., & Gallant, J. P. (2000). Bridging the gap between micro and macro practice: Large-scale change and a unified model of narrative-deconstructive practice. *Journal of Social Work Education, 38*(3), 439–458.

Walker, S. (2001). Tracing the contours of postmodern social work. *British Journal of Social Work, 31*(1), pp. 29–39.

Ward, M. (1995). Butterflies and bifurcations: Can chaos theory contribute to our understanding of family systems? *Journal of Marriage and the Family, 57,* 629–638.

Warren, K., Franklin, C., & Streeter, C. L. (1998). New directions in systems theory: Chaos and complexity. *Social Work, 43*(4), 357–372.

Washington, M. H. (1999, March). Prison studies as part of American studies. *ASA Newsletter, 22*(1), 1, 3.

Weed, E., & Shor, N. (Eds.). (1997). *Feminism meets queer theory.* Bloomington: Indiana University Press.

Weil, M. O. (1996). Community building: Building community practice. *Social Work, 41*(5), 481–499.

Wernet, S. P. (1994). A case study of adaptation in a nonprofit human service organization. *Journal of Community Practice, 1,* 93–112.

Wheatley, M. J. (2001). *Leadership and the new science: Discovering order in a chaotic world* (Rev. ed.). San Francisco, CA: Berrett-Koehler.

Wuthnow, R. (1991). *Acts of compassion: Caring for others and helping ourselves.* Princeton, NJ: Princeton University Press.

Wuthnow, R. (1993). Altruism and sociological theory. *Social Service Review, 67*(3), 344–357.

Wuthnow, R., Hunter, J. D., Bergesen, A., & Kurzweil, E. (1984). *Cultural analysis: The work of Peter L. Berger, Mary Douglas, Michel Foucault and Jurgen Habermas.* Boston: Routledge & Kegan Paul.

Zald, M. N. (1970). Political economy: A framework for comparative analysis. In M. N. Zald (Ed.), *Power in organizations* (pp. 221–261). Nashville, TN: Vanderbilt University Press.

3

The Nature of Social and Community Problems

The approaches to solving social problems can be summed up as services, advocacy and organizing. This view omits the question, "What are we trying to build?"

M. MILLER (2002, P. 36)

In a 1988 case involving the beating death of an Asian American gay man, a Broward County [Florida] circuit judge jokingly asked the prosecuting attorney, "That's a crime now, to beat up a homosexual?" The prosecutor answered, "Yes, sir. And it's also a crime to kill them." The judge replied, "Times have really changed."

N. HENTOFF (AS CITED IN JENNESS, 1995, P. 148)

CONCEPTUALIZING A SOCIAL–COMMUNITY PROBLEM

The problem-solving process was covered in our first chapter (also see Hardina, 2002). Here we explore how situations become problems. Besides the external aspects of laws and social norms captured in the epigraph from Hentoff, we want to rivet the reader's attention on internal perspectives that can help us be part of the solution. Defining and addressing social problems entails more than doing; it involves thinking, values, and discernment about culture and related concepts. Diversity is explored in every sense of the word as we present numerous examples of challenges that social workers must meet.

A Viewpoint on Problems and Their Resolution

Communities define which of many social problems they will make their own, just as nations do. This chapter will contribute to the social worker's understanding of problems—facilitating more appropriate interventions—and will suggest applications that can lead to mutual construction of problems and solutions and to coalition building. What determines whose definition prevails? Does power or passion play a part? From whose standpoint is a problem raised and whose worldview is accepted (Lopez, 1994)? Are there service consequences (underutilization, inappropriate interventions) to being oblivious to another group's culture or reality? Are new possibilities conceivable? Can problem solving be used to unite a community? We will explore such questions and rethink the conventional wisdom regarding the nature of social problems, focusing on

Definition—how problems are conceptualized;

Meaning—how problems are experienced; and

Action—how problems are kept in check or solved.

This requires exploring many-sided and fluctuating *realities.* Although reality is not fixed, trying to overcome problems is no quixotic exercise, for there are ways to frame problems and interventions (Chapin, 1995; Mildred, 2003). The crucial thing is for community members to become part of the process.

Introduction to a Complex Phenomenon

A clinician ordinarily sees but one aspect of individuals who are surrounded and sustained by a community of immense complexity. It is as if the professional stands before the open top half of a Dutch door, conversing without seeing the operations of the household or even a single whole person. The same is doubly true of our view of a social problem, many dimensions of which are veiled.

Aspiring to see the *whole view* of a community condition, Vissing and Diament (1995) set out to learn how many homeless teens lived in the seacoast area of New Hampshire and Maine. Social service providers kept telling them that "teen homelessness simply was not a problem in their communities" (p. 287). However, the 3,000 teenagers they surveyed conveyed a different story. Part of the difference in perception hinged on definitions, but Vissing and Diament decided that "adolescents are likely to be invisible. . . . Living with friends, floating from place to place, there is no one person to identify teens who 'live independently'" (p. 289). Thus, *unveiling* dimensions of community problems requires mental agility.

Understanding how specific clients and problems inhabit their social context contributes to problem clarification. We may or may not already be familiar with the problems, those linked with them, or the setting. Suppose a worker is told that a community has problems "related to family breakdown, drug and alcohol abuse, long-term health care, services for the elderly, equal opportunity in employment, and affordable housing" (Murase, 1995, p. 157). An experienced worker might feel perfectly confident about proceeding. However, if the community is Japanese American and the worker is not, more information might be needed. The same problems can take different forms within a community and between communities due to cultural variations (Greenberg, Schneider, & Singh, 1998).

Human service workers, according to Ginsberg (1994, pp. 45–47), typically contend with these problems: economic disadvantage, physical illness, mental illness, crime and delinquency, maltreatment, lack of services to special populations, and lack of resources for programs. *For now, let us view social problems as widespread, intense worries that collectively demand leadership, societal attention, and intervention.* Ginsberg says it is "the shared belief that the problem represents a serious threat to a community or the larger society which provides people with the will to do something about it" (p. 41). (See Box 3.1.)

DISTINCTIONS RELEVANT TO OUR PROFESSION

A skeptic might ask why social workers need to learn any more about problems since, after all, they work with problem families every day. It is clear that our profession assists hard-pressed families and lunges to catch society's throwaway citizens. It is less clear whether the problem is these individuals, or those who toss them aside. Unemployment and underemployment in an era of global corporate relocation illustrate this complexity. Did blue-collar workers fail to acquire information-age skills, did management focus too much on immediate profits instead of acquiring productive computer-controlled plant machinery, or will corporations always gravitate to cheap labor? How will the problem be defined? Organizer and policy advocate Makani Themba (1999) challenges us to think about problems in new ways:

> Who are you holding responsible for social problems in this country? A strange question perhaps, but each time we choose an action to address a problem, we also assign responsibility to some group for solving that problem. . . . Youth violence? Focusing on gun policy or movie violence puts the onus on one set of players and institutions, advocating for mentoring or 'scared straight' problems targets another. (p. 13)

REACHING OUR OWN UNDERSTANDINGS

When people say to social workers, "Here's a social problem—fix it," we cannot take either

BOX 3.1	WHEN DOES A CONDITION BECOME A PROBLEM?

Some Middletown residents saw a brook in their town turn red. Some workers saw their skin turn yellow. Others became fatigued and developed the "Line One Shuffle." Between 1947 and 1975, thousands upon thousands of people in this southeast Iowa town worked at the local munitions plant. Now, public health officials and university professors are attempting to locate former assembly line workers, guards, technicians, maintenance workers, and even laundry personnel.

VEILED DIMENSIONS OF THE SOCIAL CONDITION

A deadly secret was kept through the end of the Cold War. Middletown workers had been assembling atomic weapons. Even those who were told that classified secret were not told about the dangers of radiation. Workers handled radioactive substances with their bare hands and breathed deadly fumes and powders. The U.S. Department of Energy is now funding the University of Iowa to contact everyone who might have been exposed to the bomb assembly line (Line One) processes. Public health officials are interviewing workers and holding educational outreach events.

Source: Excerpts from "Trouble in Middletown," 2001, April, *Iowa Alumni Magazine*, p. 37.

---

their judgment or their command at face value. For many reasons, we must not "accept the problem definitions of others" (Glugoski, Reisch, & Rivera, 1994, p. 84). *We must establish our own understandings and agendas—and do so with those affected.*[1] From this perspective, one human service role is to be aware of how affected individuals can help frame social problems. Thus, we discover a hidden challenge in social work: how to avoid being pressured or dominated by others who would define problems for us. The better able we are to follow the amorphous nature of problem development, the more we can influence the process for professional ends. We need to have as much input as possible; one person's judgment cannot be automatically preferred, because it is limited in perspective and knowledge. To be relevant and consumer-centered (Tower, 1994) regarding social problems requires flexibility. As Castex (1993) says, "An awareness of the occasional arbitrariness of one's assumptions should lead to an openness about altering those assumptions in new situations or when more information is supplied" (p. 687).

Similarly, when everyone says a problem is impossible to solve, we cannot take that assessment at face value either. It is incumbent on us to know ways to break logjams, work around constraints, and further the interests of community members. To return to Box 3.1, the Iowa factory employees may not have believed that their work conditions could be changed—even if they faced them head on—and they may have been correct, given the combined power of industry, military, and government arrayed against them, but who in the community or the university shouted out that there was a problem?

The many *conceptions of problems* outlined in this section reveal that a problem may be promoted on the basis of self-interest or blame. While lay people believe they know a problem when they see it, social workers need to take a larger view. We do not want to disempower by adding to the chorus of those telling our clients, "You are the problem!" As Rose (1990) says poignantly: "Believing in the 'promises' while being constricted by the realities . . . countless people experience themselves as failures, as stupid or inadequate" (p. 42).

SUBTLE FORMS OF BLAMING THE VICTIM
When people unfairly attribute responsibility to individuals who have suffered harm, this pejorative practice is called blaming the victim (Ryan, 1992). This concept is cited when rapists use the victim's manner of dress as an excuse or when people with human immunodeficiency virus are blamed for acquiring their disease or when small investors get taken in the stock market. *From a blamer's viewpoint,* children who ate lead paint and became ill and their parents, who "obviously" did not exercise proper "surveillance," become the problem, as opposed to manufacturers, landlords, and housing inspectors. Ryan contends that while environmental causes are now accepted as major factors, interventions

are directed to individuals. Think about that. Moreover, blaming the victim is "the most characteristic response to contemporary social problems on the part of most citizens, many public leaders, and some social scientists" (Lowry, 1974, p. 32). Social workers and liberals fall into the same trap according to Ryan (also see Kozol, 1995).

Some in society, says Ryan (1992), simply dismiss victims, even in the face of "unalleviated distress," while "kind humanitarians" place blame on the environment, not on individual character (p. 367). Yet Ryan reproaches the "kind" people who want to be compassionate while (unconsciously) leaving their self or class interests unchallenged—"charitable persons" whose mission is to compensate or change society's victims rather than change society: "They turn their attention to the victim in his post-victimized state. . . . They explain what's wrong with the victim in terms of . . . experiences that have left wounds. . . . And they take the cure of these wounds . . . as the first order of business. They want to make the victims less vulnerable, send them back into battle with better weapons, thicker armor, a higher level of morale" (p. 372).

Ryan is thinking of survival battles. Mental health practitioners focus on psychoanalytic explanations and solutions, he suggests, rather than *facing with numerous clients* "the pounding day-to-day stresses of life on the bottom rungs that drive so many to drink, dope, and madness" (1992, p. 373). Parsons, Hernandez, and Jorgensen (1988) add that "society is more willing for social workers to work with these victims than with other components of social problems" (p. 418). Such insights are reason enough to question our assumptions about problem formulation and resolution.

History Allows Us to See Problem Patterns

PERCEPTIONS OF PROBLEMS AND SOLUTIONS

A historical perspective involving *youth* can heighten the perception of what was or is viewed as a problem (H. Miller, 2000). Conduct and circumstances addressed as social problems in sermons and editorials 100 years ago are still discussed but not regarded in the same way today. These include unregulated spare time, masturbation, truancy, and pilfering from vacant buildings (Elkin & Handel, 1978; Kett, 1977). Today, along with concerns about body piercing and tattoos, the public worries about problems involving (a) "innocent" youth, such as victims of kidnapping and child pornography; (b) "troubled" youth, such as those living on the streets or taking and selling illegal drugs; and (c) "out-of-control" youth, such as children who kill children (Ginsberg, 1994, p. 48).

It is easy to assume that our era has found the truth and to forget that *what is deemed a social rather than a personal problem continues to be fluid* (see Box 3.2). Infertility, frailty, and menopause are recent problem constructions (Greil, 1991; Jones, 1994; Kaufman, 1994; Taylor, 1992; Theisen & Mansfield, 1993).

Proposed *solutions* or timetables may capture our imagination, only to disappoint us later or make us scoff. Alcohol prohibition—the result of a century of lobbying—was disappointing as a policy *solution*. Current controversial solutions include (a) facilitated communication with autistic children, (b) recovered memory therapy, and (c) the death penalty for teenagers. Homelessness was thought to have quick solutions, but like other problems treated initially as acute rather than chronic and as urgent rather than routine, it has remained for decades, leaving

| BOX 3.2 | CHANGING PERCEPTIONS OF SOCIAL PROBLEMS |

Spector (1989) captures the historical vagaries of social problems: "People who drink alcohol to excess were thought to be sinners by the temperance movement . . . regarded as criminals by the prohibition movement . . . and as diseased addicts by the medical establishment after 1940. Homosexuality used to be both a crime and a mental disorder [before] the decriminalization movement and a particularly dramatic official vote by the American Psychiatric Association in December 1973" (p. 779).

Similarly, Gordon (1994) puts the drug problem in historic perspective, revealing how often it was promoted as a problem in the twentieth century and in what forms, and showing today's resurrection of the "dangerous classes" construction (p. 225).

emergency service providers in bad straits (Lipsky & Smith, 1989). (Today, "housing first" is a preferred solution for chronic homelessness, that is, permanent housing—even single room occupancy housing with supports—is seen as preferable to shelters.) Similarly, food banks and other hunger relief programs diverted us from policy solutions (Poppendieck, 1998).

Perceptions of Nonproblems and Nonperceptions of Problems

In an earlier period, parents and the public were affronted and outraged by boys and men who wore their hair long. This nonproblem was treated as evidence of social disintegration. Less susceptible to notice, but fascinating, is what has *not* been labeled a social problem. For instance, discrimination based on age has rarely been identified as a problem for those in the younger age brackets, except when the voting age was lowered. Similarly, prejudice based on personal unattractiveness or size differences and societal advantages flowing from beauty are considered natural. It is telling that the following statement comes not from a newspaper or a textbook but from a science fiction story: "For decades people've been willing to talk about racism and sexism, but they're still reluctant to talk about lookism. Yet this prejudice against unattractive people is incredibly pervasive. People do it without even being taught by anyone, which is bad enough, but instead of combating this tendency, modern society actively reinforces it" (Chiang, 2002, p. 282).

Or consider aid to dependent families, compared with aid for dependent corporations (Ralph Nader's term). That some low-income families receive long-term welfare is defined as a problem. That wealthy families benefit from foundation tax breaks or corporate welfare is *not* defined as a problem (Donahue, 1994).

PRACTICES NOT CONSIDERED PROBLEMATIC

In a democracy (as opposed to a country with a rigid class system), we think of all children as having an even start. Yet children are automatically of the same class as their parents, and the U.S. school experience solidifies that position in much the same way that English schools do (Apted, 1998). If a child is killed through negligence in an accident and an insurance claim or court case is being settled, lost future earnings will be projected—was this child headed for Harvard Medical School or jail?—and linked to

the family history. Thus, what one child's life is worth in actuarial terms can differ between families by millions of dollars. As Elkin and Handel (1978) say, "Newborns begin their social life by acquiring the status their families have" (p. 119). This is not raised as a problem in polls, by schools, by planners, by presidential candidates. However, a crisis brought to the surface doubts about this "nonproblematic" stance in a supposedly egalitarian society. In 2001, when people in several government buildings were exposed to anthrax, lower profile postal workers were tested long after higher profile workers and elected officials on Capitol Hill, and several postal employees died. Income, class, and status issues also were in plain view as the government determined a compensation formula for September 11th victims. In an article entitled "Who Counts?" a writer for the *National Journal* raises class and favoritism issues as problems:

> The terrorists didn't choose their victims based on income, marital status, number of children, sexual orientation, place of birth, or state of residence. But to the consternation of many Americans, the sums that victims' loved ones could expect from the federal fund varied widely depending on these factors and others. . . . Strikingly similar grumbling was heard in the aftermath of the nation's first true bio-terror attack—the spread of anthrax through the mail. (Kosterlitz, 2002)

Ideology and receptivity affect our conceptions of problems. In Tallman's (1976) astute words, "An essential element in the problem-solving process is the ability or willingness to recognize that a problem exists. . . . People will differ in both the kinds of situations they view as problems and the number of situations they are willing to consider to be problems" (p. 151).

SITUATIONS NOT NOTICED OR NOT ACTED ON

Hurtful situations exist that fail to be perceived by those who could intervene, including the social service system. Over 700 residents of Chicago died between July 14th and 20th, 1995, in a heat wave. It was equally disturbing that initially the bodies of approximately 170 victims went unclaimed by families who did not even realize they were missing (Klinenberg, 2002). Isolated, poor individuals—living without fans or air conditioning—kept their windows and doors closed because everyone had defined street crime as a *problem* but had defined extreme heat and extreme isolation as *conditions*. Netting,

Kettner, and McMurtry (1993) help us see this by defining a *condition* as a phenomenon present in the community "that has not been formally identified or publicly labeled as a problem" and a *social problem* as a recognized condition that has been "incorporated into a community's or organization's agenda for action" (p. 204). Why is one group's pain noticed rather than another's (Hodges, 1999)? For example, *USA Today* ran a lead story about the tribulations of college students and graduates with personal debt. One student enhanced her life style by racking up $20,000 on 14 credit cards (Dugas, 2001, pp. A1–A2). However, newspapers seldom describe hardships caused to young people in impoverished countries by the crushing societal debt.

Problem creation results from *human action* (Tallman, 1976, p. 5). The action involves activity to promote a problem and a response to address the problem. Kaminer (1992) provides a stark example when she contrasts two very different groups. She points out that Cambodian refugees "who survived torture, starvation, multiple rapes, and internment in concentration camps and witnessed the slaughter of their families" do not use terms like *survivors* and *trauma* loosely and do not "testify" to the distress of their childhoods, as do those who are caught up in "victimization"[2] (pp. 81, 84). Cultural values about silence and resilience characterize this immigrant group. In contrast, articulate and impassioned promotion of recovery and self-help characterize the second group, a diffuse, nationwide network of proselytizers and sincere participants. The persons who *acted* to promote a problem contributed to this outcome: being a child of an alcoholic and many forms of codependency have become defined and publicized as national *problems*, while the needs of Cambodian and other refugees remain a *condition*. (The outcome also was influenced by the fact that millions are involved in self-help programs.) Being a metaphorically wounded child has made it onto the media agenda as a problem along with physical abuse. These are now defined problems; as part of the response, programs are being designed and money is being spent to address them.

Sociological Ways to Study Problems

A *social problem* is a construct, just as *goodness, defense mechanisms, service-worthy*, and *the deserving poor* are constructs (Griffin, 2002; Loseke, 1999; Marvasti, 2002). While we are used to

thinking of problems as being revealed by objective indicators and other measurement devices, we have been seeing how difficult it is to rely on facts when there are issues of theory versus fact and lack of shared definitions. Sociologists increasingly account for such complexity in their analyses. For example, Rubington and Weinberg (1995) discuss various ways, such as labeling and critical analysis, of looking at social problems (p. 357).

LABELING

Since a single personal behavior or social phenomenon can be called many positive and negative things, those who study labeling or an interactionist approach are intrigued by the *dynamics of how the naming occurs or prevails, how it changes across time, and how attention and reaction create a problem.* (See S. Cohen, 1980; Hardcastle, 1978; and F. B. Mills, 1996, for case studies.) Changes in labels are common enough to be mocked in musical theater. For example, the song "Gee, Officer Krupke" from *West Side Story* suggests how members of youth gangs have been characterized by various helping professionals (Bernstein & Sondheim, 1957).

Labeling can be amusing but usually has serious implications. Effects of being labeled "mentally ill" or a "hyperactive child" can be studied. Think what it would be like to say that your child's track in school was the "socially advantaged" track rather than the "honors" track. Consider the difference between being labeled a high school "dropout" and "a dissatisfied preparatory school customer." There are societal as well as personal consequences. As historian Katherine Castles (2002) maintains, "It is unlikely that the large sums of money spent on special services for disabled students would be available if those students were identified as merely poor" (p. 10). Public labels such as "sex offender" and "ex-con" are conceptualizations that can create or sustain a problem. Trice and Roman note that someone entering prison is put through elaborate procedures of negative labeling but, on release, "no process delabels or relabels him" (in Lowry, 1974, p. 128) in a positive way. Social workers specializing in addictions or working in institutions are in a position to ritualize an individual's "reentry into conventional society."

CRITICAL PERSPECTIVE

A critical approach requires us to step back, examine presumptions, and figure out who benefits from maintaining a particular problem (unemployment, vagrancy, conspiracy). For instance, respected sociologist Herbert Gans (1973) has written cogently about functions of poverty that help explain poverty's persistence. *The focus of attention in this approach is on the entire social system, in particular on the ruling class.* It encompasses activist inclinations toward *exposing domination and promoting emancipation* (Rubington & Weinberg, 1995, Chapter 7). Domination reveals itself in its labels. To wit, a Salvadoran complains about the way indigenous culture is devalued and denied: "They call our art . . . handicraft; our language . . . dialect; our religion . . . superstition, and our culture . . . tradition" (Gabriel, 1994, p. 5).

A critical approach asks us to examine societal contradictions. A contradiction in a program or club aimed at socialization skills would be to call the program users "members" but then to divide the lunchroom, lounge, and bathrooms into separate member and staff facilities—reserving the preferable rooms for staff (the opposite of other kinds of clubs). A critical approach to problems requires development of "critical consciousness" (Reeser & Leighninger, 1990, p. 73). Many adherents of this perspective emphasize political activism and the need for social change (Rubington & Weinberg, 1995, pp. 234–235).

RELEVANCE FOR PRACTITIONERS

Since social workers often engage in multidisciplinary work, in team practice, and within a host agency, they must be alert to theoretical perspectives about problems held by other professions. Just as the medical model shapes what should be done, a problem perspective may undergird the workings of a program with which social workers are associated. However, that perspective may not be respectful of clients or community residents.

DEFINING AND FRAMING A SOCIAL–COMMUNITY PROBLEM

Before confronting community problems, it is important to understand in what ways social workers can define and intercede with problems. We seek analysis tools that can make clear the nature of a problem and its potential relationships to its environment and solutions. Such knowledge and understanding will inform our practice interventions.

The elements of social problems can be pulled together into a conceptual framework, the purpose of which is to organize phenomena in a manner that allows the analyst to determine (a) *if* the phenomena or conditions are problematic and, if so, (b) *to whom* they are problematic, (c)

why they are problematic, and (d) the potential for social *intervention*. Think of a fact such as this one: Alcohol-related traffic accidents kill someone every half hour. That is the phenomenon.

Framing a Social/Community Problem

Circumstances often require us to look at a phenomenon in an immediate, rational way. This, in turn, requires a framework that can be used with many situations—pediatric AIDS, use of marijuana, homicide, illiteracy. The framework we utilize here (Hardcastle, 1992) has six elements:

1. Definitions of normative behavior
2. Ideology and value configurations involved
3. Views of social causation
4. Scope
5. Social cost
6. Proposed mode of remediation

This framework is suited to social work analysis because of the profession's strong normative and ideological emphasis, although as an analytic vehicle the framework strives for ideological neutrality by making ideology explicitly a component. It assists us in understanding how others have come to their conceptualization, how we can come to our own, and how we can position ourselves to address problems.

Before discussing each element, an explanation of *normative* and *deviant behavior* may be helpful. Behavior and circumstances may be regarded as desirable, acceptable, and normal within a group or a community. Then they are normative. However, a situation may be defined as a deviation from the norms of a community, a nation, or another entity. Thus, hunger, homelessness, and mental illness are deviations from community standards. Some standards are manifest; for example, regulations are codified norms, while others are insinuated. Our great-grandparents were openly religious in their speech, letters, and diaries. In today's secular society, similar behavior may be considered deviant by the less religious (touting one's atheism is also not acceptable). To understand why a situation is or can be labeled as deviant, the analyst needs to search for the meaning of a particular deviance to certain community segments. People have their own outlooks on how things should be.

In the following section, we look at the composition of social problems. We describe six elements of problem analysis and action. A condition must be subjected to a problem definition process by *defining* groups to be *classified* as a problem by an observer.

NORMATIVE AND DEVIANT

For a condition to be labeled a problem, it must represent to the defining group an important deviation from an actual or ideal standard or norm. The norm can be statistical and the deviation quantitative, such as poverty based on deviations from standard of living indexes or poverty lines. The norm also can be a model/ guideline and the deviation qualitative—for example, quality of life standards such as income security or respect. If the group plans to take on an issue and set the stage for successful intervention, the task is to capture the broad range of standards. The community is not homogeneous in its normative conceptions, but the group can figure out what is basically shared, that is, where cooperation or at least toleration is possible. The defining group can anticipate rival depictions.

IDEOLOGY AND VALUE CONFIGURATIONS

Ideology means an internally consistent set of values and integrated system of beliefs that form a unit and shape the definer's perceptions. It suggests the ideals that determine how the world should be constructed (e.g., the United States wants everyone to adopt the work ethic). The term goes beyond limited, formal political beliefs captured by labels like *conservative*, *liberal*, or *right* to encompass the holder's sense of community, community standards and acceptable behavior, belonging, and reciprocal obligations. Ideology is not necessarily controversial, at least within the community where it arises and is articulated. Values range from permissive to punitive on such issues as casual drinking, drug use, and sex. Whether a deviance is a problem or is significant depends on perception, which is rooted in ideology. Women's control over their bodies and whether the fetus has human rights are familiar examples. When perceptions are widely held and promoted strongly enough by the defining party, the problem becomes publicly defined.

SOCIAL CAUSATION

The public attributes most problems to social factors. This attribution of cause relates to the definer's perception that the condition is not totally the result of physical or biological forces but also has social roots. It may represent a conflict between the physical or technological and the social, or between social elements within society. Social causation does not mean that problems are exclusively social; they may have strong biological elements. Drought is a function of nature, but emergency supplies are social.

SCOPE

Scope relates to the condition's social nature in terms of the number and proportion of the community affected by the condition. It is reflected in incidence and prevalence. Generally the condition has to affect more than one person. It represents costs to significant portions of the population. These costs, such as restricted choice, are more than one-time costs. If a child falls into a hole or well and is rescued by a huge collective effort, that is *not* a social problem. Thus, the number of persons affected beyond a social worker's individual client or caseload will be relevant. However, if too many are affected, it can be overwhelming, so the defining group should not overstate the deviation's scope.

SOCIAL COST

Social cost relates to the assumption that the condition, if left unattended, has economic, personal, interpersonal, psychic, physical, or cultural costs. It may be a real cost, an implied cost, or an opportunity cost, the cost compared to what it would be if the conditions were successfully remediated. There is no assumption that the cost is perceived or carried equally by all members of society. An analytical task is to determine (a) who bears the cost, (b) the perceived cost, and (c) the perception of its distribution. Defining social costs often propels parts of society toward intervention or remediation. The definitions of social costs also may be a function of affordability. Conditions are defined as problematic as the interventions become affordable. Examples are relative deprivation (the raising or lowering of the poverty line as the wealth of the society increases or decreases) and mental health (expansion of the definition of mental illness as technological gains and society's ability to treat, alter, or address the conditions expand).

REMEDIATION

For intervention to be considered, there must be a defining party that can turn a condition into a problem, and a belief that the condition is alterable and remediable. If there is no belief, there will be no search for possible remediation. The levers of change or those who can affect change cannot be totally out of range for the community. A means of remediation does not have to be known; only the belief that remediation is possible must be present. If a condition is believed to be unalterable or in the natural order of things, the condition may be defined as nonproblematic or as something that must be endured, perhaps with some attention to reducing suffering. One example is how the poor are viewed under the philosophy of Social Darwinism. Combined beliefs about cause and remediation are important in many social work situations. The initial remedial plan can be official or unofficial and commonly will be changed as interest groups react to it.

Discussion of the Interventive Problem Framework

If we notice that 30 of our clients share a similar condition or circumstance, could this be the start of a problem? Considerations will include our view and others' views of its tractability and whether circumstances (supportive media, public approbation, etc.) appear favorable for resolution (Mazmanian & Sabatier, p. 191). We are not advocating developing a formula for taking immediate action on a perceived problem but rather a means of determining what to do based on a better understanding of what needs fixing and why. Thus, if we intend to stage a problem, we figure out the factors that allow us to be most effective as interveners. We need to know the problem's scope and the community's costs if the condition remains, compared with those if it is remediated. This approach thrusts the analyst toward the specification of outcomes without assuming that all of society will benefit equally from any specific outcome or alternative social state. It does not assume that everyone perceives the problem similarly or envisions the same solution. However, a careful use of the framework should enable us to determine to some degree, a priori, to whom certain outcomes will be beneficial and to whom they will be problematic.

Other Models

Other frameworks exist for identifying conditions, distinguishing problems, and moving toward resolution. Two human service books (Kettner, Moroney, & Martin, 1990; Netting, Kettner, & McMurtry, 1998), for example, walk readers through similar processes. Tallman (1976), on the other hand, asserts that "in all social problems" there are three essential and observable elements: "(1) a demand for social change based on moral interpretations of social conditions, (2)

overt controversy and conflict between groups over the issues articulated by those seeking change, and (3) an attempt, by at least one of the opposing sides in the conflict, to mobilize support from broader segments of the population" (p. 204). Think of animal rights.

As we move toward resolution of a problem, we can consider the group empowerment framework. It comes out of collective social problem solving, a participatory process. Barnes and Fairbanks (1997) have explored problem-based learning and Paulo Freire's problem-posing model (see our Chapter 14). They suggest that common people are more likely to take part when social endeavors reflect these points:

- Relevant issues and problems drive participation.
- Participants are learners and teachers.
- Participants identify and solve problems.
- Participants learn better through self-discovery.
- There is a continual cycle of reflection and action.
- Community transformation is *by* people, not for them. (Barnes & Fairbanks, pp. 58–59)

GETTING A SOCIAL–COMMUNITY PROBLEM ADDRESSED

In this section, we continue to discuss conditions and problems from a social construction perspective.

Stages, Players, and Techniques of Construction

Once a defining group has pinpointed a troubling condition, it must get *itself* in a position to be taken seriously in making a demand. We call this *community organizing* (see Chapter 14, this volume). When the group works instead to *position the condition* so that it will be considered a problem and to create an environment in which anyone would be viewed as having a right to make a claim because the condition is so intolerable, we call that *claims making*. Claims making is not equivalent to coalition building, where many groups find common ground; it is a competitive process that tends to favor problems with pathetic victims and groups with clout. Claims-making activities can be grassroots efforts where we can affect matters. Input is possible since we are dealing with *activities of defining and demanding*.

THE STAGES AND THE CLAIMS PROCESS

How does a problem evolve? Spector and Kitsuse help us examine the claims process and how citizens and advocates can make claims. They stress "unfolding lines of activity" (1987, p. 158) and see the life of a social issue commonly going through four stages of development and resolution. To them, government responses are key in determining whether social problems become part of society's agenda.

- The critical *first stage* occurs when a public claim is made that a problem exists and should be addressed (at this point, no formal or recognized group may even exist) with an ensuing debate.

- A *second stage* of getting government engaged will follow if (a) the issue has become public, (b) the claimant has exercised power effectively, and (c) the claimant has used the various channels of recourse (such as the government and the media) well. This is the stage in which policymakers (who believe they, too, have discovered the problem) respond to the claimant and offer official recognition (if the designated agency decides to own the program).

- A *third stage* of renewed claims may follow in which the original conditions, problems, and activities for change reemerge. By now, these may be less of a focus for the claimant than the *perceived blocked or ineffective avenues of recourse, discourse, dialogue, and procedural resolution* that had seemingly opened in Stage 2. (For further detail, see Spector & Kitsuse, 1987, pp 142–155.)

- Finally, a *last stage* of return to the community may happen when claimants back away from government agencies, disillusioned with their responses, and develop alternative solutions. The problem might die during or after any of these stages.

Brief examples. Noting the high rate of suicide by the elderly is the first stage of recognition as a problem. Although documented by organizations, scholars, and even the media (*USA Today*, the *New York Times*), elder suicide has not caught on as teenage suicide did (Mercer, 1989; Osgood, 1992). In contrast, nursing home reform followed the full course. Applying the stages to concerns about quality care, the development followed this path:

1. Abuse documentation

2. Formation of resident and consumer organizations and government response units

3. Ongoing conflicts between advocates and the relevant federal agencies

4. Renewed advocacy at the community and state level

PLAYERS AND STATES OF RESOLUTION

Who and what potentially contribute to recognition of a problem? Gladwell (2002) has popularized the idea that there are three kinds of exceptional people who contribute to what he calls social and word-of-mouth epidemics, or the spread of "ideas and products and messages and behaviors" (p. 7). He calls them "mavens" (information collectors), "connectors," and "salesmen." A targeted push by such people can contribute to problem resolution. Blumer (1971) says that types of action (e.g., agitation and violence) may be factors. He also notes significant types of players: interest groups, political figures, the media, and powerful organizations that may want to "shut off" or "elevate" a problem or both (p. 302). Thus, many groups contribute to problem definition: those suffering from a condition, challenging groups, social movement participants, policymakers, and journalists. Helping professions can be important participants in the process (Spector, 1985, p. 780). Blumer puts professionals like social workers with others—such as journalists, the clergy, college presidents, civic groups, and legislators—who have access to "the assembly places of officialdom." We can *legitimate* a problem or a proposed solution through "arenas of public discussion" (Blumer, 1971, p. 303).

In what is essentially a political process, governments "respond to claims that define conditions as social problems by funding research on solutions to problems, establishing commissions of inquiry, passing new laws, and creating enforcement and treatment bureaucracies" (Spector, 1985, p. 780). In the case of resident maltreatment by some nursing homes, for example, in the discovery stage a Nader report was published that included firsthand accounts by people who had worked undercover in several facilities. The federal government began monitoring nursing homes more closely, funded reports from the Institute of Medicine, passed the Nursing Home Quality Reform Act, and created the Administration on Aging's Long Term Care Ombudsman Program. (Simultaneously, the nursing home industry has fought hard to keep reform regulations from going into effect.) As one aspect of the response stage, more social workers have been hired by facilities to upgrade quality.[3]

Concurrent with drawing attention to a condition, claims makers must interpret it. They must shape public understanding of an emerging social problem, convince the public of its legitimacy, and suggest solutions based on the new consensus and understanding (Best, 1989, pp. xix–xx). This definitional process is often conflictual, as different definitions and the solutions that flow from them compete for public favor and scarce resources (Blumer, 1971). The systems for ameliorating a problem and establishing control that result from successful staging of a problem have been studied less than the initial framing of problems. Two cases follow, in which the aftermath has been documented.

> In the morning mail of January 8, 1962, the Supreme Court of the United States received a large envelope from Clarence Earl Gideon, prisoner No. 003826, Florida State Prison. . . . [His documents] were written in pencil. They were done in carefully formed printing, like a schoolboy's, on lined sheets.
> *Source:* From *Gideon's Trumpet* (p. 3), by Anthony Lewis, 1966.

Extended Examples of Claims-Making Processes

We deliberately emphasize classic over current situations (gay marriage), so the reader can concentrate on process rather than content. Experience suggests that substantive details can distract from seeing *how* a circumstance becomes a social problem. It will be productive to focus here on problems as activities.

THE RIGHTS OF THE ACCUSED

A criminal justice example will serve as an illustration of simple, straightforward claims making. Clarence Gideon made a claim that injustice was happening and society had a problem it should remedy immediately by paying for lawyers for the indigent in all criminal cases. Gideon was a small-town, middle-aged man who had served time. He was unjustly accused of a pool hall robbery in Florida but could not afford a lawyer and had to defend himself. He asked for a lawyer, was denied one, lost his case, and was sent to jail for 5 years. He immediately appealed, though unsuccessfully, to the Florida Supreme Court, wrote the U.S. Supreme Court about the right to counsel, and started a legal revolution that ended with a new system of public defenders in our country. Gideon himself was acquitted at his second trial with the help of a local lawyer. He was an average guy who decided to make a constitutional claim and, in standing up for himself, called attention to a national social problem—the lack of legal representation in noncapital cases. Until then, only poor people facing a death sentence were provided with lawyers. Gideon's story illustrates the sociological distinction between troubles and issues. Far more than Gideon's character and criminal troubles were at stake; values and issues of fairness at a societal level were at stake because Gideon was one of thousands of poor people failed by the legal structure. A private

matter became a public matter because of "a crisis in institutional arrangements" (C. W. Mills, 1959, p. 9).

In the first phase of claims making, prisoners from many states had petitioned for years to get redress for their perceived injustice. In the second phase, for various internal reasons, the Supreme Court was ready to consider change and therefore accepted Gideon's petition and upheld his claim, which, crucially, had been buttressed by supportive briefs filed by state officials. Claims-making analysis helps us see the important role of the Supreme Court in accepting Gideon's case, providing him, as a pauper, with top-notch lawyers at that level of the legal system, legitimizing the claims of injustice put forward by a convicted felon, and setting the stage for conclusions involving new programs at the state level. Power plays a role in the definition of problems, but so do well-positioned professionals, including social workers. So can the tenacity of one individual.

PROTECTION OF THE INNOCENT

In our second example, the dramatization of missing *and endangered* children provides a complex illustration of the claims-making process. This represents another aspect of the crime and punishment saga, for it is about those who are or fear being victims of major crimes. The public career of this problem started with a number of sensational murders, peaked with milk carton and grocery store sacks printed with pictures of missing children, and continues with the "Have You Seen Us?" cards sent in the mail with the 800 number for the National Center for Missing and Exploited Children. The designation *missing children* combined into one broad conceptualization what had been three different problems—children kidnapped or abducted by strangers, children kidnapped or snatched by one parent, and runaway children who were missing but sometimes returned (Best, 1987, p. 104). When they were lumped together, the total number of children involved was higher. The commonly cited incidence figure for missing children became 1.8 million cases per year (inexact estimate), which got attention and led to public hearings but misled almost everyone into thinking that most of these children were abducted by strangers—by far the *least* prevalent circumstance (Best, 1987, pp. 106–107; Best, 2001, p. 128).[4] In actuality, approximately 100 abductions by strangers are investigated per year. By the time the advocacy campaign had lost public interest and some credibility, new organizations and television shows were attending to the problem. Many individuals were involved, but more to the point, many advocacy groups and social service organizations were part of the identification, formulation, and promotion of this problem. Parents and child advocates sought to get stolen children returned and to bring flaws in systems to the attention of policymakers and the public. A useful Web site for further information on policy concerns is maintained by the National Center for Missing and Exploited Children at http://www.missingkids.com.

To highlight aspects of the claims-making process, Best draws on the field of *rhetoric* (also see Baumann, 1989). This approach helps us see the techniques employed to get this problem on the agenda, such as repeated use of horrific stories (atrocity tales and case histories), exaggerated use of statistics, and frightening parents into having their children fingerprinted. To stage the problem and buttress its need for attention, advocates staked out the claim that no family was exempt, as this problem was not tied to size of locale, income level, or race: "By arguing that anyone might be affected by a problem, a claims maker can make everyone in the audience feel that they have a vested interest in the problem's solution" (Best, 1987, p. 108). Rationales or justifications for focusing attention on *this* problem were used: the victims were "priceless" and "blameless" (in contrast, say, to drug abusers); even runaways were portrayed as abuse victims who fled, only to face exploitation on the streets (Best, 1987, pp. 110, 114). The objectives were to force more sharing and coordination of information between states and between the FBI—which handles kidnapping cases—and local police, as well as to cut down on the waiting time before children were declared missing so that the official search could begin sooner. Preventing the murder and kidnapping of children is still deemed the highest priority (Amber alerts and Megan laws) but one a bit more in perspective today.

That some priests were exploiting children and teenagers was known to the church hierarchy 25 years before the pedophiliac behavior and its cloaking became headline news. Church officials convinced many parents and children to treat the egregious situation as a nonproblem. The transition from condition to social problem took place only after large numbers of victims were documented and hidden atrocity tales were revealed through legal suits and investigative journalism. The claims-making process involved an "innocent children" justification for the problem receiving attention and remediation. Getting a problem in the public eye does not require a consensus about causation. The sexual abuse and institutional cover-up have been attributed to many factors, for example, the church's policy of celibacy and its arrogance toward laypeople.

On a positive note, the Catholic Church is actively opposing wife abuse and the practice of using Bible passages to justify it. Thousands if not millions more church members are affected by this condition; will they deem it a problem and stage any action?

THE POLITICS OF CLAIMING

Social action experts Robert Fisher and Eric Shragge (2000), drawing on John Friedmann, urge social workers who work with community organizations to engage in strenuous claims making, not just about social problems such as sexual abuse but about the larger workings of society. Social workers should, Fisher and Shragge argue, make claims for the need for the government to engage in wealth redistribution: "Claims making needs a broader strategy, which understands the fundamental importance of raising social policy, and wider political demands which critique the dominant political economy. In an era of neoliberalism, the dominant social agenda of a relative free market with a diminished role for the state in the social and economic field cannot be accepted as inevitable. It has to be challenged" (p. 13).

Techniques Used in Claims Making

The above descriptions of claims-making processes in legal aid and child protection illustrate ways to make potent arguments and shape perceptions, as we social workers have done and will continue to do as part of our mission. We want to master convincing techniques as described below, but from the outset we should remember that individual workers are not flying solo when they make claims; they have the prestige of our field and the combined helping professions to draw on.

Examples and case histories or stories, used so effectively with missing children, are employed with charitable fund-raising (e.g., Jerry Lewis's kids) and other problems. Sexual harassment became identified with Anita Hill after she testified on Capitol Hill in the Clarence Thomas Supreme Court nomination hearings. Since a 21-year-old college student from Wyoming was murdered because he was gay, the name Mathew Shepherd is becoming linked with public opposition to bigotry. His death has sparked drives for antihate legislation and became the subject of a play called *The Laramie Project*. In shaping perceptions, "welfare advocates focus on the deserving poor, their opponents speak of welfare Cadillacs," and both sides find this a convenient "shorthand for describing and typifying complex social conditions" (Best, 1987, p. 114). The most effective stories are those that ring true to the majority of the population.

To *typify* is to exemplify. George W. Bush uses the word *evil* to denote many foes. "Typification occurs when claims makers characterize a problem's nature" (Best, 1989, p. xx; see also Kennelly, 1999). Among the forms used are providing an *orientation* or an *example*. Typification through orientation is a device used to position the problem. To illustrate orienting, or steering, think about an organization that wishes to characterize a problem such as kleptomania or prostitution. The organization could characterize it as (pick one) deviance, a crime, a self-esteem problem, evidence that society is being too materialistic, or a woman's problem. Regarding typification through examples, we are all aware of the power of the typical case as it is used in politics—from the family unable to pay its medical bills "because of" legislation opposed by the Republicans, to the rapist who has been paroled "because of" laws sponsored by the Democrats.

Social workers can operate with integrity and still provide examples that will withstand scrutiny and reveal why a problem such as racial and ethnic profiling (Gates, 1995; Meeks, 2000) is important. We can aid those who have not had a problem themselves to experience it vicariously through a telling example, so they can see the impact of profiling (or whatever) on people's lives. Typification tells society about the nature of a problem and implies the advocacy that would be needed to address it. Regarding the typification of the problem in Box 3.3, the person featured in the example (a best-selling author and professor of religion at a prestigious university) cannot be discounted, and the objected-to behavior is given the *orientation*, or spin, of being antidemocratic and unlawful, a violation of core societal values. Most of those fortunate enough to obtain taxicabs instead of West are not even conscious of their "white privilege."

PROBABILITIES AND PRECONDITIONS

Why do some conditions become problems and not others? Is there a formula? Gladwell (2002) discusses the rise and fall of social problems in terms of a "tipping point" (p. 9). If problem creation results from an organized human response, then we should be interested in the inducements for and indicators of that action. In

---

BOX 3.3	AN EXAMPLE REGARDING PERSPECTIVE

Cornel West has allowed plenty of time to make an important appointment, but he must catch a cab and none will stop for him in downtown New York City. West, a theology professor at Princeton, is dressed in a suit and tie. He is on the way to have his picture taken for the book cover of what will become his best-seller, named, appropriately, *Race Matters*. However, the taxis drivers do not know any of this and drive by West to pick up white passengers, only yards beyond him, instead. Ten cabs refuse him. West becomes angrier and angrier.

The observer would see this as an example of discrimination. Taxi drivers would highlight their fear not of West in his suit but of his destination. To the refused passenger, the unfairness goes deeper than the fact that the drivers—whatever their race—are violating their own regulations. The experience negates democracy, the "basic humanness and Americanness of each of us," as West (1994) puts it (p. 8), and causes achievement stories to seem like a mockery. To West, the increasing nihilism of minority groups results not from doctrine but from lived experience (pp. xv, 22).

collective action and social movements, terms such as *critical mass* are used. Gitlin (1991) speaks of "critical social thought, oppositional energy," and "a vision of social change." Goldberg (1991) talks about an "energizing event" (p. 14). Netting et al. (1993) think that "a condition becomes a problem when it receives enough attention that it can no longer be ignored by community leaders, or when one or more leaders declare a condition unacceptable and decide that something must be done" (p. 210). Is there a *threshold* that must be met or a *trigger* that puts a condition over the top? Must a critical mass experience the problem or get involved in promoting a solution? Netting et al. argue against a threshold notion because they see no precision "in terms of time of appearance, size, or severity" (p. 210). (They still believe that such factors, along with urgency and duration, should be analyzed.)

The number of those having a condition is not sufficient because those affected may not act and because other factors may be involved—perceived costs and who bears them. For example, numerous people have sarcoidosis, a disease that does not spread and threaten public health and that is more common in African Americans, a less influential group in medical circles. Consequently little research money is spent on this somewhat mysterious, incurable—albeit rarely fatal—condition. *Intensity of effects*, or the suffering, of many individuals, is also not a criterion; lupus and arthritis are not treated as problems. Even the *death* of many individuals annually may be treated as just a condition. We can contrast the relative lack of action regarding the safety of space heaters, despite many deaths, with decisive action on lawn darts, on the basis of two deaths, due to the efforts of the determined father of a child who died. We can identify the *process* of organizing a response, *factors* (as in the missing-children example), and *techniques*, but there is no one precipitant.

THE MEDIA AND SOCIAL PROBLEMS

People interpret the information they receive on the basis of their own experience. Thanks to the expanding media role in our society, more and more people get their "experience" from the media picture of the world. We are what we watch—which is just as true for the Arab public as the U.S. public (El-Nawawy & Iskandar, 2002)—especially since people are often too busy to have developed their own understanding of an event or a condition and have no other competing picture.

Agenda

We need to know about short- and long-term media effects, how to use the media to advance an agenda regarding individual and social problems, and how to counter the way the media reinforce destructive individual and societal tendencies. An obvious case is the massive and extended attention that the media focus on violent people (school and workplace shootings, bombings). A century-long debate has raged over media's role in creating some social problems (e.g., effects of television violence) and media's potential to resolve others (e.g., documentation of police violence or the promotion of safe sexual practices or birth control). Today we believe the media's reality-shaping capacity and their ability to set or stall an agenda give them a great deal of influence.[5]

One role played by the media is to introduce us to a parade of problems until we are saturated. Humorist Art Buchwald once compared this process to the Miss America pageant; instead of Miss Georgia, Miss South Dakota, and so on, each year brings us such contestants as Miss English-Only, Miss Pollution, and Miss Global Warming, all competing for attention until one is crowned. We have a multiyear hit parade of social problem favorites: "Here she comes," Miss Hunger in America. ("There she goes" is the accompanying verity.) This hypothetical competition comes to life, in a political context, when first ladies select the winning problems, such as drug addiction, illiteracy, or lack of health care; or spouses of vice-presidents back winning solutions, such as emergency preparedness and mental health coverage. Lucky the problem that wins the contest or receives a sponsor!

Accountability

On a serious note, although media coverage can be superficial or deplorable, some investigations are exemplary, such as *Time* magazine's extended photo spreads on subjects social workers care about: gun deaths and deaths in foster care. We should look for ways to take advantage of such media-borne public attention to our issues, so we can turn that attention into action or public campaigns. It is also imperative for us to pay attention when the finger of blame is pointed at our field, documenting, say, the failings of the foster care system. Since we want citizens to take ownership of community problems, our own credibility will be higher if our profession takes ownership of human misery in our bailiwick (Bernstein, 2001; Klinenberg, 2002; Roche, 2000).

News coverage often lets powerful responsible parties off the hook. Iyengar (1996) puts it this way, "By obscuring the connections between political problems and the actions or inactions of political leaders, television news trivializes political discourse and weakens the accountability of elected officials" (p. 59).

Aileen O'Carroll (2001) analyzed television coverage of a Group of Eight (G-8) meeting and its attendant protest. She detected the following assumptions by television professionals:

Assumption 1. Members of the ruling class are peaceful. The protestors are violent.

Assumption 2. It is shocking when journalists are attacked by the police, because they are innocent; by implication, all protestors, if not guilty, then at least are suspect.

Assumption 3. It is the right of the G-8 powers to meet; the protestors have no right to be there.

Assumption 4. The protests aren't political. Real politics is conducted by the world leaders only (excerpts from pp 1–6)

Popular magazines also shape problems for us as do various tidbits served up on the Internet. The following clever piece ran in *BusinessWeek Online* (July 23, 2001). It suggests how we can reframe situations to provide a new perspective.

The List: Think Gas is Expensive?

To put the price in perspective, remember these fluid numbers the next time you're at the pump:

Snapple (16 oz., $1.29)
Price per gallon: $10.32
Evian water (9 oz., $1.49)
Price per gallon: $21.19
Scope (8.6 oz., $3.19)
Price per gallon: $47.48
Pepto-Bismol (4 oz., $3.85)
Price per gallon: $123.20
Liquid Paper (0.6 oz., $1.99)
Price per gallon: $424.53 (p. 3, para 2)

This brief but effective piece probably pleased both gas and oil executives and environmentalists, who want high prices for different reasons, while displeasing those concerned about low-income people and those seeking to hold Vice President Cheney—with his corporate ties—accountable on energy policy. People pass along something fun; so, after publication, the clever piece began circulating on the Internet. By now, the source reference to *BusinessWeek* magazine has long since disappeared, and it seems to be the original idea of individuals who post it. What is the logical fallacy in comparing gasoline to bottled water or mouthwash?

Journalists also need to be held accountable. As activists long have argued, profit-driven media owners and arrogant media personalities sitting astride emerging news stories play a role in the disaffection of people from public life. Now, some journalists agree. The public journalism movement hopes to prod cynical or fractious journalists and citizens to *solve* social problems. Proponents of public journalism believe that dialogue about solutions is impossible so long as not caring reigns in journalism, and everyone else is drowning in information overload (Merritt, 1995, pp. 262–264). A number of media outlets are experimenting with new approaches (Rosen, 1996). One newspaper ran a series on projects underway to improve the city. Instead of focusing on the awfulness of the problems, journalists focused on the awesomeness of the efforts being put forth by community-based organizations. For once, none of the published quotes were from government officials; they were all from townspeople. Social workers and other problem solvers may want to be part of such reforms.

We can ask community outlets to assist with community education. For instance, the media can help assimilate newcomers to the country, and even Native Americans who were here first, by teaching the public how to pronounce their names. Basic respect is lacking when radio or television personalities make fun of a name that is unfamiliar or has many syllables.

WORLDVIEWS AND SOCIAL PROBLEMS

Multiple Realities

Many of us know the non-Western world primarily from photographs in *National Geographic*. Yet that publication's pictures have "rarely cried out for change" (Lutz & Collins, 1993, p. 280). Our mental pictures of social problems in other lands are shaped and incomplete, and we have little sense of how non-Westerners who move to North America have lived or how they think. We must come to know intimately others' worldviews to be relevant in interventions and to es-

BOX 3.4	SEPARATE SOCIAL REALITIES

The following scene was recorded, by Erik Baard, a *Village Voice* reporter, at 9:50 p.m. on September 11, 2001, when it seemed possible that crowds would turn on neighbors and store owners as news spread of who had crashed the passenger planes into the World Trade Towers.

In one of three Arab-run delis in Queensboro Plaza, a Latino boy of maybe 10 years enjoyed grilling the nervous thirtyish man behind the counter at the Plaza Deli and Grocery. The gap-toothed boy glowed the way a child does when he finds he's got one over on an adult, watching the grownup sputter silly denials, like denying a bad toupee.

"Are you an Arab?"
"No, I'm a Gypsy."
"You're an Arab."
"No, I'm a Gypsy."
"No you're not, you're an Arab."
"I am a gypsy. Next person?"

The only Gypsy on Queens Plaza is a palm reader upstairs from the fishmongers [*sic*] and check cashers [*sic*]. The workers at the three delis studding Queensboro Plaza South are largely Yemeni. But one man already knew to hide, from even a child. (Baard, 2001, paras. 4–11)

tablish a (partial) shared reality. We should strive to broaden our take on situations until we can include the viewpoints of constituencies with whom we work and communicate and understand what they face. Events have very different meanings for our varied citizenry, some of whom experience foreigner discrimination and post–September 11 suspicion (see Box 3.4).

DIRECT PRACTICE AND REALITY CONCEPTIONS

Our field emphasizes the potential for shared meaning with clients and community members (Lum, 2003; Saari, 1991; Stringer, 1999), but some differences go deep. To be effective practitioners, we must become attuned to systems of meaning. For example, cultural and religious assumptions about the nature of reality may skew results on our standard psychological tests. After all, normalcy is a construct, not an independent truth (Pardeck, Murphy, & Choi, 1994, pp. 343–344). What do concepts such as *normalcy* and *psychosis* mean to a particular group (Richeport-Haley, 1998)? Does the group have alternative concepts for health and illness—such as energy balance and imbalance? When we avoid elevating our own reality, we remember that there "is no privileged position, no absolute perspective" (Rabinow & Sullivan, 1987, p. 8).

Imagine the experience of being a "patient" (Sacks, 1984) or a "crip" (Milam, 1993). Professionals and service users cannot presume to understand each other—another reason for checking things out—until a common vocabulary develops. "It is imperative that social workers ensure that their manner of speaking is similar

enough to the client's manner of speaking so as to be part of a shared discourse" (Pozatek, 1994, p. 399). This entails avoiding professional jargon. As Wells (1993) points out regarding emergency rooms, "Choice of words is an important consideration when dealing with a patient's family. Excessive use of medical terminology [such as *intubation*] may escalate anxiety" (p. 339). It's equally important to listen carefully and verify that key ideas are not misunderstood. During crises and commonplace activities, there are numerous and distinct realities.[4] No one can be in the know about all of them. To illustrate, substitute *social services* for *Medialand* in the boxed anecdote about gang members (next page). Everyone's world is rich and complex. As professionals, we can have more confidence in later actions if we first explore multiple conceptualizations about people and their situations, a step toward culturally competent practice.

Inside Our Heads

Flexibility in our thinking enhances problem solving. This means reexamining taken-for-granted assumptions, engaging in self-reflexivity, and being aware of possible paradigm shifts: "What if what was needed was not a bridge at all but a tunnel under the water or a ferry to cross the river?" (Martin, 1992). In *The Nurture Assumption,* Judith Harris likewise challenges accepted wisdom about childrearing (as cited in Gladwell, 1998, p. 55), making a strong case that *peers matter as much as parents.* Such a paradigm shift could broaden clinicians' hereto-

A journalist met with five teenaged boys, wards of the state of Illinois, to hear their stories but became lost in trying to understand the world of a former gang member. "He tried to explain the economy to me, the drugs and the colors and the beepers. He got me so confused I felt like I was in history class in the seventh grade, unable to even raise my hand to ask a question because I didn't quite know what the words meant. It occurred to me, then, just how remote those of us in Medialand are from our neighbors. So many realms of reality" (Laskas, 1994, p. 6).

fore nearly exclusive focus on matters inside the home to one that incorporates more outside influence. For example, clinicians working with youth might take more workshops on conflict resolution such as peer mediation, disputes and peacemaking, and community conferencing processes.

SOCIETAL THOUGHT STRUCTURES

The way we (and clients) conceive problems and solutions depends on systematic ways of thinking and frames of reference. Thought structures can set limits and shape whether and how we discern something (Witkin, 1998). If we have no way to place something mentally or lack a cognitive structure to which we can tie our thought, we are not likely to consider it. By way of illustration, a columnist points out that, in one fell swoop, our nation could nearly eliminate crime, teenage pregnancy, and drug abuse by "sequestering," or putting on "reservations," all males "between the ages of 15 and 19" (Allen, p. C5). While the columnist was joking, we might add that because research shows gay males are less violent and more altruistic, in this scenario they could be exempted (Nimmons, 2002).

We may avoid considering ideas that would anger or threaten those in power. Getting around such avoidance can require tactics, such as bumper stickers, that gradually shift perceptions; the Movement for Economic Justice used the slogan "Robin Hood Was Right." The Web can also give provocative ideas a voice. An example is the movement to redesign corporations: to take away their personhood, roll back their rights to early days, and revoke charters or seize assets when corporations misbehave.

MONEY AND PROPERTY EXAMPLES

Thought structures affect how (or if) we look at phenomena. In a rich country, it shocks us to hear that people in poor countries sell their body organs for transplant, because we lack the framework—desperate poverty—to consider it. Politicians could easily improve human conditions (drinkable water, health supplies) and save lives through forms of wealth sharing such as overseas aid. But *ideological unthinkability* stops most U.S. leaders from pursuing international or domestic sharing, even ideas considered by close allies. For example, to give young people a more promising future, Prime Minister Tony Blair persuaded the British government to set up Baby Bonds to guarantee that at age 18 every child will receive a fund of about $4,500 to $7,500 (a self-help account). The poorest children receive the most money (Boshara & Sherraden, 2003). This is not to say that ours is the only culture that finds some ideas unthinkable. In most cultures, for instance, abolition of inheritance is unfathomable.

Most Americans entertain new thoughts about money only after being exposed to ideologies other than capitalism, to worldviews other than those held in the Western developed world, and to utopian novels and communities. However, even a little exposure to a contending thought structure can put new possibilities on the table. Why does any of this matter in our practice? First, we must start from the premise that we have certain cognitive blinders. Second, if a way of thinking is unfamiliar—or even a bad idea or based on error—a social worker still must take notice and be able to stand in the shoes of those who use it. For example, a practitioner who discounts *collectivism* will fail to see the pluses when a religion requires its members to avoid loans and interest payments (Noguchi, 1999) or when a religious or immigrant community pools its capital and decides who will use it in which order for what. We may have heard of immigrant burial societies, but we may be unaware that "savings and credit associations are common to many cultures" (Sun, 1995, p. 22) and that money pools, which make payouts based on need or a lottery, operate for practical and social bonding reasons. Ethiopians call this arrangement an *ekub*, Bolivians refer to it as *pasanau*, Cambodians as *tong-tine*, and Koreans as *keh* (Sun, pp. 1, 22). Suppose family money is held in common, yet the practitioner urges the young adults to become independent and use their savings to buy a house for themselves, their spouse, and child. Reciprocal obligation and the family safety net are being ignored. The mainstream U.S. worldview puts the *individual* at the center, with "family, community, and society as the environmental context"; many immigrants and refugees, however, operate out of a worldview "in which the family, community, or society, not the individual, is central" (Glugoski et al., 1994, p. 83).

PROPOSING A DIFFERENT THOUGHT STRUCTURE

While we often attempt to see the total picture, we rarely attempt to propose a different picture. Brandwein (1985) does just that by outlining the feminist thought structure that currently contends with the dominant Western white male thought structure. The dominant structure is rational and materialistic, while one feminist construct places value on emotional and intuitive knowing (p. 177). Instead of asserting a strictly gender-based conflict, Brandwein juxtaposes two philosophies and ways of seeing the world or thinking—for example, contrasting feminism's *both/and* with the dominant *either/or*, and feminism's *collaborative* with the dominant *competitive*. Brandwein argues that true change comes only when a new thought structure is introduced and gains acceptance and ascendancy (p. 174). Debates over pay equity do not take place so long as women are deemed to be possessions—whether as slave or wife. Brandwein is adamant that most movements, although "advocating social and economic justice," stay stuck in old thought patterns, that is, they adhere to "the dominant thought-structure in our society" (p. 169).

Thought structures can be contested (VanSoest & Bryant, 1995). For example, those in critical legal studies (a critical approach to law) ask whether it makes sense to continually take a rights approach to law reform or social change. Yet allegiance to individual rights goes so deep that it is hard for us to conceive of alternatives. The gay/lesbian movement (Tully, 1994; Warner, 1993) has challenged the way normal human behavior and development and couples counseling is taught.

CULTURE AND SOCIAL PROBLEMS

Culture is "that which makes us a stranger when we are away from home," according to anthropologist John Caughey (1984, p. 9), who connects culture with a set of beliefs, rules, and values, with a way of life, with an outer and an inner world.

Reality in a Cultural Context

"Because we are each a product of our culture(s), culture provides the filters through which we each interpret reality," explain Kavanagh and Kennedy (1992, p. 23), but they add that approaches flowing from many cultures can have merit. Saari (1991) says, "Culture has often been referred to as if it were a singular and static thing. It is not" (p. 52). Nor is it solely about language and racial differences. Indeed, Swidler describes culture as a tool kit (Forte, 1999).

EXPECTATIONS REGARDING CULTURAL AWARENESS

Social workers are expected to acquire multicultural awareness and cultural competence in dealing with discoverable differences. It is discoverable, for instance, that godparents are a resource in many Hispanic families (Vidal, 1988). We also must learn to interpret less obvious or apparent differences. A study of older rural African Americans found that many of them believe receiving help in old age is a reward for having lived a good life. Acquiring such cultural knowledge allows helpers to market or program services in more appropriate ways to address problems (Jett, 2002).

To grasp the hidden, a social worker, like an ethnographer, must search for the "meaning of things" that a full participant in a separate culture "knows but doesn't know he knows" (Spradley & McCurdy, 1972, p. 34). For instance, cultural participants have a tacit understanding of the conventions and values associated with public speaking. Conklin and Lourie (1983) point out that not all speeches use the form taught in school of previews, reviews, summaries, and evaluations. An alternative form is topic chaining, shifting from one topic to the next. Moreover, many Native Americans "offer all known facts, regardless of how they apply to their own personal opinions. . . . The interactional goals of Anglo-Americans and American Indians—the one to convince the listeners, the other to submit information for their private deliberation—lead to two radically different oratorical structures (Conklin & Lourie, p. 274).

Ethnocentrism makes us feel that our way is right because it is what we know, even though facts can give us a broader view (e.g., Americans hold silverware differently from most other Westerners). As professionals, we must know our biases, how we see the world, and how we take the measure of others. Do we grasp our own ethnic bias about what constitutes an effective speech, an appropriate–acceptable human body, or the best way to eat a formal meal? Those who must learn a new culture become more accepting of multiple traditions. Cao O. is Chinese, born in Vietnam. Now a social worker in the United States, he describes his transition as his family became more American, acquiring new habits and new wants, such as privacy: "Now what I use to eat with depends on who I am eating with. . . . At home we don't use the small rice bowls any more. We use the American soup bowls to eat with. Yet my family would use chopsticks to go with that. We don't pick up the bowl anymore. . . . Before my family all lived and slept in one big room. Now I have to have my own room" (quoted in Lee, 1992, p. 104).

It sometimes takes a jarring twist for conventional Americans to notice either *different practices* (such as not automatically smiling) or *competing perspectives* (such as thinking of oneself as "temporarily able-bodied" or differently-abled rather than thinking of some fellow citizens as "mobility impaired" or "handicapped"). Oliver (1990) describes a survey of adults with disabling conditions that included questions such as "Can you tell me what is *wrong* with you?" and "Does your health problem/disability mean that you *need* to live with relatives or someone else who can help *look after* you?" (emphasis added) (p. 7). According to Oliver, "the interviewer visits the disabled person at home and asks many structured questions. . . . It is in the nature of the interview process that the interviewer presents as expert and the disabled person as an isolated individual inexperienced in research, and thus unable to reformulate the questions" [which never focus on the environment, just the person] (pp. 7–8).

No matter how pleasant the interviewer, niceties cannot overcome his or her built-in power and control, yet the professional may not think of this or the competing realities. A *disabled identity* that affects the thinking of everyone with every degree of ableness, in Oliver's view, is constructed through medicalization personal tragedy theory, dependency expectations, and "externally imposed" images of disability (Oliver, 1990, p. 77).

There can be rival perceptions. Many oppressed groups and persons out of the mainstream have identification considerations. Native Hawaiian children do not identify with either Japanese or white (Haole) people. With any given group, social workers must grasp whether messages from the dominant group are "accommodated, negotiated, or resisted" (Grace & Lum, 2001, p. 421).

DIFFERENT STANDPOINTS

The concept of communitarianism, discussed in chapter one, helps us avoid getting stuck in tribalism, balkanism, victimization, and martyrdom. However, *differences and history cannot be ignored*, whether one is working in a military community, with its tendency to reject homosexuals, or in a *gay* (even the language is different) community, where the 1978 murder of San Francisco city supervisor Harvey Milk and the 1969 Stonewall battle in Greenwich Village still have meaning (Duberman, 1993; Simon, 1994, p. 150). Similarly, those who want blacks to get over it and quit bringing up the topic of slavery are ignoring other debasing moments in *white* history. Hideous tortures before lynchings were public entertainment as recently as 70 years ago (R. Cohen, 2000). If the Great Depression still affects people, then lynchings will still affect people. A caseworker takes a social history; a community worker digs out a social history. A practitioner involved with the community in capacities such as child adoption needs to know personal and communal social histories and their accompanying worldviews.

Once again, we can best communicate across social boundaries when we realize that ours is not the only reality (Green, 1998). Service users and community residents can better share their stories if they realize that we know something about their world. If a sixth grader in a self-esteem group says that she sleeps in the same bed as a parent, we do not presume incest when the problem may be poverty. Greif (1994) observes that "working with these parents [from public housing] has taught me to rethink many of my basic assumptions about therapy with poor families and African American families. Twenty years ago I had been trained, for example, that parents should never share a bed with children. Yet these mothers have little choice" (p. 207). Awareness of multiple realities keeps us from making premature assessments. Feminist standpoint theory takes a similar position. "Members of each group must work to understand the standpoint of others to construct views of our shared reality that are less partial," says Swigonski (1994, p. 392). For direct and indirect practice, the "key to successful intervention is communicative competence" (Pardeck et al., 1994, p. 344).

DIFFERENT CLASSES

Saari (1991) asserts that "members of traditionally disadvantaged minority groups are by no means the only persons in society who must participate in more than one culture. . . . In a complex society, the individual normally participates in a number of somewhat different cultures or shared meaning systems in the course of an average day" (pp. 53–54). Some of these cultures or systems play a greater role than others. For example, it is easy to underestimate class differences if the focus is solely on race and ethnicity.

Those who are more privileged and better educated, with certain tastes, have the idea that they see things as they really are and are sure that Others lag, without drive, stuck in their provincial or limited realities and behaviors. Less privileged and less educated people of the same heritage, with certain tastes, consider themselves down-to-earth people who see things as they really are but view Others as fixated on striving and appearances, uptight and stuck-up, limited by snobbish realities and behaviors. Each view is ethnocentric. These views are internalized at quite a young age; children know about subtle distinctions, as this telling story shows: A little girl was shown a card depicting five bears who looked exactly alike, but one bear was being shunned by the other four. When she was asked what was happening in the picture, her quick reply was, "He's not our kind of bear."

Insider/Outsider Perspectives on Reality

Children gain cultural knowledge from a variety of sources, ranging from parental commands ("leave your nose alone") to peer teaching. They also develop a perspective of their own. Sixth-grade girls can "distinguish nearly one hundred ways to *fool around*," including "*bugging other kids, playing with food, and doodling*" (Spradley & McCurdy, 1972, pp. 18–19). Adults have a different perspective on such activities.

We must be aware of how the other person views experience. "The effective communicator learns to acquire and to understand, to the greatest extent possible, both insider (emic) and outsider (etic) perspectives" (Kavanagh & Kennedy, 1992, pp. 45–46). *Etic analysis*, which is observer oriented, gives us the ability to see similarities and differences and to compare or find commonalties across systems. Such a level of analysis might further a communitarian view by pointing out categories that all humans relate to, such as kinship. In social work, planners and organizers build on such a perspective. In contrast, *emic analysis*, which is actor oriented, allows us to become immersed in a worldview or lifestyle and its minutiae as a participant or a participant-observer. Emic analysis takes us into a collective, culture-specific mindset. Kavanagh and Kennedy see trade-offs: "The emic view provides the subjective experience but limits objectivity, whereas the etic perspective is more ob-

jective, but is farther from actual experience of the phenomenon" (p. 23).

Uniting with Consumers and Community Residents

Often it seems as if there is a world of clients, communities, and causes and also a social worker world, while for practice purposes the ideal is a joint one. Three key ideas derived from the etic–emic discussion are as follows:

- *Those experiencing the social problem have an emic or insider view.* Therefore, "Instead of asking, 'What do I see these people doing?' we must ask, 'What do these people see themselves doing?'" (Spradley & McCurdy, 1972, p. 9). Kavanagh and Kennedy (1992) urge that we "assess from the client's perspective what the most appropriate goals are in a given situation" (p. 24).

- *Social workers and clients may not share the same context or realities during an interaction.* What we say may not be what clients hear and vice versa. "It is essential," writes Pozatek (1994), "for practitioners to be aware of this phenomenon, and to socially construct, through dialogue with the client, a shared reality that they agree is a representation of their interaction" (p. 399).

- *Clients have reasons for what they do or decide.* We must individualize (Al-Krenawi & Graham, 2000). Green (1998) warns that if social workers view intervention modes as having universal applicability, such thinking constitutes applied ethnocentrism.

One area in which we want to build a shared reality is in constructing *the story of the problem* as it is told by individuals, families, groups, or community residents (Chrystal, 1999; Donaldson, 1976; Finn, 1998; Marcus, 1992; Saleebey, 1994). We may be the experts on resources and options, but our clients are the experts on their own needs and problems (Hartman, 1992). We must convert the question "What can I as a social worker do to help out those poor people?" to a question to mull over: "What are they saying to me?"

The second way to build a shared reality is through *mutual hope, mutual expectation,* and *a shared sense of efficacy.* Saleebey (1994) sees narrative and the building of hope as connected. If only negative tales are being told (e.g., by residents in public housing), then *counterstories* of success or "grace under pressure" might be spread and "scenarios of possibility" might be opened up (pp. 356–357). Most individuals and advocates have such stories to tell. Since "meaning . . . can inspire or oppress," suggests Saleebey, "why not take the time to work with individuals to articulate those meanings, those stories, those possible narratives that elevate spirit and promote action?" (p. 357).

In terms of self-efficacy, we can "help make possible different stories that clients . . . tell about themselves" (Saleebey, 1994, p. 357) and we can approach our work in new ways. Clinicians can allow clients to direct their therapy (Pardeck et al., p. 343; Wyile & Paré, 2001). At the macrolevel, we should make an equally strong commitment to those directly involved: their interpretations should determine the agenda of community development. Community organizers might see it as getting the people who are most affected by the change involved in the process (see Chapter 14, this volume).

If we have an etic view while simultaneously trying to gain an emic perspective, what is our role? We should not give ourselves short shrift, especially since we have resources and options. As practitioners, we have much to offer. We take our own reality for granted and forget how much we know that our service users do not know about how systems work or the ways certain aspects of the community function. We know how to manipulate our own and other organizations to get them to serve clients better. Our function at times is to connect one world to another. As a shelter and employment director for chronically mentally ill adults puts it, "There are all these homeless people who have fallen out of the larger system. They almost can't get back without someone to be a bridge and to help them access all those systems and services that they may be able to get." This social worker does not operate from a superior position—she talks of kinship with her clients—but rather from another reality, with different knowledge, where both perspectives are validated. She believes that success for a social worker is predicated on "being somebody that can deal with diversity of backgrounds and *functioning* levels and cultures, if you will."[6]

TOWARD SOLVING A SOCIAL–COMMUNITY PROBLEM

As sociologists Eitzen and Zinn (2001) state, "Solutions come from the bottom up—that is, people organize through human agency to change social structures. Solutions also come

from the top down—social policies determined by the powerful" (p. 17). While later chapters analyze power, advocacy, and intervention methods, here we consider ways to move the problem remediation process forward. To concur with VeneKlasen (2002), the process of citizen-centered advocacy involves looking inward, understanding the big picture, identifying and defining problems, analyzing problems and selecting priority issues, and mapping advocacy strategies.

Problem Solvers Must Be Supported

Problem solvers are those who identify, develop, and accelerate the reaction to social problems (Tallman, 1976). A community survey called Voices of Rural America was conducted in 2000. It found that those living in places of 2,500 or fewer persons ranked obtaining living-wage jobs and affordable health care as their most serious problems and reported usually turning to friends and neighbors for assistance in solving problems. The survey also determined that "in urban communities, nonprofits along with local ministries and the local police department were viewed as the most effective problem solvers. Rural residents were significantly more likely to view their civic and service clubs as more effective problem solvers than those in urban communities (Pew Partnership, 2000, p. 5, para 1).

Problem solvers include citizens in social distress, the many players in problem solving, and those local heroes—professionals and community leaders alike—who stay engaged in problem solving for decades, often taking on one problem after another. They include a "cloud of witnesses," community and social heroes proceeding us who faced social injustice (Brueggemann, 2002, p. 430). The luckiest problem solvers engage out of choice or professional commitment, but as Tallman (1976) points out, "others are forced to take action either by circumstances or by confrontations which they cannot avoid" (p. 150). It is outside our scope to discuss the many influences that give individuals the capacity to act, but Tallman's emphasis on vision and values is noteworthy: "One of the most important elements influencing the development of social problem solvers is the expectations they hold for how society should treat its members" (p. 172). (See Box 3.5.)

Rather than calling themselves problem solvers, some people think of themselves as pro-

---

BOX 3.5   A PROBLEM SOLVER STARTS A MONTHS-LONG PROCESS

Asherah Cinnamon is the director and sole paid staffer of the East Tennessee chapter of the National Coalition Building Institute (NCBI), an organization that addresses intergroup tensions. This social worker, who coordinates 20-30 local volunteers, demonstrates sensitivity to her community:

Three days in January, though not routine for me, nevertheless represent the culmination of three years of local organizing and relationship-building. At 8 p.m. on a Monday night, I hear that a black church [and its radio station and day care center] in our city has been burned to the ground in the early morning hours. Recovering from shock, outrage, and grief about this, I begin making phone calls to find out more about it and learn that the church is one of more than 20 that have burned to date in the Southeast USA in the past 16 months. . . . That same night, we put together a statement of support to present to the congregation of the burned out church as quickly as possible. Calls go back and forth at 10 p.m. with the first draft of the statement, to check with the NAACP president and several chapter members to make sure that the statement is appropriate and will indeed be seen by the African community as a genuine offer of support.

Early the next morning I begin faxing the statement out to key community leaders, especially white church and synagogue leaders, for their signatures. . . . I make more phone calls to encourage other local leaders to sign

the statement. . . . The vast majority of people I speak with thank me for giving them the opportunity to show their support. Many say they did not know what to do, and their shock kept them immobile until I called.

That evening, I meet with the Methodist minister who helped me draft the statement, to attend the prayer service in the parking lot of the burned out church. It is a freezing January night . . . and our toes feel frozen soon after we arrive. We are introduced to the presiding minister, who welcomes us and invites us to read our statement of support after the service. I do so and then list some of the community leaders who have signed. I notice the faces of the 50 or so congregants who are gathered in this place of violent destruction. As I read, I see one woman elbow her friend with an excited air as she hears the names of the signers. . . . One woman's eyes sparkle with unshed tears. . . . It is a small thing, really, to put words together and send around a statement of support. But for these people, it is a sign of hope, and a contradiction to their isolation as victims of violence and their isolation as members of a minority group in the midst of a majority culture which has too often let them down.

Source: From "Community Organizing for Social Change" (pp. 295–300) by Asherah Cinnamon, 1999, in L. M. Grobman (Ed.), *Days in the Lives of Social Workers: 50 Professionals Tell Real Life Stories From Social Work Practice* (2nd ed.), Harrisburg, PA: White Hat Communications. Copyright 1999 by White Hat Communications. Reprinted with permission of the author and White Hat Communications.

---

testors or social movement participants. Originally, people experiencing a problem might not have identified themselves as advocates or activists. Mansbridge (2001) found—in studying such groups as sexually harassed women, Chicano workers, and gay men, and lesbians—that their "outrage at their situation had at one point been kept under control by a dominant set of ideas that portrayed their situation as natural, normal, or in any case not unjust" (pp. 1–2). Mansbridge also notes,

Oppositional consciousness as we define it is an empowering mental state that prepares members of an oppressed group to act to undermine, reform, or overthrow a system of human domination. . . . At a minimum, oppositional consciousness includes . . . identifying with members of a subordinate group, identifying injustices done to that group, opposing those injustices, and seeing the group as having a shared interest in ending or diminishing those injustices. . . . Oppositional consciousness takes free-floating frustration and directs it into anger. It turns strangers into brothers and sisters, and turns feelings for these strangers from indifference into love. (p. 5)

Here, the important support is peer support from others in a subordinated group or from others in an action group seeking to end the domination.

Those of conviction who are already empowered clearly can help empower others. Still, those out in front pushing on for the rest of society must be valued by professionals in their quest to provide solutions to social problems. Their intensity of emotion should engender some reciprocal passion in us (Tallman, 1976, p. 6; Weaver, 2000). Furthermore, for political reasons, we had better back up our allies.

Issues Must Be Cut Strategically

To recapitulate, we can analyze the nature of a social problem by

- knowing our own minds and ideas and learning how clients or consumers of services see the problem's implications for them;
- figuring out which significant actors or community segments can potentially provide resources;
- on any issue, finding out our profession's stance, reading in other disciplines and studying the media, and reviewing past and present general views regarding solutions, as well as conservative/liberal positions; and
- discovering the collective definition process this problem has undergone to date and an appropriate role, if any, for our agency. If we plan to intervene, we must also look at what others have done and consider what we can do.

Once we or those we work with get started addressing problems, we are not eager to take time out to do this type of analysis. One of the first impulses after recognizing and discussing the seriousness of a problem is an intuitive attempt at "often ill-advised" reform, which James Bossard calls the "Well, let's do something, folks" stage (as cited in Spector & Kitsuse, 1987, p. 138). However, doing just anything to satisfy others' or our own sense of frustration is unprofessional and fruitless. Also, simply because we have finally defined a condition as a problem does not mean that others have done so. We have to look for support or mutual understanding in the wider world, and we have to think logically about the elements of problems so that our emotions and actions will be purposeful and successful. To start, we need to find out how many others are morally indignant (Tallman, 1976). How many hold our point of view or see a situation our way?

Our problem-framework components relate to intervention as much as to definition. We must work toward a shared construction of a problem. The way a group's purpose is characterized will expand or narrow the number and variety of people who will join the action. It has become clear, for example, that *right to life* was successful as a recruitment and umbrella term for diverse constituencies, while *antiabortion* was more limiting. In the same way, *proabortion* was not something many wanted to endorse, in comparison with the idea of *prochoice*. Community organizers sometimes call this cutting the issue (Staples, 1997; Mizrahi, 2001). If we are clear that we will be working with people of many minds, our appeals can be better directed to reach a broad group. The same holds true as we try to build an action coalition. To lobby with the community requires us to find core beliefs that unify. Problems create common denominators for citizens even while being distinctively experienced.

How does a strategic grasp of problems influence our practice? The practitioner becomes clear about what community members understand to be social problems and achieves a joint vision with them, then looks for ways to get forces in the community to work toward desired outcomes. The practitioner may strive to get defined as a problem something the community cares about or wants to change, or could strive to get something currently seen as a problem to be viewed as a nonproblem or, more typically, a different kind of problem. Suppose that the current understanding of the problem is adverse to community interests or siphons off resources that should go toward solving problems in the community's interests. The effort to stop terrorists from injuring U.S. citizens is an example. The current understanding is that immigrants, foreign visitors, and men from the Middle East are risks. Social workers who work with immigrants and refugees may be able to reframe the problem, at the community level, to protect those we serve. Certainly, all the money put into military and security programs represents money that could have been used to meet community goals and to solve social problems.

Inertia Must Be Confronted

After perception comes action (Tallman, 1976, p. 29), but most people are going to be inactive. It is within the range of normal to be indifferent to aspects of one's personal life (jobs, schools, spouse), so naturally many will be indifferent to social distress. Still, why don't those of us who do care "get off the dime"? Perhaps it is numbness, self-preservation, being fed up, or a lack of leadership. It takes effort to pay attention, and yet political attending is necessary for democracy (Bellah, Madsen, Sullivan, Swidler, & Tipton, 1991, p. 254). What sometimes stops us from taking personal or collective action is uncertainty or lethargy induced by beliefs or myths. This point will be covered more in Chapter 8. Lowry (1974) cites Robert Claiborne, who said that such myths and "schlock" research lead to the following conclusions:

- Nothing can be done about the problem; it is an inherent aspect of humanity and nature.
- Nothing needs to be done about the problem; things aren't that bad; enjoy things as best you can.
- Nothing much needs to be done; a little cosmetic reform of the system will suffice. (p. 40)

Here is a starting point for our profession, which has firsthand experience with the personal pain and social costs involved in these supposedly inconsequential problems. We can renounce such myths and bear witness to the need for a community-based system of social care. We can play a role in community education. We can make sure that the burdened and oppressed reject such myths and do not get tricked into adopting positions that are in conflict with their own self-interests. We can study reasons why people finally act. For instance, E. P. Thompson has written about how the English working class "overcame the dominant ideas of its time and began to see itself as a distinct class whose interest conflicted with those of factory owners" (as cited in Mansbridge, 2001, p. 2).

Organizers spend their days helping citizens frame social problems in ways that reflect the interests of the community rather than the powerful. However, organizers are keenly aware that first they have to overcome years of socialization that teaches people to be passive and oriented solely to the personal. To quote Si Kahn (1991): "We are taught to act as individuals, not as groups. . . . Individual problems can be handled without making major readjustments in the system. . . . Another reason for encouraging individual solutions is that they tend to make people blame themselves for their own problems. . . . It makes us believe that we are really not as good as the people who run the country, the factories, the schools" (p. 16).

If professionals are not careful, we can add to this sense of powerlessness. We must not skip past clients' attitudes. How do those with whom we work view themselves and life? Success frequently follows when community residents make a simple adjustment in their thinking, a cognitive action equivalent to cleaning one's glasses. While many want to see change, they cannot imagine it happening or themselves being involved in the process. An activist makes this point quite eloquently:

The initial problem that any community organizer has to overcome is a sense among people that (a) there's nothing I can do to make a difference in the way things are, or (b) even if I tried, I wouldn't be successful. It's what a lot of people call apathy. I don't think it is apathy. A lot of folks haven't really looked at their environment with a goal of changing it. It's a new idea for many people. Quite a few people go through life thinking that *life is happening to them*. What you do in organizing is help people see that life isn't something that necessarily happens to you, it's something that you can change as a group. The trick in the beginning is having enough hope in people's hearts that doing something will work.[7]

The phrase *making a difference* became a personal mantra for advocates, a successful volunteer and activist recruitment pitch, and a popular advertising theme because most people hunger for meaning and quietly hope that their lives indeed count for something. Freire (1994) says poetically, "I do not understand human existence, and the struggle needed to improve it, apart from hope and dream. . . . Hopelessness is but hope that has lost its bearings, and become a distortion of that ontological need" (p. 8).

By nature, social problems seem initially overwhelming but, with engagement, emerge as fairly resolvable. Personal passivity can change to action before or after this perceptual conversion, as those who are affected by a social problem get angry enough about how they are being treated to face the problem squarely. Once they have moved from a feeling of futility to one of self-efficacy, they may try to recruit us, the mayor, or the governor as an ally.

Putting Oneself in the Picture: Exercises

1. In her empowerment guide for people engaged in social action, Katrina Shields (1994)

proposes ways to connect the personal and the political.[8] We adapted some exercises she suggests:

(a) Relax, close your eyes and remember a time when you felt that some action you took made a positive difference. What happened? Who was involved? What was the setting? Remember as vividly as possible your feelings at the time.

Share your memory in small groups or pairs, or write about the incident in your journal.

(b) If you were totally fearless and in possession of all your powers, what would you do to heal our world (or do about a social problem that concerns you)? With whom would you like to join forces?

Share in a circle in pairs, or write your thoughts in your journal.

(c) How do you disempower yourself? How do you perceive others as doing this? Do you have a myth, belief or story that helps you put the current times in perspective, and to persist when the going gets rough?

Ask yourself these questions or discuss them with others (see Shields, 1994, pp. 19, 23, 77, for the original exercises).

2. Mainstream media ignore positive changes brought about by grassroots groups. Start a scrapbook of success stories about community problems and issues.

Discussion Exercises

1. Did you disagree with any of the premises or arguments set forth in this chapter? Over which sections do you think you and your parents or you and your neighbors would have the most disagreement?

2. On what basis should social workers take action regarding social problems? Consider these possibilities: stopping the spread of AIDS in Africa; condemning Islamophobia in the United States; legalizing marijuana or euthanasia; replacing old, faulty voting equipment; regulating violent content in video games; rewarding never married welfare recipients who marry; stopping abortion. Review the elements in framing a condition. What are your first three steps?

3. For a study of alternative realities, watch *Rashomon* (1951), the classic Japanese film about a lady, a gentleman, and a bandit; consider their widely differing points of view about whether there was a sexual assault and about virtues such as bravery. How can we take differing realities into consideration without losing confidence that there is any solid ground on which we can stand to practice?

4. Discuss similarities and differences in societal perspectives over time regarding honor and respect. Think about deaths resulting from "being dissed" (disrespected) and from dueling.

5. Imagine a different society. Parents only have their children with them for 4 years; then the children go to live with a series of other families, randomly selected. Eventually, parents and children are reunited for 4 years. In general, children would spend about 10 of their first 26 years with their birth parents (based on Sandra Feldman's "Child Swap Fable" in Eitzen & Zinn, 2000, p. 547). Discuss what difference this would make in what families care about and in the U.S. budget.

6. Spector and Kitsuse (1987) suggest a rudimentary approach to analysis and action: cut out community newspaper clippings; put down fundamental ideas and your own beginning knowledge about a situation that should be addressed for personal or professional reasons. The requisite activities are these: (a) describe a condition; (b) tell why it is annoying, disturbing, harmful, unethical, destructive, or unwholesome; (c) identify what causes the condition; (d) describe what should be done about it; and (e) explain how one would begin to accomplish this (pp. 161–162). Experiment using this exercise in the field with a client. If you're working with an organization, examine an issue collectively with your group.

7. Do not forget collecting data and obtaining a firm grasp on specifics. As a young labor organizer, Eugene Debs endeavored to protect the rights and lives of firemen on U.S. railways. To orient himself, "He set up a sheet of brown wrapping paper on one wall of his room and drew it off into squares. On the left-hand side he put the job the worker was doing; in the first column he set up the hours, in the next the wages, in the next the ratio of employment to unemployment, in the

next the proportion of accidents, and what responsibility the employer took for them; and in the last column the conditions under which the men worked" (Stone, 1947, p. 44). He also learned the realities for the wives and children, "He knew to an eighth of a pound and half of a penny how much of the poorest grade of hock meat and bones they could buy, to the last pint of milk and thin slice of bread how much nourishment could go into each of the children; how much longer the threadbare clothing on their backs could endure" (p. 81). Find documents that pinpoint such data about a problem and about a group that are of grave concern to you.

8. Brief research: Is rape of females viewed as a condition or as a problem in the United States, Mexico, Canada, and England? What about rape of males, especially in prison, in the same countries? Content analysis: Check to see if newspaper accounts about this act of violence use passive voice, that is, "A woman was raped last evening," or active voice "A man raped a woman last evening" (Blezard, 2002). Does wording matter?

Notes

1. Gowdy (1994) quotes an intriguing statement by a consumer: "Throw away the textbooks and let me teach you about being mentally ill. I have a Ph.D. in mental illness!" (p. 362).

2. Empowerment expert Simon (1994, Chapter 1) discusses the terms *healer* and *survivor* as *positive* metaphors. By contrast, victimization cultivates a "sense of resignation" rather than a desire to act (Kaminer, 1992, p. 158).

3. Most social work jobs are a result of a problem creation process. Think of positions in houses for battered women or mental health centers.

4. Pozatek (1994) provides an illuminating example of traditional Hispanic differences and realities (p. 397). Different worlds are powerfully depicted in Michael Moore's movie on Flint, Michigan, called *Roger and Me* (1989) and in Anna Deavere Smith's book and film on Crown Heights, Brooklyn, called *Fire in the Mirror* (1993).

5. For an overview, see McQuail (1994). See the "Glossary" in Lull (1995). On controlling the agenda, psychological abuse of any group is hard to sell as a problem to market-driven television because there is nothing to see, just as in the women's movement, consciousness raising was not observable (Tuchman, 1978, p. 139). Regarding culture–media connections, see Schiller (1989) and Stevenson (1995).

6. Mary Slicher, executive director of Project PLASE (People Lacking Ample Shelter and Employment), was interviewed by Sally Dailey for *Stirring People Up* (Powers, 1993).

7. Susan Esty of the American Federation of State, County, and Municipal Employees in a 1992 videotape by Lesley Bell and Michael Garcia, University of Maryland at Baltimore School of Social Work, entitled "Action Adventures in Our Own Backyard." A separate interview with Esty by Rebecca Smith appears in *Stirring People Up* (Powers, 1993).

8. Exercises from *In the Tiger's Mouth, An Empowerment Guide for Social Action*, a delightful manual by Katrina Shields (1994, New Society Publishers; ordering information retrieved May 30, 2003, from http://www.newsociety.com/bookid/3722).

References

Al-Krenawi, A., & Graham, J. R. (2000). Culturally sensitive social work practice with Arab clients in mental health settings. *Health and Social Work, 25*(1), 9–21.

Allen, J. T. (1995, February 19). Throw away the key: Locking up every young guy (for a while) can save America. *The Washington Post*, p. C5.

Apted, M. (1998). *42 up: Based on the award-winning documentary series.* New York: The New Press.

Baard, E. (2001, September 11). Listening to the Arabs of New York. *The Village Voice.* Retrieved May 29, 2003, from http://www.villagevoice.com/issues/0137/baard.php

Barnes, M. D., & Fairbanks, J. (1997). Problem-based strategies promoting community transformation. *Family and Community Health, 20*(1), 54–65.

Baumann, E. A. (1989). Research rhetoric and the social construction of elder abuse. In J. Best

(Ed.), *Images of issues: Typifying contemporary social problems* (pp. 55–74). New York: Aldine de Gruyter.

Bellah, R. N., Madsen, R., Sullivan, W. M., Swidler, A., & Tipton, S. M. (1991). *The good society.* New York: Vintage Books.

Bernstein, L., & Sondheim, S. (1957). Gee, officer Krupke! [Song from *West Side Story*]. New York: Leonard Bernstein and Stephen Sondheim.

Bernstein, N. (2001). *The lost children of Wilder: The epic struggle to change foster care.* New York: Pantheon.

Best, J. (1987). Rhetoric in claims-making: Constructing the missing children problem. *Social Problems, 34*(2), 101–121.

Best, J. (Ed.). (1989). *Images of issues: Typifying contemporary social problems.* New York: Aldine de Gruyter.

Best, J. (2001). *Damned lies and statistics.* Berkeley: University of California Press.

Blezard, R. (2002, Fall). It takes a man: The epidemic of rape won't end until males own up to its causes. *Teaching Tolerance, 22,* 24–30.

Blumer, H. (1971). Social problems as collective behavior. *Social Problems, 18,* 298–306.

Boshara, R. & Sherraden, M. (2003, July 23). For every child, a stake in America. Op-ed. *New York Times,* p. A19.

Brandwein, R. A. (1985). Feminist thought-structure: An alternative paradigm of social change for social justice. In D. G. Gill & E. A. Gill (Eds.), *Toward social and economic justice: A conference in search of social change* (pp. 169–181). Cambridge, MA: Schenkman.

Brueggemann, W. G. (2002). *The practice of macro social work.* Belmont, CA: Wadsworth/Thomson Learning.

Business Week Online (2001, July 23). Upfront regular feature. The list. Retrieved July 8, 2002 from http://www.businessweek.com/magazine/content/01_30/c3742013.htm.

Castex, G. M. (1993). The effects of ethnocentric map projections on professional practice. *Social Work, 38*(6), 685–693.

Castles, K. (2002). *Measuring children's futures: Intelligence testing and the search for a cure for poverty in Head Start and Special Education.* Unpublished paper. Contact klc3@duke.edu.

Caughey, J. L. (1984). *Imaginary social worlds: A cultural approach.* Lincoln: University of Nebraska Press.

Chapin, R. K. (1995). Social policy development: The strengths perspective. *Social Work 40*(4), 506–514.

Chiang, T. (2002). Liking what you see: A documentary. In T. Chiang, *Stories of your life and others* (pp. 281–323). New York: Tom Doherty Associates.

Chrystal, S. (1999). Out of silence. *Journal of Teaching in Social Work, 19*(1/2), 187–195.

Cinnamon, A. (1999). Community organizing for social change. In L. M. Grobman (Ed.), *Days in the lives of social workers: 50 professionals tell real life stories from social work practice* (2nd ed., pp. 295–300). Harrisburg, PA: White Hat Communications.

Cohen, R. (2000, April 26). Not just "black history": Yesterday's lynchings help explain today's reality. *The Washington Post,* p. A35.

Cohen, S. (1980). *Folk devils and moral panics.* New York: St. Martin's Press.

Conklin, N. F., & Lourie, M. A. (1983). *A host of tongues: Language communities in the United States.* New York: Free Press.

Donahue, J. (1994, March 6). The fat cat freeloaders: When American big business bellies up to the public trough. *The Washington Post,* p. C1.

Donaldson, K. (1976). *Insanity inside out.* New York: Crown.

Duberman, M. (1993). *Stonewall.* New York: Dutton.

Dugas, C. (2001, February 13). Debt smothers young Americans. *USA Today,* pp. 1–2A.

Eitzen, D. S., & Zinn, M. B. (2000). *Social problems* (8th ed.) Boston, MA: Allyn & Bacon.

Elkin, F., & Handel, G. (1978). *The child and society: The process of socialization.* New York: Random House.

El-Nawawy, M., & Iskandar, A. (2002). *Al-Jazeera: How the free Arab news network scooped the world and changed the middle east.* Cambridge, MA: Westview Press.

Finn, J. L. (1998). A penny for your thoughts: Stories of women, copper and community. *Frontiers, 19*(2), 231–249.

Fisher, R., & Shragge, E. (2000). Challenging community organizing: Facing the 21st century. *Journal of Community Practice, 8*(3), 1–19.

Forte, J. A. (1999). Culture: The tool-kit metaphor and multicultural social work. *Families in Society: The Journal of Contemporary Human Services, 80*(1), 51–62.

Freire, P. (1994). *Pedagogy of hope: Reliving pedagogy of the oppressed.* New York: Continuum Books.

Gabriel, J. (1994). Initiating a movement: Indigenous, black and grassroots struggles in the Americas. *Race & Class, 35*(3), 1–17.

Gans, H. J. (1973). *More equality.* New York: Pantheon.

Gates, H. L., Jr. (1995). Thirteen ways of looking at a black man. *New Yorker, 71*(33), 56–65.

Ginsberg, L. (1994). *Understanding social problems, policies, and programs.* Columbia: University of South Carolina Press.

Gitlin, T. (1991). The politics of communication and the communication of politics. In J. Curran & M. Gurevitch (Eds.), *Mass media and society* (pp. 329–341). New York: Edward Arnold.

Gladwell, M. (1998). Do parents matter? *New Yorker, 74*(24), 54–64.

Gladwell, M. (2002). *The tipping point: How little things can make a big difference.* Boston, MA: Little, Brown, & Company.

Glugoski, G., Reisch, M., & Rivera, F. G. (1994). A wholistic ethno-cultural paradigm: A new model for community organization teaching and practice. *Journal of Community Practice, 1*(1), 81–98.

Goldberg, R. A. (1991). *Grassroots resistance: Social movements in twentieth century America.* Belmont, CA: Wadsworth.

Gordon, D. R. (1994). *The return of the dangerous classes.* New York: W. W. Norton.

Gowdy, E. A. (1994). From technical rationality to participating consciousness. *Social Work, 39*(4), 362–370.

Grace, D. J., & Lum, A. L. P. (2001). "We don't want no haole buttholes in our stories": Local girls reading the Baby-Sitters Club books in Hawaii. *Curriculum Inquiry, 31*(4), 421–452.

Green, J. W. (1998). *Cultural awareness in the human services.* Englewood Cliffs, NJ: Prentice Hall.

Greenberg, M., Schneider, D., & Singh, V. (1998). Middle class Asian American neighborhoods: Resident and practitioner perceptions. *Journal of Community Practice, 5*(3), 63–85.

Greif, G. L. (1994). Using family therapy ideas with parenting groups in schools. *Journal of Family Therapy, 16*(2), 199–208.

Greil, A. L. (1991). *Not yet pregnant: Infertile couples in contemporary America.* New Brunswick, NJ: Rutgers University Press.

Griffin, S. P. (2002). Actors or activities? On the construction of "white-collar crime" in the United States. *Crime, Law, and Social Change, 37*(3), 245–276.

Hardcastle, D. A. (1978). Negative label attribution: A community study. *Arete, 5*(7), 117–127.

Hardcastle, D. A. (1992). *SOWK 631: Social work practice with communities and social service networks: A manual of readings, concepts and exercises.* Unpublished. University of Maryland at Baltimore School of Social Work.

Hardina, D. (2002). *Analytical skills for community organization practice.* New York: Columbia University Press.

Hartman, A. (1992). In search of subjugated knowledge. *Social Work, 37*(6), 483–484.

Hodges, M. H. (1999). Someone to watch over me. *Out, 70,* 102–105, 177.

Iyengar, S. (1996). Framing responsibility for political issues. *Annals of the American Academy of Political and Social Science, 546,* 59–70.

Jenness, V. (1995). Social movement growth, domain expansion, and framing processes: The gay/lesbian movement and violence against gays and lesbians as a social problem. *Social Problems, 42*(1), 145–170.

Jett, K. (2002). Making the connection: Seeking and receiving help by elderly African Americans. *Qualitative Health Research, 12(3),* 373–438.

Jones, J. (1994). Embodied meaning: Menopause and the change of life. *Social Work in Health Care, 19*(3/4), 43–65.

Kahn, S. (1991). *A guide for grassroots leaders.* Washington, DC: National Association of Social Workers Press.

Kaminer, W. (1992). *I'm dysfunctional, you're dysfunctional: The recovery movement and other self-help fashions.* Reading, MA: Addison-Wesley.

Kaufman, S. R. (1994). The social construction of frailty: An anthropological perspective. *Journal of Aging Studies, 8*(1), 45–58.

Kavanagh, K. H., & Kennedy, P. H. (1992). *Promoting cultural diversity: Strategies for health care professionals.* Newbury Park, CA: Sage.

Kennelly, I. (1999). That single-mother element: How white employers typify black women. *Gender and Society, 13(2),* 168–192.

Kett, J. F. (1977). *Rites of passage: Adolescence in America, 1790 to the present.* New York: Basic Books.

Kettner, P. M., Moroney, R. M., & Martin, L. L. (1990). *Designing and managing programs: An effectiveness-based approach.* Newbury Park, CA: Sage.

Klinenberg, E. (2002). *Heat wave: A social autopsy of disaster in Chicago.* Chicago, IL: University of Chicago Press.

Kosterlitz, J. (2002, May 3). Who counts? *National Journal, 34*(18), 1296–1302.

Kozol, J. (1995). *Amazing grace: The lives of children and the conscience of a nation.* New York: Crown.

Laskas, J. M. (1994, July 17). Cut from the chase. *The Washington Post Magazine,* p. 5.

Lee, J. F. J. (1992). *Asian Americans: Oral histories of first to fourth generation Americans from China, the Philippines, Japan, India, the Pacific Islands, Vietnam and Cambodia.* New York: New Press.

Lewis, A. (1966). *Gideon's trumpet.* New York: Vintage Books.

Lipsky, M., & Smith, S. G. (1989). When social problems are treated as emergencies. *Social Service Review, 63*(1), 5–25.

Loseke, D. R. (1999). *Thinking about social problems: An introduction to constructionist perspectives (social problems and social issues).:* Aldine de Gruyter

Lopez, S. (1994). *Third and Indiana.* New York: Viking Press.

Lowry, R. P. (1974). *Social problems: A critical analysis of theories and public policy.* Lexington, MA: D. C. Heath.

Lull, J. (1995). *Media, communication, culture: A global approach.* New York: Columbia University Press.

Lum, D. (Ed.). (2003). *Culturally competent practice: A framework for understanding diverse groups and justice issues* (2nd ed.). Pacific Grove, CA: Brooks/Cole—Thomson Learning.

Lutz, C. A., & Collins, J. L. (1993). *Reading National Geographic*. Chicago: University of Chicago Press.

Mansbridge, J. (2001). The making of oppositional consciousness. In J. Mansbridge & A. Morris (Eds.) *Oppositional consciousness: The subjective roots of social protest* (pp. 1–19). Chicago, IL: University of Chicago Press.

Marcus, E. (1992). *Making history: The struggle for gay and lesbian equal rights*. New York: Harper Perennial.

Martin, M. (1992). Assessment: A response to Meyer. *Research on Social Work Practice, 2*(3), 306–310.

Marvasti, A. B. (2002). Constructing the service-worthy homeless through narrative editing. *Journal of Contemporary Ethnography, 31*(5), 615–651.

Mazmanian, D. A., & Sabatier, P. A. (1981). The implementation of public policy: A framework of analysis. In D. A. Mazmanian & P. A. Sabatier (Eds.), *Effective policy implementation* (pp. 3–35). Lexington, MA: Lexington Books.

McQuail, D. (1994). *Mass communication theory*. Newbury Park, CA: Sage.

Meeks, K. (2000). *Driving while black*. New York: Broadway Books.

Mercer, S. O. (1989). *Elder suicide: A national survey of prevention and intervention programs*. Washington, DC: American Association of Retired Persons.

Merritt, D. (1995). Public journalism and public life. *National Civic Review, 84*(3), 262–265.

Milam, L. W. (1993). *CripZen: A manual for survival*. San Diego, CA: MHO Works.

Mildred, J. (2003). Claimsmakers in the child abuse "wars": Who are they and what do they want? *Social Work, 48*(4), 492–503.

Miller, H. (2000). Researching a law: "Stubborn children" then and now. *Focus on Law Studies, XVI*(1), 3, 9, 12.

Miller, M. (2002). The meaning of community. *Social Policy, 32*(4), 32–36.

Mills, C. W. (1959). *The sociological imagination*. New York: Oxford University Press.

Mills, F. B. (1996). The ideology of welfare reform: Deconstructing stigma. *Social Work, 41*(4), 391–395.

Mizrahi, T. (2001). Community organizing principles and practice guidelines. In A. R. Roberts & G. J. Greene (Eds.), *Social workers' desk reference*. New York: Oxford University Press.

Moore, M. (Writer/Director/Producer). (1989). *Roger and me* [Motion picture]. United States: Warner Bros.

Murase, K. (1995). Organizing in the Japanese American community. In F. G. Rivera & J. L. Erlich (Eds.), *Community organizing in a diverse society* (2nd ed., pp. 143–160). Boston: Allyn & Bacon.

Netting, F. E., Kettner, P. M., & McMurtry, S. L. (1993). *Social work macro practice*. New York: Longman.

Nimmons, D. (2002). *The soul beneath the skin: The unseen hearts and habits of gay men*. New York: St. Martin's Press.

Noguchi, Y. (1999, October 28). Matching faith and finances: Alternatives to loans cater to area Muslims. *The Washington Post*, pp. E1, E15.

O'Carroll, A (2001). What did you hear about Genoa? Review of TV coverage of the Genoa G8 protests. Retrieved July 14, 2003 from http:flag.blackened.net/revolt/wsm/news/2001/genoaTV_july.html

Oliver, M. (1990). *The politics of disablement*. New York: St. Martin's Press.

Osgood, N. J. (1992). *Suicide in later life: Recognizing the warning signs*. New York: Lexington Books.

Pardeck, J. T., Murphy, J. W., & Choi, J. M. (1994). Some implications of postmodernism for social work practice. *Social Work, 39*(4), 343–346.

Parsons, R. J., Hernandez, S. H., & Jorgensen, J. O. (1988). Integrated practice: A framework for problem solving. *Social Work, 33*(5), 417–421.

Pew Partnership (2000). Voices of rural America: National Survey results. Retrieved on July 14, 2003 from http://www.pew-partnership.org/pubs/voicesOfRuralAmerica.html

Poppendieck, J. (1998). *Sweet charity? Emergency food and the end of entitlement*. New York: Penguin Books.

Powers, P. (Ed.). (1993). *Stirring people up: Interviews with advocates and activists* [Monograph]. Baltimore: University of Maryland at Baltimore, School of Social Work.

Pozatek, E. (1994). The problem of certainty: Clinical social work in the postmodern era. *Social Work, 39*(4), 396–403.

Rabinow, P., & Sullivan, W. M. (Eds.). (1987). *Interpretive social science: A second look*. Berkeley: University of California Press.

Reeser, L. C., & Leighninger, L. (1990). Back to our roots: Toward a specialization in social justice. *Journal of Sociology and Social Welfare, 17*(2), 69–87.

Richeport-Haley, M. (1998). Approaches to madness shared by cross-cultural healing systems and strategic family therapy. *Journal of Family Psychotherapy, 9*(4), 61–75.

Roche, T. (2000). The crisis of foster care. *Time, 156*(20), 74–82.

Rose, S. M. (1990). Advocacy/empowerment: An approach to clinical practice for social work. *Journal of Sociology and Social Welfare, 17*(2), 41–51.

Rosen, J. (Ed.). (1996). Rethinking journalism, rebuilding civic life [Special issue]. *National Civic Review, 85*(1).

Rubington, E., & Weinberg, M. S. (1995). *The study of social problems: Seven perspectives* (5th ed.). New York: Oxford University Press.

Ryan, W. (1992). Blaming the victim. In P. S. Rothenberg (Ed.), *Race, class and gender in the United States: An integrated study* (pp. 364–373). New York: St. Martin's Press.

Saari, C. (1991). *The creation of meaning in clinical social work.* New York: Guilford Press.

Sacks, O. (1984). *A leg to stand on.* New York: Harper & Row.

Saleebey, D. (1994). Culture, theory, and narrative: The intersection of meanings in practice. *Social Work, 39*(4), 351–359.

Schiller, H. I. (1989). *Culture Inc.: The corporate takeover of public expression.* New York: Oxford University Press.

Shields, K. (1994). *In the tiger's mouth: An empowerment guide for social action.* British Columbia, Canada: New Society Publishers.

Simon, B. L. (1994). *The empowerment tradition in American social work: A history.* New York: Columbia University Press.

Smith, A. D. (1993). *Fires in the mirror.* New York: Doubleday.

Spector, M. (1985). Social problems. In A. Kuper & J. Kuper (Eds.), *The social science encyclopedia* (pp. 779–780). New York: Routledge.

Spector, M., & Kitsuse, J. I. (1987). *Constructing social problems.* New York: Aldine de Gruyter.

Spradley, J. P., & McCurdy, D. W. (1972). *The cultural experience: Ethnography in complex society.* Chicago: Science Research.

Staples, L. (1997). Selecting and "cutting" the issue. In M. Minkler (Ed.), *Community organizing and community building for health* (pp. 175–194). New Brunswick, NJ: Rutgers University Press.

Stevenson, N. (1995). *Understanding media cultures: Social theory and mass communication.* Thousand Oaks, CA: Sage.

Stone, I. (1947). *Adversary in the house.* New York: New American Library.

Stringer, L. (1999). *Grand Central winter: Stories from the street.* New York: Washington Square Press.

Sun, L. H. (1995, February 17). Traditional money pools buoy immigrants' hopes. *The Washington Post*, pp. 1, 22.

Swigonski, M. E. (1994). The logic of feminist standpoint: Theory for social work research. *Social Work, 39*(4), 387–393.

Tallman, I. (1976). *Passion, action, and politics: A perspective on social problems and social problem solving.* San Francisco: W. H. Freeman.

Taylor, B. C. (1992). Elderly identity in conversation: Producing frailty. *Communication Research, 19*(4), 493–515.

Theisen, S. C., & Mansfield, P. K. (1993). Menopause: Social construction or biological destiny? *Journal of Health Education, 24*(4), 209–213.

Themba, M. N. (1999). *Making policy, making change: How communities are taking the law into their own hands.* Berkeley, CA: Chardon Press.

Tower, K. D. (1994). Consumer-centered social work practice: Restoring client self-determination. *Social Work, 39*(2), 191–196.

Trouble in Middletown. (2001, April). *Iowa Alumni Magazine*, p. 37.

Tuchman, G. (1978). *Making news: A study in the construction of reality.* New York: Free Press.

Tully, C. T. (1994). To boldly go where no one has gone before: The legalization of lesbian and gay marriages. *Journal of Gay and Lesbian Social Services, 1*(1), 73–87.

Van Soest, D., & Bryant, S. (1995). Violence reconceptualized for social work: The urban dilemma. *Social Work, 40*(4), 549–557.

VeneKlasen, L. (with Miller, V.). (2002). *A new weave of power, people and politics: An action guide for advocacy and citizen participation.* Oklahoma City, OK: World Neighbors.

Vidal, C. (1988). Godparenting among Hispanic Americans. *Child Welfare, 67*(5), 453–458.

Vissing, Y., & Diament, J. (1995). Are there homeless youth in my community? Differences of perception between service providers and high school youth. *Journal of Social Distress and the Homeless, 4*(4), 287–299.

Warner, M. (Ed.). (1993). *Fear of a queer planet: Queer politics and social theory.* Minneapolis: University of Minnesota Press.

Weaver, H. N. (2000). Activism and American Indian issues: Opportunities and roles for social workers. *Journal of Progressive Human Services, 11*(1), 3–22.

Wells, P. J. (1993). Preparing for sudden death: Social work in the emergency room. *Social Work, 38*(3), 339–342.

West, C. (1994). *Race matters.* New York: Vintage Books.

Witkin, S. L. (1998). Chronicity and invisibility. *Social Work, 43*(4), 293.

Wyile, H., & Paré, D. (2001). Whose story is it, anyway? An interdisciplinary approach to postmodernism, narrative, and therapy. *Mosaic, 34*(1), 153–172.

4

The Concept of Community
in Social Work Practice

They hang the man and flog the woman
Who steals the goose from off the Common,
But let the greater criminal loose
Who steals the Common from the goose.

ENGLISH RHYME

It is hard to imagine a more elusive concept than the idea of community. Fraught with meaning, the word *community* conjures up memories of places where we grew up and where we now live and work, physical structures and spaces—cities, towns, neighborhoods, buildings, stores, roads, streets. It evokes memories of people and relationships—families, friends and neighbors, organizations, associations of all kinds: congregations, PTAs, clubs, teams, neighborhood groups, town meetings. It evokes special events and rituals—Fourth of July fireworks, weddings, funerals, parades, and the first day of school. It evokes sounds and smells and feelings—warmth, companionship, nostalgia, and sometimes fear, anxiety, and conflict as well. We all grew up somewhere; we all live in communities somewhere; we all desire human associations, some degree of belonging to a human community; we all carry around some sense of community within us. It goes deep into our souls (see Box 4.1).

The elusiveness of the concept of community derives from its multidimensionality. Accord-

ingly, for this book, we have adopted Fellin's (2001) formal definition of communities as "social units with one or more of the following three dimensions:

1. a functional spatial unit meeting sustenance needs

2. a unit of patterned interaction

3. a symbolic unit of collective identification (p. 1)."

This chapter establishes the basic concepts, variables, and changes related to community life. The following two chapters examine ways of studying communities and methods for hearing community concerns. To change community, their parts, processes, and particularities must be understood.

The common elements in sociological definitions of community are geographic area, social interaction, and common ties. However, while connection to a territorial base is frequent so that neighborhoods, villages, or cities fit the defini-

| BOX 4.1 | MR. BIRTHDAY MAKES HIS ROUNDS |

On the morrow, she will turn 7. On every birthday of her life, she has awakened to find a festooned sign planted in her front yard and signed at the bottom, "Mr. and Mrs. Jerry Engert." Annie has no blood tie to Mr. Engert. Nor do Johanna and Greta Pemberton, nor Robert and Emma Speiser, nor Wendy and Lisa Bauman, nor any of the 18 neighborhood kids whose names and birth dates appear in a 3-by-5 index file in Mr. Engert's basement. But each gets a lawn sign every year, individually crafted and bearing a bag of goodies. . . .

What Mr. Engert does, though, isn't only about birthdays. It's about neighborhood. . . . Mr. Engert lives on Luzerne Avenue, a shaded lane of delightful bungalows in North Woodside, not far from downtown Silver Spring. . . . On Easter in North Woodside, there's an egg hunt. On Mother's Day, a softball game. On Labor Day, Luzerne has a block party. And all year long, Luzerne has birthday signs.

Source: From "Mr. Birthday Makes His Rounds," by Steve Twomey, June 19, 1995, *The Washington Post*, p. 81. Copyright 1995, *The Washington Post*. Reprinted with permission.

tion, functional and cultural communities or "communities of interest" without clear geographic bases (such as the social work community, the Chicano community, or the gay and lesbian community) are also included. Spatial units with clearly defined geographic boundaries are seemingly becoming less necessary to communities because of rapid electronic communication technology, ease of physical mobility, and economic globalization.

Most of us have connections to several communities, in part because we are geographically mobile and increasingly tied together though electronic and other media, and in part because the smaller communities we affiliate with are usually embedded in larger communities that also affect our lives. As social workers, we need to understand the multiple communities of our clients as well as our own communities. Communities provide us with a rich social and personal life. They shape the way we think and act. They surround us with values and norms of behavior, explicit laws, and unwritten rules of conduct. They furnish us with meanings and interpretations of reality, with assumptions about the world. They provide resources and opportunities, albeit unevenly—places to work, to learn, to grow, to buy and sell, to worship, to hang out, to find diversion and respite, to be cared for. They confront us with traumas and problems; they intrude on our lives, and they hold out the possibilities for solutions. In keeping with the social work ecological model's emphasis on person in environment, communities must be the object of social work intervention as much as individuals, families, and groups. Social workers can help expand community resources. A competent community, according to Fellin (2001), is a community that "has the ability to respond to

the wide range of member needs and solve its problems and challenges of daily living" (p. 70). Community competence is enhanced when residents have (a) a commitment to their community, (b) self-awareness of their shared values and interests, (c) openness in communication, and (d) wide participation in community decision making.

BASIC COMMUNITY CONCEPTS

Community, Neighborhood, and Public Life

Community enterprise zones, community control, community partnership abound in policy discussions. Community and grassroots have a kind of social currency. They are buzzwords in politics and ideologies of the left and right. By *grassroots*, we mean a bottom-up approach, starting with common people. *Community* and *neighborhood* are sometimes used interchangeably to mean a local area (e.g., a section of a city or a county, where many residents share, over time, a common world view). Residents unite, on a short-term basis, in their roles as indignant utility ratepayers or exuberant sports fans in ways that can facilitate community action and transcend deep differences.

Community suggests people with social ties sharing an identity and a social system, at least partially, while *neighborhood* suggests places that are grounded in regional life where face-to-face relationships are possible. See Fellin (1995, 2001) for an in-depth discussion and definition of community and neighborhood. *Public life* refers to the civic culture, local setting, and institutional context that also are part of the "environment-surrounding-the-person" (Johnson, 2000). Lappé

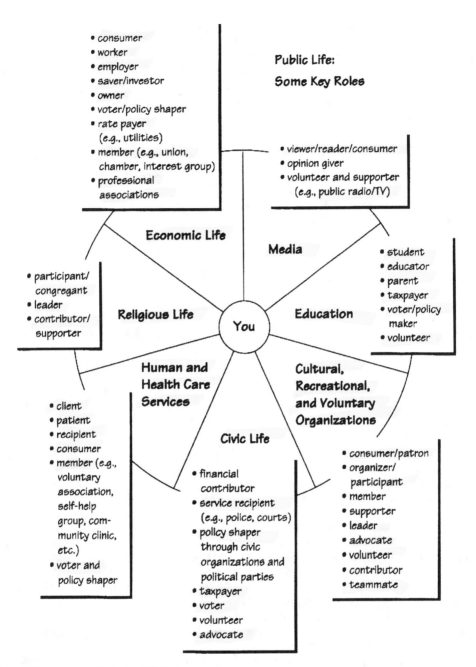

- consumer
- worker
- employer
- saver/investor
- owner
- voter/policy shaper
- rate payer
  (e.g., utilities)
- member (e.g., union,
  chamber, interest group)
- professional
  associations

**Public Life:
Some Key Roles**

- viewer/reader/consumer
- opinion giver
- volunteer and supporter
  (e.g., public radio/TV)

Economic Life

Media

- student
- educator
- parent
- taxpayer
- voter/policy
  maker
- volunteer

- participant/
  congregant
- leader
- contributor/
  supporter

Religious Life

You

Education

**Human and
Health Care
Services**

**Cultural,
Recreational,
and Voluntary
Organizations**

- client
- patient
- recipient
- consumer
- member (e.g.,
  voluntary
  association,
  self-help
  group, com-
  munity clinic,
  etc.)
- voter and
  policy shaper

Civic Life

- financial
  contributor
- service recipient
  (e.g., police, courts)
- policy shaper
  through civic
  organizations and
  political parties
- taxpayer
- voter
- volunteer
- advocate

- consumer/patron
- organizer/
  participant
- member
- supporter
- leader
- advocate
- volunteer
- contributor
- teammate

Figure 4.1   Public life: Some key roles. From *The Quickening of America: Rebuilding Our Nation, Remaking Our Lives* (p. 25), by F. M. Lappé and P. M. DuBois, 1994, San Francisco: Jossey-Bass. Copyright 1994 by John Wiley & Sons, Inc. Reprinted with permission of John Wiley & Sons, Inc.

and Du Bois (1994) provide a delineation of some roles in the various sectors of public life (see Figure 4.1).

Let's illustrate these three concepts with Dixie County, Florida, a real rural neighborhood near the Gulf of Mexico. As one index of its public life, residents vote at the lowest rate in Florida. They may trust each other. They don't trust rich politicians. A 41-year-old worker in Cross City,

Dixie County, reported (concerning politicians), "I don't think they think about people like us, if they do care, they're not going to do anything for us. . . . Maybe, if they had ever lived in a two-bedroom trailer, it would be different. I don't think either one of those men running for president has ever had to worry about where their next paychecks are coming from" (Bragg, 2000, p. 18).

Other residents wished for a political champion who would talk sincerely about poor people. During a national economic boom, people in this rural locality were preoccupied with hard times, low-paying jobs and a lack of neighborhood factories and work places. They worried about gas prices at least four months before the rest of the country. They felt and were ignored by Washington.

Geographical communities evolve in many forms and have been classified in numerous ways such as *enclave, edge, center, retreat* (Brower, 1996); white versus blue-collar; and boom versus bust. These descriptive structural ideas cannot substitute for the community narrative. Community is more than just local space, especially in urban areas, and needs social identity (Fellin, 2001). Residents can share the same geographic space, such as in rural Arizona (McCormick, 1997), and hold widely differing ideologies and particularistic religious, ethnic, and class identities. Gays and Cuban Americans inhabit the same territory in Key West without sharing the same language, political agenda, history, or social institutions. A London resident may think about himself more as a businessman or an immigrant from Pakistan than as a Londoner. People not in physical proximity, that is, international travelers or guest workers or undocumented aliens, can still share more cultural affinity with those back home than with the new neighborhood. Those in our caseload also have complex allegiances and affiliations. Think of a child who has a father in urban Michigan and a mother in rural Montana and, in either state, bounces from one relative's neighborhood to the next—bringing along clothes, attitudes, haircuts, and slang from the last school that never quite fits at the new school.

We often bemoan the loss of community with its fragmentation, alienation, and increased mobility accompanied by a decline in public life with fewer residents involved in voting and volunteering. Today, many people *choose* their degree of commitment to their neighborhoods and towns. Using length of stay as a variable, Viswanath, Rosicki, Fredin and Park (2000) found four types of residents:

> *Drifters:* Less than 5 years of stay and a high likelihood of moving away from the community.
> *Settlers:* Less than 5 years of stay and less likelihood of moving away from the community.
> *Relocators:* More than 5 years of stay but likely to move away from the community.
> *Natives:* More than 5 years in the community and unlikely to move away. (p. 42)

Natives often blame problems on new arrivals. When we plan with families or create new programs, both length of stay *and* level of involvement and commitment are crucial factors.

Place and Nonplace Communities

A mantra for real estate agents is *location, location, location,* the mantra for community practitioners is *context, context, context.* Where do people come from? Who do they relate to? Where is their identity? What gives meaning to their lives? Social workers should learn about their clients' place and nonplace communities. Locational communities in a definable area, with boundaries that often constitute a political jurisdiction, where many inhabitants have familial roots (Ginsberg, 1998), focuses attention to a physical and social environment surrounding providers and consumers of services. However, within and outside such spatial and structural communities are other influential nonplace groupings based on identity, profession, religion, and other social bonds that comprise another type of community. Social workers must pay equal attention to an individual's or family's diffuse nonplace social networks and solidarity bonds. Place and nonplace communities represent two forms of *we-ness* and *identity.* Box 4.2 compares the two types of communities.

A social worker's complete social history on a client or case ought to include a community history and a client's experiences in communities as well as personal or family history: Where was a person born? What did the person gain from living in prior locales? Social workers also will want to get a complete picture of how both types of communities—place and nonplace—figure into an individual's present life. We discuss these needs more fully in Chapter 15.

THE CHANGING U.S. COMMUNITY

To understand the modern community as a context for social work practice, we will briefly review some important changes in U.S. life that have occurred over the last 50 years. The contemporary U.S. community as the context for social work practice has undergone significant changes in the past half century. Change is American, and the past two decades' changes have been dramatic. Perhaps it is because we are living through these changes. The United States has vast resources and ambitious people with the freedom and energy to invent, to explore, to develop, and to challenge. The changes are sometimes positive and sometimes, unfortunately, exploitative.

BOX 4.2	DIFFERENCES AND SIMILARITIES BETWEEN PLACE AND NONPLACE COMMUNITIES

Differences

Place—Bounded Location	Nonplace—Bounded Interest
Collective territorial identity	Relationship identity and dispersion
Intertwined processes	Specialized processes
Empathetic connections	Mixed allegiances

Similarities

Traditions
Mutual constraints
Lack of absolute boundaries

During most of the last half of the twentieth century, the U.S. economy expanded and especially boomed to end the millennium. But the new millennium was welcomed by economic recession, corporate greed, and collapse. We were clear about the constellation of a good family and family values, even if not always faithful to them. Per capita income and consumption grew, and Americans worked harder and longer. The new millennium was accompanied by threats to retirement income and Social Security with an expanding work life for an aging population. College education, seen as an American birthright until the 1980s and 1990s, was becoming inordinately expensive. World peace, on the horizon with the end of the cold war and breakdown of the Soviet Union, appears to have collapsed in the ethnic strife and terrorism that characterizes so much of the world. And on September 11, 2001, global terrorism came to the United States. It seemed apparent to some observers that a future can't be predicted on a past. Americans, "accustomed by our historical training to expect mastery over events," could no longer remain uncritically optimistic about the future (Heilbroner, 1960, p. 208).

The social movements of the 1960s—civil rights, community action, women's liberation, peace—together with the Vietnam War—did much to shake the complacency of the 1950s in the United States. However, the radicalism of the 1960s was followed by a conservatism since the 1970s. It's still with us.

The 1980s saw a necessity for two wage earners to support a family; burgeoning health care costs; expansions of unemployment, welfare rolls, homelessness, and crime; and a growing income and wealth disparity between the wealthy and the poor and middle classes. The 1990s and the beginning of the twenty-first cen-

tury have reversed some of these trends and accelerated others. Welfare, crime, and taxes decreased while income inequality, corporate power, and the influence of money in politics increased. Privatization of social welfare and public services become trendy. Prisons became a growth industry, with many of the prisons operated by proprietary corporations. These all spoke of complex forces at work in U.S. society, seemingly unresponsive to easy fixes. Let's now consider some of the more important forces and trends to deepen our understanding of social work practice for the twenty-first century. The changes reviewed in the following paragraphs reflect our views of what seems significant. They are not presented in any particular order of importance.

- Urbanization, or more accurately, suburbanization continues (Scott, 2001). Most U.S. citizens (over 80%) live in 39 metropolitan statistical areas (MSAs) of 1 million people or more, more than in smaller cities or rural communities (U.S. Census Bureau, 2001). Population continues to shift from the old Rust Belt, mill towns, and smokestack cities of the Northeast and Midwest to the Sunbelt of the South and Southwest, especially California, Florida, and Texas. Reflecting the population shift is a change in the economy from manufacturing and farming to information, personal, and entertainment services, technology, and e-businesses. Most MSA growth is in the new outer ring suburbs beyond the old suburbs. Even with periodic energy crisis and chronic dependence on foreign energy sources, the automobile and high-energy single-family homes are preferred. Metropolitan area growth hasn't brought metropolitan government to coordinate the multiple jurisdictions within MSAs.

Probably the greatest resistance to metropolitan governments comes from suburbanites' not wanting to mingle their public amenities and tax resources with the poorer neighboring core cities in the MSAs. The metropolitan areas are becoming increasingly balkanized and hypersegregated. with more centers of ethnic minorities and poverty, while the suburbs are less ethnically diverse and more affluent (Scott, 2002).

- Rural-urban and suburban differences will increase with rural problems, as with central city problems, which will be neglected for at least the first part of the twenty-first century.[1] Poverty will continue to be greater in rural areas than in metro areas, with most of the poor counties in the United States being rural. While most rural poor are white and non-Hispanic, a disproportionate number of poor families are African American, Hispanic, and headed by females. The natural resources base of rural areas continues to decline, and low-skill jobs face increasing global competition. The metro–rural wage gap continues to widen, as does the gap in college completion rates. Distance and a lack of sufficient density hinder rural economic development. Rural localities will continue to lose population, especially the young and more educated (Economic Research Service, 1995). The proportion of the nation's population that is nonmetropolitan decreased from 20.2% in 1990 to 19.7% in 2000 (U.S. Census Bureau, 2001, pp. 30). Agriculture is becoming more corporate, with farm sizes increasing (U.S. Census Bureau, 2001, pp. 523–524). The exceptions to these trends are the high-amenity rural areas with mild climates and scenic environments that are becoming gentrified and gaining populations (Economic Research Service, 1995).

- The 90s and beyond have seen an escalating economic inequity in the work force. There has been an extensive loss of well-paying, stable manufacturing blue-collar jobs, with job growth in lower paying service jobs. One result has been high *and* persistent rates of unemployment and *underemployment* among older industrial workers and unskilled men and women of all ages. A rising retirement age is reversing a decade-long trend (Walsh, 2001). Later retirement ages will be accelerated with the decline in value of stock-based retirement plans and the increasing age requirements for Social Security benefits.

- Even with recession, the Enron and World-Com fiascos, and other corporate failures and shenanigans, executive and management salaries and bonuses have rapidly increased. From 1980 to the end of the century, the average pay of ordinary working people increased by 74%, while the average compensation to corporate CEOs exploded by a gigantic 1,884%. The compensation increased during the last quarter century for CEOs from 10 to 45 times as much as the average worker to 400 times as much (Executive Pay Watch, 2003; Executive Pay, 2002; Executive Pay, 2003; Johnston, 2002c). The median CEO annual salary in 2000 was $6.2 million, supplemented by $14.9 million in stock options, up 50% from 1999, for a total average annual compensation of over $20 million. The increases in managerial compensation are not linked to managerial or corporate performance. Many executives eased out for poor corporate performance received huge bonuses and severance packages (Leonhardt, 2002; McGeeham, 2003; Pearlstein, 2000). Investors, on the other hand, typically lost, as illustrated by an average 12% reduction in total shareholder return value in 2000 and 2002. Managerial compensations increased by 22% although managers often were dumping their stock ownership of their company's failing stock (Banerjee, 2002; Leonhardt, 2001b). Graef Crystal, an analyst of corporate executive compensation observed that if this trend continues, by the year 2015 the gap between workers' and executives' pay "will approach that which existed in 1789, when Louis XVI was King of France" (as cited in Day, 2000). The French Revolution also began in 1789.

- The average worker's salaries increased by only between 3 to 4% in 2000, compared with the 22% increase in managerial compensation (Leonhardt, 2001a, 2001b). These workers had increased their work year by over 2% during the decade of the 1990s, so most worker gains are explained by their working more. The U.S. worker now works more hours a year than workers in other industrial countries. We are increasing the hours in the work year while it's decreasing in other countries (Greenhouse, 2001).

- Unfortunately, social work's salaries did not even keep up with inflation during this era (Gibelman & Schervish, 1996, p. 166). The average salary for direct service social workers according to Kerger and Stoesz (2003), combined social work salary, the average for BSWs and MSWs was $32,010 in 2000. This was less than 0.15% of the average CEO compensation (Executive Pay, 2002).

- As would be expected from the earnings and compensations differences, the United States now is more income unequal, with a greater concentration of income at the top than any other industrialized nation. The middle 60% of U.S. society have seen their share of the national income fall from 53.6% in 1980 to 48.5% by 1999 (U.S. Census Bureau, 2001). Some 47% of the total real income gains between 1983 and 1998 accrued to the top 1% of income recipients, 42% to the next 19%, and only 12% to the bottom 80%. Only people at the very top made any real economic improvements (Johnson, 2003). Tax policies, economic policies and recession, and a devolving welfare state has led to increasing poverty for the first years of a new millennium (Pear, 2002). According to some economists, including a founding father Adam Smith (1922, p. 17), one's position in the unequal income distribution is largely a matter of birth. James Hechman, a libertarian University of Chicago economist, as quoted by Stille (2001), asserts, "Never has the accident of birth mattered more. If I am born to educated, supportive parents, my chances of doing well are totally different than if I were born to a single parent or abusive parents. . . . This is a case of market failure: Children don't get to 'buy' their parents, so there has to be some kind of intervention to make up for these environmental differences" (p. A-17).

- The 1990s saw the U.S. economy and world economy globalize and the nation-states and welfare states begin to devolve. This trend should continue despite the growing unilateralism of the United States. Economic globalization treats the world as a single economic system. Globalization's intent is to reduce state sovereignty and the constraints of national borders and any social and cultural arrangements and relationships as economic hindrances (Deacon, 1997, p. 34; Gray, 1998; Park, 1999, p. 34). Globalization weakens the economy's basic social partnership by shifting the balance of power to capital and corporations, and it reduces the power of labor and the state (land) (Gray, 1998; Mishra, 1999, pp. 100–101). Transnational corporations have reduced public regulation and responsibilities for community social welfare and any ecological agenda. As seen by the environmental unilateralism of the United States, setting sustainable global growth limits need not be heeded by a single nation or global corporation transnationally (Deacon, 1997, p. 54). Competing nation-states pursuing global corporations in a global economy discard social obligations to their citizens with a subsequent erosion and downward spiral of social provisions *that can lead to the lowest social welfare denominator* (Deacon, 1997, p. 196). The economic upheavals of the globalized turboeconomy may be as dramatic as the industrial revolution. A global economy encourages cheap labor, lower or no taxes on the rich and on corporations (Gray, 1998; Johnston, 2002b, 2002c), corporate welfare, tight money, market deregulation, protection of capital over labor and antilabor policies, and a decline in welfare state provisions and benefits for labor as employees and as citizens of a welfare state (Freudenheim, 2002; Gray, 1998; Johnston, 2002a; Mishra, 1999; Pear, 2002; Wagner, 1997). The G7 nations, the globe's top economic powers, national marginal personal tax rates declined in all seven countries with the greatest decline in the United States. Globalization increases aggregate national wealth, poverty, and social and income inequality within and between nations (Deacon, 1997, pp. 34–35; Halsey, Lauder, Brown, & Wells, 1997, p. 157; Hokenstad & Midgley, 1997, 3; Room, 1990, p, 121). Globalization cultivates national fragmentation and a civic decay manifested by increasing income and social inequality, poverty, fear, violence, family breakdown, fundamentalism and intolerance, social and economic ghettoization, social isolation and social exclusion, political and social marginalization, and political authoritarianism (Berry & Hallett, 1998, pp. 1–12; Dahrendorf, 1995; Hokenstad & Midgley, 1997, p. 45; Passell, 1998; Thurow, 1995). We have seen an increase in the number of nation-states and a growth of separatist movements within nation-states since the advent of globalization.

- The welfare state is devolving in the United States and globally (Dodds, 2001). We commented on the growing political conservatism in the United States in Chapter 1. Liberal government's traditional function in a market economy—to help communities manage and protect themselves from the excesses and vagrancies of the market economy—is reduced with global deregulation. Globalization's logic undermines the Keynesian welfare state as a means of mutual communal support and a first line of defense against poverty. It creates downward pressures on the welfare state and its social protections, undermines the ideology of social protection under girding the welfare state, subverts national community solidarity, and legitimizes inequality of rewards. The results are "welfare reform's" punitive and austere approaches. The welfare state's devolution is to motivate the poor to accept and depend on marginal, low-wage employment, and to reduce and keep taxes low on corporations and the extremely affluent. First instigated by conservative government, devolution has been subsequently embraced and expanded by traditionally liberal or left political parties of the United Kingdom and the United States (Deacon, 1997; Kramer & Braum, 1995; Gray, 1998; Mishra, 1999; Morgan, 1995; Mullard & Spicker, 1995; Park, 1999; Room, 1990, pp. 106–111; Wagner, 1997).

- Privatization, proprietarization, and commercialization are currently trends and shibboleths in the welfare state's rollback. These also are manifestations of the conservative trend. The privatization movement assumes a primacy of economic market forces as the best means of allocating and conducting services (Gibelman & Demone, 1998; Moe, 1987; Morgan, 1995, Salamon, 1997). A privatization ideology forces government to be more businesslike and efficient as well as smaller— leaner and meaner. It reduces public sector costs and competition for money either through taxes or by borrowing. Privatization diminishes public sector involvement in enterprise decision making through deregulation (Morgan, 1995). Privatization takes the focus and political pressure off government for poor services, places a buffer between the public and politicians, and transfers any onus of poor services and inefficiency to the market resolvable by market forces. Privatization of government-financed vendor services also provides political spoils to the government's backers in contingent employment and contracts (Berstein, 1997; Metcalf, 2002), as with the proposed, and as of 2003 only a proposal, privatized U.S. Social Security retirement accounts. Privatization and commercial enterprises are increasing their share of the education, health, and human services. In the United States, the profit sector has over a third share of the social services market with a 50% growth projected over the next few years. Proprietary firms are global involving mammoth, vertically integrated global companies such as Lockheed Martin, Magellan Health Services and Crescent Operating, Inc. (health and mental health), Wachenhut (corrections), and Xerox (for context, see Berstein, 1996; Fein, 1996; Freudenheim, 2002; Kuttner, 1996; Levenson, 1997; Myerson, 1997; Nordheimer, 1997; Rose, 1997; Salamon, 1997; Swarns, 1997, pp. A1, A12; Strom-Gottfried, 1997; Uchitelle & Kleinfield, 1996). The business model of social welfare transforms social workers into producers and clients into consumers. As with most public policy pronouncements, privatization's efficiency claims have neither been rigorously tested nor supported (Morgan, 1995).

- United Way giving in the United States is down, especially in urban centers, and agencies are forced to increase revenue from other sources (Johnston, 1997, pp. 1, 28). Foundations also are retaining more of their funds during this high market growth era (Domini & Van Dyck, 2000). Corporate contributions to health and human services have dropped and constitute less of total giving than prior to the tax reductions (Marx, 1998, p. 34). Philanthropic giving largely serves the donor community's social and political ends and cultural institutions. The socially marginalized are effectively excluded from benefit (Abelson, 2000; Marx, 1998). The very affluent traditionally donate smaller portions of their income to philanthropy than do the middle-income ranges (Phillips, 1993, p. 143; Salamon, 1997). Donations deterioration will continue as income concentrates at the top of the income distribution, a sense of a general community declines, and tax codes make giving less financially attractive (Freudenheim, 1996, p. B8; Phillips, 1993, p. 143).

- The United States is becoming more ethnically and socially diverse and is moving toward greater ethnic heterogeneity, with no ethnic majority population. California currently has no ethnic majority, with over a quarter of its population foreign born (Haub, 1995; Scott, 2002).

Table 4.1 illustrates more than a lack of a national majority ethnic population by 2060. It also points up the absurdity of ethnic classifications (Patterson, 2001). The total *white* population, including *white Hispanics*, remains the majority population into the next century. *Non-Hispanic whites* are projected to decline to less than 50% by 2060, as Hispanics increase to over a fourth of population. Non-Hispanic whites, however, will remain dominant in political and economic power.

Appiah (1997) thoughtfully observes the inconsistencies in our obsession with race, multiculturalism, and diversity:

Some groups have names of earlier ethnic cultures: Italian, Jewish . . . Some correspond to

TABLE 4.1 United States Population Grouping in Percentages: 2001, 2006, and 2060

Population Grouping	2001	2006	2060
Foreign-born	9.9	10.8	13.1
Total white	82.0	81.3	73.8
White, non-Hispanic	71.0	68.9	49.6
Total black	12.9	13.1	14.8
Black, non-Hispanic	12.2	12.4	11.8
Total American Indian	0.9	0.9	1.1
American Indian, non-Hispanic	0.7	0.8	0.8
Total Asian and Pacific Islander	4.2	4.7	10.3
Asian and Pacific Islander, non-Hispanic	4.0	4.4	9.8
Total Hispanic	12.1	13.5	26.6

Note. Data in this table are adapted from *National Population Projections: I. Summary Files, Total Population by Race, Hispanic Origin, and Nativity*, U.S. Census Bureau, November 2, 2000. Retrieved June 19, 2003, from http://www.census.gov/population/www/projections/natsum-T5.html

the old races—black, Asian, Indian; or to religions. . . . Some are basically regional—Southern, Western, Puerto Rican.. Yet others are new groups modeled on old ethnicities—Hispanic, Asian American—or are social categories—women, gay, bisexuals, disabled. . . . Nowadays, we are not the slightest bit surprised when someone remarks on a feature of the 'culture' of groups like these. Gay culture, Deaf culture . . . but if you ask what distinctively marks off gay people or deaf people or Jews from others, it is not obviously the fact that to each identity there corresponds a distinct culture. (p. 31)

An increased emphasis on the constructions of race and culture is misplaced and leads to greater balkanization, social marginalization, and challenges to a cohesive community (Longes, 1997, p. 46). There are no trends to indicate that an increasing emphasis on multiculturalism leads to less hypersegregation and balkanization. Appiah (1997) again provides some insight:

To an outsider, few groups in the world looked as culturally homogeneous as the various peoples—Serbs, Croats, Muslim—of Bosnia. (The resurgence of Islam in Bosnia is a result of the conflict, not a cause of it.) . . . And the trouble with appeal to cultural difference it that it obscures rather than illuminates this situation. It is not black culture that the racist disdains, but blacks. There is no conflict of visions between black and white cultures that is the source of discord. No amount of knowledge of the architectural achievements of Nubia or Kush guarantees respect for African Americans. . . . Culture is not the problem, and it is not the solution. . . . So

maybe we should conduct our discussions of education and citizenship, toleration and social peace, without the talk of cultures. (pp. 35–36)

The United States is becoming more diverse. We have done relatively well in our diversity during the last two decades, compared with the rest of the world, if nondiversity is measured by genocide, ethnic cleansing, and outright violence. However, if we are to avoid these plagues, we should emphasize community rather than differences.

• Despite advances in civil rights, communities still remain highly ethnically and economically segregated, especially within urban areas and between urban and suburban areas. This creates a significant barrier to upward social mobility (Massey, 1994). Poverty of women and children has also increased since the 1960s. Single parent, female-headed families now make up nearly half of the households living below the poverty line. Forty-four percent of these are black families, and most live in central cities due to historic, still extant patterns of racial segregation and economic entrapment.

• Often touted as the most significant change in the United States as part of globalization is its vulnerability to terrorism, and a *war on terrorism* has been declared. The drama and fear following September 11, 2001 (9-11), was powerful. After that day, it has seemed that nothing is the same. The popularity of war movies has increased. The United States has become the *Homeland*, an appellation coined for political purposes after September 11, 2001, and rarely if ever used before. Flags and other patriotic symbolism are everywhere: in office and home windows, on cars and lapels, and especially in commercial and political advertising. Politicians wave flags at every opportunity. The political scientist Robert Putnam touted, based on an October 2001 poll, that one positive consequence of 9-11 was that "whites trust blacks more, Asians trust Latinos more, and so on, than did these very same people did a year ago" (as cited in Morin & Dean, 2002). The impact, unfortunately, on the U.S. sense of community has been more jingoistic than profound in producing solidarity and cohesion. The increase in trust from 22% to 29%, a 7% gain, was probably a function of social desirability responses brought on by a near-universal emphasis on *united we stand*. Even in the face of universal media efforts to create national unity after 9-11, 71% indicated no increase in trust. Other polls and indicators are less optimistic than Putnam (Clymer, 2002). Since 9-11, hypersocial segregation has been maintained. Devolution of the welfare state with decreasing government general welfare services and increasing privatization continues unabated (Pear, 2002b). The affluent continue to receive disproportionate relief from taxes and public responsibility for the nation's welfare (Johnston, 2002b). Corporate flag waving is accompanied by relocations to offshore tax havens to avoid paying taxes in support of the war against terrorism and other assumed enemies of the homeland (Johnston, 2002a, 2002c). Rules of secrecy are imposed and due-process protections weakened in the name of homeland security, recalling a dark Vietnam War–era slogan *of destroying the village to save it* (Broad, 2002; Ignatieff, 2002).

- The United States and the world are aging. Americans are getting older and working longer. The growth of an aging population between 65 and 85 and a frail elderly population over 85 is a significant factor in health and welfare spending. The frail elderly, in particular, require costly in-home and institutional support, as well as more complex and expensive medical care (Ginsberg, 1990). With a devolving welfare state and a privatization ideology, despite the political power of the elderly, the security of Social Security and an improvement of elderly health care are at risk (Mitchell, 2002).

- The spiraling, totally pervasive, unbounded technological revolution in the United States and our love of it will continue. The widespread increase in the use of computers and other communication equipment for information access, data processing, and communication has decreased the virtual time and space between people, organizations, and communities. As we balkanize, we are simultaneously served by national economic franchises, shaped by national and global media, and connected internationally by a high-tech information superhighway. Use of computer and electronic technologies can allow human and social services to be more widely distributed. A single professional can serve more people, and fewer professionals can serve more people. E-mails and Web pages provide more opportunity for public information distribution, marketing, and case coordination. Internet chat rooms are used for information sharing and emotional support groups (Finn, 1996). Networks, Web sites, and online chat rooms also can be used for community organizing.

PERSPECTIVES FOR PRACTICE

As social workers become involved in developing new programs and services and redesigning old ones, as they provide community education and client advocacy and help structure support networks, the models that follow suggest the kinds of information, contacts, and activities we should consider in our practice.[2]

The Community as People: A Sociodemographic View

The U.S. Census Bureau collects, compiles, and distributes a huge quantity of information about the characteristics of the U.S. people and their activities. The annual *Statistical Abstract of the United States*, for example, contains aggregate information about the numbers of people, births, deaths, homeownership, occupations, income and expenditures, labor force, employment and earnings, health and nutrition, business enterprise, manufacturing, and more. In addition, the Census Bureau disaggregates information by census tract, its smallest spatial unit at the local level. The local municipal or county planning department and local libraries usually have census tract information that reveals a good deal about the composition and character of the local community. Thus one can learn about the ages, nationalities, average income, and educational levels of people in different local areas, for example, and the data are available for comparative purposes across census tracts and municipalities. Comparisons can also be made for geographic areas over time, so that community changes can be examined. Social indicators of the relative well-being of a community can be developed, for example, by tracking crime statistics, infant mortality rates and various other health statistics, and so on. The utility of sociodemographic information for social planning purposes and to understand the community is readily apparent. And, as indicated above, how the U.S. Census Bureau chooses to divide people tells us something about the American community's perception of itself.

The Community as a Social System

The community as a social system essentially views a community as a system of interrelated subsystems that perform important functions for their members. What differentiates the community as a system from an organization that can also be construed as a system of systems is that a community's subsystems are not rationally organized by a centralized authority and coordinated with each other to achieve a common goal. Even if we think of the American community as a political jurisdiction, a city with a mayor and a city council, there are important subsystems that are not subject to central control, such as the nonprofit sector, the economic sector where multiple business firms produce and distribute necessary goods and services, or the underground economy.

We use Warren's (1978) conception of community. It best serves our purposes of understanding community for purposes of intervention on both micro- and macrolevels. Following Warren's system analysis of the U.S. community, we may view the community as "that combination of social units and systems that perform the major social functions having locality relevance" (p. 9). Warren conceived of community functionally as the organization of social activities to afford people daily local access to those broad areas of activities and resources necessary in day-to-day living. A community, in this definition, has a locality but needs no well-defined geographic boundaries. Social work is concerned with where people live and, more important, with the influences of where they live on how they live. Social work is immersed in people, families, social relationships and networks for education, jobs, and values, and how people acquire and maintain their social relationships and networks. Communities can be compared on the dimensions of (a) the relative degree of dependence of the community on extracommunity

(vertical patterns) institutions and organizations to perform its locality-relevant functions (autonomy), (b) the extent that the service areas of local units (stores, churches, schools, manufacturing, and so on) coincide or fail to coincide, (c) the psychological identification with a common locality, and (d) the relative strength of the relationships between local units (horizontal pattern Warren, 1978, pp. 12–13).

Warren proposes five critical locality-relevant social functions: (a) production-distribution-consumption, (b) socialization, (c) social control, (d) social participation, and (e) mutual support. These social functions are required for survival and perpetuation of a community and its members. A community fulfills the functions through a pattern of formal and informal organizations and groups. It should be kept in mind, however, that while an organization or entity can be identified with a primary social function and are discussed in terms of the primary function, such as a school system with the socialization function, the same social units generally perform more than one function. For example, a school provides socialization but also provides jobs, opportunities for social participation, and social control. The units that provide these functions may have local physical sites but may not necessarily be controlled by members of the community or be truly of a community. A supermarket can serve several different communities and belong to a regional, national, or international supermarket chain with interests adverse to the local community. A child protective service unit may serve several neighborhoods, but the number of workers it can hire to meet the local needs and even its conception of child abuse and neglect are controlled by state laws, the state's child welfare department, and federal grant-in-aid funding limits.

The community as a social system operates systemically, with its entities interacting and affecting one another. The entities and institutional structures interact, shape, and contribute to shared purposes and support the capacity of the others to accomplish their social functions. Each component of a system is necessary for the system to achieve its purposes. All of the social functions and social structures are interdependent and impact on our well-being or welfare. A school system's capacity to educate, to socialize, is affected by its community's economic viability. In turn the school system contributes to the community's economic and social viability. A poor community has greater demands for mutual support, the welfare structures, but has less capacity to provide mutual support. An affluent community has a capacity, but it may provide mutual support only if its commonly socialized values support public welfare and voluntary giving.

Before we consider each of the five functions in more detail, we need to lay a foundation by examining the concepts of *vertical* and *horizontal* integration, *reciprocity*, and *social exclusion*. These are critical to understanding the great changes within the functions and to community.

Changes in Communities From Horizontal to Vertical Systems

Communities have undergone great changes over the past half century, transforming from locality-focused and horizontally organized communities emphasizing primary and holistic relationships and responsibilities to vertical integrated communities. The terms *vertical entity* and *horizontal entity* describe the relationship between the entity or organization and the local community, and not their internal structure. It is important to determine whether an organization has a vertical or a horizontal relation to the community. *Horizontal* organizations share the same geographic domain with a community and coincide or fit within the community. Their ultimate locus of authority situs is within the community, and their relationship with community is *horizontal*. They are on the same plane. The *locality limited horizontal community* was a community where people lived and got their needs met by structures and institutions that existed in the same community. Their hierarchical structure of authority and locus of decision making were at a community level horizontal to one another and their constituencies. The *locality limited horizontal community* is becoming antiquated as the community functions become global and increasingly specialized in their divisions of labor, complex and fragmented, and without congruence with one another or for a locality.

Vertical entities, organizations, and structures are characterized by hierarchical levels of authority and decision making beyond the local community to regional, state, federal and national, and international levels. The *verticality* of the entity refers to its relationship with the local community and the community's capacity to influence its decisional authority and rule making capacity. The decision making for a particular social function is beyond a local community and has little interest in a particular horizontal local community. Decisions that affect one community social function may not correspond geographically or socially with decisions affecting another social function. This creates greater community complexity and makes decision making more remote from the individual. The local community and its welfare are unimportant to the vertical entities. A particular local community is simply one of many communities in its domain. Interests are specialized by functions. Economic entities are concerned with their economic interest rather than with the local community's economic and social well-being. *Vertically integrated communities* have few definable geographic and social boundaries for functions, fragmented social relationships based on more explicit social contracts, extensive divisions of labor, and secondary and tertiary modes of social interaction. Individuals have a growing sense of isolation and increasing anomie with a loss of community values to guide behavior. With alienation and normlessness comes a loss of local social control and a growth of splintered life style and social identity with a growth of special interests enclaves in an effort to recreate community within the amorphous national and global social ecology (Bellah, Madsen, Sullivan, & Tipton, 1985, 1991; Etzioni, 1993).

Although our current political rhetoric is for smaller, more local government and more individual responsibility, our nongovernmental economic organizations are becoming larger; global; more remote from the individual; more intrusive on and dominant over the community; and more unregulated, controlled, and controllable. The community hospital and the independent family doctor have been supplanted by the proprietary and distant profit-driven national health maintenance organization operating under managed-cost principles. The mom-and-pop family business has been replaced by the multinational megacorporation. The global multimedia entertainment industrial conglomerate has deposed the local newspaper. Decision making for all these structures is generally distant from the local community of living and is based on narrowing economic self-interest rather than a consideration of community well-being. We are concerned with vertical and horizontal relationships because they influence the relationships within and between communities: cohesion, power, dependency and interdependency, community commitment, and the capacity and willingness of the organization to respond to local community change. Vertically related structures usually have less community interdependence and cohesion.

As communities have become more vertically integrated, larger in terms of the base for fulfilling the functions, the conception of locality has expanded. Today the community for some of the functions is national and often global. Not only is the economy global, but social welfare, socialization, and social control entities are also global. With the expansion and complexity of community, unfortunately, as Nisbet (1953, p. 52) has stated, "For more and more individuals the primary social relationships [of community] have lost much of their historic function of mediation between man and the larger ends of our civilization." A primary criterion in assessing whether an organization or agency has a vertical or horizontal relation is the ultimate locus of authority and a local unit's decision-making ability to commit resources to local community interests. A practice task for the community practitioner, in addition to assessing whether the entity is a vertically or horizontally related entity, is to develop a relationship with more horizontal character with greater power equivalency and interdependence, with these vertically related entities.

RECIPROCITY

Community cohesion requires reciprocity and responsibility commensurate with individual rights and benefits. People need to give to the community on the basis of what they get from the community. This extends beyond the simplistic, though important, notion that public welfare recipients should reciprocate for the assistance received from the community. It includes obligations of the affluent to reciprocate the community for their prosperity. Global corporations have an obligation to all the communities where they operate at least equal to the gains they make. Adam Smith (1922), hardly a collectivist, advocated proportionate reciprocal community responsibilities:

> The expence [sic] for defending the society . . . are laid out for the general benefit of the whole society. It is reasonable, therefore, that they should be defrayed by the general contribution of the whole society, *all the different members contributing, as nearly as possible, in proportion to their respective abilities. The subjects of every state ought to contribute towards the support of the government, as nearly as possible, in proportion to their respective abilities; that is, in proportion to the revenue which they respectively enjoy under the protection of the state.* [italics added] (pp. 300, 310)

SOCIAL EXCLUSION

The growth of the global turboeconomy and vertically structured communities is accompanied by increasing social exclusion in the United States and Europe. Social exclusion "restrict[s] or den[ies] people participation within society. . . . Individuals or groups are wholly or partially excluded from full participation in the society in which they live . . . [and represent] a failure or inability to participate in social and political activities" (Berry & Hallett, 1998, p. 2).

Social exclusion relates to individual social marginalization and alienation. Social exclusion is the flip side of the French concept of social solidarity. Social exclusion can affect others besides the poor if they are prevented from integrating themselves within the community, but the poor tend to be the most structurally socially excluded. Social exclusion appears to be a by-product of the globalization by which most of us are excluded from its economic and political decisional processes (Room, 1990; van Deth, 1997).

COMMUNITY FUNCTIONS

Production-Consumption-Distribution

Production-distribution-consumption (P-D-C) is the system of organizing individuals and other resources for the production and distribution of goods and services for their consumption. P-D-C is the economy. It is the most basic community function. Heilbroner (1962, p. 5) has pointed out that societies and communities must meet only two fundamental and interrelated needs to survive in the short run:

1. They must develop and maintain a system for producing the goods and services needed for perpetuation, and
2. They must arrange for the distribution of the fruits of production among their members, so that more production can take place.

A community must meet its current and the next generation's need for goods and services. If the next generation doesn't have consumption needs met, there will be no succeeding generation of producers and hence no continuation of community. Without production and its distribution, there is no consumption. Without production there is no mutual support. Without consumption there is no energy for socialization, social control, social participation, or production. P-D-C therefore is necessary for a community's survival, but it is not sufficient. Communities are so much more than economic systems.

P-D-C doesn't require a particular economic system or model. Economic systems are social inventions to support the production, distribution, and consumption of goods and services by the community. P-D-C's organization is highly flexible. The models can range from a wide variety of collectivist approaches ranging from the family through to nation-state collectivism on one hand to individualistic laissez-faire and wanton corporate capitalism on the other. The extremities and all the models in-between are social inventions. Any single model does not represent the natural order of things or a higher progression of humankind. Laissez-faire and corporate capitalism are social inventions of fairly recent historical vintage. Adam Smith's classic and seminal work on capitalism, *An Inquiry Into the Nature and Causes of the Wealth of Nations*, was first published in 1776. In passing, it must be noted that Dr. Smith's concern was the wealth of nations as communities, and not with individuals or corporate wealth. A P-D-C system is to serve a community's needs, rather than as it currently often appears, for a community to serve an economic system's needs. This axiom is ignored by an unbridled market economic system that fragments, if not destroys, community cohesion and values.

P-D-C is becoming increasingly vertical with a concurrent distancing of decision making from the community and the individual. Decisions are made without much regard for the community's interests and needs. As we move more totally to global, highly vertical, economic structures, we should keep in mind several propositions:

1. Economies are social creations and are not created by nature.

2. No economic system has greater inherent morality than other systems. Its morality is determined by how well it serves its communities.

3. Economies serve communities rather than communities existing for economies.

4. While the structures for production-distribution-consumption—the economic system— are necessary for community viability, economic systems alone are insufficient for a viable community. The other functions also must be fulfilled.

Socialization

Socialization is a process "through which individuals, through learning, acquire the knowledge, values and behavior patterns of their society and learn behaviors appropriate to the various social roles that the society provides" (Warren, 1978, p. 177). Socialization is necessary for people to gain a shared set of values. It's a lifelong formal and informal process of learning social values, constructions, roles, and behaviors. It's how we learn how and what to think and do. The community is the primary arena that instructs in the particular structures and strictures of social behavior for that community.

Socialization initially was the responsibility of such primary and secondary social entities as the family, religious bodies, informal peer groups, and, historically more recent, the tertiary institution of schools. However, these primary and secondary associations now have lost their grip on socialization. Control of socialization in the contemporary community has moved beyond the local community and its structures to becoming the province of vertical, privatized, and proprietary structures. Education, religion, entertainment, and information are no longer local but national, global, and proprietary. The commercial, monopolistic, and global media, the Web, and the Internet are now significant instruments of socialization. Young people spend more time with television and video/computer games than with family, religious groups, or schools. The values imparted are the values of the media's proprietors and not necessarily a community's values. These values will become the community's values as young and not-so-young Americans learn them (Stein, 1993). Television and the other components of an increasingly monopolistic global media ("The Big Media," 2002) are most concerned with attracting viewers for advertisers and with shaping public opinion to support their sponsors' ideology. Socializing to community values, educating, or transmitting information has given way to tactics for luring viewers. If ready random sex, frontal nudity, frequent violence, *reality television*, and entertainment news attracts viewers, so be it regardless of their socializing implications. Schools sell information systems, use commercially sponsored closed circuit television for instruction and fast food franchises for food service, sell naming rights to national corporations, and buy commercially packaged teaching packages and tests (Metcalf, 2002). Privatized and proprietary profit-driven school systems are touted as educational reform. The goal of public education of creating community has been replaced by pecuniary motives.

Without strong socialization to a congruent and shared set of values, there is no internal control of behavior based on these values. Without internal behavioral control, there is a greater need for an imposition of external social control to regulate behavior.

Social Control

Social control is those processes communities use to obtain compliance with their prescribed and proscribed social roles, norms, and behaviors. Social control is inherent in the community and society. They enter every aspect of organized human activity. The concept is inherent in the notion of social living. Without social controls, there is chaos. The question is not whether a community will regulate and control its members' behavior, but how it will regulate and control and for what reasons?

Behavioral control can be done in two ways: (a) by internal controls developed through socialization processes and (b) by external social controls with a system of allocating rewards for ascribed and acceptable behaviors and punishments for forbidden behaviors imposed by the community. Most social institutions perform some social control function. Trattner (1999) includes social work and social welfare as social control agents. Trattner sees social control as "those processes in a society that supported a level of social cohesiveness sufficient for a society's survival, including measures that enabled the needy and the helpless to survive and function within the social order—the very things we now call social work or social welfare" (p. xxvii).[3]

Etzioni's (1993) communitarianism discourse offers that when external social control is necessary, it is done best by primary groups in the community:

> We suggest that *free individuals require a community,* which backs them up against encroachment by the state and sustains morality by drawing on the gentle prodding of kin, friends, neighbors and other community members rather than building on government controls or fear of authorities. . . . *No society can function well unless most of its members 'behave' most of the time because they voluntarily heed their moral commitments and social responsibilities.* (pp. 15, 30, italics original)

If socialization and civic society are weakened, more demands are placed on social control structures external to the individual in an extremely heterogeneous and differentiated community. As solidarity wanes, external social controls must be maintained for social order. These controls are most represented by the regulatory powers of the state's legal system and extragovernmental groups usurping the power of the community. External social controls represent a failure of socialization. The growth of external and imposed social controls is an argument for improving socialization to a common set of community values.

But as we have seen, socialization by communities has weakened and they have become more vertical, more sophisticated, more interdependent, and more pluralistic. The rules of contract and law have replaced the more informal means of social control through socialization. Tertiary and vertical social control systems have led to formal limits on individual freedom and an expansion of government and corporations into people's personal lives justified as a community good and security. Constraints on personal freedoms and local community authority have been constrained by a national government since 9-11, excused by and claiming that they are protecting us from terrorism and preserving the American way of life. Again, we are burning villages to save them. The state too frequently reneges on its social responsibilities for the public good and—as a creature of the community—is abandoning its socialization responsibilities. Instead, it is using draconian social control approaches such as the ineffectual "three-strikes-and-you're-out" prison sentencing, a ready use of capital punishment, imprisonment for mental illness and drug use, limiting constitutional protections, and commercializing social control with the privatization of police and prisons. Law enforcement and corrections are growth industries.

SOCIAL PARTICIPATION

Social participation is the essential community function that allows and *requires* its citizens to participate in the life and governance of the community if they and their community are to be socially healthy and competent. Fellin (2001, pp. 70–71) defines community competence as "the capacity of the community to engage in problem-solving in order to achieve its goals." Various parts of a community collaborate, share decision making and power and work together to address community needs. Community competence is enhanced when there is community-wide participation in decision making. Social participation is the core of community practice and the social component of social work practice. It is essential to participatory democracy. Social participation is indispensable to ameliorating possible adverse and arbitrary effects of a community's social control institutions and policies. It is the restorative to social marginalization. The very concept of community entails direct and unbuffered social interaction and involvement by its members to develop communal character and to transmit and implement communal values.

Social participation entails social structures that develop, maintain, and regulate communal life and the other community functions of P-D-C, socialization, social control, and the next community function of mutual support. It ranges from participation in informal primary and secondary group activities to civic participation in the community's more formal tertiary rule making and governance.

Civic participation has become more remote and fragmented with industrial society's separation of work from home, extension of the community's physical-geographic boundaries, and movement to a contract society. Social interaction and participation is more complex and distant, intricate, socially isolating, and detached. Tertiary social structures of larger and more impersonal communities have replaced direct, integrating, and bonding social interactions. Town meetings, informal face-to-face discussions and debates as consensus-building modes of political interacting have been replaced by political parties, extensive media political advertising, political action committees (PACs), public opinion polls, impersonal media talk shows, and the virtual reality and chat rooms of the internet. These allow politicians to bypass the mediating structures of associations, include grassroots political parties, and appeal directly to the voters. The mass marketing approach reduces the mediating function, reciprocity, and community accountability mechanisms. Participation in these more impersonal and technological modes may be virtual but contribute little to the social investments, social capital, and reciprocity necessary for a community's social cohesion.

The current decline in social participation and engagement within communities and an impotence of the political system are a cause of serious social problems. The decline of civic participation, including voting, by the poor, the working class, the middle class, and the young is accompanied by a diminished government interest in and responsiveness to the interests of these community strata. This decline enhances their social marginalization and eventually social exclusion. It also accompanies the relative economic decline of these groups. Governments generally favor the economic interests of the elites who control both government and the economic institutions.[4]

Full social participation requires civic participation in the governance of local and national communities. The core and necessary trait or concept is primary and secondary participation rather than just checkbook membership (Ladd, 1999, p. 16; van Deth, 1997).

Social and civic participation is especially critical in democratic communities. Democracies, especially in a diverse megastate, depend on their many organizations to influence policy. If people do not participate in this process, they are essentially excluded and not considered in the rule-making processes of government. In democracies, as Phillips (1990) has observed, the government's interests and policies reflects the interests of those who select the government: "Since the American Revolution the distribution of American wealth has depended significantly on *who controlled the federal government, for what policies, and in behalf of which constituencies*" (p. xiv, italics original).

Democracies depend on multiple levels of organizations. An individual voter exerts very little political influence in the act of voting, although an individual with great economic and social resources can have influence in other ways. The individual voter can share political influence through mediating organizations. The totalitarian danger of mass society, according to McCollough (1991), lies less in a dictator's seizing control of the governmental apparatus than in atomizing effects of mass society arising from the vacuum of community where nothing stands between the individual and the state. Social and civic groups are an important influence on government. These structures and interests compete for resources. They differ in influence on a variety of factors, not the least being a willingness to develop and use influence.

VOLUNTARY ASSOCIATIONS

A remedy against social atomization and social disintegration characteristic of mass societies is, of course, the active membership of individuals, especially including our clients, in all kinds of voluntary associations (van Deth, 1997, p. 5). Voluntary associations provide the opportunity to meet and network with new people, learn to work with them, expand reciprocity that integrates society, develop social and civic engagement skills, and expand social supports that reduce the impact of mass society. Participation breeds participation. People who participate tend to participate even more and have more social and political participation opportunities. Without participation on the level of association, an individual is limited in most forums of civic participation. Associations provide the individual with a network of contacts, whether or not the associations are overtly political. Van Deth's metaresearch led him to conclude that social participation and political behavior had a clear and direct relationship, "even when socioeconomic status or political orientation are taken into account" (1997, pp. 13–14). Political and social participation reinforce one another (Dekker, Koopmans, & van den Broek, 1997; Moyser, 1997, p. 44).

MEDIATING STRUCTURES

Increasing social participation is a critical social work task. It is vital to countering complexity and size. Community-based associations are *mediating structures* and act as buffers between the individual and the uncongenial, complex megastructures. They are necessary to protect the individual and democracy from the imposition of the megastate and megacorporations of a global turboeconomy. They provide the individual with protective zones (P. L. Berger & Neuhaus, 1977, p. 2; Nisbet, 1953; van Deth, 1997, p. 6). Voluntary associations as mediating structures are an anodyne to the social fragmentation, atomization, and social disintegration characteristic of our mass societies. Ladd (1999) points out that "joining face-to-face groups to express shared interests is a key element of civic life. Such groups help resist pressures toward 'mass society.' They teach citizenship skills and extend social life beyond the family" (p. 16). People who participate in voluntary organizations have more civic trust (Moyser, 1997, p. 43). Examples of mediating structures are family, churches, advocacy groups, labor unions, support groups, and neighborhood associations.

Individual → Mediating structure →
Society's megastructures and institutions

With a global turboeconomy populated and dominated by megatransnational corporations, individual, independent consumer competition becomes less relevant to market functioning. Just as an individual voter in a megademocracy is essentially powerless to influence the political marketplace, an individual consumer has little power to shape the marketplace. Competition in the classic sense of no single or few vendors or purchasers able to highly influence or control a market is an archaic concept. Individuals as consumers have no influence. A single, multinational and multifunctional corporation has great influence. Without mediating structures, an individual is relatively powerless compared to the megainstitutional structures of government and commerce. With mediating structures, individuals can aggregate influence. The organizations, associations, and coalitions serve as mediators as well as action groups in dealing with megacorporations and the megastate.

Mediating structures need to be as continuous as are the megastructures. They need to parallel the megastructures. However, there is a risk that a continuous mediating structures will follow a developmental course similar to that of the megastructures and become impersonal, imposing megastructures themselves (Maloney & Jordan, 1997). This seems to be the path of mediating structures such as labor unions, political parties, and large voluntary checkbook membership associations such as the Red Cross.

Social participation's relevance for social work practice is explored more fully in the practice areas of community organization, networking and coalition building, and community social casework. Clients need social participation and to be brought into civic associations and coalitions. Integrating clients into community-based social support networks and organizations allows clients to be in contact with a range of social support resources, provides social structures for reciprocity, and provides opportunities for social and political empowerment. Grassroots community organizations need to coalesce and form mediating structures for individuals to manage a global economy. Social workers need to promote local and national participation of communities/constituents as social and political actors rather than as customers or consumers. Socially marginalized clients need linking to local and global networks of organizations (van Deth, 1997, p. 3). Social welfare organizations and social welfare professionals hold some potential as positive mediating forces if they can develop the fortitude and skills to intervene against the excesses of corporate and social conservatism that has captured the state and community.

Mutual Support

The mutual support function, the social welfare function, is the community's provision of help to its members when their individual and family needs are not met through family and personal resources. Mutual support is helping one another in time of need. Primary and secondary groups—family, neighbors, friends—traditionally provide the first line of social support and protection. As communities have become more complex, more secondary groups and tertiary formal organizations have been developed to perform these functions, such as governmental agencies, for-profit and nonprofit health and welfare agencies, other proprietary organizations such as insurance companies and day-care centers, and a host of voluntary, nonprofit organizations such as burial societies, credit unions, and child care co-ops. The helping structures may be temporary or permanent. Mutual support helps to delineate a community from a simple aggregation of people. Under this conception of mutual support, social welfare is caring for others by virtue of their membership in the community.

The functional and systemic questions of membership are embedded in the construction of community and its cohesion. Fullinwider (1988) argues, "We almost never encounter people, even strangers, whom we think of as 'simply humans'; we encounter fellow citizens, coreligionists, neighbors, historic kinsmen, political confederates, allies in war, guests. Our typical moral judgments and responses are almost always made in the context of some connection between us and others that goes beyond being members of the same species" (p. 266).

The community citizenship question for mutual support is whether a membership requirement is that one be a citizen of the political entity such as the United States, Maryland, or Baltimore, or that a member of the community is someone identifying with and identified by the community as one of them. The question relates to conception of community and the community cohesion requirement for mutual support with minimum coercion. If membership is legal citizenship of a state and not simply functional membership in a community, then coercion probably plays a part in the process of mutual support. If functional citizenship in a community is required of welfare recipients, then community responsibility and reciprocity is inferred. California's 1994 proposition and 1996 federal welfare reform excluding illegal aliens, and in some cases legal aliens, from public mutual support and the Bush administration's denial of constitutional protections to aliens emphasize the legal citizenship definition over functional citizenship conundrum.

We are back, again, to the importance of civic participation by all in a community, especially the poor and welfare clients. Civic participation creates networks and social bonding necessary for social support. It provides an opportunity for reciprocity and gives them a claim and mechanisms for exercising the claim based on reciprocity.

Inherent in the development of cohesion necessary for mutual support is trust and bonding between people. People need trust to avoid the *free riders and the sucker's challenge* (de Jasay, 1989). The 2001–2002 Northeastern United States drought illustrates a *free riders and suckers* quandary. The drought was the area's worst in over 60 years. The region needed to conserve water. Individuals were asked to sacrifice for the sake of the community and limit all water use. However, the logic of individualism versus community interest presented the following quandary: It is in my individual interest to shower daily, water my yard, and wash my car. My use will only marginally decrease the region's supply. I am better off and no one else is appreciably worse off, *if all others follow the rules.* I'm, however, a free rider. If they don't follow the rules and I use the water, I did not make the situation appreciably worse. I'm only following the behavior of the collective, and the collective made it worse. I'm temporarily better off and the collective no worse off. But if most others don't follow the rules and conserve water and I do, I'm the worst off. They are better off in the short run, although probably worse off in the long run than if they had conserved. Me, I'm worse off both in the short and long run. I'm a sucker.

The free riders and suckers quandary is the tragedy of the commons argument made against the welfare state (Schmidtz, 1991). The tragedy of the commons argument, simply stated, is that if we all can have our needs met by doing nothing—the use of the commons or communally held resources such as the water—there is little motivation for each of us to develop either individual or collective property or exercise constraint. We individually will be no better off. If the individual does not get his or her needs and preferences met from the commons, someone else may use or consume the property, thus leaving nothing for the first individual or for future generations. Personal denial ensures that our current needs will not be met, and it doesn't ensure that our future needs will be met or that future generations' needs will be met. The commons can perpetuate itself only when all are in harmony and act in common. In other words, there must be strong community.

The fear of a tragedy of the commons is evident in our public health and welfare policies and programs. We do not feel responsible either as donors or as recipients. As donors, we resent the intrusion of the state on our resources and its making us share them with people who contribute little to our well-being. We have little bonding with the recipients as individuals or concern about them as fellow community members. If recipients have little sense of communal responsibility, they are marginalized and excluded. If mutual support recipients, whether from welfare, education, health, or disaster relief, fulfill no public or common good, if they demonstrate no communal responsibility and make no contributions to the commons or prudently use it, then they are free riders. And if recipients are free riders, then donors—the taxpayers and those who are communally responsible by not exploiting the commons—are suckers. If we as donors view recipients as free riders, then we must view ourselves as suckers. If we do not wish to remain suckers or to view ourselves as suckers, we must rid the community of free riders. This is called welfare reform in current political rhetoric.

Trust is imperative in avoiding the free riders/suckers dichotomy and tragedy of the commons. Trust and bonding are dependent on some mutual identity. Trust stems from community. It involves commitment to others (Haley, 1999). Trust and mutual identity are diminishing factors in the relationship between U.S. citizens and people globally.

A welfare state exists where state or public appliances provide mutual support. The welfare state provides a public structure and resources for mutual support and community building in response to the impersonal social contract of an industrial society. When there is a reliance on state appliances for mutual support without an underlying sense of community, community cohesion, and trust, there is a general increase in using social control for and in implementing mutual support. Vertical approaches relying on taxes and transfers instead of community cohesion are used.

Communities as Local, Global, or Virtual Networks

Bennett Berger (1998) provides a contrast to the traditional idea of integrated, broadly supportive, tight-knit communities with our modern sense that people have "limited, partial, segmented, even shallow, commitments to a variety of diverse collectivities—no one of which commands an individual's total loyalty" (p. 324).

This presents the issue of cohesion discussed above. We live in many communities and feel totally a part of none. Barry Wellman's (1999, pp. 97–100) analysis leads him to conclude that we in the Western, largely urban world live in a new type of world of *loosely coupled* communities. Its new community characteristics are as follows (Wellman, 1999, pp. 97–100):

1. Community ties are narrow and relationships are specialized and not broadly supportive;

2. People float in sparsely knit, loosely bounded, frequently changing networks and not wrapped up in traditional cohesive, tightly bound communities;

3. Communities are not neighborhood bound and have become dispersed networks that continue to be supportive and sociable;

4. Private intimacy has replaced public sociability, for example, homes have replaced pubs as a place to see people;

5. Communities have become domesticated, for example, women have replaced men at the center of community life.

6. Political, economic, and social milieus affect the nature of communities; and

7. Cyberspace supports globalized communities.

The implications for societal changes is that as we lose the cohesive traditional community, new models of communities are being formed. Proponents argue that rather than lament fewer bowling leagues and a loss of a pub-culture camaraderie, we should appreciate coming together in new ways through the Web, use the Internet to find each other, and recognize that we participate differently in civic and community life (Kirchhoff, 1999; Ladd, 1999: Oldenburg, 1999). Electronic linkage in a cyberspace community reduces isolation (Uncapher, 1999). Internet support groups whose members are dispersed geographically but share narrow interests provide some of the functions of natural helpers and community face-to-face support groups (Wellman & Gulia, 1999). The proponents of the loosely coupled new community conception hearken back to Nisbet, who, over a half-century ago in *The Quest for Community* (1953), argued that freedom came from multiple associations and authorities. Thus, "while the best life was to be found within community, people should not limit themselves to one community. They should experience many communities" (Brooks, 2000, pp. 244–245).

The Community as an Arena of Conflict

Viewing the community as a social system has some built-in biases that make it insufficient by itself to serve as a framework for social work practice in the community. The systems perspective's basic bias assumes a set of integrated subsystems working together for the benefit of the whole. But what happens when there is disagreement between powerful groups in different subsystems or when the whole and some of its subsystems disagree? We know, for example, that it is often the case that minority groups' fundamental interests are not acknowledged or taken adequately into account by the majority group. The good of the system as a whole—that is, the inclusive community—does not necessarily mean the good of all of its subsystems. How is the conflict perceived, and how should it be resolved (Warren, 1978)? The perspective of community as an arena of conflict suggests that conflict and change are characteristic of U.S. communities and that the process of determining the public interest therefore involves conflict and negotiation as much as it does rational planning, collaboration, and coordination. Issues of power do not seem to enter into the systems perspective, but viewing the community as an arena of conflict brings power and politics to the fore. We are forced to ask a variety of questions. What does it mean to say that the community has a collective identity? How do we take into account community differences in values and beliefs, goals, and interests? Does the community have an overriding public interest, and, if so, how is that public interest determined? Who is influential? Is the public interest synonymous with the interests of the most powerful people in the community? To answer these questions, we must turn to conceptions of *power* and *power structure*.

POWER AND COMMUNITY

Most definitions of power stem from the Weberian notion that power is "the chance of a man or of a number of men to realize their own will in a communal action even against the resistance of others who are participating in the action" (Gerth & Mills, 1958, p. 180). In other words, power is the ability to get what you want when you want it, despite the opposition of other people, and in this case the *you* is a decidedly masculine pronoun. *As Box 4.3 indicates, power is varied.* Generally people exercise power to gain more and give less than those over whom power is exercised. Power is about gaining and losing, about control (Willer, 1999, p. 2). Power

is the capacity to produce *intended* and *foreseen* effects on others. Power has the *intent* of change in a *particular* way with the expectation of particular results (Willer, Lovaglia, & Markovsky, 1999, p. 231; Wrong, 1979). Some social scientists use *influence* as a more inclusive and nuanced concept than power. Willer, Lovaglia, and Markovsky (1999, p. 230–231) define *influence* as the socially induced modification of beliefs, attitudes, or expectations without a use of sanctions and regardless of intent or effort to make change. We can influence behavior in certain directions even when it is not our intent to do so.

Even for very powerful individuals and groups, however, power is seldom unlimited. Some authors therefore suggest that power can be usefully viewed as a medium of exchange, a commodity that can be invested or consumed depending upon gains or losses (Banfield, 1961). Jean Baker Miller (1983) offers a more feminist conception of power. She defines power, similar to influence, as "the capacity to produce a change—that is, to move anything from point A or state A to point B or state B. This can include even moving one's own thoughts or emotions, sometimes a very powerful act. It can also include acting to create movement in an interpersonal field as well as acting in larger realms such as economic, social, or political arenas" (p. 4).

In this view, fostering another's growth or increasing another's resources, capabilities, and effectiveness to act exercises power. People who nurture, socialize, and educate—parents, teachers, social workers—hold and can exercise a great deal of power. This is quite different from a masculine conception of power that often involves limiting or controlling the behavior of others.

Most theorists distinguish *power* from *authority*, defining *authority* as legitimated power that has been legally, traditionally, or voluntarily granted to the holder of a particular position, such as a corporate CEO, an elected governmental official, or royalty in traditional societies. In the U.S. form of democracy, authority is granted to various elected officials to enact laws; to executives to carry out the business of the state; and to the courts to interpret, arbitrate, and enforce the laws in a tripartite system of balanced powers. In traditional societies with caste and class structures, higher classes and castes have authority over lower classes and castes by virtue of their positions. The distinction between authority and power notes that, while authority is a form of power, not all persons in authority are powerful, and powerful persons exist apart from authorities in any social system. Other than

BOX 4.3	FACETS OF POWER IN OUR WORK

Power is the ability to control one's own destiny and the ability to form support systems that affect one's life. Power has three dimensions: personal, interpersonal, and political. The work of psychologist Robert White [enhances] and understanding of personal power. . . . [He] has suggested that all human beings have a basic drive, which he calls the *effectuance drive*, a drive to experience oneself as a cause, to interact effectively with the environment—in other words, to experience oneself as having power.

Interpersonal power is closely related to personal power because it carries it into the social domain. [Inter]personal power is the ability to influence the human surround, and it is dependent upon social competence, on the ability to interact effectively with others. Political power is the ability to alter systems, to bring about some change in social structure or organization, to redistribute resources.

Source: Excerpts from a speech by Ann Hartman, then editor of *Social Work*, at the Integrating Three Strategies of Family Empowerment, School of Social Work, University of Iowa, 1990.

---

formal authority, the sources of power are multiple, including access to and control of strategic information, economic resources, connections to other powerful people, charisma, intelligence, wisdom, age, and more.

Finally, some theorists differentiate between *reputed* or *potential* power and *actual* power. We argue that power exists in its use. Potential power is only powerful in the threat to exercise it. If a threat to use it serves to constrain the actions of others, it is power. The classic example is the labor union, which has the power to strike. The potential for a strike often acts as a stimulus to negotiation and a resolution of differences. An actual strike, should it occur, is sometimes difficult to sustain and is often costly, so in this case a threat may be more potent than the reality. Or the capacity of bosses to fire can keep a workforce docile, even though workers may rarely be fired.

POWER DISTRIBUTION

Turning now to the matter of public interest, the question of whether there is such a thing as community decisions and who makes them is complicated. Communities can seldom express a clear and overwhelming pubic interest because they are composed of competing interests and because resources are limited. The public policy process invariably favors some interests, those of the elites, over others. The question, though, is "Does the process always favor the same interests?"

The gist of *elitist theory* is that community life is dominated by a small group of people with sufficient economic and political power to con-

trol public decision making in their own interests. Citizen participation, in this conception, is limited or ineffectual, or both. We cover this theory more fully in Chapter 5.

Mills (1956) contends that the structure of power in the United States resembles a pyramid with three levels (Kornhauser, 1968). At the top is the *power elite*, a group composed of the leaders of (a) giant corporations, (b) the executive branch of the federal government, and (c) the military. This group controls large national and multinational corporations and their corresponding public organizations. They control the means of political power, production, and destruction. Those who make the big decisions are almost exclusively male and white, especially in economic and foreign policy. They have the power, through the control of dominant institutions and the media, to manipulate public opinion and ensure that the rest of society accepts their decisions. The 2000 presidential election with the U.S. Supreme Court intervention and national politicians in the service of corporate and economic elites lends support to this version of elite theory.

Although this group is not an economic class in the traditional Marxist sense, it does share common values, interests, and experiences and does comprise a U.S. and global ruling class. Surrounding this power elite is a circle of syncopates who are advisers, technical experts, powerful politicians, regional and local upper classes, and celebrities. Some eventually may be elevated to the top level.

The second tier of the pyramid, at a middle level of power, consists of a variety of special interest groups, such as labor unions, media, religious and professional associations, and farm organizations that struggle with modest influence only within the parameters established by the power elite.

Unorganized mass society falls into the bottom level of the pyramid—the majority of the populace—with little power over the decision makers at the top; it is those in this level to whom the top leaders send orders, information, and interpretations of events. This base is becoming more socially marginalized and excluded. From an elitist perspective, top leaders determine the fundamental direction of public policy and shape the public interest to coincide with their interests.

A number of studies using *reputational methods* (Hunter, 1953) have found evidence of an elitist power structure in both smaller and larger communities, although the makeup of these structures does not strictly follow Mills's conception. Numerous studies have also found the members of this group to be related by social class (Domhoff, 1967, 1974, 1990). The reputational method essentially involves asking many people (who are in a position to know) who they think the top community leaders are. Names that frequently recur are selected as the top leaders. Then, through interviews and further community investigation, the researcher begins to sort out the extent of these leaders' influence, how they exercise power in the community, and their patterns of interaction with each other.

A variation of the reputational approach, the *positional method,* has also been used in studying community power structures. This approach identifies power in terms of the positions that various people hold in the community. Essentially the researcher identifies the major organizations active in the different sectors of community life, then identifies the occupants of the top positions in these organizations, and finally checks for overlap to pinpoint the most powerful individuals (Meenaghan, Washington, & Ryan, 1982).

Pluralist theorists have strongly criticized the elitists along three lines. First, they argue that the basic premise of an ordered system of power in every human institution is faulty. Researchers who begin their studies by inquiring, "Who runs this community?" are asking a loaded question. The question assumes that there is a particular structure of power, and therefore that the researchers are sure to find it. Second, it argues that the power structure is not stable over time, as elitists suggest, but rather is tied to issues that can be transitory or persistent. Therefore the assumption of a stable coalition or set of coalitions in the community is inaccurate. Third, they contend that the elitists wrongly equate reputed (and positional) power with actual power. Power does not exist until it is actually exercised successfully.

In contrast to the elitists, the *pluralists* propose that power is distributed among many different organized groups, with control shifting depending on the issues. Citizens participate in the public policy process through a variety of interest groups. Because individuals potentially have the freedom to organize a group and compete in the policy arena, differences can be resolved amicably. The political system therefore operates much more democratically than the elitists would have us believe, the public interest being whatever comes out of the pluralistic melting pot after the process is completed.

David Riesman (1951) argued that the power structure pyramid has only two levels, corresponding roughly to Mills's bottom two tiers. There is no power elite. "The upper level of the Riesman's pyramid consists of 'veto groups': a diversified and balanced body of interest groups" (Kornhauser, 1968, pp. 39–40). Each group mainly wants to protect its own power and prerogatives by blocking the efforts of other competing groups. There is no dominant ruling group. Instead there are multiple power centers, thereby creating a much more amorphous structure of power. The lowest level of the pyramid, as with Mills, consists of an unorganized mass public, but in this case the public is pursued as an ally rather than dominated by interest groups in their struggles for power (Kornhauser, 1968). Therefore pluralist power figures are potentially more responsive and accountable to the majority of citizens than are elitist power holders.

Elitist theories imply that democracy is at best a weak institution or at worst a sham altogether, because the public interest is basically determined by a relatively small (though not necessarily conspiratorial) group of powerful leaders. Pluralist theories suggest that the political process is complex and increasingly remote due to the large number of interest groups protecting their turf and struggling for power. Because it is so hard to get anything done, leadership is weakened and political alienation begins to set in. Whether an issue involves the community (or the country) as a whole, no individual or group leadership is likely to be very effective due to the presence of entrenched veto groups. Consider, for example, the battles to enact health care legislation during the Clinton administration. For Banfield (1961), this struggle leads to public decision making that is seldom the result of deliberate planning. For Lindblom (1959), it leads to "disjointed incrementalism."

In order to demonstrate how power is exercised in the community and by whom, pluralist theorists turn to the analysis of concrete issues under lively contention (*issue analysis method*). Thus the pluralist researcher goes about the investigation by (a) selecting a number of key issues, as opposed to routine political decisions, to study; (b) identifying the people who took an active part in the decision-making process; (c) obtaining an account of their actual behavior while the policy conflict was being settled; and (d) analyzing the outcomes of the conflict to determine who won.

There are several lines of criticism of the pluralistic approach. One main criticism is that the pluralists present a rather idealized version of the political process. Since interest groups cannot be easily organized and sustained without many resources, a large part of the community cannot participate. Furthermore, the notion that the pluralist process operates amicably and effectively by a set of institutionalized political rules does not conform to the experience of challenging groups who have succeeded primarily by using norm-violating, disruptive tactics (Gamson, 1990).

Another main line of criticism is that pluralist theory does not recognize a hidden face of power (Bachrach & Baratz, 1962, 1963, 1970). That is, by assuming that power is played out solely in relation to concrete issues, pluralists omit the possibility that in any given community there may be a group capable of preventing contests from arising on issues that it considers important. Power may well be at work in maintaining the directions of current policy, limiting the parameters of public discourse to fairly safe issues—in short with the power elite controlling an increasingly media prevents some items from ever reaching the community agenda and becoming issues. Moreover, as the pluralist methodology offers no criteria for adequately distinguishing between routine and key political decisions, by accepting the idea that in any community there are significant, visible issues, the researcher is only examining what are *reputed* to be issues. Hence the pluralists are guilty of the same criticism they level at the elitists. Pluralism appears to exist only on less vital issues than on fundamental community welfare concerns.

Although both elitist and pluralist theories talk about groups in the political policy process, most of the early theories tended to focus on powerful individuals rather than powerful organizations. As communities become larger, more complex, and their institutions vertically integrated, power is exercised by a loose network of compatible interests rather than a small, tight cabal. Powerful corporations and their need to maintain a stable business market and the growing power of government in American life have led power structure theorists to focus on networks of organizations as sources of widespread and enduring power (Perrucci & Pilisuk, 1970; Perrucci & Potter, 1989). Through such arrangements as interlocking boards of directors and government-corporation executive exchanges, interorganizational (IO) leaders can mobilize the resources of a network of organizations (including governmental-military-media) to influence public policy. With the vertical structuring of society, these sorts of IO arrangements operate on the local level as well as state, national, and global levels. In the final analysis, it is not the specific people who occupy the organizational linking roles that are critical. The people change. It is the elite interests that shape the IO networks that represent the enduring structuring of community power.

Mediating Structures and Community-Sensitive Social Work Practice

This chapter argues that there is value in strengthening the local community to meet the onslaught from larger forces outside its control. As discussed earlier, we agree with Berger and Neuhaus (1977) and propose a strengthening of mediating structures. They have great value for linking and empowering ordinary people. They stand between and protect individuals in their private lives from the alliance of global meta-corporations and the state. Berger and Neuhaus argue that "public policy should protect and foster mediating structures and wherever possible, public policy should utilize mediating structures for the realization of social purposes" (p. 6). In general, we support these propositions. But neither of them is simple to fulfill. As always, we have to find a balance between individual rights and community rights and between the protective functions of the state and the defensive functions of the mediating structures. It is easy to imagine, for example, that some public social services might be better received and more effectively utilized if local religious and voluntary associations were involved in the service delivery. It is also harder to decide whether a neighborhood is right in preventing a church-sponsored homeless shelter from locating in its midst. We can say, though, that the community has a legitimate claim to being involved in the location decision. A fair process is at least a step toward democratic decision making.

It is also not hard to imagine that mediating structures themselves, due to size and patterns of decision making that are not truly participatory, may have difficulty in building a strong sense of community among their participants. In a study of Baltimore's black community, Harold McDougall (1993) made a potent argument for the need for even smaller, informal community building blocks called *base communities*:

> Mediating institutions, such as churches, schools, and community organizations, are essential to this task [of community strengthening, institution building, and networking], but small base communities of one or two dozen people, spun off from mediating institutions or growing independently, are essential to counterbalance the tendency of mediating institutions to mirror the hierarchical character of the public and private bureaucracies with which they contend. (pp. 186–187)

CONCLUSION

The crucial premise of this chapter is that, for social workers to be effective, we need to understand how community affects our lives and the lives of the people we work with. We live and work and play in multiple, overlapping local communities of different kinds. These communities are often culturally diverse and potentially quite different from the communities where we ourselves grew up and now live. The importance of community calls for a community-based social work practice. Some examples of how community may bear on practice will help clarify this idea.

Consider the social worker employed by a church-sponsored nonprofit social work agency. In her practice she has begun to see more and more clients who are HIV positive or who have AIDS. How should she deal with this problem? Suppose that the church has strong antigay sentiments and sees AIDS as a gay problem. Suppose that the church reflects values that are prevalent in the community. What kinds of services can be provided for these new clients? How do clients themselves feel about their circumstances, given the community's values? What kinds of services are needed in the community? How might the social worker begin to address that need? (Obviously many other kinds of problems, such as homelessness, substance abuse, and teenage pregnancy, might raise similar questions.)

To take another example, assume that, as a school social worker, you have encountered a child who appears abused. You are obligated to involve Child Protective Services (CPS). Do you need to know how the community views CPS workers or the nature of the relationship between the school and the community? How will the situation be handled if the police become involved? How do the school authorities feel about CPS and potential disruptions of the school day? How would you approach the family and the child? How can you get CPS to work with you to manage the situation in the most helpful fashion for all parties involved?

A third example supposes that you are a social worker in a large university hospital's department of family medicine. You suspect that the children in the family you are seeing have been poisoned by lead paint from their substandard apartment house. How can you prevent further damage? What about the children who live in other units in that building? Might there be legal or political issues that you should know about? What are some of the different professional roles you might have to play to help your clients and their neighbors?

There are no simple answers to the questions posed in these illustrations. The answers require a sound understanding of community.

Discussion Exercises

1. How have vertical and horizontal changes in community functions affected social work practice? Give examples.

2. Select a client and describe the specific institutions and organizations in the client's life that are used to fulfill the five locality-relevant functions. How much do the organizations coincide in their service areas? What is the locus of decision making for the organizations? Repeat the exercise for yourself. How many of the specific structures are the same for yourself as for your client? Do any serve as mediating organizations?

3. In a small group discussion, consider the examples and questions posed in the "Conclusion" section and try to answer them. Identify the mediating structures and their roles in your answer.

4. Identify an issue in your community relevant to the provision of social services, and try to follow it through a public policy process. Identify the stakeholders for various sides and facets of the issue. What are the roles of the media, elected officials, public agency representatives, leaders of voluntary associations, and corporation leaders in the process? Is the process democratic? Who has power? Who is left out? Is there a hidden face of power influencing the process?

5. What is the best community you have even lived in? Why do you select it? What made it the best? List the characteristics of this place. How can that community be made even better?

Notes

1. Note that even an official definition of *rural* is lacking. It is generally defined as "not an urban area." For more information, see the U.S. Department of Agriculture Rural Information Center's Web site at http://www.nal.usda.gov/ric/faqs/ruralfaq.htm (retrieved May 23, 2003).

2. In proposing these approaches, we are mindful that the literature offers many other useful models, such as the community as a system of interaction (Kaufman, 1959), as a system of human ecology (Fellin, 2001; Poplin, 1979), as shared institutions and values (Warren, 1978), and as an ecology of games (Long, 1958).

3. For a more sinister description of social control and public welfare, see Piven and Cloward (1971, 1982).

4. For a review of the use of the state's police powers and policies to create wealth for particular classes and community interests, see Barlett and Steele (1992, 1994) and Phillips (1990, 1993).

References

Abelson, R. (2000, May 8). Serving self while serving others. *The New York Times,* p. A16.

Appiah, K. A. (1997, October 9). The multiculturalist misunderstanding. *The New York Review of Books,* pp. 30–36.

Bachrach, P., & Baratz, M. S. (1962). The two faces of power. *American Political Science Review, 56,* 947–952.

Bachrach, P., & Baratz, M. S. (1963). Decisions and nondecisions: An analytical framework. *American Political Science Review, 57,* 641–651.

Bachrach, P., & Baratz, M. S. (1970). *Power and poverty: Theory and practice.* New York: Oxford University Press.

Banerjee, M. (with Dewan, S. K.). (2002, February 15). For executives of Enron Unit, the skill was in leaving. *The New York Times,* pp. C1, C6.

Banfield, E. (1961). *Political influence.* New York: Free Press.

Barlett, D. L., & Steele, J. B. (1992). *America: What went wrong?* Kansas City, MO: Andrews and McMeel.

Barlett, D. L., & Steele, J. B. (1994). *America: Who really pays the taxes?* New York: Simon and Schuster.

Bellah, R. N., Madsen, R. D., Sullivan, W. M., Swidler, A., & Tipton, S. M. (1985). *Habits of the heart: Individualism and commitment in American life.* Berkeley: University of California Press.

Bellah, R. N., Madsen, R. D., Sullivan, W. M., Swidler, A., & Tipton, S. M. (1991). *The Good Society.* New York: Vintage Books.

Berger, B. M. (1998). Disenchanting the concept of community, *Society, 35*(2), 324–327.

Berger, P. L., & Neuhaus, R. J. (1977). *To empower people: The role of mediating structures in public policy.* Washington, DC: American Enterprise Institute.

Berry, M., & Hallett, C. (Eds.). (1998). *Social exclusion and social work: Issues of theory, policy, and practice.* Dorset, UK: Russell House.

Berstein, N. (1996, September 15). Giant companies entering race to run state welfare programs. *The New York Times,* p. A1.

Berstein, N. (1997, May 4). Deletion of word in welfare bill opens foster care to big business: Profits from poverty. *The New York Times,* pp. 1, 26.

The big media and what you can do about it: How the "Big Ten" shape what you think and know. (2002). *The Nation, 272*(1), pp. 11–43.

Bragg, R. (2000, Sept. 17). In a working-poor town, candidates are dismissed as being out of touch. *The New York Times*, p. 18.

Broad, W. J. (2002, February 17). U.S. is tightening rules on keeping scientific secrets: Terrorist threats cited. *The New York Times*, pp. A1, A13.

Brooks, D. (2000). *Bobos in paradise: The new upper class and how they got there*. New York: Simon & Schuster.

Brower, S. (1996). *Good neighborhoods: A study of in-town and suburban residential environments*. Westport, CT: Praeger.

Brown, P., & Lauder, H. (1997). Education, globalization, and economic development. In A. H. Halsey, H. Lauder, P. Brown, & A. S. Wells (Eds.), *Education: Culture, economy, society*. (pp. 172–192). New York: Oxford University Press.

Clymer, A. C. (2002, May 20). U.S. attitudes altered little by Sept. 11, pollsters say. *The New York Times*, p. A14.

Dahrendorf, R. (1995). A precarious balance: Economic opportunity, civil society, and political liberty. *The Responsive Community: Rights and Responsibilities, 5*(3), 13–39.

Day, K. (2000, August 27). Soldiers for the shareholders. *The Washington Post*, p. H5.

Deacon, B. (with Hulse, M., & Stubbs, P.). (1997). *Global social policy: International organizations and the future of welfare*. Thousand Oaks, CA: Sage.

de Jasay, A. (1989). *Social contract, free ride: A study of the public goods problem*. New York: Oxford University Press.

Dekker, P., Koopmans, R., & van den Broek, A. (1997). Voluntary associations, social movements and individual political behavior in Western Europe. In J. W. van Deth (Ed.), *Private groups and public life: Social participation, voluntary associations, and political involvement in representative democracies*. (pp. 220–239). London: Routledge.

Dodds, I. (2001). Time to move to a more peaceful and equitable solution. *IFSW News, 3*, p. 2.

Domhoff, W. G. (1967). *Who rules America?* Englewood Cliffs, NJ: Prentice Hall.

Domhoff, W. G. (1974). *The Bohemian Grove and other retreats*. New York: Harper & Row.

Domhoff, W. G. (1990). *The power elite and the state: How policy is made in America*. New York: Aldine de Gruyter.

Domini, A., & Van Dyck, T. (2000, March 21). Generous to a fault. *The New York Times*, p. A31.

Economic Research Service. (1995). *Understanding rural America: Agriculture information bulletin no. 710*. Washington, DC: United States Department of Agriculture. Retrieved May 31, 2003, from http://www.ers.usda.gov/publications/aib710/

Etzioni, A. (1993). *The spirit of community: Rights,* responsibilities, and the communitarian agenda. New York: Crown.

Executive Pay: A special report (2003, April 6). *The New York Times*, pp. 8–9.

Executive pay: A special report. (2002, April 7). *The New York Times*, pp. 7–9.

Executive Pay Watch, retrieved July 9, 2003, from http://www.aflcio.org/corporateAmerica/paywatch/ (2000, August).

Fein, E. B. (1996, July 5). A move to hospitals for profit seems inevitable in New York. *The New York Times*, pp. 1, B2.

Fellin, P. (1995). Understanding American communities. In J. Rothman, J. L. Erlich, & J. E. Tropman, with F. M. Cox (Eds.), *Strategies of community organization: Macro practice* (5th ed., pp 114–128). Itasca, IL: F. E. Peacock.

Fellin, P. (2001). *The community and the social worker* (3rd ed.). Itasca, IL: F. E. Peacock.

Finn, J. (1996). Computer-based self-help groups: On-line recovery for addiction. *Computers in Human Services, 13*(1), 21–41.

Freudenheim, M. (1996, February 5). Charities say government cuts would jeopardize their ability to help the needy. *The New York Times*, p. B8.

Freudenheim, M. (2002, May 10). Companies trim health benefits for many retirees as costs surge. *The New York Times*, pp. A1, C4.

Fullinwider, R. K. (1988). Citizenship and welfare. In A. Gutman (Ed.), *Democracy and the Welfare state* (pp. 261–278). Princeton, NJ: Princeton University Press.

Gamson, W. (1990). *The strategy of social protest*. Belmont, CA: Wadsworth.

Gerth, H. H., & Mills, C. W. (1958). *From Max Weber: Essays in sociology*. New York: Oxford University Press.

Gibelman, M., & Demone, H. W., Jr. (Eds.). (1998). *The privatization of human services*. New York: Springer.

Gibelman, M., & Schervish, P. H. (1996). *Who we are: A second look*. Annapolis Junction, MD: NASW Press.

Ginsberg, L. (1990). Selected statistical review. In L. Ginsberg, S. Khinduka, J. A. Hall, F. Ross-Sheriff, & A. Hartman (Eds.), *Encyclopedia of social work* (18th ed., 1990 suppl., pp. 283–285). Silver Spring, MD: National Association of Social Workers.

Ginsberg, L. (Ed.). (1998). *Social work in rural communities* (3rd ed.). Alexandria, VA: Council on Social Work Education.

Gray, J. (1998). *False Dawn: The delusion of global capitalism*. London: Granta Books.

Greenhouse, S. (2001, September 11). Report shows Americans have more "Labor Days": Lead over Japan in hours on the job grows. *The New York Times*, p. A5.

Haley, J. (1999). Inside Japan's community controls: Lessons for America? *The Responsive Community, 9*(2), 22–34.

Halsey, A. H., Lauder, H., Brown, P., & Wells, A. S. (Eds.). (1997). *Education: Culture, economy, society*. New York: Oxford University Press.

Haub, C. (1995). Global and U.S. national population trends. *Consequences, 1*(2).Retrieved May 31, 2003, from http://www.gcrio.org/ CONSEQUENCES/summer95/population.html

Heilbroner, R. L. (1960). *The future as history*. New York: Harper Torchbooks.

Heilbroner, R. L. (1962). *The making of economic society*. Englewood Cliffs, NJ: Prentice Hall, Inc.

Hokenstad, M. C., & Midgley, J. (Eds.). (1997). *Issues in international social work: Global challenges for a new century*. Washington, DC: NASW Press.

Hunter, F. (1953). *Community power structure*. Chapel Hill: University of North Carolina Press.

Ignatieff, M. (2002, February 5). Is the human rights era ending? *The New York Times,* p. A29.

Johnson, A. K. (2000). The community practice pilot project: Integrating methods, field, assessment, and experiential learning. *Journal of Community Practice,* 8(4), 5–25.

Johnston, D. C. (1997, November 9). United Way, faced with fewer donors, is giving away less. *The New York Times,* pp. 1, 28.

Johnston, D. C. (2002a, February 7). More get rich and pay less in taxes. *The New York Times,* pp. A13.

Johnston, D. C. (2002b, February 18). U.S. corporations are using Bermuda to slash tax bills: Profits over patriotism. *The New York Times,* pp. A1, A12.

Johnston, D. C. (2002c, May 20). Officers may gain more than investors in move to Bermuda. *The New York Times,* pp. A1, A13.

Johnston, D.C. (2003, June 26), Very richest's share of wealth grew even bigger, date show. *The New York Times,* pp. A1, C2.

Karger, H. J. & Stoesz, D. (2003). The growth of social work education programs, 1985–1999: It's impact on economic and educational factors related to the profession of social work. *Journal of Social Work-Education,* 39(2), 279–295.

Kaufman, H. F. (1959). Toward an interactional conception of community. *Social Forces, 38*(l), 9–17.

Kirchhoff, S. (1999, November 20). Disability bill's advocates rewrite the book on lobbying. *Congressional Quarterly Weekly,* 27, 62–66.

Kornhauser, W. (1968). "Power elite" or "veto groups"? In W. G. Domhoff & H. B. Ballard (Eds.), *C. Wright Mills and the power elite* (pp. 37–59). Boston: Beacon Press.

Kramer, D., & Brauns, H. J. (1995). Europe. In T. D. Watts & N. Mayedas (Eds.), *International handbook on social work education* (pp. 103–122). Westport, CT: Greenwood.

Kuttner, R. (1996). *Everything for sale: The virtues and limits of markets*. New York: Alfred A. Knopf.

Ladd, C. E. (1999). Bowling with Tocqueville: Civic engagement and social capital. *The Responsive Community,* 9(2), 11–21.

Lappé, F. M., & Du Bois, P. M. (1994). *The quickening of America: Rebuilding our nation, remaking our lives*. San Francisco: Jossey-Bass.

Leonhardt, D. (2001a, April 1). For the boss, happy days are still here. *The New York Times,* Sec. 3, pp. 1, 8–11.

Leonhardt, D. (2001b, April 1). Leaving shareholders in the dust: Executives sold stock while the sun shone. *The New York Times,* Sec. 3, pp. 1, 9.

Leonhardt, D. (2002, June 4). A prime example of anything-goes executive pay. *The New York Times,* pp. C1, C10.

Levenson, D. (1997, Summer). Online counseling: Opportunity and risk. *NASW News,* p. 3.

Lindblom, C. E. (1959). The science of "muddling through." *Public Administration Review, 19,* 79–88.

Long, N. E. (1953). The local community as an ecology of games. *American Journal of Sociology,* 64, 251–261.

Longes, J. F. (1997). The impact and implications of multiculturalism. In M. Reisch & E. G. Gambrill (Eds.), *Social work in the 21st century* (pp. 39–47). Thousand Oaks, CA: Pine Forge Press.

Maloney, W. A., & Jordan, G. (1997). The rise of the protest business in Britain. In J. W. van Deth (Ed.), *Private groups and public life: Social participation, voluntary associations, and political involvement in representative democracies* (pp. 107–124). London: Routledge.

Marx, J. D. (1998). Corporate strategic philanthropy: Implications for social work. *Social Work, 43*(1), 34–41.

Massey, D. S. (1994). America's apartheid and the urban underclass. *Social Service Review, 68*(4), 471–487.

McCollough, T. E. (1991). *The moral imagination and public life: Raising the ethical question*. Chatham, NJ: Chatham House.

McCormick, P. J. (1997). Ethnography and a sense of place: Alternative measures for quality of life in Eastern Arizona small towns. *Small Town, 27*(4), 12–19.

McDougall, H. A. (1993). *Black Baltimore: A new theory of community*. Philadelphia: Temple University Press.

McGeehan (2003, April 6). Again; Money follows the Pinstripes. *The New York Times,* pp. 3,7.

Meenaghan, T. M., Washington, R. O., & Ryan, R. M. (1982). *Macro practice in the human services*. New York: Free Press.

Metcalf, S. (2002). Reading between the lines. *The Nation, 274*(3), 18–22.

Miller, J. B. (1983). Women and power. *Social Policy, 73(4),* 3–6.

Mills, C. W. (1956). *The power elite.* New York: Oxford University Press.

Mishra, R. (1999). *Globalization and the welfare state.* Northampton, MA: Edward Elgar.

Mitchell, A. (2002, February 6). Social Security pledges may haunt both parties. *The New York Times,* p. 18.

Moe, R. C. (1987). Exploring the limits of privatization. *Public Administration Review, 47,* 454–460.

Morgan, P. (Ed.). (1995). *Privatization and the welfare state: Implications for consumers and the workforce.* Aldershot, UK: Dartmouth Publishing.

Morin, R., & Deane, C. (2002, January 15). The ideas industry. *The Washington Post,* p. A17.

Moyser, G., & Parry, G. (1997). Voluntary associations and democratic participation in Britain. In J. W. van Deth (Ed.), *Private groups and public life: Social participation, voluntary associations, and political involvement in representative democracies* (pp. 24–46). London: Routledge.

Mullard, M., & Spicker, P. (1995). *Social policy in a changing society.* London: Routledge.

Myerson, A. R. (1997, October 7). The battle for hearts and tonsils: Hospitals specialize to enhance profits. *The New York Times,* pp. D1, D4.

Nisbet, R. (1953). *The quest for community: A study in the ethics of order and freedom.* New York: Oxford University Press.

Nordheimer, J. (1997, March 9). Downsized, but not out: A mill town's tale. *The New York Times,* pp. F1, F13.

Oldenburg, R. (1999). *The great good place.* New York: Marlowe & Co.

Park, K. S. (1999, Spring). Internationalization: Direction of social welfare policy education in the future. *Arete, 23*(2), pp. 33–45.

Passell, P. (1998, June 14), Benefits dwindle along with wages for the unskilled: Even less for the have-nots. *The New York Times,* pp. 1, 28.

Patterson, O. (2001, May 8). Race by the numbers. *The New York Times,* p. A31.

Pear, R. (2002a, September 25). Number of people living in poverty increases in U.S. *The New York Times,* p. A1.

Pear, R. (2002b, February 5). Upon closer look, Bush budget cuts include risks. *The New York Times,* p. A19.

Pearlstein, S. (2000, August 30). Giving the golden handshake. *The Washington Post,* p. 9.

Perrucci, R., & Pilisuk, M. (1970). Leaders and ruling elites: The interorganizational bases of community power. *American Sociological Review, 3*(5), 1040–1057.

Perrucci, R., & Potter, H. R. (Eds.). (1989). *Networks of power: Organizational actors at the national, corporate, and community levels.* New York: Aldine de Gruyter.

Phillips, K. (1990). *The politics of rich and poor: Wealth and the American electorate in the Reagan aftermath.* New York: Random House.

Phillips, K. P. (1993). *Boiling point : Republicans, Democrats, and the decline of middle-class prosperity.* New York: Random House.

Piven, F. F., & Cloward, R. A. (1971). *Regulating the poor: The functions of public welfare.* New York: Random House.

Piven, F. F., & Cloward, R. A. (1982). *The new class war.* New York: Pantheon Books.

Poplin, D. E. (1979). *Communities: A survey of theories and methods of research.* New York: Macmillan.

Riesman, D., Denny, R., & Glazer, N. (1951). *The lonely crowd.* New Haven, CT: Yale University Press.

Room, G. (1990). *"New poverty" in the European community.* London: Macmillan.

Rose, N. (1997). The future economic landscape: Implications for social work practice and education. In M. Reisch & E. G. Gambrill (Eds.). *Social work in the 21st century* (pp. 28–38). Thousand Oaks, CA: Pine Forge Press.

Salamon, L. M. (1997). *Holding the center: America's nonprofit sector at a crossroad, a report for Nathan Cummings Foundation.* New York: The Nathan Cummings Foundation.

Schmidtz, D. (1991). *The limits of government: An essay on the public goods argument.* Boulder, CO: Westview Press.

Scott, J. (2001, June 18). Increasing diversity of New York is building islands of segregation: The census. *The New York Times,* pp. A1, A18.

Scott, J. (2002, February 7). Foreign born in U.S. at record high. *The New York Times,* p. A18.

Smith, A. (1922). *An inquiry into the nature and causes of the wealth of nations*(Vols. 1 & 2; E. Cannan, Ed.). London: Methuen.

Stein, B. (1993). Work gets no respect on TV. *The Responsive Community, 3*(4), 32.

Stille, A. (2001, December 15). Grounded by an income gap. *The New York Times,* pp. A15, A17.

Strom-Gottfried, K. (1997, Winter). The implications of managed care for social work education. *Journal of Social Work Education, 33*(1), 7–18.

Swarns, R. L. (1997, October 25). In a policy shift, more parents are arrested for child neglect. *The New York Times,* pp. A1, A12.

Thurow, L. C. (1995, September 3). Companies merge: Families break up. *The New York Times,* p. C11.

Trattner, W. I. (1999). *From poor law to welfare state: A history of social welfare in America,* (7th ed.). New York: Free Press.

Twomey, S. (1995, June 19). Mr. Birthday makes his rounds. *The Washington Post,* p. 81.

Uchitelle, L., & Kleinfield, N. R. (1996, March 3–8). The downsizing of America: A national headache [Series of seven articles]. *The New York Times.*

Uncapher, W. (1999). Electronic homesteading on the rural frontier: Big Sky Telegraph and its community. In M. A. Smith & P. Kollock (Eds.), *Communities in Cyberspace* (pp. 264–289). London: Routledge.

U.S. Census Bureau. (2000, November 2). *National population projections: I. Summary files, total population by race, Hispanic origin, and nativity.* (http://www.cinsus.gov/population/www/projections/natsum-T5.html)

U.S. Census Bureau. (2001). *Statistical abstract of the United States: 2001* (121st ed.). Washington, DC: Government Printing Office.

van Deth, J. W. (Ed.). (1997). *Private groups and public life: Social participation, voluntary associations, and political involvement in representative democracies.* London: Routledge.

Viswanath, K., Kosicki, G. M., Fredin, E. S., & Park, E. (2000). Local community ties, community-boundedness, and local public affairs knowledge gaps. *Communication Research, 27*(1), 27–50.

Wagner, A. (1997). Social work and the global economy: Opportunities and challenges. In M. C. Hokenstad & J. Midgley (Eds.). *Issues in international social work: Global challenges for a new century* (pp. 45–56). Washington, DC: NASW Press.

Walsh, M. W. (2001, February 26). Reversing decades-long trend, Americans retiring later in life. *The New York Times,* pp. A1, A13.

Warren, R. L. (1978). *The community in America.* Chicago: Rand McNally.

Wellman, B. (1999). From little boxes to loosely bounded networks: The privatization and domestication of community. In J. L. Abu-Lughod (Ed.), *Sociology for the twenty-first century: Continuities and cutting edges* (pp. 94–114). Chicago: University of Chicago Press.

Wellman, B., & Gulia, M. (1999). Virtual communities as communities: Net surfers don't ride alone. In M. A. Smith & P. Kollock (Eds.), *Communities in cyberspace* (pp. 167–194). London: Routledge.

Willer, D. (Ed.). (1999). *Network exchange theory.* Westport, CT: Praeger.

Willer, D., Lovaglia, M. J., & Markovsky, B. (1999). Power and influence: A theoretical bridge. In D. Willer (Ed.), *Network exchange theory* (pp. 229–247). Westport, CT: Praeger.

Wrong, D. H. (1979). *Power: Its forms, bases, and uses.* New York: Harper Colophon.

5

Community Intervention and Programs: Let's Extend the Clan

Cynicism or hope. That's the real question, the choice all of us face.

P. LOEB (1999, P. 340)

One goal of community practice is to expand the circle so that more and more people will be embraced by others as an integral part of the human family. Chapter 4 presented environmental factors and the context of community practice. The purpose of this chapter is to convey a sense of what much of community work is like today, in terms of goals, approaches, and preoccupations. Through concrete examples, this chapter will showcase contemporary community intervention modes and successes.[1] It will describe the kind of programs underway to address some of the problems outlined in Chapters 3 and 4. It will show how direct service practitioners can be part of activities such as building capacity, identifying assets, creating caring connections, and joining with others to promote community cohesion and individual and group self-respect. Community intervention encompasses the ability to tap community strengths and the skills of including, linking, engaging, and empowering citizens. (See Chapter 14 for advanced skills in connecting and organizing people and communities.)

COMMUNITY UNDERTAKINGS

Current Burst of Activity

After decades of pessimism about the quality of community life, phrases such as *community resiliency* and *comeback cities* suggest a new societal atmosphere. Community practice also has increased status in our profession and workplaces. *U.S. News* labels social work a "hot job" and says being a community practitioner is part of that hot track: "Elected officials are hiring these organizers as a liaison to the community, tracking problems facing constituents. Labor unions employ them to do fieldwork, and nonprofits bring them aboard for local issues, like organizing low-income neighborhoods against hospital chains said to be unsympathetic to the poor. More groups are bringing them on to do good work" (U.S. News & World Report, n.d.).

Such positions involve working beside people of varied backgrounds to create a culture of change, identify assets, and link groups. Thousands of neighborhood associations have been started in the United States in the last 20 years, and other nations such as Brazil seem to be experiencing similar trends. Spirited organizations can make the crucial difference between a vital community and a stagnant one, between a community run for controlling corporations or the moneyed class and a community run for ordinary people. Community workers are increasingly being celebrated as creators of social capital and sustainers of social infrastructure (Couto, 1999). *Social capital* can be thought of as social networks or connections; *social infrastructure* can be thought of as institutions supportive to residents and as underlying foundations of a community. See Box 5.1 for overview of community change lingo and outpouring of activity.

Earlier Burst of Activity

Some view contemporary community intervention strategies and programs as a rebirth of the community-focused efforts of the 1960s with new auspices, rhetoric, and without the federal encouragement and fiscal involvement provided by the earlier Economic Opportunity Act. Former executive director of the National Association of Social Workers Mark Battle called it the "first substantive federal-to-community-to-people program.... Its design and operation had

facilitated it to have a flow of money from the federal government to the man on the street." From his vantage point as a key player at the U.S. Department of Labor during this period, Battle asserted that the War on Poverty "enriched democracy" and gave "worth in the larger public mind to poor people" (Battle, n.d., para. 7, 15; also see Dellums & Halterman, 2000). When social work publications refer to community programs in the 1960s, we are thinking of the Peace Corps abroad and a range of domestic programs, such as Mobilization for Youth in New York, Great Society and War on Poverty programs (ranging from Community Action Agencies and Head Start to Job Corp and Neighborhood Youth Corp), Model Cities, Volunteers in Service to America (VISTA), and federal public benefit programs. Head Start was not the only program to survive; today there are 1,000 Community Action Agencies across the nation (See Ceraso article via National Housing Institute at http://www.nhi.org/online/issues/100/caas.html). Some of those agencies were created recently in places such as small farm towns. Concerns about the poor continue, given that in the U.S. more than 30 million people still live in poverty.

Exciting and relevant jobs for social workers were available then and are today. Contemporary intervention is more community based and grounded.

BOX 5.1	CURRENT MODUS OPERANDI

Disparate groups are coming together to stir members of their communities. With mandates requiring resident-driven planning, ordinary folks are finally getting a voice in local and regional decision making. Successes associated with grassroots efforts are crowding out somber talk of alienation and bleak pictures of slums and farm foreclosures. Without ignoring such problems, hope and a new vitality are associated with community improvement. No single ideology or approach prevails. Web sites, media stories, and professional articles are filled with write-ups of community change success (or failure) based on one or more of these concepts or topics:

action research	citizen participation
coalitions	collaboratives
community capacity development	community organizing
community revitalization	comprehensive initiatives
constituency building	cultural strategies
empowerment zones	faith-based groups
healthy cities	holistic approach
local regeneration	interorganizational networks
participatory planning	neighborhood issues
resident involvement	partnerships
sustainable development	social entrepreneurship

WHAT IS COMMUNITY BUILDING?

Definitions

Much of the activity listed in Box 5.1 relates to *community building*, engaging a community to improve itself. Minkler (2002) defines community building as "an orientation to community that is strength based rather than need based and stresses the identification, nurturing, and celebration of community assets" (pp. 5–6). Chaskin, Brown, Venkatesh, and Vidal (2001) define community building as "actions to strengthen the *capacity* of communities to identify priorities and opportunities and to foster and sustain positive neighborhood change" (p. 1). Fabricant and Fisher (2002a, 2002b), who call community building the most significant social service work of the twenty-first century, view it as a process based on principles of reciprocity, respect, inclusiveness, and accountability. Some authors use the terms *community building* and *community empowerment* interchangeably. Perhaps it matters not what the process is called, so long as it facilitates collective change (Checkoway, 1997) and empowers "disadvantaged citizens to more effectively define and advance their own life chances" (Turner, 1998, p. ix).

Two distinguishing features of community building are (a) collaboration, to tap strengths of both displaced and well-placed citizens (Martinez-Brawley, 2000), and (b) engagement by the community itself, in contrast to the use of peripatetic professional organizers (Minkler, 1997) or remote social service providers. When professionals are involved, ideally they become partners with community groups. Many community building initiatives have four elements:

- Focus on geographically defined target areas
- Planning based on a recognition of community assets and available resources as well as needs
- Community participation in the governance, planning, and implementation of development activities
- Comprehensive development, including an attempt to integrate economic, physical, and human development activities (Chaskin, Joseph, & Chipenda-Dansokho, 1997, p. 435)

This requires community practitioners to "work across multiple systems simultaneously" (Mulroy & Matsuoka, 2000, p. 229). Community building helps traditional social work clients, people who have fallen on hard times, by surrounding them with the potent village that it takes to nurture and sustain humankind. There is a need for social cohesion, social infrastructure, and social capital (see Chapters 2 and 11, this volume). These have inherent civic and political repercussions.

Community capacity building often happens through either established or new organizations. Chaskin et al. (2001) point out that organizations in communities often

- produce needed goods and services,
- provide access to resources and opportunities,
- leverage and broker external resources,
- foster development of human capital,
- create or reinforce community identity and commitment, and
- support community advocacy and exertion of power. (pp. 63–64)

Such roles are a functional starting place for the thousands of community projects being carried out today. (For a description of key efforts, see Appendixes A and B in Chaskin et al., 2001; for other case examples, see Murphy & Cunningham, 2003; Putnam & Feldstein, 2003.)

Cautions

It should be noted that community building and regeneration is usually broader than community organizing, which will be discussed in more depth in Chapter 14. The now widely used community-building concept does not necessarily involve altering power relationships (Bricker-Jenkins, 2001; Cart, 1997; Walter, 1997) or income disparities (Phillips, 2002). There is less rhetorical emphasis on acquiring power or renting buses to go down to City Hall to demonstrate. Fisher and Shragge (2000) argue emphatically that, "Social welfare programs are replaced by poorly funded community-based activity, without a political agenda to challenge the growing disparities of income and wealth" (p. 9). Mark Warren (2001), who is in favor of building social capital "at the level of local community institutions," does point out that

> building such social capital may not be sufficient, if those community institutions remain detached from our political system. What has largely been overlooked in the debates about social capital is the growing disconnection between politics and what remains of American community life. . . . The political efficacy of turn-of-the-century political parties and twentieth-century cross-class federations both promoted civil participation and benefited from it.

. . . Revitalizing democracy, then, requires community building, but also something more: creating institutional links between strong communities and our political system. (p. 19)

Johannesen (1997) would say that this is important because vital social development is not possible without political development and action. Social development inherently involves a redistribution of political control and capacity that is needed to accompany economic redistribution. These are the empowerment and social integration functions of social work. (See Chapters 13 and 14 of this textbook for more on the inherently political nature of social action, organizing, and social participation; van Deth, 1997.)

RECENT COMMUNITY INTERVENTIONS: EXAMPLES

Having celebrated a new climate of hope at the chapter beginning, we now back up and look more closely at this turn of events. Although professionals always have worked in and with communities as enablers, organizers, and consultants (O'Neill & Trickett, 1982; Wenocur & Soifer, 1997), increasingly the horizons of change agents are widening, and there is more stress on the community context of social services and institutions such as hospitals and schools. The focus is also on collaboration and linkages within the community, identifying and using the strengths of the community, and community engagement.

Quiet Successes

In the 1970s, Britain established a system of community assistance called the patch approach that deploys teams of human service workers to neighborhood-sized geographic catchment areas or "patches." Field-workers or case managers, who often live within their assigned patches, support and build "on the resources of informal networks of kin and neighbors" and join with other local organizations and institutions "to solve both individual and community problems" (Adams & Krauth, 1995, p. 89). In other words, a patch makes use of natural helpers and community networks. Creating a patch team is a decentralized but unified way of providing flexible personal social services to people in an immediate geographic area, often with a single point of entry. However, a locality-based patch is not as small as it sounds, since it often includes 4,000 to 20,000 people (Martinez-Brawley & Delevan, 1993, pp. 171, 181). The patch can be general or specialized and may be focused on a particular clientele or broad-based (p. 9). This responsive community intervention approach, which has been experimented with in Iowa and Pennsylvania, has influenced community-based service delivery (see Chapter 15, this volume). Two additional examples follow, showing how linkages and collaboration are used in both urban and rural settings to focus on the community and develop services or policies.

Focused Community Intervention

One hundred residents live in a building owned by the Colorado Coalition for the Homeless. It took 2 years of intense collaboration to build the Forum Apartments building, which houses formerly homeless people with their attendant substance abuse problems, mental illness, and disabilities. Coordinators had to get funding from seven sources or partners for the construction phase and had to repeat the process to fund a permanent program. Eventually, this enormous effort won an award for community problem solving.

Broad-Based Community Intervention

The Southern Rural Development Initiative works with Southern and Appalachian communities, pulling together such resources as land-based centers, statewide community development corporations, comprehensive community development organizations, community development financial institutions, and community-based philanthropies. It has an interesting project called Parables to Policy, stories with a message that "prominently position the voices of rural people in the policy deliberations that influence their lives (Southern Rural Development, n.d.)." Interviews with average citizens from community-based organizations and legislators can be heard in Real Audio clips at the program's Web site (http:www.srdi.org). That project is funded by the Kellogg Foundation's Managing Information With Rural America (MIRA) program.

Successes seldom involve the entire rural or metropolitan community. Community builders know how to focus on the *community of solution,* a concept that means boundaries can be established by problem-definers, actors, and solvers. A community of solution usually crosses jurisdictional lines of governmental and voluntary agencies to resolve problems; it may function at any level, even internationally. In health and social services, a typical community of solution involves those organizations and people who want to address an identified problem, perhaps an alliance that gets together because the problem affects everyone in the group. As nursing professors Allender and Spradley (2001) elaborate, "Recently communities of solution have formed in many cities to attack the spread of HIV infection. Public health agencies, social service groups, schools, and media personnel have banded together to create public awareness of the dangers present and to promote preventive behaviors" (p. 5).

A Well-Known Example of Comprehensive Community Building

Infamous since the 1950s for widespread blight, the South Bronx was a place that Presidents Carter and Reagan visited to wring their hands. Then, in 1977, some impoverished families rehabbed three abandoned apartment buildings slated for demolition. "Following this restoration, each apartment was sold for $250 to those who had invested 600 hours of labor in restoring the building. . . . In addition, the families created a grassroots self-help organization known as the Banana Kelly Community Improvement Association" (Abatena, 1997, p. 28).

Major resurrection started in 1986 with new housing built by community development corporations (CDCs), which gave themselves monikers such as Mid-Bronx Desperadoes (Grogan & Proscio, 2001). Still, the schools and other services remained pathetic. Much of the later progress is owed to Anita Miller, a leader who convinced the Surdna Foundation to underwrite massive changes: "A one-time banker . . . Miller had been intimately involved with South Bronx CDCs as a program officer at the Ford Foundation and later as program director at the Local Initiatives Support Corporation. Well connected to everyone who mattered in both the public and private sectors, Anita Miller not only recognized the paradox [of physical renaissance with inadequate human supports] but was bursting to do something about it" (Schorr, 1997, pp. 329–330).

Collaborative community building does not always go smoothly or solve every problem (Meyer, 2002), but the South Bronx as an environment now has new resources (day care, senior services, retail services) and is more livable. We can see that successful community builders must function well in their local community ecosystem and be cognizant of the interface between it and larger societal institutions (Bowen & Richman, 2002, p. 68).

Many other communities, such as the empowered Dudley Street neighborhood 2 miles from downtown Boston (see the Dudley Street Neighborhood Initiation Web site at http://www.dsni.org), have taken a comprehensive approach to development with good outcomes (Walljasper, 1997). Out of a shared community vision to end deteriorating neighborhoods, one community initiative, the Marshall Heights Community Development Organization (see its Web site at http://www.mhcdo.org) in Washington, D.C., has created affordable housing and shopping centers while simultaneously providing employment services, general equivalency diploma (GED) programs, drug and alcohol treatment programs, and emergency assistance. Started in 1979, the group has received millions in the last decade from the Robert Wood Johnson and Annie E. Casey Foundations (Greene & Woodlee, 2002). Loretta Tate, president and CEO of Marshall Heights, has been praised for good management and results compared to other community development corporations in the District. According to the *Washington Business Journal*, the organization has "been lauded for its formula: taking on fewer projects and relying less on government dollars. One third of the nonprofit's $4.5 million operating budget comes from government grants" (Madigan, 2002, para. 4).

These community undertakings demonstrate that, despite the shameful national neglect of the poor and their hardscrabble neighborhoods, an array of professions has become involved in meaningful local work and partnerships (Borgsdorf, 1995). These undertakings also demonstrate that community building is an antipoverty effort.

CURRENT THEMES: ASSET-BASED COMMUNITY BUILDING

After years of disinvestment and disinterest in low-income and inner-city neighborhoods (Naparstek & Dooley, 1997), assets, resources, and strengths have become a central revitalization focus. For instance, after banks and insurance companies refused to do business in desperately poor neighborhoods, activists secured the passage and enforcement of the Community Reinvestment Act to stop this practice of "redlining." The spectacular long-term results of the implementation of this law led to more interest in tangible personal and community assets. Beginning with building tangible assets such as housing and small businesses, activists and other change agents became equally intrigued by intangible assets (spiritual, character) and practical talents of people in impoverished neighborhoods. It became clear that potential for political influence and the ability to build relationships also counted in community building. Not all asset agendas involve public policy changes or grassroots organizing; a variety of asset-related activities are available for the social worker to consider. Both tangible and intangible assets are discussed here.

Asset assessment is part of good patch analysis. The British patch approach was explained above. As social workers focus on a particular geographic area, look for the social networks in that area, and establish communication between groups and between agencies, they are beginning to look for structural and personal assets. Full use of the opportunities and resources available to a community requires a broad, inclusive understanding of the community's assets.

The following are five ways in which assets play a role in urban and rural community practice:[3]

1. Asset building
2. Asset claiming
3. Asset identifying and mobilizing
4. Individual leadership assets
5. Cultural assets

Many articles, if not entire books, are available on each of the topics to be discussed. The abbreviated discussion here is meant as an introduction to a multifaceted practice approach and a chance to see what these efforts reveal about community and community building. Given that the most current information appears on the Internet, numerous Internet cites and sites are provided.

Asset Building

Asset-building programs focus on the development of tangible assets such as housing, small business ventures, and savings accounts. They have the potential to change impoverished communities in many ways. In their positions as program developers and nonprofit managers, macropractitioners will want to be familiar with the range and success rates of programs in order to further broad progress. Those engaged in direct practice will want to be aware of opportunities as they help families navigate the path to dignity and economic security.

HABITAT FOR HUMANITY

This well-known nonprofit organization, based in Georgia, is a self-help, sweat-equity program in which volunteers help families build their own houses and houses for others like themselves. Each family usually puts 300 to 500 hours of labor into their own house as it is being built in order to receive a no-interest mortgage. The idea for Habitat for Humanity International came from minister Clarence Jordan, but the organization was founded in 1976 by Millard Fuller, a business partner of Morris Dees, who started the Southern Poverty Law Center (Walls, 1993). Former President Jimmy Carter's volunteer work with this organization has given it invaluable publicity. The Habitat for Humanity organization has built 150,000 simple but sound homes in 3,000 communities (see http://www.habitat.org). In some places, one house will be built with the help of dozens of volunteers, while in another place 18 houses may be built with the assistance of thousands of volunteers. The local staff locate skilled construction supervisors and coordinate with many local organizations. The interaction that can occur between social classes is one strength of the program. Former corporate executives work side by side with church groups and low-income families.

MICROENTERPRISE

Small loans and credit can foster microenterprise, and approximately 300 programs now exist in the United States (Jansen & Pippard, 1998), where microentrepreneurship is sometimes integrated with programs stemming from national welfare changes. However, the concept of using groups or centers to encourage financial independence started abroad. Economics professor Muhammad Yunus established the Grameen (rural) bank in Bangladesh and began making minuscule loans to women who wanted to start or expand local or home businesses such as refilling ballpoint pens or making bamboo stools. The women repaid the money; most received second or third loans and are thriving, as are their children. By now, a million people have participated in the program (Papa, Auwal, & Singhal, 1997). This concept is being tried in hundreds of variations in the U.S. (Banerjee, 2001; Raheim, 1996).

ACCION New York provides access to credit for people such as Carlos Aldana. When Aldana first emigrated from Columbia, he worked three jobs, 7 days per week, to buy a used car to start a delivery service business.

After he brought his wife and children to New York, money was even tighter, but with an ACCION loan of $1,000 Aldana was able to slowly expand his business to include another car and driver. Today, with the help of several more loans from ACCION, Aldana has also opened a small arepas restaurant business, while his delivery service business continues to thrive. Says Aldana, "My children see a dad who is happy and feels proud of himself—and that is good for them" (Acción New York, n.d.).

INDIVIDUAL DEVELOPMENT ACCOUNTS

Robert Friedman (2002) of the Corporation for Enterprise Development puts it this way: "To work for, earn, and own an asset gives one a stake in one's own future. The very process leading to ownership builds the capital, competence, and connections to keep people reaching toward and building dynamic and promising futures" (p. 1). For years, Michael Sherraden of the Center for Social Development and his colleagues have promoted individual development accounts (IDA), an asset-based policy innovation. The idea is to encourage the asset poor to get in the habit of saving, even $25 to $30 a month, by matching savings for the first few years. The goal is usually to own a home or acquire an education. Programs have been established in 500 communities, legislation has passed in 34 states, and national facilitating legislation for IDA tax credit and match money is possible (for information see http://www.idanetwork.org/assets). Tangible wealth creation, such as property and financial holdings, and economic literacy can jump-start individual and community engines of opportunity (Page-Adams & Sherraden, 1997) and tribal self-sufficiency in Indian Country.

Asset Claiming

Asset claiming can be for individuals, families, categories of workers, or populations. Of course, social workers will want to help eligible households to obtain various forms of public assistance and to identify sources of money such as the earned income tax credit and child tax credits. Just as important, social workers can explain to the general public how such supplements and tax reductions lift people out of poverty. We can also provide emotional support during the long process of obtaining a very different type of asset to be discussed here.

Tangible wealth that has been withheld has the potential to benefit place and nonplace communities. When exploited people live in reduced circumstances while others exhibit indifference, it is a social justice practice concern. The examples that follow involve campaigns and lawsuits rather than programs.

LIVING WAGE MOVEMENT

In the view of those in the living wage movement, big business not only fails to share resources with its labor counterpart but also fiercely fights attempts to promote economic democracy. Nevertheless, working people continue to claim a right to fairness in their economic relationships with their employers. Building custodians and contract workers argue strongly that local governments give businesses huge public subsidies such as tax abatements during development and downtown revival projects, but those businesses never share financial assets with the low-income workers who run, clean, and maintain their buildings and stadiums. They question what workers get in return for taxpayer investments. Such sentiments have launched community organizing campaigns to secure this type of asset. Although a living wage benefits a smaller number of people than an increased minimum wage that would cover all workers in a city, state, or our nation, the federal government has been unconscionably slow in raising the minimum wage, and therefore organizers have looked for leverage to help workers who are paid under city contracts or under large government contracts to for-profit firms.

The first policy agreement to pay a living wage was negotiated with Mayor Kurt Schmoke in Baltimore, Maryland, by a coalition of labor (led by the American Federation of State, County, and Municipal Employees) and community groups (led by Baltimoreans United in Leadership Development, the Industrial Areas Foundation, and the Solidarity Sponsoring Committee). It required city service contractors and government suppliers to raise the pay of 4,000 low-wage workers (Uchitelle, 1996). The agreement resulted in resetting the starting wage for such workers to $2.65 above the minimum wage. Similar ordinances have been passed in St. Louis, Boston, Los Angeles, Tucson, San Jose, Portland, Milwaukee, Detroit, Minneapolis, and Oakland—bringing the total to 83 living wage ordinances, a fact that inspired economist Robert Kuttner to describe the movement as "the most interesting (and underreported) grassroots enterprise to emerge since the civil rights movement . . . signaling a resurgence of local activism around pocketbook issues" (as quoted by

ACORN, n.d., "The Living Wage Movement," para. 1). Campaigns to help the working poor have spread from city to city, led by a coalition of progressive, labor, and mass-based organizations such as the Association of Community Organizations for Reform Now (ACORN). Critics have argued that living wage protections will destroy jobs. However, a recent report by a conservative economist for the Public Policy Institute of California documented a net benefit, that is, that more workers benefit from the higher wages that take them out of poverty than lose from job reductions (Wood, 2002). Tactics such as organizing tenants in downtown buildings to pressure their building owners and managers to back legislation or ordinances for living wages have been used. For other tactics and advice on the nuts and bolts of these types of assets and organizing activities, see Reynolds and Kern (2002). Also see Chapters 13 and 14 in this text.

HISTORICAL FAIRNESS CLAIMS

Specific populations residing in the United States are owed money by our government that they have never received. As a first example, the U.S. government has been the worst kind of trustee, banker, and money manager for over half of a million American Indians, an abuse that was admitted but went unchecked until lawsuits were filed. Due to "screwed-up records" and disinterest from officials, for over 100 years certain Native Americans suffered blatant loss and theft of assets belonging to generations of families. These assets, such as proceeds from grazing leases, timber sales, and royalties from oil, gas, and coal production, were generated in payment for use of Indian lands and were held in trust in Individual Indian Money accounts. The Bureau for Indian Affairs has received stinging criticism for gross mismanagement of Indian assets, in part because documents have been lost on an unprecedented scale. Three cabinet secretaries have failed to produce results and have been held in contempt (Gehrke, 2002; Summers, 2003). About 500,000 trust fund beneficiaries are owed around 10 billion dollars, and the judge is sympathetic to their class-action lawsuit, *Cobell v. Norton* (for more information, visit the Blackfeet Reservation Development Fund, Inc., Web site at http://www.indiantrust.com/). The lead plaintiff in the suit is Eloise Cobell of the Blackfeet Tribe. This case has been an organizing catalyst for indigenous peoples.

As a second example, most of us have heard that, during Reconstruction, there were good intentions by a few Civil War leaders to see that freedmen received something, such as 40 acres and a mule, but elected officials from top or bottom immediately ignored this promise. African American leaders argue that reparations are due to slave descendants—whether in the form of cash payouts for unpaid labor, a trust fund, or another vehicle. This is an issue capable of galvanizing minority (and majority) communities. The possibility of compensation has also been explored with local or state governments in locations such as Tulsa, Oklahoma where race riots destroyed people and property (for more on reparations, see Magagnini, 2002). Now that Japanese Americans who were interned in camps during World War II have received federal compensation and European workers are being reimbursed by corporations for forced (slave) labor during the same war, there is precedent for African Americans to receive promised but never-delivered assets. Lawsuits have been filed against two railroad companies, two insurance companies, and two financial institutions whose predecessors profited from slavery and its attendant horrors—forced breeding, torture, and so on. A plaintiff in one suit, Deadria Farmer-Paellmann, argues that it is wrong for these companies to benefit monetarily from stealing and raping human beings. In August 2002, there was a Millions for Reparations Mass Rally held in Washington, D.C.[4]

Asset Identifying and Mobilizing

In their book *The Art of Possibility*, Zander and Zander (2000) argue that those in leadership and authority roles need a shift in attitude, need to stop viewing others in terms of school grades—as *C* or *F* types. The authors (an orchestra conductor and a family therapist) have discovered that giving an *A* early on allows individuals to realize themselves and allows their assets to become manifest. Moreover, in a collective endeavor such as an orchestra performance, the "freely granted *A* expresses a vision of partnership, teamwork, and relationship" (Zander & Zander, p. 36).

Many professionals find the emphasis on intangible assets such as strengths and resiliency to be a better way of working with communities than the deficits orientation emphasizing problems and deficiencies (Ammerman & Parks, 1998). The community builds on what is in its midst already. Tangible assets such as housing, financial resources, and living wages were discussed previously. The next three sections present ways of identifying and using intangible assets. Once identified, these assets become tools in community building. This approach is illustrated by a brief example of identifying and mobilizing personal strengths and a brief example of identifying a community resource.

> *"The nurse was impressed with me because I was so young [17] but yet I had my shot records and I had my children up to date. She was so impressed with that that she would come to me and ask me if I would walk around to talk to the other mothers in the [migrant] camp."*

> *An asset approach need not focus on individuals or on money. For instance, community radio stations in Africa and Latin America where "both the process of communications and the content of the messages are controlled by the receiving communities" are community assets (Gray-Felder & Deane, 1999).*

Social workers are well positioned to intuit intangibles (reciprocity, trust, a sense of civic identity), to notice those currently lacking the networks necessary for a social life, and to promote active membership in voluntary associations (Onyx & Bullen, 2000). See Appendix A on skills.

EXISTING COMMUNITY ASSETS ASSOCIATION

Some communities such as the Boyle Heights and Vernon Central neighborhoods of Los Angeles have linked asset mapping with the Web, but most asset identification and mobilization is face-to-face or face-to-organization in nature. Although cities and towns are composed of masses of people, populations, and aggregates, the typical loosely coupled interactions between people can evolve into actual ties or bonds as community members interact in clubs, leagues, support groups, or networks (see Chapter 11, this text). Existing associations and the relationships they represent typify potential personal and community resources (Fuller, 2002).

"We're talking to local people about what skills they have," write Jody Kretzmann and John McKnight (1993, p. 19), who endeavor to identify hidden assets and then mobilize those assets, including people's time, energy, and willingness to pitch in, for community improvement. They point to the Adopt-A-Highway program—in which local associations take responsibility for a stretch of road—as evidence that groups are willing to take on more civic activity than we would expect. Their Asset-Based Community Development Institute (ABCD) helps organizations identify, nurture, and mobi-

lize individual and neighborhood assets—underused social capital—such as choirs and softball teams. Kretzmann tells the story about a capacity inventory conducted in a housing complex where others repeatedly named two women as the best cooks, yet these women had never met. The women were introduced, traded recipes, and eventually started a soul-food catering business on the west side of Chicago, employing 15 people.[5] Utilizing community assets in rural areas also requires the "ability of people to exchange information" (Fesenmaier & Contractor, 2001, p. 61). Social workers can network clients in this manner.

Kretzmann and McKnight (1993) suggest that, before starting to change any sector (e.g., libraries, police), we make an inventory of assets (e.g., empty space in library basements) already available in that sector. For example, one team conducted an inventory in a 24-square-block neighborhood and located 223 associations, including Toastmasters, La Leche League, a Golden Diners Club, and a Norwegian Women's Group. To create this long impressive list, the team used newspapers, directories, and other print sources; talked with people at local institutions; and conducted a telephone survey with a sample of residents (Kretzman & McKnight, pp. 113–132). They found evidence of productive community life. Even more dramatically in pure number terms, asset-oriented people in the Phillips neighborhood of Minneapolis, which is comprised of 17,000 people who speak 82 languages, have so far done 1,700 capacity inventories to create relationships and conversation guides as part of community building (Mádii Institute, n.d.). According to observers Kingsley, McNeely, and Gibson (1997), "the act of jointly inventorying assets is itself a powerful community organizing device that, by evidencing opportunities to change things, motivates collaboration and commitment to action" (p. 7). The next step of *linking* and mobilizing those discovered assets is, of course, a true organizing challenge.

Individual Leadership Assets

Sparkplug individuals, "even idiosyncratic ones," are more likely than plans or ideologies to yield change, according to The Rensselaerville Institute (TRI, n.d.). Organizers certainly emphasize leadership development (Mondros & Wilson, 1990). There are many ways to solicit and refine individual assets (Lazarri, Ford, & Haughey, 1996; Rodriquez, 1998). Among the programs created for that purpose are Union

Summer, which develops new talent for the labor movement, and a program that locates women who direct development organizations—the idea being that "women's contributions have been neither widely acknowledged nor explicitly credited" (McAuley Institute, 1999, p. 7). In other words, despite the wealth of personal assets in communities, most are not currently being applied to social goals, because people are scattered and not directed. An individual may embody valuable assets such as knowing the community and being nurturing of others but may lack an asset such as confidence. Gathering and orienting are the key tasks. This is important in terms of creating an effective team: The social worker can either help nurture confidence in an individual or can recruit a person with confidence. (For fascinating examples of recruiting strengths and getting the best out of weak people, see Morrell and Capparell, 2001.) Local action can pinpoint assets; for instance, spearheading civic initiatives can boost grassroots leaders into local office (Saegert, Thompson, & Warren, 2001). This is not to say that only potential leaders count. Since each individual has strengths and weaknesses, practitioners can "connect citizens through the exchange of their talents and shared interests, and build lasting multiple associations capable of incorporating both the capacities and fallibilities of everyone" (Rice & Seibold, 2001).

DEVELOPING ORGANIZATIONAL LEADERSHIP

To identify potential leaders, community builders ask, Who cares about the issue? Who has had problems with the issue, if anyone? Who is known on the issue? What people have ideas to contribute? They keep track of the names of those mentioned most often and of any groups with which the potential leader is associated. Leadership assets include personal qualities (like being trustworthy, having emotional intelligence) and professional skills (like raising money). Organizer Si Kahn writes about cultivating, supporting, spotting community leaders: A leader is "someone who helps show us the directions we want to go and who helps us go in those directions" (1991, p. 21). He designed a workshop exercise to transform people's sense of power and cohesion and to affirm that individual assets can make anyone a leader. Each person stands up, states his or her name, and says, "I am a leader because . . ."—for example, "I am a leader because I'm a facilitator for other people to be in leadership positions" (Kahn, 1997, p. 132). Then participants tell about elders from their neighborhoods or families who helped them become the leaders they are today:

"I am a leader because my grandfather wore a red tie and did exactly as he pleased" (p. 130). A candid discussion follows, which Kahn finds is a better way to learn about resourcefulness than writing ideas about leadership on a flip chart.[6]

Cultural Assets

Any culture—Armenian, Nigerian, Welsh—can give its members a sense of community, identity, history, and ability. Culture can provide intangible and sometimes tangible assets. Even though competence in dealing with those from cultures different from our own has become a professional social work goal, our understanding of cultural processes and of inference and implication in cross-cultural exchanges remains limited. Fortunately, with effort, we can quickly identify many positive factors in cultural worlds.

> *A historical example illustrates the potential of a cultural asset. When immigrants came to Florida from Cuba, cigar makers brought along an interesting institution: the lector. As factory workers rolled cigars, an educated person with a loud voice sat on a stool and read to them from newspapers and novels. Some workers even went outside after their shifts and listened to the next chapter through the open windows. The lector's choice of thinly disguised political materials often upset management, but workers would strike if the lector were fired (National Public Radio, 1999). Today's community workers are eager to locate comparable assets. Thus, people need to be linked with service assets but they themselves can also be assets for others.*

CELEBRATING GROUP STRENGTHS

Melvin Delgado (1998) educates us about the indigenous resources that exist in cultures and institutions outside of social services and government sectors. He describes *nontraditional* assets such as herbal shops, laundromats, and murals; settings such as malls; and networks such as arts, humanities, and sports that can become part of the help-seeking and help-giving system. This method goes beyond providing culturally specific services (Z. P. Henderson, 1992) and culturally competent staff. For example, Delgado (1997) says "gender-based natural supports" such as beauty parlors can be used for outreach or recruitment: "The Latina owners expressed willingness to involve themselves in leadership roles on social agency boards, advisory committees, task forces, and so forth. None of the owners, however, had ever been approached. . . . All of the owners indicated a willingness to collaborate with local human services agencies in an effort to help the community in a variety of social service areas, most notably alcoholism and family violence" (p. 449). Thus, natural helpers and indigenous leaders are assets. By learning the ins and outs of a Pentecostal church or a botanical quasi-pharmacy shop (Delgado, 1996), social workers become more at ease and effective in nontraditional settings.

Wrap-Up

Our extended discussion shows how assets of many types are being utilized as part of community building, community organizing, and other change approaches. The wonderful programs and projects just described did not spring up by chance. Skillful people nourished them. In additional, such programs are not a brand-new phenomenon. In many ways, assets-based community work resembles traditional community organization and development of the 1950s and 1960s. While today's community building approach is more rhetorically contemporary and interdisciplinary, its heritage has social work roots. For example, Habitat for Humanity reflects the rural self-help housing program of the U.S. Department of Agriculture (USDA) and the U.S. Office of Economic Opportunity (OEO) of the 1960s.

CARING CONNECTIONS AND PRINCIPLES

As the previous sections have shown, to establish a successful assets program, we must make a regular practice of finding out who knows what and who knows whom. We must be on the lookout for knowledge linkages (Fesenmaier & Contractor, 2001) and social-emotional linkages between individuals, groups, associations, and social institutions. We also must be on the lookout for those who are not attached. An important element of community building is the connection in and to a community. Even work to secure tangible assets is usually done through connections (Horwitt, 1989, Chapter 12).

We know that social and organizational connections are much more powerful when reinforced by emotional bonds. Faceless or neglected individuals need to be *beheld* by fellow human beings and to experience that connection. For this reason along with practical considerations, the late Maggie Kuhn, organizer of the Gray Panthers, promoted the concept of the "healthy block." It makes sense for people to care about and watch after each other in times of crisis. If neighbors would spare a little time to become familiar with the needs of those in the immediate neighborhood, we could move beyond neighborhood crime watch and into true community. Similarly, Elma Holder, founder of the National Citizens Coalition for Nursing Home Reform, advocates the "total community approach" to connect nursing homes. Rather than once-a-year visits from Brownies, Boy Scouts, and women's clubs, many organizations and networks of people could work out permanent interactive arrangements and caring relationships. Such community and institutional transformations require a "culture change" (E. Holder, personal communication, November 2, 2002).

Solidarity Within a Community: The Ideal

THE CIRCLE OF INCLUSION

"Solidarity works" is a belief that has fueled numerous successful social action interventions. This belief also has united people with different characteristics toward common ends and unity. Underlying the sentiment is an imperative for citizens to unite rather than divide, to further one's self-interest but not at the expense of other "little guys." Similarly, community-building initiatives try to solidify friendships and mutual trust. One goal is to bring out those facets of human beings that are accepting rather than rejecting of others. But what furthers acceptance? Robert Putnam (2000) describes an intriguing experiment about a stranger falling ill, to show how even polite, beginning encounters can lead to communal caring: "Experimental social psychologists have uncovered striking evidence that even the most casual social interaction can have a powerful effect on reciprocity. When a confederate 'stranger' speaks briefly to an unwitting subject, the subject is quicker to provide help when she subsequently 'overhears' the confederate having an apparent seizure than if there had been no previous contact" (p. 93, footnote). Much attention has been paid to incidents in which people failed to come to the rescue of fellow citizens, but, on a more positive note, the research (conducted by Latane and Darley) cited by Putnam makes us think about why a person would be more apt or likely to give assistance to another individual.

Communal caring must be cultivated or the circle of inclusion will not be expanded. See Box 5.2 for ways to grow communal caring.

BOX 5.2	CONNECTING AND DISSIMILARITY

As human service professionals, we support social processes that create community and embrace differences. Altruism researchers believe that humans can have personal and group attachments and still include others, that is, we can extend the clan. According to Oliner and Oliner (1995), expressions of communal care grow out of eight processes:

Promoting attachments with those in our immediate settings:

1. Bonding
2. Empathizing
3. Learning caring norms

4. Practicing care and assuming personal responsibility

Promoting caring relationships with those outside our immediate settings and groups:

5. Diversifying
6. Networking
7. Resolving conflicts
8. Establishing global connections

Source: Excerpts from Toward a Caring Society (pp. 6–7), by Pearl M. Oliner and Samuel P. Oliner, 1995, Westport, CT: Praeger Publishers. Copyright 1995 by Pearl M. Oliner and Samuel P. Oliner. Reproduced with permission of Greenwood Publishing Group, Inc.

A classic ethics and altruism research question has been why certain Europeans helped Jews and Gypsies survive the Holocaust, while most did not? After all, everyone was afraid. The answer illustrates one of the benefits of a connected, caring community. Examining the personalities and situational factors of non-Jews who took the risk, researchers learned they had expressed a bit more commitment to the broader society before the war, such as showing more inclusiveness in their friendships. For some of them, their concern for specific individuals led them to take more risks for other Jews (Batson, Ahmad, & Tsang, 2002). Research also showed that those who helped save Jewish people felt more obligation toward groups besides their own. Moreover, in the crisis, a sense of futility did not sidetrack them.

The concepts of *caring connections* and *solidarity*, underlying community intervention enterprises, also have moral and political implications. Organizer Arnie Graf puts it this way: "There's a drive in us to have a life of meaning that transcends the day in and day out of what we do." He is drawn to the work of Victor Frankel, who survived the Holocaust and developed *logotherapy* to help people find meaning in their lives. Graf has worked for the Industrial Areas Foundation since 1971 to build the power, organization, and economic security of low-income people. He discerns the importance of organizing around something larger than ourselves for both organizers and constituencies: "The human being is more than economics, more than the need to make money to survive out there."[7]

Philosopher and theorist Richard Rorty "emphasizes that the burden of liberal political morality is *to extend the sense of community in order to include hitherto neglected or despised social groups* [italics added]. . . . This too proceeds through radical redescription, the telling of stories which alter our self-understandings so that we come to see ourselves as sharing a common predicament with strangers" (Festenstein, 2003, p. 236). Influential moral and political philosopher John Rawls (1971) conceives of justice as *fairness*, an egalitarian approach to individual rights and community solidarity. Like Plato and other philosophers, he is thinking in abstract terms of the ideal as he designs justice principles and a framework to evaluate specific behavior or positions. The familiar statement "There but for the grace of God go I" implies that "community" partly is based upon empathy and compassion for the unlucky and less fortunate. Still—to complicate things even more—those who repeat the familiar statement know that in fact they have been spared and are not the murdered Jews or the people across town whose house burned down. That may be one reason why, above, Rorty speaks of mentally sharing a common predicament with strangers. Rawls goes further asking us to consider a situation where we will enter a meta-ethical community where we will not know whether we will be the one saying or *triggering* the phrase "There but for the grace of God go I."

THE CIRCLE OF JUSTICE, RIGHTS, AND DUTIES
Rawls believes that if humans could choose to start from scratch and delineate a fair system of

justice for the world, then those establishing principles would need to have a "veil of ignorance." This means that those in the group, the parties who are figuring out what principles would constitute fairness, should know nothing about their own race or nation. None of the parties would know if they are Swiss or German or Palestinian. Even if the parties think of themselves as Caucasian Americans, they would not know whether they have the childhood, temperament, ability, and situation of Bill Gates, Bill Clinton, Bill O'Reilly, Billy the Kid, or Billie Jean King. They would not know whether they are the bedridden neighbor who needs chores done or the fun-loving adolescent next door who is resisting additional responsibilities, whether they are the owner of the nursing home or the newest nursing assistant hired. The initial situation is hypothetical. Rawls (1971) explains his idea this way:

> Among the essential features of this situation is that no one knows his place in society, his class position or social status, nor does any one know his fortune in the distribution of natural assets and abilities, his intelligence, strength, and the like. I shall even assume that parties do not know their conceptions of the good or their special psychological propensities. . . . Since all are similarly situated and no one is able to design principles to favor his particular condition, the principles of justice are the result of a fair agreement or bargain. . . . For example, if a man knew that he was wealthy, he might find it rational to advance the principle that various taxes for welfare measures be counted unjust; if he knew that he was poor, he would most likely propose the contrary principle. One excludes the knowledge of those contingencies which sets men at odds and allows them to be guided by their prejudices. (pp. 12, 18–19)[8]

By being totally ignorant of any self-interest, the public interest or the ideal would be created at an abstract level. In keeping with the desire of contemporary community builders to enhance all human capital, over 30 years ago Rawls stated that *only the weakest in the community should be given advantages.* To quote him, "Thus the principle holds that in order to treat all persons equally, to provide genuine equality of opportunity, society must give more attention to those with fewer native assets and to those born into the less favorable social positions" (Rawls, 1971, p. 100). Social workers strive to keep ever in mind this deeper level of connection discussed by Graf, Rorty, and Rawls.

PRACTICES AND APPLICATIONS

Joining with a Community—The Realities

It is one thing to preach community and another thing to build it against great odds. Practitioners quickly learn that there are as many orientations to communities as counseling approaches to individuals (Blank, 1998). Yet, for all the variety and innovations, the keys to empowerment and success are the same: (a) treating community people as valued human beings, (b) getting to know them, and (c) establishing a bond.

What does it mean to treat community people as valued human beings? Social worker Nathaniel Branson, who grew up in Chattanooga as the youngest of 11 children and later worked in poverty programs, puts it this way: "How do you bring about community and institutional change? How do you work with people to help them take control of their own lives? I approach things this way—you don't talk down to people, people are intelligent, poor people can size you up in 20 seconds. Because they are poor does not mean they are stupid. And a part of what happens in our [social work] training, what happens in our development is involving a sense of being authentic. Not phony, you don't have the social smile pasted on your face. People will see through that. The connection that we make . . . through the feeling tone as we communicate with each other . . . 'Is this person really for real?' "[9]

What does it mean to get to know community people? As Baltimore housing organizer Ralph Moore recalls, "Down the line, I started to feel as if I was one of the family, that I had become part of the fabric of the neighborhood. I had knocked on most people's doors and I knew by name all the children of a woman who had 15 kids."[10]

What does it mean to establish a bond? In the civil rights movement, bonds began when the organizer would knock on the door of a house and ask for a glass of water. The transaction allowed the resident to generously meet a human need, and provided the organizer with an opportunity to begin a conversation. Even at a distance, some Internet communities or peer networks have started with shared personal tragedies, another humanizing context. It is important to clarify that caring connections are more than sentimental connections. Organizer Bob Moses describes entering a small town this way: "The organizer becomes . . . aware of its strengths, resources, concerns, and ways of doing business. The or-ganizer does not have . . . comprehensive plans for remedying a perceived problem. The orga-nizer wants to construct a solution with the community. He or she understands that the com-munity's everyday concerns can be transformed into broader questions of general import" (Moses & Cobb, 2001, p. 112).

Joining Without Taking Over

For new practitioners, it can be hard to bond with people, build things together, construct so-lutions together, and then let committees or members of the community proceed on their own. Yet, almost as soon as the joining process and the building of social capital begin, the trust-ing in people's strengths must also begin. The excerpts below, from a community worker's di-ary, make vivid such emotions.

Tonight the first meeting of the neighbor-hood action group (Operation Upgrade) is to take place at 8:00 P.M. in the Methodist Church. I didn't want the group to lean too heavily on me, or foster the idea that what they needed all the time was a professional to rescue them. I told the [seven-person] Steering Committee two weeks ago to decide if they wanted me to come to the neighborhood meeting, and if they de-cided, they would have to invite me. This has really been a troublesome, trying day for me. I kept hoping they would have strength and con-fidence enough to handle it without me. Each time the phone rang today, I hoped it would be an invitation. At 4:30 P.M., Mr. Halley came to tell me the Steering Committee had decided to let me rest for tonight. They will invite me at a later date. He thanked me for my help and promised a report soon.

At home, I caught myself feeling a little re-sentful and trying to think through this thing. Who do these people think they are? I gave them the idea, coached them, and met with the Steering Committee, and now they think they can handle a meeting without me. Have I let them go too fast with this program? What if something goes wrong at this crucial point?

A week had gone by, and I had not had a re-port from Mr. Halley. At 11:30 A.M., he came in and he made a report that sent my enthusiasm sky high.

There were at least 60 people at the meeting. They chose to keep the Steering Committee in-tact. They talked about needing a recreation center. One lady had a building she would do-nate. (Cohen, 1971, pp. 341–342)

Joining When There Are Competing Demands

Joining with the larger community is harder when that community is fragmented; but valu-ing others, getting to know them, and bonding through common tasks are still the keys. Com-munity developer Allison Gilchrist's (1992) anal-ysis of her organization in Bristol, England, shows the universality of this process. Partici-pants in the community association and its cen-ter programs where she worked were white. Most members of the over-60 club wanted things to stay as they were, but others in the associa-tion wanted to be more communally oriented, to involve Afro-Caribbeans. Meanwhile, Asian neighbors asked for a parallel over-60 group for their parents. Even though the last idea sounded simple, Gilchrist predicted that religious sectar-ianism, cultural and language differences, sex-ism, and racism would complicate the building of connections and her organization's transition.

The community developer's initial actions ad-dressed a mixture of task and process steps. Gilchrist decided to

1. meet with representatives and establish the program requested by the previously ex-cluded Asian immigrants;

2. deal with the resentment this generated in the existing seniors group (in fact, to referee or mediate disputes arising from any change);

3. change the organization's white image in out-reach and publications and through diversity hiring; and

4. start a new effort to involve black neighbors, including meetings for dialogue and dealing with old grievances.

Step 1 brought the challenges anticipated by the community developer. According to Gilchrist (1992), she had to "ensure that the group was for all Asian people (mainly Muslim and Sikh), and that it would be welcoming and accessible to women. . . . It proved vital to implement posi-tive action measures, such as transport, separate meeting space for women, equal representation on the management committee, and vegetarian refreshments acceptable to both religious com-mittees" (p. 177). Gilchrist succeeded, but het-erogeneous communities do tug professionals in many directions, as her complex situation illustrates.

Joining Through Thick and Thin

Another point about joining with communi-ties should be made here. When associations have been operating for decades, staff and neighbors can be joined at the hip or can have worked together so long that they are sick of each other. Even after many successes and a long time of working together toward constructive change, it can be challenging and demanding to attend to community people's concerns.

Let us be more specific about this aspect of community intervention. Neighborhood association employees often spend half their time dealing with government bureaucracies to make things happen and half their time with difficulties of individuals in the organization (such as when someone is ill or in jail). An association in Philadelphia with a budget of about $60,000 provides a real-world example. It has long been located in a transitional neighborhood, a place with glass on the street, visibly vacant buildings, and yet some houses selling for $300,000. Ten to twenty neighbors with political savvy are involved in a blight initiative, taking possession of city land and maintaining model people and dog parks. Along with addressing such macrolevel concerns, the paid staffer receives many calls a day from neighbors who are sobbing or screaming and whose concerns must be addressed. The staffer and governing board members also mediate disputes between valued neighborhood leaders who annoy each other.

Patience becomes critical when distractions, tension, fatigue, or factionalism threaten to undermine problem solving and collective unity. In short, attention must be given to tasks and issues, such as tackling property abandonment (Accordino & Johnson, 2000), but also to process and people.[11]

JOINING WITH ENDANGERED RESIDENTS

There can be unintended consequences to community intervention and community improvement. Despite community policing programs and other positive developments, the advocate, the organizer, the community builder cannot make things turn out right all the time. Safety must be considered—the safety of the professional and the safety of the community residents involved in an improvement effort. Whose block is it? We tend to think of groups, populations, or aggregates in a geographic area as if they were a unified whole or, at least, of one mind about addressing problems. However, neighbors do not necessarily think alike about disorder or want the same problems addressed. Many home owners and renters want local drug dealers off the porch, off the street corner, off the block. But some area residents do not want the

drug corners cleared, do not want the police coming into the neighborhood.

A horrifying example from East Baltimore makes the point. Seven members of the Dawson family were murdered when arsonists struck. The row house fire was apparently in retaliation against 36-year-old Mrs. Angela Dawson. She repeatedly called the police about loitering and drug activity around her home. The neighbors took differing approaches and did not unite to confront those they feared. If such a tragedy can have a lesson, it is to continue Angela's cause and our on-the-ground social work, but with caution. In deteriorating or gang-ridden neighborhoods, in buildings filled with drug dealers, it may be too risky to intervene alone even with the blessing of the police. It works better when a cadre of community practitioners approach, work in, and join with a neighborhood group in facing dangers and opportunities together.

Ongoing Challenges

Successful community-building projects have been completed in every state. Without a doubt, such projects have contributed to citizen engagement and to reinvigorated social capital (Putnam, 2000, p. 22; Putnam & Feldstein, 2003). Social workers have used their perspectives and talents to examine the macrosystem and to benefit community members through this process. The heritage of community intervention successes from the 1960s and 1970s is being brought to bear in a new century, with one essential difference. Projects today are more community motivated than stimulated by federal funding. The philosophy behind today's projects is that building social cohesion is critical to economic advancement and civic transformation. Social workers involved in today's and earlier approaches share a belief in human "improvability" and a belief that "responsibility and initiative are more readily acquired in the active meeting and solving of problems together than in verbal learning alone" (Biddle & Biddle, 1979, pp. 374–375). This chapter has discussed but a few of the community programs and associations that are attempting to make life better for community residents. They are a hopeful sign but there is always more to do.

CONCLUSION: ON TO SKILL DEVELOPMENT

"Community Intervention and Programs" concludes Part I of our textbook, which is about how to examine the current social environment and social interaction. This chapter illustrates ways that community workers are expanding the circle and involving communities in achieving their own success. It anchors the chapters in Part II by previewing how the methods and skills to be taught will further program development and associational life.

The next chapters cover principles drawn out of practice. They show how to study, investigate, and assess communities; how to build capacity; how to help people mobilize, organize, and plan (Arches, 1999); and how to advocate and "take action for the benefit of a wider constituency" (P. Henderson & Thomas, 1987, p. 7, pp. 25–26). Most of the practice methods that community workers need will be covered in these chapters, along with an introduction to an array of skills. *To be competent is to be aware of the multiple sets of skills that can be used.*

- Community practice involves a set of cognitive, analytic, and sorting skills, plus the ability of the worker to secure commitments and establish partnerships. Think of priority setting, delegation and problem sharing, problem solving, assessment, and contracting.

- There is also the set of skills of looking, listening, finding, and proffering surmises (testing one's hunches against another's perspective). Think of issue identification and pattern recognition, investigation, documentation, interviewing, and observation.

- Community practice entails a set of persuasion, representation, and reframing skills that allow social workers to deal with different agendas as we work with individuals and groups and in community affairs. Think of mediation, conflict management, negotiation, and facing authority figures.

- There is a set of interactive, responsive, and socially oriented skills with a focus on public information and on collaboration and interorganizational tasks such as networking and linking. Think of media skills and think of facilitation, coordination, coalition building, outreach, and social marketing.

- Skills are used to hold government entities and service providers accountable for action or inaction, to reform systems to benefit users, and to augment the potential of needy or powerless people to act for themselves. There are ways to let those marginalized by society know that they are valued as persons and as community members. Think of protecting individuals, protecting categories or classes of people, relating, advocating, asserting, and empowering.

- Finally, there is a set of skills focused on bringing the plight of individuals, families, and populations onto the social agenda and administering the programs that result from proposed reforms. Think of lobbying, institutional reform, organizing and mobilizing, fund-raising, changing agencies, and management skills.

Community intervention, like clinical intervention, is complex in terms of the circumstances of those needing help and in terms of professional performance challenges or use of self. Appendix A shows a community worker in action—listening, relating, facilitating.

APPENDIX A: COMMUNITY SKILLS EXAMPLE

I am a community worker hosting a meeting in the basement of a neighborhood museum center. It is important to arrive early, put up signs, and create a welcoming environment. Instead of standing at the door, though, I set up refreshments and let anyone help who wanders over. In this casual manner, I learn their names and how they heard about the meeting. Some individuals sit by themselves. I go over, offer them coffee, and introduce myself. They tell me their names; several share more information. As I put out nametags and written materials, I unobtrusively jot down the names and where everyone is seated in case I forget. One woman avoids my gaze and I leave her alone. At most gatherings, at least two people arrive early. Tonight, I use that time to determine their needs and interests. Notably, one of them asks me for my story—why do I care about women's health concerns (HIV/AIDS, abortion, pregnant teenagers)? Usually several people arrive late after things start; I ask someone seated near the door to greet them.

My "crowd" turns out to be seven women. I suggest forming a circle and talking. Several residents are uncomfortable with this; they have come to hear a lecture. So I say I will address the group and lead a discussion afterwards. I cut the presentation in half. As I speak, I look at or refer to each person. Where possible (and respecting privacy), I use their stories to authenticate the message.

Here is how that works. I say, "Access to services is vital. By access, we mean getting medical services easily. Yet, Mrs. Beaubrûn was telling me earlier that the mobile health unit has stopped coming to this area." I look for heads to nod and they do. "Access also means having someone knowledgeable to answer questions. Mrs. Paul, for example, had a good question. She wondered if a certain type of cancer was catching because three people she works with have the same kind."

I join the group before taking questions; this way people do not leave because the meeting is over. I let the group set the discussion agenda. Since two dominate, after a while I go around the circle, which allows each person to speak, starting with the quiet late arrival. I remember to obtain all seven attendees' names, addresses and telephone numbers. Finally, I invite the group to teach me: "I have only lived here a year. Tell me about this museum. Were all of you born in this town?" The point is to gain a sense of each other. I ask a woman with burning questions to stay afterward, so I can provide concrete answers and find out what information to mail. I make sure everyone leaves with our agency brochure, my card, and leftover cookies. One insight: Never disrespect those who did

come by expressing disappointment about the turnout. I note who walked or drove together and which strangers hit it off with each other. I ask myself questions: Was there a natural leader? Who articulated her concerns well? To what associations do they already belong?

Within a week, I telephone each woman— another opportunity to listen and relate. I feel confident. She cared enough to come to a meeting. Her personal story connects with this issue. I make another call to ask about the original and recent history of the neighborhood museum where our group met.

PRACTICE WISDOM

During a group discussion, one intent is to understand what community residents know and to determine why they do not know some things while knowing others. Do they understand the issue, or has mythology, gossip, or misinterpretation sprung up around the issue? Keep in mind people's needs and respect their concerns. Ask them what they want and let their feedback about the subject and agency priorities be a guide. Remember that few of your participants have experienced a sense of respect or empowerment from local social and health agencies. When appropriate, use humor to project affable vibes and help reinterpret your status as the expert. Before the next meeting, review materials on group work, organizations, and networks.

Discussion Exercises

1. After serving as U.S. Treasury Secretary, Robert Rubin became chairman of the board of a nonprofit giant with community building programs in 38 cities and 66 rural areas (Swope, 2000). Since Rubin is one of the most respected players on Wall Street and in the federal government, what does it say about the vitality and momentum of community building that he decided to serve on that particular board? Using the bibliography, determine what other professionals are involved in community building besides social workers and bankers.

2. Which way of creating or better using assets (asset building, asset claiming, asset identification and mobilization, individual leadership assets, cultural assets) most interests you and why? Do you have personal or professional experience with any of the described programs?

3. Is your agency engaged in community building? Does it give annual hero awards to those improving community life, to make the work of such people known to everyone?

4. Who funds the change-oriented programs of your organization? Who conducts training for staff, area denizens, and service users?

5. Why are associations as important as individuals to social work practice? In your view, are communities "bowling alone" in the sense of disengagement or "bowling along" in the sense of building anew and muddling through? Look up Robert Putnam on the Internet regarding civic participation and association (try *American Prospect* at (http://www.movingideas.org/links/civiclinks.html).

6. Using the Internet and other resources, research government funding sources for commu-

nity projects. Start with the U.S. Department of Housing and Urban Development's revitalization HOPE VI funds and the Community Outreach Partnership Centers.

7.   The epigraph at the beginning of the chapter speaks of hope. Oral history author Studs Terkel says we should remember that note of hope and focus on success. Folk singer Pete Seeger projects hope about action and the future. List three social workers you know who convey hope and describe how their hope is manifested. In contrast, certain places symbolize hopelessness; on the Internet, look up Pruit Igo in St. Louis and Davis Inlet, Labrador, in Canada. How did the government try to bring hope back to residents of the housing project and the village?

8.   Here is a community resident's profile: She has a job. She has a home, five dogs, and one cat. Young men have beaten her up. She videotapes drug transactions and prostitution and has worked for years to get more law enforcement on the streets. Finally, an undercover officer came but was killed—and she still feels guilty. Some see Gina Johnson as bold, others as prickly, some as reclusive. This 45-year-old woman has come to your community office wanting help with crime and in forming some type of action group. How can you learn more about Ms. Johnson as an individual in relationship to the neighborhood? How could she be an asset? A liability? What is your obligation to her?

9.   Many people who die in storms live in manufactured housing. A proposed solution is to require owners of trailer parks to install huge storm cellars that can accommodate residents.

(a)   Debate the issues (costs that will be passed on to residents versus saving lives).

(b)   If the trailer park population is divided, how can the positions be reconciled, or can they?

(c)   Draft statements to give before a state legislative committee. How does it *build community* to consider the well-being of a portion of the populace? If the trailer park residents must hire experts, what associations might help with fund-raising?

Notes

1. This chapter gives examples of positive communities (the glass half full) and serves as a counterpoint to the negative political and societal trends addressed elsewhere in our text (the glass half empty). Acting as resources on community intervention, several universities provide online information about skills, community projects, and justice vocations. Look up Community Toolbox (http://ctb.ku.edu) and also the On-Line Conference on Community Organizing and Development (http://comm-org.utoledo.edu/), a comprehensive set of examples, resources and syllabi. See, for example, on the Toledo site courses on community practice or organizing by Marshall Ganz, Megan Meyer, Randy Stoecker, Moshe ben Asher, and Dick Schoech.

To browse the Library of Congress Web site for publications on related topics, go to http://lcweb.loc.gov/. Also see studies on (a) organizing as an occupation (O'Donnell, 1995) or as part of social movements (Hyde, 2000; MacNair, Fowler, & Harris, 2000), (b) social workers with social change careers (Mizrahi & Rosenthal, 1998; Mondros & Wilson, 1994), and (c) teaching community practice (Gardella, 2000; Hardina, 2000; Johnson, 1998). See Walljasper (1997) for an important success story.

2. Social work is a hot career. Today, according to Nili Tannenbaum and Michael Reisch from the University of Michigan, "social workers comprise the largest percentage of professionals working in the fields of mental health and family services. It is estimated that by 2005, there will be about 650,000 social workers, more than a 30% increase over 10 years" (Reisch & Tannenbaum, 2001, conclusion, para. 1).

3. For a comprehensive glossary on assets and community capacity building terminology, see the Connecticut Assets Network's Web site (http://www.ctassets.org/library/glossary.cfm).

4. It should be noted by social workers that con artists are running scams by pretending that tax refunds, a reparation tax credit, and other potential restitution benefits already exist. Many African American taxpayers have filed claims that were not only rejected by the Internal Revenue Service but could bring penalties to those who filed them.

5. Speech given by John Kretzmann at the National Conference on Community Systems Building and Service Integration, U.S. Health and Human Services, September 4, 1997. For more examples, see Cheryl Bardoe's article, "Asset Management: Chicago Communities Find Hidden Strengths," which originally appeared in the January/February 1996 issue of *The Neighborhood Works* and is now available in *Urban Parks Online*. For client-community linkages, see Gretz (1992).

6. Concerning risk and shared leadership, see Burghardt, 1982, chap. 5. For a comparison of three church leaders in Saul Alinsky's Woodlawn organization, see Horwitt (1989, pp. 415–420).

7. Arnie Graf started BUILD, a Baltimore community action group. From an interview by Cathy Raab in Powers (1994).

8. G. Moore (1999) explains that Rawls's most famous book, *A Theory of Justice* (1971), is a "seminal treatise of relevance to political scientists, economists, philosophers, and legal theorists alike," and adds that critics oppose Rawls by arguing that "man is in reality intolerant and cannot be abstracted from his material circumstances" (Moore, 1999, pp. 397–399). Rawls died at age 81 in 2002.

9. Dr. Nathaniel Branson was interviewed by Maria Luisa Tyree on March 27, 2001, for an oral history course taught by social work professor Betsy Vourlekis, University of Maryland, Baltimore County campus.

10. Ralph Moore in a 1992 University of Maryland at Baltimore School of Social Work videotape by Lesley Bell and Michael Garcia, "Action Adventures in Our Own Backyard."

11. Janet Finegar of Northern Liberties Neighborhood Association (interviewed by Patricia Powers on March 13, 2002) reminds us not to idealize neighborhood work. In other words, wacky individuals, that is, "crazy neighbors," are as difficult to tolerate as crazy coworkers and crazy clients.

References

Abatena, H. (1997). The significance of planned community participation in problem solving and developing a viable community capability. *Journal of Community Practice, 4*(2), 13–34.

ACCIÓN NEW YORK (n.d.) Our clients. Carlos Aldana, El Gran Pan de Queso. Retrieved July 11, 2003 from http://accionnewyork.org/ourclients.asp

ACORN. (n.d.). *Introduction to ACORN's living wage web site.* Retrieved June 12, 2003, from http://www.livingwagecampaign.org/

Accordino, J., & Johnson, G. T. (2000). Addressing the vacant and abandoned property problem. *Journal of Urban Affairs, 22*(3), 301–331.

Adams, P., & Krauth, K. (1995). Working with families and communities: The patch approach. In P. Adams and K. Nelson (Eds.), *Reinventing human services: Community and family-centered practice*, pp. (87–108). New York: Aldine de Gruyter.

Allender, J. A., & Spradley, B. W. (2001). *Community health nursing.* Philadelphia: Lippincott.

Ammerman, A., & Parks, C. (1998). Preparing students for more effective community interventions: Assets assessment. *Family and Community Health, 21*(1), 32–45.

Arches, J. L. (1999). Challenges and dilemmas in community development. *Journal of Community Practice, 6*(4), 37–55.

Banerjee, M. M. (2001). Micro-enterprise training (MET) program: An innovative response to welfare reform. *Journal of Community Practice, 9*(4), 87–107.

Bardoe, C. (2002). Asset management: Chicago communities find hidden strengths. *Urban Parks Online.* Retrieved May 29, 2003, from http://pps.org//topics/community/engagecomm/assetmgmt

Batson, C. D., Ahmad, N., & Tsang, J. (2002). Four motives for community involvement. *Journal of Social Issues, 58*(3), 429–445.

Battle, M. (n.d.). Reflections. 1960's "Into the Community." Interview highlights on department website: http://www.umbc.edu/socialwork/Rbattle.html.

Biddle, W. W., & Biddle, L. J. (1979). Intention and outcome. In F. M. Cox, J. L. Erlich, J. Rothman, & J. E. Tropman (Eds.), *Strategies of community organization*, 3rd ed. (pp. 365–375). Itasca, IL: F. E. Peacock Publishers.

Blank, B. T. (1998). Settlement houses: Old idea in new form builds communities. *The New Social Worker, 5*(3), 4–7.

Borgsdorf, D. (1995). Charlotte's city within a city: The community problem-solving approach. *National Civic Review, 84*(3), 218–225.

Bowen, G. L., & Richman, J. M. (2002). Schools in the context of communities. *Children & Schools, 24*(2), 67–71.

Bricker-Jenkins, M. (2001). The slippery slope of civil society. *ACOSA Update, 15*(2), 14–15.

Burghardt, S. (1982). *The other side of organizing.* Cambridge, MA: Schenkman.

Cart, C. U. (1997). Online computer networks. In M. Minkler (Ed.), *Community organizing and community building for health* (pp. 325–328). New Brunswick, NJ: Rutgers University Press.

Chaskin, R. J., Brown, R. J., Venkatesh, S., & Vidal, A. (2001). *Building community capacity.* New York: Aldine de Gruyter.

Chaskin, R. J., Joseph, M. L., & Chipenda-Dansokho, S. (1997). Implementing comprehensive community development: Possibilities and limitations. *Social Work, 42*(5), 435–444.

Checkoway, B. (1997). Core concepts for community change. *Journal of Community Practice, 4*(1), 11–29.

Cohen, M. H. (1971). Community organization

practice. In A. E. Fink (Ed.), *The Field of Social Work* (6th ed., pp. 333–361). New York: Holt, Rinehart & Winston.

Couto, R. A. (with Guthrie, C. S.). (1999). *Making democracy work better: Mediating structures, social capital and the democratic prospect.* Chapel Hill: University of North Carolina Press.

Delgado, M. (1996). Puerto Rican elders and botanical shops: A community resource or liability? *Social Work in Health Care, 23*(1), 67–81.

Delgado, M. (1997). Role of Latina-owned beauty shops in a Latino community. *Social Work, 42*(5), 445–453.

Delgado, M. (1998). *Social work practice in nontraditional urban settings.* New York: Oxford University Press.

Dellums, R. V., & Halterman, H. L. (2000). *Lying down with the lions: A public life from the streets of Oakland to the halls of power.* Boston, MA: Beacon Press

Fabricant, M., & Fisher, R. (2002a). Agency-based community building in low-income neighborhoods: A praxis framework. *Journal of Community Practice, 10*(2), 1–22.

Fabricant, M., & Fisher, R. (2002b). *Settlement houses under siege: The struggle to sustain community organizations in New York City.* New York: Columbia University Press.

Fesenmaier, J., & Contractor, N. (2001). The evolution of knowledge networks: An example for rural development. *Journal of the Community Development Society, 32*(1), 160–175.

Festenstein, M. (2003). Richard Rorty. In A. Elliott and L. Ray (Eds.), *Key contemporary social theorists* (pp. 232–238). Oxford, UK: Blackwell Publishing.

Fisher, R., & Shragge, E. (2000). Challenging community organizing: Facing the 21st century. *Journal of Community Practice, 8*(3), 1–19.

Friedman, R. (2002, summer). A call to ownership. *Assets: A quarterly update for innovators,* 1–12.

Fuller, R. (2002). "I'm a social work student and I'm here to observe an AA meeting," *Journal of Social Work Practice in the Addictions, 2*(1), 109–111.

Gardella, L. G. (2000). The group-centered BSW curriculum for community practice: An essay. *Journal of Community Practice, 8*(2), 53–69.

Gehrke, R. (2002, September 17). Interior Secretary held in contempt. Retrieved from Yahoo latest news, Associated Press.

Gilchrist, A. (1992). Struggles for new thinking and new respect. *Community Development Journal, 17*(2), 175–181.

Gray-Felder, D., & Deane, J. (1999). *Communication for social change: A position paper and conference report.* (p.12, para 6) Rockefeller Foundation. Retrieved May 16, 2001 from http://www.devmedia.org/documents/Position%20paper.htm)

Greene, M. S., & Woodlee, Y. (2002, February 25). World takes notes as nonprofit lifts its District neighborhood. *The Washington Post,* p. A13.

Gretz, S. (1992). Citizen participation: Connecting people to associational life. In D. B. Schwartz, *Crossing the river: Creating a conceptual revolution in community and disability* (pp. 11–30). Newton Upper Falls, MA: Brookline Books.

Grogan, P. S., & Proscio, T. (2001). *Comeback cities: A blueprint for urban neighborhood revival.* Boulder, CO. Westview Press.

Hardina, D. (2000). Models and tactics taught in community organization courses: Findings from a survey of practice instructors. *Journal of Community Practice, 7*(1), 5–18.

Henderson, P., & Thomas, D. N. (1987). *Skills in the neighbourhood.* London: Allen & Unwin.

Henderson, Z. P. (1992). Educating multicultural groups. *Human Ecology Forum, 20*(3), 15–19.

Horwitt, S. D. (1989). *Let them call me rebel: Saul Alinsky, his life and legacy.* New York: Vintage.

Hyde, C. (2000). The hybrid nonprofit: An examination of feminist social movement organizations. *Journal of Community Practice, 8*(14), 45–68.

Jansen, G. G., & Pippard, J. L. (1998). The Grameen bank in Bangladesh: Helping poor women with credit for self-employment. *Journal of Community Practice, 5*(1/2), 103–123.

Johannesen, T. (1997). Social work as an international profession: Opportunities and challenges. In M. C. Hokenstad & J. Midgley (Eds.), *Issues in international social work: Global challenges for a new century* (pp. 146–158). Washington, DC: National Association of Social Workers Press.

Johnson, A. K. (1998). The revitalization of community practice: Characteristics, competencies, and curricula for community-based services. *Journal of Community Practice, 5*(3), 37–62.

Kahn, S. (1991). *Organizing: A guide for grassroots leaders.* Washington, D.C.: National Association of Social Workers Press.

Kahn, S. (1997). Leadership: Realizing concepts through creative process. *Journal of Community Practice, 4*(1), 109–136.

Kingsley, G. T., McNeely, J. B., & Gibson, J. O. (1997). *Community building: Coming of age.* Washington, DC: Development Training Institute, Inc. and the Urban Institute.

Kretzmann, J. P., & McKnight, J. L. (1993). *Building communities from the inside out: A path toward finding and mobilizing a community's assets.* Chicago, IL: ACTA Publishing.

Lazzari, M. M., Ford, H., & Haughey, K. J. (1996). Making a difference: Women of action in the community. *Social Work, 41*(2), 197–205.

Loeb, P. R. (1999). *Soul of a citizen: Living with conviction in a cynical time.* New York: St. Martin's Griffin.

MacNair, R. H., Fowler, L., & Harris, J. (2000). The diversity functions of organizations that confront oppression: The evolution of three social movements. *Journal of Community Practice, 7*(2), 71–88.

Mádii Institute (n.d.). See organization section. The VOICE in Phillips, p. 1, para 3. Retrieved July 12, 2003 from http:www.madii.org/html/voice.htm

Madigan, S. (2002, April 26). Marshall Heights CDC launches $1M capital campaign. *Washington Business Journal.* Retrieved from http://washington.bizjournals.com/washington/stories/2002/04/22/daily56.html.

Magagnini, S. (2002, October 22). Another way to fix past wrongs? Reparations are in order for the black underclass, Says a Harvard professor. Retrieved November 4, 2002 from http://www.sacbee.com/content/news/story/4896938p-5909094c.html

Martinez-Brawley, E. (2000). *Close to home: Human services and the small community.* Washington, DC: National Association of Social Workers Press.

Martinez-Brawley, E., & Delevan, S. M. (1993). *Transferring technology in the personal social services.* Washington, DC: National Association of Social Workers Press.

McAuley Institute. (1999). *Women as catalysts for social change.* Silver Spring, MD: Author.

Meyer, M. (2002). Review of "Civic Innovation in America," *Social Services Review, 76*(2), 341–43.

Minkler, M., Ed. (1997). *Community organizing and community building for health.* New Brunswick, NJ: Rutgers University Press.

Mizrahi, T., & Rosenthal, B. (1998). "A whole lot of organizing going on": The status and needs of organizers in community-based organizations. *Journal of Community Practice, 5*(4), 1–24.

Mondros, J. B., & Wilson, S. M. (1994). *Organizing for power and empowerment.* New York: Columbia University Press.

Mondros, J. B., & Wilson, S. M. (1990). Staying alive: Career selection and sustenance of community organizers. *Administration in Social Work, 14*(2), 95–109.

Moore, G. (1999). John Rawls. In E. Cashmore & C. Rojek (Eds.), *Dictionary of cultural theorists.* London: Arnold.

Morrell, M. , & Capparell, S. (2001). *Shackleton's way: Leadership lessons from the great Antarctic explorer.* New York: Penguin Books.

Moses, R., & Cobb, C. E., Jr. (2001). *Radical equations: Math literacy and civil rights.* Boston: Beacon Press.

Mulroy, E. A., & Matsuoka, J. K. (2000). The Native Hawaiian children's center: Changing methods from casework to community practice. In D. P. Fauri, S. P. Wernet, & F. E. Netting, *Cases in macro social work practice* (pp. 228–242). Boston: Allyn & Bacon.

Murphy, P. W., & Cunningham, J. V. (2003). *Organizing for community controlled development: Renewing civil society.* Pittsburgh, PA: University of Pittsburgh.

Naparstek, A. J., & Dooley, D. (1997). Countering urban disinvestment through community-building initiatives. *Social Work, 42*(5), 506–514.

National Public Radio. (1999, May 14). *Lost and found sounds: Cuban stories.*

O'Donnell, S. M. (1995). Is community organizing "the greatest job" one could have? Findings from a survey of Chicago organizers. *Journal of Community Practice, 2*(1), 1–19.

O'Neill, P., & Trickett, E. J. (1982). *Community consultation: Strategies for facilitating change in schools, hospitals, prisons, social service programs and other community settings.* San Francisco, CA: Jossey-Bass.

Onyx, J., & Bullen, P. (2000). Measuring social capital in five communities. *Journal of Applied Behavioral Science, 36*(1), 23–42.

Oliner, P. M., & Oliner, S. P. (1995). *Toward a caring society.* Westport, CT: Praeger.

Page-Adams, D., & Sherraden, M. (1997). Asset building as a community revitalization strategy. *Social Work, 42*(5), 423–434.

Papa, M. J., Auwal, M. A., & Singhal, A. (1997). Organizing for social change within concertive control systems: Member identification, empowerment, and the masking of discipline. *Communication Monographs, 64*(3), 219–249.

Phillips, K. (2002). *Wealth and democracy: A political history of the American rich.* New York: Broadway Books.

Powers, P. (Ed.) (1994). *Challenging: Interviews with Advocates and Activists* [monograph]. Baltimore: University of Maryland at Baltimore School of Social Work.

Putnam, R. D. (2000). *Bowling alone: The collapse and revival of American community.* New York: Simon & Schuster.

Putnam, R. D., & Feldstein, L. M. (with Cohen, D.) (2003). *Better together: Restoring the American Community.* New York: Simon & Schuster.

Raheim, S. (1996). Macro-enterprise as an approach for promoting economic development in social work. *International Social Work, 39*(1), 69–82.

Rawls, J. (1971). *A theory of justice.* Cambridge, MA: Harvard University Press.

Reynolds, D., & Kern, J. (2002). *Living wage campaigns: An activist's guide for organizing living wage campaigns.* (Available from ACORN, 739 8th St. SE, Washington, DC 20003)

Reisch, M., Tannenbaum, N. (2001). *From Charitable Volunteers to Architects of Social Welfare: A Brief History of Social Work.* Retrieved on July 31, 2003, from University of Michigan, School of Social Work web site: http://www.ssw.umich.edu/ongoing/fall2001/briefhistory.html

Rice, D., & Seibold, M. (2001, May). *Redefining community: Using agency resources differently to build relationships and promote inclusion.* Paper presented at National Institute of Disability meeting, New York.

Rodriquez, C. (1998). Activist stories: Culture and continuity in black women's narratives of grassroots community work. *Frontiers, 19*(2), 94–112.

Saegert, S., Thompson, J. P., & Warren, M. R. (Eds.). (2001). *Social capital and poor communities.* New York: Russell Sage Foundation.

Schorr, L. B. (1997). *Common purpose: Strengthening families and neighborhoods to rebuild America.* New York: Anchor Books.

Southern Rural Development Initiative (n.d.). A new voice for the rural South. Retrieved July 6, 2002 from http://www.srdi.org/info-url1806/info-url.htm

Summers, C. (2003, August 25). The great American land row. *BBC News* world edition (http: news.bbc.co.uk/2/hi/americas/3108713.stm).

Swope, C. (2000). Robert Rubin's urban crusade. *Governing, 13*(11), 20–24.

TRI (n.d.). The Rensselaerville Institute principles. Retrieved June 23, 2001 from http://www.tricampus.org/principles.htm

Turner, J. B. (1998). Foreword. In P. L. Ewalt, E. M. Freeman, & D. L. Poole (Eds.), *Community building: Renewal, well-being, and shared responsibility* (pp. ix–x). Washington, DC: National Association of Social Workers.

Uchitelle, L. (1996, April 9). Some cities pressuring employers to raise wages of working poor. *The New York Times*, p. A1, B7.

U.S. News & World Report (n.d.). Hot job: Social work. Retrieved on April 5, 2001 from http://usnews.com/usnews/nycu/work/wohot20.htm

van Deth, J. W. (Ed.). (1997). *Private groups and public life: Social participation, voluntary associations, and political involvement in representative democracies.* London: Routledge.

Walljasper, J. (1997). When activists win: The renaissance of Dudley Street. *Nation, 264*(8), 11–17.

Walls, D. (1993). *The activist's almanac: The concerned citizen's guide to the leading advocacy organizations in America.* New York: Simon & Schuster.

Walter, C. (1997). Community building practice: A conceptual framework. In M. Minkler (Ed.), *Community organizing and community building for health* (pp. 68–83). New Brunswick, NJ: Rutgers University Press.

Warren, M. R. (2001). *Dry bones rattling: Community building to revitalize American democracy.* Princeton: Princeton University Press.

Wenocur, S., & Soifer, S. (1997). Prospects for community organization. In M. Reisch & E. Gambrill, *Social work in the 21st century* (pp. 198–208). Thousand Oaks, CA: Pine Forge Press.

Wood, D. B. (2002, March 15). "Living wage" laws gain momentum across U.S.: New study shows higher incomes from "living wage" outweigh the cost in job losses. *Christian Science Monitor*, p. 1.

Zander, R. S., & Zander, B. (2000). *The art of possibility.* Boston: Harvard Business School Press.

II

COMMUNITY PRACTICE SKILLS FOR SOCIAL WORKERS: USING THE SOCIAL ENVIRONMENT

6

Discovering and Documenting the Life of a Community

The "inner life" of communities is bubbling away all the time.

J. Armstrong and P. Henderson (1992, p. 189)

THE LANDSCAPE OF OUR LIVES

Overview of Chapter

How enjoyable it is to learn what makes a town tick—whether a quiet town with one grain elevator or a toddlin' town like Chicago. The process takes us into libraries (research) and along thoroughfares (experience).

A library provides facts and analyses about urban areas. We can learn that the largest concentration of Filipinos in the United States is near San Francisco (Eljera, 2000). We can analyze what underlies changes in the urban neighborhood of Kibby Corners in Lima, Ohio (Li, 1996). However, conventional publications do not convey daily life for new Hispanic residents along the thoroughfares of Wisconsin and New Jersey—that entails footwork and a reading of ethnic newspapers. Similarly, libraries allow us to delve into rural areas (Homan, 1994, p. 100). For instance, nonmetropolitan areas can be classified; they can be manufacturing dependent, mining dependent, persistent poverty counties, retirement destinations, and so forth. Certainly, we want to identify a place's economic base and population characteristics (Davenport & Daven-

port, 1995, p. 2077). On the other hand, we want details about how this rural place functions and affects people, and that entails probing. Question: What is the current concern of the local planning board? Answer: Whether sidewalks should be added downtown. Question: How does local law enforcement plan to mount an antidrug program here? Answer: By asking residents to write down the names of suspected users and dealers and slide the paper under the town hall door (R. V. Demaree, personal communication, January 2, 1995).

It is a professional obligation to understand service consumers' communities. The first reason is <u>responsibility</u>. Knowing the whole picture is mandatory, regardless of our intended level of intervention. The second reason is <u>credibility</u>. Knowing a cross section of people and their histories gives us believability and access. The third reason is <u>versatility</u>. Knowing the players and systems provides us with more options. The fourth reason is <u>accountability</u>. Knowing what residents want gives us direction and makes us answerable. We talk about these responsibilities throughout this book.

Opportunities abound to experience community life, indirectly through reading (Boyle, 1995;

145

Cleage, 1997; Grisham, 1999; Kidder, 1999; Kotlowitz, 1997; Kozol, 1995) and directly through fieldwork. As one example, Martin (1995) makes sure students experience Tampa's ethnic make-up, which includes Seminole Indians, Vietnamese, Haitians, and Jewish people. Her students eat in those communities' restaurants and tour Spanish and African American newspaper offices; Spanish, Cuban, and Italian clubs; and cigar factories. Seasoned practitioners continue to familiarize themselves with community sectors. For example, Morales (1995) has coordinated with community groups in Bridgeport, Connecticut, to find out why Puerto Rican teenagers drop out of school. Similarly, to learn about the world of 12 British working-class boys, Willis attended classes with them and worked alongside them; he also acquired a detailed knowledge of their locality (Turner, 1992, p. 170).

This how-to-do-it chapter delineates strategic ways of unearthing facets of communities and gives detailed guidance on conducting or acquiring such studies. Learning about communities and engaging in a communitywide study (or an in-depth study in one sector) are satisfying challenges.

Four Types of Community Studies

This chapter presents four types of community studies and the relevant history, values, variables, and methodologies associated with each. Since social workers may well end up conducting or contributing to one of these studies, we also cover the broad topic areas usually included, distinct knowledge sought, and available sources.

From among many varieties of broad community studies, we will consider the (a) *fieldwork study* (original research), (b) *community power structure study* (original research, compared with a previous study of community power if available), (c) *community analysis study* (secondary sources plus original data from informal interviews and observation), and (d) *problems and services study* (secondary sources plus input from meetings, interaction with service providers and users, and surveys). All of these studies help us learn more about community settings, structures, processes, and functions.

Sociologists, anthropologists, and political scientists favor the first two types of studies, which focus on geographic area or place communities; elements of both are utilized by social workers as well. Journalists appreciate the third type because community analyses provide useful information for a broad audience. The last two varieties, which permit investigation of a place or nonplace community, are most commonly used by social workers. In fact, social workers sometimes move too swiftly into the fourth type of exploration. Readers may be more familiar with problems and services studies than with the other three types, but keeping an open mind and paying close attention to all four options permits us to make more informed judgments about applicability.

Learning about community studies will assuredly be helpful to macropractitioners and organizers, who will likely *initiate* comparable projects. Those in direct service are more likely to *help* with such studies, but they still need to be familiar with all the ways to learn more about who and what is out there in their localities. Practitioners should inquire as to whether such community studies have been completed by others and are available locally. Such knowledge can be useful in situations such as the following:

- In the hospital outpatient clinic where he works, Jason notices that different health beliefs create communication problems between staff and patients. He wonders if anyone has studied the culture of the immigrant patients or made meaningful contacts in the surrounding neighborhoods, and he decides to seek out field studies that can help to inform the work of his department.

- Elsa heads an interagency project to recruit and train spouses of local corporate leaders to be board members for service and advocacy organizations ranging from mentoring programs to food kitchens. She wonders how to attain the names of such people and hopes that someone has already done a community power structure study.

- Chandra is to supervise two AmeriCorps volunteers, from another area and with no rural experience, assigned for a year to her outreach agency. She will find out if any type of community profile has been completed—say, for a grant application. If not, she and the volunteers might do a community analysis together to give them an overview so that they can be of more use much sooner.

- A church in a working-class neighborhood proposes to start an after-school program. The minister calls Charlie's child welfare department for advice. Delegated to work with the church, Charlie wants to track down recent studies about current and needed neighborhood services.

Since we believe students and practitioners benefit from experiential as well as intellectual understanding, we have also included a number of suggested ways to appraise your area first-hand. There is an old expression about people being from many walks of life. We want you to come to appreciate your community in all the diversity that this phrase implies, not just as an abstract system, and to understand what holds it together.

FIELD STUDIES

Definition

A community *field study* is a case study with a holistic perspective that uses methods such as informal interviewing and observation to describe from firsthand acquaintance a particular locality, culture, or network. Out of a concern with society and with individual identity, the investigator interacts face-to-face with a group of people (informants) over time in order to understand life from their perspective (see Edgerton, 1967). Eventually, the field worker should be able to write up lived moments that help introduce this group to the outside world.

History

Such studies are closely linked with an interest in being where the action is and a willingness to meet people where they are in both the geographic and cultural senses. To illustrate, the purpose may be to record and interpret the "lower class life of ordinary people, on their grounds and on their terms" (Liebow, 1967, p. 10; see also Ramas, 1998). However, field studies can also be conducted of rich people. Field-study trailblazer Robert Park's broad background familiarized him with many aspects of city life. He believed his "tramping about"

helped him gain "a conception of the city, the community and the region, not as a geographical phenomenon merely but as a kind of social organism" (as cited in Bulmer, 1984, p. 90).[1]

The first such studies conducted in Chicago employed a multimethod approach, using newspapers as a source to study certain types of public behavior and using participant observation— "following Park's injunction to get the seat of one's pants dirty with *real* research" (Bulmer, 1984, p. 108). These sociologists valued the subjects or informants and their environment. They also attempted to explain subgroups and their environments to outsiders, which is one way social workers employ field studies today. Along with the Middletown study by Robert and Helen Lynd (1929) and the Street Corner Society study in 1943 by William Foote Whyte (1943/1993), the Chicago studies set parameters for the in-depth study of a community, neighborhood, or sector of the population (Abbott, 1997). While the Lynds studied people in general in Muncie, Indiana, plus the leading family in town, Whyte looked at particular people and situations and the social structure of an Italian slum. (See Box 6.1 for the types of questions asked in field studies.)

Traditionally, community organizers are required to get to know the neighborhood first off, not only families door-to-door but also commercial establishments and hot spots, and to make connections before calling any meetings. For example, back in 1960, new organizer Bob Squires acquired knowledge as he scratched around the Woodlawn area of Chicago for a project he had been hired to do with money from a foundation, the Presbyterian church, and the Catholic church. He recalls, "Sixty-third Street from Stoney Island to Cottage Groove, I knew every son of a bitch in that area. I knew every bookie, every whore, every policy runner, every cop, every bartender, waitress, store owner, restaurant owner" (Horwitt, 1989, p. 398). Squires was expected to synthesize his impressions of

BOX 6.1	REPRESENTATIVE QUESTIONS FOR FIELD STUDIES

Would you show me around your [town, neighborhood, school]?

Tell me about your typical day.

What's the best way around here to [rent a cheap room, get a free meal, get a truck, . . .]?

What kind of neighborhood would you say this is?

If I needed a [passport, green card, box at the opera, . . .], what would I have to do to get one?

Describe the sorts of things I shouldn't do at this meeting we are going to.

What do you mean? [as a response]

everyone he met, how they fit into the community, their motivations and activities, and what issues they cared about. Squires's field study of the neighborhood led to the formation of a strong neighborhood association which, six years later, was able to send 46 buses with more than 2,500 African American passengers to City Hall for voter registration (pp. 398–408).

Terminology

The anthropological field study approach—which we connect with scholars like Margaret Mead—has been of interest lately, in part because of its effectiveness in making us aware of our own ethnocentrism and cognizant of the logic and wholeness of others' cultural perspectives. This approach of experiencing another culture or racial/ethnic/age group from its own viewpoint is labeled *ethnography* (cultural description). It also uses participant observation methods. Elliot Liebow (1967, 1993) and James Spradley and David McCurdy (1972) pioneered in applying methods originally used in places outside our borders to groups within our nation. The goal is to acquire exhaustive knowledge of a group, including its inner experience. Recent studies of relevance include one on the homeless as a community (Wagner, 1993) and another on a continuing-care retirement community. Rachelle Dorfman (1994), for example, is a clinical social worker specializing in gerontology who included an examination of psychotherapy with the elderly as part of her community study. She moved into the retirement community she studied for 3 months (*immersion*).

Sometimes such qualitative work is referred to as *naturalistic inquiry* (Rodwell, 1987), and sometimes grounded theory is used instead of ethnographic theory (Brandriet, 1994). Regardless of the label, these approaches to field studies entail a humanistic approach and an empathetic stance, as advocated by Emilia Martinez-Brawley (1990): "Practitioners need to understand the tangible and intangible factors that shape the character of their communities. They need to be skilled applied ethnographers . . . able to see the world and assess its problems as members of their constituencies would, not necessarily to agree with them, but to define clearly the practitioner's point of view in the sociocultural mosaic" (p. 13).

Anthropologists stress the need to incorporate *local knowledge,* also referred to as indigenous knowledge, into plans. In general terms, people have tacit knowledge that they are barely able to verbalize but that provides them with a working knowledge of the world, for example, how to treat sick animals and children. It requires a deep understanding of a way of life. Mocking the distance that many professionals keep from indigenous and common people, British anthropologist Paul Sillitoe (1998) entitled one of his articles "What, Know Natives?"

Methodology

Very occasionally, social workers hear for the first time about the existence of a subgroup such as a gang or an immigrant group when an incident makes the news. Here is a pertinent example. A mother is caught on a surveillance camera videotape seemingly beating her child in a car parked in a Mishawaka, Indiana, department store lot. She reveals that she is affiliated with the Irish Travelers, a nomadic group of people unknown to most of us. Different and contradictory descriptors begin floating around. Some say that Irish Travelers are a large national band of people, but others say they are a small clan. Some assert that the Travelers descend from potato-famine Irish immigrants and are of common ethnicity, while others argue that they are of many nationalities. The stereotypes and descriptors continue: scam artists with assumed names, isolated, family-oriented, secretive. It is suddenly incumbent upon Mishawaka child welfare workers to find out more about these traveling people and to avoid rash judgments. Such an abrupt need for a ministudy is unusual. Fortunately, more accurate information from anthropologists and others can be found on the Internet (although not everything one reads online is reliable) and by contacting the Irish Association of Social Workers. The Indiana caseworkers put the child in foster care until trial, rather than with another Traveler family as the mother wanted, and then mother and daughter were reunited. Community workers must be able to put such a case into context—for judges, journalists, and the general public.

If we study traveling groups, such as migrant workers, Gypsies, carnival personnel, and Irish Travelers, we discover that mobile groups are negatively compared with settled societies. Alan Katruska of the University of Pittsburgh did a field study in Ireland of Travellers (spelled there with two *l*s) and learned about their culture, their "unique identity, lifestyle and heritage." Katruska (2000) explains, "Based upon what I have learned from Travellers in Ireland (if I am permitted to speak for Travellers at all), life becomes very depressing if one stays in one place for too long. Looking at the same landscape or same furniture or same boots for too long is not mentally healthy. It is better to be changing. It is better to be crowded together in the constant company of relatives and friends than to be isolated in a house with walls. When the first bee starts buzzing, it is time to move on. Travelling offers families and friends a chance to meet up together, it lets people share news and work with each other."

Most of the time, social workers are aware that there are groups in our geographic area that we know only by reputation, which is to say not at all. The field study gives us a chance to meet face-to-face and under better circumstances. Those who study the community in this way have willingly shared their methods (e.g., listening, keeping careful notes on details of daily life, and forming relationships with insiders). While any member or resident is a potential informant, this method relies on those willing to initiate us into their world. Green (1995) calls them "cultural guides" (p. 102). _Key respondents or informants_ are well-positioned insiders who can and will act as interpreters for the outsider. They could be indigenous people, elected leaders, or professional observers such as newspaper reporters. They may be amateur historians, people with connections, or networkers who do everything from matchmaking to transporting people to vote. If we can establish a working relationship with key informants, they are potentially valuable because they can "act as . . . de facto observer[s] for the investigator; provide a unique inside perspective on events . . . serve as a 'sounding board' for insights, propositions, and hypotheses developed by the investigator; open otherwise closed doors and avenues to situations and persons" (Denzin, 1970, p. 202). They sometimes read and comment on draft study reports to help maintain insider input (Duneier, 1992, 1999).

According to Whyte (1943/1993), the first question his key informant Doc asked him was, "Do you want to see the high life or the low life?" (p. 291).[2] Social workers familiarizing themselves with a place should ask to see both facets of the community, for they need to understand both the X-rated moviegoer and the churchgoer. We need to keep in mind that one common insider reaction is to put a good face on things and another is to try to deliberately freak out the outsider.

If we begin to understand a culture well enough, we can interpret aspects of it for others (Schwab, Drake, & Burghardt, 1988). Circum-stances often require social workers to make a case for client or citizen participation in decision making or for hiring a paraprofessional from the community. The more we understand and can convey the worldview of another class or culture, the more logical it will seem to have that viewpoint represented. Social workers are also asked to explain the behavior of particular groups of community residents. Since we want to do so from their perspective as much as possible, it is helpful if we learn to write what has been called _thick description_ "about a specific phenomenon and its surrounding environment" (Karabanow, 1999).[3]

Examples

To illustrate field studies and give the flavor of the study process, we look at the physical and social worlds of three groups as depicted by a planner, an anthropologist, and a sociologist. They describe their first looks at a place and a people and the means they used to conduct their studies. Joseph Howell, the planner, portrays life on an urban block he calls Clay Street. His study of the blue-collar community opens with a long list of details he noticed, including "old cars jacked up on cinder blocks . . . the number of dogs and 'beware of dogs' signs . . . the chain link fences . . . the small gardens . . . old folks rocking on their porches . . . a few old, shabby houses, with excessive amounts of debris and junk out front—old toys, bedsprings, tires, and old cars. In one of these houses lived the Shackelfords" (Howell, 1973, p. 8). Later, documenting lifestyles, Howell discusses this family's relationship with helpers. He noted that "Bobbi had her first visit from the caseworker. When she had been notified that the caseworker was coming to visit, she became very excited. She spent the preceding day cleaning and straightening the house, and when the caseworker arrived, Bobbi was ready. Everything was picked up and the house was very clean" (pp. 125–126).

As these two excerpts show, behavior and values are revealed to be complex. We cannot presume or assume after seeing one piece of the picture, like the yard. Howell assesses coping patterns and, eschewing stereotyping, distinguishes between "hard living" and "settled living" residents. He lets us hear directly from those in the area through reconstructed scenes and dialogue, which makes us care about those on the street. Such an orientation to a particular place makes us curious, rather than judgmental, about the Shackelford family and their "intense,

episodic, and uninhibited" approach to life (Howell, 1973, p. 6). Thus, one purpose of a community study has been achieved—to highlight the life ways and values of a group. Of special interest to us, this study pinpoints how family events, crises and problems can "fall outside the orbit of community service systems and how service systems are often insensitive to life situations of those they seek to serve" (p. xi). This represents a different way of examining service adequacy. Field studies demonstrate that knowing more completely even a few families helps us better understand a community.

Barbara Myerhoff, the anthropologist, studied a community within a community—a neighborhood in Venice, California, populated with Eastern European Jewish immigrants, many concentration camp survivors of advanced age. The focal point for the residents was the cultural community connected with a senior citizen center which she introduces by noting that "the front window was entirely covered by handlettered signs in Yiddish and English announcing current events" (Myerhoff, 1980, pp. 12–13).

Rather than looking at a community in terms of demographics or 5-year plans, we look through the eyes of particular individuals. The

words of encouragement on the signs say a good deal about those being beckoned. Social workers can use this method too and learn by looking at details that accrue to become the physical environment and cultural life of those with whom they work.

Rebecca Adams, the sociologist, studied a nonplace, affinity community. For over a decade, she inquired into the lives of fans of the rock band the Grateful Dead. Those "Deadheads" who followed the band around the country comprised one element of a loose national community; Adams observed by traveling with them. She reached the nontraveling element through questionnaires and dialogue in the Grateful Dead's newsletter and magazines. Many Deadheads stayed in touch with Adams by telephone, letter and e-mail; for example, after the death of Jerry Garcia (the Dead's lead guitarist/singer), 150 fans wrote to Adams. Local and nearby concerts provided a setting for studying the world of fans. Adams (1998) explains, "I began my field research project by standing in line at Ticketmaster and at the Greensboro Coliseum, by spending time in the parking lot before the shows, and by attending all the shows in the run. I also interviewed police officers who were on duty at the concerts, people cleaning up the parking lot the morning after the run was over, and staff members at nearby hotels and restaurants" (p. 10).

Sometimes, field researchers act as interpreters for a community that is unknown to or misunderstood by the public. In such a liaison role, Adams gave interviews to radio stations, television stations, newspapers, magazines, and independent film companies.

Regarding methodology, Howell (1973) believes that participant observation consists of making friends, being where the action is, writing it all down, and pulling it all together: "I had three things going for me. I lived in the neighborhood. I had a southern accent, and I had a family. . . . The approach I decided to follow consisted of . . . involvement with families on my block and . . . with community groups and community activities" (pp. 367, 372).

Like Howell, Myerhoff (1980) worked with individuals and an area. She knew 80 center members and spent time with 36. She describes her method, with the reminder that there is no definitive way to "cut up the pie of social reality. . . . I tape recorded extensive interviews . . . ranging from two to sixteen hours, visited nearly all in their homes, took trips with them from time to time outside the neighborhood—to doctors, social workers, shopping, funerals, visiting their friends in old age homes and hospitals. . . . I concentrated on the Center and its external extensions, the benches, boardwalk, and hotel and apartment lobbies where they congregated" (p. 29).

Immersed in the lives of those who attended the center, Myerhoff spent time in nursing homes and hospitals and at funerals or memorial services. She probed for their viewpoint, asking questions such as "Do you think that being a Jew makes the life of a retired person easier or harder in any way?" (p. 46).

Some parts of any community are harder to reach than others. Like Howells and Myerhoff, Adams needed guides. But, prospective key informants viewed her as unsympathetic or as an undercover police officer (a "narc"). She had to prove herself by mastering the community's special language and grasping its value system. For instance, Deadheads felt that the federal government was engaged in a "war on some drugs." Adams writes about identifying a guide: "Two groups that were particularly difficult for me to approach were drug dealers and members of a Deadhead cult known variously as the Church of Unlimited Devotion, the Family, or simply the Spinners. It was particularly important that I gain the trust of these two groups, because they tended to be the most orthodox of Deadheads. . . . [One Spinner eventually] commented on drafts of chapters, challenging my interpretations of data and steadfastly reminding me that Deadheads are not all affluent" (1998, pp. 18–19).

To generalize, the right guide can explain to us how to enter a community and can coach us about community terminology. This holds true for more than the three fieldwork examples described in this section. In the world of tramps, for example, there are variously named types such as "bindle stiff," "mission stiff," and "boxcar tramp" (p. 76) that have favorite "flops" (p. 99) (J. Spradley, 1970). In popular neighborhood hangouts or pubs, there is an order of welcome. Prodigal regulars who have been away are greeted most enthusiastically, then regulars, then strangers who arrive with a regular, and finally lone newcomers (Oldenburg, 1999). Awareness of such language, categories, social typing (Faircloth, 2001), and traditions allows us to function more effectively within a locality or an identity community (see Box 6.2).

We are learners, not experts coming in. We will share and our informants will share, affecting each other and the process, so there is emphasis on interchange, "mutual learning," and "respect" (Daley & Wong, 1994, p. 18).

Applications to Our Own Work

Inquiry conducted in a natural setting introduces us to groups and individuals who help us see life in nonmainstream communities with new eyes. The experience teaches us how to avoid being irrelevant or condescending. Such studies may assist us in speaking the same language as our involuntary clients or give us a clearer sense of their worlds. They allow us to see the lack of fit between one of our clients and his or her culture. Abbreviated versions of such studies may be appropriate in work with marginalized populations or before doing outreach to new communities. Because social scientists are more likely to conduct surveys to learn about community ideas, even modest face-to-face studies can be a valuable counterbalance.

Few of us can move into a neighborhood or retirement community or spend years hanging around a service center, but faster ways exist to enhance our understanding of neighbors, fellow citizens, and service users. We can seek out anyone who has conducted such studies in our area

BOX 6.2	TRAMPING ABOUT: A COMMUNITY WALK, DRIVE, JAUNT

The goals are to discover people, places, and rituals; to build relationships with informants; and to talk with persons often avoided. Exploring alleys and byways on foot or bicycle takes time, but main thoroughfares can be covered in several hours; stroll through an area again and again. *Learn* via speaking with, sitting with, and accompanying those encountered: mail carriers, shopkeepers, delivery drivers, individuals sitting on stoops. Ask them about their communities; listen to the tales. What generalizations do residents make about themselves? Learn their names. Traffic court, public benefit office waiting rooms, and blood banks can be used for resting and observing. Riding the subway in new directions makes sense; riding a bus provides an opportunity to ask passengers natural questions. Someone in a wheelchair might take an excursion through a barrier-free retirement community, spending time with many residents. *Write-ups* of such outings (*field notes*) include particulars, observations, and inferences, and one might start as follows:

I live in a popular neighborhood. When I take my child to day care, I walk past Rafael's Cuban restaurant—supposedly owned by militant exiles (scuttlebutt says its neon sign was used years ago to signal clandestine meetings), the grocery store, the apartment building with the circular drive, and the park. When we walk home at 6, I always notice which parents and children are at the playground. In the mornings, I've noticed three men in the opposite corner of the park. Maybe I am seeing in new ways, because recently I observed them washing in the fountain and today I realized that they are living in the park.

and ask for a briefing. We can borrow from field methods, such as observation, listening, and ethnographic interviewing, and we can embrace accepting attitudes. When we develop a deep understanding of communities, we bring fresh insights to counseling, case management, and other interactions. More important, engaging in such studies makes us want to keep working, to do more, because the rich pastiche we discover is so intriguing and the individuals we meet are so reassuring.

COMMUNITY POWER STRUCTURE STUDIES

Definition

If field studies give us the essence and variety of a community, power studies help us identify those who exert influence, "can produce intended effects," and affect community decision making in the political, economic, or communications sphere (Dye, 1993, p. 4; see for example Gaventa, 1980). A *community power structure study*—using surveys, interviews, and library investigation methods—explores the configuration and dynamics of the system of influence at the local level and the characteristics of dominant individuals; it results in a list of names and rankings of persons who are perceived to exercise power in the locality where they live or work. As discussed in Chapter 4, this power may be exercised by a small circle or by different and sometimes competing blocs or interest groups.

History and Terminology

The beginning of the *community power structure* study as a methodology is usually linked to a 1953 book of that title by Floyd Hunter, a social worker in Atlanta. In 1961, critical of Hunter's approach, Robert Dahl (a political scientist) did a famous study of the role of power in community decision making in New Haven. These pioneering studies came up with different models of local power systems or types of power constellations: *elite* (business community) in Hunter's study and *pluralistic* in Dahl's study. The current focus of attention is on how the wealthy control elected officials through contributions (Bates, 2001; "The Mother Jones 400,"; Rothman & Black, 1998).

The concepts of power and social class tend to intermingle. One book suggests that the following class groups exist in the United States: very poor, poor, working class, middle class, upper-middle class, upper class, ruling class, and mixed class (Mogil & Slepian, 1992, pp. 160–161). The very poor, poor, and working classes have no power except in numbers; they have been called everything from the *underclass* to the *silent*

BOX 6.3	REPRESENTATIVE QUESTIONS FOR POWER STUDIES

Who runs this city? Who are the most economically powerful persons?

Who controls the resources?

Who determines local taxes such as real estate taxes? Who benefits?

Tell me about the power brokers in this county that everyone knows about. Is there anyone operating behind the scenes?

Does anyone with connections at the county or state level live in your subdivision, neighborhood, or town?

Who is influential due to the high regard people have for him or her, or because of his or her clout with politicians?

Do you know any family that sends their children to an excellent boarding school?

majority, depending on their income level. Nevertheless, others in society are very interested in the leaders of these groups. Most individuals and families who are in positions of power or who can exert power are currently upper-middle, upper, or ruling class, regardless of their original background and social standing. Who do we want to locate? The terms *the powerful*, *dominants*, *influentials*, and *elite* are used fairly interchangeably to describe individuals who exercise power or are widely regarded by perceptive people as having that option (Ostrander, 1995). Admittedly, such questions as those in Box 6.3 may not elicit information about the power elite in the community; the upper class is not necessarily the ruling class. To determine those who are at the *core* of the entire community power structure, we need access to formal power structure reports.

Methodology

Different approaches for studying the powerful include reputational, positional, and decisional (sometimes called *issue analysis* or *event analysis*) studies. These studies ask, "Is this person perceived to be powerful, occupying a position that confers authority and power, or actually involved in specific decision making?" If all three are employed, a social worker can feel assured that those leaders whose names reappear often are "likely to exert influence in an array of decisions and in a variety of areas" (Martinez-Brawley, 1990, p. 75).

Although full-blown studies using any approach may take a year, modest exploratory or shortcut studies can be completed in 2 months, especially if an earlier study is available. Newspaper offices and political science, economics, or sociology departments at colleges or universities are starting places to unearth such a study.

Examples

To illustrate how successful power structure studies are conducted and what they tell us, we look at studies undertaken by a journalist, social workers, and a human services fund-raising expert. We provide three examples, but the social workers employed two different methodologies in the second example.

JOURNALISM STUDY

Our first example shows how a newspaper study of local power can be useful to our field. A journalist conducted a survey of 27 community leaders, often called a *panel* in power structure literature, to elicit names of "folks with real clout" in a large, mostly metropolitan county (Sullivan, 1994, p. 1). The leaders were asked to name "influential individuals . . . not necessarily those with the big jobs or titles, but the 10 people they would want on their side if they were trying to get something big accomplished" (p. 1).

The runaway winner in the survey turned out to be fairly similar to county influentials in other informal studies (who are often concerned with growth), because he was a developer. His family connections also fit the picture—a father who had been acting governor and a grandfather who had run a political dynasty in the county. That the winner was also a political columnist and cable-TV talk-show host illustrates a newer route to influence. The school superintendent, county executive, and a U.S. representative ranked second through fourth. Public service does not equate automatically with power; in this study, not one of 9 county council members was in the top 10 with real clout or sway. Influence can also be wielded by those who serve the community outside of office; the former president of the National Association for the Advancement of Colored People (NAACP) ranked eighth.

To the surprise of many, the person ranked fifth most influential in the county was not a household name and was active in social service causes. He had involved 100 congregations in an interfaith effort to feed and house low-income residents. The newspaper described him as "a Presbyterian minister who devotes his life to outreach programs for the poor and hungry, through the Community Ministry." As the reporter quipped, "That's hardly a Boss Tweed formula for power and influence, but [he] makes the list hands down."(Sullivan, 1994, p. 8) The reporter did not know the minister/executive director but planned to call on him in the future for opinions, which had the unusual result of putting a social service type into the mass communications loop. Social work managers and practitioners must also reach out to someone like that minister, who is positioned to know the thinking of the least and most powerful, both as a key informant and for help with needs assessment and planning.

Inclusion of one of us on the list of county influentials is astonishing to social service students or practitioners. Yet to our surprise, almost invariably when the results of local power studies are in, we know, an acquaintance knows, or someone in our family knows an individual on the long list, if not the top 10 list, fairly well. Reading community power studies makes it clear that we have more access to influentials than we realize.

Social Work Study

Even if studies are already available, it may still be worthwhile to do a study of one's own. *Our second example illustrates steps in the process and the payoffs for learners when they conduct power studies themselves.* Social workers need to figure out who to go to for what, who to hold accountable on various issues, and who to approach as decision makers in a community. Such objectives were pursued as a class project by undergraduate social work students located in a low-density area encompassing a city of 25,000. The students divided into two teams, each with a graduate student mentor. Since the teams used different approaches, both will be described, along with a brief report on the integrated results of the studies. These class project results were then compared and contrasted with an existing newspaper study. Some names were predictable; others on both lists evoked surprise. The student findings and the daily newspaper findings overlapped for 21 people. In a medium-sized community, knowing the names of that many decision makers is extremely useful to our

profession. How did the students locate those significant to our field?

Team 1, using a *positional* approach, sought to identify decision makers in public affairs and the human services field. It searched for a list of city and county boards, committees, and appointed citizen panels; found out which members were appointed and which were volunteers; obtained the names of members on each board and committee; and compiled a comprehensive list. This step took longer than expected, about a month. By asking questions, Team 1 informally determined which boards or committees were considered most important in city and county affairs (e.g., those bodies dealing with zoning, the airport, land, water resources, and natural resources were important to businesspeople).

Unlike investigators in other disciplines, these social work students also included the names of government service boards and committees affecting social services and low-income citizens, such as the community planning and development committee, human services board, community action board, and law enforcement advisory board. (Team 1 could also have added influential voluntary sector boards such as United Way's board of directors.) Even if many were not countywide influentials, they were power actors in the social service world.

With the results in hand, Team 1 noted the names of those who served on multiple committees and those with the same last names. Team 1 also talked with long-time residents, who pointed out other family connections the team would have missed. This method of looking at those in authority can reveal an elite or pluralistic power structure.

Throughout the 2-month process, students on this team learned about city and county government operations, the appointments process, board volunteer possibilities, the types of citizens who do and do not participate in civic activities, the individuals and families who are extremely involved in such activities, professionals in the social service community with government connections, and finally, those in the client community who serve on one or more boards. This represents quite an informational payoff, apart from the way the findings may help.

Team 2 employed a modified *reputational* approach, with the aim of identifying those in power behind the scenes. This approach requires nominations and meeting with those nominated. The students wondered if anyone would talk with them, but they learned that busy, powerful people open their doors when they learn that others consider them to be influential, perhaps because they hope to discover who nominated them, if nothing else, although the students did not disclose that information. As a starting point, Team 2 asked their field supervisors for names of community influentials; since this was a town of 25,000 with mostly local service providers, the field instructors had more community knowledge than might be true elsewhere. Team 2 compiled a list, and those persons mentioned most frequently were interviewed and asked for additional names. All of this was accomplished in less than a month.

As another way of seeking local elites, Team 2 checked traditional places where those with money and position might be identified, such as the university, for evidence of founders and large donors (e.g., names of buildings), and town banks, for the plaques that list the founders and the current directors. Team 2 noted any family names of local funds and charities and obtained the names of current chamber of commerce officers. There were no country clubs (however, country club presidents could be used in studies elsewhere). In cities, the boards of prestigious hospitals might be important (Ollove, 1991). Finally, Team 2 obtained the names of the largest employers (factory owners) in the city, county, and region. Team 2 compiled a larger list from its three sources: those nominated early on, those suggested by influentials (who were interviewed after they were nominated), and names culled from other places (see Box 6.4).

Throughout this process, this second group of students (Team 2) interacted personally with several people considered important in the area, and thus made contacts. The team also enjoyed sleuthing to find the moneyed families in a town where none were obvious. They did not conduct library research; in a bigger locale, such research might save time while making findings more reliable and would teach different skills (Warren & Warren, 1984).

To finish up, the names from Team 1 and Team 2 were combined and compared with those appearing in a reputational study published in the local newspaper of the 50 most influential people in the city. Neither the student city-and-county study nor the newspaper city study was scientific, but they provided leads to influentials and to power actors with the potential to exert influence, who were certainly the right people to contact for many purposes. *For social work purposes, the longer the list the better. Our purpose is not to prove who is on top but to involve as many influential people as possible in our work.*

Every student researcher turned out to know someone who was considered influential. In one instance, such awareness proved useful for lobbying purposes; at the request of an advocate, an influential arranged and attended a meeting with a state representative. Before the study, the advocate was unaware that this person, well-known to the advocate, had broad influence.

We profit from doing power studies, which introduce social workers to important community figures and to people with resources who might help with community assessment and other tasks. We can use our studies for advocacy or exposé purposes, or for assessment or administrative purposes. Thus we benefit, and so do our constituents.

BOX 6.4	THE POWERS THAT BE: A COMMUNITY WALK, DRIVE, JAUNT

The goal is to identify old, moneyed, or revered families in the area. Drive around the oldest and best-kept cemeteries, stopping by the mausoleums and largest stones to record the names (this doesn't work for all religions). Find the oldest building or the administration building at any college or university, look for the wall that lists the institutional founders, and record names. See if there is a foundation center in town and find out which families, if any, have their own foundations; otherwise, seek out planning offices or multimillion-dollar real-estate sellers (often promoted in newspapers and on office windows) who are likely to know about land holdings; ask the chamber of commerce about family enterprises that have continued for more than 100 years. In a small town or suburban community, track down the town historian and see if any historical or genealogical books have been published on the area. For a swift walk, go straight to the public or university library and seek help in identifying big law firms and banks in town. In cities, look at the Social Register, if available. Review available telephone books and other directories.

FUND-RAISER STUDY

Our final example suggests additional ways to use power studies to further an organization's self-interest. Learning the names of powerful persons behind the scenes and influentials at the city and neighborhood levels can be useful for your own agency's board of directors recruitment process and for resource development (Useem, 1995). If power studies are being undertaken for direct, obvious agency purposes such as fund-raising, they probably should be contracted out and conducted by a consulting group or university—not directly by the agency—to put some distance between the requests for information and the later use of that information. Advocacy groups could do the studies themselves.

Emenhiser (1991) writes convincingly about how we can make fund-raising approaches to the influential, spot long-term corporate mentors who can assist nonprofit organizations, and link power structure members to a low-power population in a mutually beneficial way. This is why we need to identify the powerful by name. Emenhiser gives a clear explanation of how to do this.

Who is or is not an elite or influential continues to be debated, but among those who are usually *not* part of the power structure, according to Emenhiser (1991, p. 11), are politicians, plant managers, women and minorities, professionals (except for lawyers from large firms), university presidents, civic association executives, media executives, and ministers. Look at Box 6.5.

Applications to Our Own Work

The type of decision making dominant in a community has implications for practice. If there is equilibrium among competing groups, then social workers want to become part of the field of exchange and to influence local policy through bargaining. If there is centralization of power and local government responds to a set of elites with a shared set of interests, then workers need to bargain with elites, get elites to propose policy alternatives, and keep elites from controlling the public, which, after all, has distinct and dissimilar interests from the elites. Finally, workers can look for common interests in the community and try to link groups to expand their influence.

The type of decision maker dominant in a community also has implications for practice. A remote circle of people unknown to workers presents less of an opportunity than known influentials whom workers have direct or indirect means of contacting. Either way, specific names are helpful. If key decision makers turn out to be generally hostile to social services, we can still find out which influential has a personal situation that may open a door. According to Martinez-Brawley (1990), "a thorough knowledge of people and structures that promote or interfere with community decision-making is essential to [social workers'] understanding of community units and to their professional functioning" (p. 52).

BOX 6.5	FUND-RAISERS HAD BETTER KNOW ABOUT ELITE POWER STRUCTURES: A REPUTATIONAL STUDY METHOD

Emenhiser (1991) describes a reputational method in simpler fashion than most authors. He conducted a study in Indianapolis to identify and rank influentials by following these steps:

1. Put together a base list of potential influentials (from research on the corporate 5% club, banks, etc.).

2. Ask seven or eight respected members of the community to review the list, to rank order the 30 most influential names on the base list, and to add names (these experts must be well connected or positioned to know).

3. Compile a new list, weight the names according to the ranks given, and reorder them.

4. Interview the 30 to 40 on the final list, asking these questions:

a. If a project were before the community that required decisions by a group of leaders, which 10 leaders could obtain its approval?

b. Place in rank order, 1 through 10 with 1 being the most influential, those individuals who in your opinion are the most influential in the city—influential from the point of view of their ability to lead others.

5. Weight and compile the rankings by interviewees to get the names of the 7 to 12 persons at the top.

Source: Based on Emenhiser (1991), pp. 9–14. Copyright 1991. NSFRE Journal. Used with permission; all rights reserved.

It is imperative to know who is on the board of directors of the agency with which we are associated, as well as any parent organization, what each person's background is, and why he or she was chosen. Those working in a government agency should be similarly aware of citizen advisory boards or other influentials who might be swayed by staff concerns.

As in field studies, conducting and discussing local power structure studies turns out to be an antidote to burnout. Community power studies seem to heighten our desire to critique results and methodology and to pursue new leads because they activate our juices and kindle our curiosity.

COMMUNITY ANALYSES

Definition

Community analysis can be a task, an orientation method, and a particular type of report write-up. To illustrate, Haglund, Weisbrod, and Bracht (1990) look on analysis as a critical first step before any intervention, and as a "profile [that] includes a community's image of itself and its goals, its past history and current civic changes and its current resources, readiness, and capacity for [activity]" (p. 91). A *community analysis* will be discussed here as a broad interpretive study based on factual documents, interviews with officials and natural leaders, observation, and search methods; a once-over-lightly examination of many aspects of a particular area or group; and a process of refining initial impressions.

A *natural leader* is a person respected and often listened to by others. The online Community Tool Box provides an unalloyed example: "A community coalition had as a founding member a veteran who had been shot down as a fighter pilot in Vietnam. When he got home, the whole town watched for agonizing months as he learned, through obvious pain, to walk and function despite crippling injuries that were supposed to confine him to a wheelchair for life. He was an ordinary guy without wealth or position but he had credibility in that town" (Who should be involved; influential people in the community, para 3).

Community or neighborhood analyses have many forms. While the analysis helps us differentiate, comprehend, and respond to a certain population or neighborhood and determine who generally runs things in town, it is also designed to grasp intangibles such as ethos, morale and town character. Although it may sound more ambitious, traditionally this type of analysis is done in fleet fashion as a preliminary procedure. "Neighborhoods are different," assert Warren and Warren (1984), who state, "Identifying the sources of this uniqueness is the first step in designing effective outreach programs and organizing for citizen action" (p. 27). And, we would add, a first step in determining whether your agency does the job it is supposed to in aiding the community. Time must be set aside to reflect; otherwise, says Cox (1977), "Practice is apt to be governed entirely by preconceived ideas, expedience, past habits of work, stereotyped attitudes, the insistent demands of a vocal minority, and accidental encounters with atypical situations. . . . There is no real substitute for first-hand knowledge of people and their problems, their needs and hopes" (pp. 15–16).

History, Terminology, and Purpose

This type of study has a less definite history. Robert Lamb's 1952 widely used shortcuts to gain a comprehensive picture of the life of one's hometown and Roland Warren's book on studying the community may be the progenitors; their suggestions have been employed by practitioners ranging from salespersons to organizers. Compared with the first two, this type of study is less well defined, in part because of its many names and descriptions. It is viewed alternatively as getting the pulse of community life, profiling one's community setting, doing a first approximation of an official community survey, gaining enough knowledge to allow one to function effectively in a community, and sizing up a situation. We believe *community analysis* is an appropriate designator.

Journalistic community profiles published over many decades are the closest popular equivalent. These include in-depth examinations of places published in the housing section or Sunday supplement of a large newspaper, city magazines such as *Pittsburgh*, or national publications such as *The New Yorker*. Such pieces, historical or current, are worth reading, if available, because they provide names of centrally important individuals and thoughtful analysis of economic ups and downs, of civic strengths and problems. Think of the Atlanta or Albuquerque of 40 years ago compared with the Atlanta or Albuquerque of today. Such articles help orient us to changing communities, but it will be our task to add assessments of a social work nature. For example, a magazine featuring the fishing past and picturesque present of a small town will not note a dearth of hospitals, clinics, and physicians within its borders, which requires residents to drive 30 minutes to the next larger town.

Why do we, as professionals, begin such an analysis? An analysis helps us get our bearings and avoid false starts in our practice. Warren and Warren (1984) put it extremely simply: "When you first arrive in a community, it's a good idea to spend a short time getting a feel for the city *as a whole* [italics added]" (p. 27). Since we want to root ourselves in the social fabric, we must go beyond the Welcome Wagon plane of information for ourselves and those we serve—for example, by attending some city council or town hall meetings or watching the cable television channel that covers civic meetings. The next steps in analyzing a community, even if easy, may not be as obvious or apparent as they first seem.

Methodology

While a field study often starts with certain individuals and families, and through their lives and activities works up to the city level, analyses start with countywide and citywide institutions and then move down to the neighborhood, suburban, or smaller unit level. Thus, one might start with city librarians and the census and later interview the corner druggist and the head of the elementary school PTA. Among the reasons for starting with a wide focus are that maps usually portray a broad geographic area, many planning studies look at a region, and histories are seldom written on small residential enclaves. Cook County and Chicago are too huge to analyze, but if we want to put into perspective the area around the University of Chicago, called Hyde Park, then statistics and demographics for the whole area can be used as a basis of comparison for data on Hyde Park. Sometimes the opposite is true: A village is too small to study in a vacuum because data are collected at the county or consolidated school district level.

How do we begin such an analysis? Cab drivers, ambulance drivers, fire fighters, and police officers are expected to quickly become familiar with various areas and with names of places. Lamb (1977) recommends these first steps for analyzing a town: Buy a map, including a street directory; look up local history; review *Rand-McNally's Banker's Register*, *Moody's Banks*, and *Standard and Poor's Directory of Directors* at the library to obtain the names of local bank and corporate manufacturing directors (today we might

also look at the names of the directors of the largest service and information businesses); and read census data and area studies by social workers detailing the citywide distribution of types of cases and social problems. To study a neighborhood, Warren and Warren (1984) suggest the following process: The observer should first walk around city hall or central government buildings, pick up pamphlets on city services, and visit the central business district; obtain maps, the telephone book, and local newspapers; go by the library and chamber of commerce to get a list of community organizations and their contact persons; and then drive and walk around the neighborhood, chat with people on the street, and ask them to define the boundaries of the area. After getting more settled, the observer should precisely identify key informants and various networks and generally figure out "how the neighborhood operates" (Warren & Warren, p. 34).

Obtaining an introduction to a small town can be accomplished with brief stops at the most conspicuous gas station and most noticeable church, the real estate office, pizza parlor, and elementary school. At this point, we do not need to speak with business owners, principals, or ministers; anyone working in the establishment who has time will do fine. In fact, sometimes others will be better initial guides to the area. Every place is different, so the social worker has to explore. In Carlinville, Illinois, a key person to contact would be a school janitor who has been around for 14 years and knows many families. He is also "a city alderman . . . a volunteer fireman, deputy coroner, a member of the Macoupin County Historical Society, American Legion, and the Elks" (Browning, 1995). If one of our stops is an elementary school, we might be lucky enough to run into him (or someone like him in another town) outside the building. Although the community itself will take a long time to know, newcomers can quickly start familiarizing themselves with the town. What does one say at such stops besides "I'm interested in this area"? See Box 6.6 for typical questions asked at this and later stages of the analysis.

Exactly what are we talking about here in terms of a community analysis process and product? A social work study of an inner-city area conducted one summer covered these topics: sociodemographics; history; political life; drugs, crime, and law enforcement; the revitalization process; community impressions; and notable community programs. Appendixes in the report included a list of contacts, a commu-

BOX 6.6	REPRESENTATIVE QUESTIONS FOR A COMMUNITY ANALYSIS

What are the boundaries of this area or community? What do you call it? Do old-timers call it something else?

Where do people stop to chat, hang out, or relax around here?

Have you ever seen anything written up about this area? Should I read it?

What are the good and bad points about living here?

What special problems or central issues does your [network, area, neighborhood, community of common interest] have?

Who are important civic leaders in your community and why?

Who are the chronic gripers in the area? What is their complaint?

What kind of games do children play around here?

---

nity survey by another university, a "community-building" report from another organization, census tract data, crime statistics, and descriptions of three social agencies involved with the community.

The bottom line is that one should gather information on one's neighborhood before it is needed. A sudden turn of events can make a prior study invaluable, as a Washington, D.C., urban improvement group learned. Logan Circle was being transformed from a rundown area where prostitutes congregated into a family neighborhood. Still, the place lacked basics such as grocery and hardware stores. Then someone heard that an outstanding food company was seeking a downtown location. Quickly, a cadre of neighbors prepared a pitch for locating it in Logan Circle. The group had just 48 hours to (a) identify and contact local landowners who might rent or sell to the store; (b) write and polish a report containing demographics, crime statistics, and anecdotes meant to personalize and market their neighborhood; and (c) recruit and brief credible negotiators who could influence the store owners. A completed analysis would make all three tasks easier. Fortunately, they made the deadline and recruited the store.

Kathleen Hirsch's (1998) examination of a neighborhood outside Boston exemplifies other methodologies. Yes, she secured facts from the Census and learned that a third of the households in Jamaica Plain were below the poverty line and 46% of households owned no car. And she did her homework about the community's economy. Jamaica Plain, it turned out, had these business sectors: "hardwares, bodegas, clothing, used book, ice cream and thrift shops (small-scale commercial); check cashing, real estate, restaurants (service); beer making, pretzels (light industry); small-scale agriculture" (Hirsch, 1998, p. xii). But, going beyond fact gathering to ob-

servation, Hirsch discovered the following gathering places:

Lockhorn's
Bob's Spa
Costello's
El Charro
The Midway
3M Market
Old Stag Tavern
Eddy's Market
Rizzo's Pizza
Fernandez Barber Shop
Franklin's CD
J. P. Record Shop
Cafe Cantata
Black Crow Caffe (pp. xiii–xiv)

The variety on this list may spur us to think more broadly about hangouts in our own communities.

Details about community life are invaluable to the social worker. Thus, besides reading and creating social reports, we want to focus on those places (besides home and work) that nourish personal connections, that is, we want to look for core settings "where one is more likely than anywhere else to encounter any given resident of the community" (Oldenburg, 1999, p. 112). Everette Dennis suggests that we observe gathering places and monitor other "touchstones" to keep tabs on community realities: "Learn how people live and work by observing housing standards, neighborhoods, and primary work places. Monitor such public gathering places as laundromats, beauty parlors, restaurants, and bars. Use public transportation at various times during the day and night. Watch facilities such as emergency rooms, jails, and shelters for the homeless—action at these sites helps the observer understand the community's pressure points" (as cited in Ward & Hansen, 1997, p. 70).

Examples

Perhaps our clients come from many different neighborhoods; however, many may live in a few areas that we could visit, and we all meet in a certain place—where the office is located. Without much effort, we can walk to different places for lunch and use new routes to drive to and from work until we have seen the 10-square-block area surrounding our urban office or the 10-mile radius surrounding a rural office. If our agency has satellite offices or scattered service delivery sites, we can visit each of them and, where possible, again move out in concentric circles to get the lay of the land.

We should pinpoint the central area of the suburbs or towns or neighborhoods, from which the majority of our service users come, and pick a central point, such as a key street corner, to make some instant but ongoing observations. These may not be surprising snapshots but rather *written observations* that prove useful regarding such subjects as who might need what services. Here are notes from one student who observed in a gentrified section of a large city:

Tuesday, 11 A.M. Many walking by are elderly (counted nine older people in 5 minutes I stood here). I also noted five women pushing baby carriages—a couple looked like young mothers; the rest looked older and may have been babysitters. I saw a group of Hispanic women waiting for the bus but not any black people. I saw a handful of people, casually dressed, coming up out of the subway.

Tuesday, 6 P.M. People with briefcases and wearing running shoes pour out of subway exits—in 5 minutes, at least 50—almost everyone white adults. Bumper-to-bumper traffic.

Saturday, 2:30 P.M. From same vantage point, I saw large numbers of couples with small children, but very few older people. Again, almost everyone was white. The bus stop by the 7-Eleven appeared to be a meeting place for young people hanging out.[4]

A number of possibilities can be explored if further observation reveals similar patterns. Among these are (a) potential needs of the elderly, and of house cleaners and baby-sitters who come into the area, such as day care for their children (or for residents' children); (b) whether play space is safe and adequate; and (c) possible discrimination in housing in the area, which could be checked out by testers.

Observers can be surprised by what they see while observing more closely than usual. For example, students noticed a number of Asian American families grocery shopping in a suburban area that was thought to have a totally homogeneous population (Box 6.7). Their finding might have program development implications. (It is surprising how accurate such informal observations can be sometimes. Within 6 years,

BOX 6.7	ANALYZING: A COMMUNITY WALK, DRIVE, JAUNT

Speedily discover if an area is heterogeneous. Look through the telephone book (as many named Kim as Kelly, Nguyen as Nash?), stop by unisex hair-cutting places in neighborhood shopping areas and by the motor vehicle center in your immediate vicinity—and take the answer into consideration in planning a walk. The goal is to identify small worlds within the geographic area.

A walk just beyond an urban university campus and a few blocks around the environs might reveal multiple communities of a sort: the campus, ranging from professors to security guards, a yuppie neighborhood, a public housing project, and an enclave of medical-related residential services flanking a hospital (e.g., a Ronald McDonald House). Find specific places where people congregate in a locale. Explore neighborhoods and walk in or around local centers of activity like these: pool hall, video arcade, casino, skating rink or good roller blading areas, bingo hall, tattoo parlor, swimming pool, coffee shop, jazz or other night spot, bowling alley, karaoke bar, the Royal Bakery downtown, Starbucks at the suburban mall, the Country Store at the crossroads, the small-town Dairy Queen. Look for other places where residents interact, such as a central bus stop, the high school parking lot, the lobby of the post office, the corner where day laborers are picked up, a storefront check-cashing place, or the farm implement store. Record who (in a demographic sense) is found where and at what time. How are you greeted along the way?

there were many new Asian American specialty food stores and restaurants within a 2-mile radius of that grocery store.)

Martinez-Brawley (2000) has figured out a rather easy way of identifying many kinds of linkages. To gain a "colloquial understanding" of her hometown in Maine, she scrutinizes obituaries: "Here I find the heritage and connections of families . . . the organizations, lodges, and service groups that provided purpose and membership, the churches that offered spiritual respite, their favorite pets, and even the simple leisure activities that gave meaning to individual lives" (p. xiii).

Noticing newspaper stories about incidents in one's community of interest is another way to be observant. The idea here is to check things out: What does the community think about this incident? What is a problem for them? For example, one student read about a hate crime in which two young white men doused an African American woman with lighter fluid and tried to set her on fire. The student began interviews to learn more about the suburban area where it happened and to determine whether this event indicated that skinheads or other organized groups had moved into the neighborhood. Here is part of her report: "According to police who attended a meeting to discuss the incident, this neighborhood does not have a greater propensity for this type of violence than others, and every person I interviewed felt that this was an isolated incident. However, I got an interesting perspective from G, a black man who works in the shopping center. He was not surprised and felt that if the woman had been lit on fire, the whole area would have exploded. He feels relations between blacks and whites are strained. He added that there were more media at the neighborhood rally than participants, and as far as he could see, there were no civic leaders in attendance." It would be foolish to rely on scattered interviews for truth, but ordinarily we get only one version of reality, while a community analysis reports on multiple versions and perceptions.

Ways to dig deeper exist that can take us beyond observations and a few interviews. The *rural method*, which Meenaghan et al. (1982) recommend for large areas with scattered populations, nicely fits our notion of a community analysis. We particularly like the emphasis of Meenaghan et al. on figuring out "smaller social worlds within the larger arbitrary unit" (p. 99) to be served by entities such as multicounty community mental health programs, hospital planning boards, or rural legal services.

To take the suburbs as an example, the *interactional approach* operates from the premise that place does not necessarily dominate the lives of those living in such communities (Meenaghan et al., 1982). In this interactional model, to look for community *isolates*, who are not part of the community, we can note the person who drives alone to work in the city and goes to the same bar most nights, we can observe at the unemployment center, or we can inquire at beauty shops about patrons who seldom venture out except to get their hair done. To search out *neighbors*, we can research car pools into the city, or to and from day care centers or schools or lessons on weekends, or we can track down ongoing poker games; these may be the start of at least "weak-tie" social networks (Flanagan, 1993, p. 22). To seek *key actors* in the suburbs, we can obtain the names of those who started the Neighborhood Watch group, as well as those who serve as block captains and those who started the children's soccer league or the adult softball league, along with current coaches.

Robert Putnam (2000), an expert on social bonds and social capital, reminds us that individuals can engage in formal and informal ways in their communities: "In Yiddish, men and women who invest lots of time in formal organizations are often termed *machers*—that is, people who make things happen in the community. By contrast, those who spend hours in informal conversation are termed *schmoozers*" (p. 93). We can consider whether we and those around us are machers or schmoozers or both, but more important, we want to note what linkages if any are occurring. Inevitably, people exhibit varying *degrees* of local involvement and leadership. How does a family or association fit into the community? Equally important, where do we as professionals fit—or do we?

The Write-Up

We began our community analysis by seeking out logical resources. We finish by writing a report and having it double-checked by our key informants.

1. A sample of topics to cover in a community analysis includes the following:
   Geographic, corporate, jurisdictional boundaries
   Demographics, statistics, subgroups
   History, community strengths today
   Political structure, governance
   Economic structure, major or key employers

Social services structure

Mutual aid, community action organizations

Potential or actual civic and service problems

Power relations

2. A sample of approaches to use in a community analysis includes the following:

Interviewing, "hearing" the community in new ways

Observing, analyzing

Collecting illuminating anecdotes, stories

Following methods used by social scientists

Providing orientation materials (map, photographs)

Being aware of personal bias, limits of analysis

Sometimes an innocuous topic such as transportation or community boundaries, or a basic step such as identifying those boundaries, turns out to be difficult, rewarding to capture on paper, and quite helpful for practice purposes. One student determined which political ward his community was in and located the names and telephone numbers of political block captains and neighborhood advisory board members. As part of a study of an affluent subdivision, another student examined schools and the boundaries that dictated which children went to what school. She learned that the influential subdivision's elementary school prevailed more often in school politics than a buffeted-around elementary school (that received the children nobody wanted) located quite close by in a noninfluential neighborhood. The student said that seeing how physically close to each other these schools were opened her eyes to power, influence, and class.

Applications to Our Own Work

Agencies and organizations need the information contained in a community analysis. At a minimum, they must know community indicators in their own specialization (Mitchell, 1998). If we cannot conduct one ourselves, we should ask librarians and newspaper editors if they know of a community profile that has been published recently; an economic development office might also be a place to check. By doing it ourselves, we will learn more, target it more precisely to our concerns, and become known to significant people in the process. We will be on top of things and in a position to make better judgments about social service and justice interventions.

Once we have successfully conducted a community analysis, we will be ready for the day the mayor calls to ask our advice or the day we need a detailed understanding of several elements in our town or city or county. This type of study also generates many ideas that allow us to do our jobs better and more easily (Cruz, 1997).

At a more mundane level, we are wise to keep abreast of even simple community developments—if only to avoid embarrassment. Can we give accurate and easy directions to clients on how to reach the office and where to park? Will we be aware when clients may be late due to a parade, baseball traffic, or a political demonstration (not to therapy resistance)? Do we realize when the buses or subway go on strike? Do we know when the school holidays occur? Do we know where clients with modest incomes can purchase cheaper medicine? The more specific we can be about resources and the more knowledgeable we are about how systems work, the easier we can make life for the users of our services.

PROBLEMS AND SERVICES STUDIES

Definition

Social problems and services/programs can be studied separately or in combination. We will call a *problems study* the kind needed to determine the extent and severity of specific problems or to give an overall diagnosis of the range of problems; we will call a *services/programs study* one that looks at provision and utilization of services (affordability, suitability, effectiveness). Both fall under our umbrella term *problems and services studies*, the fourth type of community study.

According to Siegel, Attkisson, and Carson (1987), anyone living or working in a community forms impressions about human service needs; thus, we want to obtain community residents' perspectives on the accessibility, availability, acceptability, and organization of services because their reactions give us "indispensable clues about the human service needs of the community as a whole" (pp. 86–87). (See Box 6.8 for questions that might be asked in such studies.) When a problem of great magnitude has occurred, a researcher may conduct a "social autopsy" to see what factors contributed to the natural disaster or human failure.

History

Power and influence studies look at one dimension of community—structure—while social welfare studies emphasize the values facet of

BOX 6.8	REPRESENTATIVE QUESTIONS ASKED IN SERVICES STUDIES

How do you get here? How many buses or transfers does it take?

What types of needs go unaddressed in your community?

What are some differences between your group and others in the community? Are those differences a problem for any of you?

Who are the various players who are trying to solve these problems and meet these needs? If the community is not being responsive, what do you think is the reason?

Have you received mail, telephone calls, or in-person calls about [how you obtain dental care, etc.]?

Please answer the following about your child care arrangements: [from a questionnaire with open- or closed-ended questions]

Have any social or health indicator analyses or surveys been conducted for this area? [asked of planners or officials]

---

community; that is, meeting common needs, caring for others (Morris, 1986). Sociologists are more likely to take a problem slant—what is breaking down society? And social workers usually take a services slant—what can reintegrate society? Some of the earliest social work endeavors involved this type of community study or social survey—obtaining necessary facts for planning and for documenting the numbers of child laborers and other social conditions or problems (Garvin & Cox, 1995).

Terminology

The most common approach used by helping professions when they undertake a community inquiry is to spotlight a target population or targets for change or a population at risk. Also mentioned are related service delivery problems, the responsiveness of the community to the target or at-risk population, and the community's capacity to respond (Menolascino & Potter, 1989). Less common but connected are a concentration on a "solution environment" (Rothman, 1984), a "human services system" (Netting, Kettner, & McMurtry, 1993), or even players, procedures, and linkages affecting human services (Hahn, 1994). These studies help bridge the gap between community and agency analysis. Such investigations may be utilized when an organization has to prove to others that a problem exists, believes some problems are unaddressed, or resolves to move toward community-based services.

Our agency can originate a study, but first we should locate relevant studies conducted in our locale or in similar communities—to discover the variables that define problems and their solutions. We are looking for multidimensional and systematic studies of (a) social problems, (b) private

and public sector programs addressing problems (that have been field tested) and other solutions for these problems, and (c) implementation critiques (issues, cost/benefit analyses, evidence of consumer satisfaction).

In many community-oriented versions of problems and services studies, such as general population or target population surveys, the perspectives of potential and current participants in the service delivery system must be solicited and valued equally with the advice of peers, funders, professionals, and service providers (Meenaghan et al., 1982). Potential and actual service users have opinions on the types of services they want and can suggest priorities for skills they desire.

Methodology and Examples

APPROACHES AND GOALS

The problem or service oriented community study varies in subject matter, research methodologies, and purposes, as shown by these representative examples:

- Bergman studied physical, sexual, and verbal violence that occurs on dates by having students fill out questionnaires. She selected high schools from rural, suburban, and inner-city locations and found that community setting had more influence than, say, racial make-up, with "the percentage of white collar workers positively correlated with the incidence of violence" (Bergman, 1992, p. 26). That surprising result from this *problem study* might change the focus or location of youth programs.

- Icard, Schilling, El-Bassel, and Young (1992) explored the "complex cultural, economic, and social factors obstructing the reduction of the

AIDS rate" in the African American community (p. 440). In their *problem and solution* study, they noted regional and subgroup differences within a demographic group: "An effective AIDS prevention effort must respond to differences among black gay men, black gay men who are IV drug users, and black heterosexual male IV drug users" (p. 444).

- A *services/programs* study can aid disaster preparation. To avoid chaos in the future requires coordination within the community and with outside organizations. Murty's study (1999), in a rural county in Missouri, identified 75 formal and informal organizations that could comprise a system for planning and responding to disasters. This identification was accomplished through network analysis and interviewing. As a result, relevant but peripheral organizations could be better linked.

- Following up on the circumstances of workers who had lost their jobs, Wagner (1991) used union peer counselors to telephone 495 workers and conduct 20 minute interviews pertaining to their job status and how they had coped. One goal of this *problem and solution study* was to learn more about the disruptions to mill workers and their communities; another was to follow up with appropriate service, organizing, or advocacy options.

- Following up on a horrendous death toll from extreme heat, Klinenberg (2002) used ethnographic fieldwork, in-depth interviewing, archival research, map-making, and statistical analysis to, among other things, contrast areas of Chicago that were hard hit by a heat wave with those that were not (some next door to each other). Among his findings were that busy streets made safe neighborhoods, that changes in social service delivery and privatization trends contributed to the calamitous effects, that the media treated the tragedy as a social spectacle, and that the mayor was predisposed to blame the elderly victims rather than Chicago's social service agencies.

Scope and Cost

Analyzing sectors of communities can be expensive and citywide studies often require federal or foundation support. For example, for his project on social characteristics of neighborhoods, Chow (1998) received grants from the Rockefeller and Cleveland Foundations. He examined 10 social problems and the level of social distress by census tract and used agency and census data to distinguish four types of neighborhoods for planning purposes. Fortunately, most problem-oriented studies are affordable, in part because a study's parameters can be limited by an agency's specialization. The dislocated worker study described above used volunteers and cost only $8,000.

Klinenberg's study took 5 years; thus, problem-oriented community studies can—but need not—require years to complete. Sometimes simply gathering and focusing on changing demographic information helps those in human services understand new community dynamics and needs. To use another example from the Midwest, meat-packing jobs have lured sizable numbers of immigrants to certain towns and small cities—a development that has created education, labor, intergroup, and service problems requiring attention (Wells & Bryne, 1999). As next steps, social workers could become better informed by interviewing, participant observation, and contacting towns undergoing similar changes. This immigration example illustrates a study that puts the focus on the *solution environment* and the community's capacity to respond.

New Tools

To start a community problem study, we want to check with geography, public administration, and business departments at local universities and with police, transportation, health, recreation, and other government offices. Professionals there may have conducted research in relevant areas or have capacities to pinpoint problems such as domestic violence by neighborhoods or wards that our organization lacks.

Numerous offices such as city planning departments have acquired a technology called Geographic Information Systems (GIS), a type of management information system that can provide new insights for community situations through sophisticated graphics and information maps (Elwood, 2001). For instance, human service workers and organizers can use GIS to link data to the target group's environment, e.g., to examine patterns of arson (McNutt, 2000). Telephone complaints about rodents can be mapped so the neediest neighborhoods quickly and regularly receive rat traps and other interventions (Richards & Croner, 1999). Students in Raleigh, North Carolina, created a school archive using GIS in combination with oral histories of its graduates and discovered how the community surrounding the school changed over time (Alibrandi, Beal, Candy, & Wilson, 2000). Hoefer, Hoefer, and Tobias (1994) suggest several reasons to use this study tool:

One of the key theoretical viewpoints of social work is that the clients must be viewed in the context of his or her environment. Yet, as clients' environments frequently differ from our own, we may overlook or misunderstand the effects of their environments on their problems. GIS can help us keep track of both the physical and social aspects of those environments. . . .

GIS easily addresses such questions as: Where do our clients come from? Are we accessible to our clients by public transportation? Are there geographic concentrations of particular client problems? And, if we need to change location or add satellite offices, where are the best areas to be? (p. 117)

The Republican and Democratic parties are additional sources of GIS technical expertise. They may have created digital maps on such subjects as values or attitudes, residential density, and voting participation that could be of use. According to Novotny and Jacobs (1997), "What makes GIS so appealing to political campaigns is that it allows a small group of people to take a multitude of geographic and demographic data, from marketing and consumer research to property tax information and U.S. Bureau of the Census statistics, and render them all on a colorful multilayered map that is far more accessible to use than a mere spreadsheet of tables and numbers" (p. 268). Computer graphics can enhance community studies through the generation of show-and-tell materials for political meetings, fund-raising efforts, and so on.

New Roles

We can combine forces with professionals trained to use new technologies. They might have statistical capacities or visual displays that will be effective with policymakers and philanthropists, while we on the other hand have the case or environs examples that humanize their numbers and graphics. Or we can empower others by giving training in GIS and other systems to resource-poor organizations (Ghose, 2001).

Quantitative Versus Qualitative Studies

Some studies of problems and services have an appropriately narrow focus. Suppose that someone working in the employee assistance program (EAP) of a huge corporation has determined the annual number of cases of alcohol abuse that come to the attention of his EAP office; he now *wants to put those numbers into per-*

spective by looking at a community study on alcoholism, particularly among employed individuals. If such a study does not exist, the social worker can propose one and coordinate it with other agencies in the addictions field.

Keep in mind, though, that formulating sensitive study questions, gaining access to study participants, interpreting results, and ensuring reliable findings can be difficult. *Even seemingly cut-and-dried problems and services studies sponsored by human service agencies are affected by community and cultural dynamics.* If the agency has conducted a prior field study or community analysis, these steps will be easier to take. Members of the target population—who may or may not know us already—often are affiliated with a number of subgroups, some of which are wary of us as researchers or service providers. "Disempowered consumers view providers through the prisms of history, contemporary inequities and their previous experiences with health and other human service providers—often negative. . . . Part of diversity competence with disempowered people is anticipating distrust, accepting it, and knowing how to build trust" (Rauch, North, Rowe, & Risley-Curtis, 1993, p. 23).

To address such multiple interwoven concerns, social workers may benefit from combining qualitative research methods, ethnographic approaches, and ethnocultural awareness with the conventional quantitative methods usually employed in problems and services studies. A *qualitative approach* is especially useful in exploratory studies, in follow-up studies that bring to life existing data on the incidence and prevalence of a disease or social problem, and in studies to design and promote services for special populations (Delgado, 1979; Hughes, 1998; Rounds, Weil, & Bishop, 1994). For example, Rauch and her colleagues believe that learning about genetic illnesses requires sensitive questioning about personal issues surrounding health and genetic inheritance. Using open-ended kinds of questions, as in conducting a careful social history, they find they can probe a family's experiences with an inherited disorder much more deeply than with typical survey questions. Furthermore, the qualitative approach enables the researcher to enlist the cooperation of the study participants who are coping with the illness (hence, the real authorities). Without this cooperation and without exploring solutions acceptable to the consumers, research findings would be much less reliable and services designed to respond to the problem would be of little value (see Box 6.9).

BOX 6.9	WALKING IN THEIR SHOES: A COMMUNITY WALK, DRIVE, FORAY

Choose a population (teenage parents, dually diagnosed adults in group homes, Haitian immigrants) in the area that is underserved. Arrange to spend the day with a member of that group. Someone who has work that takes him through the *residential or place community* of this population (if one exists), such as a pizza deliverer, meter reader, pest control employee, local transit worker, or activities director, would be a good choice. If this is a *scattered or nonplace community*, ferret out members of this population whose work takes them on rounds involving this group, such as public health workers, job coaches, English-as-a-second-language tutors, and Head Start outreach workers. Better yet, on a weekend, take a walk with two clients or community residents. This may be easier and more natural for case managers and community-based practitioners than for clinicians, but it would be useful for all in better understanding relationships; obtaining basic information on errands, shopping, transportation, and missing resources; and soliciting opinions informally about service adequacy and other delivery dimensions. (Avoid being intrusive, be humble, and make clear your desire to understand.)

Applications to Our Own Work

Many federal agencies collect data on social problems and service utilization, and even on the quality of services, but by necessity most such studies are quantitative. We social workers must be familiar with the ongoing studies conducted in our field of interest. We also have an obligation to stay informed on events at the local level, consulting with planners and interagency task forces that prepare relevant reports. If we are unable to do studies of our own, we can seek them from hospitals, the United Way, government planning departments, urban or rural centers that specialize in social demography, and universities or colleges that do social-problem or program-evaluation studies. Our special role is our commitment to involving clients, service users, and the general public. We seek input less for magnanimous reasons and more because of our growing awareness that research alone is insufficient and that we need input from consumers, other providers, demographers, and other experts. As we shift our emphasis from broad study to focused assessment, the problems and services theme will continue to be addressed in the next chapter.

INTEGRATING METHODS TO SUIT THE PROJECT

When practitioners wish to get to know their clients' worlds better, or when program development or another course of action is underway, several of the studies discussed here can be combined or elements of all four can be mixed to fit the situation. Community studies can be as personal as ethnography and as impersonal as computer analysis. Approaches are mixed and matched to fit the situation and available resources.

Illustrative Example

Your Juneau office has been successful at community building and has received money to open an office in Sitka, a town of 7,800 residents about 70 miles away by air. You know little about Sitka except that it is a small coastal area that has lumber, salmon, and halibut fisheries; tourism; a college; and a naval air base. You know that much only because one of your friends (Mike S., who runs Juneau's port) frequently talks about Sitka.

Under terms of the grant, the first step is to conduct a community study. Your director asks you to move to Sitka early to start this study, which may provide guidance on hiring and programming. He gives you the names of three townspeople whom he has met: George P. of the Alaska Marine Conservation Council, Nancy F. of the nonprofit Island Institute, and Lesley A., who runs day tours for cruise ships. The director tells you to investigate the area in four ways and report back in a month.

1. Conduct a field study to learn more about the culture of any minority, low-income, fringe, or disreputable groups in the area that might be overlooked in the community building process. Your first steps will be _____

   _____

   _____

2. Conduct a power structure study to find out who openly and who quietly controls the community. Your first steps will be _____

_____

_____

3. Conduct a community analysis to gain an overview and a sense of town character. Identify community strengths. Your first steps will be _____

_____

_____

4. Find out who has recently conducted problem-oriented community studies. Try to prioritize community concerns. Your first steps will be _____

_____

_____

5. Would you do the studies in this order or another order? Explain your rationale. _____

_____

_____

For a metropolitan, multicultural version of the exercise, focus on Raleigh, North Carolina; Atlanta, Georgia; Greensboro, North Carolina; Charlotte, Virginia; Orlando, Florida; Las Vegas, Nevada; or Nashville, Tennessee, all of which have rapidly increasing Latino populations. For cultural background, see Rodriguez (2002).

Conclusion: Unpretentious But Necessary Outings

We conclude this overview, of how to study and size up communities and learn more about the day-to-day realities of residents and members, with these summarizing points:

- To be aware of local mores and clients' assumptions about reality, we must involve ourselves as much as possible in their worlds with the aim of gaining cognitive and affective knowledge.

- There are many ways to recognize and analyze communities; therefore, one must decide on appropriate variables (you can't find it if you don't look for it) and methodologies (how to find it).

- Practitioners can learn more about any of the four approaches described by exploring their particular areas. We suggest that readers review the suggestions for the four walks—designed to capture the flavor and other aspects of each type of study (review Boxes 6.2, 6.4, 6.7, and 6.9). If you are still not sure what to look for, think of yourself as a filmmaker depicting aspects of your community that you are discovering and want to document or share with your office.

- We also suggest that readers review carefully the possible questions to ask community residents or clients. Those who anticipate conducting a study should think of additional relevant questions and then recruit a small focus group of individuals from the community to help refine suggested questions and additions.

- Even if inexperienced practitioners use such unpretentious methods as looking, asking questions, and listening, they can be more relevant and helpful in their future work.

Ultimately, we must look beyond needs and differences to see what pulls a community together. Residents of rural Arcadia, Indiana, for instance, came together to throw a farewell party for the United Parcel Service driver when he retired. Each store in town had handmade signs inviting the public to a potluck dinner held in his honor. He had been a link between various communities.

Discussion Exercises

1. Conduct a professional development workshop for your agency addressing the question, What sort of community is this? Bring in service users. What kind of community does this seem to be from a resident's viewpoint? Bring in staff and the board. What kind of community does this seem to be from your organization's viewpoint? Bring in experts. What kind of community does this seem to be from a societal viewpoint? Do not anticipate or judge answers from anyone.

2. Has your field agency conducted a neighborhood or community study? The community study might be of the larger metropolitan area or of a particular population (e.g., the gay community or the drug community). If so, determine

whether it fits one of these types. (Needs assessments are covered in Chapter 6.)

3.   It is incumbent on practitioners in small communities to know about the *local*, the person who has always resided in the town and is respected as an authority or role model by other community members. Martinez-Brawley (1990) puts it this way: "The community-oriented social worker needs to know a great deal about these residents and their unique claims, not only because they are often part of the power structure, but because they are also part of the community's fibers" (p. 222). Referring to three of the methods presented in the chapter, discuss how you would go about identifying such locals.

4.   Do you know the names of the newspapers in each community you serve, especially the weekly ones?

5.   After we learn about a place, we can play many roles. An example: Local enterprise facilitator Ernesto Sirolli (1999) sends out feelers to anyone in town who is thinking of setting up a business. Many people want to improve their lot in life and Sirolli has the expertise and advocacy skills to help make their dreams happen but he waits for them to ask for help (Chapter 6). What is different if the dreamer initiates?

6.   Secure a large map of your county to the wall. For each locale (neighborhood, town) depicted, using red pushpins, put up a name of someone who *lives* there; using blue pins, put up names of someone who *works* there; using yellow pins, put up names of elected representatives. The project may take awhile; in the meantime, enter the locales and names in a database for your office. Additional relevant names will be added later.

Notes

1. The beginnings of the community study, as a vehicle for firsthand inquiry and as a research methodology, are linked to the Chicago school of sociology. The reports of that 1920s era, such as *The Unadjusted Girl* and *The City*, were descriptive and ethnographic, utilized personal observation and documentary sources, and built on an urban ecology model. Researchers studied diverse and marginal groups such as homeless men, waitresses, department store saleswomen, gangs, and African Americans.

2. The appendix to the 1993 version of *Street Corner Society* (especially from p. 288 to the end) gives a wonderful introduction to street work and field work. That edition also includes materials on controversies over the original portrait of Boston's North End.

3. See Clifford Geertz, 1987; A. Hunter, 1993; Rodwell, 1987; and Spradley and McCurdy, 1972.

4. From a community analysis by Faith Little.

5. From a community analysis by Michele Feder.

References

Abbott, A. (1997). Of time and space: The contemporary relevance of the Chicago School. *Social Forces, 75*(4), 1149–82.

Adams, R. G. (1998). Inciting sociological thought by studying the Deadhead community: Engaging publics in dialogue. *Social Forces, 77*(1), 1–25.

Alibrandi, M., Beal, C., Thompson, A., & Wilson, A. (2000). Reconstructing a school's past using oral histories and GIS mapping. *Social Education 64*(3), 134–39.

Armstrong, J., & Henderson, P. (1992). Putting the community into community care. *Community Development Journal, 27*, 189.

Bates, E. (2001, March/April). Campaign inflation. *Mother Jones*, 46–55. Retrieved June 12, 2003, from http://www.motherjones.com/web_exclusives/special_reports/mojo_400/

Bergman, L. (1992). Dating violence among high school students. *Social Work, 37*(1), 21–27.

Boyle, T. C. (1995). *The tortilla curtain.* New York: Penguin.

Brandriet, L. M. (1994, July). Gerontological nursing: Application of ethnography and grounded theory. *Journal of Gerontological Nursing, 20*(7), 33–40.

Browning, T. (1995, February 28). For the children. *The Springfield (Illinois) State Journal-Register*, p. 9.

Bulmer, M. (1984). *The Chicago school of sociology: Institutionalization, diversity, and the rise of sociological research.* Chicago: University of Chicago Press.

Chow, J. (1998). Differentiating urban neighborhoods: A multivariate structural model analysis. *Social Work Research, 22*(3), 131–42.

Cleage, P. (1997). *What looks like crazy on an ordinary day.* New York: Avon Books.

Community Tool Box (n.d.). Who should be involved in a participatory planning process? Influential people in the community. Retrieved August 1, 2003 from http://ctb.ku.edu/tools/en/sub_section_main_1143.htm

Cox, F. M. (1977). What's going on: Addressing the situation. In F. M. Cox, J. L. Erlich, J. Rothman, & J. E. Tropman (Eds.), *Tactics and techniques of community practice* (pp. 15–16). Itasca, IL: F. E. Peacock.

Cruz, B. C. (1997). Walking the talk: The importance of community involvement in preservice urban teacher education. *Urban Education, 32*(3), 394–410.

Dahl, R. A. (1961). *Who governs? Democracy and power in an American city.* New Haven, CT: Yale University Press.

Daley, J. M., & Wong, P. (1994). Community development with emerging ethnic communities. *Journal of Community Practice, 1*(1), 9–24.

Davenport, J., & Davenport, J., III. (1995). Rural social work overview. In R. Edwards (Ed.-in-Chief), *Encyclopedia of social work* (19th ed., pp. 2076–2085). Washington, DC: National Association of Social Workers.

Delgado, M. (1979, Summer/Fall). Health care and Puerto Ricans: A consultation and educational program. *Patient Counseling and Health Education, 1*(1), 164–168.

Denzin, N. K. (1970). *The research act: A theoretical introduction to sociological methods.* Chicago: Aldine.

Dorfman, R. A. (1994). *Aging into the 21st century: The exploration of aspirations and values.* New York: Brunner/Mazel.

Duneier, M. (1992). *Slim's table: Race, responsibility and masculinity.* Chicago: University of Chicago Press.

Duneier, M. (1999). *Sidewalk.* New York: Farrar, Straus & Giroux.

Dye, T. R. (1993). *Power and society: An introduction to the social sciences.* Belmont, CA: Wadsworth.

Edgerton, R. B. (1967). *The cloak of competence: Stigma in the lives of the mentally retarded.* Berkeley: University of California Press.

Eljera, B. (2000). Filipinos find home in Daly City. In T. P. Fong & L. H. Schinagawa (Eds.), *Asian Americans: Experiences and Perspectives* (pp. 110–114). Saddle River, NJ: Prentice Hall.

Elwood, S. A. (2001). GIS and collaborative urban governance: Understanding their implications for community action and power. *Urban Geography, 22*(8), 737–759.

Emenhiser, D. (1991, Spring). Power influence and contributions. *National Society of Fundraising Executives Journal,* pp. 9–14.

Faircloth, C. A. (2001). "Those people" and troubles talk: Social typing and community construction in senior public housing. *Journal of Aging Studies, 15*(4), 333–350.

Flanagan, W. G. (1993). *Contemporary urban sociology.* New York: Cambridge University Press.

Garvin, C. D., & Cox, F. M. (1995). A history of community organizing since the Civil War with special reference to oppressed communities. In J. Rothman, J. L. Erlich, & J. E. Tropman with Fred M. Cox (Eds.), *Strategies of community intervention* (5th ed., pp. 64–99). Itasca, IL: F. E. Peacock.

Gaventa, J. (1980). *Power and powerlessness: Quiescence and rebellion in an Appalachian valley.* Urbana: University of Illinois Press.

Geertz, C. (1987). Deep play: Notes on the Balinese cockfight. In P. Rabinow & W. M. Sullivan (Eds.), *Interpretive social science: A second look.* Berkeley: University of California Press.

Ghose, R. (2001). Use of information technology for community empowerment: Transforming geographic information systems into community information systems. *Transactions in GIS, 5*(2), 141–163.

Green, J. W. (1995). *Cultural awareness in the human services: A multi-ethnic approach* (2nd ed.). Boston: Allyn & Bacon.

Grisham, V. L., Jr. (1999). *Tupelo: The evolution of a community.* Dayton, OH: Kettering Foundation.

Haglund, B., Weisbrod, R. R., & Bracht, N. (1990). Assessing the community: Its services, needs, leadership, and readiness. In N. Bracht (Ed.), *Health promotion at the community level* (pp. 91–108). Newbury Park, CA: Sage.

Hahn, A. J. (1994). *The politics of caring: Human services at the local level.* Boulder, CO: Westview.

Hirsch, K. (1998). *A home in the heart of a city.* New York: Northpoint Press.

Hoefer, R. A., Hoefer, R. M., & Tobias, R. A. (1994). Geographic information systems and human services. *Journal of Community Practice, 1*(3), 113–128.

Homan, M. S. (1994). *Promoting community change: Making it happen in the real world.* Pacific Grove, CA: Brooks/Cole.

Horwitt, S. D. (1989). *Let them call me rebel: Saul Alinsky, his life and legacy.* New York: Vintage.

Howell, J. T. (1973). *Hard living on Clay Street: Portraits of blue-collar families.* Garden City, NY: Anchor Books.

Hughes, M. (1998). Turning points in the lives of young inner-city men forgoing destructive criminal behaviors: A qualitative study. *Social Work Research, 22*(3), 143–151.

Hunter, A. (1993). Local knowledge and local power: Notes on the ethnography of local community elites. *Journal of Contemporary Ethnography, 22*(1), 36–58.

Hunter, F. (1953). *Community power structure.* Chapel Hill: University of North Carolina Press.

Icard, L. D., Schilling, R. F., El-Bassel, N., & Young, D. (1992). Preventing AIDS among black gay men and black gay and heterosexual male intravenous drug users. *Social Work, 37*(5), 440–445.

Karabanow, J. (1999). Creating community: A case study of a Montreal street kid agency. *Community Development Journal, 34*(4), 318–327.

Katruska, A. (2000). Irish travelers in the U.S. Retrieved on November 25, 2002 from http://www.pitt.edu/~alkst3/USA.html

Kidder, T. (1999). *Home Town.* New York: Washington Square Press.

Klinenberg, E. (2002). *Heat wave: A social autopsy of disaster in Chicago.* Chicago: University of Chicago Press.

Kotlowitz, A. (1997). Where was the village? In S. R. Shreve and P. Shreve (Eds.), *Outside the law: Narratives on justice in America* (pp. 106–110). Boston: Beacon Press.

Kozol, J. (1995). *Amazing grace: The lives of children and the conscience of a nation.* New York: Crown.

Kretzmann, J. P., & McKnight, J. L. (1993). *Building communities from the inside out.* Chicago: ACTA.

Lamb, R. K. (1977). Community life: How to get its pulse. Suggestions for a study of your hometown. In F. M. Cox, J. L. Erlich, J. Rothman, & J. E. Tropman (Eds.), *Tactics and techniques of community practice* (pp. 17–23). Itasca, IL: F. E. Peacock.

Li, Y. (1996). Neighborhood organization and local social action: A case study. *Journal of Community Practice, 3*(1), 35–58.

Liebow, E. (1967). *Tally's corner.* Boston: Little, Brown.

Liebow, E. (1993). *Tell them who I am: The lives of homeless women.* New York: Penguin.

Lynd, R., & Lynd, H. (1929). *Middletown.* New York: Harcourt Brace.

Maguire, L., & Biegel, D. (1982). The use of social networks in social welfare. In *Social Welfare Forum, 1981* (pp. 140–159). New York: Columbia University Press.

Martin, R. R. (1995). *Oral history in social work: Research, assessment, and intervention.* Thousand Oaks, CA: Sage.

Martinez-Brawley, E. E. (1990). *Perspectives on the small community: Humanistic views for practitioners.* Washington, DC: National Association of Social Work Press.

Martinez-Brawley, E. E. (2000). *Close to home: Human services and the small community.* Washington, DC: National Association of Social Workers Press.

McNutt, J. (2000). Organizing cyberspace: Strategies for teaching about community practice and technology. *Journal of Community Practice, 7*(1), 95–109.

Meenaghan, T. M., Washington, R. O., & Ryan, R. M. (1982). *Macro practice in the human services.* New York: Free Press.

Menolascino, F. J., & Potter, J. F. (1989). Delivery of services in rural settings to the mentally retarded–mentally ill. *International Journal of Aging and Human Development, 28*(4), 261–275.

Mitchell, A. (1998). The rewards of getting to know the community. *Caring Magazine, 17*(4), 58–60.

Mogil, C., & Slepian, A. (with Woodrow, P.). (1992). *We gave away a fortune: Stories of people who have devoted themselves and their wealth to peace, justice, and a healthy environment.* Philadelphia: New Society.

Mondros, J. B., & Wilson, S. M. (1994). *Organizing for power and empowerment.* New York: Columbia University Press.

Morales, J. (1995). Community social work with Puerto Ricans in the United States. In F. G. Rivera & J. L. Erhlich (Eds.), *Community organizing in a diverse society* (pp. 77–94). Needham Heights, MA: Allyn & Bacon.

Morris, R. (1986). *Rethinking social welfare: Why care for the stranger?* New York: Longman.

The Mother Jones 400. (1998, November/December). *Mother Jones,* 49–63.

Mowry, D. D. (1994). Mentoring the Hmong: A practice outlet for teaching faculty and a possible community development tool. *Journal of Community Practice, 1*(1), 107–112.

Murty, S. A. (1999). Setting the boundary of an interorganizational network: An application. *Journal of Social Science Research, 24*(3/4), 67–82.

Myerhoff, B. (1980). *Number our days.* New York: Simon & Schuster.

Netting, F. E., Kettner, P. M., & McMurtry, S. L. (1993). *Social work macro practice.* New York: Longman.

Novotny, P., & Jacobs, R. H. (1977). Geographical information systems and the new landscape of political technologies. *Social Science Computer Review, 15*(3), 264–285.

Oldenburg, R. (1999). *The great good place: Cafes, coffee shops, bookstores, bars, hair salons and other hangouts at the heart of a community.* New York: Marlowe & Co.

Ollove, M. (1991, February 17). Johns Hopkins Hospital: The board to be on. *The Baltimore Sun,* Sunday magazine, p. 8.

Olsen, M. E., & Marger, M. N. (Eds.). (1993). *Power in modern societies.* Boulder, CO: Westview.

Ostrander, S. A. (1995). "Surely you're not in this just to be helpful." In R. Hertz & J. B. Imber (Eds.), *Studying elites using qualitative methods* (pp. 133–150). Thousand Oaks, CA: Sage.

Putnam, R. D. (2000). *Bowling alone: The collapse and revival of American community.* New York: Simon & Schuster.

Ramas, R. (1998). Anatomy of a drive-by: What can we learn from an unexpected death? *Sociological Quarterly, 39*(2), 271–288.

Rauch, J. B., North, C., Rowe, C. L., & Risley-Curtis, C. (1993). *Diversity competence: A learning guide*. Baltimore: University of Maryland at Baltimore School of Social Work.

Richards, T. B., & Croner, C. M. (1999). Geographic information systems and public health: Mapping the future. *Public Health Reports, 114*(4), 359–373.

Rodriguez, R. (2002). *Brown: The last discovery of America*. New York: Penguin Books.

Rodwell, M. K. (1987). Naturalistic inquiry: An alternative model for social work assessment. *Social Service Review, 61*(2), 231–246.

Rothman, J. (1984). Assessment and option selection [Introduction to Part 1]. In F. M. Cox, J. L. Erlich, J. Rothman, & J. E. Tropman (Eds.), *Tactics and techniques of community practice* (2nd ed., pp. 7–13). Itasca, IL: F. E. Peacock.

Rothman, S., & Black, A. E. (1998). "Who rules now?" American elites in the 1990s. *Society, 35*(6), 17–20.

Rounds, K. A., Weil, M., & Bishop, K. K. (1994). Practice with culturally diverse families of young children with disabilities. *Families in Society, 75*(1), 3–15.

Schwab, B., Drake, R. E., & Burghardt, E. M. (1988). Health care of the chronically mentally ill: The culture broker model. *Community Mental Health Journal, 24*(3), 174–184.

Siegel, L. M., Attkisson, C. C., & Carson, L. G. (1987). Need identification and program planning in the community. In F. M. Cox, J. L. Erlich, J. Rothman, & J. E. Tropman (Eds.), *Strategies of community organization: Macro practice* (4th ed., pp. 71–97). Itasca, IL: F. E. Peacock.

Sillitoe, P. (1998). What know natives? : Local Knowledge in development. *Social anthropology, 6*, 203–220.

Sirolli, E. (1999). *Ripples from the Zambezi: Passion, entrepreneurship and the birth of local economies*. Gabriola Island, British Columbia: New Society Publishers.

Specht, H., & Courtney, M. (1994). *Unfaithful angels: How social work has abandoned its mission*. New York: Free Press.

Spradley, B. W. (1990). *Community health nursing: Concepts and practice* (3rd ed.). Glenview, IL: Scott, Foresman.

Spradley, J. (1970). *You owe yourself a drunk: An ethnography of urban nomads*. Boston: Little, Brown and Company.

Spradley, J. P., & McCurdy, D. W. (1972). *The cultural experience: Ethnography in complex society*. Chicago: Science Research.

Sullivan, K. (1994, April 14). The power people: Government, corporate, community and media figures who stand out. *The Washington Post*, Maryland section, pp. 1, 8.

Turner, G. (1992). *British cultural studies: An introduction*. New York: Routledge.

Useem, M. (1995). Reaching corporate executives. In R. Hertz & J. B. Imber (Eds.), *Studying elites using qualitative methods* (pp. 18–39). Thousand Oaks, CA: Sage.

Wagner, D. (1991). Reviving the action research model: Combining case and cause with dislocated workers. *Social Work, 36*(6), 477–482.

Wagner, D. (1993). *Checkerboard square: Culture and resistance in a homeless community*. Boulder, CO: Westview.

Ward, J., & Hansen, K. A. (1997). *Search strategies in mass communications* (3rd ed.). New York: Longman.

Warren, R. B., & Warren, D. I. (1984). How to diagnose a neighborhood. In F. M. Cox, J. L. Erlich, J. Rothman, & J. E. Tropman (Eds.), *Tactics and techniques of community practice* (2nd. ed., pp. 27–40). Itasca, IL: F. E. Peacock.

Warren, R. L. (1977). *The community in America* (3rd ed.). Chicago: Rand McNally.

Wells, B., & Bryne, J. (1999). The changing face of community in the Midwest. US: Challenges for community developers. *Community Development Journal, 34*(1), 70–74.

Whyte, W. F. (1993). *Street corner society: The social structure of an Italian slum* (4th ed.). Chicago: University of Chicago Press. (Original work published 1943)

7

Using Assessment in Community Practice

Although it generally is understood that people live in complex social milieus that dramatically affect them, assessment rarely takes into account larger social variables.

A. WEICK, C. RAPP, W. P. SULLIVAN, AND W. KISTHARDT (1989, P. 351)

Some years ago in California, Erin desperately needed a job. Divorced, she had three children to support; a car accident had created even more severe financial difficulty for her. Somehow Erin wrangled work from the lawyer who represented her in the accident. Since she only had a high school education, it was an entry-level filing job. But this newest staffer at the law firm was a curious person, a thinking person, and she noticed incongruities in one obscure case. Her initial hypothesis was that something was wrong with the file itself.

Erin showed initiative. Besides asking her boss about those irregularities, she left the office, drove to the Mojave Desert, and talked directly to the family involved. Their health and housing situation made her suspicious of a nearby corporation. She revised her assessment, deciding something was wrong in the community. Gathering facts, she investigated the Hinkley area, population 1,000, and Pacific Gas and Electric. She gradually introduced herself and made a point of meeting everyone in the neighborhood and hearing their stories. As she attended picnics and sat in homes, she compiled evidence and learned people's strengths. She built trust because she knew that, before she could help, she and the community had to become allies. Erin rolled up her sleeves and dived in, and that was appreciated by residents and plant workers who slipped her secret documents.

Even though she had no legal training, Erin refused to be intimidated by technical records, and she copied what seemed relevant. She insisted on her right to use public records and gathered soil and water samples. Eventually, this paralegal was able to document widespread medical problems caused by chromium 6 contamination in the drinking water. Erin's investigation led to a $333 million settlement for 600 residents who sued the corporation with the help of her law firm. Erin Brockovich's determination to secure justice for these folks became the subject of a popular movie starring Julia Roberts. All this, because Erin developed skills in assessing and aiding communities (Dawson, 1993; Denby, 2000; Rogge, 1995).

This advocate moved from a micro- to a macrofocus when she discerned that the first family she contacted might be the tip of the iceberg. She proceeded beyond casework. Her story illustrates that community assessment can entail intensive examination or investigation of a community sector. By continually appraising the situation, the advocate assisted hundreds of families with serious ailments and medical disorders. Her hands-on, collaborative assessment brought success.

ASSESSMENT AS A BASIC SOCIAL WORK PROCESS

We must know how to include community factors in any case assessment and how to analyze the community itself. Assessment frameworks can serve as a means of planning or inquiry, as a vehicle for information exchange, as part of formal problem solving, and as a way to determine which services are needed by whom. This chapter includes types, philosophies, and methods of assessment; reflection on assessment; and a look at the transition to action. It is meant to be a guide to *preparation* for client assistance, program development, and community-based services.

Assessment Before Strategy and Intervention

Assessment serves as an umbrella term for a figuring-out process that can have a wide or narrow, general or targeted focus. Communitywide study methodologies can be employed to understand and assess *any* community, anywhere, anytime (see Chapter 6). Assessment also indicates a cognitive process used with particular clients, situations, or problems *that pays attention to uniqueness* (Meyer, 1993, p. 9; see also All, 1994; Stiffman & Davis, 1990). In line with this thinking, Johnson (1995) views assessment in broad terms, as including (a) social study analysis and understanding and (b) resource-oriented needs assessment. More narrowly, Johnson views it in the sense of (c) fitting the pieces together for particular individuals or systems. To Lauffer (1984), assessment focuses on "the examination of what is, on what is likely to be, or on what ought to be" (p. 60).

Until recently, we spoke of *diagnosing* individuals and neighborhoods, that is, looking for what is amiss. Today we say *assessment*, whatever the unit of attention. Thus, for insight into a community, we shift from an emphasis on a need-deficiency-problem assessment to one on *asset-capacity-problem-solving*, that is, to strength assessment (Cowger, 1994; Kretzmann & Mc-Knight, 1993; Meyer, 1995; Rosenthal & Cairns, 1994; Sharpe, Greaney, Royce, & Lee, 2000). Most people are less accustomed to thinking of competence and assets at a community level. For example, someone concerned with economic development who walks through a dusty town populated by American Indians—or that matter, residents of India—will quickly note the lack of material goods. However, someone interested in the arts might also spot sand painting in the U.S. Southwest and painted prayer decorations made by women in the villages in India. Social workers are as capable as folklorists and art collectors of seeing strengths in villages, towns, and cities.

Assessment Frameworks

It is valuable to understand the methods commonly used to assess service and advocacy needs (Moxley & Freddolino, 1994). Whether examining the situations of clients or of community residents, we first must identify relevant variables. Then assessment can serve as "a way to bring order out of the chaos of a melange of disconnected variables" (Meyer, 1993, p. 3). Hepworth and Larsen (1993) refer to these dimensions of assessment: the *nature of the problems*, the *coping capacities* of those involved, the *relevant systems* involved, the *available or needed resources*, and the *motivation* to resolve problems (p. 192). To know the best approach to community work, Ann Jeffries (1996) from the United Kingdom maintains that practitioners want to be able

- to size up the extent of change that is needed;
- its feasibility given the resources likely to be available in the community;
- the likely resistance to or support for such change both within the community and from powerful decision makers who could be involved;
- and how much scope the community and the workers have to make decisions about actions

needed to achieve that change, either through participation in organized decision-making processes or through community organizations—in other words, the community's state of empowerment. (p. 107)

Auspices and Context

When we assess X (e.g., the adequacy and effectiveness of a given program), the question becomes, from whose point of view? Are we a consultant for the system in question, do we represent an advocacy group, or are we a disinterested party? Do we share affinities and perspectives with those who are being assessed? We should keep in mind our predispositions toward individual cases and programs. Basic decisions underlie *any* assessment. Who do we listen to? Who will we trust? How will we decide? Whose views count most? Answers can be influenced by the auspices under which we proceed—be it a county government, a nonprofit organization, a credentialing body, a university, or an agency. We are also influenced by our education and training (Robinson & Walsh, 1999; Worth, 2001).

INDIVIDUAL IN SOCIETY ASSESSMENT

Delineating an Individual's Ties to the Community

Public health workers, community psychologists, teachers, community police officers, and social workers are expected to know how individuals and families fit into their communities and if their communities accept them (see Box 7.1). The community provides resources to its members and social workers. Discovering not only the clients' internal strengths but also their "external strengths"—networks, organizations, institutions with resources—is "central to assessment" (Cowger, 1994, p. 266). There are ways and tools to determine whether someone is isolated or attached to an area or a network.

We can delineate ties through conversation and observation. Social work involves us with others in many ways: by e-mail or telephone, in person, at meetings, in the field. As we interact with community residents, professionals, prospective and current service users, each point of contact is an opportunity to discover or assess an aspect of the person's community ties.

We can delineate ties through questioning. We want to know the types of bonds clients and citizens have with their locality. Many people will have given this topic little thought. *Question-*

naires allow us to explore psychological and practical attachments to the community. Appropriate questions also can be integrated into social histories and focus groups. Like those used by Viswanath, Kosicki, Fredin, and Park (2000), the questions can be straightforward:

- How many years have you lived in the area?
- How likely do you think it is that you would move away in the next one or two years?
- Do you own or rent the housing unit you are living in?
- In how many community groups are you active?
- Have you registered to vote in the county?
- Do you read the local newspaper?

We can delineate ties through mutual exploration. For example, there are assessment tools that can capture micro-macro linkages. If we want to see *lived geographies*, all that is needed is a map, the client's calendar, and a piece of paper to do an everyday environment analysis. We ask, "Where are the primary environments in her life located: her home, child care setting, place of employment, church, the homes of extended family members and friends, or other key places and activities?" (Kemp, 2001, p. 25).

To learn who and what is part of a household's environmental context, an *ecomap* can be drawn. The process involves asking families, partners, or close friends to list resources and to describe energy exchanges. For instance, they designate people to whom they can turn such as a brother-in-law who fixes cars or a former daughter-in-law, as well as people by whom they are oppressed or drained such as a lonely widowed mother or a brother who is becoming addicted to Ecstasy (Cournoyer, 2000, pp. 40–43). The resulting chart diagrams human relationships, for instance, a family or friendship group, and may include formal and informal resources and natural helpers (Miley, O'Melia, & DuBois, 1998, pp. 243–244).

Another way of finding out about individual and family ties with community organizations is to utilize a *social network map*. The end product here is another graphic, but one that lists social supports such as neighbors, businesses, churches, self-help groups, or clubs that our individual or family does or could access (Miley et al., 1998, pp. 340–341). From it we may be able to see links to social institutions. With immigrant families and others, we can use a *culturagram* to learn more about contact with cultural institutions, as well as

BOX 7.1	WHAT IS OUT THERE?

School social worker Chris is aware of a child with a facial disfigurement who is teased callously by classmates and by neighborhood children whose parents apparently never intervene. A practitioner must take account of the negative affects of this community and simultaneously explore it as a positive resource. Ponder how you would approach this if you were Chris.

You will start with the child's definition of the problem so that you can mutually shape the assessment. You will make factual inquiries. You will discover the history of the child's family with the school. You will assess child and parent attitudes. However, before settling on discipline for the teasers, support for the teased, or anything else, you must assess both the intensity of the teasing and the neighborhood. Are other children being derisive or merely turning away from what makes them uncomfortable? Does this child experience normal grade school teasing as torment due to unresolved feelings about the disfigurement? Or are the playground, hallway, and journey to and from home a living hell by anyone's estimate? A janitor or playground aide might shed light on this issue. Until you know more about the situation, you do not know whether strengthening the client will work.

Is the child's condition correctable? Could the child's appearance be improved by plastic surgery? What are the family's religious beliefs regarding medicine? Does the family have insurance? If not, are you aware of public and private resources if the child wants medical intervention? While we must always consider whether it is possible to eliminate a problem, practitioners who aim solely for a medical solution, even if successful, may not solve the problem. If the child is being scapegoated due to a neighborhood situation, the harassment might be aimed at something else if the disfigurement disappeared. What resources within the child, family, and environment do we draw on in that eventuality? Who might mediate?

What information do you want about the neighborhood before seeking allies there? Is the family out of step with the community? Perhaps the family is hated for some reason (e.g., re-

sponsible for the death of someone on the block) and the child is a scapegoat. How might this situation be related to the values and traditions of the community? Perhaps the family or neighbors view deformities as punishment for religious or cultural reasons. To which neighborhood leaders do young people listen?

Regardless of the origin of the teasing, what might you do to stop it or, failing that, to balance it? Besides talking to the teacher, finding out which children from the same neighborhood might be reasoned with, and checking to see if a priest, scout or band leader, or relative can be helpful, you can assess larger systems. Does the principal realize that individuals with disfigurements are protected under disability discrimination laws? Are the parents part of an informal network (a food co-op, people who go fishing together) or a formal organization (Masons or a labor union) that can be useful? For instance, if the parents participate in folk dancing, the child could go with them and master a skill in a friendlier environment. What talents does the child possess?

How can school and community assets be used? What might the principal do to place the child in a more positive light? Is there a coveted student role (e.g., making announcements over the loudspeaker) that this child could assume, becoming known in a new way? What community programs might fit? Are there individuals in town who could be role models? Do disability or veterans groups know of adults who have coped with similar problems, who might share their stories?

Chris has been assessing individual and social factors and making inferences and can now make a formal assessment. Let us assume that neighborhood conflict was apparent. A concise, focused individual assessment report should be shared with the child, the family, and the teacher. The community assessment may be in the form of a memo to colleagues in the school or to a neighborhood civic association. It should share observations and recommendations while protecting confidentiality, although privacy is admittedly difficult to maintain in this particular example.

family and ethnic history (Brownell, 1997; Congress, 1994). Finally, we should delve into our client or group's precise exposure to various forms of mass communication, a *mediagram* if you will. Social workers often overlook the role that media plays in connecting some residents with community events, happenings, issues, and essential information. At home, work, or in the car, is your client an active user of local radio, television, cable, newspapers? While local media tell us about community knowledge, national media shape people's ideas on social behavior (Rosenzweig, 1999). The goal of any of these five explorations is to see the "full complexity of client situations" (Mattaini, 1990, p. 237). Moreover, identifying linkages leads to alliance building and community building. (For analysis of agency linkages rather than individual ties to the community, see Appendix A.)

Problems in the Interface

Classification schemes associated with assessment, such as the *Diagnostic and Statistical Manual of Mental Disorders* (*DSM*) series, often fail to individualize people and to take into account their societal context. However, there are assessment processes that balance and synthesize person-environment relations and avoid the trap of assuming that the problem resides solely in the individual. This is important because, as health professor Gary Kielhofner (1993) insists, "We must not only seek to make members good for the social collective, but also to make the social collective good for individuals" (p. 251).

Let us explore the difference between a routine assessment of an individual that takes the environment into consideration and an assessment where individual and society are given equal weight: Sergio is 40 years old and has worked at a local plant for four years. Drinking beer and eating barbecue, Sergio and his buddies gripe their way through lunch. Upon his return to the floor of the factory, Sergio lurches into some equipment and is injured. Ordinarily, the first goal would be to get him medical attention and rehabilitation, and the second would be to get him back on the job.

Germaine and Gitterman (1995) say to look for interacting personal, environmental, and cultural factors. Bisman (1999) recommends building a case theory to explain the case and create a framework that will lead to the most appropriate and mutually satisfying intervention for the case. Very likely, a conventional assessment will center on Sergio's drinking. An EAP professional making an assessment might ask these questions: What do his supervisors say—was this an isolated incident? Has Sergio frequently been absent or late? Is his supervisor ready to fire him? Is he having other problems such as anger or credit management? Which addiction resources (alcohol, drugs, gambling) should be explored? Has he sought help before? Or, a counselor unconnected with his work might ask these questions: What is Sergio's personal, marital, and psychiatric history? His ethnic background? His educational level? Does he have community resources (church, buddies)? Such professionals are engaged in a practical assessment to help Sergio by seeing what he is doing to himself and what services are needed.

Kielhofner would have us shift the emphasis so the assessment pays more attention to what Sergio is up against. This means considering variables such as worker alienation (Did Sergio want to escape his particular workplace?), occupational hazards (Was the machine that Sergio fell on a safe piece of equipment?), and whether work is good for blue-collar workers (Garson, 1994). Kielhofner thinks professionals seldom ask broader questions: Can the person do the work? Is the work environment a place in which any reasonable person would want to work? How do social-environmental conditions affect Sergio? According to Kielhofner (1993), "Issues of environment or workplace conditions and incentives are largely ignored. In fact, the worker who does not wish to work, or whose behavior suggests disincentive to work, is socially identified as malingering. . . . We have as much responsibility to be agents of social change and institutional transformation as we have to help persons to change" (pp. 249, 251).

Kielhofner's expertise is in functional assessment. He analyzes situations where a determination is made about what a person is capable of, that is, whether individuals can work or live on their own, or have any quality of life left: think of those in nursing homes and institutions. Many of these transactions take place at a mezzo or middle level. Kielhofner (1993) believes professionals in such lines of work "sit at the politically loaded juncture between the individual and surrounding institutions" (p. 248). Whether they know it or not, they exercise social control and have the power to affect rights, lives, and how the public views the "moral worth" of individuals (p. 248), in part through the assessments they write. This causes us to ask, do social workers gather information about maladapted persons or maladaptive conditions? *The interface focus would have us consider our angle of vision before we start an assessment.* Perhaps this will result in gathering different data or connecting with different offices than usual, for example, the Occupational Health and Safety Administration rather than a consulting psychiatrist. (Box 7.1 illustrates the interface between a child and her school and neighborhood environment.)

Two phrases are often invoked in the discussion of assessments: "consider community context" and "avoid hasty judgments." As we evaluate others, Kielhofner challenges us to transcend preconceptions and pigeonholing. He tells of a time when the renowned Carl Jung was asked to examine the drawings of a 50-year-old man. After making extensive negative comments, Jung concluded that the man was schizophrenic. It should give pause, to all who diagnose, to learn the drawings were by Picasso (see Kielhofner, 1993, p. 248).

FORMS OF COMMUNITY ASSESSMENT

Over the past decades, many localities were asked by state planners to engage in futurist studies to prepare for the new century. That is one form of community assessment. Here four different types of more immediate community assessments will be introduced and described briefly. Then attention will be given to what they require of professionals. Resource and collaborative assessments are also discussed in this section.

One Assessment Typology

Barbara Spradley (1990) categorizes community assessments by their purview as

1. *comprehensive* assessments;
2. assessments of a *familiarization* nature;
3. *problem-oriented* assessments; and
4. *subsystem* assessments. (p. 388)

COMPREHENSIVE ASSESSMENT

Assessments can be comprehensive in the sense of encompassing the entire community, being methodologically thorough, and generating original data. To Martinez-Brawley (1990), assessment starts with abstract questions of a high order such as "How does the community rate in terms of cohesiveness, engagement and interdependence among its members?" (p. 23). Such questions require in-depth examination. Typically, a comprehensive assessment or audit

launches planning or development projects (Guterman & Cameron, 1997; Murtagh, 1999). Many communities utilize the "civic index" to systematically identify strengths and take ownership of weaknesses. Designed by the National Civic League, it facilitates self-assessment of civic infrastructure, for example, how well does the community share information? how willing is it to cross regional lines to find a solution? To illustrate results, officials in Lee's Summit, Missouri pulled together bickering interest groups to work on growth issues. Afterwards, the community stopped defeating tax initiatives and, feeling part of the agenda, voted for a dozen straight ballot initiatives (National Civic League, 1999).

> *What reason would we have to assess something as large as a community? Think of someone who organizes migrant farm workers— someone who has many locations from which to choose to begin work, since the workers need help wherever they live. An assessment would help the organizer to select a community where townspeople and media outlets are somewhat sympathetic, other occupations have a history of collective bargaining, unemployment is relatively low, interaction among minority groups is positive, and numerous residents speak the migrants' language.*

FAMILIARIZATION ASSESSMENT

Some community assessments, based on available data with some firsthand data added, entail a more cursory *examination of the entire community, with the goal of achieving a general understanding.* An abbreviated version of community analysis (see Chapter 6, this volume) falls into this category. The vignette about Chris, the school social worker, illustrates the start of a neighborhood familiarization process. Another example could flow from acquainting oneself with community and client concerns, such as by inviting those with similar problems to come together for a speak-out session. For instance, those from rural areas who must travel to receive radiation therapy or dialysis might share their needs and frustrations about their care or transportation. These patients could provide a more complete picture of the adequacy of their hometown supports. Follow-up assessments of rural towns could be of this type.

PROBLEM-ORIENTED ASSESSMENT

Problem-oriented assessments *involve the entire community but center on one problem*, such as the uninsured or child abuse. Here is one example. The town of Conne River in Canada decided to assess family violence in their community (Durst, MacDonald, & Parsons, 1999). Here is another. In upstate New York, professionals assessed poverty and social pathology in rural mobile home parks—some of which function like private, isolated low-income housing projects (Fitchen, 1998). Kettner, Moroney, and Martin (1990) astutely observe that problem analysis includes "analysis of the political environment, an assessment of a community's readiness to deal with the problem, and a measure of the resources the community is willing to commit to its solution" (p. 41).

SUBSYSTEM ASSESSMENT

Assessing a subsystem means *examining a single facet of community life*, such as the business sector, religious organizations, service agencies, non-English speaking populations, or the school system (Spradley, 1990, p. 388). A subsystem has a structure that must be demarcated and should be diagrammed. To illustrate, board and care homes are one of many subsystems on which clients rely. These care facilities are part of a multilevel provider–regulator subsystem (which is part of the long-term care system, which, in turn, is part of the health care system). The interests and concerns of immigrant communities can be assessed through analysis of print and electronic media outlets geared to ethnic groups, another subsystem. Frederick Wiseman (1968, 1994), the acclaimed documentary filmmaker, has captured internal dynamics in portrayals of multiple subsystems. Twice he has filmed high schools as a way of learning about communities. He is famous for examining without judging.

We too must initially set aside preconceived ideas to become attuned to those affiliated with whatever slice of the community we are examining (Bloom & Habel, 1998; Weiner, 1996). This often requires wide reading. We want to be able to show the operations of a subsystem, such as the world of deaf Americans, from both the participants' and our viewpoints (see Box 7.2). Eventually, if appropriate, we can make judgments (e.g., for advocacy purposes).

BOX 7.2	MULTIFACETED ASSESSMENT VIGNETTE

To comprehend a subcommunity or network, we often must increase our knowledge of that entity. We may need to particularize our assessments as well.

A social worker in a speech and hearing clinic is about to meet with the deaf parents of a preschooler with a profound hearing loss, who are coming in to talk about the child's schooling needs. We will use this vignette to look at a subsystem. This is an opportunity to study a system and, as a by-product, our preconceptions (reflexive assessment).

- Assessment of supportive service systems will be influenced by how professionals conceptualize persons with differences. Assessment of the educational needs of this child will be influenced by whether the worker views a disability as a personal tragedy, a variable to consider, something culturally produced by society, or a target of social oppression (Oliver, 1990, Chapter 1; Reagan, 2002).
- Cultural diversity (ethnic and other cultures viewed as existing at the periphery of our society) must be factored into the design and implementation of assessment.

- Examination of past change efforts and perceptions of the problem by others significant in the arena or subsystem will be important (Cox, 1995).

Many assessment variables exist at the societal level, where there are competing views. Talk of multiple perspectives may strike us merely as semantics or rhetoric until we apply the idea in this case and confront the huge, ongoing debate as to whether deafness is (a) a medical condition causing social isolation compensated for with signing, "a poor substitute for language," or with mainstreaming; or (b) a fact conveying one into a special culture that communicates with a different but equally rich mode of language expressed by the hands and face instead of the tongue and throat (Dolnick, 1993, p. 40; see also Sacks, 1989, p. ix). Some in the self-identified Deaf community see themselves as "a linguistic minority (speaking American Sign Language) and no more in need of a cure for their condition than are Haitians or Hispanics" (Dolnick, p. 37). Describing the controversy, Dolnick points out *dis*similarities to such ethnic minorities, since "90 percent of all deaf children are born

BOX 7.2   (CONTINUED)

to hearing parents" (p. 38). These various splits illustrate why assessments must consider social context, current theories (Cox, 1995, p. 155), and various tensions beneath the surface.

Many challenges come to the fore in a subsystem analysis. When we learn that our taken-for-granted assumptions are in question, we have no easy answers, but we can list pros and cons. The *implications of these differing perspectives* for treatment, schooling, and living arrangements, for medical intervention with cochlear implants or nonintervention, for identity and reality, are heightened by the fact that a decision about a baby's first language needs to be made very early. Having so much at stake in making the best decision makes the situation more pressing. One camp alleges that Deaf culture has an antibook bias and that without reading skills, dead-end jobs are common; the other camp argues that signing introduces children to language much earlier (see for example, Dolnick, 1993, pp. 46, 51; Sacks, 1989, p. x).

An educational assessment must take note of these differing philosophies. What did the parents decide to do with their baby? How far have they gone down a certain path? Do they want to turn back or continue? How do they view their child's *degree of hearing loss*: (a) as a personal problem (e.g., child's temperament), (b) as a social problem (e.g., child's future), (c) as no problem at all (e.g., child can communicate satisfactorily), or (d) as affecting a decision to be made? Luey, Glass, and Elliott (1995) warn that "social workers must look at the complicated and interrelated dimensions of hearing, language, culture, and politics" (p. 178). Social workers may be dealing with the emotional upset of hearing parents who have a deaf child or the disappointment of deaf parents who have a hearing child.[1] Just as likely, they may need to gain acceptance for a particular child or for the Deaf community. Thus, this social worker must establish the family's self-definitions, listen to the *experiencer* (Oliver Sacks's word—the child in this case), and weigh community and societal factors. Practically, the community and the world beyond must be assessed for resources; the family may decide to move to a community with a public school system featuring mainstreaming, may decide on a particular bilingual approach, or may find the local Deaf community and move in a different direction. The worker also must figure out what the agency has to offer. Linking this family with community organizations may be as therapeutic as personal counseling. If the problem for the child is acceptance and the clinic does not engage in advocacy, then the worker must join with those who do on the family's behalf (Harris & Bamford, 2001).

An assessment process should attune us to the realities of a given subsystem. Did the worker arrange for someone to sign or interpret whenever the deaf parents come in to talk over options? Is that service wanted by the consumer (McEntee, 1995)?

The Range and Flavor of Community Assessments

Community assessments and expectations surrounding them will be further explicated through human service illustrations, for instance, professional responses to official requests, community responses to rape, and service responses to public housing tenants during relocation.

SCOPE, REQUEST INITIATOR, AND PRACTITIONER ROLE
Social workers ought to be able to conduct and provide full-blown, long-term problem assessments such as health status documents and neighborhood crime status reports, but also quick ones. We can expect to receive *targeted* *questions from journalists and public officials*. We might be asked, "Who will use public toilets if they are installed along sidewalks in our city, and what is the prediction for nontraditional use?" or "What is the capacity of our community and its service network to absorb more refugees?" Assessing the coping capacities of a client and of a social service network have much in common (see Box 7.1). Public officials like to involve those with firsthand experience. A group set up to assess the portable potty issue could be comprised of those providing direct services to the homeless; a Travelers Aid–type organization; a Women, Infants, and Children program representative; someone from a methadone clinic; and officials from the city's tourist bureau and police and sanitation departments.

The refugee question could be addressed to church sponsors, job placement and housing location groups, public welfare staff, civic leaders, and representatives of (and translators for) the refugee/immigrant community already in the area.

We must organize our knowledge in a form that can be pulled together and used by others. As Covey (1991) says, "Decision makers need to see a balanced picture and to receive information in user-friendly ways" (p. 229). Journalists or politicians come to the front-line worker neither for statistics nor diatribes, but rather for cases and insights that make sense of statistics. They also want easily remembered points on both sides of the question. To illustrate: If refugee wives and parents can join men already here, there might be less crime and alcoholism, but because housing in the community for large families is in short supply and there is a waiting list, tensions could be heightened if refugees are given preference. While this may seem mere common sense, it is our role to inject common sense, facts, and ethics into political decision making.

A Beginning Point for Analysis

A social problem can be a starting point to learn more about community responsiveness and how different systems interrelate. We can examine problems and responses to them (a) from a flowchart perspective, tracing those entities involved after the fact to those involved before the fact or vice versa, and (b) from an overview of the "quality and comprehensiveness of local services" for a problem (Koss & Harvey, 1991, p. 115).

Box 7.3 illustrates resources a community may or may not have, to use in responding to rape. This simple resource inventory can be used to assess local services, give guidance on a range of community actions that can be taken, and look for gaps or problems. It provides a sample assessment form that could be adapted to the reader's own subject area. (However, each community problem will require a different list.) Assessment helps with more than research, planning, and evaluation; it gives us a quick look at areas of difficulty within the system.

Service Providers and Users

Assessments often involve direct service practitioners. In one city, for example, a huge public housing complex was to be entirely rebuilt; therefore, residents had to relocate to other sites in town for 2 to 3 years. Part of the overall analysis of residents' needs included questionnaires and planning sessions with social workers and housing officials to identify services and programs wanted by residents in their temporary location and in their remodeled housing complex. The degree of importance of each option— from mentoring programs to general equivalency diploma (GED) classes—was examined. An assessment of relevant service providers and other civic entities was also made to identify programs already in place at the new sites, services that could be transferred with the residents, and gaps that existed. All of this involved an elaborate assessment of organizations serving low-income people.

However, a separate survey of residents revealed worries not just about the continuity and predictability of services but also about the transition itself—how they would be accepted in the receiving neighborhoods. This meant that (a) the overall assessment needed to encompass residents as well as agencies, and (b) neighborhood civic associations also needed to be contacted as part of the assessment.

Resource Assessments

Looking at types of assessments from another angle, resources and collaboration are important.

Knowing Community Resources

There are "four realms of resources that are available in a community: power, expertise, funding, and service" (Whitworth, Lanier, & Haase, 1988, p. 574). In this section, we wish to focus on the realm of service resources. To grasp a *human service system*, Netting, Kettner, and McMurtry (1993) would have us inspect three types of "service-delivery units"—informal, mediating, and formal—and identify the sponsoring organizations or auspices for each. (Self- or mutual help groups and associations are examples of mediating delivery units.) Netting et al. believe that an "astute practitioner will carefully assess all avenues of service delivery to the target population" (p. 102).

We want to be aware of informal resources within particular communities that can be helpful. Melvin Delgado (1996) explains that *bodegas* (grocery stores) do more than sell native food in their neighborhoods. They also provide seven services:

1. Credit
2. Banking—cashing of checks
3. Community-related news and information
4. Counseling customers in distress

BOX 7.3	ASSESSING A COMMUNITY'S RESPONSE TO RAPE

Service Component	Criteria				
	Availability	Accessibility	Quantity	Quality	Legitimacy
Victim Services					
Crisis					
1. Hot line	_____	_____	_____	_____	_____
2. Counseling	_____	_____	_____	_____	_____
3. Hospital accompaniment	_____	_____	_____	_____	_____
Hospital care					
1. Emergency	_____	_____	_____	_____	_____
2. Follow-up	_____	_____	_____	_____	_____
Police services					
1. Rape unit	_____	_____	_____	_____	_____
2. Investigatory procedures	_____	_____	_____	_____	_____
District attorney's office/ court procedures					
1. Rape unit	_____	_____	_____	_____	_____
2. Victim advocacy	_____	_____	_____	_____	_____
3. Court accompaniment	_____	_____	_____	_____	_____
Mental health/social service					
1. Short-term	_____	_____	_____	_____	_____
2. Long-term	_____	_____	_____	_____	_____
3. Special services	_____	_____	_____	_____	_____
Offenders					
Police and district attorney					
1. Investigation	_____	_____	_____	_____	_____
2. Arrest	_____	_____	_____	_____	_____
3. Prosecution	_____	_____	_____	_____	_____
Court systems					
1. Trial practice	_____	_____	_____	_____	_____
2. Sentencing by judges	_____	_____	_____	_____	_____
Alternative treatment					
1. Juvenile	_____	_____	_____	_____	_____
2. Adult	_____	_____	_____	_____	_____
Community Intervention					
Social action					
1. Victim advocacy	_____	_____	_____	_____	_____
2. Law and policy reform	_____	_____	_____	_____	_____
Community education					
1. Avoidance	_____	_____	_____	_____	_____
2. Prevention	_____	_____	_____	_____	_____

Note: For availability: Y = Yes; N = No.
For other measures, use 1–5 rating scale (1 = Excellent; 5 = Poor) for individual services and categories of service.
Source: Copyright © 1991 by Sage Publications, Inc. Reprinted by permission of Sage Publications, Inc.

5. Assistance in filling out or interpreting government forms

6. Information and referral to social service agencies

7. Cultural connectedness to homeland (Delgado, p. 63)

Narrower resource assessments can be undertaken before or at the time of need. We can conduct such assessments ourselves or stay aware of others who make them and learn to interpret their conclusions. At any time, we may face a situation that requires knowledge of previously unexplored facets of the community.

ENSURING GOOD REFERRAL MATCHES

In the future, the public may be able to reach a central telephone number, 211, to get information and assistance regarding social, medical, housing and other services. Such a local or regional service could be a cooperative venture between nonprofits, telephone companies, and governments. To date, few states provide a unified or seamless system of assistance through 211. Instead, there are dozens of unrelated service directories that lead unsophisticated people from one number to the next until they fall through the cracks.

The practitioner's job in assessing resources for a particular problem or referral starts with the directories, references, and tools available in a community to locate a potential resource and then becomes one of understanding its nature, effectiveness, and the quality of its match to the needs at hand. For a college student in crisis, a where-and-when pamphlet listing the Alcoholics Anonymous (AA) meetings in the area is probably available from AA's local center. In most areas, the list is surprisingly long, and the meetings differ greatly in their format. Would this person benefit from a small discussion meeting giving a strong sense of personal support? Or a less personal, lecture type of AA meeting that might not intimidate a shy newcomer?

Schneider and Lester (2001, pp. 155–156) provide a detailed example of a resources directory, that is, an inventory of available services available to meet identified needs. However, such lists, directories, and other formal tools achieve their value in combination with understanding and experience. Good users of these resources work to develop their own skills and to develop a network of persons who can help with selection and interpretation of this information. It is the combination of information from documents and computers and understanding from experi-

ence and advice that leads to the effective selection of community resources.

Most practitioners engage in *brokerage* or *linkage* activities. When the focus is on the *individual*, tasks include "locating appropriate community resources; connecting the consumer to the resource; and evaluating the effectiveness of the resource in relation to the consumer's needs" (J. Anderson, 1981, p. 42). However, if the focus is less on "a clear statement of the consumer's need" and more on "an investigation of the nature, operations, and quality of available resources" (pp. 42–43), then we are engaged in *community* assessment. Netting et al. (1993) would say that we must know not only what agencies are available but also how well they work together and if they make the linkages they should: "whether these interacting units truly comprise a system that is responsive to multiple needs" (p. 110).

Tasks. Kettner et al. (1990, pp. 61–64) suggest developing resource inventories for a particular clientele or subpopulation. Social workers survey other providers to obtain an understanding of "what actual services are available, which services are most often utilized and why (location, quality, staff attitudes?, and different uses of key terminology" (p. 63).

Assessing service integration and utilization for a population, such as HIV/AIDS-related services, can do more than ensure good matches; it can lead to new agency directories, service coordination, and community empowerment (Mancoske & Hunzeker, 1994). To do such tasks, we must be organized (see Box 7.4).

Collaborative Assessments

So far, we have looked at the scope, purpose, and multidimensionality of assessment from the perspective of professionals acting generally on their own. In contrast, assessments can be made of the community or in the community in conjunction with service users and community residents, or even by residents alone. (For real world examples, see http://pps.org/topics/community/engagecomm/). Rothman (1984) reminds us that whatever the form or method, one of the first decisions to make concerns who will do the community assessment and where:

"Assessment can be a fairly technical and solitary professional activity carried out in an office surrounded by computer printouts and area maps. On the other hand, it can be conducted on a collaborative basis in neighborhood clubs, and

BOX 7.4	VALUABLE OFFICE RESOURCES

The information and referral directory lying around the office is invariably out-of-date, requiring practitioners to supplement it. City, county, and neighborhood telephone directories provide telephone numbers such as those of housing inspectors, polling places, elected officials, blood banks, and police–community relations offices. Some localities also have specialized directories listing such organizations as mutual help (e.g., grief) or neighborhood self-help groups (e.g., recycling or mural painting) or resources for a particular population. Social workers with handheld Palm Pilots or other computers can build their own database of names, addresses, and numbers. Such technology is convenient, not imperative. A resourceful practitioner keeps a number of handy references and lists. These include the basics—emergency numbers pasted on the telephone and a tickler file of contact people and key deadlines or time frames. As the Rolodex grows, the professional adds the names of individual and organizational contacts (who can be contacted about the soup kitchen, etc.). The practitioner should also *obtain organization charts for state and city governments and for key agencies*; without the precise name of the agency with jurisdiction, a telephone book will be less useful. Some cities and states maintain a list of key agencies and personnel on their Web sites. Big organizations often have a (more or less) permanent chart with division names and job titles and a parallel (constantly changing) chart with the names of those who currently occupy those slots. They readily provide the general chart and often send outdated copies of the name-specific chart. Be persistent. Call the governor's office and ask for a list of constitutional or cabinet officers, department secretaries or agency directors, and staff cabinet attendees.

meeting halls, with the professional and the constituency taking joint responsibility as partners" (p. 8).

Since the citizenry rarely initiates systematic assessment, such an assessment may begin with a professional, civic leader, or elected official. Unfortunately, outsiders seldom get it right, so input from residents is needed and solicited. Many residents want their preferences taken into consideration, but naturally they resist tedious, unfathomable, time-consuming assessment exercises. When the process is meaningful, the community can be appreciative, even to the extent of throwing a fiesta at the end of the experience (Elliot, Quinles, & Parietti, 2000). Typically, co-inquiry is modest and experimental; for example, 15 young people in Baltimore worked closely with an assessment team to help define youth health issues using photographs (Strack, Magill, & Klein, 2000). This Photovoice approach encourages people to assess their own situations and communities. Cameras are passed out to young, homeless, or mentally ill people—or to illiterate villagers—who take photographs, talk about them, look for themes, and make assessments and recommendations as a group. Program creator Caroline Wang (1999; 2003) says, "Photovoice is a method that enables people to define for themselves and others, including policy makers, what is worth remembering and what needs to be changed" (p. 3, para 2). Such a mutual learning experience can advance sound decision making and trust before action steps are taken (Abatena, 1977; Colby, 1997).

Apart from professionals, citizens must learn to deliberate with each other and express their disagreements about problems and priorities: "People who can not choose together can not act together" (Mathews, 1994, p. 401).

ASSESSMENTS OF, IN, AND BY THE COMMUNITY

Community participants can be involved as full partners most easily when community assessment is the first stage of a funded project, as illustrated by a project in Richmond, California, where community members of an informal planning group not only helped plan surveys and field observations but even hired the project coordinator (Hunkeler, Davis, McNeil, Powell, & Polen, 1990). Participation continued from analysis through the design initiation and implementation phases. In Eagle Pass, Texas, program staff ran seven focus groups to learn about grassroots health concerns. Five involved members of the community and two were with "prominent figures" who could influence the community (Amezcua, McAlister, Ramirez, & Espinoza, 1990, p. 259). The political dynamics of communities often surface during assessment and are more easily integrated into the process when local people rather than outside consultants are running the show.

Rapid rural appraisal and *participatory rural appraisal* (PRA) are used globally to solicit views and to elicit local knowledge about cultural, social, and ecological resources. They are viewed by some authors as collaborative assessments and by others as research tools, project development methodologies, or implementation strategies. PRA is increasingly used in urban and rural social development (Bar-on & Prinsen, 1999; Berardi, 1998) because of its stress on community ownership of both data and the project. Reporting on efforts to involve people in remote areas of Australia who require rehabilitation and disability services, Kuipers, Kendall, and Hancock (2001) say that PRA was adopted because it had "been reported to foster the participation and decision making of community members in community projects" (p. 22). PRA epitomizes an assessment that is of, in, and by the community. However, as a process and program, it will fail if those adopting it just walk away when the communal assessment is over. For such projects to be successful, the problems identified and ranked as most important by townspeople must be those that can actually be changed at a community level (to avoid frustration and feelings of powerlessness). In addition, the PRA team must get back to community participants not only with results but to engage in active follow-through with them on their stated priorities.

Besides dialogue, PRA practitioners utilize interesting task-based methods. Community residents and an outside team (ideally multidisciplinary and gender balanced) hold group discussions and work together on tasks. In one small village, a team worked with everyone and, in four days, inventoried social services, conducted a household census and wealth ranking, formulated a seasonal calendar, charted how men and women spent their time, and completed a territory map and a transect (Gallardo, Encena, & Bayona, 1995, p. 263). A village transect records what falls along a diagonal line drawn through the community and highlights natural resources or human activities, needs and problems. Meitzner (2000) describes it as a quick sketch, sometimes made during a "transect walk" in which the terrain is drawn by villagers as they take outsiders on a "guided tour" (pp. 3–4). Other activities also encourage illiterate people to participate; for instance, a map can be drawn in the dirt with each household repre-

sented and flowers used to depict the living or the dead, or both.

PRA has found a home in applied anthropology and sociology; in the natural resource and agriculture disciplines; in education, health, and other fields. Social workers will want to make more use of this assessment approach and program. Multiple tools can be viewed at Participatory Avenues, an electronic resource (http://www.iapad.org/).

Community assessments can take many forms. Before launching one, we should consider such elements as collaboration, scope, focus, and purpose.

PHILOSOPHIES BEHIND ASSESSMENT

A listening, learning, exploring style and philosophy should guide an initial assessment interaction with an individual or a community.

Attitude of the Professional

Our philosophy of assessment matters because assessment is a first step in establishing our relationship with a community. The stance taken at the beginning will affect all of the operations that come later. Underpinning these efforts must be the belief that we have the capacity to assist individuals and groups (and that they, in turn, have the same capacity) and that we can solve social problems (Huber & Orlando, 1993). Otherwise, there is little point—besides complying with paperwork requirements—in doing assessments at any level. We also must believe in the potential of the community as a living system to nourish, to grow, and to change.

Sullivan (1992) states that "the manner in which assessment is conducted and the choice of data gathered set the tone for future intervention" (p. 205). Using the mentally challenged as an example, he stresses how workers describe, assess, and work for this population. He is quite persuasive about the negative ramifications of an assessment process that requires clients "exclusively to recount previous hospitalizations [and] illness episodes" (p. 206). Even if it requires modification of current assessment tools used by agencies, he believes, workers must also ask about:

"abilities, interests and past accomplishments. . . . Information should be gathered on client interests and aspirations; resources currently or previously used; and needs in various life domains including living arrangements, employment, leisure-time activity, and health" (p. 206).

We want to avoid simply asking people if they are taking their medicine. We establish a different relationship with a person if we ask: "What place were you born? Reared?" "Do you ever go back there?" "What have been important events during your life?" "Do you have any special interests, skills, hobbies, interesting possessions?" (Jackson, 1987, p. 35).

Rural expert Emilia Martinez-Brawley (2000) gives an intriguing example of four families, only distantly related, who "lived in rented trailers but always moved together, even if only one family was dissatisfied or was experiencing problems with housing arrangements" (p. 263). At first blush, a practitioner may consider this practice to be weird or simply unimportant because the practitioner would not view this as a real relationship. And yet, the families have chosen to intertwine their lives in a form of social glue which probably empowers them. An open-minded assessment could be very worthwhile.

Analyzing Community Needs and Resilience

We must avoid self-fulfilling prophecies. By focusing on weaknesses, social work and other professions may inadvertently create a *client neighborhood*. Human services, urban studies, and community development too often have had deficiency-oriented policies and programs responses. Consequently:

"many lower income urban neighborhoods are now environments of service where behaviors are affected because residents come to believe that their well-being depends upon being a client. They begin to see themselves as people with special needs that can only be met by outsiders. . . . Consumers of services focus vast amounts of creativity and intelligence on the survival-motivated challenge of outwitting the 'system,' or on finding ways—in the informal or even illegal economy—to bypass the system entirely" (Kretzmann & McKnight, 1993, p. 2).

This suggests that everyone is telling a "one-sided" story of the community (O'Looney, 1996, p. 232). Meyer (1993) would ask why assessment is limited to "what is the matter," in an individual or community situation, when it should also include *how people are doing* with what is the matter (p. 36).

Practitioners are urged to identify the capacities of local individuals, citizen associations, and institutions and to build connections and strong ties with and among them. This method of assessment looks for *problem solvers*, not problems. Embodying affirmative community assessment, Kretzmann and McKnight depict the same community as it looks on paper mapped by assets in contrast to needs (see Figure 7.1).

ALTERNATIVE PERCEPTIONS

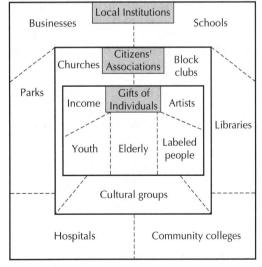

Figure 7.1   Source: *From Building Communities From the Inside Out: A Path Toward Finding and Mobilizing a Community's* (pp. 3, 7), by J. P. Kretzmann and J. L. McKnight, 1993, Evanston, IL: Northwestern University. Copyright 1993 by Neighborhood Innovations Network. Reprinted with permission of Neighborhood Innovations Network.

Values, Preferences, and Mutuality of Interest

AGENCY, COMMUNITY VALUE DIFFERENCES

Assessment involves more than points of view (e.g., a strengths perspective) and how we behold things. It involves values and variation. Given differing perspectives, an agency and a community may not share philosophies or opinions about behavior. Yet, as workers we easily forget this fact because we take so much for granted—things like what mental health is and how it should be maintained. We value self-insight, facing up to adversity, and talking things over, for instance. Atkinson, Morten, and Sue (1993) provide good suggestions for clinicians on how to "hear" clients with beliefs about mental health different from their own. For example, some Asian Pacific Americans believe that mental health is "maintained by the avoidance of morbid thoughts" (p. 212). Clients who put off treatment would not regard themselves—as some workers might—as hiding their heads in the sand, but rather as being appropriately stoic about a family member's condition. Thus, we note knowledge and philosophical differences that might affect outcomes, because being oblivious can lead to an unstated conflict that could hamper mutual assessment.

Awareness may not suffice. The hardest situations are those in which our professional values are in conflict with those of most community residents. Such situations require decisions about when and where to substitute professional values for the values of the community, when to adhere to the community's values, and when to strive for compromise or consensus. A subcommunity or the town as a whole may feel imposed on or affronted by our program, whether it distributes condoms in schools or clean needles on the streets, arranges for birth control implants, or makes controversial recommendations regarding releases from mental hospitals. We must develop means of finding out where residents and potential users of services stand and judging the intensity of feelings, opposition, and resistance. Such facts could determine whether we would be better off going public (on talk shows, for instance) to educate and give our point of view, or lying low.

RESPECT AND RESPONSIVENESS

We will follow this principle: Respect community residents enough to seek and listen to their views on the subject at hand (Julian, 1999). In the previous chapter, we grounded ourselves in social science approaches as a means of understanding. Here we highlight tapping current and potential service users and others in our network as sources of information and insight. Along with doing or reading formal studies, we must integrate intelligence gathered from our environments into our operations. How might we do this? We must know who and what to ask. As one form of inquiry, Mitroff and Linstone (1993) urge us to list all *stakeholders* connected with our organization, that is, "any individual, group, organization, institution that can affect as well as be affected by [our] policy or policies" (p. 141). Then, after discovering through interaction all the assumptions each player has about the nature of the problem at hand, we mutually analyze the fundamental differences in our assumptions. For more on stakeholders, see Marley & Rogge, 2000; Sacken, 1991. Moving further out in our environment, Greever (1983) defines *intelligence* as what we need to know in advance of an action. He speaks of "gathering broad pieces of information (Military Intelligence calls them 'EEIs—Essential Elements of Information') and working with them until some sort of pattern emerges" (p. 1). In our context, intelligence can also involve keeping an ear to the ground regarding client concerns and colleague concerns (Proenca, 1998).

We must circulate. Peters (1987) gives an example of a Lutheran minister in a small Pennsylvania town who built relationships through his philosophy of "Ministry by Wandering Around" and was the "first minister in over *twenty years* to stop by the corner coffee shop to sit down and have coffee with the local farmers" (p. 148). Peters believes that listening and being receptive to customers are fundamental guidelines. This philosophy underlies current business preoccupations with quality and management innovation (Moore & Kelly, 1996). We could wander around our waiting rooms, checking out the ambience to see if we have humanized our organizational presentation. We can ask those who have used our services: "How are we doing? What did you think?" We can reach out to those in our vicinity: "Do you know who we are? Where we are located? Are our hours convenient for you?" This is no public relations game. We must assess who we are serving well and who we are not because social workers are accountable to community residents and clients (Maluccio, 1979, p. 199) and can learn from them in the same way that the minister in Peters's story learned from the farmers at the coffee shop.

LISTENING TO FEEDBACK

Feedback will figure heavily in this learning process. Agencies can experiment with anonymous satisfaction-with-services evaluations, on-premise suggestion boxes, a newsletter written and controlled by clients to be read by practitioners, formal evaluation by users of services through an outside evaluator, and serious analysis of any complaints received. *Services* is used here in a broad sense, because feedback can be given on training, group therapy, oversight of homemaker services, psychodrama, and many other activities.

Although we will concentrate on feedback from those outside our programs, we should not forget coworkers with community ties who receive few opportunities to give feedback. When asked, staffers such as receptionists, cooks, house parents, drivers, aides, and work crew leaders can provide valuable information on service users. They can also provide feedback on program functioning and *community reactions*—yet professionals rarely ask them for such information.

People working in organizations of all types—businesses, government agencies, nonprofits—should "use every listening post [they] can find" (Peters, 1987, p. 152). We identify three possible ones here. First, we should encourage *case managers* to give honest performance feedback—based on client statements with due regard to confidentiality—to each office on quality of services and responsiveness of personnel. They can tell us about desired new programs as well. Case managers focused on client strengths may be particularly attuned to agency limitations (Sullivan & Fisher, 1994). Second, since *self-help and mutual support meetings* are places where grievances against professionals are aired regularly, we should ask groups related to the work of our office to give us summaries of common complaints. Third, we should identify *service providers, entrenched in the community* and plugged into different networks, who will be blunt with us.

Independent Assessments from Service Users

ACCEPTING FORMAL SERVICE CRITIQUES

More surprising perhaps to wary agencies, we want to encourage formal critiques of us (Stoesz, 2002) and to legitimize the consumer's voice (Thompson, 1999), even if the critique is sometimes unrestrained or irritatingly insistent. Our organizations should have consumer advisory boards, democratically selected, whose advice is carefully heeded during strategic planning and at other times. We must welcome the presence of advocates—for example, for the mentally challenged and their families (who often have different viewpoints from each other)—and others who question our actions as a professional group or with particular clients. This questioning may be verbal or written. Our worries about accreditation, funding sources, and staying out of trouble with bureaucracies cause us to avoid collecting potentially negative documents. There is a trend, however, toward the legitimacy of *independent* service user evaluation. Consumers can now complain to state occupational licensing boards about practitioners such as physicians and social workers; information about physicians is gathered from malpractice insurance claims and disciplinary actions and fed into the National Practitioner Data Bank. Moreover, the government is beginning to require the input of users; for example, federal law requires nursing home inspectors to talk to residents, not just staff and management. It is natural for us to be excited about citizen efforts to assess another institution but threatened if the target is our own agency. However, we should still listen (see Box 7.5).

ADVOCACY RECOMMENDATIONS

Our assessment philosophy must embrace openness and willingness to integrate input from many sources because it is of critical importance to learn what people want from service providers and their communities.

- We can encourage individuals and advocacy groups to explain, face-to-face, how the environment can become more responsive to their needs.
- We can use oral histories to solicit views of a service, an association, or an organization.
- We can also seek out state and national publications with relevant recommendations about our area of work. Advocacy publications may be sophisticated guides to citizen involvement or one-page flyers.

Consumer-oriented assessments of problems and their discussions of appropriate responses deserve our attention. Such discussions may focus on (a) how community life affects particular sectors or groups, (b) practical tips that might be implemented within a reasonable length of time, and (c) citizen participation or rights. For instance, older people and their advocates have

---

| BOX 7.5 | ASSESSMENTS TO ASSIST SERVICE USERS: TWO EXAMPLES |

Brief descriptions of two consumer critiques will illustrate (a) how members of the public can be informed about availability and quality of services in a form they can easily utilize, and (b) how providers can get valuable input from independent assessors. Two different groups rated long-term care facilities and made the results available to the public in simple formats. A metropolitan area and an entire (different) state were studied.

1. The *metropolitan advocacy group* visited each facility but relied more on official reports about nursing homes and board and care homes. The group compiled the results of local fire, state health, and state social services reports and compared federal Medicare inspections over a period of time. Their critique showed clearly which homes were always, sometimes, or never in compliance with various regulations (e.g., the most luxu-

rious nursing home had been noncompliant). Facilities had preferred to keep such information hidden, but now the compliance information was public.

2. In the *statewide survey*, an interdisciplinary team, composed of a nurse and students of social work and gerontology, asked questions of administrators designed to help families understand the variety of services available in different facilities. While in the facility, they also made careful note of such things as odor, morale, and treatment of residents. In the end, whether or not the administrators agreed with the final guide, the facilities did learn how people representing service users would compare them with their competitors. Detached consumer advocates had provided an assessment from which the providers could take suggestions. Such rare events should be welcomed rather than resisted.

---

suggested that communities *assess their livability* and make traveling easier. They argue for traffic lights to be set to allow sufficient time for pedestrians to cross the street. They point out that bells or other sounds permit those with visual impairments to know when it is safe to cross. They also suggest the creation of large, separate paths to accommodate safely those walking, along with those using conventional two-wheeled bicycles and three-wheeled electric vehicles (Parker, Edmonds, & Robinson, 1989, p. 8). This illustrates how community assessments by citizen advocates may differ in emphasis from those prepared by professionals.

An assessment philosophy establishes our attitudes, organizes our approach, and directs many of our applications. It even dictates whether assessment should be a two-way process. Information gathering provides a foundation for more elaborate assessment and research.

TRADITIONAL ASSESSMENT: INFORMATION-GATHERING METHODS

Disciplines usually evolve a few specialized assessment methods but adapt most of their methods from sources such as sociology, political science, or planning. In community health, for instance, surveys and descriptive epidemio-

logical studies are common methods used to carry out an assessment (Spradley, 1990, p. 382), just as needs identification and assessment methods, including surveys, are common in social work. In the view of organizer Makani Themba (1999), community-focused methods of listening include surveys, canvassing, focus groups, one-on-one interviews with key players and walkabouts (p. 89). Having discussed nontraditional ways to learn from and be more interactive with the public, we now turn to established methods used to assess community or client needs, launch program development, and update strategic plans (Ross & Coleman, 2000). Focus groups, public meetings, needs assessment, and outreach methods can bring results helpful to providers and to those who will ultimately be served. Since focus groups and public meetings are more narrowly defined than needs assessment and outreach, we will look at them first (Butterfoss, Houseman, Morrow, & Rosenthal, 1997).

Focus Group Methods

PROTOCOL AND PARTICIPANT SELECTION

Agencies can conduct focus groups for assessment purposes on their own or with assistance. A *focus group* is a qualitative data collection process in which a small number of individuals meet together with a trained facilitator to discuss a narrow topic in a detailed, guided way. Sometimes this is done with a written, predetermined agenda or set of questions. The point is not to reach a consensus but to air many ideas; members of the group react to each other, and the process builds to refinement of opinions. The session may be recorded for later study. Broadcast and print media use this form of opinion gathering during political campaigns; a heterogeneous group of 8 to 12 people is generally shown reacting to a debate or commenting on issues. Any results must be qualified because we cannot generalize from small samples.

We will describe focus groups made up of strangers, although social service personnel or acquaintances can be used (Martinez Brawley & Delevan, 1993, p. 177; also see Hopkins, Mudrick, & Rudolph, 1999). A cross section of the community is sought in terms of income, race, education, and other factors unless a particular segment, such as women or teenagers, is targeted. The more targeted the group, the more expensive the process of finding a representative sample through telephone solicitation. Ideally, several groups are run in different parts of the community. Most focus group sessions meet one time only for about 2 hours. Working people find it hard to arrive early in the evening. Older people prefer daytime hours and are more likely to expect to have transportation money provided. Sometimes participants are given a modest sum; more often, they are provided with a meal or refreshments because they are volunteering their time. The goal of bringing people together in this way is to encourage them to give their candid opinions. If we interrogate them or ask them questions calling for a yes or no answer, we will learn little. We are trying to create the atmosphere of a study group, not a courtroom or research laboratory.

PURPOSE: TO PROVIDE VALUABLE INFORMATION

Individual and group reactions provide insights into issues of comprehension, suitability, and acceptable phrasing. (Thus, politicians test campaign themes on focus groups.) Let us explore focus group methodology by understanding how a group can serve as a test audience. In the recent past, federal regulators and the apparel industry were considering voluntary warnings for sleepwear. A focus group of middle-aged and older participants was asked their preferences regarding flame-resistant fabric, warning labels, or both, to protect themselves or frail, older parents with cognitive or physical

limitations. (Older people have high mortality rates associated with fires involving apparel, especially nightwear.) The meeting opened with a videotape documenting a burn hazard. The group then examined and discussed several proposed wordings for a cautionary label in sleepwear. Participants examined handouts of alternative warnings, which were also printed on big signs and displayed at the front of the room. The discussion that followed made clear a common misconception among the participants: that a labeled product must be more dangerous than an unlabeled product. Without more education, honesty might backfire in the marketplace. The advocates involved had failed in many ways to anticipate how members of the public would react, *which is precisely why focus groups can be helpful.*

PURPOSE: TO TEST THE WATERS

This flexible methodology also can be applied in clinical settings. A social worker at a sexual assault center wants to start a group for males who experienced sexual abuse as children. Uncertain about how to reach prospective members, he sends letters to potential referral sources and places free advertisements in community newspapers. After receiving five responses, the worker asks if these individuals would be willing to come in and discuss perceived needs and how to reach others. Since this is not a randomly selected group—which would have been impossible in this case—the worker has to note ways in which the group may be atypical (e.g., race, sexual orientation). Instead of using an outside facilitator, the worker moderates the session himself and explores topics such as where and how to reach out, wording of the invitation, appropriateness of the agency location and hours, and the most effective descriptors for a group. Because the participants have experience with this problem, they can share (a) their personal states of mind about seeking help (embarrassed, relieved), (b) what they had responded to and what others might want (opportunity to talk? get help? pursue redress?), (c) how they regard themselves or identifiers they find acceptable (incest victims? sexual assault victims? abused children? adults struggling with childhood traumas?), and (d) what type of outreach slogans they might best respond to ("Angry today about what happened yesterday?" "Never talked about it before?") During the focus group meeting, the social worker listens for themes and key words that can be used in outreach and as a basis for the therapeutic group. Having taped the session with permission, he has a coworker listen, because he admits to himself that he already has notions about the best means of reaching out to this group. The professionals then reassess the original plan for the group.

Purpose: Specialized Assessment

Our planning should take into account the subject matter, the task to pursue, and the literacy level of the population. To assess what types of sensory devices Deaf and Hard of Hearing (D/HH) people would like to have developed, Gallaudet University used focus groups "because both mail and telephone communication would require reading and writing. A survey involving prelingually D/HH would be biased toward those who had excellent reading and writing skills. Among D/HH persons with marginal literacy, it would be difficult to ascertain whether the questions were understood. . . . [Also] the subjects were required to think creatively about communication problems and possible technological solutions. . . . Probing on the part of the researcher is needed to bring out this thought process, something which would be extremely difficult to do by mail or by telephone" (Harkins & Jensema, 1987, p. 2).

Society's increased use of intercoms was one communication problem that surfaced: "Repeated mentions were made of difficulty in using the drive-through service in fast-food restaurants. Secure buildings which require a visitor to use the security system's phone also present problems" (Harkins & Jensema, 1987, p. 7). Details such as this, along with a process that allows other participants to jump in and say "me, too" (instant, albeit limited, confirmation), make focus groups with facilitators popular assessment tools.

Methods of Data Gathering From Community Events

Public Participation

The title says it all: "Taking the Pulse: A Community Exchange to Gather Information About _____ Needs in _____ County." Our profession supports civic involvement, open government, and public participation in decision making. We can learn through community meetings and events. Realistically, few participants at such an event will read the write-up of the recommendations, but they have the opportunity to talk, to hear the options, and (later) to read the report. Today many open meetings are mandated public hearings (Kettner et al., 1990, p. 69). In various fields, for obligatory and democratic rea-

sons, individuals are allowed more say. A citizen could travel from forums about cable television rate hikes to sound-off meetings about animal control. The current competition for everyone's time must be kept in mind as our agency plans opportunities for participation.

Community residents often take these meetings more seriously than we do. Current and potential service users envision something tangible coming out of such interchanges and expect their recommendations to be taken seriously. To be credible and ethical, we must not falsely raise expectations, and we should want input if we ask for it. (Regarding doing it right through planned town meetings, see Alcorn & Morrison, 1994; Luckey, 1995.) Town meetings must be accessible (transit, building, audio loops, interpreters, etc.), too.

Meeting Protocol

Suggestions for running any meeting are covered in Chapter 10. The warnings here involve only those matters that may color or cloud the assessment process. The trend to give more say to the community means that meetings can be taken over by a group with an especially obdurate agenda—such as those on either side of the abortion rights, capital punishment, gun control, or immigration issues. One smooth-talking person can also take a group off the agenda. This requires being alert but open. For example, a meeting to discuss the perceived need for more day care might be attended by parents who oppose day care, prefer after-school care, or want help in coordinating relief time for families teaching their children at home. Genuine needs may exist, making it inappropriate to tell these parents that they came to the wrong meeting. We may not agree with or like everyone who comes to public meetings, but worthwhile information can often be found in the unexpected or the unreasonable.

To avoid disruption, some people who run meetings make a show of letting everyone take part but actually regulate the proceedings tightly to ward off or reject unwanted input. We should anticipate that community people will organize and try to control meetings; this is part of the process. We want to be sure that in small gatherings each person present is offered equal time, and that in big gatherings access to the microphone is handled fairly. Moderators can set time limits and establish ground rules ("Avoid arguing with someone else's statement; just make your own") without squelching participants. It is common for sensible ideas to appear garbled or self-serving in their delivery; therefore, input is properly measured by the usefulness of the suggestion, not the speaking skills and demeanor of proponents or their stance on issues.

FOLLOW-UP ANALYSIS AFTER THE MEETINGS

During a forum, an agency staffer and someone who lives in the community should take notes on each point made and who said it. He or she can then organize the notes, using tentative headings, and have the moderator check them for errors. We must sort out what we heard, using these notes and our own memories, or, better yet, listening to a tape and noting the intensity of feelings expressed on given topics—from represented groups in particular. Next, we must separate needs from preferences and gripes, not by how participants characterized what they were saying but by customary use of the following terms:

1. *Need:* Essential, necessity, requirement
2. *Desire, wish,* or *preference:* Want, choice, longing
3. *Complaint:* Gripe, grievance, objection, protest

Despite a focus on the need for day care, complaints may have poured out about a particular caseworker or about how a current program is being run because constituents may mix needs, desires, and gripes. Perhaps there should be a period of time in which participants can air complaints and preferences before beginning constructive discussion about agency mission and community needs.

OTHER WAYS TO LISTEN TO THE COMMUNITY

To gather *community impressions,* practitioners can go to those sectors believed to have the most intense needs—whether served, underserved, or unserved to date—interview key informants, and use the target group to validate objective data (Siegel, Attkisson, & Carson, 1987, p. 93). Newer possibilities involve electronic networks and interactive media. Those interested in needs and preferences can monitor sectors of a community via Web pages and e-mail mailing lists.

Although practitioners and managers must know how to put on successful forums, they may be better off attending already scheduled community events than holding their own. We may hear better from the back rather than the front of the room when we do not have to be in charge. Getting out into the swim of things is something we know we should do, but we often lack time. Professionals neglect communitywide celebrations and specialized events where they can gain

information and exposure: Hispanic International Day, Strawberry Festival, Ice Carnival. We must look for opportunities to interact with the public and other providers. For example, if it is our turn to oversee our office's booth at the mall, then we should visit every other organization's table to gather information (to check service gaps and overlaps) and renew contacts.

Informal Need Assessment Processes

Assessment occurs regularly as we discuss the needs of our locality. Informal problem solution assessment takes place each time a vague if valid concern is thrown at an agency—for example, "You must do something about fatherlessness!" Everyone has an immediate opinion about the problem, the solution, and the perfect program, but this is reaction, not need analysis. We must sort out the basics of a target problem or system and an action system before we can say that we have identified a need (see Chapters 1 and 3, this volume). See Box 7.6 on the first steps in case sorting.

Need assessment also happens informally because it is interwoven with the skills of identification (size of the problem or population) and intervention (Whitman, Graves, & Accardo, 1987). As Box 7.6 illustrates, need is an elastic concept, so we must review each situation.

Formal Need Assessment Processes

Program evaluation, needs assessment, community assessment, and research overlap in ways that may be confusing. For instance, Bayne Smith and Mason (1995) employ focus groups and surveys to understand a Caribbean American community that may need services for residents with developmental disabilities; they use the terms *need assessment, field study,* and *descriptive research* to describe their study. Need studies can be designed to show us the *big picture of need* in the community. For instance, communities forced to undergo economic conversion from military to other economic endeavors must plan and reevaluate. Their need assessments provide an example of a big-picture look and macrolevel involvement (Mary, 1994). Here we examine, instead, assessments undertaken to provide tailored guidance to an agency or a multiagency team whose scope of work is already fairly well determined but could change in the future (Marley & Rogge, 2000; Soriano, 1995; Whitworth et al., 1988; Witkin & Altschuld, 1995).

BOX 7.6	CONSTRUING THE SITUATION

When a problem or case is brought to your official notice, you must decide how narrowly or broadly to interpret it. For example, Rosenthal and Levine (1980, p. 401) point out that an individual complaint about discrimination in a local government's handling of a job promotion might be investigated in one of the following ways:

• As an individual complaint only: Did the government agency discriminate against this person?

• As a class complaint: Does the government agency discriminate against all persons in certain categories?
• As a broadly construed class complaint: Does the entire government discriminate against all persons in certain categories?

COMMUNICATION ABOUT NEED

To oversimplify, if a neighborhood group says, "We need better housing," a worker might hypothesize that members of that group live in substandard housing, and the worker would want to know whether that is true. If we look up census figures to learn how many homes in the area lack running water or indoor toilets and find that the answer is none, that information redirects our assessment. Are there multiple housing violations in apartments? What is the average rent people are paying, and what percentage of their income does that represent? Is the problem housing or security? The worker returns to the group with questions that show interest, concern, and some knowledge.

Neuber (1980) defines *need assessment* as "a communication medium between consumers and service providers," which can affect "the planning and evaluation of the various services to be delivered to the community and consumers" (pp. 62–63). Need assessment is also an ongoing process that involves the community in a form of continuous quality improvement (D. Menefee, personal communication, June 1995). Need assessments may be *client oriented* (population at risk) or *service oriented* (addressing gaps and fit). To give an example of the latter, a graduate student thinks she has identified a need. Her dream is to start her own agency after she leaves school to provide housing for post-high-school-age youth. She wishes to find a niche in the transitional housing market and has several communities in mind, but she wants to find out if such a service is essential, in the opinion of local practitioners, and desired by decision makers in the area. The student believes a service-oriented need assessment will help her to

determine in which locality there will be a positive fit and where her plan will most likely succeed.

Multiple Approaches

Assessment processes involve compiling available information, developing new information, or integrating relevant new information with the old. Neuber and associates urge us to obtain data from *demographic-statistical profiles*, *key informants*, and *random community members* in order to define needed services, develop programs, enhance interagency cooperation, and improve accountability. Among the traditional methods used to do this are *indicator* approaches, *social area survey* approaches, and *community group* approaches (Siegel et al., 1987, pp. 76–77). While it is beyond the scope of this book to explain all these methods fully, in general, social indicator approaches are oriented to available data, while surveys gather new data. Both are quantitative in nature (Jacob & Willits, 1994), whereas the community approaches are more qualitative. The community approaches include forums and community impressions, the Delphi method (Raskin, 1994), and the nominal group technique (Alcorn & Morrison, 1994; Wiatrowski & Campoverde, 1996).

As we have seen, need assessment methods involving the community are used to obtain ideas from current and potential service users. *Social service practitioners may attend forums*, but the community approaches focus primarily on people with a direct stake in any outcome(s) of the information-gathering, planning, and priority-setting process. Community representatives are asked what is and is not working, and what they are satisfied with, proud of, and afraid of concerning the future of their community.

In contrast, the *Delphi method* involves input from experts—more detached and not usually directly affected by the outcomes of the process—who refine and synthesize ideas on a topic. "It is axiomatic with the Delphi method that the respondents need not be a random sample of the population" (Molnar & Kammerud, 1977, p. 325). When an *environmental impact study* is done, for instance, decision makers want to hear from those who study similar situations, have informed judgments, and can suggest new options, rather than merely supporting or opposing what is on the table. Johnson (1995) describes a parallel *social impact assessment* (p. 275).[2] Typically, with this method, a question is put to a panel. The Delphi process involves several rounds in which anonymous experts look at each other's ideas (or the range as summarized) in writing (Nartz & Schoech, 2000). It is an "inquiry system" for moving toward "agreement or consensus" (Mitroff & Linstone, 1993, p. 29).

A *nominal group* is a structured exercise in which each participant works silently alongside other individuals and then answers questions when called on until the meeting is opened to free discussion. A moderator might pose a question and ask each participant to list ideas. Each would give one answer from these lists when it is her or his turn until each participant has reported each response. Thus, 8 to 10 people sit in a group but talk in rotation as a facilitator records all ideas; eventually these will be discussed and may be ranked. The initial round-robin sharing format prevents individuals from taking over the brainstorming session (Siegel et al., pp. 88–90) and gives equal voice to usually reticent members (Alcorn & Morrison, 1994, p. 36). This technique can help to avoid disruption—for example, when groups holding different stakes in a particular question, such as rent control reforms, are together. Nominal group meetings can also be held consecutively; landlords could give their opinions in one group and tenants in another at an earlier or later time.

Survey Options

Common types of social or community surveys include citizen surveys (Murtagh, 1999; Siegel et al., 1987) or general population surveys, target population surveys, and service provider surveys (Meenaghan, Washington, & Ryan, 1982). The time and expense involved can discourage our use of any of these formats, but we can learn to use and interpret others' surveys. A practitioner wanting to supplement a huge survey with some special questions or to do a limited survey should contact a trained researcher, survey expert, or pollster. Such people can usually be found in a city or county planning office or a local college. Some public service agencies have such experts in-house.

Our information needs may be simple and our target easy to reach. Suppose that an adolescent unit wanted to find out the literacy level of parents of adolescent clients, that is, the families of current service users. Case records could be examined to discover how long adults currently in the household attended school, but that does not necessarily reflect literacy. We would need to determine whether a telephone or face-to-face survey of parents would get the fullest results at the least cost. *Alternatively, our information goals may be less clear and our target harder to reach.* We may start with service providers to reach potential service users. For example, one study wanted to determine the needs of mentally challenged adults and their children. The directors used an *agency informant method* to identify individuals in the target group and then interviewed a subset of them. Since the "actual prevalence of intellectually limited parents is unknown," Whitman et al. (1987) instead "attempted to identify those retarded parents in a large metropolitan area who had come to agency attention and to survey a sample of these parents in order to determine their perceived service needs" (p. 636).

We may decide that we can benefit from any information about certain potential service users' needs/preferences or their knowledge of available services. Let us say that the target group is women whose lives are threatened by their weight—a small number compared to the many women who would potentially be noticed or experience rejection due to their size (Wiley, 1994). A physician survey will run into confidentiality issues and miss women who avoid doctors. A questionnaire can be designed to be administered on a given Saturday in front of department stores, factory outlets, and shops selling large-size women's fashions. The challenge would be to get the stores' cooperation; they may want to screen the questions for potential offensiveness. Surveyors would have to be trained. Results could serve as a pretest, since responses would help us design a more relevant (and perhaps less fatphobic) questionnaire that could be administered outside diet stores, the clothing stores again, and so on. Shoppers are not a random group, and obese women who stay at home (of whom there are probably many) will be missed, which is one reason why such a survey would be unscientific.

However, surveys can have a value that goes far beyond their scientific validity. For assessment purposes, they are often revealing no matter how limited they are in sophistication, subject, or sample, as the following letter (sent to the Gray Panthers) shows:

Sir/Madam:

My name is Troy Moore. I am in the fourth grade. I am doing a project on older people.

I recorded some answers on older people. I got some answers from children in my school. My results were that old people have gray hair and wrinkle skin, are mean, are unhealthy and are smart. We want to know if they are true. Do you have information about old people? Would you please send me information?

Sincerely,

Troy Moore

c/o Mrs. Beeson

1415 29th Street East

Palmetto, FL 34221

One group of graduate students practiced the skills listed in Box 7.7 and may have benefited the community by conducting a quick survey for an urban community association. The goal or larger objective was to find out about problems, use of public services (e.g., the local recreation center), and so on. The study population consisted of residents of an older, racially and ethnically mixed area of about 1,000 households in the north-central and western part of the city. The immediate objective was to complete 100 household interviews in order to provide information on concerns and some sociodemographics. The students designed the survey instrument and cleared it with the association. Using a large city planning map, they randomly divided the neighborhood into quadrants, then streets, and then select houses. They organized into teams.

After they completed 118 face-to-face interviews, the data were processed and the frequency distributions, along with anecdotal information, were reported to the director of the association. The results gave direction for action. Elderly residents were afraid to go out and were trapped in houses they could not sell because the market value was going down. Drug dealers were moving into the area; residents identified particular crack houses.

Outreach Methods

Outreach and assessment intertwine in two ways. Community assessment may help determine the best means of outreach. Assessment can be made possible through outreach to less well-known segments of the population.

A BROAD DEFINITION

Typically, *outreach* involves systematically contacting isolated people in their homes or wherever they reside (institutions, streets), or in the neighborhoods where they congregate, and linking them to services and financial programs for which they are believed to be eligible. For example, in Nogales, Arizona, the community health center hires *promotoras*, lay health educators and outreach workers who can translate both language and cultural issues (Slack & McEwen, 1997). Outreach involves efforts to include those often left out (such as absent fathers). Directories can be part of outreach, as can 800 or 888 telephone numbers. Outreach is also used to expand an agency's program (a) into new settings and communities, thus making a service or resource immediately and more widely available; (b) into new time periods to reach a target group, as has been done with midnight basketball; and (c) into client "linkage" with institutions, the community, or other clients to enhance "peer support" (Wells, Schachter, Little, Whylie, & Balogh, 1993).

BOX 7.7	HOW TO RUN A SMALL SURVEY

1. Determine the objectives.
2. Define the study population.
3. Determine data to be collected.
4. Select the sampling unit.
5. Select the contact method.
6. Develop the instrument.

7. Organize and conduct the survey.
8. Process and analyze the data.
9. Report the results.

Source: Based on G.E.A. Dever, in *Community Health Nursing: Concepts and Practice* (pp. 382–383), by B. W. Spradley, 1990 (3rd ed.), Glenview, IL: Scott, Foresman. Based on G.E.A. Dever in Spradley (1990, pp. 382-383.)

Sometimes we fail to recognize the *information-gathering and assessment potential* of outreach efforts or programs because we think of them as a satellite operation, a customer recruitment strategy, or an obligation. Takoma Park, Maryland hired organizers to canvass wards full of newcomers—to register people to vote in city elections but also to learn about immigrant concerns; for instance, to learn whether illegal immigrants were being taken advantage of in their everyday transactions (Becker, 2001). We should be aware that outreach involves an interesting mix of giving and *getting* knowledge (Glogoff & Glogoff, 1998).

VARIETIES AND METHODS

Outreach methods vary. Some government agencies are mandated to alert potential service users or beneficiaries—for instance, regarding food stamps or Supplemental Security Income. They often perform outreach through public service announcements. In contrast, around 10 P.M., homeless shelter director Mitch Snyder used to take hamburgers and blankets out to individuals who chose to stay on the streets rather than come in from the cold. While distributing the food and blankets, he gained intelligence from those on heat grates about specific fears people had about coming indoors and who on the streets were the sickest or most violent. A continuing education program on mental health, on the other hand, employed more conventional but equally important ways of reaching out to older people: selecting *accessible community sites*, allowing registration at the first class so that frail people did not have to make an extra trip, and printing materials in large type (Blackwell & Hunt, 1980). Telephone *hotlines* offering legal assistance to the poor or elderly have been tried in several localities as a way to make information more available, as well as a means of collecting information on the types of requests received over time. The University of Maryland at Baltimore has a Social Work Community Outreach Service that links university resources with community groups and residents (Cook, Bond, Jones, & Greif, 2002). *Support groups* can be initiated, in either a public or a circumspect manner (D. B. Anderson & Shaw, 1994), as a form of outreach.

As shown in a newspaper story by Susan Levine (2002) entitled "Word Gets Out on Children's Insurance," methods of outreach can be direct or indirect:

> It is advertised during back-to-school nights and baseball games, in beauty parlors and liquor stores, on yo-yos and toothbrushes. The creative lengths to which state and local officials go in publicizing the Maryland Children's Health Program know few bounds. At the local bowling alley? On a Frisbee? Why not?
>
> Their work has paid off by the tens of thousands since the program began in 1998. Nearly 95,000 previously uninsured children have health coverage—a yield more than 50 percent greater than officials originally predicted and success that these days draws applause from outside policy experts. (pp. 3, 6, reprinted with permission of the *Washington Post*)

Methods of outreach can be expected or unexpected: If skywriting in Spanish were the best way to identify a service and encourage its use for a particular target group, and resources were not at issue, then it would be an appropriate mechanism. Direct, personal outreach . . . must, of course, be made as non-threatening and nondisruptive as possible.

Successful outreach through direct contacts in a Texas program revealed some specific, nonthreatening steps that can be taken to serve a previously unserved group (Watkins & Gonzales, 1982). The plan sounded easy enough: a Mexican American counselor was hired to spend time in an isolated neighborhood and in homes, gaining trust, and later to provide mental health counseling. However, much assessment of, and with, the community went on concurrently with hiring and initial outreach. *Research was studied* and community leaders and referral sources were contacted regarding the perceived need for services by the target group, the compatibility between counselor and client regarding culture and decision making, and the best site for services. Initially, counseling was done in homes. Later, it was done at a community center in the barrio. In addition, an original play in Spanish was performed to facilitate discussion of pressing issues. Interaction was key to assessment and action. The agency saw more of a need for marriage counseling services than did militant community leaders, who wanted economically oriented help. The leaders ended up being more accepting of the services than they anticipated, and the services rendered were more resource and advocacy oriented than the agency had anticipated. This variety of outreach can overlap with case finding. Auerswald (1968) describes case recruitment—in contrast to acceptance of referrals—as part of an integrated service approach to a "so-called disadvantaged community" (p. 206).

The philosophy is to meet people where they are in every way we can—through their own language or their own stores (e.g., botanical shops in Puerto Rican communities), accommodating them in their own environment and in ours (getting rid of barriers such as stairs), providing services or programs in a way and at a time that is convenient, and conveying messages at an appropriate level of comprehension. It is important to assess the informational requirements of the public. We can be creative in community education: comic books, for instance, are part of adult education and advocacy efforts. (See the discussion of readability in Chapter 12). The Migrant Clinicians Network and other organizations that serve non-English speakers use graphics to reach out to women dealing with such problems as domestic violence. The women can point to a picture of a face with comic strip stars rising from the jaw. A mental health handbook could use pictorial graphics to direct less educated readers to the right services. It could contain pertinent information on emergency psychiatric evaluation, designated government agencies, community rehabilitation services, resident grievance systems in psychiatric hospitals, and related assistance such as pharmacy programs. Sullivan (1992) believes that personal commitment also is required: "Helpers can best assist mentally challenged individuals in reclaiming the community through daily work on the street and in the community" (p. 208). The idea behind the methods discussed is to look for practical ways to facilitate our discovery of who and what is out there and to identify what we may have to offer that others in the community can use.

THOUGHTFUL ASSESSMENT

The act of assessment covers an astonishingly wide range of activities, from technical analyses, to preparation for massive programmatic intervention in a community, to judgments about a society itself. We must be familiar with methods and prescriptive rules. However, it would be a pity if the purposes of our profession were submerged by the practical. We must also heed the evocative in the assessment process—that is, what is indicative of what—and consider values.

An Allegorical Aside

How do we include self-reflection in community-based research (Murphy & Pilotta, 1983)? We will benefit from imaginative exploration, a willingness to face complexity, an ability to contemplate that which is not seen or heard yet still applies, and an awareness of our own mental processes. A task so nuanced, yet so audacious, is hard to describe. Therefore, we draw on the imagery of Edward Bellamy's *Looking Backward* (1960), and on Ursula K. Le Guin's short story "The Ones Who Walk Away From Omelas" with its description of an imaginary place (1975). For the latter, see Box 7.8.

Bellamy and Le Guin provide us with societal extremes to consider. Bellamy, writing a novel in 1888 about the year 2000, made no pretense about neutral observation. He wrote about his vision of the perfect society of the future, contrasting it with the war and poverty of his era. In a famous comparison, Bellamy likened our society to a "prodigious coach which the masses of humanity were harnessed to," with hunger as the driver, while the rich had the seats up on top, where they could "critically describe the merits of the straining team." He continued: "Naturally such places were in great demand and the competition for them was keen, every one seeking as the first end in life to secure a seat on the coach for himself and to leave it to his child after him. . . . For all that they were so easy, the seats were very insecure, and at every sudden jolt of the coach persons were slipping out of them and falling to the ground, where they were instantly compelled to take hold of the rope. . . . Commiseration was frequently expressed by those who rode for those who had to pull the coach. . . . It was a pity but it could not be helped" (pp. 27–28). Various explanations were developed to explain why society had to operate the way it did (the innate abilities of the pullers and the pulled, etc.).[3]

Most notions of better societies are built on the idea that we know what is right but must take the next steps to do it. Bellamy's assessment was that inhumanity grew out of failure to even comprehend what could be. Le Guin helps us look at the constant trade-offs. In her story, Le Guin paints a related but prettier picture than Bellamy. No class of people in the fictional town of Omelas struggles in the dust and mud, pulling the rich up on a coach.

Sometimes when the macrolevel and the collective good are stressed, practitioners worry that the individual will get lost. Le Guin's story is one reason that social work must never lose sight of the good of the individual. Bellamy's coach metaphor reminds us, though, that if we look only at individuals pulling the coach or at those inside it or those on top of it, we may miss the big picture, the connections. We hope social

BOX 7.8	A FANTASTIC FICTION?

Someone arriving to do an assessment of Omelas, would find a picturesque world without our woes—a land of bright towers and bells, meadows and dance, and "faint sweetness of the air". If the visitor looked for social problems, he or she would find that the people lead full lives of prosperity, beauty, and delight. If the residents were analyzed, they would be found to be not simple but happy, content. The residents are appreciative of what they have. The visitor would realize how rare it is elsewhere to observe "mature, intelligent, passionate adults whose lives [are] not wretched" Author Ursula K. Le Guin (1975) asks, "Do you believe? Do you accept the festival, the city, the joy?".

An observer would soon learn about a small locked room in which a "feeble-minded" child of about 10 is kept, fed but uncared for, miserable, whining but unanswered, alone most of the time. A professional doing a diagnosis would say, "Aha, the negative side of the community finally shows through." And it is true that the child is a scapegoat or sacrifice, for if this pitiful being receives as much as one kind word, then all the ordinary woes of mortal life—infirmity, fatal disease, and cruelty—will be inflicted on all the citizens and the beauty, wisdom, and abundance of the harvest will disappear from Omelas. Is the child hidden? No, all children are brought to encounter the child when they are between 8 and 12. The knowledge of this child's existence rips into each citizen who experiences feelings of outrage and impotence, who weighs the suffering of the many against the suffering of the one, and who fears throwing away the "happiness of thousands for the chance of the happiness of one" (p. 335).

The citizens of Omelas understand the terms of this world. Moreover, theirs is "no vapid, irresponsible happiness. . . . It is because of the child that they are so gentle with children" (p.355–356).

What does this have to do with assessment? If positives are focused on exclusively, the distress will never be revealed. If positives are ignored in the search for negatives, then the story ends with the discovery that the community is letting a child suffer. Instead, a full assessment might compare this imperfect community with other imperfect communities. The unusually limited amount of suffering would be remarked on, as well as the fact that every single citizen acknowledges human suffering. Even when we are most horrified during an assessment, we do not ignore positives; we persevere, trying to understand more. Le Guin ends her story with a reference to exceptions. "At times one of the adolescent girls or boys who go to see the child does not go home to weep or rage. . . . Sometimes also a man or woman much older falls silent for a day of two, and then leaves home. . . . They leave Omelas, they walk ahead into the darkness, and they do not come back" (p. 356). They will not agree to the terms, those who walk away from Omelas; each one goes alone. An assessment of this community will include what keeps the system in place, what permits individuals to fortify their resolve and give up their community ties to adhere to different values, and what keeps collective protest from taking place. This material gives us a warning: If we come to assessment with a single view of what we will measure, we prejudge the question and miss complex meanings.[4]

workers can believe in happiness and festivals and not look compulsively for what is in the closet or cellar, but that they will do something when misery is found. Our ethics tell us that the happiness of the many must never come at the expense of even one, but if we blithely condemn the people of Omelas for their Faustian bargain, we condemn ourselves. Finally, it is to our benefit that the "narratives of humanists discuss a variety of communal, social, and psychological dilemmas" (Martinez-Brawley, 1990, p. xxiv).

We not only assess at the individual and communal levels, but we also care about the states of existence of persons and classes of persons. Despite this concern, we seldom take a planetary perspective when we assess dire human needs.

MOVING FROM ASSESSMENT TO ACTION

What will be the outcome of all this self-scrutiny, community examination, and assessment? Using the data, insights, and community contacts gained from study and assessment, appropriate steps become more apparent. Possible action plans include

- finding community connections for service users,
- mobilizing community resources for clients,
- selecting appropriate community interventions (development, problem reduction, education, sector mobilization, prevention, promotion), and
- organizing sectors of the community around an issue.

Look back to the beginning of the chapter to see a prime example of mobilizing legal resources and organizing a community around an issue. Erin Brockovich's story depicts the progression from assessment to action quite well.

Problem Solving and Intervention[5]

MANAGING COMPLEXITY

Activation of citizens and amelioration of problems can be an outgrowth of the community assessment process. The overriding task of the community practitioner is to help groups respond to the vicissitudes of life while keeping long-term community welfare on the agenda. A need for community problem solving usually exists when (a) there are many individuals or a class of people involved, with problems that are viewed as being large or serious enough to pose some threat, real or imagined, to the well-being of the community; or (b) the community experiences pressure due to problems in the operation of a system, such as problems in communication or socialization (see Chapter 4, this volume).

The practitioner intervenes, on behalf of an agency or organization or as part of a coalition, in the workings of the community system and its parts. Since the magnitude, complexity, and responsibility of the task of addressing either type of problem are almost overwhelming, what is needed is a way to think about the job. A guide that points up difficulties and charts ways of overcoming obstacles is helpful.

Here are 10 ideal steps that seek to explicate the thinking and behavior of a community practitioner engaging in problem solving:

1. Problem intake (identification, delineation of a social problem)
2. Selection of potential problem-solving actors (construction, location of the action group or system)
3. Determination of desired goals and potential consensus

4. Specification of types of action outcome (e.g., alleviate condition, control, rehabilitate, prevent, innovate)
5. Analysis of the facets of the anticipated intervention
6. Inventory and evaluation of resources
7. Specification of means/actions to attain goals
8. Selection of priorities (among problems, needs, and services)
9. Implementation of decisions made to reach solutions (allocation of resources)
10. Evaluation (ongoing and feedback)

We will collect data for our organization's own use to learn what should be done and, later, after a decision is made about how to proceed, we will collect additional data to support what we want from third parties who can effect solutions. During this process, we look to agency stakeholders for *insight intelligence* and look to community people who have a stake in a problem and its solution for *action intelligence*.

Community problems, public concern for those problems, and the authority to do something about them cross institutional, geographic, and special interest boundaries (Turner, 1963a). This makes community work and problem solving interesting and challenging. There are no clearly detailed road maps; worse, there is an absence of well-marked roads and the existence of many potholes. Any guide simply specifies the points of the compass that we need to chart our daily practice excursions.

Based on community problem-solving steps (see Chapters 1 and 3, this text), the emphasis may seem to be on all head and no heart. However, that view overlooks the emphasis on spirit found in actual practice. Belief in a cause and commitment are necessary because, in the final analysis, we must recognize that disturbances of the status quo are inherent in community organizing and planning. Resistance is to be expected. A second aspect of spirit requires that the practitioner learn to be comfortable with uncertainty. This is the companion of change and development. A third requirement is for the practitioner to master *feasibility management*. Practitioners must work with what is feasible at the moment they need to take action. Thus, the task of the community problem-solving practitioner is to constantly stretch the parameters of what is feasible and determine the moment for action. This, then, is the spirit of purpose and determination.

The knowledge gained from the activities described so far helps us to better understand all sectors and to comprehend the stated and unstated needs of our community; enables us to be better "curbstone caseworkers" (Ecklein & Lauffer, 1972, p. 133); and allows us to do a better job in handling our regular tasks. It helps us determine how much and how well our organization is in touch with the community (see Appendix A). This is essential if community-based programs are to be established. For example: Are materials available in each language extensively used in the area? Is the agency supposedly knowledgeable about issues concerning diversity yet still requiring adoptive mothers to stay home for the baby's first 2 years in a working- or middle-class area? Martinez-Brawley (1990) reminds us that community-oriented services are "as much an attitude as a collection of techniques" (p. 239).

Decisions must be made about whether to gear projects to a target audience or area or to the community at large. Some believe that it is misleading for an agency to say it has a community-based program unless it has a large reach (Rakowski, 1992). A satellite office does not necessarily mean a community emphasis.

A CONTINUOUS CYCLE

Assessment, problem solving, and intervention processes flow together. As a prime example, Bracht and Kingsbury (1990) conceive of community organizing in five overlapping stages: "community analysis, design and initiation, implementation, maintenance and consolidation, and dissemination and reassessment" (p. 74).

Box 7.9 illustrates the cycle of assessment, intervention, and reassessment. It provides an example of the use of a community-oriented viewpoint in planning a specific program. Note how closely the steps correspond to the fundamentals emphasized in this chapter.

This section has sketched the later phases of the assessment process. Additional forms of intervention will be addressed in subsequent chapters.

Community Reengagement

In Chapters 6 and 7, we have urged commitment to community study, analysis, and interaction. We end this unit with hopeful signs that activation of residents and professionals is increasing, as discussed in Chapter 5, which may result in more widespread use of community assessment and community social work.

HITTING THE BRICKS

Certain trends are appearing, such as home visits by some physicians and a requirement of community service or service-learning at public and private high schools. Bloomfield College in New Jersey requires students to take "a course called Social Responsibility and another called Society and Culture, as well as complete at least 30 hours of community service" (Sanchez, 1995). Nationwide, professors and students are being urged to become more engaged in the community around the campus, whether through work in new empowerment zones, outreach, or new partnerships (Ruffolo & Miller, 1994; Intercom, 2002). Political and community pressures drive some administrators in that direction. A sense of obligation to

BOX 7.9	STEPS TO ESTABLISHING SUCCESSFUL WORK SITE HEALTH PROMOTION PROGRAMS

1. Build community support.
   a. Assess community norms, culture, and activities.
   b. Establish community advisory board.
2. Assess work-site culture and social norms.
   a. Capitalize on opportunities to facilitate the program.
   b. Identify and modify existing barriers.
3. Solicit top management and union support.

4. Use employee input in planning.
   a. Conduct employee surveys.
   b. Appoint employee steering committee.
   c. Appoint work-site liaison.
5. Provide ongoing programming with environmental and social supports.
6. Conduct periodic program evaluation.

Source: Sorensen, Glasgow, and Corbett (1990, p. 160). Copyright © 1990 by Sage Publications, Inc. Reprinted by permission of Sage Publications, Inc.

assist and interact with have-nots motivates some professors. This hitting-the-bricks philosophy tries to ensure that the real listening and responsiveness, which can be by-products of concrete experience, will inform future assessments made by sensitized citizens as well as present assessments made by professionals.

Fields from library science to engineering are taking a second look at their relationship with the communities they serve and at new modes of assessment. As one facet of an aging-in-place community support program in California, Cullinane (1993) notes that: "a social worker walks a 'beat' in an inner city neighborhood. Through her contacts with merchants, bankers, pharmacists, and barbers, the social worker and the resources she represents become known to the community. In turn, she gains the confidence of the merchants, who refer their customers who need her assistance in maintaining independence" (p. 135).

Community policing requires officers who usually react to individual incidents and complaints to become "proactive in resolving community problems," to use a problem-and-prevention approach, and to work more closely with community residents (Greene & Mastrofski, 1988, p. xii). The idea is to get out from behind a desk, even if on a part-time basis, and interact with citizens, update one's sense of the place, and experience the area's problems and struggles but also its strong points and vitality. In *community* or *public health nursing*, the focus is on the needs of populations rather than on individual psyches or ailments. Since social work has already had community programs, this trend may not seem relevant, except that we know that we, like the police, had begun spending more and more time indoors, in relative calm and safety, avoiding "bad weather" on the "beat." Now we need to join hands with those in social ministry and other fields that care about community.

Professions such as dentistry and psychology add a community component to the individual component in order to further the goal of promoting the common welfare or to express their fundamental concern for the collective good. Current providers of community-based services and community care are already out on the front lines, as is now being advocated for others. However, some are struggling to make a niche for themselves, so they are working more closely with community associations.

Domestic and international programs can provide models for our engagement and service delivery efforts in this direction. England has community-based programs that make legal and counseling help and review more readily available through the use of volunteers. Social benefit tribunals, dominated by lay people, are one example. Citizen Advice Bureaus, which are lay advisory agencies, are another. Rural and isolated areas are less well served by these mechanisms (M. L. Levine, 1990), but England's programs point up that social work can tune in to the community.

APPENDIX A   ASSESSING OUR LINKS AS PROFESSIONALS WITH THE COMMUNITY

HOW ENGAGED AM I IN THIS COMMUNITY? WHAT IS MY/OUR PLACE IN THIS COMMUNITY?

Professionals need to make and use contacts. To analyze contacts we already have and to find out the degree of our engagement as human service workers in our community, we can start by listing who knows us, and who we know. For example, our agency Web page or annual report should reveal part of the local and regional professional network that we maintain. In whose newsletter is our agency mentioned? The *organization chart* (see Chapter 9) sketches our agency's organizational ties to governing, oversight, and funding bodies and a *task environment analysis* (see Chapters 2 and 11) can delineate our professional linkages with parallel and competing agencies. This process will help identify informal community partnerships. We can trace formal linkages, but personal ties are equally noteworthy; after all, social movements and other change efforts are built on networks of friends. Since a variety of people are connected with an agency, from fund-raisers to secretaries, multiple informal local networks of relationships exist. One way to tap such links and explore relationships among social actors is with a social network survey (Cross, Borgatti, & Parker, 2002).[6]

Capturing factual information about community links is a matter of becoming more systematic in identifying ties:

- Inventory community groups and organizations with which agency staffers are affiliated personally and professionally. Which of these could you call upon for assistance? For example, one social worker may have links with the National Guard, an Alzheimer's support group, and a youth gang, plus the usual memberships in professional associations.
- Look at a list of social institutions and mark those where you have some type of in due to knowledge, connection to staff, and so on.
- Have members of the agency's client and community boards also engage in this exercise; you may see different ties.
- List the organizational representatives in each coalition to which your agency or organization belongs.
- Do a *media audit*: Write down each media outlet that you rely on for information and star the ones you could tap for coverage.
- In the above evaluations, state whether the nexus is significant or superficial.

- If staffers are willing to do a collective exercise, Mattaini (1993) suggests an *ecomap*, substituting your agency for the family at the center of the graphic.
- Another group exercise has everyone who is part of the agency draw individual *sociograms*, a picture of who is connected to whom. These will graphically display the relationships and interactions within the group of agency employees and volunteers (Johnson, 1995). Results can be revealing; weak linkages or active dislike among subgroups within the agency may reflect weak ties and subgroup tensions within the community. See Chapters 9 and 11 of this volume and Valdis Krebs's "An Introduction to Social Network Analysis" Web site (http:/www.orgnet.com/sna.html).

Ultimately, we seek to be in right relationship with our community collaborators. We want to be accountable to the public and to truly involve service users in decision-making: that means actual input, not just ratification of staff plans (see Chapter 14). In summary, determining whether agencies are effectively and strategically involved in community and have a community orientation requires many mechanisms and must be an ongoing assessment procedure.

Discussion Exercises

1. Despite the many different parts of your community, what are the ties that bind? (a sports team, a widespread love of the outdoors, or a tendency to be stoical)?

2. Who or what do you view as the best source of information about community needs and why?

3. How might we give something back to a community (written observations, volunteer help, etc.) as part of any study in which we take the time of residents and leaders?

4. Compare Le Guin's "wretched one" (Box 7.8) with the Sudanese child described in critical theory in Chapter 2. Obtain a copy of the 2002 *St. Louis Past-Dispatch* week-long series "Neglected to Death" and compare the pictures of abused and neglected nursing home residents with Le Guin's description of the child.

5. What role, if any, do you think IQ plays in *justifying* who pulls the coach of society (a la Bellamy)? How do values and assessment fit together?

6. Discuss program accountability and assessment.

7. Construct a graphic of a subsystem relevant to your agency. This will require many telephone calls and much consultation with old-timers in the field.

8. Using Box 7.3 as a model, draw up a similar chart to evaluate the quality and comprehensiveness of social services for a social problem of your choice.

9. Using Figure 7.1 as an example, evaluate the needs and strengths of the area where you currently reside or where a parent or grandparent resides.

Notes

1. In the documentary *The Land of the Deaf*, a sign language teacher and deaf rights crusader refers to his hearing daughter and sighs, "I had dreamt of having a deaf child—communication would be easier. But I love her all the same" (review by Richard Harrington, *The Washington Post*, October 7, 1994, p. B7).

2. Johnson (1995) gives an example of a social impact statement: The local office of the human services department is closing, so a social worker decides to "determine the impact of such a change" (p. 276). National Park Service staffers use Rapid Ethnographic Assessment Procedures (REAP) to conduct social impact assessments, including the solicitation of community views about alternative courses of action. An excellent study on social impact and outreach in the case of epidemics or bioterrorism, commissioned by the Colorado Department of Public Health and Environment, lists many at-risk groups that should be considered. In alphabetical order, the outreach target population categories are African-Americans, Blind, Deaf, Developmentally Disabled, Elderly, Homeless, Isolated Rural Residents, Latchkey Children, Low income/Single Parent/Low Literacy, Mentally Ill, Migrant Farm Workers, Native Americans, Non-English Speaking, Physically Disabled, Tourists, and Undocumented Immigrants. Judith Cohen (2003) who has a background in social work prepared this study on emergency communications. See the Susskind profile in Kolb (1994, p. 317) on the impact of assessment, citizen participation, and public disputes. Also see Goldman (2000) and Barrow (2000).

3. Ironically, in our own era, conservatives often succeed in convincing the middle class that it is the poor (the have-nots) who sit on top of the coach snapping the whip—because of all the programs designed for them—while rich tax payers and hard-working capitalists (the haves) strain to pay their benefits and pull them along. For instance, radio talk show host Rush Limbaugh (1992) has said, "The poor in this country are the biggest piglets at the mother pig and her nipples. The poor feed off the largess of this government and they give nothing back. Nothing." (p. 40)

4. "The Ones Who Walk Away From Omelas," copyright 1973 by Ursula K. Le Guin; from the author's collection, *The Wind's Twelve Quarters* (1975); first appeared in *New Dimensions 3* (1973); Quotes are used by permission of the author and the author's agent, Virginia Kidd. For a different version of this theme of benefits to the many at the expense of the few, see Steven Spielberg's 2002 film *Minority Report* (Twentieth Century Fox Film Corporation and DreamWorks Productions, LLC, based on a story by Philip K. Dick). The film is set in the year 2054, when three humans called "precognitives" are exploited by the precrime unit to prevent murders. Leading political philosopher John Rawls (1971) sums up the principle in these words, "Each person possesses an inviolability founded on justice that even the welfare of society as a whole cannot override" (p. 3).

5. This section is based on work by Hardcastle (1992) and Turner (1963b). Also see Cox (1995).

6. See Chapter 11 in our text, plus Valdis Krebs's InFlow Software Web site (http://www.orgnet.com/).

References

Abatena, H. (1997). The significance of planned community participation in problem solving and developing a viable community capability. *Journal of Community Practice, 4*(2), 13–34.

Alcorn, S., & Morrison, J. D. (1994). Community planning that is "caught" and "taught": Experiential learning from town meetings. *Journal of Community Practice, 1*(4), 27–43.

All, A. C. (1994). A literature review: Assessment and intervention in elder abuse. *Journal of Gerontological Nursing, 20*(7), 25–32.

Amezcua, C., McAlister, A., Ramirez, A., & Espinoza, R. (1990). *A su salud*: Health promotion in a Mexican American border community. In N. Bracht (Ed.), *Health promotion at the community level* (pp. 257–277). Newbury Park, CA: Sage.

Anderson, D. B., & Shaw, S. L. (1994). Starting a support group for families and partners of people with HIV/AIDS in a rural setting. *Social Work, 39*(1), 135–138.

Anderson, J. (1981). *Social work methods and processes.* Belmont, CA: Wadsworth.

Atkinson, D. R., Morten, G., & Sue, D. W. (1993). *Counseling American minorities: A cross-cultural perspective.* Dubuque, IA: Wm. C. Brown.

Auerswald, E. H. (1968). Interdisciplinary versus ecological approach. *Family Process, 7,* 202–215.

Bar-on, A. A., & Prinsen, G. (1999). Planning, communities and empowerment: An introduction to participatory rural appraisal. *International Social Work, 42*(3), 277–294.

Barrow, C. J. (2000). *Social impact assessment: An introduction.* New York: Oxford University Press.

Bayne Smith, M. A., & Mason, M. A. (1995). Developmental disability services: Caribbean Americans in New York City. *Journal of Community Practice, 2*(1), 87–106.

Becker, J. (2001, April 26). Activists, politicians court minorities: Changing demographics could influence elections. *The Washington Post,* p. T16

Bellamy, E. (1960). *Looking backward.* New York: New American Library. (Original work published 1888)

Berardi, G. (1998). Application of participatory rural appraisal in Alaska. *Human Organization, 57*(4), 438–446.

Bisman, C. D. (1999). Social work assessment: Case theory construction. *Families in Society: The Journal of Contemporary Human Services, 80*(3), 240–246.

Blackwell, D., & Hunt, S. (1980). Mental health services reaching out to older persons. *Journal of Gerontological Social Work, 2*(4), 281–288.

Bloom, L. A., & Habel, J. (1998). Cliques, clans, community, and competence: The experiences of students with behavioral disorders in rural school systems. *Journal of Research in Rural Education, 14*(2), 95–106.

Bracht, N., & Kingsbury, L. (1990). Assessing the community: Its services, needs, leadership, and readiness. In N. Bracht (Ed.), *Health promotion at the community level* (pp. 66–88). Newbury Park, CA: Sage.

Brownell, P. (1997). The application of the culturagram in cross-cultural practice with elder abuse victims. *Journal of Elder Abuse and Neglect, 9*(2), 19–33.

Butterfoss, F. D., Houseman, C., Morrow, A. L., & Rosenthal, J. (1997). Use of focus group data for strategic planning by a community based immunization coalition. *Family & Community Health, 20*(3), 49–59.

Cohen, J. (2003, July 8). Colorado demographics and effective risk communication. Prepared by Market Views for the Colorado Department of Public Health and Environment. Retrieved July 12, 2003 from http://www.cdphe.state.co.us/bt/focusf/

Colby, I. C. (1997). Transforming human services organizations through empowerment of neighbors. *Journal of Community Practice, 4*(2), 1–12.

Congress, E. P. (1994). The use of culturagrams to assess and empower culturally diverse families. *Families in Society, 75*(9), 531–40.7777

Cook, D., Bond, A. F., Jones, P., & Greif, G. L. (2002). The social work outreach service within a school of social work: A new model for collaboration with the community. *Journal of Community Practice, 10*(1), 17–31.

Cournoyer, B. (2000). *The social work skills workbook.* Belmont, CA: Brooks/Cole.

Covey, S. R. (1991). *Principle-centered leadership.* New York: Summit.

Cowger, C. D. (1994). Assessing client strengths: Clinical assessment for client empowerment. *Social Work, 39*(3), 262–268.

Cox, F. M. (1995). Community problem solving: A guide to practice with comments. In J. Rothman, J. L. Erlich, & J. E. Tropman with F. M. Cox (Eds.), *Strategies of community organization: Macro practice* (5th ed., pp. 146–162). Itasca, IL: F. E. Peacock.

Cross, R., Borgatti, S. P., & Parker, A. (2002). Making invisible work visible: Using social network analysis to support strategic collaboration. *California Management Review, 44*(2), 25–41.

Cullinane, P. (1993). Neighborhoods that make sense: Community allies for elders aging in place. In J. J. Callahan, Jr. (Ed.), *Aging in place* (pp. 133–138). Amityville, New York: Baywood.

Dawson, S. E. (1993). Social work practice and technological disasters: The Navajo uranium experience. *Journal of Sociology and Social Welfare, 20*(2), 5–20.

Delgado, M. (1996). Puerto Rican food establishments as social service organizations: Results of an asset assessment. *Journal of Community Practice, 3*(2), 57–77.

Denby, D. (2000, March 27). Hell-raising women: And the men who love them. *The New Yorker,* 135–36.

Dolnick, E. (1993, September). Deafness as culture. *The Atlantic Monthly,* pp. 37–40, 46–53.

Durst, D., MacDonald, J., & Parsons, D. (1999). Finding our way: A community needs assessment on violence in native families in Canada. *Journal of Community Practice 6*(1), 45–59.

Ecklein, J. L., & Lauffer, A. A. (1972). *Community organizers and social planners.* New York: John Wiley & Sons and the Council on Social Work Education.

Elliot, N., Quinles, F. W., & Parietti, E. S. (2000). Assessment of a Newark Neighborhood. *Journal of Community Health Nursing, 17*(4), 211–224.

Fitchen, J. M. (1998). Rural poverty and rural social work. In L. H. Ginsberg (Ed.), *Social Work in Rural Communities* (pp. 115–133). Alexandria, VA: Council on Social Work Education.

Gallardo, W. G., Encena, V. C., II, & Bayona, N. C. (1995). Rapid rural appraisal and participatory research in the Philippines. *Community Development Journal, 30*(3), 265–275.

Garson, B. (1994). *All the livelong day: The meaning and demeaning of routine work.* New York: Penguin Books.

Germain, C. B., & Gitterman, A. (1995). Ecological perspective. In R. Edwards (Ed.-in-Chief). *Encyclopedia of social work* (19th ed., pp. 816–824). Washington, DC: National Association of Social Workers.

Glogoff, L. G., & Glogoff, S. (1998). Using the World Wide Web for community outreach. *Internet Reference Services Quarterly, 3*(1), 15–26.

Goldman, L. R. (Ed.). (2000). *Social impact analysis: An applied anthropology manual.* Oxford, UK: Berg.

Greene, J. R., & Mastrofski, S. D. (1988). *Community policing: Rhetoric or reality.* New York: Praeger.

Greever, B. (1983). Tactical investigations for people's struggles. In *Advocacy and the new federalism* manual. Washington, DC: National Public Law Training Center. (Original work published 1971)

Guterman, N. B., & Cameron, M. (1997). Assessing the impact of community violence on children and youths. *Social Work, 42*(5), 495–505.

Hardcastle, D. A. (1992). *Social problems, needs and social policy: A conceptual review.* Baltimore: University of Maryland at Baltimore School of Social Work.

Harkins, J. E., & Jensema, C. J. (1987). *Focus-group discussions with deaf and severely hard of hearing people on needs for sensory devices.* Washington, DC: Gallaudet University.

Harris, J., & Bamford, C. (2001). The uphill struggle: Services for Deaf and Hard of Hearing people—issues of equality, participation and access. *Disability and Society*, 16(7), 969–979

Hepworth, D. H., & Larsen, J. A. (1993). *Direct social work practice.* Pacific Grove, CA: Brooks/Cole.

Hopkins, K. M., Mudrick, N. R., & Rudolph, C. S. (1999). Impact of university/agency partnerships in child welfare on organizations, workers, and work activities. *Child Welfare, 78*(6), 749–773.

Huber, R., & Orlando, B. P. (1993). Macro assignment: Think big. *Journal of Social Work Education, 29*(1), 19–25.

Hunkeler, E. F., Davis, E. M., McNeil, B., Powell, J. W., & Polen, M. R. (1990). Richmond quits smoking: A minority community fights for health. In N. Bracht (Ed.), *Health promotion at the community level* (pp. 278–303). Newbury Park, CA: Sage.

Intercom. newsletter. (2002, Summer). *Wild Bill's Coffeeshop: A diversity initiative* (p. 7). Iowa City, IA: University of Iowa, School of Social Work.

Jackson, B. (1987). *Fieldwork.* Chicago: University of Illinois Press.

Jacob, S. G., & Willits, F. K. (1994). Objective and subjective indicators of community evaluation: A Pennsylvania assessment. *Social Indicators Research, 32*(2), 161–177.

Jeffries, A. (1996). Modelling community work: An analytic framework for practice. *Journal of Community Practice, 3*(3/4), 101–125.

Johnson, L. C. (1995). *Social work practice: A generalist approach* (5th ed.). Boston: Allyn & Bacon.

Julian, D. A. (1999). Some ethical standards to guide community practice and an example of an ethical dilemma from the field. *Journal of Community Practice, 6*(1), 1–13.

Kemp, S. P. (2001). Environment through a gendered lens: From person-in-environment to woman-in-environment. *Affilia, 16*(1), 7–30.

Kettner, P. M., Moroney, R. M., & Martin, L. L. (1990). *Designing and managing programs: An effectiveness-based approach.* Newbury Park, CA: Sage.

Kielhofner, G. (1993). Functional assessment: Toward a dialectical view of person-environment relations. *American Journal of Occupational Therapy, 47*(3), 248–51.

Kolb, D. (1994). *When talk works: Profiles of mediators.* San Francisco: Jossey-Bass.

Koss, M. P., & Harvey, M. R. (1991). *The rape victim: Clinical and community interventions* (2nd ed.). Newbury Park, CA: Sage.

Kretzmann, J. P., & McKnight, J. L. (1993). *Building communities from the inside out: A path toward finding and mobilizing a community's assets.* Institute for Policy Research; Neighborhood Innovations Network. Evanston, IL: Northwestern University (now available at ABCD Institute).

Kuipers, P., Kendall, E., & Hancock, T. (2001). Developing a rural community-based disability service: Service framework and implementation strategy. *Australian Journal of Rural Health, 9*(1), 22–28.

Lauffer, A. (1984). Assessment and program development. In F. M. Cox, J. L. Erlich, J. Rothman, & J. E. Tropman (Eds.), *Tactics and techniques of community practice* (2nd ed., pp. 60–75). Itasca, IL: F. E. Peacock.

Le Guin, U. K. (1975). The ones who walk away from Omelas. In U. K. Le Guin, *The wind's twelve quarters* (pp. 345–357). New York: HarperCollins.

Levine, M. L. (1990). Beyond legal services: Promoting justice for the elderly into the next century. In P. R. Powers & K. Klingensmith (Eds.), *Aging and the law* (pp. 55–79). Washington, DC: American Association of Retired Persons.

Levine, S. (2002, January 3). Word gets out on children's insurance. *The Washington Post*, Montgomery Extra, p. 3, p. 6.

Limbaugh, R. (1992). *The way things ought to be.* New York: Pocket Books

Luckey, I. (1995). HIV/AIDS prevention in the African American community: An integrated community-based practice approach. *Journal of Community Practice, 2*(4), 71–90.

Luey, H. S., Glass, L., & Elliott, H. (1995). Hard-of-Hearing or Deaf: Issues of ears, language, culture, and identity. *Social Work, 40*(2), 177–182.

Maluccio, A. N. (1979). *Learning from clients: Interpersonal helping as viewed by clients and social workers.* New York: Free Press.

Mancoske, R. J., & Hunzeker, J. M. (1994). Advocating for community services coordination: An empowerment perspective for planning AIDS services. *Journal of Community Practice, 1*(3), 49–58.

Marley, M., & Rogge, M. (2000). Lee and the amazing multifaceted community needs assessment. In D. P. Fauri, S. P. Wernet, & F. E. Netting (Eds.), *Cases in macro social work practice* (pp. 139–156). Needham Heights, MA: Allyn & Bacon.

Martinez-Brawley, E. E. (1990). *Perspectives on the small community: Humanistic views for practitioners.* Washington, DC: National Association of Social Workers Press.

Martinez-Brawley, E. E. (2000). *Close to home: Human services and the small community.* Washington, DC: National Association of Social Workers Press.

Martinez-Brawley, E. E., & Delevan, S. M. (1993). *Transferring technology in the personal social services.* Washington, DC: National Association of Social Workers Press.

Mary, N. L. (1994). Social work, economic conversion, and community practice: Where are the social workers? *Journal of Community Practice, 1*(4), 7–25.

Mathews, D. (1994). Community change through *true* public action. *National Civic Review,* 400–404.

Mattaini, M. A. (1990). Contextual behavior analysis in the assessment process, *Families in Society, 71*(4), 236–45.

Mattaini, M. A. (1993). *More than a thousand words: Graphics for clinical practice.* Washington, DC: National Association of Social Workers Press.

McEntee, M. K. (1995). Deaf and Hard-of-Hearing clients: Some legal implications. *Social Work, 40*(2), 183–187.

Meenaghan, T. M., Washington, R. O., & Ryan, R. M. (1982). *Macro practice in the human services.* New York: Free Press.

Meitzner, L. (2000, September). Now that I'm here, how do I begin? *ECHO Development Notes 69,* 1–4.

Meyer, C. H. (1993). *Assessment in social work practice.* New York: Columbia University Press.

Meyer, C. H. (1995). Assessment. In R. L. Edwards (Ed.-in-Chief), *Encyclopedia of social work* (19th ed., pp. 260–270). Washington, DC: National Association of Social Workers.

Miley, K. K., O'Melia, M., & DuBois, B. L. (1998). *Generalist social work practice.* Needham Heights, MA: Allyn & Bacon.

Mitroff, I. I., & Linstone, H. A. (1993). *The unbounded mind: Breaking the chains of traditional business thinking.* New York: Oxford University Press.

Molnar, D., & Kammerud, M. (1977). Developing priorities for improving the social environment: Use of Delphi. In N. Gilbert & H. Specht (Eds.), *Planning for social welfare: Issues, models, and tasks* (pp. 324–332). Englewood Cliffs, NJ: Prentice Hall.

Moore, S. T., & Kelly, M. J. (1996). Quality now: Moving human services organizations toward a consumer orientation to service quality. *Social Work, 41*(1), 33–40.

Moxley, D. P., & Freddolino, P. P. (1994). Client-driven advocacy and psychiatric disability: A model for social work practice. *Journal of Sociology and Social Welfare, 21*(2), 91–108.

Murphy, J. W., & Pilotta, J. J. (1983). Community-based evaluation for criminal justice planning. *Social Service Review, 57*(3), 465–476.

Murtagh, B. (1999). Listening to communities: Locality research and planning. *Urban Studies, 36*(7), 1181–1193.

Nartz, M., & Schoech, D. (2000). Use of the internet for community practice: A Delphi study. *Journal of Community Practice, 8*(1), 37–59.

National Civic League. (1999). *The civic index: Measuring your community's civic health* (2nd ed.). Denver, CO: Author.

National Public Law Training Center. (1981). *The advocacy spectrum training manual.* Washington, DC: Author.

Netting, F. E., Kettner, P. M., & McMurtry, S. L. (1993). *Social work macro practice.* New York: Longman.

Neuber, K. A. (with Atkins, T. A., Jacobson, J. A., & Reuterman, N. A.). (1980). *Needs assessment: A model for community planning.* Newbury Park, CA: Sage.

Oliver, M. (1990). *The politics of disablement.* New York: St. Martin's Press.

O'Looney, J. (1996). *Redesigning the work of human services.* Westport, CT: Quorum.

Parker, V., Edmonds, S., & Robinson, V. (1989). *A change for the better: How to make communities more responsive to older residents.* Washington, DC: American Association of Retired Persons.

Peters, T. (1987). *Thriving on chaos: Handbook for a management revolution.* New York: Knopf.

Powers, P. (Ed.). (1993). *Stirring people up*: Interviews with advocates and activists [monograph]. Baltimore: University of Maryland at Baltimore, School of Social Work.

Proenca, J. E. (1998). Community orientation in health services organizations: The concept and its implementation. *Health Care Management Review, 23*(2), 28–38.

Rakowski, W. (1992). Disease prevention and health promotion with older adults. In M. G. Ory, R. P. Abeles, & P. Darby (Eds.), *Aging, health, and behavior* (pp. 239–275). Newbury Park, CA: Sage.

Raskin, M. S. (1994). The Delphi study in field instruction revisited: Expert consensus on issues and research priorities. *Journal of Social Work Education, 30*(1), 75–89.

Rawls, J. (1971). *A theory of justice.* Cambridge, MA: Harvard University Press.

Reagan, T. (2002). Toward an "archeology of deafness": Etic and emic constructions of identity in conflict. *Journal of Language, Identity & Education, 1*(1), 41–66.

Robinson, K., & Walsh, R. O. (1999). Blunders of interdisciplinary education: Our first experience. *National Academies of Practice Forum, 1*(1), 7–11.

Rogge, M. E. (1995). Coordinating theory, evidence, and practice: Toxic waste exposure in communities. *Journal of Community Practice, 2*(2), 55–76.

Rosenthal, S. J., & Cairns, J. M. (1994). Child abuse prevention: The community as co-worker. *Journal of Community Practice, 1*(4), 45–61.

Rosenthal, S. R., & Levine, E. S. (1980). Case management and policy implementation. *Public Policy, 28*(4), 381–413.

Rosenzweig, J. (1999). Can TV improve us? *The American Prospect, 45,* 58–63.

Ross, L., & Coleman, M. (2000). Urban community action planning inspires teenagers to transform their community and their identity. *Journal of Community Practice, 7*(2), 29–45.

Rothman, J. (1984). Assessment and option selection [Introduction to Part 1]. In F. M. Cox, J. L. Erlich, J. Rothman, & J. E. Tropman (Eds.), *Tactics and techniques of community practice* (2nd ed., pp. 7–13). Itasca, IL: F. E. Peacock.

Ruffolo, M. C., & Miller, P. (1994). An advocacy/empowerment model of organizing: Developing university–agency partnerships. *Journal of Social Work Education, 30*(3), 310–316.

Sacken, D. M. (1991). And then *they* go home: Schools, reform, and the elusive community of interest. *Urban Education, 26*(3), 253–268.

Sacks, O. (1989). *Seeing voices: A journey into the world of the deaf.* Berkeley: University of California Press.

Sanchez, R. (1995, March 15). Western studies no longer sufficient: More colleges requiring education in other cultures. *The Washington Post,* pp. A1, 12.

Schneider, R. L., & Lester, L. (2001). *Social work advocacy: A new framework for action.* Belmont, CA: Brooks/Cole.

Sharpe, P., Greaney, M., Royce, S., & Lee, P. (2000). Assessment/evaluation: Assets-oriented community assessment. *Public Health Reports, 115*(2), 205–211.

Siegel, L. M., Attkisson, C. C., & Carson, L. G. (1987). Need identification and program planning in the community. In F. M. Cox, J. L. Erlich, J. Rothman, & J. E. Tropman (Eds.), *Strategies of community organization: Macro practice* (4th ed., pp. 71–97). Itasca, IL: F. E. Peacock.

Slack, M. K., & McEwen, M. M. (1997). An interdisciplinary problem-based practicum in case management and rural border health. *Family and Community Health, 20*(1), 40–53.

Sorensen, G., Glasgow, R. E., & Corbett, K. (1990). Involving work sites and other organizations. In N. Bracht (Ed.), *Health promotion at the community level* (pp. 158–184). Newbury Park, CA: Sage.

Soriano, F. I. (1995). *Conducting needs assessments: A multidisciplinary approach.* Thousand Oaks, CA: Sage.

Spradley, B. W. (1990). *Community health nursing: Concepts and practice* (3rd ed.). Glenview, IL: Scott, Foresman.

Stiffman, A. R., & Davis, L. E. (Eds.). (1990). *Ethnic issues in adolescent mental health.* Newbury Park, CA: Sage.

St. Louis Post-Dispatch. 2002, October. *Neglected to Death: Preventable Deaths in Nursing Homes.* Week-long series. Retrieved on July 31, 2003, from St. Louis Post-Dispatch web site: http://www.stltoday.com/stltoday/news/special/neglected.nsf/front?openview&coun%20t=2000

Strack, R., Magill, C., & Klein, M. (2000, November 15). Engaging youth as research partners in a community needs/assets assessment through the Photovoice process. Paper presented at 128th Annual Meeting of the American Public Health Association, Boston, MA.

Stoesz, D. (2002). From social work to human services. *Journal of Sociology and Social Welfare, 29*(4), pp. 19–37

Sullivan, W. P. (1992). Reclaiming the community: The strengths perspective and deinstitutionalization. *Social Work, 37*(3), 204–209.

Sullivan, W. P., & Fisher, B. J. (1994). Intervening for success: Strengths-based case management and successful aging. *Journal of Gerontological Social Work, 22*(1–2), 61–74.

Themba, M. N. (1999). *Making policy, making change: How communities are taking the law into their own hands.* Berkeley, CA: Chardon Press.

Thompson, A. (1999, April 8–14). User friendly? *Community Care,* 14–15.

Turner, J. B. (1963a, May). *The continuing debate: Community organization or community planning?* Paper presented at workshop on planning, group work, and recreation. Cleveland, OH.

Turner, J. B. (1963b, February). *Guidelines to a search for a theory of priority determination.* Paper presented at the Inter-Community Staff Conference, Case Western Reserve University, Cleveland, OH.

Viswanath, K., Kosicki, G. M., Fredin, E. S., & Park, E. (2000). Local community ties, community-boundedness, and local public affairs knowledge gaps, *Communication Research, 27*(1), 27–50.

Wang, C. (1999). PHOTOVOICE: Method. Retrieved July 15, 2003 from http://photovoice.com/method/index_con.html

Wang, C. C. (2003). Using Photovoice as a participatory assessment and issue selection tool. In M. Minkler & N. Wallerstein (Eds.), *Community based participation research for health* (pp. 179–196). San Francisco: Jossey-Bass.

Watkins, T. R., & Gonzales, R. (1982). Outreach to Mexican Americans. *Social Work, 27*(1), 68–73.

Weick, A., Rapp, C., Sullivan, W. P., & Kisthardt, W. (1989). A strengths perspective for social work practice. *Social Work, 34*(4), 350–354.

Weiner, A. (1996). Understanding the social needs of street-walking prostitutes. *Social Work, 41*(1), 97–105.

Wells, L. M., Schachter, B., Little, S., Whylie, B., & Balogh, P. A. (1993). Enhancing rehabilitation through mutual aid: Outreach to people with recent amputations. *Health and Social Work, 18*(3), 221–229.

Whitman, B. Y., Graves, B., & Accardo, P. (1987). Mentally retarded parents in the community: Identification method and needs assessment survey. *American Journal of Mental Deficiency, 91*(6), 636–638.

Whitworth, J. M., Lanier, M. W., & Haase, C. C. (1988). The influence of child protection teams on the development of community resources. In D. C. Bross, R. D. Krugman, M. R. Lenherr, D. A. Rosenberg, & B. D. Schmitt (Eds.), *The new child protection handbook* (pp. 571–583). New York: Garland.

Wiatrowski, M. D., & Campoverde, C. (1996). Community policing and community organization: Assessment and consensus development strategies. *Journal of Community Practice 3*(1), 1–18.

Wiley, C. (Ed.). (1994). *Journeys to self-acceptance: Fat women speak.* Freedom, CA: Crossing Press.

Wiseman, F. (Director, Producer, and Editor). (1968). *High school* [Film]. U.S.: OSTI, Inc.

Wiseman, F. (Director, Producer, and Editor). (1994). *High school II* [Film]. U.S.: Zipporah Films.

Witkin, B. R., & Altschuld, J. W. (1995). *Planning and conducting needs assessment.* Thousand Oaks, CA: Sage.

Worth, A. (2001). Assessment of the needs of older people by district nurses and social work: Changing culture? *Journal of Interprofessional Care, 15*(3), 257–266.

8

Using Self in Community
Practice: Assertiveness

When people see that you can get things done, they line up behind you.

D. KESSLER (AS CITED IN L. THOMPSON, 1990, P. 1)

Tiny steps . . . contribute to the making of the "hardy spirit."

S. PHELPS AND N. AUSTIN (1987, P. 227)

USE OF SELF

This chapter discusses competency and cognition in social work and then focuses on assertiveness as a pivotal skill.

Effective Use of Self

CORRESPONDING SKILLS
Consider how dancers and social workers are alike. Both respect highly developed use-of-self[1] abilities that contribute to professional accomplishments and benefits for others. Initiative and persistence also are basic to any success. While ballet and modern dance both require the same mastery over the body and an ability to relate to an audience, each requires specialized abilities; similarly, clinical work and community work draw on the same aptitudes while requiring the refinement of specific proficiencies.

The fact that we can draw on the same core skills means that elements of practice learned in one social work job, such as casework, are eas-

ily transferred to quite different employment settings, such as community organizations. Interviewing and information gathering, for example, are used in innumerable types of social work. Direct service workers might use these skills to elicit knowledge to improve a client's condition or to run a group more effectively, while community practitioners might synthesize information from interviews to undergird an exposé as part of social justice work. Dealing with an upset patient or community resident by telephone requires corresponding skills.

Social workers develop competence in relating to a variety of people and build on that competence in different aspects of practice. Coordination and advocacy are as basic to community practice as active listening and counseling are to clinical practice; assertiveness is vital to both. All five of those skills—coordination, advocacy, active listening, counseling, and assertiveness—involve communication. Social workers also attempt to heighten their self-awareness, that is, to become aware of skills and limitations in shift-

208

| BOX 8.1 | DRAWING ON RESOURCES, INCLUDING OURSELVES |

At a respite center for parents of totally dependent children, one child was deaf, mute, mentally challenged, and in a wheelchair because of cerebral palsy. Rick's mother communicated with him through story boards. He communicated with others through squeals and jerky arm movements. A social worker drawn to this eager youth attempted to find ways in which Rick could play and express himself. Wooden puzzles were tried successfully. As Rick mastered difficult ones, the worker began to suspect that he had more cognitive ability than had been detected during years of testing and residential programs. She contacted the hospital school, which he had attended, and the public schools for guidance—but to no avail. She spoke to the founder of the respite center and recommended,

on the basis of her observation and assessment, that a special education tutor be found for Rick. Her advice was followed. Within a year, the "retarded" child was reading.

The worker found other ways to open up Rick's world. At home, he often sat on the porch and waved to the traffic. He was particularly pleased when a driver for Pepsi began waving back. The mother and worker contacted the company to thank the driver and ask if he would be allowed to stop and see Rick. The driver not only came to call but also brought a miniature company truck and tiny cases of bottles that fit on the wheelchair tray. Thereafter, Rick whooped and waved his truck whenever the Pepsi truck passed his corner.

ing settings (Burghardt, 1982, p. 51). Direct service practitioners can apply their interpersonal skills (e.g., awareness of others' feelings, body language, and attentiveness) in their community work. They can tap into their feelings (Weick, 2000).

More basically, use of self implies that a social worker must be able to perform solo, because he or she may be the only person on the scene who can and will act. Principal dancers are thrown roses or presented with bouquets at the end of performances. Nobody brings roses to social workers at the end of a job; even so, we know when we have used our minds, hearts, and training to change lives. See Box 8.1.

SKILLS FOR CLIENTS AND COMMUNITIES

We integrate our abilities and experiences and apply them as needed. This is not just self-knowledge and development for its own sake. Social workers are engaged with individuals and with the larger community. Would a ballet be meaningful if the dancers simply performed the steps without regard to creative interpretation or audience appeal? Community connections are integral to our practice, as is making the community itself a better place. To do this effectively, practitioners need certain attitudes and a broad array of abilities. Attitudinally, community social work practice calls for a vision of communal life and the collective good. It also requires knowledge of human and social problems, of the social forces that keep many of them in place,

and of the interventions needed to address them. The decision to *consider the community* and to draw on all facets of our field does not mean a lessening of interest in or commitment to individuals. After all, all good social work must connect the personal to the social, and vice versa (Weiss, 1993). Considering community does mean getting a better sense of who we are serving and which of their needs we have not addressed, as well as discovering who we are not serving and why and forming new partnerships for service delivery and advocacy. It requires a set of skills, which will be covered in this and subsequent chapters, ranging from assertiveness to case management.

We want to be able to follow a concern rising out of our work wherever it leads us, confident that our skills are flexible enough to meet most of the challenges of venturing into new professional territory. We want to be able to follow clients and community residents into facets of their lives outside social services. We need to hear their pride: "It was me and Jack that stopped the train." See Box 8.2.

Expansion of Self

NEW ROUTINES—POLITICAL ASPECTS

Problems call us into the community if we allow ourselves to hear them. Ann Hartman (1990), former editor of *Social Work*, worries that we will use "psychic numbing to protect ourselves from the pain of seeing what is going on

| BOX 8.2 | WANTED: MORE THAN REHABILITATION |

Jack lost his legs from a slate fall in the mines. . . . [At the hospital] they were trying to rehabilitate him. . . . When the disabled miners first went out on strike with the active miners, Jack was out there in his wheelchair on the picket line. The disabled miners was out to get their hospital cards and their pensions. . . . It was me and Jack that stopped the train during the strike. We didn't have a 12-gauge shotgun like some folks say. . . . We had a sign with us that said *Hospital and Pension Card* on it. And we just held it up. We was beside the tracks, over on the edge, we didn't really block the train. But they saw our sign and they stopped the [coal] train. They pulled it back into the company's yard.

Source: Della Mae Smith, as quoted in *Hillbilly Women* (pp. 40–43), by K. Kahn, 1973, New York: Avon.

around us" (p. 4). She is concerned that we can tune in to one youth like Rick (see Box 8.1) but cannot deal with a junior high school where many students are on drugs. Yet, to tune out is to tune out the community, and we have trained our emotions, minds, and beings for a public purpose.

Dancers who have mastered floor work must still learn to jump and soar to be professionals. To some social workers, becoming proficient in larger systems may seem like leaps into the stratosphere; for them, a fear of falling or failing hampers their ability to address more complex problems head on. However, the transition for many social workers should be uncomplicated. Building on superior skills in relating, interacting, and listening, we can move on readily to collective interaction, political talk, and citizen action.

Social workers must enter the political world of civic and community participation, of self-governance and responsiveness to larger problems.[2] In this regard, Barber (1984) urges universal participation in public action, politics, and the "realm of we." He believes that most U.S. citizens see "politics as a thing or a place or a set of institutions—as, at best, something done by others," which means that we undervalue "the degree to which action entails activity, energy, work, and participation" (pp. 122–123).

Achieving true community and strong democracy requires a kind of talking and listening to which social workers can uniquely contribute. Barber (1984) believes that the talk on which democracy builds "involves listening as well as speaking, feeling as well as thinking, and acting as well as reflecting" (p. 178)—principles totally compatible with social work. He wants us to understand the political functions of *talk* for democratic and community-strengthening pro-

cesses. Barber lists "features of talking and listening in public," that is, an inventory of civic interactions and obligations:

1. The articulation of interests
2. Bargaining and exchange
3. Persuasion
4. Agenda setting
5. Exploring mutuality
6. Affiliation and affection
7. Maintaining autonomy
8. Witness and self-expression
9. Reformulation and reconceptualization
10. Community building as the creation of public interests, common goods, and active citizens (pp. 178–179)

Strong democratic *talk*, according to Barber, involves "deliberation, agenda setting, listening, [and] empathy," while strong democratic *action* involves "common work, community action, [and] citizen service" (p. 266).

We single out Barber's basic community activities and political talk because they seem more within our reach than legislative advocacy or getting an initiative on a ballot, but also because such civic engagement is a moral imperative. If we do not have the confidence and willingness to engage as citizens, then it is more difficult for any course of training to transform us into strong professionals.

Neither dancers nor social workers can stay in the wings and watch. To develop one's capacities and yet be afraid to get out on the stage of life would be a sad waste of ability, which—fortunately—seldom happens. However, some social workers are reluctant to go on tour (to perform away from their home base).

Some practitioners have not yet experienced using themselves in a way other than that demanded by the direct service part of their jobs, so they are untested in macropractice tasks. Too often, apprehension or inexperience restrains them from making the contributions they are capable of making at the board, association, service delivery system, neighborhood, or city level.

Since social workers have core aptitudes and solid competence in skills that are transferable, why are some of them uneasy about moving outside their current sphere of work? Like the ballet dancer who joins a modern dance troupe, a clinician faces discomforts when easing into collective endeavors. Confidence was established within a particular niche, and new proficiencies will have to be developed. To make the best use of one's professional self is difficult at any time, but especially when engaging in new aspects of social work.

In addition, the clinician may be uncomfortable utilizing new types of assessment or with the manner in which work in the community commonly is discussed. For example, a person accustomed to determining diagnoses using a manual or intuition and experience may be uncomfortable switching to weighing and calculating variables. Some persons making such a transition in practice express discomfort with the analytical language of *trade-offs*, *bottom lines*, *bargaining chips*, and *best practices* because they say they value openness, empathy, and doing the right thing for its own sake. Yet social work's very emphasis on genuineness, authenticity, and getting in touch with feelings may lead us to simplify ideas and follow impulses too easily at the community level (O'Neill, 1989). Mastering a full repertoire of skills will make us more thoughtful and confident practitioners.

Although we often have an uneven sense of our power and competence as practitioners, we see ourselves as capable of effective action. The question is "What action?" We may stick closely to what we have done—the familiar—and resist areas where we anticipate failure. Yet, by analyzing our anxieties and watching our behavior, we can deal with our attitudes and improve our performance (Drucker, 1999). "Knowing how to work with one's personal and emotional capacities is a fundamental skill in social work practice," states Burghardt (1982, p. 49).

ENHANCED AWARENESS

Cognition and Intuition

Social workers can become "pathfinders," to employ Leavitt's (1989) word. He compares and contrasts, "While effective problem solving requires mental rigor and hard analysis of the environment, and while effective implementing requires competence in getting things done through and with other people, effective pathfinding requires soul, imagination, personal commitment, and deep belief" (Leavitt, p. 40). Social workers must be visionaries and risk takers, able to formulate fresh approaches and challenge the status quo. Walz and Uematsu (1997) describe how some people, unfortunately, circumscribe themselves: "A fearful person may shut off many important interior messages and thus refrain from pursuing certain questions. . . . Or the person may lack the will or the energy to venture. In maintaining their carefully bounded existence, they will inevitably limit the range and volume of ideas, concepts, and metaphors that they would need to draw upon" (p. 24). Such professionals miss the freedom to experience the calling, the science, and the art of social work. Social workers who meld courage with creativity, on the other hand, can escape boredom and make valuable contributions to their profession and community.

Critical Thinking

Use of self includes use of one's mind—for example, self-examination, making judgments, taking actions beneficial to service consumers and community members (Berkman & Zinberg, 1997). The ability to think clearly is basic to effective community practice, service or advocacy endeavors, and public policy initiatives. Yet, too often promising projects are halted or misdirected by conventional wisdom and slipshod or slippery justifications—within our own agencies and from our adversaries.

According to Gibbs and Gambrill (1999), who describe reasoning errors that everyone confronts, the logical fallacies include the following:

1. *Ad hominem* (at the person): Attacking (or praising) the person, or feeling attacked (or praised) as a person, rather than examining the substance of an argument

2. *Appeal to authority* (*ad verecundium*): An attempt to buffalo an opponent into accepting

a conclusion by playing on the opponent's reluctance to question the conclusion of someone who has a high status or who is viewed as the expert

3. *Diversion* (red herring): An attempt to sidetrack people from one argument to another so as to never deal effectively with the first

4. *Stereotyping*: Oversimplifying about a class

5. *Manner or style*: Believing an argument because of the apparent sincerity, speaking voice, attractiveness, stage presence, likability, or other stylistic traits of an argument's presenter

6. *Groupthink*: The tendency for group members (e.g., of interdisciplinary teams, task groups, service-coordination groups, staff) to avoid sharing useful opinions or data with the group because they fear they might be put down, hurt the feelings of other group members, or cause disunity

7. *Bandwagon* [going with the crowd]

8. *Either-or* (false dilemma): Stating or implying that there are only two alternatives open to the group, which denies the chance to think of other options

9. *Straw man argument:* Misrepresenting a person's argument and then attacking the misrepresentation (pp. 116–119)[3]

Advocates who encounter these logical fallacies for the first time during meetings or debates can be waylaid. Even national experts can be thrown off track. The nation's best chance for comprehensive health reform was scuttled by television commercials paid for by self-interested insurers. Several fallacies were used by the typical couple, Harry and Louise, who bemoaned the overly complex bureaucracy and limited choice of doctors they said the Clinton plan would engender (West, Heith, & Goodwin, 1996). Reasoning errors and propaganda must be rebutted quickly because have-nots, in this case the uninsured, are hurt by misrepresentation.

Praxis: Self and Others

Whether engaged in clinical, community, or management work, social workers can be even more effective when they combine the creative and critical thinking just discussed with monitoring of their cognitive and affective reactions to others. Suppose the social worker is intense or unable to accept grumpy people or has not worked through feelings about authority (Falck, 1988); how will this influence community practice? *We react to others and others react to us.* If the social worker is known by a nickname such as "Uncle Roy," as Royal Morales of Los Angeles was, how could that effect community practice? More factors come into play than we usually discern. Consider how universally, even if subliminally, humans react to hairstyles (e.g., pigtails, dreadlocks, "old-lady blue hair") and to hair coverings (e.g., stocking caps, yarmulkes, babushkas) that differ from their own.

Reactions may have nothing to do with personality or appearance. Mulroy and Cragin (1994) describe an incident in which several students were given a field placement with a city agency where there were new supervisors who had not been part of the planning. Moreover, tensions in the agency were running high because of financial and top management problems. Two students, one Hispanic, did not feel welcomed or part of the team. According to Mulroy and Cragin, the other social work student "pulled out a notebook to take notes at a staff meeting, a behavior he considered routine and benign. . . . [He later reported,] 'Staff members jumped all over me. They asked me why I was taking notes. They accused me of being a spy for central office. Was I sent to take notes in order to report back to the Executive Director? They never trusted me'" (p. 28).

Use of self includes awareness and positive use of one's experiences, background, and characteristics (Christensen, 2002; Lee, McGrath, Moffatt, & George, 2002). To explain more fully, we will examine ideas from Alvarez (2001) and Gilson (2000) about critical reflection and attending to oneself as well as to the other party. Gilson suggests that we consider what will happen if we do or do not speak about our person and life. Alvarez suggests that we systematically explore—in a process-recording mode—how others perceive even our nonverbal communication. See Table 8.1.

PERCEPTIONS: HOW OTHERS SEE US

Alvarez stresses the "centrality of personal attributes and the perceptions of other actors, and the need to understand interactions in order to maximize personal and professional effectiveness" (2001, p. 197). Why are attributes and demographic characteristics so consequential, according to Alvarez? Because "class, use of language, sexual orientation, religion, and physical and mental abilities influence interactions, perceptions and results" (p. 199). The way we view

TABLE 8.1 PRACSIS Grid

CHARACTERISTICS of Practitioner:	Perceived by Practitioner	Perceived by Others (evidence?)	Effects of (describe, + or −)	Implications for Strategy and Practice
— Mental Abilities				
— Sexual Orientation				
— Religion				
— Ethnicity				
— Other (specify)				
—				
—				
—				
—				
ACTIONS (of practitioner):	Perceived by Practitioner	Perceived by Others (evidence?)	Effects of (describe, + or −)	Implications for Strategy and Practice
—				
—				
—				

Reprinted with permission of Haworth Press.
Source: From "Enhancing Praxis Through PRACSIS: A Framework for Developing Critical Consciousness and Implications for Strategy," by A. R. Alvarez, 2001, *Journal of Teaching in Social Work, 21*(1/2), pp. 216–218. Copyright 2001, *Journal of Teaching in Social Work.* Reprinted with permission of Haworth Press.

ourselves will not always be the same as how others view us, so proceeding can be tricky, and differences of many types may influence relationships with service consumers and/or our ability to deliver services. Think of the many meanings of wearing sunglasses (being old, having just had post-cataract surgery, being cool, being criminal).

Alvarez (2001) has developed a framework called PRACSIS, which stands for Practitioner Reflection on Actions, Characteristics, and Situation, by Impact and Strategies (see Table 8.1 for parts of her grid). She urges us to pause and reflect. The method involves taking a hypothetical, historical, or actual situation and applying impact analysis. For example, suppose you have been working in an Arab American neighborhood (situation). Is your religion or skin color more of a factor since the start of the wars in Afghanistan and Iraq (community perceptions, evidence of this)? What might be the effects of such factors? What are the implications for strategy and practice? Alvarez's framework is an invitation to think about how others perceive us. It can be used to anticipate or to analyze an interaction with clients or community members. After writing a succinct scenario, an exploration begins of how specific practitioner actions were perceived and affected the situation and how particular characteristics of the practitioner (race, gender, age, class, physical abilities, professionalism, facial hair) were perceived and affected the situation.

Disclosures: What We Reveal

Gilson (2000) counsels professionals to think broadly about self-disclosure and sense of purpose. Given specific circumstances, there are positives and negatives to letting others learn more about us. There needs to be general consciousness of others and of one's options, as opposed to automatically divulging or screening facts. Practitioners might ask themselves the following types of questions. If we are involved in community or advocacy organizations, do we share our experiences in a professional situation? What if our involvement stems from something of a personal nature such as having been a battered spouse? Should a professional share that she is a lesbian or that he is a religious minority? As a person who has used forearm crutches and a wheelchair himself, Professor Gilson discusses the pros and cons of personal sharing. Gilson finds, in his experience, that through "effective use of self, I am able to address and mediate against negative biases directly and by example. Students do not study me as an object, as might occur in a less direct relationship, but are able to view a disabled person as a source of power and knowledge. This phenomenon is very unusual for people with disabilities since we are most commonly studied as in need of services" (p. 127).

Nevertheless, Gilson maintains that there are multiple issues to consider in relationships. Should a social worker discuss a hidden condition (such as epilepsy or cancer) or a family situation (such as having suicide losses in one's family or having family members of different races)? What about some professionals' desire for privacy? Or conversely, what about someone from a marginalized group's desire to model a struggle with injustice? Is the professional overstepping boundaries or burdening others if he stresses his circumstances to a captive client or audience? What if others want to understand the professional's experience? Can venting or keeping the attention on oneself be detrimental to a client, a community group? Are we self-indulgently taking someone else's time with our story? There is much to mull over.

Becoming More Mindful

We must manage ourselves in every situation in every venue. This includes being aware of our public behavior. Since we are connected to and observed by the larger world, how we come across matters. A highly successful human service professional once offered this canny advice, "Never say anything negative on the elevator. Don't grouse or whine. When people ask how your work is going, respond briefly and positively." In other words, put the best face on things because one never knows who is listening. Social workers are taught, rightfully, to be genuine about their feelings. Still, there is a time and place for candid expression about one's job, bosses, colleagues, and community spokespersons. It is especially important for professionals to be affirmative about the group they are serving, regardless of any frustrations. Others rarely embrace the mission, cause, or projects of practitioners who undermine their operation's reputation. Therefore, affirm what can be affirmed and be aware of the public impression one is creating. The self-discipline to be composed and upbeat in public is part of effective use of self.

BELIEFS THAT SHAPE BEHAVIOR

Background

Use of self also involves understanding belief systems, including those about professional relationships (Locust, 1995). As we use the phrase, *belief systems* means deep-seated convictions about what is true and what can happen. Beliefs may involve ideology or expectations. For example, medical researchers discuss a *placebo* effect in which people improve after treatment that they believe helps them, and a *nocebo* effect in which people presume the worse and their expectations becomes self-fulfilling prophecies. Change agents should become aware of limiting beliefs and myths and seek empowering insights (Lappé & Du Bois, 1994, Chapter 2). One limiting community belief is this: Society is in sad shape and there is not one blessed thing anyone can do about it. Much of the pessimism in the United States about its youth, schools, or inner cities stems from citizens' sense of powerlessness. Anyone who pays attention and cares will feel overwhelmed at times, but societal cynicism and personal beliefs such as "I can't stand to deal with it" limit others and us.

When we read about a declining town or a dysfunctional foster care system, it is hard to imagine making a dent in the causal conditions, let alone the accompanying societal defeatism and the inertia that stops reorganization. However, we can face facts and still engage in mental processes that help us shift to considering what can be done. Sometimes to see the way clear involves reframing the problem. Sociologist Brenda Eheart reframed a problem and created a village for approximately 50 "unadoptable" children. She obtained money from the Illinois legislature for a comprehensive approach to foster care (Smith, 2001), with results that have been reported in *Mother Jones* and *Parade* magazines. In 1994, according to Walker (2002), "after 2,000 calls and a fax to the White House, Eheart received permission to buy part of a decommissioned Air Force base in Rantoul. She named the town-within-a-town Hope Meadows and set about placing newspaper ads for older people willing to work as volunteers with foster children in exchange for roomy, attractive homes at reduced rents. She also advertised for families who would take in foster kids with the goal of providing adoptive homes. Then she contacted the Illinois Department of Children and Family Services and requested hard-to-place kids— those who were older, more troubled, or in sibling groups" (p. 10).

Successful use of self includes a belief in one's ability to affect positive outcomes. Those with such confidence have no illusions about easy victories against foster care bureaucracy nationwide, against terrorism, against recession, against AIDS in Africa. Those with confidence do reject limiting beliefs about inability and embrace beliefs about capability.

Beliefs and Outcomes

Declarations such as "I'm okay, you're okay" and slogans such as "we can make a difference" are belief statements. It is hard to function with doubts about ourselves and the efficacy of our actions. Similarly, we must trust others. Let us explore the topic of beliefs and outcomes in more depth.

Others' Belief in Practitioner

Belief bonding is a shared belief by a social worker and a client, community cadre, or other action system that "the worker is competent, can practice social work, and has knowledge about the problems presented" (Bisman, 1994, p. 79). Belief bonding appears essential to effective social work and community practice. It is a necessary, although not sufficient, condition for psychological, social, and political interventions that require active participation by service consumers or community members. It is a critical component of compliance and of systematic, extended intervention. The social worker must not only be regarded as an expert but must also actually possess expertise and commitment. As Schilling (1990) asserts, most people prefer to be helped by someone who believes in the efficacy of his or her intervention (p. 256; see also Patterson, 1985, p. 205). When a client has the expectation that a worker is competent and the worker communicates self-confidence and fulfills a client's expectations, the client is more likely to fully engage with the worker in an intervention (Patterson, pp. 202–203). There is a correspondence at the group or community level: Confidence in a leader and a leader's methods and programs is critical. Yeich and Levine (1994) state that "high perceived personal competence and a high degree of political awareness can be seen as an important dimension in understanding mobilization of people" (p. 266).

Whether a client, group, or community association likes the worker is not at issue and may be important only to the extent that it initially allows for the formation of bonding and a relationship. The bonding also is more than a worker's empathy with a client. It is an active and *shared* belief by a client and worker in the worker's efficacy, the rightness of goals and actions, the proper division of responsibility for tasks, and that accomplishing tasks will achieve the goals (Johnson, 1995, p. 37; Kirst-Ashman &

Table 8.2 Relation Between Successful Outcome and Worker/Client Belief That Intervention Will Be Successful

	High Worker Belief	Low Worker Belief
High Client Belief	Best probability of success.	Success only if intervention can be mechanistically implemented
Low Client Belief	Success only if client involvement in intervention is unnecessary	Least probability of success

Hull, 1997, p. 33). Clearly, it is hard to proceed in an adversarial process between supposed allies. A joining of intent, if not affection, is required. Thus, workers must develop competency, believe that interventions will work, and convey a belief to their individual and group partners of the efficacy of the change process and the client's capacity to engage in it. Belief bonding also implies a shared belief by worker and client that the client has the capacity and strength to change and achieve the objectives (see Table 8.2).

PRACTITIONER'S BELIEF IN OTHERS

Similarly, the professional must have a belief that the group with which he or she works (whether drug addicts or people on probation) is worth the attention and capable of achieving goals. In social work, some professionals opposed welfare reform because they believed that recipients about whom they cared very much had little capacity to obtain or hold jobs. There is growing evidence that expectations influence outcomes. Absent teacher anticipation that their inner city or Indian reservation students will succeed, most such students will not. Research suggests that those who are served by teachers and other professionals achieve results only when the professionals believe the consumers of their services have potential (Furstenberg & Rounds, 1995). A teacher's beliefs can make him or her more effective—regardless of buildings, equipment, and other supports (Agne, Greenwood, & Miller, 1994). Recovering the notion that a teacher has the capacity to affect student performance has been an empowering insight (Greenwood, Olejnik, & Parkay, 1990). In comparison with belief bonding, there is less emphasis in this conceptual framework on the student, client, or recipient buying into the change process. Biddle and Biddle (1979), who write about the "encourager role," make this statement: "People respond to their perception of attitudes as these are expressed in gesture, word, and deed. If the worker acts as though he believes people are unworthy, not to be trusted, or

selfishly motivated, his influence is not likely to awaken generous initiative. . . . The beliefs he holds about human beings and his intentions, stated or implied, are important to the outcome in people's lives" (p. 365).

PRACTITIONER'S BELIEF IN SELF

Moving to action. Anyone can be overconfident and act when he or she should not, but just as frequently, people are timid about acting, which they regret later. Gambrill (1997) suggests filling out the following form as a way to reflect on a previous failure to act (p. 47).

Failing to Act

Just as we may act when we should not . . . , we may fail to act when this results in more harm than good. Research suggests that we often overlook ethical concerns related to not acting (omissions) (Baron, 1994). This exercise provides an opportunity for you to consider the consequences of an omission.

Situation:
_____

Omission (what was not done):
_____

Consequences:
_____

Discussion:
_____

Suggestions for discussion:

1. Would you act differently in the future? If so, what would you do and why?

2. What factors influenced your decision (e.g., agency policy, feared risks)?

3. Can you think of other examples of failing to act when you think you should have acted?

4. What could be done to prevent omissions that limit opportunities to help clients?

Barriers to action. Belief in oneself is not conceit but knowing one's strengths. It is requisite for belief bonding. You may make friends easily or you may be known for your persistence or physical stamina. Such talents or character traits can be pivotal as you take action. For instance, social work pioneer Vida Scudder founded the College Settlements Association but lost heart as family and social problems repeated generation after generation. Historian Spain states, "It may have been Jane Addams' prodigious staying power in the face of such adversity that propelled her, rather than Scudder to the forefront of the settlement movement" (2001, p. 118). Belief in oneself often grows with experience. A professional learns when it is helpful to be authoritative, such as during fund-raising functions and when testifying in court, and when it is harmful to be authoritative, such as during community feedback forums.

Discussions about overcoming fearfulness and negative thoughts about self usually are handled in counseling contexts, and yet getting stuck is just as relevant in macrosettings. At the community level, such insecurity translates as "Society is in sad shape and someone else more capable than I am should do something." Another limiting belief is that we or others are so deficient that nothing can change: "I would just make things worse." Social workers have to recharge their batteries and then turn to energizing others. Only those who have kindled themselves can kindle others. A first step for igniting one's own fires is to remember what energized us before—perhaps music, a newspaper story, or looking at photographs of street people.

Experiential Pointers on Moral Courage

Try these queries:

• "What words best describe the emotions you feel when hit with all of today's negative news?" (Lappé & Du Bois, 1994, p. 4)

• "If I were feeling strong and powerful, what I'd like to speak out about is . . ."

• "Where do you feel most capable of acting on this issue?" (Shields, 1994, pp. 8–11)

Try this visualization exercise from Katrina Shields (1994), who designed it for "those who want to act but are anxious or afraid of giving way under pressure" (p. 64). "The purpose is to give yourself a bodily sense of calm, groundedness and determination," (p. 64), says Shields. Here is the exercise:

Become aware of the soles of your feet . . . aware of the sensation of contact with the ground. . . . Imagine yourself growing roots down into the earth from the soles of your feet. . . . Imagine these roots drawing strength from the earth. . . . Now let that sense of strength travel right up your spine. . . . Be aware of your backbone, feel its strength and also its flexibility. . . .

Now think of those people you are representing here whom you care for; think of their faces, names . . . perhaps also beings of the future generations. . . . Feel the presence of all these standing firmly behind you, lending strength and conviction to what you need to express. . . . Be aware that you may be their only advocate in this situation. . . .

Open your eyes and keep that feeling in your body. . . . Now you are ready to face what comes from a calm and strong position. (Shields, 1994, pp. 64–65)

Belief in Community

Every community, every narrative needs a note of hope. In our own fields and our own ways, we must convey hope, as Rudy Giuliani did after 3,000 people were killed. Terrified citizens needed to believe in their mayor and themselves. No matter what he expressed at home, the citizens needed their leader in public to be authentic about pain and affirmative about courage. A columnist impressed by New York City's "spunk and soul" in the attack aftermath put it this way: "Leadership is a mystical quality, a combination of personal skills, innate magnetism and a heavy dose of circumstance. In this time of need and grief, the New York mayor—through personal presence, an overflowing heart and just the right words—has stepped forward to lead his city from despair to determination" (Fisher, 2001). Believing that it can be done, that we can move forward, that people will care, and that we will turn things around is contagious.

ASSERTIVENESS OVERVIEW

Background and Orientation

How does assertion fit into social work? Wakefield (1988) views it as "properly within social work's natural domain" (p. 361). A psychological or professional trait—like self-respect, confidence, problem-solving and social skills—assertion facilitates the fulfillment of our "intentions" (p. 361). Obstacles are external as well as internal: "Clearly, not all obstacles to minimally effective goal-oriented activity originate within the person. Environmental obstacles, especially in difficult environments where a person does not possess great power or social connections, can be a constant source of frustration and despair. Some degree of assertiveness is necessary in dealing with these obstacles, or actions would rarely be carried to completion" (p. 365).

The history, theory, and practice of assertiveness are linked with the *human potential movement, encounter groups,* and *sensitivity training; the women's movement and consciousness raising* (Enns, 1992); *business success ideas* (Siress, 1994); and *behavior therapy and social learning theory* (see Chapter 2, this volume). Although different terms—*taking charge, sticking up for yourself* (Kaufman & Raphael, 1990), or *empowering oneself* (Harris & Harris, 1993)—may now be utilized, ideas about assertiveness have entered into both the popular culture and the specialized training of professionals.

Assertiveness is a learned social skill and a communication style frequently discussed in terms of three response patterns: passive/ nonassertive, aggressive, and assertive. Before discussing these frameworks, we will examine assertiveness in a more personalized way.

The Psychology of Assertion

ASSERTIVENESS STARTS WITH US

Competent involvement in the processes of conflict and change, which lie at the heart of the social work enterprise, begins with articulation, with the overcoming of apprehension, with assertion. *Assertion* "is the act of standing up for one's own basic human rights without violating the basic human rights of others" (Kelly, 1979) in an "interpersonal context in which there is some risk of a negative reaction by the recipient" (Rakos, 1991, p.10).

From childhood, human beings engage in a process of sorting out the right to refuse from stubborn resistance, the desire to please from passive acquiescence, tact from timidity, circumspection from cowardice, and assertion from aggression. They learn to understand their motivations and behavior in this realm and to interpret signals and signs from family, acquaintances, and strangers. With difficulty, people learn to stand up for themselves and others and to deal with the consequences. To be a mature, assertive person means taking risks. The story in Box 8.3 speaks to a universal challenge: standing up to adults as a child (Sears, 1990, 1993).

A related predicament for adults is standing up when one feels like a child. In adulthood, Bower and Bower (1991) say, "lack of assertiveness makes millions of people feel uneasy and inadequate" (p. 2). Thus, assertiveness has been recommended for anxiety reduction (Cotler & Guerra, 1976, p. 3). Although circumstances may require anything from saying no to curbing abuse, the essence is similar: "When you assert yourself, you communicate your positive or negative feelings honestly and directly" (Zuker, 1983, p. 12). See Box 8.4.

BOX 8.3	WORKING UP NERVE: CHILD

Grace said we had to go get a chicken for dinner. [She] walked around in the yard, looking at all the birds, and finally spied one she liked. She chased it until she caught both the wings flat, with the chicken squawking the whole time. . . .

I didn't never think on killing nothing to eat and didn't want to do it. . . . Now Grace wanted me to kill the chicken and I didn't want to, so I tried to back away, only she said, "I know you are strong enough to do this, Jodi."

She stuck out the handle to the hatchet, but I couldn't take it. *I shook my head no and said, real quiet, "I don't want to, ma'am"* [emphasis added]. . . .

I ran into the barn. I climbed the ladder and went behind some hay and pulled it all over me till nobody could see me and stayed real quiet. I sucked in air and didn't give it back. Grace came and called out, "Jodi, I'm sorry if I scared you. It's all right if you don't want to help. Jodi? You don't have to hide. It's all right."

But *I was thinking on how I told a grown-up no and didn't do what she said* [emphasis added]. I knew I was going to get whipped. Paul and Grace would send me and Brother back because I was bad. . . .

I watched Grace real good the rest of the time before bed, but she never said nothing about the chicken or me not being good. She never said nothing about it ever again.

Source: Vickie Sears, "Grace" in *Simple Songs* Firebrand Books, Ithaca, NY. Copyright © 1990 by Vickie Sears.

BOX 8.4	WORKING UP NERVE: ADULT

Midnight. You sit in a hospital waiting room with someone who called you in a suicidal state and needs a consult and probably a prescription. The police arrive with a woman, high on drugs, who twists to get away. They handcuff her to a leg of the couch near you. She shrieks and tries to free herself. One officer slaps and kicks her. "Shut up," he yells. She makes a scene—cursing and ripping off her blouse—as the receptionist routinely goes over paperwork with the other officer. As the policeman stands over her, you are silent, sickened. You are concerned for the woman but also about the effects of all this on your client. You know things like this go on but a part of you wants out of there—you are not,

after all, the woman's advocate. You try to make sense of the situation. You consider waiting things out, covering the woman up with your jacket, pointing out to the policeman that she is defenseless even though behaving obnoxiously, going outdoors with your client, telling off the brutal cop, appealing to the receptionist, and asking the other officer to simmer things down.

"There are five key steps in assessing a situation and becoming aware of what you intend to do: your sensations, interpretations, feelings, desires, and intentions," says Zuker (1983, p. 56). Thus, I see → I think → I feel → I want → I will. However, we need not act on everything we become aware of.

FACING THE DRAGON

What should we do? Such elemental emotions and basic quandaries remind us of archetypes for stances people take in such situations. Pearson (1989) writes about six archetypes or ways of seeing the world that we live by: the innocent, orphan, wanderer, warrior, martyr, and magician. Each is appropriate sometimes as part of human development and life's quests. In professional life, we are no longer innocents, but the other archetypes remind us of states of assertion and nonassertion. In response to a dragon, the orphan "denies it exists or waits for rescue"; the martyr "appeases or sacrifices self to save others"; the wanderer "flees"; the warrior "slays"; and the magician "incorporates and affirms" (Pearson, 1989, p. 20).

Each of these reactions makes sense as we think about the varying responses one could have to the chaotic scene in the waiting room. *Looking at archetypes* (in simplified fashion) *purely from the dimension of how threats are met*, we suggest that the passive person approaches life as an orphan, martyr, or wanderer; the aggressive person approaches life as a warrior; and the assertive person approaches life as a magician. (A wanderer's independence also might allow assertion.) The assertive person, the magician, visualizes what he or she wants, develops tools, and takes action to make it happen while keeping all elements in balance.

An increase in assertiveness involves a more rational approach to occurrences previously dominated by uneasiness, if not fear. Depending on the person, becoming more assertive may re-

quire reevaluating a lifelong stance (e.g., martyr, warrior) or simply learning new scripts for specific situations. Ordinarily assertion, even assertion involving potential conflict, as in Box 8.4, is *not* as "dangerously risky" as nonassertive people are prone to think (Rakos, 1991, p. 66). We tend to make the other person into a dragon, as shown in Box 8.3. Training allows us to face realistic "negative consequences" while knowing that the probability is that "appropriate" assertion will actually lessen risks (Rakos, p. 66).

The Boundaries of Assertion

COMMUNICATION RESPONSE STYLES

Alberti and Emmons (1990) believe that *assertive behavior* "promotes equality in human relationships" (p. 26). Those acting assertively, according to Drury (1984), "make clear, direct, nonapologetic statements" about expectations and feelings and criticize in "a descriptive rather than a judgmental way" (p. 3)—for example, "I'd like you to hear me out." They describe their own reactions to a situation. We can see that this would be important to act effectively in the waiting room incident. Assertiveness is a strong, steady style, not a formula for automatic success.

When assertive people meet resistance, Drury (1984) says they persist in "following through on issues"; they also negotiate, compromise, and listen to others respectfully (p. 3). They are accountable and responsible for their behavior. Such a style is illustrated by *The One-Minute Manager*, which urges truth telling rather than wounding, not using feedback as an excuse to tell someone off, and getting to the point (Blanchard & Johnson, 1982).

Basic assertiveness includes such nonverbal behaviors as animation, maintaining appropriate eye contact and an upright stance, and verbal behaviors such as using "I" rather than "you" messages (e.g., "I am uncomfortable that we have not reached a decision"). This does not mean that the word "you" is forbidden but rather that the response is not an attack. Phelps and Austin (1987) illustrate a request for information as follows:

Boss: I want those reports to be more efficient and better looking next time.
You: What specifically do you mean . . . ? Can you show me an example or describe a report? (p. 227)

More advanced assertiveness might include working a room during a huge meeting reception (RoAne, 1988).

Nonassertive or passive behavior can result from being overly deferential to authorities or those established and well positioned in society. In the waiting room incident, nonassertion could involve doing nothing. Or a comment could be prefaced by "I know none of this is any of my business, but . . . " Eberhardt (1994) provides two examples of this style:

"I'm sorry to take up so much of your time."
"It doesn't matter, whatever you want to do." (p. 133)

A *person's real position* may be hidden by nonassertive behavior when expressions such as "I guess," "I wonder if you could maybe . . . ," "It's not really important," and "Maybe I'm wrong" are used. Such expressions aim to disarm the recipient by presenting a weakened picture of the speaker or writer. Tannen (1994) gives another motive: "Many people (especially women) *try to avoid seeming presumptuous* [italics added] by prefacing their statements with a disclaimer such as, 'I don't know if this will work, but . . .'" (p. 279). Nonverbal passive responses resulting in the same effect include don't-hurt-me stances, downcast eyes, shifting of weight, a slouched body, whining, hand wringing, a childish tone of voice, and the poor-me seduction of others. Both passive and aggressive responses can be manipulative.

Aggression appears in many forms. In the waiting room, it could take the form of a shouting match or speaking to the police officers as villains without acknowledging the drug reaction with which they are contending. Aggressive people, interested in winning and dominating, may want to prove themselves to the client and fail to check out the client's feelings in this situation. Aggressive behavior can go so far as to injure, demean, or diminish another person through words with an implied threat such as "you'd better" and through behavior such as using a raised, haughty, snickering, or snarling tone of voice or pointing. Some white-collar aggression is layered under propriety or disguised by parliamentary procedure. Such "indirect aggressiveness" or passive aggressiveness is often mentioned as another communication style (Phelps & Austin, 1987, p. 25) or "flavor" ("Life Would Be Easy," 1995).

ACTORS AND APPLICATIONS

Situations calling for assertion permeate all facets of practice and intimate life. We need assertion skills, and so do those with whom we work (e.g., welfare recipients who are seeking jobs). The prospective uses of assertiveness will differ greatly.

Assertiveness and Behavior

ACTING ASSERTIVELY

The basics of assertiveness, to Phelps and Austin (1987), are "saying no, expressing anger, recognizing the Compassion Trap, shedding the need for approval, giving up excessive apology" (pp. 1–2). (For example, we may, out of compassion, feel that we must always be on call or helpful.) Even though conflict is more commonly discussed, Rakos (1991) points out that "assertiveness comprises interpersonal expressiveness in both positive and negative contexts." A literature review by Schroeder, Rakos, and Moe (as cited in Rakos, 1991, p. 15) delineated seven categories of assertive responses: admitting shortcomings, giving and receiving compliments, initiating and maintaining interactions, expressing positive feelings, expressing unpopular or different opinions, requesting behavior changes by other people, and refusing unreasonable requests. For many people, the first hurdle is handling praise and criticism, not conflict. Therefore, in assertiveness groups—as in encounter groups—individuals learn to accept strokes and to give positive and negative opinions or reactions.

An assertive act may be quite simple:

- You ask questions of a lecturer.
- A colleague says you are good with protective service clients, and you respond with a "thank you" instead of disclaimers, false modesty, or a return compliment.
- Your coordinator asks you to review a paper. You thoughtfully mark up the draft to suggest reorganization.

Or an assertive act may be tricky to perform: Parents of a medically fragile infant feel that they are not getting straight answers on home care options and risks, and they want you to force the doctor to spend time with them.

TAKING THE LEAD

Assertiveness is not, at heart, simply a matter of demeanor, accepting praise, or adroit handling of social predicaments. It is *self-advocacy*:

- A social worker with seniority on an interdisciplinary team suggests that team leadership rotate, rather than having only the psychiatric staff be leaders.
- Parents of seriously emotionally disturbed children raise the point that they need respite care, not a proposed party, during the holidays.
- A frail person says to a volunteer, "Let me hold on to you instead of you holding on to me," thus asserting a modicum of control over her life.

Assertiveness is a *tool* to use in our work lives (Ryan, Oestreich, & Orr, 1996). It enables a quiet staffer to ask a vocal colleague to stop talking over him at staff meetings. It helps a social worker to sell her project to the rest of the staff at a meeting. It helps supervisors. Drury (1984) asks what an appropriate assertive statement would be under these circumstances: "The group has just spent 15 minutes of a 1-hour staff meeting complaining about clients, the agency, and the newspapers. Four items need to be discussed at the meeting." Drury suggests saying, "I'm concerned because we have four items we need to discuss at this meeting. I would like to move on" (pp. 171–172).

Assertiveness can be expected of us. Suppose that the head of your section asks you, as a lower level manager, to arrive at a staff retreat prepared to discuss your unit's strengths and weaknesses. Modesty and rigorous self-scrutiny seldom carry the day in a public forum; they also

can lower subordinates' morale. You need to draft forceful comments about the positives and give convincing specifics regarding what works in your unit, such as "We present technically complex information, that is easily understood by nonexperts and the media, in interviews and through fact sheets and issue briefs." Taking the lead or spelling out capabilities may be hard for people who have been conditioned not to boast (Tannen, 1990, pp. 218–224; 1994, pp. 38–39), but internal agency success can have benefits for the community.

Assertiveness and Gender

There is no formula for assertiveness. Still, some people are listened to more than others— and it is important to be heard.[5] Two people can say the same thing quite differently, according to Tannen (1994): "They may speak with or without a disclaimer, loudly or softly, in a self-deprecating or declamatory way, briefly or at length, and tentatively or with apparent certainty. They may initiate ideas or support or argue against ideas raised by others. When dissenting, they may adopt a conciliatory tone, mitigating the disagreement, or an adversarial one, emphasizing it" (p. 280). Tannen's comments are descriptive, not prescriptive. Assertion experts would call those whose behavior consistently and noticeably fits an extreme form of those patterns *passive* or *aggressive*.

More than communication skill can be involved. Tannen's communication research reveals differences by gender, race, culture, and context. Rakos, summarizing assertiveness research, concurs that content and style of communication will vary "according to situational, social, and cultural norms and values" (1991, p. 18). Regarding context, our behavior as individuals varies according to the situation (e.g., are we at the office picnic or a meeting?). Regarding diversity, there will be a continuum of assertive behavior for those of similar background or those of the same gender and striking differences between various groups. For example, one small study of faculty meetings found that men speak more often and longer than women. Tannen says that women are more likely to "speak at a lower volume, and try to be succinct so as not to take up more meeting time than necessary." In the study, the "longest contribution by a woman was still shorter than the shortest contribution by a man" (1994, pp. 279–280). There is no ideal length of time to talk, so long as everyone is getting a turn. "There is no *a priori* correct assertive response, though there are general behavioral guidelines for effective expression of feelings and desires," explains Rakos (1991, p. 24; Stevens, Baretta, & Gist, 1993).

In another study, personnel officers listened to tapes of prospective female employees—half with "unassertive speech features." Those *without* such features were "described as more likely to succeed in the workplace, more likely to be chosen for management positions, and more likely to be respected by coworkers" (Knotts, 1991). Examples of powerless language that makes speakers seem indecisive, tentative, and lacking in authority are tag questions ("John is here, isn't he?"), hedges ("I'd kind of like to go"), hesitations ("Well . . ."), and intensifiers ("Really . . ."). Men also are perceived negatively when they use unassertive speech features. Drawing from other studies, Knotts states that "men use speech to report, to compete, to gain attention, and to maintain their position in a social hierarchy," while "women use speech to gain rapport, maintain relationships, and reflect a sense of community" (pp. 1–32).

Tannen (1990) makes an intriguing, controversial contention along these lines: "Sensitivity training [and therapy] judges men by women's standards, trying to get them to talk more like women. Assertiveness training judges women by men's standards and tries to get them to talk more like men" (p. 297). She believes that learning each other's strategies and habits increases our flexibility as communicators. The authors of this text take the position that both men and women in social work can benefit from increasing their assertiveness. Assertiveness in its basic form, Phelps and Austin (1987) remind us, was never gender specific but rather a way of pushing past blocks or "confronting the unpleasant or difficult without getting squashed (or squashing others) in the process" (p. 80). Mele (1999) tells the true story of women in public housing who had felt squashed but mastered the Internet in order to push on past their local housing authority.

Assertiveness and Class or Minority Status

Analysis or assessment of assertive behavior requires an awareness of individual, gender, and cultural differences (Lordan, 2000; Ohbuchi & Takahashi, 1994; Zane, Sue, & Kwon, 1991). *Differences in what constitutes assertiveness* speak to the *emic* (culturally specific) nature of assertion, according to Marianne Yoshioka (1995). She

> When a request or demand must be made of a friend, Hispanics in the study were more likely to preface their assertiveness with a positive affirmation of the friendship.

studied differences in styles and values associated with assertiveness in African American, Caucasian, and Hispanic (mostly Mexican) *low-income* women living in north Florida. (Contrary to expectations, the Hispanic women were found to be the most assertive by conventional and Hispanic criteria.)

Yoshioka (1995) makes a number of useful observations:

1. Besides linguistic differences, there may be value differences between cultures. "Mainstream" assertiveness rests on rights, individualism, personal control, and self-reliance—values not necessarily equally endorsed by other cultural communities. There are differences regarding an individual's connections and obligations to others.

2. The basic message of a response must be identified apart from the language chosen to convey it. Responses may differ in word construction and intensity of language from the way a practitioner speaks but may still be considered a culturally appropriate, assertive response within the community.

3. There are differences within a population, just as there are between racial and ethnic groups.

4. People from varied backgrounds differ in where they place the boundaries between passivity, assertiveness, and aggressiveness.

> Language such as "Any time you push on me, I'm going to push you right on back" is viewed as assertive, not aggressive, by African Americans in the study. Hispanics placed more emphasis on correctly addressing the other party and using good manners. Caucasians and African Americans more often referred to consequences or obligations to elicit compliance from the other party.

Individual Caucasian reactions in one role-play in the study went from inability to formulate a response to threats to kill. Individual African Americans had fewer types of aggressive acts but used behaviors that other groups defined as aggressive. They were more direct and forthright in their strategies than were Caucasians and Hispanics.

Even if other studies find different particulars about these cultures, Yoshioka's conclusion is germane: Understanding specific ways a culturally different client may approach a given situation could enhance social work effectiveness.

Assertiveness and Being

Regardless of our background, for assertiveness or self-advocacy to be effective, we must learn to manage situations and ourselves (Lee, 1983; Lerner, 1991; Rivera, 1990; Zunz, 1998). Shoma Morita posits three principles (developed from Zen Buddhism) that appear relevant to effective assertive behavior:

- Know your purpose: Know what you want to accomplish, as (perhaps) distinct from what others want you to accomplish or what you want others to believe (i.e., you simply want to get through the meeting or encounter looking as though you care, not communicating information or having others adopt your position).
- Accept your feelings: Accept being angry, scared, and so on, but recognize that while you are not responsible for feelings, you are responsible for how you manage them and your behavior.

Each group of women in the study could stand up for themselves, but they acted according to different notions of appropriate personal conduct. This was particularly true when the other party in the role-play mistreated them. Would they accept an apology? Shove back?

- Do what needs to be done: Put your energy into developing and using the skills needed to deal with a situation, not avoiding or being anxious over it. Actively choose the strategy for managing the situation. (Morita, as cited in Clifton & Dahms, 1993, pp. 164–165)

PURPOSES AND BENEFITS OF ASSERTIVENESS IN SOCIAL WORK

Human service professionals must be able to communicate forcefully with clients and other providers, advocate their point of view, and obtain what they need from authorities. They can learn to be emphatic and avoid being wimpy.

Philosophy and Character

Assertion can be based in (a) security about ourselves; (b) confidence about our facts, research and homework; and (c) our knowledge that we have examined the situation carefully and have much to offer. While there are many points of view to which we should listen, ultimately we should share our perspective.

ASSERTION: A FLEXIBLE VEHICLE

To Hartman (1990), "there is no effective way of intervention that does not cut across all levels of possible resources and possible places of intervention" (p. 4). She envisions a social worker as "one who moves with competence across system boundaries and who follows the problem wherever it leads" (p. 1). Assertiveness is a particularly useful skill for such integrated practice, since it is applicable in expressive therapies, casework, group work, administration, community work, and social reform. It also relates to other key concepts—empowerment, personal power, advocacy, client self-determination, behavior modification, personal comfort level, and ethics. Those in human services see applications in specialized areas ranging from corrections to rehabilitation (Lange & Jakubowski, 1976, p. 241) and in the community. Alberti and Emmons (1974) discuss helping youth leaders apply assertiveness principles in working with young people in camp programs and as part of leadership training for community organizations (p. 87).

Social workers have a reason to acquire assertiveness skills, too (Butler & Coleman, 1997). Sometimes sticking up for our own place of work (e.g., family planning center) requires assertion due to the opposition's force. It is fairly common today for social service agencies to be rebuked publicly in front of elected officials by neighbors resistant to group homes. Assertive comebacks may need to be practiced for such moments. Equally important, we want to be able to promote public interests as well. A social worker may feel an obligation to argue for a teen center in an isolated hamlet even during a time of budget cutbacks. In such situations, though, as Rakos (1991) says, "assertive behavior is only one option for coping with difficult or problematic circumstances" (p. 5).

A MEANS TO IMPORTANT ENDS

Assertiveness may well be a prerequisite for working in the community, an experience that almost immediately requires us to interact with strangers, officials, and competitive organizations. *Assertiveness* is an umbrella term for many positive attributes: initiative, persistence, poise, spunk, alertness, responsiveness, the ability to defend oneself or being at the top of one's form. The development of assertiveness is meant to enable the social worker to

- identify, be in command of, and be comfortable with personal power and the assertion of basic human rights;
- provide a model for and teach assertiveness to the client and the client/citizen system, and help them realize and use their power; and
- use personal power appropriately in advocacy and other interpersonal, organizational, and political situations.

Although the emphasis is usually on *personal* assertion, the importance of examining *political* assertion (i.e., being the squeaky wheel that gets greased) has been urged as well. Alberti and Emmons (1990) believe that if we become "expressive enough, governments usually respond. . . .

The growth and successes of assertive citizen lobbies—minority/homeless/children's/gay and other rights movements, Common Cause (for political reform), AARP and Grey Panthers (for older Americans), the various tax reform movements—are powerful evidence: assertion does work! And there may be no more important arena for its application than overcoming the sense of 'What's the use? I can't make a difference'" (p. 15).

DISTINCTIVE NATURE OF ASSERTION IN SOCIAL WORK

Being personally or professionally assertive is viewed in human services as a respectful act, one implying that the other person can be (at least somewhat) trusted to behave responsibly, not to retaliate, and to remain open to a closer relationship. Lange and Jakubowski (1976) add two other aspects: respect for oneself and for the other person's needs and rights (pp. 7–8). The more difficult implementation of this philosophy focuses on interactions with involuntary clients, where respect and an awareness of clients' strengths are important but where issues of control and structure play a part in most communication transactions (Cowger, 1994, p. 263).

Professions that countenance tougher behavior, such as law and journalism, do not discuss assertive behaviors by that designation, with the exception of business management. Assertive, persistent business people are expected to "raise the muscle level when necessary" (Drury, 1984, p. 76). Moreover, few occupations outside human services emphasize respect as part of assertiveness. Good will does not necessarily underlie assertive transactions as they are defined and practiced in business. Other professions deemphasize authenticity and use assertiveness to obtain clients, information, or tactical advantages. Trial lawyers must be persuasive (Simons, 1976) and assertive—but not "boorish" (Magladry & Macpherson, 1994). For our profession, service users, and community residents, we are looking for "hardiness" (Lee, 1983).

Why Are Assertiveness Skills Important for Social Workers?

The query "What is the point of learning to be more assertive?" must be addressed before the practical problem of how to learn this mind-set and skill is outlined. We have just seen one reason—we have to be able to deal effectively with persons from other fields. There are even more important reasons. Assertiveness employed by those in our field can contribute to the interests of clients and citizens, the social worker's mental health, the social worker's physical safety, the social worker's success rate, and the voicing of social work values.

CLIENTS AND CITIZENS

Increased assertiveness benefits more than individual social workers. Those with whom we interact and those we assist (directly or indirectly) also benefit. When we are stronger, there is a valuable ripple effect. In addition, assertive people are more likely to speak up to government and nongovernment operations that have an obligation to serve citizens. After mastering assertiveness principles and skills themselves, some clinicians will engage in training with community groups, as well as assertiveness therapy with individuals and groups with special needs.

SAYING NO TO PROTECT STAFF AND SERVICE USERS

Angel and Petronko (1983) discuss such consequences as danger, "inferior patient care and consumer complaints" when nurses fail to say no (p. 142). Sherman and Wenocur (1983) relate the social worker's ability to say no to high-quality casework. One reason, then, to increase our assertiveness involves our concern for clients; our workload and our professional autonomy affect them. Another reason, pure and simple, is *mental self-preservation*, managing our own attitude and stress level by establishing fair but firm limits.

The following example of saying "No, you can't" to an employee illustrates how we need to be assertive to protect service users behind the scenes. Sharon Bower created a system for being assertive by describing, expressing, specifying, and spelling out consequences (Bower & Bower, 1991, Chapter 5). Using a modified version of Bower's format, Jonathan Smith (1991) gives an example of what a supervisor might say to a new professional:

DESCRIBE: "Bill, patient record files are confidential. When you are finished writing a report, please return the file to the cabinet and lock it. Last Tuesday and Wednesday I found three of your patients' files on the work table. I had to refile them."

EXPRESS/INTERPRET: "I was a little startled and concerned when I noticed you weren't doing this."

REQUEST: "Starting this week, please refile a file immediately after you are finished with it."

CONSEQUENCES: "This way I can be sure it gets done and you won't have to worry about a possible reprimand . . . if a file gets lost." (p. 231)

BALANCING SAFETY AND SERVICE

Learning to be more assertive can also contribute to *physical self-preservation*. Self-defense calls for decisive acts—running out into the street, for instance, or stopping a passing stranger. Practitioners are becoming increasingly worried about their safety in dealing with clients and the community. In response to this concern, there are workshops on "Street Smarts for Social Workers" and "The Intimate Terrorist" (National Association of Social Workers—Maryland Chapter, 1995) and the *Encyclopedia of Social Work* includes an entry on "Social Worker and Agency Safety" (Griffin, 1995). A recent study found that social work students are more likely to be exposed to verbal or physical violence *within* the agency than outside (Tully, Kropf, & Price, 1993, p. 195). As more students come from suburbia, with little experience of urban life, their sense of danger in field placements and on the job may be heightened. Increased confidence and competence will help quell irrational fears and prevent injuries in times of actual danger (Weisman & Lamberti, 2002). See Box 8.5.

From the District of Columbia to Hawaii, people feel or are in peril; therefore, professionals must develop "peacemaking" skills to deal with potential violence (Colburn, 1994, p. 399). Social work training allows us to help protect *others* from danger—for example, in the workplace, where we can plan ahead using threat assessment teams (Masi, 1994, p. 23). Assertiveness is needed to implement precautions, as well as to continue working effectively when precautions are not possible.

INCREASING SUCCESSES

Becoming more assertive in our outreach to the community includes believing that we are worth listening to, as the following experience reveals:

"I was invited to a dinner of the Board of the Department of Social Services, and I was the last agenda item. The president announced that we would be finished in time for the football game. I thought by the time they got to me I'd have 10 minutes. I spoke about the local jurisdiction putting an extra fee on the cost of issuing a marriage license and using that fee to help fund domestic violence programs. By providing them with this information, I got their attention. They stayed past 9:00 and that was the vehicle they ended up using. . . . That was the beginning of a community effort and we also established a rape crisis center, so it all worked out well" (Heisner in Powers, 1994). Because she resisted the impulse to cut short her remarks, this social worker helped create a new funding stream to support two additional community services.

Success may follow the discomfort associated with being invited to speak to a large or important group. Advocates can be asked to speak on their area of expertise and still be unnerved by short notice, the type of audience (highly visible leaders or unfriendly participants), or fear of failure. Many individuals dread being the center of attention. To overcome stage fright, we need to

BOX 8.5	PERSONAL SAFETY IN THE FIELD

A thoughtful student responded to the dilemma of serving the neediest while exercising caution by taking hold of the situation; the following is her advice.

"I feel strongly that social workers (and doctors and lawyers and . . .) have an obligation to work where our clients are. If I am unwilling to visit an elderly, homebound woman because I fear her neighborhood, how can I be comfortable, as her social worker, if she continues to live in such a dangerous place? For home visiting, I take several commonsense, precautionary steps. These include

- bringing a second person along when I feel a need for additional support (One older woman took her labrador retriever along for the ride);
- always telling someone exactly where I'm going, how to reach me (if there is a phone), who I'll be meeting, and when I'll be back;

- if possible, having the client or another known person watch for my arrival and even come out to escort me into the apartment/house;
- limiting visits to daytime hours, preferably mornings; and
- driving to appointments, so I can park close to the place I'm going and control when I leave. (I went through a period without a car and felt more vulnerable, although nothing actually happened.)

There is recognition in the surrounding area that we are a place worth having around. Our clients are a part of the overall organization, and they are also our neighbors. My sense is that we are protected by our reputation and our role in the community."

Source: Sara Cartmill, social worker.

go beyond mere speaking to assertively making a case for action—or inaction.

For those of us who help with charity auctions, annual and capital-giving campaigns, and phone-a-thons, a third difficult area could be asking others to volunteer or to give money; yet, success is vital to our organizational survival. Resource development requires networking and meeting with contacts and is highly reliant on using assertiveness skills (Klein, 1996, Chapter 12).

IMPLEMENTING VALUES

Being assertive allows us to implement values in many spheres—from how our office should operate to how society should operate. We think of organizers as being assertive on behalf of a community; however, psychiatric social workers, group workers, and other direct service practitioners do this too. A few years ago, in a conservative western state, community mental health services were being denied to the populace of one county because a few individuals did not want "crazy people to move to Happy Valley." Thus, although millions of federal dollars were available, the region had only two private psychiatrists and no services for low- or moderate-income people until the local National Association of Social Workers (NASW) chapter

worked with planners to write a grant and successfully crusaded to get county officials to approve the development of a mental health center. Once underway, that center served hundreds of local people, through the services of social workers with bachelor's and master's degrees, among others.

Operationalizing our values continues to require assertive stances. A church decides to feed the hungry, and neighbors object vigorously. To match the voting power of objectors, social workers associated with shelters and subsidized housing have had to learn to articulate the needs and reasons for their work. "Not in my backyard!" or "We have enough of those here already!" must be met with caring but persuasive counterarguments that property values are not negatively affected by nonprofit and community projects. We must protect individual citizens who are being humiliated and programs that are being discredited while dealing fairly with neighbors and listening to them (Gilbert, 1993; Plotkin, 1990). Assertiveness can be a resource for building collective and community endeavors.

BROADER CONCEPTIONS OF ASSERTIVENESS

Assertiveness is competent communication and more. Beyond learning new techniques, we want to increase our own competence and that of those we serve, as well as elevating our aspirations and theirs.

Becoming More Hopeful

Jansson (1990) links assertiveness with power and winning. He argues that assertiveness is "undermined" by fatalism and a victim mentality, which deny individual potency. These ideas are similar to the *irrational* beliefs that assertiveness training (AT) tries to overcome, such as that "one's past dictates one's future" (Lange & Jakubowski, 1976, p. 135). Fatalism contributes to societal cynicism and to our own passivity and submission. Jansson (1990) says it well: "The effective use of power requires people to decide in the first instance that they possess power resources, that they can use them effectively, and that they want to use them. The word *assertiveness* describes this proclivity to test the waters rather than to be excessively fatalistic" (p. 154).

To illustrate an assertive orientation to power *within* an agency, Jansson (1990) gives the example of a hospital social work administrator who learned to make successive requests for increased funds, even though a number of her entreaties were fruitless. Her justifications educated the decision makers and sent a signal of confidence. "Unlike departments with more timid executives, her department gained in size and stature as she assertively sought resources for her department," points out Jansson (p. 155). Expectancy can replace fatalism, a sense of potency can replace a sense of victimization, and hopefulness can replace helplessness (see Chapter 2). An assertive orientation to power *outside* an agency might involve governmental funding. Social workers must make regular personal contact with policymakers and test the waters by assertively stating what problems should receive priority attention, what services should receive full funding, and what cuts should be made in other sectors of the economy to protect social service resources. Here, as elsewhere, we must guard against fatalism, that is, thinking that our efforts are useless.

Phelps and Austin (1987) believe that "broadscale social issues . . . [cruelty to animals, drunk driving] can be influenced with assertive attention" (p. 243). They encourage such action but add a realistic caution:

Public and social issues are amenable to change through assertive action. It's also important not to regard assertion as a cure-all for every social

ill or as a simplistic way to achieve personal strength and self-worth. Real problems are stubborn and significant change requires patience and power. Speaking out on a subject you believe in will invite criticism or even censure—it is not easy. (p. 244)

Becoming a Client Ally

While empowering ourselves, we can work together with service users to increase their options. Within health care settings, for instance, assertive people will "perform a valuable function" if they acknowledge, support, and protect patients' rights (Angel & Petronko, 1983, p. 94; Knee & Vourlekis, 1995). Providers such as social workers can actively aid and abet patients in getting their rights in the concrete ways outlined by Angel and Petronko (1983), who note that providers can

- educate patients in the knowledge that they have both basic human rights and more specific rights as health care consumers.
- provide written information.
- help patients to evaluate the advantages and disadvantages of asserting their rights.
- assist patients in planning for successful assertion.
- promise and deliver support if patients decide to exercise their rights.
- if required, help the patient to navigate through the complaint process.
- when necessary, assist the patient in enlisting the help of an ombudsman or consumer group. (p. 95)

Becoming Open to Challenge

Another arena for assertiveness involves the relationship of service users to the experts in their lives. Angel and Petronko (1983), for example, suggest that nurses should apply their assertiveness to patients' rights, organizational and societal change, and new directions to influence the future. According to these authors, assertive skills can be part of "changing nursing's public image, influencing legislation, and influencing the health care system" (p. 233).

During the last few decades, advocates have worked to demystify law and medicine and to highlight the right to challenge lawyers, psychiatrists, and other traditional authority figures in a respectful, polite, and cordial manner. At a behavioral level, if a patient-consumer goes to another physician to get a second opinion without telling the first, that shows independence of mind and constitutes an *indirect challenge* (Haug & Lavin, 1983), but patient-consumers who are able to tell the original physician they are seeking a second opinion are assertive and capable of *direct challenge*. Assertiveness comes into play because the patient has a goal or agenda that should not have to be subordinated to the physician's personality or expectations. Those who become preoccupied with the doctor's feelings or get trapped by timidity may never get that second opinion; here nonassertiveness can have life-and-death consequences.

This trend has relevance in our field for three reasons. First, social workers are the beneficiaries of a new relationship between professions, and between consumers and professionals, that supports us as equal players on an intervention team. Second, however, we must stay alert to ways in which our service users are "consumers" and treat them the way we like to be treated by the professionals in our lives (Tower, 1994). Third and most important, we should encourage service users and citizens with whom we work to be assertive with *us*, not just with others; we need to be strong enough to engage in mutual participation, with initiative coming from either party (Gutierrez, 1990; Simon, 1990; M. J. Smith, 1975, Chapter 7, on prompting criticism). As a logical outgrowth, some social workers encourage the formation of client, resident, or user groups to play a watchdog role.

Becoming Bolder

Those who care about professional ethics may face situations that precipitate *voicing* or *exiting*. *Voicing* is another term or vehicle for being assertive.[7] A social worker cannot function effectively as a client advocate, a legislative advocate, or a community advocate without standing up for what is necessary in the circumstance. *Most books emphasize an individual's right to be assertive without discussing the responsibility to be assertive,* although integrity and responsibility while being assertive have been discussed (Angel & Petronko, 1983; Rakos, 1991, p. 8). See Box 8.6 on sticking one's neck out.

Communities often hide the existence as well as the nature of problems. Close examination is necessary to deal with this and to find out what actions can be taken to eliminate the problems. Social workers may have a duty to be impolite when politeness is keeping a social misery in place. Politeness can be a tool used by the powerful to evade challenges or hide venal purposes. An investigative reporting text by Williams includes skills to overcome secrecy and hostility. The author calls for guts and warns against gullibility. (He does not discuss psychological barriers or behavior modification techniques—common subjects in human services.) The focus is on *will* and willingness. Williams gives permission to go against societal norms to accomplish professional goals: "If you are afraid to argue, if you dread being shoved around, if you hate to go back after your polite requests for information have been refused—then you probably will not be a successful investigative reporter. If you believe something is true simply because a person in authority says it is true, you are in trouble" (Williams, 1978, p. 8). You probably will not be successful in our field either, although we may too easily permit passiveness in providers, consumers, and citizens. Then, when advocacy is required, not even the first step—assertiveness—has been mastered. Even popular magazines are beginning to reflect a broader view of bold assertiveness. Box 8.7 gives pointers on having "moxie."

BOX 8.6	IN PRAISE OF GIRAFFES

Chancing rejection and embarrassment, a staffer for World Vision went up to a conservative member of Congress from Virginia who was making a campaign stop in a shopping mall. She recruited him, on the spot, to take a trip to a famine site across the globe. This trip permanently committed him to eradication of hunger and misery (Harden, 1995). Many individuals risk far more, and their valor is honored by activists of different types. Senator Paul Wellstone of Minnesota risked his political career to stay true to his principles. Corporate and FBI whistle-blowers have risked their jobs to tell the public about covert practices of their organizations.

BOX 8.7	IT IS NOT ALL RIGHT WITH ME!

- Stating your needs unequivocally, with the sense that you have a right to state them, is half the battle.
- Sometimes, the truth hurts. Get used to it.
- You can be blunt without being a tactless cretin.
- When necessary, be just as ballsy on behalf of others as you are [on behalf] of yourself.
- Standing up for what you believe in isn't convenient? Sorry, you gotta do it anyway.

- Pick your fights carefully.
- Being assertive with people who can't fight back isn't being assertive, it's being a bully.
- If you're trying to make a stand just for the sake of making a stand, it'll be particularly obvious.

Source: From "Assertiveness Training," by comedian Rosie O'Donnell (*Know How*, 1995, p. 62)

THE CONTEXT AND THE SETTING FOR ASSERTIVE BEHAVIOR

Immediate Situation

A professional considers the immediate conditions. The necessity of stepping up to the plate occurs in varied ways. What would be considered aggressive physical behavior in ordinary circumstances could be quite appropriate in an emergency. Suppose that a social worker accompanies an adolescent to a medical appointment and the individual suddenly blacks out in the waiting room. This is hardly the time to wait one's turn or to be assertive with the receptionist—but it is a time for calling out. *Overcoming one's hesitancy* is a type of assertiveness that goes beyond *expressing one's opinion and desires*, as this and the next example show. A mental hospital in St. Louis had a fire requiring the evacuation of all patients to the auditorium, even those unwilling to leave their rooms. Social workers helped attendants and nurses to get downstairs individuals who, up to that time, had not left their floor in years and did not want to go. Holding the hands of the terrified patients and whispering consolation, the assertive social workers pushed and tugged dozens of hysterical residents to a safe location.

The Other Party

A professional is alert to potential misunderstandings. Is assertiveness appropriate to the circumstances? Forgoing assertive expression can be a matter of safety. Think about the protective service worker who is overseeing an office visit between a child and the parent who did not get custody. There are times when we should not try

to have our way through conspicuous assertion, particularly if the other person is going to feel disrespected or manipulated. We have to consider how our behavior will be interpreted and what other people's life experiences teach them to expect. As one advocate put it: "There is the risk of being misunderstood by people with whom you're trying to be in partnership. A lot of bruised and hurting people don't have the advantage of meeting, what we call, 'authentic persons.' So, the first shot they get, they're gonna take you because they have to react to somebody, and they react many times with violence. Or they not only act out on you all of these latent pains, but seek to beguile you . . . test you out. They've got a street keenness. They deal with you from their learnings, and their learnings are always 'people do you in, so you do them in before they do you'" (Dobson in Powers, 1994).

Limitations Rather Than Universality

A professional distinguishes legal rights from preferences. Although assertive rights can and have been stated, these do not have the force of law, as do the rights of airline passengers in our country to smoke-free flights. Our "rights" are culture and nation bound, (e.g., a visitor from the United States can request, but not require, someone in Spain to stop smoking in a restaurant). Typical AT stresses rights as if they should be available everywhere, but it may not acknowledge that our assertive requests will be *denied* more frequently, the further we get from our own social circles. A related criticism is that even within our own networks, some AT professionals do not caution trainees and fail to "alert them to and/or prepare them for the possibility of retaliation or other highly negative reactions from others" (Alberti & Emmons, 1990, Appendix C).

Internal Reactions to Situation

A professional considers interpersonal factors. The willingness to use assertion, and the resulting success of having used it, are usually situation or person specific. Think back to the child trying to stand up to her foster mother, Grace, over killing a chicken (Box 8.3). One professional can be appropriately directive with the cranky office receptionist but not with the kindly consulting psychologist. A support group facilitator handles the most difficult group members but turns obsequious around the church officials who grant the group free space. Social workers who have mastered most aspects of their life successfully may nevertheless doubt their ability to handle particular difficulties or demands: insurance companies refusing to honor certain bills, conflicts with suitemates over the use of space, negotiations with a client's landlord, responding to an angry community improvement association, or appearing on television to explain the death of someone in their agency's care. Those from outside a community will differ from the inside practitioners (Lee et al., 2002). Some of us appear totally unassertive with peers yet are fearless on behalf of clients and causes. Because of human and cultural variation, we will be more successful in some circumstances than others and should be comfortable with this fact in advance. We can continue to expand our competency.

Power Nuances to Consider

A professional considers political and sociological factors. Success in assertiveness does not depend solely on personality characteristics; gender, race, and social status play a role, too. Assertiveness is more likely to be "accepted from those who have traditionally had power, while it may not be accepted from those who have not had power" (Drury, 1984, p. 133). Thus, those who are part of the dominant culture more easily master assertiveness. In fact, Yoshioka (1995) argues, "Assertiveness as it has been defined is reflective only of the dominant sociocultural group." Put another way, assertive behavior— as usually described—is largely a white, upperclass, well-educated mode of expressing one's preferences (Rakos, 1991, p. 78). Still, assertiveness is something that is readily acquired, un-

like power, which could be described similarly. Transactions with persons from different backgrounds require us to be adaptable, considerate of the way their preferences are expressed, and aware of power differentials between us.

For practical reasons, Rakos (1991) suggests, many minorities will need and want to be biculturally assertive. They will benefit from knowing (a) what is considered assertive in two distinct worlds, (b) how to function effectively in the dominant system, and (c) what norms will be violated in their (sub)culture if standard assertiveness is applied without adaptation. Rakos also exhorts *trainers* to plan and "consider relevant cultural, ethnic, and religious variables" when they train people with distinctive backgrounds or work with special populations (p. 89).

Cultural Nuances to Consider

A professional considers the uniqueness of those with whom he or she will work. This topic was discussed more narrowly earlier, but it is worth reiterating that while we are all one extended community, unless differences are accommodated, true communication and bonding rarely happen. For example, if members of Group A speak in a subdued way and emphasize correct enunciation, and members of Group B speak with force and emotion and incorporate more slang, then B language may be perceived as inappropriate by listeners from the A group (Yoshioka, 1995). Certain religious, ethnic, racial, or urban subcultures are freer in expression, and their members may argue, interrupt, criticize, or laugh loudly. They are viewed as aggressive by those from other regions or backgrounds in our society. Conceivably, it may be more difficult to tone down to be acceptable—if that is desired— than to speak up.

Salcido (1993) describes culturally insensitive behavior that will alienate many who reside in Latino barrios, such as violations of preferred protocol; interviews with Mexican American social workers suggest that an emphasis "towards a task orientation, urgency, and lack of courtesies can lead toward cultural misunderstandings." The act of cutting off someone is fraught with possible misunderstanding, anger, and withdrawal in many cultures. An Anglo feminist who has finally learned to speak up to men may have to readjust once more in a home visit involving Latino or Muslim men, at least in an initial interview. Part of the bicultural challenge

Since assertiveness can take many forms and people speak in their accustomed ways, it is better to focus on intent, not communication rules. One evening in New York City, two passersby—"ordinary working stiffs en route to dinner and the tube"—see a policeman on Eighth Avenue manhandling and hurting a druggie or dealer already in handcuffs.

. . . a man in a gray suit, briefcase in hand, obviously no friend of the street drug culture, calls out: "Hey! Hey!" He hollers angrily. "Is that necessary?"

Then another voice rings out.

"You've got witnesses here," says a man who, in his manner and dress, could have been the first one's twin.

Spectators begin to gather and "getting the message, the cop finally lets up" (Springer, 1999, pp. 230–232).

involves negotiating new conceptual and behavioral parameters for assertiveness in any bicultural interchange.

The physically challenged and other differently abled individuals frequently are assumed to be passive; therefore, they are ignored in conversations or decision making as if they were invisible. Or they may be condescended to, whether they are service users, citizens, or peers. Busy professionals trying to be expeditious may not take time to listen to a slow-speaking person with cerebral palsy or a developmental disability who is making an assertive point.

Age, gender, and other factors affect the perceptions of those served by social workers, so we must be alert to what will be considered appropriate assertiveness. An older service user or volunteer may respond more to a commanding presence or be more attuned to civil but declarative sentences than to direct, firm "I" messages. We need to pay attention to how others communicate as we observe service users, volunteers, community residents, and institutional residents. Apologizing is especially common among older women who grew up in another era—tentativeness, overreliance on experts, and meekness may mask a strong personality underneath—and older men may feel expected or obligated to steer the conversation. Assertive attitudes and skills of our own allow us to be more proficient and mindful practitioners.

MODES OF ASSERTIVE COMMUNICATION

Human service professionals can be direct and straightforward in various modes of communication.

Being Assertive in Writing

Assertive writing is simple, to the point, communication. Even if it must be formal, it has no hint of obsequiousness. The advocate appropriately uses forceful or powerful words but the tone stays pleasant, not bullying.

WRITTEN EXAMPLES: INFLUENCING LEGISLATORS
Letters to allies and opponents—whom we want to support or kill a bill—can be expressed in a positive but potent manner. Below are actual letters sent by an influential social worker to a U.S. representative and a senator. Very civil and succinct, they contain powerful words such as *abandoned*. Words and phrases that establish their assertive tone are italicized.

Part of a sample letter to an ally. I am aware that you are in favor of this amendment and that you are working to have it included in the bill. As [title of professional position], I wish to add my support to the fight to ensure that people with mental illness are not *abandoned*. Please include my name in the list of people who call for a halt to the separation between mental and physical illness.

Part of a sample letter to an opponent. We cannot truly say we are a country "for the people" *unless we act* on behalf of the entire nation . . . [statistics and argument]. You play a *pivotal role* with respect to the inclusion of this option in the bill. As [title of professional position], I *urge* you to include this option in the final bill. We *must* stop separating mental and physical illnesses in our patient population.

WRITTEN EXAMPLES: TESTIMONY
Written or public testimony, in legislative and regulatory forums, provides a notable instance in which assertiveness is structurally built into the form of the communication and is less dependent on the writer's attitudes and skills. A shortened version of testimony is often read, and a longer version is submitted for the record. Those reading testimony stick to the script: "On behalf of Consumers Union, AARP-Texas, ACORN, the Texas Association of Community

Development Corporations and the Texas Low Income Housing Information Service, I appreciate the opportunity to provide testimony to the Senate Business and Commerce Committee . . ." No matter how timid the writer or deliverer, by tradition the opening and closing paragraphs of testimony are strong.

Testimony usually starts with an introduction of the group being represented and its organizational position on the issue at hand, such as this:

> Mr. Chairman and members of the committee, I am Mrs. Alice Willer, President of L. R. Vincent Homes for Children, Inc. The L. R. Vincent Homes is a nonprofit service offering substitute care for children, organized by a statewide federation of local agencies, each of which is guided by a citizens' board of directors. We thank you for giving us this opportunity to present our views on House Bill 5293.
>
> The member agencies of L. R. Vincent Homes across the state strongly oppose in principle the practice of surrogate parenthood and strongly oppose the Surrogate Parenthood Bill. (Flynn, 1985, p. 270)

Because testimony is time limited, those testifying are compelled to make a point and to skip unassertive asides. Weasel words and phrases and tentative or wishy-washy opinions are out of place in public testimony. Testimony does not hedge or bully. The tone and the choice of words are expected to be assertive, as the following excerpt illustrates:

> Thank you for this opportunity to offer our recommendations regarding reauthorization of the Low Income Home Energy Assistance Program (LIHEAP). LIHEAP is extremely important to low-income older persons who are exceptionally vulnerable to extremes in weather conditions. The Association strongly supports both LIHEAP reauthorization and certain modifications that we believe will improve program administration and funding security." [testimony March 25, 1990]

Aggressive language might be tucked into the longer version, but the oral version is careful; the cameras may be on. No matter how angry the testimony writer or presenter, the language is civil and respectful, in part because those calling hearings are often allies. One would never know from the following opening that women's groups had been endeavoring for over two decades to get a United Nations treaty ratified by the United States, as 169 countries had done before us:

> Good morning. I am Jane Smith, Chief Executive Officer of Business and Professional Women/USA. . . . I applaud Senator Biden for holding this hearing and Senator Boxer for chairing it. I welcome the opportunity to represent the working women who are members of my organization to discuss the importance of ratifying the Convention on the Elimination of All Forms of Discrimination Against Women, often called the Treaty for the Rights of Women. [testimony June 5, 2002]

Being Assertive in Speaking

SOME ARE ALREADY ASSERTIVE

By the time we train for a professional career, we have had many life experiences and have attended many workshops, perhaps even ones on assertiveness, so it is not surprising that a high percentage of workshop attendees or students are good with people and often able to stand their ground professionally. While some leaders- or professionals-in-training are aware of their shyness or timidity, others view themselves as "mouthy" or quite professional already. The latter sometime believe they are as assertive as they will ever need to be. However, confidence in attitude is not always matched by competence in skills.

OTHERS CAN LEARN THROUGH ROLE-PLAYING

Role-playing can highlight assertion strengths and weaknesses. Directions frequently stipulate that one person must present a claim or request an action for the other person to perform. Lange and Jakubowski (1976) emphasize that it is "OK for people to make reasonable requests and it is also OK to refuse them" (p. 102). Asking for a pay raise is a simulation with universal relevance and appeal. (In real life, a busy employer often appreciates directness.)

Employee: Thanks for seeing me.
Boss: Now what do you want?
Employee: I am here to ask for a $2,000 raise.
Boss: No one is getting one. Money is tight.
Employee: I am entitled to more money next year because of my recent contributions to the company.
Boss: We applaud your efforts. Maybe we can talk about salary in the future.

Employee: That's your call, but I'd like to talk about it now.

Boss: You still fall asleep at your desk. On the other hand, your suggestion did save the firm thousands of dollars.

Employee: Yes, that's correct.

Boss: OK, I'll take it under advisement.

Employee: That's great. I appreciate your considering the raise. When might you make a decision or contact me for further discussion?

Assertiveness is a skill available to micro- and macropractitioners. A switch-hitter in baseball is able to adapt batting skills to match left- or right-handed pitchers. We may not think about it, but as was discussed earlier, social workers also acquire skills that can be adapted to most levels and places of intervention. However, it takes practice.

PUTTING ONESELF TO THE TEST: ILLUSTRATIVE EXAMPLES OF ASSERTIVE COMMENTS

Example 1

Introducing oneself can reveal any of the three basic communication styles. Imagine yourself knocking on the door of the building manager to resolve a problem for a member of your organization. Imagine walking in, shaking hands, and saying: "My name is _____. I am from _____ agency. I am Mrs. Brown's advocate. She lives in your building." Your knock, walk, handshake, voice, and demeanor will convey passive, aggressive, or assertive attitudes.

Example 2

Here are varying responses to the comment, "I don't think family preservation programs work. Earlier positive research findings haven't held up." Read them all and then devise your own assertive response.

ASSERTIVE RESPONSES

1. "I think the results are mixed but tell me your thoughts on the subject."
2. Write one of your own: _____
   _____

NONASSERTIVE OR PASSIVE RESPONSES

1. Disagreeing, but not saying so.
2. "Usually we agree, but not this time. I don't mean to make you mad, but I think family

preservation is the way to go—not that I know the research."

AGGRESSIVE RESPONSE

"That shows how little you've read about it."

Example 3

You'll find this example more demanding. Read the two questions and four types of responses.

- The head of your community advisory board says, "How do you people [meaning "you African Americans," "you Jews," "you Asian Americans," or whatever is applicable to you] celebrate this holiday, anyhow?"
- An exasperated person says: "Why is it that you people [meaning "you men," "you women," "you secretaries," "you members of the cleaning staff," or whatever is applicable] always mess up our lunchroom?"

ASSERTIVE RESPONSES

1. Spoken deliberately, in response to the question about holidays: "Well, first, let's find a better phrase than *you people*. I'd suggest _____."
2. Spoken pleasantly, in response to the comment about the lunchroom: "I won't respond to that."
3. You decide that the person is naive or sincere, not hostile, and you answer the question in that spirit.

NONASSERTIVE OR PASSIVE RESPONSES

1. Smilingly changing the subject: "Don't generalize, now . . ."
2. Answering content of question while ignoring its form or tone: "It strikes me that the important thing about what you are asking is . . ."
3. "Not that I care about political correctness, but don't you think some people might react negatively to 'you _____ are always'? I admit that it bothers me."

AGGRESSIVE RESPONSES

1. Coldly: "I don't appreciate your tone."
2. "Some people around here think they can ask anything [or control everything]."
3. "Well, you people are worse, [swear word]."

1. "What's with you? Did you have burned toast for breakfast?"

2. Turning your back on the questioner and muttering to a peer: "I get so *frustrated* with this song and dance."

> *A young assembly-plant worker who considers himself hip places a call to obtain an appointment with his assigned employee assistance counselor. However, the counselor's next 2 weeks are already fully scheduled, according to the rather stuffy receptionist. Here are four possible responses to that news.*

1. "Say what? I'm serious. This here appointment is important. Don't give me grief. Check that book again. Then make him come to the phone. I ain't got all day, though. What, you'll call back?"

2. "Yo, girl, whass hapnin? Already booked! If the brother has a cancellation, my telephone number is. . . . Look, I'm not tryin' to give you attitude. I can only go to work again after I've seen the counselor."

3. "I need to see. . . . Sorry, sorry . . . my English. Maybe I not explain right. Tiempo is money. I can't get paid—and my family needs money—until the counselor sees. . . . How you say? I beg. Por favor."

4. "Tell the dude I need to bend his ear. You're damn right I'm raising my voice. Don't dog me."

> *Distinguish assertion from politeness and other factors in these telephone conversations. Note that assertiveness does not require a formal communication style. The same principles apply with slang, Spanglish, African American Vernacular English (AAVE), ungrammatical English, and exaggerated examples such as those above. Which response is assertive? Passive? Aggressive? Why?*

Gamble and Gamble (1990) suggest that we stop "automatically asking permission to speak, think or behave" and "substitute declarative statements for permission requests." They would say, "I'd like to know" such and such instead of asking, "Do you mind if I ask to have this point clarified?" (p. 222). As social workers, we need to be able to state our case firmly. Yet, a recent trend toward ending sentences with a

raised inflection when the person is *not* asking a question makes it even more challenging to speak in a manner that does not sound tentative. We can learn to make declarative statements and to make statements said without explanation or justifications. Both the first illustrative example given previously and Example 4 below provide samples of this form of assertive communication.

Example 4: Declarative Statements

Advocate: I want to look at the campaign finance records for the mayor's race.
City hall employee: Who are you? Why do you want to see them?

A nonassertive response would be: "I'm just a student. But can't I see them anyway? I'm writing a paper." But use of declarative statements would sound like the following:

Advocate: The report of contributions to each candidate's campaign is to be filed here. Are the reports kept in this office?
City hall employee: Yes, but we can't show them to just anyone.
Advocate: As you know, it is public information. I would like to see the reports.
City hall employee: Are you with the media?
Advocate: Please direct me to a place where I can read the reports or bring them to me. Thank you.

The advocate could cite a law that gives the public access, if necessary.

AT has specialized techniques. One of these, called the "broken record" (M. J. Smith, 1975), is an accepted and easily understood idea of persistent, calm repetition so that one's point cannot be ignored. Sometimes people feel odd practicing it because they normally do not talk that way, but exaggeration and repetition allows them to internalize this technique. The script in Example 5 can be read aloud by two individuals while a third critiques how assertive the "advocate" role-player is, with regard to tone of voice and ability to convey resolve.

Example 5: Broken Record Technique

Advocate: I need to speak to the principal about the Jones brothers he dismissed from school on Friday morning.
Receptionist: Mr. Markman is busy right now. Why don't you go down the hall and speak to those boys' classroom teachers?

Advocate: Thank you, but it is the principal I need to see. Here is my card. I represent the Department of Children and Family Services.

Receptionist: Maybe the guidance counselor is around this morning. She is usually pretty busy on Mondays, but I can try to find her for you.

Advocate: Thank you for your offer. However, I must speak to Mr. Markman himself.

Receptionist: You should have made an appointment. He never sees anyone off the street.

Advocate: I can appreciate that policy. I did call repeatedly Friday afternoon and was never put through to him. I'll wait until he has a break in his schedule.

Receptionist: Those boys were causing everyone headaches. I know why they were suspended indefinitely.

Advocate: Would you please call the principal and let him know their caseworker is here?

Receptionist: I couldn't bother him during a staff meeting.

Advocate: When will it be over?

Receptionist: In about five minutes, but he has other things after that.

Advocate: Please give him my card. I will wait over here until I can get 10 minutes of his time.

Left to their own devices, some would change the tone drastically. They would make friends with the receptionist and say something like this:

Advocate: Aren't you nice to suggest that? I'll bet you've been with the school for years and have seen everything. So you are probably familiar with our agency and what we need. Maybe I can sit with you and wait.

An ingratiating approach feels right but (a) risks getting caught in stalling, (b) drops the broken record strategy, and (c) loses the high ground—the emphasis on the right of the children to be in school and of the worker to deal directly with the decision maker.

Assertiveness comes into play when we have a goal or agenda, such as getting the boys back into school, and we adapt our behavior to that goal rather than to another person's personality or expectations. *Aggressiveness* arises when we subordinate the goal to a desire to respond forcefully to another person, such as the receptionist or principal. *Passivity* occurs when we allow the

goal to be overridden by intimidating signals (internal or as received from another person).

Selective ignoring means that we do not have to respond to every element or nuance of a remark made to us. *Fogging* is another technique. "Like a fog bank, you remain impenetrable. You offer no resistance or hard striking surfaces" (Zuker, 1983, pp. 134–135). If those in Ian's car pool tease him about losing his hair, he may tell them to knock it off. But there are times when we must listen calmly to annoying comments and criticism—say, from a state trooper giving us a ticket. Lange and Jakubowski (1976) call fogging and selective ignoring "protective skills" to use in response to "nagging" (p. 115). A fogging *rejoinder* to a crack such as "Ian, you're about as bald as they get, aren't you?" is designed to dampen potential confrontation. Ian can say lightly, without affect, "I probably am" or "You could say that." Assertion is about self-control more than controlling others. See Example 6. Another fogging response would be "You have a point."

Mentioned by M. J. Smith (1975), fogging is criticized by Cotler and Guerra (1976), who view it as passive-aggressive in psychological situations. Drury (1984) uses it at work to prevent arguments: "You [agree] with the criticism in principle without necessarily agreeing with the implied judgment" (p. 227). But she limits its use: "The technique stops communication and interaction rather than uncovering and solving problems. Humor, ignoring, and fogging are all techniques that should be used only for responding to teasing or attempts to start an argument, not for cases in which someone is criticizing to solve a problem" (Drury, p. 227).

Example 6: Selective Ignoring and Fogging

Client's boss: You are wearing an earring.

Client: Yes, I am. [not "So what?"]

Boss: Why would you do that? You know what people are going to think. I'll bet your parents are upset.

Client: It's possible they are.

Boss: I don't think men should pierce their ears.

Client: _____ [Act as a coach. What should your client say here?]

What was selectively ignored? What was fogged?

Two people can read the script below, with a third person giving feedback. Notice that the social worker does not give in and does not make matters worse.

Example 7: When Fogging May Be Useful

Advocate: Hello. This is Community Action.

Hostile caller: Is this Erin/Aaron _____?

Advocate: Speaking.

Hostile caller: Are you the person who has been out looking for housing deficiencies?

Advocate: Who is calling, please?

Hostile caller: I happen to be a property owner in this community.

Advocate: And your name, sir?

Hostile caller: Name's Ross Gibson. But never mind that. I wanted you to know that we landlords don't appreciate your actions.

Advocate: I see. Do you care to be more specific? [Taking the call seriously; not sure what the problem is]

Hostile caller: You're stirring up trouble with the county for no reason without talking with me first.

Advocate: I could have contacted you personally. [Starts fogging because the caller wants to ventilate, not communicate]

Hostile caller: That group of yours is against free enterprise, you're trying to help a bunch of lowlifes, and you're going about it all wrong.

Advocate: Perhaps you're right.

Hostile caller: I checked up on you and found out you're just a student. I bet that school of yours does not even realize what you are up to.

Advocate: I am a graduate student; you're correct.

Hostile caller: I have been checking with my lawyer, and I think we can get you jailed for disturbing the peace with some of your activities.

Advocate: _____

_____

Read the script to the end and then invent a fogging-style response (one that does not involve your supervisor, who is working under a deadline). The caller is not a client and need not be treated in the same way that a client would be treated. The idea is to avoid taking the bait, to let Mr. Gibson run down, and to get off the phone without getting an immediate return call from him.

Assertive Response Options

Standard assertiveness is a firm comeback without explanation or apology. "Assertions that contain explanations, acknowledgment of feelings, compromises and praise have been termed *empathic assertions*" (Rakos 1991, p. 31; Lange & Jakubowski, 1976, pp. 14–15).

Example 8: Handling a Power Imbalance Situation

The head of your interdisciplinary health team says, "You social workers always think you know better than physicians when the patient is ready to leave the hospital. Where did you study medicine?" Possible responses include the following:

- *Empathic assertion—contains an explanation:* "There's more than a medical dimension to knowing when a patient is ready to leave."
- *Standard assertion:* "You seem to like giving me a hard time, Dr. _____."
- *Fogging response:* "It's true that social workers have professional opinions about diagnostic related groups and the length-of-stay issue."
- *Timid response:* "Doctor, I don't know what to say. Maybe my supervisor should explain social work's concern to you."
- *Hostile response:* Looking up from your notes, you ask, "How do you spell anal-retentive?" (Clever, but say goodbye to your social work internship.)
- Your response: _____

Example 9: Another Role-Play

You work as a development director for a religious group that sponsors nonprofit institutions. You have been asked to be on the board of one retirement center. At the first meeting, you notice that there are no residents on the board and are told that there is no interest on their part. Later, you learn that the residents council of the retirement center has no real decision-making powers and functions as a social club. What will you say at the next board meeting? Remember, if you voice your concerns, you are being assertive—even if you cannot phrase everything in perfect assertive fashion.

APPENDIX A: ASSERTIVENESS TRAINING

Beliefs concerning who will benefit from assertiveness training (AT) and who should become assertive vary according to the type of practice. In community organizing, much of AT is part of leadership training. In direct practice, assertiveness is viewed primarily as a social skill tool to be taught to service users, often in a group context. There is less focus on a professional need for assertiveness or on serving as models for service users. In management and conflict resolution, emphasis is placed on the professional's ability to use assertiveness.

Working With or Being an AT Instructor

AT instructors commonly review spurs and blocks to assertion—inhibitors and other psychological and sociological factors (Angel & Petronko, 1983; Phelps & Austin, 1987). Much of the discussion of inhibitors focuses on *perceptual and cognitive obstacles* (Alberti & Emmons, 1990, p. 13; Rakos, 1991). Hepworth and Larsen (1986) suggest that feeling *overly* obligated to others, *overly* concerned with pleasing or impressing others, and *overly* fearful about negative reactions to being assertive are ways in which our irrational beliefs stymie action (p. 445).

Cognitive restructuring involves changing misconceptions and stopping self-defeating thoughts. Exercises are designed and used to

- change cognition (e.g., modify thoughts—ending patterns of always expecting the worst—and attitudes),
- pinpoint areas in need of upgrading (e.g., dealing with difficult people or handling putdowns), and
- practice new behaviors (e.g., refuse an unreasonable request or respond to criticism).

Following an exercise, coaches give positive or constructive feedback to participants. Lange and Jakubowski (1976) say that coaches

- describe the behavior,
- offer a possible way of improvement (in a tentative manner), and
- ask for a reaction to the suggestions. (p. 195)

For examples, see Alberti and Emmons (1990), Hepworth and Larsen (1993, Chapters 14 and 15), and Spolin (1983, p. 28).

One methodology for change involves keeping a log of situations and recording the types of behavior usually employed (Bower & Bower, 1991, pp. 64–65), then practicing the recommended assertive behavior until it becomes an available response for the situation. Logging

helps us focus on the behaviors and words, not imputed motives, of the other party; one examines what, not why. For this to work, we must examine behavior concretely in terms of the specific time, place, frequency, and situation.

The popular literature stresses remedies for specific weaknesses—for example, learning "how to avoid speech patterns that make you seem like a lightweight" (Siress, 1994, p. 49). A telling example is "This may be a dumb question, but . . . " The increasingly assertive person, this literature suggests, masters specific behaviors, such as making requests and eliminating mannerisms (Bower & Bower, 1991, p. 176); gives up particular behaviors, such as "gunnysacking," that is, saving up anger and frustration (Drury, 1984, p. 24); overcomes inhibitions (Phelps & Austin, 1987, p. 229); and gains inner strength and hopeful attitudes toward life's possibilities.

AT for Clients and the General Population

In seeking to enhance social functioning and self-esteem, AT may be combined with *problem solving, communication, stress reduction, coping, relaxation,* and *changing thought patterns* (Hardy, 1989; Hawkins, Catalano, & Wells, 1986; J. C. Smith, 1991) and, less often, with a social skill such as *networking* or a personal release skill such as *improvisation* (Spolin, 1983) or *humor* (Ventis, 1987). Persons in many different age, income, and cultural groups have had AT (Hsu, 1992; Planells-Bloom, 1992; Sue, Sue, & Ino, 1990; Wood & Mallinckrodt, 1990).

The diversity of groups with which AT has been tried is striking. A distinction is sometimes made between standard training for a general population concerned primarily with self-presentation and AT for those with clinical disorders, adjustment problems, or special needs. Professionals often view AT as a resource that can benefit clients. For instance, groups dealing with the aftermath of sexual abuse, sexual assault and rape trauma, incest, and spousal abuse often employ skill-focused activities, including assertiveness. It is interesting that assertiveness is recommended for both victims of abuse and abusers. Some would argue that batterers can learn to handle the outside world better through AT and hence take frustrations out less often on their partners. Other client groups that have received benefits include chronic pain patients (Subramanian & Rose, 1988), developmentally disabled adults (Bregman, 1985), mothers (Wayne & Fine, 1986), pregnant teenagers (Vardi, 1992), maltreated children (Howing, Wodarski, Kurtz, & Gaudin, 1990), and alcoholics (Orosz, 1982).

Many clients face daunting challenges. Kaysen (1993) tells of steps she took in leaving a mental hospital after 2 years: The hospital had an address . . . to provide some cover. . . . It gave about as much protection as 1600 Pennsylvania Avenue would have. . . . Applying for a job, leasing an apartment, getting a driver's license: all problematic. The driver's-license application even asked, Have you ever been hospitalized for mental illness? "You're living at One-fifteen Mill Street?" asked a . . . person who ran a sewing-notions shop in Harvard Square where I was trying to get a job. . . . "I guess you haven't been working for a while?" (p. 123).

Vague or sarcastic responses do not work in such circumstances. An assertiveness technique called *fogging* (M. J. Smith, 1975)—agreeing with what we can without letting the jab get to us emotionally—may protect the client emotionally while she summons a firm response about her qualifications for the job. A fogging response would be "You are correct," followed by the assertion, "I would do well at this job, however, because I have had time to practice many sewing techniques that I could teach to others." AT attempts to strengthen coping skills for those at a disadvantage in society (Glueckhauf & Quittner, 1992).

A few authors caution (a) that AT was evaluated as only moderately effective in a particular case (Nezu, Nezu, & Arean, 1991; Pfost, Stevens, & Parker, 1992); (b) that when overdone, AT has some negative associations in the public's mind that must be addressed (Ruben & Ruben, 1989); and (c) that AT can sometimes be faked by compliant individuals who go along by acting assertive (Kern & Karten, 1991).

AT for Professionals

Assertiveness also is targeted to service providers, who must be able to confront and speak to the point (Castle, 1995). Police and correctional staff and counselors—pastoral, youth group, and crisis types—are among those who have been trained in assertiveness. Providers may want to enhance their professional skills, but in some cases they are learning it to help their client groups. For instance, rehabilitation counselors have led groups for the differently abled, focusing on how to "deal assertively with persons who treat them in an overly protective or solicitous manner" (Lange & Jakubowski, 1976, p. 241). A consensus among helping professionals is that "the positive nature of assertion training and its focus on maintaining personal strengths and improving less effective qualities leaves many participants with a greater sense of self-worth" (p. 241).

Assertiveness in practitioners is often presumed but not mentioned in social work. In counseling sessions, practitioners must be able to say no, to set limits, and to relate assertively to clients by making requests and giving directives ("Will you please turn your chair . . . ?"), maintaining focus and managing interruptions, interrupting dysfunctional processes, and "leaning into" clients' anger (Hepworth & Larsen, 1993, pp. 131–135). The parallels with community work, where representatives must be able to make requests and talk precisely with county officials, are evident. Angel and Petronko (1983) and Drury (1984) provide useful discussions on implementing assertiveness on the job after completing AT.

AT for Students

Standard social work education alone apparently does not guarantee increased assertiveness (Pardeck et al., 1991), which is our rationale for including this topic. Several authors address the need for students to receive AT (Healey, Havens, & Chin, 1990; Richan, 1989). Cournoyer (1983) argues that "professional social work practice requires assertive self-expression skills of a high order" (p. 24). Hardina (1995) provides rationales for expanded skills in this realm: "Social workers may not be adequately prepared either to advocate on their own behalf or to improve access to services for consumers. . . . Without confrontation, it may not be possible to develop the power resources necessary to fight for social change that will benefit members of oppressed groups. Assertiveness training for social work students is an essential component of such education" (p. 13).

Advocacy, administrative, and community applications highlight the theme of breaking free of conventionality and can't-do thinking. Cummerton (1980) works with students to establish positive expectations because "an assumption of a negative response from the target system undermines our confidence: "Expecting a 'no' we act on this assumption and get the response we expect. . . . To get practice in reversing this negative chain of events, students were asked to reach out in a positive way to people they ordinarily viewed in a negative way, in order to create a 'yes' climate and develop ability to deal positively with a potential adversary" (pp. 4–5).

Cummerton asks students to think about a coworker they have been avoiding and then arrange a meeting or encounter with that person. Similarly, Garvin and Gruber (1978) note that as students enter a community, they are "quite concerned about rejection of themselves and their ideas: This can lead to presenting one's

position in either an overly aggressive or timid manner" (p. 5). They describe an exercise in which students involved in community organizing "identify organizing situations in which they experienced difficulty in expressing their positions" (p. 10) and role-play these many times until they feel able to handle them in the field. This type of training teaches students to think on their feet, according to Hardina (1995).

Discussion Exercises

1. Assume that you will be working temporarily with a health service delivery system on Native American land. Besides learning about tribal and federal leadership systems, you want to know this tribe's customs before you challenge anyone in your standard assertive manner. You once read a parable about a Native American who wanted to be on equal terms with every person he encountered, so he either brought individuals up to or down to his level, depending on their station in life. How can outsiders learn what is myth or

reality regarding assertion beliefs for Native people or members of any other culture unfamiliar to us?

2. Our work lives are saturated with phrases about impotence, such as *falling through the cracks*, *bogged down in the bureaucracy*, and *a half loaf is better than none*. What is our field's equivalent to *going for the gold* (sports), the cure (medicine), the scoop (journalism), or the Nobel Prize (science)?

Notes

1. Conscious *use of self* refers to honing and maximizing practice skills and being aware of matters that could cloud judgment. As one social worker put it, "Probably the most important thing they teach you in social work school is the conscious use of self; that will serve you extremely well as an administrator and as a community organizer. Whether it's with your staff, your community support, or with policymakers, you have to pose your language in ways to bring about the outcome that you want. . . . If you can put what you want them to know in ways that they are able to hear, you have a much better chance of getting them to do what you want them to do." (Judith Vaughan Prather, executive director of the Montgomery county Women's Commission) interviewed by Barbara Bikoff for *Challenging* in Powers, 1994. Regarding women's use of self in leadership roles, see Healey, Havens, and Chin (1990). Spolin (1983) described how to use oneself (e.g., "physicalization," p. 15).

2. A full skill repertoire includes the ability not only to perform but also to sustain our performance by securing needed resources. Those in the arts and in social welfare have to be concerned with national politics in regard to government funding.

3. Reprinted with permission of Sage Publications, Inc.

4. From *Social Work Practice: A Critical Thinker's Guide* by Eileen Gambrill, 1997. Copyright 1997, Oxford University Press, Inc. Used by permission of Oxford University Press, Inc.

5. Attitudes of the sender and receiver influence whether someone is listened to, but we focus on the sender. Status differences and differences between social work and other professions echo gender differences. Some have no desire to move toward their opposite and defend noncompetitive stances. Similarly, no matter how assertive someone is, some hearers will experience him or her as aggressive or passive because of their own mind-sets or because they do not even bother to tune in.

6. Linda Heisner, director of the Maryland Office of Family and Children Services, interviewed by Cathy Raab for *Challenging*, in Powers, 1994.

7. *Voice* and *exit* are terms used by Albert Hirschman to illustrate two responses to a perceived wrong. Laura Nader (1980, p. 41) applies them to the way we deal with complaints and small injustices.

8. The Reverend Vernon Dobson discussing people in and out of the justice system, in an interview by Paul Collinson Streng for *Challenging*, in Powers, 1994.

References

Agne, K. J., Greenwood, G. E., & Miller, L. D. (1994). Relationships between teacher belief systems and teacher effectiveness. *Journal of Research and Development in Education, 27*(3), 141–152.

Alberti, R. E., & Emmons, M. L. (1974). *Your perfect right: A guide to assertive behavior* (2nd ed.). San Luis Obispo, CA: Impact.

Alberti, R. E., & Emmons, M. L. (1990). *Your perfect right: A guide to assertive behavior* (6th prof. ed.). San Luis Obispo, CA: Impact.

Alvarez, A. R. (2001). Enhancing praxis through PRACSIS: A framework for developing critical consciousness and implications for strategy. *Journal of Teaching in Social Work, 21*(1/2), 195–220.

Angel, G., & Petronko, D. K. (1983). *Developing the new assertive nurse: Essentials for advancement.* New York: Springer.

Barber, B. (1984). *Strong democracy: Participatory politics for a new age.* Berkeley: University of California Press.

Berkman, C. S., & Zinberg, G. (1997). Homophobia and heterosexism in social workers, *Social Work, 42*(4), 319–329.

Biddle, W. W., & Biddle, L. J. (1979). Intention and outcome. In F. M. Cox, J. L. Erlich, J. Rothman, & J. E. Tropman (Eds.), Strategies of community organization (pp. 365–375). Itasca, IL: F. E. Peacock.

Bisman, C. (1994). *Social work practice: Cases and principles.* Pacific Grove, CA: Brooks/Cole Publishing Co.

Blanchard, K., & Johnson, S. (1982). *The one-minute manager: The quickest way to increase your own prosperity.* New York: Berkley.

Bower, S. A., & Bower, G. H. (1991). *Asserting your self: A practical guide for positive change* (Updated ed.). Reading, MA: Addison-Wesley.

Bregman, S. (1985). Assertiveness training for mentally retarded adults. *Psychiatric Aspects of Mental Retardation Reviews, 4*(1), 43–48.

Burghardt, S. (1982). *The other side of organizing.* Cambridge, MA: Schenkman.

Butler, S. S., & Coleman, P. A. (1997). Raising our voices: A macro practice assignment. *Journal of Teaching in Social Work, 15*(1/2), 63–80.

Castle, A. (1995). A review of assertion skills training, *Radiology Today, 61*(692), 23–24.

Christensen, P. (2002). An eye-opening diversity assignment. *The New Social Worker, 9*(4), 13, 17.

Clifton, R. L., & Dahms, A. M. (1993). *Grassroots organizations: A resource book for directors, staff, and volunteers of small, community-based nonprofit agencies* (2nd ed.). Prospect Heights, IL: Waveland.

Colburn, L. (1994). On-the-spot mediation in a public housing project. In D. M. Kolb (Ed.), *When talk works: Profiles of mediators* (pp. 395–425). San Francisco: Jossey-Bass.

Cotler, S. B., & Guerra, J. J. (1976). *Assertion training: A humanistic-behavioral guide to self-dignity.* Champaign, IL: Research.

Cournoyer, B. R. (1983). Assertiveness among MSW students. *Journal of Education for Social Work, 19*(1), 24–30.

Cowger, C. D. (1994). Assessing client strengths: Clinical assessment for client empowerment. *Social Work, 39*(3), 262–268.

Cummerton, J. M. (1980, March). *Empowerment begins with me.* Paper presented at Council on Social Work Education meeting, Los Angeles.

Drucker, P. (1999). Managing oneself. *Harvard Business Review, 77*(2), 64–74.

Drury, S. S. (1984). *Assertive supervision: Building involved teamwork.* Champaign, IL: Research Press.

Eberhardt, L. Y. (1994). *Working with woman's groups: Structured exercises in: Consciousness raising, self-discovery, assertiveness training.* Duluth, MN: Whole Person Associates.

Enns, C. Z. (1992). Self-esteem groups: A synthesis of consciousness raising and assertiveness training. *Journal of Counseling and Development, 71*(1), 7–13.

Falck, H. (1988). *Social work: The membership perspective.* New York: Springer.

Fisher, M. (2001, September 22). From New York, a stirring lesson in leadership. *Washington Post,* p. B1.

Flynn, J. P. (1985). *Social agency policy: Analysis and presentation for community practice.* Chicago: Nelson-Hall.

Furstenberg, A. L., & Rounds, K. A. (1995). Self-efficacy as a target for social work intervention. *Families in Society, 76*(10), 587–595.

Gamble, T. K., & Gamble, M. (1990). *Communication works* (3rd ed.). New York: McGraw-Hill.

Gambrill, E. (1997). *Social work practice: A critical thinker's guide.* New York: Oxford University Press.

Garvin, C., & Gruber, M. (1978, February). *Raising the consciousness of community organization students: The personal and professional identity issues for an organizer in the 1980's.* Paper presented at Council on Social Work Education meeting, New Orleans.

Gibbs, L., & Gambrill, E. (1999). *Critical thinking for social workers: Exercises for the helping profession.* Thousand Oaks, CA: Pine Forest Press.

Gilbert, D. (1993). Not in my backyard. *Social Work, 39*(1), 7–8.

Gilson, S. F. (2000). Discussion of disability and use of self in the classroom. *Journal of Teaching in Social Work, 20* (3/4), 125–136.

Glueckhauf, R. L., & Quittner, A. L. (1992). Assertiveness training for disabled adults in wheelchairs: Self-report, role-play, and activity pattern outcomes. *Journal of Consulting and Clinical Psychology, 60*(3), 419–425.

Greenwood, G. E., Olejnik, S. F., & Parkay, F. W. (1990). Relationships between four teacher efficacy belief patterns and selected teacher characteristics, *Journal of Research and Development in Education, 23*(2), 104–106.

Griffin, W. V. (1995). Social worker and agency safety. In R. Edwards (Ed.-in-Chief), *Encyclopedia of social work* (19th ed., pp. 2293–2305). Washington, DC: National Association of Social Workers Press.

Gutierrez, L. M. (1990). Working with women of color: An empowerment perspective. *Social Work, 35*(2), 149–152.

Harden, B. (1995, July 16). A one-man human-rights crusade. *The Washington Post*, pp. B1, B6.

Hardina, D. (1995, March). *Teaching confrontation tactics to social work students.* Paper presented at Council on Social Work Education meeting, San Diego, CA.

Hardy, A. (1989). In vivo desensitization: Action and talking therapy. In C. Lindemann (Ed.), *Handbook of phobia therapy: Rapid symptom relief in anxiety disorders* (pp. 261–267). Northvale, NJ: Jason Aronson.

Harris, C. C., & Harris, D. R. (1993). *Self-empowerment: Reclaim your personal power.* Carmel, CA: Carmel Highlands.

Hartman, A. (1990). *Family-based strategies for empowering families.* Paper presented at the "Integrating Three Strategies of Family Empowerment" conference sponsored by School of Social Work, University of Iowa.

Haug, M. R., & Lavin, B. (1983). *Consumerism in medicine: Challenging physician authority.* Beverly Hills, CA: Sage.

Hawkins, J. D., Catalano, R. F., & Wells, E. A. (1986). Measuring effects of a skills training intervention for drug abusers. *Journal of Consulting and Clinical Psychology, 54*(5), 661–664.

Healey, L. M., Havens, C. M., & Chin, A. (1990). Preparing women for human services administration. *Administration in Social Work, 14*(2), 29–94.

Hepworth, D. H., & Larsen, J. A. (1986). *Direct social work practice* (2nd ed.). Pacific Grove, CA: Brooks/Cole.

Hepworth, D. H., & Larsen, J. A. (1993). *Direct social work practice* (4th ed.). Pacific Grove, CA: Brooks/Cole.

Howing, P. T., Wodarski, J. S., Kurtz, P. J., & Gaudin, J. M. (1990). The empirical base for the implementation of social skills training with maltreated children. *Social Work, 35*(5), 460–467.

Hsu, C. J. (1992). Assertiveness issues for Asian Americans. In I. G. Fodor (Ed.), *Adolescent assertiveness and social skills training: A clinical handbook* (pp. 99–112). New York: Springer.

Jansson, B. S. (1990). *Social welfare policy: From theory to practice.* Belmont, CA: Wadsworth.

Johnson, L. D. (1995). *Psychotherapy in the age of accountability.* New York: W. W. Norton & Company.

Kahn, K. (1973). *Hillbilly women.* New York: Avon.

Kaufman, G., & Raphael, L. (1990). *Stick up for yourself: Every kid's guide to personal power and positive self esteem.* Minneapolis: Free Spirit.

Kaysen, S. (1993). *Girl interrupted.* New York: Vintage Books.

Kelly, C. (1979). *Assertion training.* La Jolla, CA: University Associates.

Kern, J. M., & Karten, S. J. (1991). Fakability of two different role-play methodologies for assessing assertion. *Psychological Reports, 69*, 467–470.

Kirst-Ashman, K. K., & Hull, G. H. (1997). *Generalist practice with organizations and communities.* Chicago, IL: Nelson-Hall Publishers.

Klein, K. (1996). *Fundraising for social change,* 3rd ed. Berkeley: CA: Chardon Press

Knee, R., & Vourlekis, B. (1995). Patient rights. In R. Edwards (Ed.-in-Chief), *Encyclopedia of social work* (19th ed., pp. 1802–1810). Washington, DC: National Association of Social Workers Press.

Knotts, L. S. (1991). *Characteristics of "women's language" and their relationship to personnel decisions.* Paper presented for departmental honors in psychology, Hood College, Frederick, MD.

Lange, A. J., & Jakubowski, P. (1976). *Responsible assertive behavior: Cognitive/behavioral procedures for trainers.* Champaign, IL: Research Press.

Lappé, F. M., & Du Bois, P. M. (1994). *The quickening of America: Rebuilding our nation, remaking our lives.* San Francisco, CA: Jossey Bass, Inc. Publishers.

Leavitt, H. J. (1989). Educating our MBAs: On teaching what we haven't taught. *California Management Review, 31*(3), 38–50.

Lee, H. L. (1983). Analysis of a concept: Hardiness. *Oncology Nursing Forum, 10*(4), 32–35.

Lee, B., McGrath, S., Moffatt, K., & George, U. (2002). Exploring the insider role in community practice within diverse communities. *Critical Social Work, 2* (2), 69–78.

Lerner, M. (1991). *Surplus powerlessness.* Atlantic Highlands, NJ: Humanities Press International.

Life would be easy if it weren't for other people. (1995). *Trial, 31*(1), 82.

Locust, C. (1995). The impact of differing belief systems between Native Americans and their rehabilitation service providers. *Rehabilitation Education, 9*(2), 205–215.

Lordan, N. (2000). Finding a voice: Empowerment of people with disabilities in Ireland. *Journal of Progressive Human Services, 11*(1), 49–69.

Magladry, J., & Macpherson, J. E. (1994). Now cut that out! Extremes of boorish behavior. *Trial, 30*(7), 43.

Masi, D. A. (1994). Violence in the workplace: The EAP perspective. *EAP Digest, 14*(3), 23.

Mele, C. (1999). Cyberspace and disadvantaged communities: The Internet as a tool for collective action. In M. A. Smith & P. Kollock (Eds.), *Communities in Cyberspace.* New York: Routledge.

Mulroy, E. A., & Cragin, J. (1994). Training future community-based managers: The politics of collaboration in a turbulent urban environment. *Journal of Teaching in Social Work, 9*(1/2), 17–35.

Nader, L. (1980). *No access to law.* New York: Academic Press.

National Association of Social Workers—Maryland Chapter. (1995, March). *Violence—Caught in the crossfire—Implications for social work practice.* Program meeting.

Nezu, C., Nezu, A. M., & Arean, P. (1991). Assertiveness and problem-solving training for mildly mentally retarded persons with dual diagnoses. *Research in Developmental Disabilities, 12*(4), 371–386.

O'Donnell, R. (with Newman, J.). (1995, Summer). Assertiveness training with Rosie O'Donnell. *Know How, 5*(2), 60–63, 101.

Ohbuchi, K., & Takahashi, Y. (1994). Cultural styles of conflict management in Japanese and Americans: Passivity, covertness, and effectiveness of strategies. *Journal of Applied Social Psychology, 24*(15), 1345–66.

O'Neill, P. (1989). Responsible to whom? *American Journal of Community Psychology, 17*, pp. 323–341.

Orosz, S. B. (1982). Assertiveness in recovery. *Social Work With Groups, 5*, 25–31.

Pardeck, J. T., Anderson, C., Gianino, E. A., Miller, B., Mothershead, M. S., & Smith, S. A. (1991). Assertiveness of social work students. *Psychological Reports, 69*(2), 589–590.

Patterson, C. H. (1985). *The therapeutic relationship: Foundations for eclectic psychotherapy.* Monterey, CA: Brooks/Cole Publishing.

Pearson, C. S. (1989). *The hero within: Six archetypes we live by.* New York: HarperCollins.

Pfost, K. S., Stevens, M. J., & Parker, J. C. (1992). The influence of assertion training on three aspects of assertiveness in alcoholics. *Journal of Clinical Psychology, 48*(2), 262–268.

Phelps, S., & Austin, N. (1987). *The assertive woman: A new look* (2nd ed.). San Luis Obispo, CA: Impact.

Planells-Bloom, D. (1992). Latino cultures: Framework for understanding the Latina adolescent and assertive behavior. In I. G. Fodor (Ed.), *Adolescent assertiveness and social skills training: A clinical handbook* (pp. 113–128). New York: Springer.

Plotkin, S. (1990). Enclave consciousness and neighborhood activism. In J. M. Kling & P. S. Posner (Eds.), *Dilemmas of activism* (pp. 218–239). Philadelphia: Temple University Press.

Powers, P. (Ed.) (1994). Challenging: Interviews with advocates and activists [monograph]. Baltimore: University of Maryland at Baltimore, School of Social Work.

Rakos, R. F. (1991). *Assertive behavior.* New York: Routledge.

Richan, W. C. (1989). Empowering students to empower others: A community-based field practicum. *Journal of Social Work Education, 25*(3), 276–283.

Rivera, F. G. (1990). The Way of Bushido in community organizing teaching. *Administration in Social Work, 14*(2), 43–61.

RoAne, S. (1988). *How to work a room: Learn the strategies of savvy socializing—for business and personal success.* New York: Warner Books.

Ruben, D. H., & Ruben, M. J. (1989). Why assertiveness training programs fail. *Small Group Behavior, 20*(3), 367–380.

Ryan, K. D., Oestreich, D. K., & Orr, G. A., III. (1996). *The courageous messengers: How to successfully speak up at work.* San Francisco, CA: Jossey-Bass Publishers.

Salcido, R. M. (1993, February). *A cross cultural approach for understanding Latino barrio needs: A macro practice model.* Paper presented at Council on Social Work Education meeting, New York.

Schilling, R. F. (1990). Commentary: Making research usable. In L. Videka-Sherman & W. J. Reid (Eds.), *Advances in clinical social work research* (pp. 256–260). Silver Spring, MD: National Association of Social Workers.

Sears, V. (1990). Grace. In *Simple Songs* (pp. 139–159). Ithaca, NY: Firebrand Books.

Sears, V. L. (1993). Grace. In P. Riley (Ed.), *Growing up Native American* (pp. 279–298). New York: William Morrow.

Sherman, W., & Wenocur, S. (1983). Empowering public welfare workers through mutual support. *Social Work, 28*(5), 375–379.

Shields, K. (1994). *In the tiger's mouth: An empowerment guide for social action.* Philadelphia, PA: New Society Publishers.

Simon, B. L. (1990). Rethinking empowerment. *Journal of Progressive Human Services, 1*(1), 27–39.

Simons, H. W. (1976). *Persuasion: Understanding, practice and analysis.* Reading, MA: Addison-Wesley.

Siress, R. H. (with Riddle, C., & Shouse, D.). (1994). *Working woman's communications survival guide: How to present your ideas with impact, clarity and power and get the recognition you deserve.* Englewood Cliffs, NJ: Prentice Hall.

Smith, J. C. (1991). *Stress scripting: A guide to stress management.* New York: Praeger.

Smith, M. J. (1975). *When I say no, I feel guilty.* New York: Dial.

Smith, W. (2001). *Hope meadows: Real-life stories of healing and caring from an inspired community.* New York: Berkeley.

Spain, D. (2001). How women saved the city. Minneapolis: University of Minnesota Press.

Spolin, V. (1983). *Improvisation for the theater: A handbook of teaching and directing techniques.* Evanston, IL: Northwestern University Press.

Springer, L. (1999). *Grand Central winter: Stories from the street.* New York: Washington Square Press.

Stevens, C. K., Bavetta, A. G., & Gist, M. E. (1993). Gender differences in the acquisition of salary negotiation skills: The role of goals, self-efficacy, and perceived control. *Journal of Applied Psychology, 78*(5), 723–735.

Subramanian, K., & Rose, S. D. (1988). Social work and the treatment of chronic pain. *Health and Social Work, 13*(1), 49–60.

Sue, D., Sue, D. M., & Ino, S. (1990). Assertiveness and social anxiety in Chinese American women. *Journal of Psychology, 124*(2), 155–163.

Tannen, D. (1990). *You just don't understand: Women and men in conversation.* New York: William Morrow.

Tannen, D. (1994). *Talking from 9 to 5: How women's and men's conversational styles affect who gets heard, who gets credit, and what gets done at work.* New York: William Morrow.

Thompson, L. (1990, November 20). Finally, a new chief for the FDA. *The Washington Post,* Health section, pp. 11–12.

Tower, K. D. (1994). Consumer-centered social work practice: Restoring client self-determination. *Social Work, 39*(2), 191–196.

Tully, C. C., Kropf, N. P., & Price, J. L. (1993). Is the field a hard hat area? A study of violence in field placements. *Journal of Social Work Education, 29*(2), 191–199.

Vardi, D. (1992). Assertiveness training for pregnant and parenting high school teenagers. In I. G. Fodor (Ed.), *Adolescent assertiveness and social skills training: A clinical handbook* (pp. 249–268). New York: Springer.

Ventis, W. L. (1987). Humor and laughter in behavior therapy. In W. F. Fry, Jr., & W. A.

Salameh (Eds.), *Handbook of humor and psychotherapy: Advances in the clinical use of humor* (pp. 149–169). Sarasota, FL: Professional Resource Exchange.

Wakefield, J. C. (1988, September). Part 2: Psychotherapy and the pursuit of justice. *Social Service Review 62*(2), 353–382.

Walker, L. A. (2002, July 7). A place called Hope. *Parade,* 10, 12.

Walz, T., & Uematsu, M. (1997). Creativity in social work practice: A pedagogy. *Journal of Teaching in Social Work, 15*(1/2), 17–31.

Wayne, J., & Fine, S. B. (1986). Group work with retarded mothers. *Social Casework, 67*(4), 195–202.

Weick, A. (2000). Hidden voices. *Social Work, 45,* (4)395–402

Weisman, R. L., & Lamberti, J. S. (2002). Violence prevention and safety training for case management services. *Community Mental Health Journal, 38*(4), 339–348.

Weiss, J. O. (1993). Genetic disorders: Support groups and advocacy. *Families in Society: The Journal of Contemporary Human Services, 74*(4), 213–220.

West, D. M., Heith, D., & Goodwin, C. (1996). Harry and Louise go to Washington: Political advertising and health care reform. *Journal of health politics, policy, and law, 21*(1), 35–68.

Williams, P.N. (1978). *Investigative reporting and editing.* Englewood Cliffs, NJ: Prentice-Hall.

Wood, P. S., & Mallinckrodt, B. (1990). Culturally sensitive assertiveness training for ethnic minority clients. *Professional Psychology: Research and Practice, 21*(1), 208–214.

Yeich, S., & Levine, R. (1994). Political efficacy: Enhancing the construct and its relationship to mobilization of people, *Journal of Community Psychology, 22,* 259–271.

Yoshioka, M. (1995, March 5). *Measuring the assertiveness of low income, minority women: Implications for culturally competent practice.* Paper presented at Council on Social Work Education meeting, San Diego, CA.

Zane, N. W. S., Sue, S., Hu, L., & Kwon, J. (1991). Asian American assertion: A social learning analysis of cultural differences. *Journal of Counseling Psychology, 38*(1), 63–70.

Zuker, E. (1983). *The assertive manager: Positive skills at work for you.* New York: AMACOM.

Zunz, S. J. (1998). Resiliency and burnout: Protective factors for human services managers. *Administration in Social Work, 22*(3), 39–54.

9

Using Your Agency

Organizations are necessary and important because they enable people to accomplish *collectively* what cannot be accomplished by individuals acting on their own. The maintenance of complex industrial societies is inconceivable without the existence of large-scale organizations, together with a great number of very small organizations.

H. E. ALDRICH (1979, P. 3)

As social workers, we will likely spend most of our professional lives practicing in human service organizations—governmental (public), nongovernmental nonprofit agencies, and proprietary organizations. These organizations profoundly affect our personal and professional well-being. Regardless of our talents and skills, organizational structure, culture, and management strongly influence how well and in what manner we are able to deliver services, that is, how well we are able to do the professional work for which we were trained. At the same time, our work organizations affect our self-image, our livelihoods, and our sense of accomplishment and worth as human beings. For these reasons, understanding how organizations operate is critical. We need organizational knowledge to create a personally and professionally more satisfying and capable work environment.

This chapter is written from the perspective of the direct service worker rather than the supervisor or manager. It deals with human service ınizations in general first, and then with the

formal and informal aspects of organizational life that workers should know about to understand the forces that impinge on them and the opportunities for intervention. We also remind the reader of the interorganizational context of organizational life because external economic, political, and institutional forces strongly affect *intra*organizational behavior. Throughout the chapter, we try to regard workers as organizational actors intervening on their own behalf and on behalf of their clients. As a prelude to this chapter, we encourage the reader to review the material on systems theory, exchange theory, and interorganizational theory in Chapter 2.

ATTRIBUTES OF HUMAN SERVICE AGENCIES

Social workers practice in a very broad array of human service organizations (HSOs). Although these agencies vary in such characteristics as size, complexity, auspices, domain, and whether or not social work is the dominant profession in the agency—and more, as a class of organizations—they are also alike in many ways. These similarities help to explain the organizational problems and opportunities that human service workers and service users often encounter. In briefly reviewing these shared attributes, we shall draw on Hasenfeld's (1992b) work on the nature of HSOs.

HSOs are *people-processing* and *people-changing* agencies in that "the core activities of the organization are structured to process, sustain, or change people who come under its jurisdiction" (Hasenfeld, 1992b, pp. 4–5). An HSO's primary purpose is to provide effective programs and services, now and in the future, to clients and the community. To provide services in the future, the HSO must persist. Organization and agency management activities—such as resource gathering, controlling and coordinating, reporting and accountability—ideally serve the ends of current and future service.

Organizations accomplish what an individual or an aggregation of individuals working alone cannot. If organizations simply do as well as people working alone can do, then organizations make no significant social contribution. HSO are systems. As systems, HSOs can be viewed as means-ends chains. Generally, as Figure 9.1 indicates, they are transforming systems. HSOs tend toward open systems with resources or inputs from their ecologies (people, material, ideas, knowledge, and technology) and transform or process them in some way into outputs to reach organizational objectives. Some organizational examples are job placement, information, and referral (processing); Social Security, long-term nursing home care (sustaining); counseling, school (changing).

To maximize compliance and hence control, HSOs must win their clients' cooperation and trust. Social workers employed by HSOs are agents of the HSO. Clients are first clients of the HSO and only then clients of the HSO's social workers. The HSO is the significant party in the relationship with the client. The nature of this relationship is critical and should be understood by the worker and client. The agency frames the attachment of social worker and client. It constricts such relationship components as client privacy and worker confidentiality. The organization's managerlist control of the working relationship between workers and clients is a growing characteristic of contemporary agency-based social work practice (Thompson, 2000; Walker, 2001; Webb, 2001). This relationship is vulnerable to deliberate or unwitting abuse, since HSOs typically control some of the resources clients need. Moreover, control and standardization of the services that are delivered are difficult to achieve because services, the products of professional intervention, are intangible and "inextricably bound to the person and personality of the producer" (Larson, 1977, p. 14; see also Wenocur & Reisch, 1989, pp. 9–11). Since human service "technologies" (modes of intervention) are variable and hard to reproduce (though greater reliability is the object of professional training), and since the outcomes of intervention are hard to measure and not clearly visible, HSOs, not surprisingly, have difficulty gaining support for their work.

In a market economy, HSOs are unique in that their primary funding sources are largely governmental tax dollars and philanthropic contributions, although proprietaries are becoming more numerous. If the current trend toward privatization continues, the human services proprietary sector will expand. One implication of this is that often service users are not the same people as the service funders. An increase in the numbers of clients and corresponding services does not automatically result in increased revenues. In addition, since service users are not funders, they lack a major source of power over the operations of the organizations that serve them. Nevertheless, service users are valuable assets for HSOs—no clients, no organization. Agencies compete for clients and other resources (Greenley & Kirk, 1973).

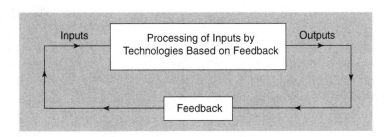

Figure 9.1   The general systems model.

The sources of funding for HSOs make them dependent on an uncertain, competitive, often turbulent political and institutional environment for legitimacy and resources. Consequently, the legitimacy of and funding for human service agencies wax and wane with changes in political administrations and the currency of new ideas that happen to be in vogue. Currently privatization, market models, and faith-based services are trendy.

Human service managers are managers of essentially political entities and need to have their political antennae up with their political hats close at hand. The political character of their work and public dependency for fiscal resources engender many challenges. HSOs', as well as social work's, emphasis on the social environment, social interactions, and social functioning make them inherently political. This does not imply *necessarily* a limited partisan profession consistently aligned with a particular political party, although they may reasonably align with partisan positions congruent with a profession's and an organization's mission and aims. A political profession and organization are concerned with influencing social policy or the rules that regulate social behavior and social relations. A political organization is attentive to public and civic affairs and the public or community's distribution of social statuses, privileges, and other resources that constitute the elements for the organization's well being. Political professions and organizations are innately ideological and moral beyond the growing ideology of economic market models. They use values and ethics in selecting social theories to develop social constructions *of how things ought to be* as well as how things are to guide their policy behavior. Political awareness is a necessary counterbalance to escalating managerialism.

Human service work is often stressful, not only because of inadequate resources, but also because it is both "moral work" and "gendered work" (Hasenfeld, 1992b). It is moral work in the sense that workers inevitably are involved in making value-laden decisions, often painful ones, that render moral judgments about the social worth of an individual or a family—for example, whether or not to make one more attempt to reach a difficult client, whether or not to cut off a service or separate a child from a family, or what kind of diagnostic label to attach. In the all too common situation where resources are scarce and clients' needs are strong, if not overwhelming, workers often agonize over requirements to ration services. In organizational settings where ˜s levels are constant and high, workers may

burn out and leave or stay and find a functional or dysfunctional mode of accommodation. In public welfare agencies, such accommodations may include (a) finding a special niche in the organization that removes the worker from the firing line, (b) capitulating to agency demands to serve only "deserving" clients, (c) openly resisting agency demands, and (d) adopting a victim mentality by overidentifying with the clients (Sherman & Wenocur, 1983).

Human service work is *gendered work*. Women make up the majority of direct service workers in HSOs, while men tend to hold positions of authority. Although this pattern is slowly changing, a study of members of the NASW (Gibelman & Schervish, 1996) and other recent NASW surveys indicate that most social workers are women and largely work in direct practice and for private organizations. Some 74% of NASW respondents work at nongovernmental employment agencies, with 36% in proprietaries. Some 17% are solo practitioners. Only 23% work for state and local governments, with another 14% employed by the federal government or military (O'Neill, 2003, p. 8). This skewed gender distribution potentially generates stressful dissonance between the workers' *feminine value orientation* of altruism, caring, and nurturing that requires nonroutine activities and the formal organization's *masculine value orientation* that requires formal procedures and standardization for efficiency's sake (Dressel, 1992; Hasenfeld, 1992b). This conflict, coupled with the lower pay attached to female-dominated occupations and industries and the fact that many of the clients of human service agencies are poor women and other "undeserving" poor, devalues human service work and demeans all human service workers. And since devalued human services attract inadequate financial resources, it is difficult to have the impact on complex social problems that might change the pattern of allocations significantly in the future (Hasenfeld, 1992, pp. 8–9).

Organizational Auspices

Having discussed some of the similarities among HSOs, we should also attend to some of the differences, as these also will have a strong bearing on service delivery and worker satisfaction. HSOs have three general auspices: (a) public, (b) voluntary not-for-profit, and (c) proprietary and for-profit. Auspice reflects to the organization's sponsorship, control, and fundamental purpose. Social welfare agencies and HSOs are moving toward proprietary, vertically integrated and extracommunity auspices along with a managerial emphasis. The proprietary or for-profit sector has an almost 36% share of the social services market, with a 50% growth projected over the next few years. Mammoth, vertically integrated companies, such as Lockheed Martin, Xerox, and HCA, have entered and may eventually control the market. Faith-based agencies in the not-for-profit sector also are expanding and serve as an exception to the commercialization trend.

PUBLIC AUSPICE

Public or *governmental* HSOs are established by federal, state, or local governmental regulations and supported by tax revenues. Examples include the Department of Health and Human Services, a county department of public welfare, a city mental health center, and a local high school. The fundamental intent of agencies with a public auspice is to govern. As Gortner, Mahler, and Nicholson (1987) state, "*It is the business of public bureaus to administer the law*. Their function is authoritarian in the deepest and most formal sense. Their role is as active and pervasive as the reach of law and government" (p. 19). Public agency accountability is broad and general and not just to a particular group of shareholders or sponsors. While claiming community accountability, public agency accountability is to the public at large as exercised by elected officials. Public agencies are neither market driven nor responsive to economic forces. They are politically driven and respond to political forces. Their marketplace is a political marketplace, and they respond to political actors and forces in that market place (Gortner et al., pp. 27–30).

Since public organizations are established by government, the top of the public sector HSO's governance structure is often a politically appointed executive officer (titles may vary), such as the secretary of a department of health and mental hygiene, appointed by the governor, or the executive director of the local department of public welfare, appointed by the mayor or county executive. Other top-level administrators may also be political appointees. Below the top echelons, federal, state, and local governmental employees are hired and fired in accordance with civil service regulations that provide job classifications, salary levels, criteria, and procedures for meritorious appointments and promotions and procedures for termination.

Some public agencies have governing boards that make major policy decisions and hire the organization's chief executive officer(s). Examples include an elected local school board, a library board, or the board of regents of a state university, which is appointed by the governor and which, in turn, appoints the university president or chancellor. Some public organizations utilize advisory boards to assist with guiding policy and making top-level appointments and decisions, but advisory boards do not have the legal authority to make the final decisions.

VOLUNTARY NOT-FOR-PROFIT AUSPICE

In this text, *voluntary not-for-profit auspice* refers to HSOs that are legally incorporated in their state as nonprofit corporations and thereby subject to state charitable laws. Their primary function and fiduciary responsibility is service to the community. In addition, these nonprofit organizations usually have been granted tax exemption by the Internal Revenue Service (IRS) under section 501(C)(3) or one of the other sections of the Internal Revenue Code reserved for religious, charitable, and educational organizations. This means they do not have to pay federal taxes on their corporate income. Usually nonprofit organizations also are exempt from state and local taxes as well, although some financially strapped local governments are challenging this policy. Clearly this auspice covers a very broad range of organizations, from huge multifunctional corporations such as the Johns Hopkins conglomerate and the Salvation Army USA, to regional family service associations, to small church-sponsored soup kitchens and everything in between.

Nonprofit organizations receive significant funding from private philanthropy (individual, corporate, and foundation donations and grants). They may also receive substantial governmental funding through purchase of service contracts, grants, and governmental insurance payments such from as Medicaid. Nonprofits frequently earn revenue from fees for its services of various kinds, including third-party private insurance payments, direct fees for a service or product, and income from other related business activities, such as the operation of a health spa by a YMCA or a blood testing lab by a medical school. Fees for service are the fastest growing funding source for social welfare (Johnston, 1997; Salamon, 1997). Private giving as a share of nonprofit revenue dropped by some 20% during the 1980s and early 90s. This deterioration of giving is expected to continue as changes in the national income distribution concentrates income at the top of the income distribution and the tax code makes philanthropic giving less financially attractive. The very wealthy donate proportionately less of their income to social welfare services than do the middle class (Freudenheim, 1996, p. B8; Phillips, 1993, p. 143). Hence the source of funding does not clearly distinguish nonprofit agencies from governmental and for-profit organizations.

The key feature distinguishing nonprofit auspices from public agencies and from for profit is that nonprofits have the primary mission of service to the community rather than governance or profit. They are self-governed. Their governing boards are an all-volunteer board of directors accountable neither to nonexistent owners or to government. They are accountable to the community. The boards are stewards for the community. The executive officer is responsible to the boards and ultimately to the community. The voluntary board is a legal requirement of incorporation as a charitable organization. Although nonprofits can earn a profit, called a fund balance, it can't be distributed to shareholders and board members. It is saved for a rainy day and reinvested in agency programs. Neither profit nor politics should be a core part of the agency's calculus.

The presence of a large nonprofit sector supports pluralistic democratic values. Nonprofits represent the essence of voluntary action by citizens to provide the services they need and want, services that government and private corporations cannot provide legally or fail to provide because they are not politically or economically viable. So, for example, many nonprofits are sponsored by sectarian and culturally distinct groups, such as a Korean Community Center, a Jewish Family Services agency, a Black Mental Health Alliance, an Associated Catholic Charities, or a Hispanic Community Council. Moreover, because nonprofits are voluntary, self-governing bodies, they can challenge the policies and practices of private corporations and governmental agencies. Most of our important social reforms came about through nonprofit activities—child welfare, civil rights, environmental protection, women's rights, workplace safety (Salamon, 1992).

Nonprofit organizations usually provide a very different work environment from governmental agencies, one that is potentially less formal and more flexible and varied. When large and complex, both types of organizations can operate quite bureaucratically, with many policies and rules to follow, a hierarchical system of decision making, and a clearly differentiated division of labor. However, many nonprofit HSOs are not very large. A study of the Baltimore area nonprofit sector, for example, found that in 1987, 72% of the nonprofits had expenditures of less than $500,000 (Salamon, Altschuler, & Myllylu-

oma, 1990). Even when they are large, nonprofits have the capacity to make decisions more quickly and to operate more flexibly than their governmental counterparts. In part, this is a function of their system of self-governance; the executive, with the approval of the board, has great leeway to make program and policy changes. In part, it is also a function of their ability to choose whom they will serve and the nature of the services they will provide. If the market is there, a nonprofit agency could decide to provide therapy only to people with three nostrils. If the market is too large, they can decide to limit their services even further or expand if they want. Governmental organizations lack this flexibility. Legally they are mandated to serve all who are eligible according to the legislation that established the organization, regardless of numbers. For example, a child welfare agency must serve all abused and neglected children in its geographic service area, ultimately an indeterminate number, and additional staffing is subject to political competition for scarce resources.

Faith-based agencies are a particular form of nonprofit organization. They are agencies sponsored or operated by a religious faith. While sharing with secular nonprofits the service mission, they are constrained by obligations to the tenets and dogma of the religion, whether those include admonitions against abortion and homosexuality (as sins) or requirements for race and family relationships and child rearing. Discrimination and inequity in hiring and services to nonadherents and persons with traits that go against dogma—such as gays and lesbians, abortion choice, "race mixing," gender role limitations—are often present in faith-based service agencies. Hiring discrimination is explicitly allowed in the Charitable Choice section, section 104 of the federal *Personal Responsibility and Work Opportunity Reconciliation Act of 1996* (PRWOR). Service giving by faith-based agencies is often a means to proselytize and strengthen the religion's community.

PROPRIETARY FOR-PROFIT AGENCIES

Proprietary for-profit auspices share the trait of having a defined ownership or proprietors—whether a single owner, a partnership of practitioners, a group of investor owners, or stockholders—and operate under the auspice of the owner(s) rather than under public or voluntary auspices. Proprietaries' fundamental intent is profit rather than service. Service provision is a means to profit. Proprietaries can provide a service only insofar as it is profitable. Someone must be willing to pay a profit margin for any services. They are a rapidly growing segment of the social work arena and social welfare field. According to a 2002 survey of a sample of NASW members, 36% of all respondents were employed by proprietary for-profits, with 17% working primarily as solo proprietary practitioners (O'Neill, 2003). Social work's private practitioners are proprietary practitioners. Proprietary practice also includes practice in the megacorporations that own hospitals, home health care agencies, counseling services, residential treatment facilities, and nursing homes. These organizations are incorporated in a state as businesses, and they pay local, state, and federal corporate income taxes. If corporations, each is required to have a board of directors with a minimum of three members. These are the main administrative officers of the company. Other board members may be added because of stock ownership or special connections and expertise they bring. The chairperson is frequently the chief executive officer of the corporation. For-profit board members, unlike not-for-profit boards, expect to be paid for their services (Houle, 1989). Proprietary organizations sell their services or products at a price sufficient to cover the cost of production plus an amount for profit. The profit that is not reinvested in the organization is divided among the owners.

For-profit organizations must be extremely sensitive to the marketplace. Services often are more flexible, client-friendly and market responsive. The claim is that proprietaries because they are profit-driven are more performance-oriented and in tune with the latest trends and knowledge than are public and not-for-profits. As yet research has not supported these claims. Competition will produce advantages for clients only if there is truly competition for clients and client choice vendors exists.

The proprietary's disadvantages are that professionals in solo or group practices must operate as entrepreneurs and generate business. Flexibility gained in one aspect of practice may be offset by the time requirements of marketing and business management in another. Profit rather than service or client welfare takes priority. Large for-profit HSOs, like their counterparts in other fields of business or government, are complex bureaucratic organizations with a highly differentiated division of labor and specialized work roles, such as marketing and public relations departments, various departments of professional services, a governmental affairs department, and so on. Individual professional authority and autonomy is lost. As businesses, the proprietaries are organized to pursue profit.

The most intrinsic disadvantage of for-profit social welfare services is that they are inherently unresponsive to the needs of poor and working-class people. Currently government through contracts and other third-party vendor arrangements pay and allow proprietaries a profit margin when serving the poor. Functionally, funders are the proprietary's most important clients. If—or perhaps more *when* and *as*—the public sector, insurance companies, and other third-party payees reduce their market participation on behalf of the poor, proprietaries (including solo proprietary social workers) inevitably will correspondingly reduce their services to the poor if the poor are unwilling and unable to directly pay for the services. The poor by definition have limited capacity to purchase services. The proprietary for-profits, to survive, have and will continue to gravitate to clients with a capacity to pay. When the economy is good, affluent people buy more personal services, including social work's services (Berman & Pfleeger, 1997). The poor, however, are unable to buy services even when the economy is good, let alone when it is not. Some observers claim that profit-seeking human services ignore social work's advocacy and social reform responsibilities.

PERSPECTIVES ON HOW ORGANIZATIONS FUNCTION: A BRIEF REVIEW

Intraorganizational Systems

The whole point of establishing an organization such as a social work agency or a private business is to do what an individual or a group of people cannot do as efficiently and effectively. The aim might be to deliver an intangible product, such as mental health services, to a needy population or to produce a tangible product, such as the all-famous widget, for an enormous market of widgetarians. In any event, the organizational founders logically set up systematic rules for organizing the work in order to accomplish their aims and then put their plans into action. In a word, they create an organization. Frequently, if the founders know what they are doing, these plans work out fairly well—but seldom exactly as intended, because there are too many variables and unknowns to contend with. Organizational rationality breaks down. Some clients do not neatly fit the image projected; some staff members do not get along with each other; some sources of funding are unexpectedly cut off; and so on. All of this is to say, as we did in Chapter 2, that organizations are open systems striving for closure. That is, by definition, organizations always try to operate rationally, but they never can do so completely because of multiple uncertainties deriving from internal organizational sources and the external political and institutional environments that they are part of and must relate to (Thompson, 1967).

Internally, uncertainty creeps into organizations through at least three different paths: structural complexity, technological indeterminateness, and human variability. When organizations are set up to serve a large, heterogeneous population that has many complicated needs, these agencies themselves necessarily become complex systems. As mentioned previously, organizational directors and managers will usually divide the work of running the organization and producing its products or services into smaller subdivisions, some of which may become quite specialized. For example, a nonprofit antihunger organization with a $3 million budget might have an emergency services department; a feeding program; a public policy unit; a community organizing and advocacy division; a resource development unit that includes fund-raising and public relations; a general administration unit that includes building maintenance, purchasing, and bookkeeping; and a management division that includes planning, personnel, volunteer oversight, and training. Even small nonprofits are likely to have subdivisions; large governmental or for-profit organizations can be infinitely more complex. The more differentiated the organization, the greater the difficulty in coordinating the work of the various subsystems to produce products and services efficiently and effectively. It is interesting that, at various times, both greater organizational centralization and greater decentralization have been proposed as ways to improve coordination in the interests of organizational efficiency and effectiveness. However, there is no simple answer. The structural solution that works best depends on the goals, needs, and managerial capacities of the particular organization (Webber, 1979), as well as the organization's technology and conditions in the external environment. An organization's technology is the things an organization intentionally does with and to the raw materials, the inputs and clients, to produce its outcomes and final products.

Technological uncertainty in HSOs comes from several sources. First, we are not always sure about how best to intervene to help deal with certain problems. What is the best approach to deal with the alcoholic, for example, or with the high incidence of alcoholism in the larger society? How about a client who is both alcoholic and mentally ill? How about the low-income, multiproblem family? In addition, many different technologies and belief systems may exist simultaneously in the same organization. A psychiatric hospital employs nurses, psychiatrists, psychologists, social workers, recreational therapists, and so on, each of whom may approach the patients quite differently. And even within the individual disciplines, professionals may have contrary intervention practices—for example, behaviorists versus psychodynamically oriented psychologists. Second, to provide assistance effectively, we often have to rely on the cooperation of other agencies and service providers over whom we have little control. And finally, since our service users are reactive, individual human beings, not inert physical materials, our interventions depend on feedback from our clients, and we cannot always predict their responses. In effect, we have to use individually customized rather than standardized technologies (Thompson, 1967) in situations, incidentally, where the external world often seems to be demanding mass solutions to widespread problems, such as crime or substance abuse.

Human variability, of course, also enters the organization through its employees, managers, and directors. While organizations seek rationality, all the people who make up the organization differ in personalities, beliefs and values, needs, goals, ideas, knowledge and skills, life experiences, cultural identity, and so on. They also tend to form informal groups and subgroups and develop organizational culture that strongly influence employee and managerial behavior. The groups and subgroups can differ greatly, for example, on goals, status, and expectations as can the culture from the official organizational governance. As various interest groups form based on shared values, norms, and predilections, some authors view the process of reaching agreements on goals and activities as an ongoing negotiation and the organization in essence as a "negotiated order," constantly in flux, rather than fixed and determinate (Cyert & March, 1963; Strauss, Schatzman, Ehrlich, & Bucher, 1963).

One consequence of the unique characteristics of HSOs is that they tend to be structured internally as *loosely coupled systems* (as opposed to tightly coupled systems). In essence, this means that the hierarchical structure of authority and clear lines of communication that one might associate with a strictly rational system of organization do not work well in HSOs. Instead, (a) strict top-down authority is likely to be weak and dispersed in multiple authority units; (b) various subunits are likely to maintain a considerable degree of autonomy and identity, and their tasks and activities tend to be weakly coordinated; and (c) there is "a weak system of control over staff activities" (Hasenfeld, 1983, p. 150). Imagine a school system with administrators (principals), teachers, social workers, guidance counselors, psychologists, and various other specialists. Despite directives from above, ultimately the teacher runs the classroom autonomously, and necessarily so, because of the great variations among students and teaching styles. Evaluation of effective teaching performance is difficult. Evaluation of successful counseling and social work intervention is even more difficult, since these activities are carried out even more autonomously than teaching. Moreover, while the principal exerts authority over the social workers, the social workers also report to the head of the school's social work department, so the principal's authority is dissipated. A similar pattern exists with guidance and psychology, adding to coordination problems between all of the different units. Without the ability to hold staff accountable for their performance through monitoring and evaluation—and unionization and civil service requirements may add to these difficulties—the administrator's authority is further weakened. One result of loose coupling is a potentially fragmented, disjointed service delivery system. At the same time, this arrangement may serve important functions for the organization, such as creating more potential for a flexible response to changes in the environment and buffering the organization from failures in any particular unit (Hasenfeld, 1983).

Interorganizational Systems

In Chapter 2 we discussed two concepts central to understanding interorganizational relations, *domain* and *task environment*. For social service agencies and community organizations, we said that organizational domain represents the territory that an organization has carved out in terms of social problems it will address, populations it will serve, and types of advocacy or services it will provide. Two points relevant to interorganizational relations flow from this concept. The first is that since every other organization also makes domain claims, turf battles and competition often crop up, particularly when resources are scarce, a condition sometimes referred to as *domain dissensus*. Over time, conflict and negotiation may lead to some reso-

lution, a state of *domain consensus,* where the different actors have basically worked out agreements about boundaries and overlaps and expectations about what each actor will and will not do (Thompson, 1967). The second point is that an organization's domain determines what other organizations and individuals it will have to relate to or pay attention to in order to fulfill its mission. This network of organizations, organizational subunits, and individuals forms the focal organization's *task environment.*

The task environment is a convenient way of conceptualizing the immediate external environment with which an organization must transact business. It consists of the following categories of actors: (a) suppliers of fiscal resources, (b) suppliers of nonfiscal resources, (c) consumers and clients and their suppliers, (d) competitors, (e) collaborators or complementary service providers, and (f) suppliers of legitimation and authority. These are not necessarily exclusive categories; organizations may be represented in more than one category at the same time. For example, a prestigious foundation that supplies funds in the form of a grant also supplies legitimacy by lending its name to the work of the organization. Competitors are the other agencies and organizations seeking the same resources from the task environment, whether the resources are fiscal or nonfiscal. Competitors are not clones of the service agency nor are they even limited to other service providers. There is always competition when a resource holder has choice as to use of a resource. Competition will be discussed again in the chapters on networking and marketing.

An organization's external environment inevitably poses uncertainty for the organization because it contains needed resources and information that the organization cannot fully control or even, in some cases, perceive. HSOs, for example, depend on having clients or members in order to obtain resources and legitimacy. While this is usually not a problem in public agencies, it can be a severe problem in nonprofit and for-profit organizations as needs change, populations shift, or new competitors enter the field. Interorganizational systems will be explored more fully in the networking chapter.

For any given organization, not only its task environment but also the structure and dynamics of the larger environment surrounding the task environment may affect organizational functioning. Structurally, the larger environment may be relatively simple or complex, or resource rich or poor, for example. Therefore the options and opportunities for finding clients and funds are quite different for rural as opposed to urban or suburban agencies. Dynamically the larger environment may be relatively stable or constantly changing and therefore highly unpredictable. Organizations providing health care seem to be in a rapidly changing, uncertain environment due to political, economic, organizational, and technological developments. Changes in health care, in turn, may have a ripple effect on many other HSOs. Health care trends may be still easier to anticipate than other distant political or economic changes that can have local short- and long-term ramifications. Foreign policy in relation to Southeast Asia, for example, has led to an influx of Asians from many different nations and their dispersal to U.S. communities often totally unprepared to serve persons with such diverse backgrounds and languages.

Uncertainty and Power

In the section on exchange and power in Chapter 2, we noted that the ability to control resources that another party needs is a major source of power in an interdependent relationship. Since any organization depends on satisfactory exchanges with the members of its task environment in order to accomplish its goals, at various points members of the task environment may hold a certain amount of power over the organization. This idea is most clearly illustrated with funding sources. Grant-making organizations usually stipulate the requirements that an organization must meet in order to receive funds. In market-based organizations, individual customers have power because the organization needs them to purchase its products or services. Customers who form a consumer organization can wield even greater influence over a target organization. Similarly, since organizations need workers to produce products or provide services, when workers form labor organizations, they, too, gain power over their employing organization.

Relating the concept of uncertainty to power and exchange, we could say that the inability to control the elements that an organization needs to accomplish its goals creates organizational uncertainty. In today's much more competitive climate for charitable dollars, for example, nonprofit HSOs experience increasingly greater uncertainty about their funding sources. In this formulation, then, within an organization, power accrues to those individuals or groups that can resolve uncertainties for the organization (Crozier, 1964). These uncertainties may

stem from internal or external environmental sources. Thus, in a HSO that needs the capacity to process a great deal of information rapidly, employees with computer-based information-management skills may have a great deal of influence and command high salaries. The employee who can get the system up when it crashes may be the most powerful of all.

In view of the pervasive uncertainty that permeates modern organizational life, administration involves an ongoing struggle to manage internal and external environmental uncertainty while keeping the organization on the path to accomplishing its goals. To succeed at this complex task, administrators and professional staff members must be able to obtain and process strategic information about every aspect of organizational life, particularly environmental trends and opportunities. A recent study by Menefee and Thompson (1994, p. 14) comparing management competencies of the early 1980s with requirements for the 1990s found a dramatic shift from roles and skills, such as supervising and direct practice, "focused primarily on internal operations to one(s) that (are) strategically oriented," such as boundary spanning and futuring, aimed at managing a complex external environment. Thompson (1967) likens this idea of *opportunistic surveillance* to natural curiosity in the individual, defining this search activity as "monitoring behavior which scans the environment for opportunities—which does not have to be activated by a problem and which does not therefore stop when a problem solution has been found" (p. 151).

Opportunistic search roles take many different forms and involve both regular staff members and managers. Because they help the organization manage environmental uncertainties, they may also carry special status and influence. One important role set focuses on *strategic planning*. Strategic planning activities engage the organization in (a) systematically scanning its internal and external environments to identify organizational strengths and weaknesses in relation to short- and long-range trends, opportunities, and threats and (b) formulating strategies to manage the issues confronting the organization and developing a vision for the future (Bryson, 1989, p. 48). Management, staff, and volunteers may all carry out strategic planning activities. In some larger organizations, strategic planning is the ongoing business of an organizational planning department. *Boundary-spanning* roles encompass a large range of activities carried out by managers and staff persons, sometimes alone and often as parts of specialized departments, such as a public relations division, a government affairs office, an admissions department, and a discharge-planning unit.

The strategic planning activities mentioned above are also boundary-spanning functions. *Boundary spanning* refers to transactions that enable the organization to manage (environmental) "constraints and contingencies not controlled by the organization" (Thompson, 1967, p. 67). Boundary-spanning roles typically involve networking skills, the ability to develop relationships with a broad array of individuals and groups in order to exchange resources and information of value to the organization. The social worker in a hospital doing discharge planning is performing a boundary-spanning role. She enables the organization to respond to the constraints placed on it by the insurance companies for length of inpatient stay. She must learn about and develop relationships with a variety of external organizations, such as home health care agencies and different types of nursing homes, in order to help patients continue their recovery after hospitalization. The job is a sensitive one, and a powerful one if no one else can perform this function effectively, because the hospital is under pressure to discharge patients but, at the same time, to ensure that the planning is sound so that patients recover appropriately and are satisfied with the services they have received. In one hospital where the number of non-English-speaking patients increased, a social worker developed a network of interpreters by scanning the community and reaching out to a host of immigrant groups, who were then linked to the hospital to lend their special assistance. An agency's government relations department speaks to an organizationally recognized need to be able to identify, promulgate, and influence legislation that affects the organization's ability to fulfill its mission. Boundary spanners may develop a good deal of power in their organizations if they help the organization manage environmental contingencies that are important to it and if others cannot easily do the job (Thompson, 1967). Organizational fund-raisers or resource developers, for example, can often bargain for much higher salaries than other staff members. In the growing culturally diverse environment of many social agencies, social workers who have skills in working with diverse populations will potentially gain leverage. Boundary-spanning roles in organizations facing complex, competitive, and highly dynamic external environments are likely to require the exercise of a great deal of personal discretion. If handled well, these positions are likely to bring influence and high compensation. In homogeneous and more stable environments where boundary-spanning roles can be routinized, influence will be correspondingly less.

EXAMINING THE FORMAL STRUCTURE AND OPERATIONS

Organizational Mandates, Mission, and Goals

In order to understand the workings of an organization, we need to examine both the rational and nonrational aspects of organizational life. On the rational side, we can begin by trying to understand the purpose for which the organization was formed, the mandates under which it is operating, and its operative goals. Straightforward as this may sound, such an examination usually moves us quickly onto the road of organizational complexity.

Organizational *mandates* indicate what the organization is required to do according to its charter or articles of incorporation or, in the case of a public agency, as codified in laws and ordinances (Bryson, 1989). A department of child protective services, for example, may be required by statute to investigate all cases reported to it of child abuse and neglect in a particular locality. A nonprofit agency may require, in its articles of incorporation, that the organization serve the poorest families in the county. Organizations may exceed their mandates and provide additional services, so any search for organizational purposes should not stop with mandates.

An organization's *mission* usually flows from the organization's mandate. An organization's mission statement "delineates the organization's reason for existing, usually in a short paragraph capturing the essence of what the organization is attempting to do" (Fisher, Schoenfeldt, & Shaw, 1990, p. 691). Two examples of mission statements are presented in Box 9.1. Such statements often appear in annual reports, agency brochures, and newsletters and provide a basis for the organization to acquire needed legitimacy and support in the community. Mandates and mission statements represent the *official goals* of an organization. These are relatively easy to discover and may be essential to understand for purposes of evaluating agency effectiveness, holding it accountable, and comprehending the underlying beliefs and values about human nature guiding the organization (Hasenfeld, 1983). However, they also tend to be rather general or vague and do not really tell us what the organi-

BOX 9.1	TWO MISSION STATEMENTS

THE CHESAPEAKE FOUNDATION FOR HUMAN DEVELOPMENT, INC.

The purpose of the Chesapeake Foundation for Human Development is to provide education and training opportunities for youth in an effort to foster positive relationships and the personal development that leads to satisfying and appropriate ways of living. Of particular interest to the Foundation are those youngsters at risk who have the greatest needs—those youth who are growing up without the benefit of adequate supervision and guidance and without a nurturing family and healthy neighborhood environment.

THE DOOR

The Baltimore Urban Leadership Foundation trading as The Door is organized and shall be operated exclusively for social, economic, educational, physical, spiritual, and charitable purposes by providing resource services and fund raising support to urban and multi-cultural community-based organizations and ministries for the purpose of promoting racial reconciliation, urban leadership development and community renewal in neighborhoods with minority and poverty concentrations.

---

zation spends its energy and resources actually doing in the face of multiple or competing interests and pressures generated from both internal and external environmental sources. Instead, to really understand an organization, according to Perrow (1961), we need to try to uncover the organization's *operative goals*. "Operative goals designate the ends sought through the actual operating policies of the organization; they tell us what the organization is actually trying to do regardless of what the official goals say are the aims" (p. 856). A corrections unit may include rehabilitation as one of its main aims, but if little of its budget goes into staff to provide rehabilitative services, we would have to conclude that its primary function is custodial. Hasenfeld's (1983) report of his study of community action agencies found that whereas the official goals stressed aims such as "linking low-income people to critical resources" and "developing in and among the poor the capacity for leadership," the centers actually functioned more like welfare departments and seemed to primarily serve "to provide jobs to the poverty workers themselves rather than to their clients" (pp. 86–87).

Operative goals are much more difficult to discern than official goals. First, any complex organization is likely to have multiple and sometimes conflicting goals. Second, organizations are dynamic systems. Therefore, goals are not necessarily fixed for all time; they shift as the organization loses and gains staff and board members and as the environment produces new threats or opportunities. How, then, might we determine what an organization's goals are? Hasenfeld (1983) provides one approach in his description

of what he did to learn about the goals of community action centers. His data-gathering strategy included participant observation, analysis of a sample of client case files, observations of client–staff transactions, and formal interviews with numerous staff members. Perrow (1961) indicates that if we know something about how the organization accomplishes its major tasks of acquiring resources and legitimacy, the skills that it marshals to deliver its services, and how the staff and clients and other external agencies are coordinated, and if we learn about the characteristics of the organization's "controlling elites," we can develop a pretty fair idea of an organization's operative goals. First, this means observations and interviews with key people in the organization, those in high positions of formal authority as well as powerful informal leaders. To this we would add analysis of the agency's budget to see where resources are allocated. Much of this information is available to organizational insiders, namely, staff members, if pursued thoughtfully and systematically.

Authority and Structure

Organizations are used to do what individuals and informal groups alone can't do. This gives rise to the defining characteristics and formal structure of organizations. They are rooted in the need for efficiency and effectiveness in production, coordination of organization units, and control of behavior. The central feature of complex organizations is the *scalar principle*. The scalar principle, illustrated by Figure 9.2, is the

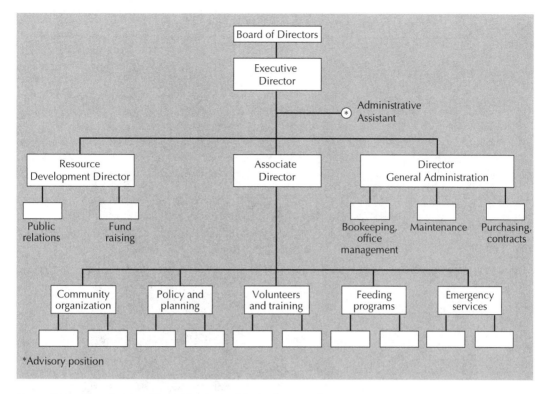

Figure 9.2   Organization Chart of a Statewide Antihunger Agency.

principle of the pyramid or a hierarchy. The flow and delegation of authority is downward from the apex and accountability and responsibility is owed upward to the apex. Authority is delegated and decentralization (diffusion) occurs downward and centralization or putting the organization into a whole occurs upward (Fayol, 1987). The other significant features of complex organizations are outlined in Box 9.2.

Organizational authority is an important form of organizational power, though not the only form, as we have seen. It derives from the formal rules and charter of the organization legitimate the power ascribed to positions of authority by its laws. It may be supported as well by tradition, expertise, and the charismatic leadership of the authority holders. The exercise of authority depends partly on the strength of the sanctions that can be applied to produce compliance. In the final analysis, however, authority rests on the consent of the governed. Persons in positions of authority who exceed their limits or whose dictates are considered unfair may breed subtle forms of noncompliance, sabotage, or even open mutiny.

The organization's hierarchical structure of authority based on the scalar principle delineates a chain of command for decision making and a span of control for all of the organization's participants. This *formal organizational structure* can be depicted graphically in an organization chart, as shown in Figure 9.2. Its logic is that "it establishes clear lines of responsibility and accountability" for decision making, "it provides for a system of controls to ensure staff compliance," and "it enables the coordination of various tasks by means of hierarchical centers of responsibility" (Hasenfeld, 1983, p. 161). Under the organizational rationality of the scalar principle, higher positions in a hierarchy have greater authority and correspondingly greater organizational knowledge and competence.

Organizational *authority* is an important form of organizational power, though not its only form. It derives from the rational or legal rules of the organization. The rules confer the authority and legitimate the power ascribed to positions. Rational or legal organizational authority often is buttressed by traditional and charismatic authority and other forms of power (Netting, Kettner, & McMurtry, 1993, p. 126).

Leaders with rational or legal authority are often given charismatic authority. Staffs frequently attribute charisma to formal leaders regardless of their personal traits, especially in times of crisis. President George W. Bush was ascribed

BOX 9.2	COMPLEX ORGANIZATION'S KEY FEATURES

1. Specialization with limited areas of authority and responsibility for each position and organization unit representing the division of labor. Each position needs well-defined authority, responsibility, and accountability (ARA).

2. Hierarchical authority structure with control and responsibility concentrated at top according to the scalar principle and delegated to subordinate organizational units and positions. Unity of command and direction is necessary for coordination, and control occurs at every level.

3. Organizational intelligence and information centralized at the top and dispersed to other units, according to need, by formal channels of communication.

4. Position specialization rooted in the needs of the organization and requires specific expertise, authority, responsibility, accountability, and compliance with organizational job descriptions.

5. Positions seen as careers that require full-time commitment contributing to organizational stability.

6. Rules and procedures for rational coordination of activities, compliance with the complex organization's division of labor, and a position's ARA established by the organization.

7. Impersonality of and secondary relationship between members rather than relating by personal traits and attractions and a separation of personal lives from organizational position to contribute to organizational stability, order, and rationality.

8. Recruitment and position assignment based on merit, ability, and technical skills as required for a position, rather than on personal traits and primary relationships.

9. Separation of the person's private and personal lives and primary relationships from the organizational position, to contribute to the organization stability, order, and rationality.

10. Promotion by seniority, merit, and contributions to production and organizational goals, rather than because of personal relations. Seniority represents merit. (Fayol, 1987; Netting, Kettner, & McMurtry, 1993, pp. 125–126)

charisma power during the period following the September 11, 2001, terrorist attacks on the World Trade Center and the Pentagon. Mayor Rudolph Giuliani during the same period was encouraged and indeed attempted to extend his time as mayor beyond the legal term limit, on the basis of charisma but not law. Charisma is especially used in the informal organization and culture when people are drawn to leaders based on their personal traits, regardless of their organizational position.

The exercise of authority depends partly on the strength of the sanctions that can be applied to produce *compliance*. Compliance refers to the ways organizations obtain adherence by organizational members to organizational goals, norms, and prescribed and proscribed behaviors. There are three general types or models of compliance: *Coercive* applies punishment to obtain compliance, *utilitarian* uses rewards and self-interest to obtain compliance, and *normative* bases compliance on values, norms, and ethics (Etzioni, 1987). The models are not mutually exclusive. Social agencies to use all three models to obtain compliance. Employees are given raises

and material rewards, sanctioned and threatened with terminations, and have their pride and professional ethics challenged. Voluntary not-for-profits (especially faith-based) organizations emphasize the normative model, while proprietaries are more likely to first employ utilitarian approaches.

Part of the organization's challenge is that *power* doesn't always correspond to the organizationally assigned formal rational or legal organizational authority. While the hierarchical structure of authority delineates a chain of command for decision making and a span of control for all of the organization's participants, it may not reflect the distribution of power. Power is the ability to act in the face of opposition to control one's self and to control or influence others. While power is rarely pure, it does exist, especially as influence or the capacity to produce *intended* and *foreseen* effects on others (Bragg, 1996; Willer, 1999; Willer, Lovaglia, & Markovsky, 1999). Influence is less than absolute power and affects the behavior of others, regardless of the intent. Influence is rooted in an ability to alter the behavior of another. Sources of power be-

BOX 9.3	FORMS OF AUTHORITY

- Traditional authority: Based on culture and customs
- Charismatic authority: Based on the personal traits and characteristics of the individual
- Rational/legal authority: Based on the organization's rules and laws and rooted in the scalar principle

yond the formally assigned organizational authority include control over resources needed by the organization such as connections to networks that can be drawn upon, personal power or charisma, expert knowledge needed by the organization, and knowledge or organizational secrets or where the figurative bodies are buried. Power and influence is enhanced when others have fewer alternatives and are dependent on the resource supplier. As Box 9.3 indicates, a knowledge of the HSO's authority has varied sources.

Other factors also affect the organization's authority structure. Authority seldom operates in a straight-line fashion. Confusion in the division of labor and organization design confuses the arrangement and distribution of authority-responsibility-accountibility (ARA) and creates uncertainty that can pervade an agency. Second, in complex organizations, authority and expertise don't always come together in a single individual sufficiently to make him or her the most effective decision maker. For example, the director of an antihunger organization may understand hunger policy and legislation quite well and have strong planning skills, but he or she may be ignorant about the whole area of resource development. To the extent that effective organizational decision making requires a unification of knowledge and authority, collective input and consultation into decision making is necessary. Third, in order to operate effectively in a turbulent external environment, organizations need flexibility more than rigid hierarchical structures to allow internally and externally an entrepreneurial organizational behavior. Another way of gaining flexibility is to use temporary structures. "Through independent, limited-life project, product, problem, or venture teams, specialists necessary to accomplish a mission are brought together for as long as necessary, but no longer" (Webber, 1979, p. 383).

Boards of Directors

Both for-profit and not-for-profit agencies have boards of directors, unless the for-profit or proprietary is not a corporation. This section primarily concerns the boards of nonprofit organizations. For-profit corporate boards may operate somewhat differently. In not-for-profits organizations, the ultimate authority for decision making about the direction of the organization rests with the board of directors or trustees, hereafter referred to as a *governing board* (Houle, 1989). Rather than flaunt this authority, the governing board normally works in partnership with the executive who oversees the operation of the organization daily and with the staff who daily carry out the actual work of the agency. The popular notion that boards establish policy and executives and staff carry it out does not work out that way in practice, for a variety of practical reasons. Board members serve only on a part-time basis and seldom have the professional expertise in the organization's service area or the necessary staff of their own to be able to make operating and even long-range policies. They are not in a good position to dictate policy from on high. If the board and the executive have developed a good working relationship, then, more typically, the executive will generate policy, fiscal, and programmatic recommendations for the board to consider and act on in a timely fashion. Usually these deal with general policies and large fiscal expenditures or programmatic changes, and an understanding of the meanings of *general* and *large* will need to be worked out between the parties involved. Boards are ultimately fiduciary responsible is to the community and not either to the agency or executive director.

The above does not imply that power struggles between executives and boards never arise, that executives always keep their boards properly informed, or that boards never try to micromanage their organizations (Kramer, 1965). In fact, in the early stages of organizational development, when an agency is starting out, board members may commonly exercise a great deal of authority over the daily affairs of the organization (Mathiasen, 1990). As the organization matures, however, governing boards evolve that recognize the need to shift from specific to general oversight.

Borrowing from Cyril O. Houle (1989, pp. 90–94), the functions of governing boards can be described briefly as follows:

1. The board should make sure that the organization remains true to its mission.

2. The board should make sure that the organization engages in long-range planning and should approve the developed plans.

3. The board should supervise the programs of the HSO to assure that objectives are being achieved in the best fashion possible. The board needs to be sophisticated enough about programs, with the help of the executive and staff, to be able to make informed judgments.

4. The board should hire the chief executive officer and establish the conditions for that person's employment.

5. The board should work closely with the executive and through the executive with staff. The executive has responsibility for administering the agency and for such functions as recruitment and deployment of staff, developing personnel policies, participatory decision making, conflict resolution, and developing effective fiscal control measures. The board is ultimately responsible for making sure that executive functions are carried out effectively.

6. The board should serves as the final arbiter and mediator in conflicts between staff members on appeal from the decision of the executive as well as in conflicts between the executive and the staff. The executive has first responsibility to resolve conflicts, but the board must serve as the court of last resort.

7. The board should establish broad policies governing the organization's program within which the executive and staff can function. These policies may originate with the board, executive, or staff. As mentioned earlier, usually such policies are drafted by the staff and executive in the form of recommendations to the board, and the board may adopt, modify, or reject them after due consideration.

8. The board is ultimately responsible to ensure that the organization's basic legal and ethical responsibilities are fulfilled.

9. The board ultimately responsible for securing and managing adequate financial resources. This is tantamount to saying that the board must secure funding for its policy decisions. The board, for example, should not decide that the organization should move into a new area of programming without attending to the resources needed to operate that program. Although securing resources is not solely the board's responsibility, it is one of the board's most important functions.

10. The board should help the organization promote a positive image with the public and with the other institutions with which the organization must transact business. The board is one of the organization's main links to the larger community. These links are very important in helping the organization establish legitimacy and find the resources it needs to operate.

11. The board should evaluate its own performance and composition to keep its membership able, broadly representative of the community, and active. It should assess its own processes and its ability to help the organization achieve its mission.

Boards of directors, in addition to their other functions, serve as important linchpins and boundary-spanning mechanisms. Board members help to network the agency with other agencies and give cohesion to the social agency community when board members serve on the boards of more than one agency. Agency policy and operations can be affected by influencing the board members. They also link the agency to important community constituencies such as client groups, holders of fiscal resources, and community economic and political power holders. The board's membership helps to give the agency community standing and legitimacy. A board's fiduciary responsibility, therefore, is to the community. These functions and contributions should be considered when constructing and using boards of directors.

THE INFORMAL STRUCTURE: WHAT'S NOT ON THE ORGANIZATION CHART

A transitional shelter for homeless men has a formal policy of not serving drug addicts. To check on their clients, a random system of urine testing is carried out, and if the test is positive, the client is supposed to be asked to leave the shelter. A new social worker tries to follow this policy with one of his clients but is overruled by his supervisor. Why? Unknown to the new staff member, the social work staff has developed an informal system for rating drug-addicted clients, so that some are given second and third chances after positive test results. He did not yet know the system; it was not part of any official agency policy. Analyzing why this unofficial policy developed and how it operates would provide a lot of insight into the workings of this particular organization. This example and our own experiences in organizations, if we think about them for a moment, remind us that the formal aspects of organizational life do not tell the whole story of how organizations function. A more complete understanding requires examination of the *informal structure* as well, that is, the associations among members of the organization that are not part of the formal organizational chart (Scott, 1973, pp. 105–106). The members of any organization form relationships with each other for many different reasons—physical proximity on or off the job, mutual interests, personal attractiveness, similar job responsibilities, shared values, social class, status, income or other social characteristics, or because of some special issue that arises. Informal associations may take on a small group life of their own with unique status and communication systems, leaders, membership requirements, and norms for behavior that associational members are expected to follow. If formal relationships provide a skeletal structure for an organization, informal relationships are the glue that holds an organization together and makes it work.

Informal associations can strongly influence organizational culture and behavior. *Organizational culture* is the informal side of organizations. Organizational culture is a pattern of basic assumptions developed by groups of organizational members to cope with problems of functioning in an organization that worked well enough to be considered valid and, therefore, to be taught to new members as the correct way to perceive, think, and feel in relation to those problems. It represents how things are and ought to be (Gortner et al., 1987, 73–75; Schein, 1987, p. 385). Organizational culture has (a) observed behavioral regularities, (b) values, norms, and rules such as *a fair day's work for a fair day's pay* or *don't be a rate buster*, (c). a philosophy, and (d) rules (or the ropes) (e) that create a feeling or climate that guides internal behavior and the ways members interact with publics (Schein, 1987, p. 384). While all organizations have formal rules to guide behavior, to understand the behavior of organizational members and understand or predict how an organization will behave under different circumstances, one must know and understand its organizational culture. Organizational culture determines the organization's *symbols and reality construction*. The organization's reality is influenced by its culture and its symbols and ideas that provide the way to interpret facts and data, The symbols are the emotionally charged words, phases, acts, and things that determines who gets what perks and privileges, who fits in, and who are the organizational heroes. The human relations and organizational development schools attempt to manage organizations by developing, manipulating, and managing the symbols and dramaturgy of organizational culture.

From a management perspective, informal groups and sometimes the organizational culture can knot up an organization in open conflict over a new policy or program, or subtly sabotage it, or sometimes even make it work well. Since such associations always develop, management would seem to do well to work with the informal organization. This involves "not threatening its existence unnecessarily, listening to opinions expressed for the group by the leader, allowing group participation in decision-making situations, and controlling the grapevine by prompt release of accurate information" (Scott, 1973, p. 107).

Nonmanagerial members of an organization also benefit from an understanding of its informal structure and culture. The formal structure tells you who has the authority to make decisions; but when that authority is remote, the informal structure and organizational culture suggests who communicates with whom, who has influence with the decision makers, and how to gain access to them. The informal system reveals alternative sources of power in the organization. In addition, the informal system often serves as the repository of organizational tradition and history, oral history actually, because much of organizational life is left unrecorded. Since formal and informal values and practices do not always agree, sometimes organizational members are faced with conflicting demands that are difficult to resolve. Better understanding of the informal system and some attention to organizational history may help an individual avoid these situations.

A Paradigm of the Competitive Culture

- Competition is good, because it brings out the best in people and makes them more productive.
- With competition, the better, more productive people will succeed.
- The people who can't stand the pressure will fail to produce.
- If they fail, they fail because they are made of lesser material.
- If we succeed, we are better than others because we do succeed.
- If we succeed, it is because we are better and therefore deserve better treatment than those who are inferior and don't succeed.

Communication is the lifeblood of any organization. Within the informal structure, communication tends to be oral rather than written. If the memo is the symbol of bureaucratic communication, the rumor could be considered the symbol of informal communication. "A rumor is an unconfirmed message transmitted along interpersonal channels" (Rogers & Agarwala-Rogers, 1976, p. 82). Since anyone can talk to someone else in the organization, rumors spread quickly through the grapevine winding under, over, and around official communication pathways. Rumors often have some truth to them, a characteristic that tends to make them credible (p. 82).

In studying organizations, the organizational chart gives us some idea of the formal structure of communications. But how do we uncover informal communication structures? Communication in organizations generally can be studied through network analysis, a *network* referring to "a number of individuals (or other units) who persistently interact with one another in accordance with established patterns" (Rogers & Agarwala-Rogers, 1976, p. 109). The basis for the interaction may be common work tasks, common attraction or liking for one another (sociometric dimension), or a topic of mutual interest. "Each network is a small pocket of people who communicate a great deal with each other, or a multitude of such pockets that are linked by communication flows" (p. 110). Informal analysis might involve observations of who spends time in whose offices, which groups eat together, regularly sit with each other at general meetings, and the like. Through careful observation it should be possible to identify cliques, opinion leaders, and individuals who seem to be able to bridge different formal and informal groupings (liaisons). Further systematic analysis is more complicated, involving the collection of sociometric and other kinds of data through surveys of the members of an organization or a subsystem therein.

COMPUTER RESOURCES AND USES IN AGENCIES AND PRACTICE

Agencies are requiring and social workers are learning how new technologies can help professionals and community residents (Giffords, 1998). Electronic and online information resources now compete with traditional paper and telephone systems. E-mail and local area networks (LANS) have greatly expanded the speed and quantity, if not always the quality, of intra- and interorganizational communication. The keyboard and monitor are replacing the water cooler and coffee room as the prime venue for office gossip. Computers, electronic information, communication management skills for the World Wide Web, videos, closed circuit telenets, interactive computer, video bases, interactive Web sites, and Internet *virtual* clinics are all critical technologies and skills for managing and conducting practice. The use of the Internet and the Web to promote social ideas, agencies, and as a venue for therapy or counseling is essential for twenty-first-century practice. E-mails and Web pages on the Internet provide expanded opportunities for public information distribution, marketing, and case coordination. Internet chat rooms are used for information sharing and emotional support groups (Finn, 1996). Computerized library reference services such as Social Work Abstracts and Psychlit allow more rapid and timely literature searches in developing case theory. Computers are most useful in performing repetitive tasks, in storing and retrieving huge amounts of qualitative and quantitative information efficiently, and in analyzing quantitative information. They can be used to retrieve specific information from extensive and complex data files or databases with relative speed and ease. Case records can be stored in computer files that allow for ease of retrieval and for the examination of traits and relationships across cases to develop treatment approaches. Spreadsheet software enables greater ease in fiscal management necessary in a competitive practice arena (Baskin, 1990, p. 6; Finn, 1988; Kreuger, 1997; Lohmann & Wolvovsky, 1979). Although sometimes employed in ways that make no real contribution in return for the effort, computers can allow access to massive amounts of information and are becoming obligatory for participation in many areas of society. Everyone used to use card catalogues at the library to research term papers on social problems. Now people use computer indexes and the Web to find out about problems, solutions, skills, resources, experiments, case studies, and arguments. They may also find that online resources are not always reliable because opinions abound in the new electronic dialogue.

Electronic mail (e-mail) is a primary computer resource and an essential communications tool. It can eliminate phone tag for professionals and allow messages to be sent with documents, lists, or pictures attached. Communication systems are enhanced with e-mail and LANS of computer stations. The use of e-mail is a reason that many small organizations and individuals have computers with Internet access. It is possible for community groups to obtain free e-mail accounts with a service on the Internet and to send and receive messages from any accessible, connected computer. If you have Internet access, you can get free e-mail through Yahoo, Hotmail, Juno, and many other companies, as well as from local governments and community organizations. In our democracy, anyone can e-mail our nation's leader (president@whitehouse.gov).

Internet access is useful to social workers in several ways. General indexing services or search engines have a number of useful resources. These include nationwide telephone directories, maps and driving directions, and local directories linked to media, government and community organizations, in addition to their primary function of finding Web pages (posted materials). State and local governments are rapidly publishing detailed information about their programs and the personnel responsible for them on the Internet.

Our agencies must be sensitive to the design of our own Web sites to make sure they are useful, interesting, and accessible to everyone (Smith & Coombs, 2000). Community education materials about general governmental activity or particular legislative bills can be obtained by electronic means (Bourquard & Greenberg, 1996; Perlman, 2000). Knowing how to use the Internet allows anyone, including disadvantaged persons, to be in instant contact with experts— lawyers, architects, and planners—from around the country for purposes of self-education, planning, or action (Blundo, Mele, Hairston, & Watson, 1999; Mele, 1999). Caring professionals have launched projects in places such as rural Florida to ensure Internet access to low-income communities.

Like most people in society, social workers are developing skills to use computers and the Internet to communicate and gather information. A number of basic texts are available for those who want to achieve computer literacy or make better use of their computer, from finding a client who has vanished to obtaining fundraising information (Basch & Bates, 2000; Ferrante & Vaughn, 1999; Martinez & Clark, 2001; Yaffe, 2001). Local libraries may be helpful to clients, to our community groups, and to us in demonstrating what can be done. Some useful Web sites are those of the Association for Community Organization and Social Administration (http://www.acosa.org); a site called "World Wide Web Resources for Social Workers" that is jointly sponsored by New York University's Ehrenkranz School of Social Work and the Division of Social Work and Behavioral Science, Mount Sinai School of Medicine (http://www.nyu.edu/socialwork/wwwrsw/); and the University of Maryland's School of Social Work Web site (http://www.ssw.umaryland.edu).

Internet users and even office LANS for e-mails are cautioned to remember that they leave a trail. Unlike the water cooler and coffee room gossiping, e-mail leaves an electronic and paper trail and is the property of and assessable to the network managers. They are not truly private. Generally, office e-mails can be monitored and read by employers and LANS managers. Internet managers can follow the electron trail of communication targets and e-mail addresses and messages.

WORKING THE SYSTEM

Formal decision-making processes in organizations are necessary for action on major policies, organizational goals, and large expenditures of resources. However, within the formal structure of goals and policies, staff members and managers must make daily operative decisions using their own discretion on a wide array of significant and insignificant but necessary matters. Some of these operative decisions fall solely within one's own jurisdiction; many also involve someone else's purview. A letter has to get out right away and your computer is down; documents must be copied to complete an important client referral; a client in crisis needs immediate attention and an exception to policy to take care of it. How do you get around the rules or get the rules bent or priorities rearranged to make the organization work better for yourself and your clients? In other words, how do you work the system to accomplish what you need to get done on your own behalf or on behalf of a client? We will consider this question in the present section, recognizing that some of the requirements for working the system also apply to broader efforts to change agency policies and priorities that will be discussed in the next section.

In considering the question of working the system or changing agency policy, let us first note our assumption that the worker is an active organizational participant, not merely a passive recipient and implementer of orders from above. As a professional social worker, you are called on to exercise judgment in your practice in accordance with the values of the profession, not merely to act out of loyalty to the organization. Sometimes this means working the system. Sometimes it means trying to change agency policy and practices altogether. Second, the question of working the system implies that organizational flexibility is necessary and desirable in the face of the myriad uncertainties that every HSO encounters.

Both working the system and changing the agency require the worker to understand formal processes for decision making, formal and informal sources of power, and formal and informal agency rules that guide decisions. This means the worker needs to understand how decision are made, who makes them, and who influences the decision-making process, since persons in authority seldom act alone without input from various subordinates or others connected with the organization (Patti & Resnick, 1972). To work the system, the worker will then have to decide whether a formal decision is necessary to pursue the particular course of action in mind, or whether the course of action merely involves some organizational tinkering (Pawlak, 1976) that can be handled informally or by exercising personal discretion. If you are new in the organization, if you have not yet established your own legitimacy and influence, or if the course of action you want to take violates a basic policy or organizational tradition, you may be wise not to act without first seeking a formal decision or the approval of an administrator.

Formal and informal organizational rules beg to be tinkered with. The reason is that "rules vary in specificity, in their inherent demand for compliance, in the manner in which compliance is monitored, and in their sanctions for a lack of compliance" (Pawlak, 1976, p. 377). Therefore workers can bend or get around the rules by exercising discretion in the case of an ambiguous or general rule or by the interpretation of the rule that they choose to make. For example, an agency rule for referring homeless persons for emergency health care can be interpreted strictly or liberally. In some cases, a sound knowledge of the rules may enable a worker to challenge an interpretation of a rule with another contradictory rule or to find the exceptions that can be used to justify one's decision. Workers also need to exercise caution in asking their superiors to interpret a rule rather than using their own judgment, lest the authority render an unfavorable decision that must then be complied with.

In working the system or trying to change it, we can increase the success rate of our efforts as advocates and change agents by developing our own "social capital" or influence in the organization (Brager & Holloway, 1977). This involves two approaches: (a) establishing positive exchange relationships with other members of the organization and (b) establishing personal legitimacy. In the former case, by offering support, assistance, approval, or favors, the worker creates an obligation to reciprocate on the part of others, hence building potential political or social indebtedness. In a reciprocal relationship, the debt that you are owed may be used to obtain assistance, reorder priorities, or take care of a problem that you need to solve—for example, getting your letter typed right away by a busy secretary or getting some inside information. As these exchanges are made, of course, you may incur debts in turn.

In order to strengthen one's legitimacy in the organization, the worker seeks to establish competence and expertise to deal with a particular problem area. Thereby, the worker gains influence in decisions affecting the problematic area. Remember, the sources of power in an organization are a function of controlling resources others need or the ability to resolve uncertainties that the organization cannot tolerate. Competence in one area may help the worker to establish a reputation for competence in other areas, thereby gradually enlarging his or her sphere of influence. Building up one's social capital is a major practice task preceding a worker's attempts at organizational change.

CHANGING THE AGENCY FROM WITHIN

Sometimes agency rules, policies, or even entire programs need to be changed in order to prevent or correct an injustice or to improve agency programs and services. For a variety of reasons, these changes may not be initiated from the top down. Line workers and middle managers often have to act as agency change agents in their own interests or in the interests of their clients and for the good of the agency. For example, a new staff member in a community mental health center found, in following up with clients, that many former mental patients were living in group homes near the agency that were little more than human warehouses. When she suggested to her supervisor that some group services might be extended to these homes, she was met with a negative response: "Our agency has no funds for outreach services of that sort." Should the matter end here? From our point of view, no. The worker, as an advocate for her clients, should try to find some way of getting them needed services, and her own agency is a reasonable place to begin. Can the worker do anything to help move the agency in a different direction? Potentially, yes. How might a worker go about acting as an agency change agent, whether in this instance or in the numerous other situations that arise?

Viewing the agency here as the client system, let us consider the change process for a moment.

As in other forms of professional social work practice, change, as we are considering it here, is purposeful change. That is, it is change that results from a deliberate process of intervention by the worker. Using a traditional problem-solving framework, then, the worker would first *study* the problem and learn as much as possible about the agency, with special attention to how power is exercised, who exercises it, and how decisions are made. Next, the worker would *assess* what needs to be done in order to bring about a change based on the information that has been generated, and a specific change goal or goals would be developed. Third, the worker would *develop intervention strategies*, or strategies for changing the client system, and implement them. And finally, the worker would *evaluate* progress or lack thereof toward achieving the goal(s) and make necessary adjustments. As Box 9.4 indicates, these are ways to "work the system."

While the internal agency change process mirrors other client change processes, the position of the worker in this process differs. Since the target system, in this case the agency, did not request assistance from the worker, and since the worker is an employee of the agency and therefore in a reduced position of power vis-à-vis the client system, the worker may be vulnerable to punitive sanctions. The risk of such sanctions depends on a variety of factors, such as the nature of the change that is being sought, the culture surrounding agency decision making, the change strategies that are selected, and the relative power of the change agent. The worker's potential vulnerability suggests two practical steps. First, the worker, as an internal change agent, must *assess the risk of punitive sanctions* and take these into consideration in planning a change strategy. A new worker who is still on probation must obviously operate more cautiously than a worker with civil service longevity or long-standing influence in the agency. Strategies and tactics that are apt to provoke a strong response from the administration should be weighed carefully. Second, the worker should try not to act alone; that is, the change agent should really be a change agent system. This means that the worker must utilize knowledge of the informal system to *identify allies* who share his or her concerns and think strategically about involving influentials in the change effort. Connections to sources of power outside of the agency may also help to decrease one's vulnerability to sanctions. Box 9.5 presents a change effort by a social worker.

To operate as an internal agency change agent it is useful, even necessary, to have a mental image of the organization as a dynamic system. (If you don't see the system as changeable, you're not likely to try to make any changes.) Kurt Lewin's (1951) *field theory* helps to provide that image. Lewin looks at organizational systems as fields of countervailing forces. Imagine a system

---

BOX 9.4   RULES OF THUMB FOR WORKING THE SYSTEM

1. Learn the decision-making process in the agency and for the particular course of action you are interested in.

2. Learn who has the formal authority for making decisions, as well as who has informal influence with decision makers in the organization and department.

3. Build your social capital by developing positive exchange relationships with other members of the organization and with organizational decision makers.

4. Build your social capital by establishing your expertise and competence in managing a particular problem area.

5. Learn as much as you can about the rules that can be bent or avoided safely by your course of action.

6. Search for loopholes, contradictory rules, or cases in which exceptions were made pre-viously, as support for your action. Remember, use the rules when they are helpful.

7. Decide if your course or action requires a formal decision or whether you are better off exercising personal discretion or handling the matter informally. Avoid formalization when it's not in your favor.

8. Decide if overloading the system will be helpful. If so, overload the old protocols and have new protocols ready to replace them.

9. Use the informal system to get necessary information and compare notes (remember reciprocity).

10. If necessary, draw on your social capital to accomplish your objective (and remember to rebuild it).

made up of different kinds of forces pushing, with varying degrees of intensity, both in the direction of system change (driving forces) and in the direction of resistance to change (restraining forces). Forces include variables ranging from external environmental factors, such as access to resources, to internal organizational factors, such as rivalries for influence or any other of the myriad variables of organizational life. When these forces are in balance, the status quo is maintained; but when the forces are out of balance, the resulting stress creates a period of disequilibrium until the forces are realigned and a new dynamic equilibrium is reestablished. With respect to a specific change, if driving forces are increased or restraining forces are reduced, or some combination thereto, then change will take place (Brager & Holloway, 1978).

After studying the problem (in this case, the problem is in the agency but the framework could be applied to an individual, a family, a group, or a community), collecting the necessary information about the agency mentioned previously, finding allies, and taking account of the workers' potential risk, a worker can systematically analyze the force field to develop a strategy for organizational change. The material that follows provides a practical set of Force Field Analysis Steps for conducting a *force field analysis* leading to a potential organizational change strategy. Follow these steps, using the Force Field Analysis Inventory located at the end of the chapter. We have partially completed the inventory using the example of the deinstitutionalized mental patients warehoused in group homes. See if you can complete it or try your own situation.

FORCE FIELD ANALYSIS STEPS

Step 1

Describe the problem or need succinctly. This is the situation you want changed. Record this on the Force Field Inventory (FFI).

Step 2

Specify the SMARRT goal or objective to be achieved. In doing this, you begin to break the problem down into smaller parts. Be as operationally specific as possible. Your goal or objective should be stated so that it can be measured. Record your goal on the FFI.

Step 3

Identify all of the restraining forces—those that contribute to the problem or work against goal achievement. Record these forces on the FFI.

Step 4

Identify all of the main driving forces—those that currently or potentially support and work for changes to achieve the goal, Record these forces on the FFI.

Step 5

Estimate the amenability to change of each force. Designate each as H (high), L (low), or U

(uncertain). Place the appropriate letter in the column to the left of the restraining forces and to the right of the driving forces.

Step 6

Identify the crucial actors and facilitators whom you feel will be best able to influence the forces you have identified as amenable to change. Record them on the FFI.

Step 7

List the driving and restraining forces that are amenable to change and identity the actors who can influence these forces. Record them on the FFI.

Step 8

Select two or more restraining forces from your diagram and outline a strategy for reducing their potency. The forces should be both important and changeable. Record your plan on your FFI.

Step 9

Select two or more driving forces from your diagram and outline a strategy for increasing their potency. The forces should be both important and changeable. Record your plan on your FFI.

Changing the agency from within, as we have presented it here, views the organization as a target of change (a target system). This perspective does not assume cooperation from management at the outset, although it by no means eliminates that possibility. In fact, to the extent that collaborative strategies, such as joint planning sessions, can be used to help change the organization, these are almost always preferable to conflict-oriented strategies. They are most appropriate in situations where the action system and the target system have good communication, and where they basically agree that a change needs to be made and that the direction of the proposed change is desirable (Brager, Specht, & Torczyner, 1987).

When the change agent is an outside consultant brought into the agency by management to help solve an agency problem or to create a particular change, such as more receptivity to an emerging client population, the organization in this context can be viewed as a client system. The agency, in effect, is the management consultant's client. Many management consultants use *organization development* strategies, which are always "cooperative, collaborative, and consensus building in nature" (Resnick & Menefee, 1993, p. 440), to achieve their aims. The interventions that are part of this discipline include such methods as "team building, intergroup activities, survey feedback, education and training, technostructural activities, process consultation, grid organization development, third-party peacemaking, coaching and counseling, life and career planning, planning and goal setting, and strategic management" (Resnick & Menefee, 1993, p. 439). Staff members who are acting as change agents

and who have had some organization development training may also use organization development methods of intervention when collaborative strategies are appropriate.

When the action system and the target system agree that a problem exists but disagree strongly on what should be done about it, change agents may have to use campaign tactics to influence the organization (Warren, 1969). "Campaign tactics include political maneuvering, bargaining and negotiation, and mild coercion" (Brager et al., 1987, p. 353). Political maneuvering is involved in all sorts of internal (and external) change efforts. It takes many forms, from persuading uninvolved agency or outside influentials to join the change effort to trading bargaining chips. However, once a campaign moves to formulating demands as the basis for bargaining and negotiation, this approach, as well as more disruptive, conflict-oriented strategies and tactics, require a well-organized action system, intensive, careful planning, and a strong commitment to the end purpose. It goes without say that all strategies are usually time-consuming and are likely to provoke angry, hostile responses from management. For these and other reasons, staff rebellions occur relatively infrequently, though they may be necessary when important values are at stake. On the other hand, successful bargaining and negotiation commonly does take place when a staff is unionized. Social workers have a long history of participation in the union movement, past and present (Alexander, 1987; Wenocur & Reisch, 1989), so that unionization still remains as a viable option for disgruntled social workers.

BOX 9.5	CHANGING AN AGENCY FROM WITHIN: CHAINIE SCOTT

Quiet and attractive, Chainie Scott[1] is an MSW with the foster care system in the District of Columbia. In 1990 she took part in a sustained effort within the agency to draw attention to huge caseloads and subsequent neglect by the system of children entitled by law to receive help from the city. First a foot soldier going to meetings and sharing her horror stories, Ms. Scott gradually became more involved and was eventually one of only two agency workers to testify against the system in the case the American Civil Liberties Union brought against the city. As a result of her leadership and as part of their change tactics, Ms. Scott was featured in several stories in

the Washington Post. The social action in which Ms. Scott participated resulted in mandates for new policies for the foster care system. (In 1995, the courts placed the system in receivership.)

The whole process we went through, myself and other social workers, I don't think we put a title to it in any set category of social activism or anything. It was a reaction of professionals. The kind of thing you do for your clients all the time, we needed to do for ourselves. It was a natural progression of events. The situations we faced were so difficult: large volume of cases, inability to visit clients, lack of basic resources like cars, and telephones that didn't work.

BOX 9.5   (CONTINUED)

I had gone to meetings, had voiced concerns, but I didn't spearhead the action that went on. I was a soldier rather than a leader, which was good because everyone needed to play their role. Working with the agency for about three years, I was very frustrated; 99 percent of the people were feeling frustration. I had reached the point where I decided it didn't matter—there wasn't anything they could do to me. It didn't seem fair, because I thought I deserved better than this as a professional. I have a graduate degree, and so I assume I should have a better working environment. Most importantly, it didn't seem fair to the children. It seemed like such a lie. Here we are, an agency that is supposed to protect and serve children, and we weren't doing either. To see the kind of suffering that happened. There was a lot of hesitancy on my part. I figured, "What the hell, what do I have to lose?" [Jokingly] Fire me! Fire me!

Q: Can you describe the social action involved in confronting the injustices in the foster care system?

A: There was definitely a plan. There were social workers who spearheaded the whole thing. Everyone else made their contribution either by comments or by coming to meetings or helping draft memos that would be sent upstairs. There was fear, too. No one wanted to risk their job, or their reputation, or their career or whatever. We tried to go through the chain of command. All the memos went to the right people. All the meetings were checked with the right people. The newspaper—Everything started gradually. There were some studies going on by the Child Welfare League looking at foster homes. The climate for foster children in the District of Columbia was such that they were not being provided the services mandated by Public Law 2-22. How not to run a child welfare system! The American Civil Liberties Union became involved. From reviewing records, they focused on the cases of Leshawn A., a child in foster care, and seven other plaintiffs, all foster children. The ACLU also began to see the problems that the system was having.

It was, for me, a feeling like somebody had to do something. There was a meeting with an ACLU attorney. The word was out that this person from the ACLU needed to talk with line-level social workers to see what's going on. I went to the meeting. I listened. There were a couple of people there, and they were saying things that didn't hit home. They weren't getting at the meat of it. So, I just started talking. I said, "Wait a second, what about this? What about that?" They, I don't know, I guess they were impressed. They kind of said, "Oh, yeah, she'd be good. Get her." [Laughing]

They asked if I wanted to do it. I said no at first. Then after some thought, I said, "Okay, I'll do it."

As a result, the ACLU decided it was appropriate to bring suit against the District of Columbia on behalf of Leshawn A. and seven other foster care children. The suit talked about the lack of continuity of care for the children, children remaining in homes that were inappropriate, children who didn't have appropriate permanency plans. The suit named all the defendants: the mayor, a director of human services, the commissioner, the administrator, and the family services division chief. We had to go to court.

It was scary! There was only two of us who gave testimony in Federal Court, Judge Hogan's courtroom. It was just matter-of-fact questions, but it was someone who was on the front line answering those questions with answers that you wouldn't get from the administration. The order came down from Judge Hogan that our child welfare system is unconstitutional to the children. After the Leshawn hearing ended and the ruling came down, we did interviews for the radio. That was still a part of the process.

I'm not sure what the process is going to be in the post-Leshawn days. I don't know how active I'll be. I'll be there, but I may not be in the front. We said early on we should be part of the remedy for change. It never happened. I read through the plan, and it's a good plan. But I think it could have had a different tilt to it had line-level social workers been involved. There's this callousness beyond the line-level social worker. Maybe as you move up and become more of the policy part of it, you're so far removed you don't feel it—because you don't see it. That's why we're having so many problems now with the plan.

That's been real difficult. Here we are now, 2 years later, and people are still leaving. The big thing our agency keeps talking about now is, we have hired 90 new social workers. I say you need to ask how many have left and why did they

BOX 9.5 (CONTINUED)

leave? I can bet you, they left for the same reasons that came out at the court hearing—lack of cars, lack of support, lack of resources, lack of direction, too many cases, overwhelmed. They're leaving for the precise reasons that folks like myself and all the others have been complaining about and crying and screaming and saying, "Hey, help us!" Nothing has changed for it! How could that possibly be?

After the lawsuit had been won and reforms were slowly underway, Ms. Scott has had time to reflect on the process and the outcome.

Professionally I say the court win was good. Personally, I say I don't think it really made a difference. Professionally it was good because it was something you have to do as a social worker. You have to be the one that says, "Oh, wait a second, this is wrong, this is not right, we're not doing this right." You have to not allow yourself to get brainwashed by your system, whatever that system is—private or government. If it's not right, then you have to say something or do something to make it different. Personally, I don't think it made a big difference because I just don't think our administration has the stomach for it, the courage, or the commitment to do it. They talk good talk, but they're not walking the walk.

When I started in 1987, we were getting cases on our unit, mommy on crack, mommy selling food stamps, mommy leaving child alone, leaving child with unwilling caretaker, child left alone, electricity about to be cut off, mother facing eviction. Every single case. Now somewhere along that line, somebody in a position of policy, of administration, should have said, "Now what kind of cases are we getting? What's going on here? Is there a trend going on out there?" There was no forecasting, no planning, no sense of how the population changes or what kinds of things we are seeing. It didn't have to get as bad as it was. What could have qualified as social action is if one of the administrators had said, "Wait a second. We have a problem here. Let's stop this." If commitment was there, why are we still where we are? I don't want to hear that it takes a while to turn the system around. I know it takes a while to turn the system around. How did it get this way? Why didn't someone do something, rather than taking the posture of business as usual?

I feel real changed by what happened in that I'm not afraid. I was afraid of them. It was like treading on water. But now, I think I have a better sense of the process. When you speak out, and if you have the commitment, you have to figure, "What can they do?" If they do something, what difference does it make so long as the change that you want comes about?

Inside themselves, social activists have to know where their commitment lies. They need to know what that battle is for them; if they have the resolve to do it; if they end up becoming a sacrificial lamb, whether that's okay with them. This is something you have to go through and not feel bitter about in the end. In the classroom you have to learn what it is to organize, how to communicate what those concerns are that you're dealing with and how you want to see those issues resolved. You certainly have to have a frame of reference. You need to understand why people didn't want to change. You bring all your knowledge together. In the process of change, you have to continue to be part of the remedy. You just can't bring it on. You have to be there to help devise the rules.

[Laughing] It was a fun process. You get all psyched up! "Yes, let's go! Oh, yeah, that's what you want to do? Grrr!" It's very exciting! I have no regrets about anything I did. As a matter of fact, I feel proud of myself. I have a sense of principle. I thought testifying, etc., was the right thing to do. Now, I want to leave district government. I can make a much more positive impact outside of a system that's restrictive and bureaucratic and censorized. So, while I'm still feeling some of those frustrations that led to wanting to change the foster care system, I made my mark when it was appropriate for me to make my mark. I don't want to continue being on the front line anymore. I have enough experience and ammunition and that thing that gets in you when you've been through a lot—that "we can't let this happen again because I've lived through it." It would be a natural progression to do advocacy for a group. I always find myself looking at this big picture. I see myself staying in social action in some capacity or another.

Ms. Chainie Scott-Jackson, largely an unsung social work hero except by those who knew her, died of leukemia and lymphoma on December 5, 2002, in Lanham, Maryland.[1]

Last, *whistle-blowing* (calling to the public or a higher authority's attention wrongdoing by an agency or its management) is a change option. Whistle-blowing often carries with it very real personal costs and doesn't always result in organizational change. Agencies tend to rally to protect their own. The potential whistle-blower should apply the guidelines set forth in Chapter 1 to be sure the action is fair, in the public interest, and is the least harmful of the available alternatives to colleagues and the agency (Reisch & Lowe, 2000).

FORCE FIELD ANALYSIS INVENTORY[2]

Definition of Terms

Critical Actors: The individuals or groups who have the power to make a change. Their support or approval is necessary in order for your SMARRT objective to be achieved.

Facilitators: A type of critical actor (1) whose approval must be obtained before the problem can be brought to the attention of other critical actors and (2) v/hose approval, disapproval, or neutrality will have a decisive impact on a critical actor(s).

Driving Forces: Forces which when increased change behavior and conditions in a desired and planned manner toward achieving the objectives.

Restraining Forces: Forces which when increased or stay the same reinforce the status quo or move conditions away from the objective.

Potency or Strength: The strength of the restraining or driving force to inhibit or promote change. It can be rated high (H), low (L), or uncertain (U, unable to assessed).

Amenability of Conditions to Change or Influence: The potential to change the potency of a force, for example, the ability to increase a driving force's or decrease a restraining force's potency.

Problem Situation or Need	SMARRT Objective
Support group services needed for mental patients in the Green Street Group Home	Have an operational support group service for the mental patients in the Green Street Group Home by January 30, 20xx.

Restraining forces against establishment of support group (Rate Potency or Strength: H - high, L - Low, U - unable to decided)	Driving forces supporting establishment of support group (Rate Potency or Strength: H - high, L - Low, U - unable to decided)
Tight budget and fiscal situation ( ) Transient caseload ( ) Clinical staff opposes ( ) No group worker on staff ( )	New Program Director wanting to establish herself ( ) Social Work Interns Available ( ) Patient Interest in Support Group ( ) Media coverage of Warehousing Mental Patients ( )

Critical Actors (CA) and Facilitators (F)

1. Program director (CA) to approve group and reduce clinical opposition.
2. Social work field practicum director (CA) to assign appropriate student intern to agency.
3. Agency director (F) needed to approve project operation
3. Media beat reporter (F) – to do a story on the facility after support group begins

4. School of social work faculty (F) to serve as a field instructor for student intern and provide legitimacy to the project.
5. Others (based on your agency experience speculate as to possible critical actors and facilitators)?

_____

Based on your agency experience speculate as to what other forces, critical actors and facilitators that might serve as driving forces?

_____

Based on your agency experience speculate as to what other forces, critical actors and facilitators that might serve as restraining forces?

_____

Change Strategies

- Strategies to reduce the potency of the restraining forces and to influence conditions to become amenable to change.
- Strategies to increase the potency of the driving forces and to influence conditions to become amenable to change.

Discussion Questions

1. If a change in client services is needed in your agency, how will you go about making the change?

2. If clients are being harmed by an agency policy or operation and the agency management appears unwilling to alter the program or operation, what is your ethical obligation? What should you do?

Notes

1. Chainie Scott was interviewed on November 6, 1992, by Brenda Kunkel, a graduate student at the University of Maryland School of Social Work for *Challenging: Interviews with Advocates and Activists*, a 1993 monograph edited by Dr. Patricia Powers. A caveat must be added to the District of Columbia Foster Care case example of organizational change from within. The situation in the agency is still problematic. Change of any large organization is complex. It requires an abiding effort if the change is to endure. Systems theory indicated that while change in one part of the system will change other parts of the system and changes in the inputs will change the system, unchanged components of a system tend to bring the changed component back to an old, prechange, state. This is especially true in large complex organizations where policymaking is remote from the operational or line level. Child welfare services, like services from most large metropolitan social agencies, suffer from inadequate funding to fulfill their responsibilities.

2. Force Field Analysis is a tried and tested analytical methodology. Its procedures and formats are available from many resources. This format was adapted from Lauffer (1982) and from Salus, Reagan, and DePanfilis (1986). Also see Brager and Holloway (1978).

References

Aldrich, H. E. (1979). *Organizations and environments*. Englewood Cliffs, NJ: Prentice Hall.

Alexander, L. B. (1987). Unions: social work. *Encyclopedia of social work* (Vol. 2, 18th ed., pp. 793–798). Silver Spring, MD: National Association of Social Workers.

Basch, R., & Bates, M. E. (2000). *Researching online for dummies*. Foster City, CA: IDG Books.

Baskin, D. B. (Ed.). (1990). *Computer applications in psychiatry and psychology*. New York: Brunner/Mazel.

Berman, J., & Pfleeger, J. (1997). Which industries are sensitive to business cycles? *Monthly Labor Review, 120*(2), 19–25.

Blundo, R. G., Mele, C., Hairston, R., & Watson, J. (1999). The Internet and demystifying power differentials: A few women on-line and the housing authority. *Journal of Community Practice, 6*(2), 11–26.

Bourquard, J. A., & Greenberg, P. (1996, March). Savvy citizens. *State Legislatures, 28*–33.

Brager, G., & Holloway, S. (1977). A process model for changing organizations from within. *Administration in Social Work, 1*(4), 349–358.

Brager, G., & Holloway, S. (1978). *Changing human service organizations: Politics and practice*. New York: Free Press.

Brager, G., Specht, H., & Torczyner, J. L. (1987). *Community organizing* (3rd ed.). New York: Columbia University Press.

Bragg, M. (1996). *Reinventing influence: How to get things done in a world without authority*. Washington, DC: Pitman.

Bryson, J. M. (1989). *Strategic planning for public and nonprofit organizations*. San Francisco: Jossey-Bass.

Chesapeake Foundation for Human Development, Inc. (1993). *Annual report*. Baltimore, MD. P.O. Box 19618, http://www.ccyd.org/untact.htm

Crozier, M. (1964). *The bureaucratic phenomenon*. Chicago: University of Chicago Press.

Cyert, R. M., & March, J. G. (1963). *A behavioral theory of the firm*. Englewood Cliffs, NJ: Prentice Hall.

The Door. (1992). *Annual report*. Baltimore, MD. 219 N. Chester St. http://nmc.loyde.edu/Door.html

Dressel, P. L. (1992). Patriarchy and social welfare work. In Y. Hasenfeld (Ed.), *Human services as complex organizations* (pp. 205–233). Newbury Park, CA: Sage.

Etzioni, A. (1987). Compliance, goals, and effectiveness. In J. M. Shafritz & J. S. Ott (Eds.), *Classics of organizational theory* (2nd ed., pp. 177–187). Chicago: Dorsey.

Fayol, H. (1987). General principles of management. In J. M. Shafritz & J. S. Ott (Eds.), *Classics of organizational theory* (2nd ed., pp. 51–81). Chicago: Dorsey.

Ferrante, J., & Vaughn, A. (1999). *Let's go sociology: Travels on the Internet* (2nd ed.). Belmont, CA: Wadsworth.

Finn, J. (1988). Microcomputers in private nonprofit agencies: A survey of trends and training requirements. *Social Work Research and Abstracts, 24*(1), 10–14.

Finn, J. (1996). Computer-based self help groups: On-line recovery for addiction. *Computers in Human Services, 13*(1), 21–41.

Fisher, C. D., Schoenfeldt, L. F., & Shaw, J. B. (1990). *Human resource management*. Boston: Houghton Mifflin.

Freudenheim, M. (1996, February 5). Charities say government cuts would jeopardize their ability to help the needy. *The New York Times, p.* B8.

Giffords, E. D. (1998). Social work on the Internet: An introduction. *Social Work, 43*(3), 243–251.

Gortner, H. F., Mahler, J., & Nicholson, J. B. (1987). *Organizational theory: A public perspective*. Chicago: Dorsey.

Greenley, J. R., & Kirk, S. A. (1973). Organizational characteristics of agencies and the distribution of services to applicants. *Journal of Health and Social Behavior, 14*, 70–79.

Hasenfeld, Y. (1983). *Human service organizations*. Englewood Cliffs, NJ: Prentice Hall.

Hasenfeld, Y. (1992b). The nature of human service organizations. (pp. 3–23). Newbury Park, CA: Sage.

Houle, C. O. (1989). *Governing boards: Their nature and nurture*. San Francisco: Jossey-Bass.

Institute for Distance Education, University System of Maryland. (1997). *Linkages, 6*(1).

Johnston, D. C. (1997). United Way, faced with fewer donors, is giving away less. *The New York Times*, pp. 1, 28.

Kramer, R. M. (1965). Ideology, status, and power in board–executive relationships. *Social Work, 10*, 108–114.

Kreuger, L. W. (1997, Winter). The end of social work, *Journal of Social Work Education, 33*(1), 19–27.

Larson, M. S. (1977). *The rise of professionalism*. Berkeley: University of California Press.

Lauffer, A. (1982). May the force be with you: Using force field analysis. In A. Lauffer, *Assessment tools for practitioners, managers, and trainers*. Beverly Hills, CA: Sage.

Lohmann, R. A., & Wolvovsky, J. (1997). Natural language processing and computer use in social work, Administration in Social Work. 3(4), 409–422.

Lewin, K. (1951). *Field theory in social science*. New York: Harper & Row.

Martinez, R. C., & Clark, C. L. (2001). *The social worker's guide to the Internet*. Needham Heights, MA: Allyn & Bacon.

Mathiasen, K. (1990). *Board passages: Three key stages in a nonprofit board's life cycle.* Governance Series Paper. Washington, DC: National Center for Nonprofit Boards.

Mele, C. (1999). Cyberspace and disadvantaged communities: The Internet as a tool for collective action. In M. A. Smith & P. Kollock (Eds.), *Communities in Cyberspace* (pp. 290–310). London: Routledge.

Menefee, D. T., & Thompson, J. J. (1994). Identifying and comparing competencies for social work management: A practice driven approach. *Administration in Social Work, 18*(3), 1–25.

Netting, F. E., Kettner, P. M., & McMurtry. (1993). *Social work macro practice.* White Plains, NY: Longman.

O'Neill, J. V. (2003. Feb.). Private sector employees most members. *NASW News, 48*(2), 8.

Patti, R. J., & Resnick, H. (1972). Changing the agency from within. *Social Work, 17*(4), 48–57.

Pawlak, E. J. (1976). Organizational tinkering. *Social Work, 21*(5), 376–380.

Perlman, E. (2000). Chief of tomorrow: Focused on digital government. *Governing, 14*(2), 36.

Perrow, C. (1961). The analysis of goals in complex organizations. *American Sociological Review, 26*, 854–866.

Phillips, K. P. (1993*). Boiling point: Republicans, Democrats, and the decline of middle-class prosperity.* New York: Random House.

Powers, P. (Ed.). (1993). *Challenging: Interviews With Advocates and Activists* [Monograph]. Baltimore: University of Maryland at Baltimore, School of Social Work.

Reisch, M., & Lowe, J. I. (2000). Of means and ends: Teaching ethical community organizing in an unethical society. *Journal of Community Practice, 7*(1), 19–38.

Resnick, H., & Menefee, D. (1993). A comparative analysis of organization development and social work, with suggestions for what organization development can do for social work. *Journal of Applied Behavioral Science, 29*(4), 432–445.

Rogers, E. M., & Agarwala-Rogers, R. (1976). *Communication in organizations.* New York: Free Press.

Salamon, L. M. (1992). *America's nonprofit sector: A primer.* New York: Foundation Center.

Salamon, L. M. (1997). *Holding the center: America's nonprofit sector at a crossroad. A report for Nathan Cummings Foundation.* New York: Nathan Cummings Foundation.

Salamon, L. M., Altshuler, D. M., & Myllyluoma, J. (1990). *More than just charity: The Baltimore area nonprofit sector in a time of change.* Baltimore: Johns Hopkins University, Institute for Policy Studies.

Salus, M., Ragan, C., & DePanfilis, D. (1986). *Supervision in child protective services.* New York: Child Protective Services Training Academy.

Schein, E. H. (1987). Defining organizational culture. In M. Shafritz & J. S. Ott (Eds.), *Classics of organizational theory* (2nd ed., rev. & exp.). Chicago: Dorsey.

Scott, W. G. (1973). Organization theory: An overview and appraisal. In F. Baker (Ed.), *Organizational systems: General systems approaches to complex organizations* (pp. 99–119). Homewood, IL: Richard D. Irwin.

Sherman, W. R., & Wenocur, S. (1983). Empowering public welfare workers through mutual support. *Social Work, 28*(5), 375–379.

Smith, M. L., & Coombs, E. (2000, Spring). Could Stevie Wonder read your web page? *The New Social Worker, 21–23.*

Strauss, A., Schatzman, L., Ehrlich, D., & Bucher, R. (1963). The hospital and its negotiated order. In E. Freidson (Ed.), *The hospital in modern society* (pp. 147–169). Glencoe, IL: Free Press.

Thompson, J. D. (1967). *Organizations in action.* New York: McGraw-Hill.

Thompson, N. (2000). *Understanding social work: Preparing for practice.* London: Macmillan.

Walker, S. (2001). Tracing the contours of postmodern social work. *British Journal of Social Work, 31*(1), 29–39.

Warren, R. L. (1969). Types of purposive social change at the community level. In R. M. Kramer & H. Specht (Eds.), *Readings in community organization practice* (pp. 205–222). Englewood Cliffs, NJ: Prentice Hall.

Webb, S. A. (2001). Some considerations on the validity of evidence-based practice in social work. *British Journal of Social Work, 31*(1), 57–79.

Webber, R. A. (1979). *Managing organizations.* Homewood, IL; Richard D. Irwin.

Wenocur, S., & Reisch, M. (1989). *From charity to enterprise: The development of American social work in a market economy.* Urbana: University of Illinois Press.

Willer, D. (Ed.). (1999). *Network exchange theory.* Westport, CT: Praeger.

Willer, D., Lovaglia, M. J., & Markovsky, B. (1999). Power and influence: A theoretical bridge. In D. Willer (Ed.), *Network exchange theory* (pp. 229–247). Westport, CT: Praeger.

Yaffe, J. (2001). *Social work on the net.* Boston: Allyn & Bacon.

10

Using Work Groups: Committees, Teams, and Boards

Sometimes it seems that all social workers ever do is go to meetings. There are staff meetings to clarify agency policies, team meetings to coordinate treatment plans, interagency meetings to work out service agreements, board committee meetings to plan fund-raising events, professional association committee meetings to do conference planning, and community meetings. These are not clinical group meetings. None of these meetings involve direct group work with clients—for example, running a treatment group for sexually abused girls, a parenting group for new mothers, or a socialization group for senior citizens. But they are social work professional groups. It is to be hoped that all of these meetings are necessary for direct service work to go forward. All of these meetings involve work with task groups of some kind—committees, task forces, boards, teams, coalitions, task forces, planning bodies, and the like. Task groups are working groups established to achieve some specific purpose or goal. The specific purpose goal or goal is usually external to the group and does not focus on changing the traits of individual group members (Kirst-Ashman & Hull, 2001, pp. 90–100; Payne, 2000).

Effective work with task groups, an important aspect of all social work practice, is essential for community practice. The task group is one of the main vehicles through which community practice is carried out. Organizing groups and committees and participating as chair, member, or facilitator of one of these bodies are the means

by which social advocacy, interagency and interprofessional planning and coordination, and community development are accomplished. Although we often participate as members of a task group, in this chapter the role of the social worker is conceived predominantly as leader, chair, or staff member. The roles' tasks can be adapted to participation as a member in work groups if we keep in mind why task groups are used. We participate in work groups because we want to get something done and need a group to get it done. Regardless of our formal position in the task group, we should assume leadership when necessary to enhance the group's effectiveness. Leadership and decision making in task groups and organizations, including social agencies, are rarely democratic with everyone having equal authority and say but should be *consultative-participatory*.

A CASE EXAMPLE

Besides the task groups in direct service agencies, social action organizations also are sustained by task groups. These may be temporary, ad hoc groups internal or external to the organization. Organization or agency members, staff, or leaders can serve a part of outside groups formed by other organizations. Organizations also support the work of task groups without members serving on the task group or controlling the task group. Organizations may also have to fight the work of task groups formed by opponents. A distinctive and critical feature of macropractice and social action task groups is involving the community. The task groups are used to recruit and train leadership, deve;lop and tailor participation for subgroups of community members, further program objectives, and empower the community members. Very small organizations use work groups to build networks and alliances by involving contributors from other organizations, and huge organizations use groups to create more intimacy for participants and get down to the grassroots level. Progressive organizations use these work groups to enable members to run the organizations.

Some established community organizations have an enormous reach geographically or in their network of institutional members (churches, unions, schools, and other community organizations). This requires an organizational structure and process that can keep association and individual members of the alliance engaged. Sociologist Mark Warren has studied the Industrial Area Foundation, particularly in the Southwest. He provides an organizational map of the units constituting one Fort Worth affiliate known as ACT (see Table 10.1). In this example, the task groups that comprise the organizational apparatus are permanent by design, even as their membership changes. ACT was formed to bring together African Americans, Anglos, and Mexican Americans in united social action on pressing issues (Warren, 2001, Chapter 4). As Warren (2001) explains, "ACT leaders from different communities have the opportunity to build bridging ties with each other through working together on action teams and on organization-wide leadership bodies. Action teams work on a variety of campaigns, like job training. Meanwhile, about 45 leaders, drawn from all member congregations, meet monthly as the organization's central decision-making body. The Strategy Team brings about 16 leaders from the three racial groups in the organiza-

TABLE 10.1 Teams and Other Ways to Involve Organization Members

Organizational Unit	Composition and Involvement
Cochairs	Two or three top leaders, including chair of Strategy Team and The Organizing Council (TOC)
Strategy Team (Executive Committee)	16 key leaders representing three ethnic groups that comprise TOC Meets bimonthly to plan strategy; sets agenda for TOC Co-opts its members from TOC

The Organizing Council (TOC)
    Steering Committee
	About 45 attendees, usually two to three leaders from each member church
	    Decision-making body
	    Meets monthly

Delegates Assembly	Size varies from 30 to 80 members Meets occasionally, usually every 3 months, to ratify important decisions
Action Teams • Job Training • Bond • Health Care • Parental Empowerment (schools) • Education Reform • Neighborhood Strategy Project • Utility Reform • Money Campaign (fund-raising)	Five to seven members, usually triracial leaders drawn from different churches
Member Church Committees	Address church/neighborhood concerns Implement ACT-wide campaigns in the church
Annual Convention	Network of all leaders (1,000–2,000 depending on year); stages ritual events that endorse agenda and leadership; conducts business with public officials

Note. Adapted from *Dry Bones Rattling,* by Mark Warren, 2001, p. 115. Copyright 2001 by Princeton University Press. Adapted with permission.

tion together to act as the executive committee" (p. 114).

What may be a complicated structure for a typical association can be very functional for sustaining an alliance involving the socially marginalized. When community organizations seek to further community participation, they create structures that seem elaborate but are designed to be inclusive and democratic (again, see Table 10.1). Grassroots organizations to build and bridge social capital may entail a different process. For instance, several regional campaigns to engage communities in social justice work have hired up to 60 organizers as organizational staff and community organizers. The intent is to unite an institutional base of civic and church organizations to fashion an infrastructure. The infrastructure consists of (a) support for the 20 to 100 organizations in the umbrella (e.g., interparish) and (b) a voluntary leadership cadre on which each participating organization depends (e.g., intraparish). Thus, community workers link different organizations as they meet with many organizations and federation members in small groups.

Like other parts of professional social work, social work practice with task groups involves a deliberate process of intervention to accomplish a goal. Just as direct service workers interact purposefully during interviews with their clients, social workers use themselves consciously and deliberately in meetings to further the aims of the task group. *No social worker participating in a task group, whether as staff, leader, or regular member, should approach a meeting unprepared.* The task group, in that sense, is an *action system* for the social worker. Members of a task group usually participate as citizens, colleagues, or representatives of larger network constuencies who come together to achieve an external purpose. They have not sought the social worker's help with an interpersonal or intrapsychic problem. The social worker's preparation is for helping them work on the task. Even when the task group is composed of agency clients, the aim of the group, as a working group, is external, not internal. Clients are part of an action system.

The worker does develop a contractual relationship with the group as with a client system. Sometimes the contract is explicit: The agency board hires a social worker to coordinate its fund-raising efforts, or the agency staff members hire a consultant to help them improve their skill in serving a population with special needs. A written job description may form the basis for a working agreement, and direct negotiation about roles and boundaries will usually take place before any substantive work begins. Frequently the contract is implicit, as with the school social worker who organizes a parents group to develop a mentoring program. Here the social worker's and members' understanding of their respective roles and responsibilities evolves out of their shared interaction and out of the worker's explanations or interpretations of the different roles in the group.

TEAMS

Teams are a specific type of task group. A team generally is a number of people working together, with each member or position on the team having a fairly unique, complementary, and essential contribution that forms a whole necessary to achieve the common and shared goal. Although each team member's contribution may not be equal, all are necessary. There is interdependence. Success or failure is defined as a collective achievement. Individuals do not achieve success without the whole team's achieving success (Payne, 2000, pp. 5–7, 55–59). Members with contributions not truly needed are not truly team members. And there can be no all-stars on losing teams.

Teams can be used to coordinate different expertise or to form networks. They are used in social services as *linchpin structures* to unite the resources of different organizations, or intraorganizationally to coordinate resources of different units in the same agency. A linchpin structure connects a network of units with its members as representatives or linking units to bring the constituencies to the team's task.

Teams, whether linchpins or composed of individual expertise require certain strategies for effectiveness and accountability (Payne, 2000):

- Boundaries between each member's expertise, contributions, and authority-responsibility-accountability (A-R-A) should be clear and understood by all team members.

- With A-R-A clarity, each member should know the contributions, the roles, of other team members and the policies, rules, and procedures for coordination.

- The team should build on the strengths inside the team and use the members to link to resources outside the team.

- The team should emphasize the use of consensus and a consultative-participatory leadership for team decisions. Consensus is defined as meaning "everyone can live with it" rather than "everyone thinks it's the best thing to do."

- Respect, extend, and work with each member's skills. While maintaining some flexibility for reorganization and recognizing that it is sometimes necessary, avoid frequent reorganization as it confuses A-R-A, weakens cohesion, and complicate coordination[1]

As teams are specific types of work groups, *task forces* are special subsets of teams (Gersick, 1988). Task forces are working groups that are action oriented, time limited, and formed administratively to deal with problems that cannot be solved by routine methods (Johnson, 1994). Their particular nature, it is argued, make them prone to a development pattern of "punctuated equilibrium" whereby the group alternates between fairly long periods of inertia and bursts of creative energy. Task forces should be used where there are especially clear, reasonably unique, and time-limited SMARRT objectives or to develop the objectives.[2] SMARRT objectives are operational goals or goals that can be translated into specific actions to achieve them. They have saliency and acceptability to members. SMARRT objectives emphasize a task orientation rather than a process of gradual development as proposed in most models of group development.

GROUP DEVELOPMENT AND THE ROLE OF THE SOCIAL WORKER

Task and Process

Professional practice with task groups requires good listening skills and keen observation of behavior. The worker is truly a participant-observer, but what should the worker attend to? The answer is that all group interactions have a *task* and a *process* dimension. *Task groups of all kinds must attend to both in order to succeed.*

A group's *task dimension* refers to the subject or content of the group's interactions. For example, when parent volunteers begin to meet with a school social worker to plan a mentoring program for their children's school, the different ideas they discuss about mentoring programs and how they should be established represent the task dimension of that interaction. In the course of the meetings, the worker will listen to alternative proposals and help the group to assess clarity, see connections between ideas, consider their merits, determine what information may still be needed, and make decisions that will eventually lead to agreement on a plan and its implementation.

A group's *process dimension* deals with the nature and dynamics of the interactions and relationships that develop within the group. In the words of Philip Hanson (1972): "Process is concerned with what is happening between and to group members while the group is working. Group process, or dynamics, deals with such items as morale, feeling tone, atmosphere, influence, participation, styles of influence, leadership struggles, conflict, competition, cooperation, etc." (p. 21).

While task and process dimensions of group interaction are conceptually distinction, operationally they are inseparable. Task groups are formed to complete tasks rather than engage in a process. Process has consequence in that it can contribute or distract from task achievement. And success on group tasks enhances process, bonds members, and makes the group more rewarding. A good process in task groups contributes to task accomplishment and is concerned with the satisfaction group members obtain from participating in successful group task accomplishments. Member morale is often a function of task success. When the members of a mentoring group become angry at a member (Mrs. Smith) who monopolizes meetings, arguments begin to break out, and attendance begins to wane. These are manifestations of the group's process dimension disrupting the group's task dimension. In observing a group for task and process, Hanson suggests that a worker think about the following questions: What signs of feeling do I see in the group members? How do the members feel about each other? Are there any cliques that seem to be forming? What's the energy level of the group? Are all of the members getting a chance to participate? How does the group make decisions? In the course of the meetings, the worker will try to facilitate interaction that strengthens the members' bonds to each other and their commitment to the group as a whole. The worker, of course, is also mindful of keeping the group on task.

In the above example, where Mrs. Smith arouses the ire of the other group members, the arguments that take place may well be about the proposals someone has offered or the procedures for reaching a decision. So, both content and process issues emerge at the same time. Or suppose that a member asks the group to review how a particular decision was made, that is, to consider the process that the group went through. For analytical purposes, we can generally assign interactions centered on issues of communication to the process dimension, and interactions centered on issues of goal implementation to the task dimension.

Stages of Group Development: When Is a Group a Group?

People who meet for the first time to do some work together, whether as a committee or a team or planning body, will vary greatly in the amount of energy they want to invest in the task and in their commitment to working with other people to do it. Yet they have come together because the task is either too complex or too difficult to do alone; it will take a group to do it. This tension between *differentiation* (going it alone, doing it one's own way) and *integration* (collaborating with others, giving up some of one's autonomy) captures the essence of the struggle involved in forming a group (Heap, 1977). *Until that collection of autonomous individuals begins to feel some allegiance to the collectivity and finds some way to work together on a common goal, a group has not yet fully formed.*

Stage theories of group development exhibit a remarkable degree of similarity despite variations in the number and names of the stages. They are useful in that they reinforce the simple but important idea of *group development over time.* Groups can do different things at different points in the course of group formation. This knowledge gives workers a frame of reference for their interventions in the group and helps them set realistic objectives for group meetings.

A few cautions are necessary before we consider the stages of group development in more detail. First, the stages of group development, presented discretely in theory, cannot be neatly separated from each other in the real world. The stages represent a continuum, perhaps a pleated continuum, with overlapping and spiraling stages. A group can sometimes loop back to a preceding stage if it was previously unsuccessful in completing that stage or if its membership changes. A group with a significantly changed composition becomes a new group for group development purposes. One phase runs into another; groups take two steps forward and one step backward, and so on. Nor can we define an exact length of time for a given phase. We cannot say, for example, that it takes a group three meetings or 3 hours to get through the formative stage. Nor does the notion of stages make group life as predictable as it might seem. In the same way that each of us is unique even though we all pass through similar stages of growth and

development, groups are unique. The dynamics of any group are influenced by many different variables —size, purpose, sponsorship, context, composition, nature of the task (complexity, emotionality, etc.), time frame, and more. To effectively practice with task groups, we need to know the theories about groups in general and about task groups. We also need to know our task groups. Group behavior is not simply a function of the group's stage of development.

With these cautions in mind, let's review the stages of group development. Tuckman (1965) synthesized a great deal of research on small groups into a developmental model that links group task (instrumental) and process (socioemotional) dimensions with stages of development. His easy-to-remember stages are *forming, storming, norming, performing, and adjournment* (Tuckman, 1965; Tuckman & Jensen, 1977). Table 10.2 presents a comparison of the main features of each stage, the characteristic behaviors one might expect along the task and process dimensions, and the role of the worker. We have augmented Tuckman's ideas with information from other models (Bandler & Roman, 1999; Toseland & Rivas, 1995) and community practice experience.

STAGE 1: FORMING

In this stage, prospective group members are trying to determine what the group and other group members are all about. They are getting oriented. They are wondering what the group will be like, what will be expected of them, whether they will be accepted, and whether or not to make a commitment. They are rather dependent on the leader, organizer, or chair to provide an orientation. They ask orienting questions and sometimes exhibit testing behaviors. Members are ambivalent about commitment and often are unwilling to volunteer for tasks. They joke around, and if not convinced of the group or task's importance, may attend irregularly. In this formative phase, the worker, either directly if there is no chairperson or working through the chairperson if there is one, helps to establish the group climate (accepting, businesslike, formal, informal, open, etc.). Leadership, whether by the formally recognized leader such as a chair or by others assuming leadership, also helps the group establish or clarify its goals into SMARRT objectives and ground rules.

SMARRT objectives and operational goals need to be distinguished from a group's inoperative goals. Inoperative goals can't be translated into action. They are generally used as part of staging or as public relations window dressing

TABLE 10.2 Stages of Group Development

Stages of Development	Main Features	Task Dimension	Process Dimension	Worker's Role
Forming	Ambivalent about commitments; dependence on leaders	Orientation to task and content; search for ground rules	Testing behaviors in performance due to ambivalent commitment	Orienting members; contracting; setting goals and rules; working through dependency issues
Storming	Conflict; struggles for power; development of structure	Obtaining agreement with content or substance	Heightened emotions; hostility; struggles for control; resistance to work	Constructive conflict resolution; fostering participatory democratic structure
Norming	Development of group cohesion; harmony	Open exchange of opinions	Acceptance of members' peculiarities; development of bonding and "we-ness"; unity	Keeping group focused on task rather than just socializing
Performing	Structuring participation for task accomplishment	Task focus; emergence of solutions	Functional role relatedness; interpersonal issues temporarily set aside	Structuring work and participation to lead to outcomes; evaluating efforts; celebrating success; developing new leadership
Adjournment	Regression to earlier patterns of behavior	Obtaining agreement on decisions and accomplishments	Appearance of emotional resistance to completing work and ending group, especially if high bonding	Discussion of winding down, closing of group as a mark of success; orienting members to future of task accomplishments and change

(Baudler & Roman, 1999; Toseland & Rivas, 1995, Tuckman, 1965) to enhance group acceptability, either internally or externally, and to promote morale (Zastrow, 1997, pp. 58–61).

In addition, a group needs to develop ground rules for interaction and to work through any issues of dependency by accepting responsibility for its functioning. Competition in a work group needs to be recognized and managed. While competition can be productive between groups, it is generally not productive within groups. It interferes with group cohesion, coordination, and a unity of resources and effort. Overly competitive members whose competitive needs can't be directed outward generally disrupt internal group processes.

The roles of the work group are negotiated, assigned, established, and accepted. Leadership needs to know these roles and their allocation. The group is structured on a preliminary basis during this phase. Considerations in structuring a group's work include agendas and seating arrangements. Agendas are the formal agendas that lay out a group's purpose and work. *Hidden agendas* reflect goals of a single individual or small clique, a cabal, in a committee or board that are often unrelated and sometimes at variance with a group's purpose and unknown to all group members. While any member of a work group can have unique reasons for participation, hidden agendas generally are destructive since their promoters manipulate the group for private, secrete, and often ends contrary to the group's goals. A leadership task is to discover and manage any hidden agendas to limit their destructiveness to group task and process.

Seating arrangements are one way to help manage hidden agendas and facilitate group process to foster the group's work. Students of history will recognize the importance of seating arrangements. During the preliminary stages of the negotiations to end the Korean War in the 1950s and America's invelovement in the Viet Nam War of the 1960s and 1970s, months were spent negotiating the shape of the table and seating arrangements prior to starting the actual peace negotiations. Seating arrangements often indicate and confer status within a group. The arrangements can facilitate or hinder both oral and visual communication, focus attention and reduce or promote member distractions, and reinforce or weaken cliques and side discussions. These are all part of developing a working contract in a group.

STAGE 2: STORMING

As the group members begin to invest their emotions and energy in the group, they initiate a stage of development often characterized by conflict and struggles for power and control. The newness of the group has worn off. Emotions may run high; disagreements over substance and procedure arise. Although conflicts may be difficult to manage, the fact that they are going on indicates that a group has formed. Members care enough about the group and each other to fight over it. This is a crucial period in the life of the group. The group members are moving toward some resolution of the tension between differentiation and integration, between having their own way and giving in to the requirements of the group. The worker or leader must help the group to resolve conflicts in a constructive manner and to foster a democratic structure for decision making. Alternatively, the group is at risk of developing an authoritarian structure or of falling apart.

STAGE 3: NORMING

Having found a workable resolution to the conflicts created in the previous stage, the group begins to gel. A sense of cohesion emerges, characterized by greater acceptance of the unique traits of each member and a willingness to express views openly. The members feel comfortable with each other and begin to get down to doing the work necessary to accomplish the group's goals. The group needs to avoid too much socializing and to keep on task.

STAGE 4: PERFORMING

In this stage, the interpersonal structure that has developed becomes the functional instrument for dealing with task activities. Roles become flexible and functional, and group energy is channeled into task completion. Structural issues have been resolved (e.g., who plays what role, rules for decision making), so that the structure can now support task performance. The group can make decisions efficiently. This period is characterized by an emergence of solutions. The work of the group is structured in order to lead to outcomes and help the group to evaluate and celebrate its accomplishments. If the group's mission is completed, it prepares for adjournment.

STAGE 5: ADJOURNMENT

As the group begins to recognize that its work is reaching a conclusion, members often feel ambivalent about ending—pleased about accomplishments, sad about ending relationships and coming to a conclusion. During this period, groups often express their ambivalence by regressing to earlier forms of nonconstructive behavior and patterns of relating. Meetings may be missed; emotions may run high again; old conflicts can break out. The group reaches a successful conclusion (a) if it encourages its members to talk openly about their feelings about ending; (b) by planning for group-appropriate closing rituals or events such as parties, testimonial dinners, and the like; and (c) by focusing on future plans and life beyond the group.

EFFECTIVE MEETINGS

How many times have you gone to a meeting and left with the feeling that it was a waste of time? Nothing was accomplished. When this happens, frequently it is because whoever was responsible for running the meeting did not think through the specific decisions to be made at the meeting or could not facilitate the decision-making process effectively. *Task group meetings all share a common purpose: making decisions or completing a task.* Whatever the larger purpose of the group, when a task group holds a meeting, it does so to make decisions that will help the group move toward achievement of its goals. The fact that meetings may also provide opportunities for socialization, networking, and education does not alter their decision-making function. Therefore, effective meetings require both planning and chairperson skills. (Members of a group who are not chairing a meeting also have responsibility for advance planning and for helping a meeting accomplish its tasks by their interventions, both verbal and nonverbal.) Let us look at the planning aspect first.

Meeting Planning: Footwork and Headwork

The main point to realize about effective meetings is that *a meeting is the culmination of a prior planning process* (Tropman, 1980). The planning process begins before the first meeting and occurs thereafter with the follow-up work after

the meeting, thereby beginning the premeeting planning process for the next meeting. Box 10.1 indicates some of the necessary pre-meeting tasks. Tropman (1980) provides some guidance to plan for good task group decision making:

- Personality is not as important in the decision-making process as are the roles of the participants.
- The formal meeting itself is an end point in a long series of premeeting activities leading to decisions rather than the beginning point in decision making. Once a meeting begins, events have largely been determined.
- It is during the premeeting phase that most opportunities for influence, bargaining, and coalition structuring and agenda setting occur. (The importance of the premeeting phase increases with a group's size, diversity, and constituent diversity.)
- The purpose of a meeting of a decision-making group is to make good decisions, not just decisions (p. 15).

When the meeting takes place, enough attention should have been paid to administrative chores and decision-making requirements ahead of time so that effective decisions can result. Since there are many different kinds of task groups (e.g., staff groups, coalitions, treatment planning teams, boards), and since meetings range in their degree of formality, premeeting planning activities will vary as well, but in all cases premeeting planning should go on. In advance of a meeting, the chair (and the staff member for the group, if assigned) should have thought about the following:

1. The dynamics of the group in light of its development
2. Task and process objectives
3. Decisions that need to be made at the meeting

BOX 10.1	**PREMEETING ADMINISTRATIVE CHORES**

1. Preparing meeting minutes
2. Getting out meeting notices
3. Reproducing agendas and other informational materials and getting them to members before the meeting
4. Arranging for and setting up meeting space
5. Arranging for refreshments

4. Information the group must have in order to make decisions

5. The various roles of the participants and how the work of the group might be carried out

6. The actual meeting agenda

In formalized groups, such as a social service agency team meeting, a board meeting, a neighborhood association community meeting, or a working coalition strategy session, typically the chair and possibly some other members plan the agenda and consider the decision-making process for the meeting far enough in advance so that the members can get the agenda and meeting materials early enough to review them before the meeting takes place. If the group has a staff member assigned, such as with a board of directors or with a community group that a social worker is forming (e.g., to do a neighborhood needs assessment), then the worker and the chair and other members would meet and plan in advance of the meeting. If a group is meeting monthly, the members should receive the agenda and materials at least a week in advance of the meeting. Every item on a meeting agenda will not necessarily lead to a decision, as for example with progress reports of a committee or subcommittee or an informational briefing by an expert in a particular substantive area. Getting member input and feedback about the business of the group and its process is important. Also, some agenda items may take more than one meeting to complete. However, for every task group meeting that is scheduled, the worker and chair (and members, too) should be asking themselves what decisions should be made at the meeting that will advance the purpose of the group. The agenda should reflect these prospective decision items.

In planning an agenda, the worker and chair will also want to consider how various agenda items will be disposed of during the meeting in light of the group's needs and dynamics. For example, to foster group participation, preplanning may include asking particular members to take responsibility for reporting on or handling an agenda item. If members have been doing work in preparation for a meeting, they must be given the opportunity to report back. Otherwise you will discourage future voluntary action. Many prospective agenda items will emerge during a meeting, with insufficient information for the group to make a decision. Usually these items need to be assigned to an existing committee for work outside the meeting, leading to recommendations for group action in the future. Of course, sometimes the best-laid meeting plans may be interrupted by a critical but unplanned issue that suddenly arises. In this situation, modifying the agenda may be a necessary and appropriate course of action. However, these issues also will often have to be assigned to an existing or newly formed committee in order to bring them to resolution at a later meeting. This should be a rarely used tactic.

The worker and chair, as Box 10.2 emphasis, must also pay attention to the process or socioemotional dimension of the group in meeting planning. Members who make an emotional investment in a group seldom go through the group experience without being aroused by the way a decision is handled, or the way some members behave, or the lack of opportunity to present their own points of view. For example, observations of unexpressed or expressed anger may be cues for follow-up phone contact to help members manage their feelings or find a way to express them constructively at the next meeting. Other premeeting contacts may be important for

---

BOX 10.2   RULES FOR EFFECTIVE TASK GROUP DECISION MAKING

✓ Give members opportunities to participate and seek to equalize participation in decision making to enhance cohesion and avoid member exclusion and marginalization.

✓ Give members opportunities to demonstrate their preferences and positions.

✓ Seek expression of diversity of opinion and interest within the group to avoid groupthink and to create cohesion from the diversity.

✓ Start with the least-powerful members of the group in seeking member expressions of opinions, to promote a full expression of opinion.

✓ Structure the agenda to promote good decisions, because the purpose of the group is to encourage good decision making.

✓ Emphasize consensus, with good decisions being what everyone can live with.

any number of reasons, such as to encourage participation, to bridge communication gaps, to lend support, or to try to understand a member's reactions. In addition, groups have the wonderful capacity to be able to reflect on their own process. If emotions are running high, a chair may need to plan for some time in a meeting for the group to look at its process and take corrective action.

The Meeting Itself

Members usually come to meetings of a working group to do business during some specified time period, usually between 1 and 2 hours. Effectiveness tends to diminish if meetings last longer than 2 hours. Although there is no guarantee that members will come to a meeting properly prepared, *if* the agenda and other materials have reached them in advance and *if* the meeting stays on track so that the agenda is dealt with in the allotted time and decision are made, the probability for meeting effectiveness increases (Tropman, 1980). The *if*s are important.

Staying on track means beginning and ending a meeting on time and covering the items on the agenda. If meetings begin late, members will start to arrive late. Soon the time for conducting the group's business will be reduced, and meetings will begin to run over the agreed-on time of closing. Inevitably some members will arrive late, so it is usually a good idea to begin the meeting with the lighter part of the agenda, such as approving minutes and making announcements. Save roughly the middle third of the meeting for the weightiest agenda items, when the members' attention is most focused and everybody is ready to get down to business. The final portion of the meeting can then be more relaxed. This is a good time to generate new agenda items, talk about the process and progress of the group, pull together the decisions that have been made, and remind the group of the next meeting date (Tropman, 1980).

The structure for decision making that task groups adopt varies on a continuum from formal to informal. Many groups fall somewhere in between. At the formal end of the continuum, the group adopts formal rules and procedures for reaching decisions based on a vote. Usually this process is guided by *parliamentary procedure*, a fair and orderly process for reaching decisions that follows *Roberts' Rules of Order*. Developed over a hundred years ago, *Roberts' Rules* is used extensively by chairpersons to preside over meetings. Revised editions are available in any

bookstore or library, and short versions are published regularly. (For a useful shortened version, see Zastrow (1997, Chapter 12). Any social worker regularly involved in task group work should become familiar with the basics of parliamentary procedure.

A formal structure for decision making can be very useful when the group is too large for easy decision making (e.g., a meeting with 25 or more community members, as compared with a committee of 8 to 10 people). The bigger the group, the more important the procedures for reaching decisions. Formal decision rules, such as those of parliamentary procedure, have the advantages of preventing a minority from controlling the group and ensuring that group decisions have been clearly ratified. On the disadvantages side, discussions may easily become bogged down in rules and in competitive parliamentary strategizing to gain advantage; a minority group can be abused; and the procedures can be handled so rigidly and mechanically that the process dimension of group life is totally ignored.

An informal decision-making structure, at the other end of the continuum, usually involves a consensus-seeking process, which can but often does not culminate in a vote. Consensus-seeking behavior tends to emphasize careful listening, the broad expression of different viewpoints, constructive conflict over ideas, and a search for creative solutions that have wide member input and approval. It places a premium on process. An informal structure tends to be most useful when the group is fairly small, when member trust is high, when creative problem solving is needed, and when time for reaching decisions is not a problem. Remember, the consensus sought is not that everyone thinks the same thing is the best thing, but that a decision is reached that everyone can live with (Payne, 2000, p. 211). The disadvantage of seeking consensus, in comparison with the *dictatorship of the majority* or a majority vote, is that it is often a time-consuming and overly complicated process, especially if a minority is allowed to control the group. Box 10.3 lays out some "dos" and don't of meeting management.

As we stated earlier, many task groups fall somewhere along the formality–informality continuum. Many groups use a modified version of parliamentary procedure to formally consider an agenda item and reach a decision through voting; at the same meeting, some decisions will be reached by consensus—a nod of the head from the participants, signifying agreement. Some meetings benefit from the best of both worlds: strict parliamentary procedure with an allotted

---

BOX 10.3   GUIDELINES FOR MORE EFFECTIVE COMMITTEE/BOARD MEETINGS

1. Agenda integrity
   a. DO always have an agenda and a reason for the meeting.
   b. DO always have necessary agenda items and address all necessary items.
   c. DO always make all necessary decisions.
   d. DON'T discuss items not on the agenda.
   e. DON'T make unnecessary, unneeded, or premature decisions.
2. Temporal integrity (time management)
   a. DO always begin and end meetings on time.
   b. DO always have and keep meeting to an agenda time schedule.
   c. DO always have a committee/board long-range schedule with preplanning to allocate agenda items to relevant meetings when decisions are needed.

3. Rule of halves
   a. DO prepare agenda items by priorities and schedule discussion and decisions by the priorities.
   b. DON'T place an item on the agenda unless it is submitted by the time one half of the period between meetings has elapsed.
4. Rule of thirds
   a. DO place and deal with the most important items in the middle third of the meeting, when group energy is highest.
   b. DO have a break at the two-thirds point, for a distraction.
5. Rule of three quarters
   a. DO make the agenda available to members sufficiently in advance to allow members time for preparation.
   b. DO avoid last-minute surprises.

(Tropman, 1980, pp. 25-31)

---

period of consensus-building time in the meeting. For example, a very formal meeting may also set aside time for a brainstorming session on a difficult agenda item, with no censorship of ideas—in fact, encouragement of even the wildest notions—and a conscious attempt to avoid reaching any decision.

There are no explicit rules on how task group meetings must be run. Much depends on the leader's and staff's assessment of a particular group's task and process needs, and their skills in these roles, and in developing saliency for members. Box 10.4 identifies why committees and task groups don't always work well. It's a responsibility of leadership to address these issues.

Chairing Meetings

Chairing a meeting well is no easy feat, because the chairperson's role is complex. Meet-

---

BOX 10.4   WHY COMMITTEES/BOARDS DON'T ALWAYS WORK WELL

- Activities have low saliency and importance for members in their lives and responsibilities. If a missed meeting does not make any difference to the committee's decision making, the absent member, or the unit that the member represents, has low saliency.
- Committee has decision overload and is spending too much time with trivia that do not contribute to or crowds out real decision making.

- High inertia in a group's and meeting's structure because of poor agenda planning, pre-meeting work, agenda clarity on needed decisions, and poor time management.
- Group's culture and history are of ineffectiveness, irresponsibility, not following through, and other behaviors not conducive to decision making. The group is unable to overcome its history and culture of ineffectiveness and irresponsibility.

(Tropman, 1980, pp. 19-20; Zastrow, 1997, pp. 58-61)

ings represent a public space, in that whatever happens at a meeting is available to all of its participants. If a participant is treated unfairly, for example, by being insulted or cut off prematurely, all other participants also observe and experience that treatment in some way. For meetings to be effective, therefore, it is incumbent on the chair to act as a neutral, objective arbiter of the group's business and to insist on sensitivity and fair play. The chair sets the tone for the meetings. If the chair in a formal meeting has very strong feelings or opinions about an issue and wants to express them, he or she usually asks someone else to preside until that agenda item is resolved.

Issues of distance arise in other ways as well. In general, the chair must be involved enough in the substance and process of a meeting to be able to engage the ideas and the people, and yet the chair must be uninvolved enough to be able to step back and guide the interchange to fruitful decisions. In that sense, *the chair operates with a split vision or dual consciousness, one aimed at understanding the ideas being expressed and the meaning of the interaction, the other aimed at using the group process to help the group members make sound decisions in which they are also invested.* This duality comes together in the various roles that the chairperson plays in a group meeting. We have identified these as *presider, facilitator,* and *administrator.*

PRESIDER

In this role, the chair makes sure that the business of the meeting is accomplished in a democratic fashion. The chair is in the position of controlling the flow of interaction in a meeting so that the agenda is dealt with effectively. The chair convenes the meeting, calls on the members to start the work (calls the meeting to order), and closes the meeting at its conclusion. Between the start and the finish, the chair regulates the discussion by calling on people to express their feelings and viewpoints. By summarizing, clarifying, repeating, and reminding the participants of the topic under discussion and the time available, the chair keeps the meeting agenda on track. The chair often synthesizes ideas for the group and determines when the group is ready to make a decision. When the group is ready to act, the chair clarifies the decision that is being made and ratifies the action by taking a vote or a reading of the degree of consensus. (Group members, of course, may also help to keep meetings on track, synthesize ideas, and clarify decisions. These roles are by no means limited to the chair, nor would you want them to be.)

FACILITATOR

As group facilitator, the chair must observe and interpret the way relationships are developing among the members, and the development of the group as a whole. In addition, the chair must intervene so that the group process supports the group's task objectives. This involves the chair in many different kinds of interventions. Four important types of intervention are the following:

1. *Providing support* (e.g., "That's really an interesting idea") helps to create a positive "climate for expressing ideas and opinions, including unpopular and unusual points of view," and to "reinforce positive forms of behavior" (Sampson & Marthas, 1981, p. 258)

2. *Mediating conflict* (e.g., "Let's see if we can get to the bottom of this disagreement") helps the group members communicate more openly and directly with each other to relieve tension and to reduce disruptive behavior

3. *Probing and questioning* (e.g., "I wonder if that idea could be enlarged") helps the group "expand a point that may have been left incomplete" and "invites members to explore their ideas in greater detail" (Sampson & Marthas, 1981, p. 259)

4. *Reflecting feelings* (e.g., "The group seems to be having a very hard time coming to grips with that decision") "orients members to the feelings that may lie behind what is being said or done" (Sampson & Marthas, 1981, p. 259)

Perhaps it should be stated again here that group members can and should also help to facilitate the group process. That role is not limited to the chair.

ADMINISTRATOR

In the absence of staff support, the chair, as administrator, basically coordinates the work of the group before, during, and after meetings. The chair, for example, attends to many of the premeeting tasks mentioned earlier, such as ensuring that information the group needs for making decisions is available in a timely manner. Before and during the meetings, with the help of other group members, the chair generates agenda items for future meetings. During the meeting, the chair usually assigns tasks and delegates responsibilities—for example, assigning a particular agenda item to a committee or subcommittee for follow-up work. The chair must also make sure that the particular agenda item is brought back to the group at an appropriate future date. The chair also serves as spokesperson for the group when the group needs to be represented (Tropman, 1980).

Staffing a Task Group

Many social workers provide staff support to task groups, as with boards of directors or board committees, community development associations, interagency teams, planning bodies, and long-term coalitions. In these instances, the role of the professional is to enable the group to function effectively by providing assistance to the group, mainly through the chair, in handling administrative tasks and coordination, preparing for meetings, and serving as process consultant and, in some cases, as strategy and substantive expert. The main point here is that the professional staff person plays a critical, but *behind-the-scenes*, role, assisting the leaders of the group (the chair and various other members who accept responsibilities) in performing their functions effectively. The staff person thus primarily carries out a *leadership development* role.

Although the paid staff person clearly has responsibility for the group, he or she is normally not a voting member of the group. In many cases, the staff person is directly hired and fired by the group. In other instances, the employment relationship with the task group is much more indirect, although the group still has influence over a staff member's status. A direct service worker who is organizing a community group to sponsor a health fair would serve as staff to the health fair steering committee and would not typically be a voting member of that body. Or, for example, in an organization such as United Way, the staff person is a member of a larger professional staff responsible to the organization's executive director. This professional staff works with a host of volunteer planning and fund-raising committees but is not a voting member. The executive is responsible to the board of directors and serves as its professional staff. The executive here is usually an ex officio board member (a board member by virtue of the office held), but again without a vote.

In working with chairpersons and other group leaders, staff must gauge their experience and sophistication and adapt the assistance they provide accordingly. In general, staff should help a chair prepare for meetings by jointly developing and reviewing the agenda, tasks to be accomplished, and a plan for accomplishing them. The plan may include preparing some group members for roles they might play in the meeting; planning how to break down a complicated agenda item into smaller decisions; considering process snags and how to handle them; and, in some cases, considering how to reach an acceptable decision in the face of the political machinations of various subgroup factions. Inexperienced chairs may need help in role-playing parts of a meeting. More sophisticated chairs may need other forms of assistance, such as sensitization to process concerns.

At community meetings, professional staff are, of course, visible and have a good opportunity to talk to the group members and get to know them better, and vice versa. Once the meeting begins, though, the staff member should take a back seat to the chair, who is directing the meeting. Since the staff member has already had input into the meeting by virtue of premeeting preparations with the chair, during the meeting the staff person should be carefully observing the group process as well as following the substance of the discourse. Sitting beside the chair, the staff person can then share comments, suggestions, and observations discreetly with the chair. This is not to say that the staff member must be totally silent. Sometimes the chair or a member will ask the staff person directly for observations or suggestions. Sometimes a meeting may be getting out of hand or straying too far off course, and the staff person may judiciously make a corrective comment or ask a question. Sometimes it may be apparent that the chair does not know how to handle a particular situation, and the staff member may have to help out. *A principle to keep in mind, however, is that while leadership, group development, task and process balance, and decision-making are staff goals, staff should be careful not to usurp the authority and leadership of the chair.*

Since professional staff members tend to spend more time on the business of a task group than do the chair or other leaders, they often tend to take over a group or at least to dominate it. Sometimes this is not even a conscious decision; staff members just find it easier to act for the group than to work through the group. The problem with this approach is that group leadership and the group as a whole have difficulty developing fully. Yet, presumably, forming a group was necessary to reach some specified set of goals. The bottom line is that the *members of the group have to own the group if it is to succeed.* For ownership to occur, staff members have to enable the group members to make their own decisions about the nature and direction of the group and to take responsibility for its work. Enabling involves a delicate balance between holding back advice and hands-on assistance and offering them at various critical points to guide a group over a rough spot. There are no simple guidelines for managing the balance, but if a group does not seem to be developing, staff members at least need to ask themselves whether they have done too much for the group. Perhaps more holding back would be appropriate.

DEALING WITH GROUP PROBLEMS

All groups experience problems; these come with the territory. For example, task groups commonly experience difficulties getting started, handling conflict, reaching decisions, dealing with disruptive behavior by an individual member (the meeting monopolizer, the angry challenger, etc.) or by a subgroup (negative bloc voting), and more. Common as these and other group problems may be, however, there is no standard recipe for how best to deal with them. Because groups differ in so many ways and because the circumstances surrounding any problem are unique, in working with groups, just as in social work with individuals, families, or communities, we prefer a general approach to problem solving rather than a set of fixed solutions. Let's look at the framework first and then apply it to some group problems one might encounter.

A Problem-Solving Framework

The now-familiar problem-solving framework used in this book has four general steps: (a) study, (b) assessment, (c) treatment or intervention, and (d) evaluation or reassessment. (See also Sampson & Marthas, 1981). The framework provides a useful guide, a kind of mind-set, for dealing with group task and process problems. The time frame involved in these steps can range from instantaneous to prolonged. As a problem arises in the group, the social worker as leader, member, or staff person may respond then and there, based on observations and some conclusions about the meaning of the behavior. Or the social worker may choose not to intervene, but instead to continue to observe and consider the nature of the problem and what to do about it, saving the intervention for some later date. (Remember that, since a group is a public space for all the participants, nonintervention may sometimes be a form of intervention, depending on how this is interpreted.) Whenever the intervention has occurred, the social worker should

assess its effect and make a decision about whether to respond further and what kind of intervention to make, again at that particular moment or at some later date. The transition from thought to action and back to reflection, sometimes referred to as *praxis*, can be seamless or spaced out.

STUDY

The study section of the problem-solving framework, then, is the period for defining and clarifying the nature and extent of the problem in the group. When a problem arises, therefore, we need to ask ourselves the following questions: What is the actual problem? What are the observable behaviors indicating that there is a problem? How is the group affected? How serious is the problem?

ASSESSMENT

Here we want to clarify what we think is the cause of the problem and what it means. We connect our observations to our theoretical knowledge in order to intervene effectively. Assessment analyzes the group's problems and builds a case theory. Assessment is an information-gathering process to understand a problem, a situation, a case, in order to effect a future change (Bisman, 1994, pp. 111–121). Assessment questions are Why is this problem occurring? What's going on outside the group or in the group that may be contributing to this problem? Am I contributing to the problem in some way? Where is the group developmentally? What role do subgroups or factions play in this problem? What part do the individual needs and personalities of the participants play in this problem? Is there any pattern to the behavior I am observing? What is my understanding of the problem?

INTERVENTION

This is the point of action. The worker needs to say or do something in the group, or sometimes outside the group, to help the group deal with the problem. When intervening, the worker may think about the following kinds of questions: How can I get the group to start to handle the problem? How will my reaction to an individual member or to the group as a whole facilitate the group process and keep the group on course? How will my intervention be perceived by the group? Are there specific techniques I can use to affect the problem?

EVALUATION

Having intervened to try to deal with the problem, the worker now needs to observe the impact of that intervention. The main questions, then, are as follows: What effect did my action have on the group? What effect did my intervention have on specific individuals and/or subgroups? Does my diagnosis seem to be correct, or do I need to modify my understanding of the problem? Do I need to take any follow-up action?

Three Common Group Problems

As we turn to some examples of problems and interventions, we should keep in mind, once again, that the responsibility for dealing with problems does not rest with the leader/chair or staff person alone. All members of a group share responsibility for helping the group to function effectively, and any member may be instrumental in helping the group address problematic behavior. Since this chapter is written from the perspective of the chairperson or leader and staff person, and since these individuals often do intervene to deal with group problems, we shall adopt that stance in the illustrations that follow. As we go through these examples, consider your own analysis of the problem and possible interventions.

THE MEETING MONOPOLIZER

Scenario. Imagine the third meeting of a treatment planning team of staff members on an acute illness unit of a large psychiatric hospital. The unit leader, who is a social worker with many years of seniority, is also the team leader. The other members of the team include a psychiatrist, a head nurse, a nursing assistant, a psychologist, an occupational therapist, and a recreational therapist. Team planning on the unit is not new, but this particular team, with three new members, represents a new team configuration. The team meets weekly. The newcomers are the psychiatrist, the head nurse, and the nursing assistant. Although the social worker, Karen Jones, chairs the meetings, the meetings have increasingly been dominated by the psychiatrist, Dr. Matthew Freud, who has a lot to say about each case before the group. Other team members have had difficulty interjecting their ideas. Some group members are beginning to grumble outside the group about their inability to be heard, and it is becoming difficult to arrive at treatment plans that everyone can accept. So far, the team leader has taken a laissez-faire approach to chairing the group, but now the time has come to intervene more directly. In this third meeting, when the second case is put before the group for

discussion, Dr. Freud immediately takes the lead in explaining the nature of the patient's illness. How might the chair intervene?

Study. At each meeting, Dr. Freud monopolizes the discussion of the cases. He usually does a lot of teaching about the nature of the illness and reviews current research before getting to his own recommendations. While the information is interesting, other members are forced to sit and listen passively. The doctor is not good at picking up cues that others want to contribute their observations. He does not maintain good eye contact with other group members. He also discounts input from other disciplines. Group members have begun to resist coming to agreement on treatment plans and are often restless. Two members have come late to the third team meeting and have expressed some resentment to the leader outside the meeting. Dr. Freud's behavior is threatening the effectiveness of team planning.

Assessment. The case theory can posit a number of factors that can contribute to this problem. The team leader has not dealt with the fact that the team has several new members who may not be familiar with the ground rules the old team had established. Her laissez-faire approach thus has not provided the group with a sufficient orientation to the team's expectations and norms. The psychiatrist is new and is trying to find his niche in the group. Other new members have a similar challenge, while older members are used to their particular format for team meetings. Dr. Freud's previous experiences as team leader himself may have led him to adopt a dominant leadership-teaching pattern. His behavior may reflect discomfort with his status on the unit and in the group. Also, Dr. Freud appears not to be a good listener, at least as far as the staff is concerned.

Intervention. The group leader has a number of options. Some possibilities include the following:

1. She could confront Dr. Freud directly about his behavior. "Dr. Freud [firmly until she has his attention], you seem to have an awful lot to say about each case before the group. Although your points are informative, I'd like to stop your discourse at this point so that other members have a chance to express their views on the case. Thank you."

2. She could reflect the group's behavior back to the group and solicit their feedback. After Dr. Freud finishes his discourse, or after politely interrupting, the leader might say, "I'd like to stop the discussion of cases for a few minutes to consider our process. As I look around the group, I see a lot of restlessness and dissatisfaction. I wonder if we could talk about what's going on."

3. She could reflect back her own behavior to the group as a means of inviting clarification of ground rules. After Dr. Freud finishes his discourse or after interrupting him politely, the leader might say, "Before Dr. Freud finishes his explanation, I need to interrupt the group for a few minutes to take care of some important business that I realize I neglected. As I've been observing the group, it seems that I never took the time to orient this team from the outset about expectations for team functioning. Since we have three new team members, maybe we could take some time now to make some decisions together about how we want to handle our cases in the group meeting."

Evaluation. The first intervention offers Dr. Freud limited support but also lets him know directly that his behavior is not acceptable, sets limits on it, and lets the other team members know that their participation is valued. Other group members may also feel freer to interrupt Dr. Freud in the future. Dr. Freud, however, may find the confrontation surprising and irritating, laboring under the notion that he was doing what he was supposed to do as team psychiatrist. He may feel that he has lost face in the group.

The second intervention potentially allows the group to express their dissatisfaction with Dr. Freud's monopolistic behavior, as well as their own expectations for participation. Since this is only the third team meeting, the members may not be willing to take Dr. Freud on. If they are willing, the leader risks a session that deteriorates into an attack on the psychiatrist.

The third intervention recognizes the group's formative stage of development, directs some of the group's anger back to the leader rather than the psychiatrist, and opens the way for the team to establish its ground rules in a constructive fashion. Once the members have negotiated the rules of the game, monopolization will be less likely to occur and easier for the team leader and other members to limit, since the group has guidelines for participation.

GROUP CONFLICT

Scenario. You are serving in your first year as an associate director of a moderate-sized non-profit family services agency. Your responsibilities include supervising the professional staff and chairing monthly agency staff meetings. Along with the director and another associate director, who is also new, the agency staff consists of 12 professional social workers, 2 immigrant resettlement workers, and 4 case aides. The agency is departmentalized into four divisions: family and children's (six social workers), single adults (two social workers), senior adults (two social workers), and immigrant services (two social workers and two resettlement workers). One case aide works in each division, handling arrangements for in-home services, transportation, respite care, and the like. Staff turnover in the agency is generally low, so that these staff members know each other quite well. Half of the professional staff members have been with the agency for more than 10 years. The agency has been trying to work out a policy on home visiting. Currently, the only staff members who regularly make home visits are the nonprofessional workers and the two social workers handling adoptions in the family and children's division. This division is within your purview. The other new associate director, Hector Gravas, has proposed that every client seen by the agency have a home visit, with the exception of single adults unless there is severe contagious illness. The professional staff is split on the policy. One faction, led by Molly Black, the head of the family and children's division and a senior staff member, is adamantly opposed. Although a subordinate of Hector Gravas, she is vocal in opposing the home visit proposal. She states that for professionals "to be gallivanting around the city making home visits" is a poor use of professional time. The other faction, led by Felice Navidad, head of immigration services under your direction and also a senior staffer, strongly favors home visits by professionals. The nonprofessional staff members, feeling caught in the middle, have tried to stay out of the line of fire.

After going round and round for nearly an hour and making no headway, rational discourse has deteriorated into simmering anger that can split the work units. How might you intervene to begin a process of constructive conflict resolution?

Study. Groups frequently experience conflict, especially as part of their development. The task is to manage the conflict effectively so that group cohesion can be enhanced rather than destroyed and an appropriate decision for the agency made. When the group has a strong sense of trust and commitment to group goals, when the conflicts represent substantive disagreements over ideas, procedures, or priorities, and when the group has a history of productive problem solving, constructive resolutions are easier to achieve. When conflicts erupt due to struggles in the group over status and power, when attacks become personalized and hostile, when there is a win/lose competitive atmosphere and the members begin to take sides, the group deteriorates into destructive conflict. With two relatively new associate directors and passed-over staff, cohesion is lacking. Constructive resolution is much harder to achieve. In the family services staff group, conflict seems to have taken a destructive turn following competitive lines that split work units into factions. The group has not been able to make any progress on coming up with an acceptable policy. Anger is running high. The professional staff has polarized into two factions. The nonprofessional staff are not participating so as not to be subjected to personal attacks or retribution from more powerful group members. The atmosphere has degenerated into a win/lose situation.

Assessment. A quick analysis and case theory conjectures that a number of factors may be contributing to this destructive climate. The members of the family and children's division, under Molly Black, see themselves as highly professional therapists with neither the time nor the resources to do extensive home visiting. Hector Gravas is viewed as something of an upstart trying to shake things up just to exert power. In addition, Molly wanted but did not get his associate director's job. Instead, an outsider was hired for the position. Her division feels slighted. Hector Gravas is aware that Molly was a candidate for his position, but as her supervisor, he has never discussed this matter with her. Felice Navidad, the senior professional staff member in charge of immigration services, already spends a lot of time seeing immigrant families in their homes. She believes the proposed policy will eventually generate more resources for her department. Her vocal support has not sat well with the family and children's division and gives the impression that you, as her supervisor, may support this position. A number of other staff members do support Hector's proposal, and they maintain that prevention, social support, and resocialization should represent the major professional goals of the agency. The nonprofessional staff have mixed feelings about the pol-

icy. Some believe that if all members of the professional staff did home visits, the nonprofessionals' contribution would be recognized and more greatly appreciated. Others fear that if all staff members did home visits, there would be less need for their services, potentially leading to cutbacks in nonprofessional positions.

Thus, a shift in agency policy could upset the existing tenuous group equilibrium. The new associate directors are being tested. Your honeymoon periods as new staff leaders are over; staff members no longer feel they have to be polite and deferential. They can take more risks in expressing their feelings and ideas and find out how the new group leader/authority figure will react and what your limits are. Will you understand them? How will you and Hector deal with anger and internal competition? He did not recognize the potential ramifications of his proposal and therefore made no moves before the meeting to get feedback on his idea and to reduce the anxiety that often accompanies change. Neither did you. Had either or both of you recognized the potential for conflict ahead of time, the staff might have been prepared more effectively before the meeting. The most important time is the premeeting time. Hector also has avoided dealing with Molly's competitive and hurt feelings about his receiving the associate director's job over her.

Intervention. The following are some possible interventions:

1. You try to legitimate differences of opinion and defuse the situation a bit. Ideally you will recognize that you, as well as Hector Gravas, are being tested, and you will not overreact. You do not want a win/lose solution or to contribute to the conflict by undermining either Hector Gravas or Molly Black. You want a win/win solution that still deals with the task, that is, the proposed policy change. In an effort to achieve this, you might propose a cooling-off period that will allow for less visible and emotion-charged negotiations. It will also allow Hector Gravas to address and work out his administrative relationship with Molly Black in a less public and volatile environment. "After an hour of hot and heavy debate, let's recognize that there are legitimate differences of opinion. I don't think there is any right or wrong solution here. Why don't we think about the policy and come back to it next week with some ideas about how to blend the different positions?"

2. You recognize that more is evidently at stake than a substantive difference over a policy option. You try to get at the underlying anger and fear by reflecting back the group's behavior. "After listening and watching the interchange about this policy, I've noticed that several people have not said anything for almost an hour, while others have taken sides without fully listening to and hearing each other. I'd really like to understand what's going on."

3. You acknowledge that the conflict goes deeper than the policy itself and try to get at this by reflecting back the group's feelings. "I think we need to stop for a minute and try to understand the anger and fear that this policy suggestion seems to have aroused. I don't think we'll make much progress if we're this tense about the proposal, and I would like to make some progress."

4. You adopt a structural approach to defuse the conflict that also incorporates a cooling-off period. "We seem to have hit an impasse on this policy for now. One group is strongly opposed, one group is strongly for, and another contingent seems stuck in the middle. I'm going to ask two members from each subgroup to meet during the week and see if they can work out a compromise proposal that everyone can live with. I'll meet with the group afterward to see what has been worked out, and we'll discuss it at the next staff meeting." This, as with as the first approach, provides time for you to act as a mediator.

Evaluation. Not every conflict that a group experiences has to be processed by the group. Otherwise, the group might spend all of its time doing that and nothing else. When a conflict has destructive qualities, as was the case in this scenario, the group probably does need to look at it in more depth. Nor are these responses necessarily mutually exclusive. For example, the fourth alternative, or something like it, might well follow a discussion generated by the second or third alternatives. The interventions identified above also are not the only possible responses. Sometimes a group may even need the assistance of an outside facilitator to get at their difficulties and resolve them.

In the first response, you recognize that the group is tired and has gone as far as it can for now. Legitimizing differences is generally a constructive approach, and allowing for a cooling-off period may be helpful. It sets a tone of calm acceptance, in contrast to the group's turmoil. In

this situation, it seems unlikely that the group will come up with a compromise policy on its own without some specific structure in place for doing the work. Since the conflict has some destructive properties, the chair needs to be sure that the situation will not be dropped, lest it fester and surface again and again in different ways. Before the next meeting, you as chair need to talk with Molly and other staff members individually to get a clearer sense of their feelings and concerns. You might want to informally mediate a discussion between Hector and Molly. You then will be more prepared to lead a discussion of the policy at the next staff meeting.

In the second intervention, you feed your observations of their behavior back to the group. In effect, you hold up a mirror and show them how their behavior appears, with the aim of opening up the discussion about their underlying concerns and feelings in a manner that can lead to some resolution. Again, the tone is calm and accepting.

In the third intervention, you openly recognize the strong feelings that the proposal has aroused and legitimates discussion of feelings and concerns. Again, the aim is to move beyond the policy itself, because the staff's anger and fear are blocking effective progress.

In the fourth alternative, you try to defuse the staff's anger by taking time to explicitly deal with the policy outside the group. This is like the first alternative, except that here you set up a structure for working on the compromise. You still have work to do between meetings in eliciting the staff's feelings and concerns.

GROUP SILENCE OR NONPARTICIPATION

Scenario. The six-member steering committee of a local homeless service provider coalition is meeting to decide on an activity that will mobilize support for a bill requiring the city to provide 24-hour mobile emergency aid teams to reach out to the homeless on cold days. The mayor has come out publicly against the proposal due to budgetary constraints. The group has met six times, and the members generally know each other because of their common work with the homeless population in the city. The discussion, chaired by the organizer/leader, has gone on for about an hour, without much enthusiasm or focus. The members don't seem to be able to come up with viable ideas or to take hold of the issue. The mayor's position has reduced the issue's saliency for the committee. Finally, the group leader, Mary Brown, enthusiastically proposes a dramatic activity to get media coverage on the issue—a demonstration in front of the mayor's private home. Nobody responds. There is an uncomfortable silence (Sampson & Marthas, 1981, p. 271).

Study. The group has shown signs of apathy throughout the meeting. The discussion has been unenthusiastic and unproductive. The feeling tone of the meeting has been apathetic. The leader has tended to carry the discussion, until finally her last proposal has been met with silence.

Assessment. There are many reasons why a group may behave apathetically or withhold participation. Some common reasons may apply to this group. Among the first possibilities a group leader must consider are reasons related personally to the leader. The leader may be out of tune with the interests and experiences of the members. Or the leader may have been monopolizing the group, creating a dependent relationship in which the members' level of participation is low. In this case, we have a group of service providers who are not accustomed to social action. Social action is outside their professional experience but not outside of the leader's interests and experience. The leader is out of step with her group.

Some members' reluctant participation may be due to a variety of unspoken fears. As homeless service providers, each member's organization receives some city funding. They are afraid that political action may result in funding cutbacks to their agencies. In this light, the proposal to challenge the mayor is particularly threatening.

Some members do not believe that social action is the purpose for the group's formation. Their primary interest and not-too-hidden agenda is better service coordination and networking with other providers. The group has never discussed its goals in SMARRT language and arrived at a consensus on the group's purpose.

The task of mobilizing support for passage of a bill in the city council may be too daunting. The providers are up to their ears in work just to keep their services operating. Even if they are interested, they may not have the time or energy to devote to this sort of project.

The leader herself is a highly respected, long-time advocate for the homeless. Some group members are uncomfortable about opposing her openly and parhaps being viewed as anti-the-homeless.

Intervention. Again, a variety of interventions are possible, depending in part on the leader's diagnosis of the problem.

1. If the leader has had a flash of insight about being out of step with the group, she might say, "Judging from the unenthusiastic discussion over the last hour and your silence, maybe I've been pushing for social action too hard. What do you think?"

2. The leader might tune in to the lack of clarity about the group's purpose. "I can see that there is not too much excitement about a campaign to pass the city council bill. I guess this is pretty different than the other work the group has done. Maybe we should go around the room and check on what we see as the purposes of the group. John, could you start us off?"

3. The leader might open up further discussion about the group's purposes by zeroing in on the underlying fears of the members of exposure and loss of funding. "Since nobody is saying anything, I'm guessing that the idea of going after the mayor is pretty scary. How do you all feel about our coalition getting involved in social action?" She can also explore social actions that doesn't embarrass the mayor.

Evaluation. In the first intervention, the leader reflects back the behavior of the group and tries to solicit feedback, starting with responses to the direction of her own leadership. In the second intervention, the leader is fairly direct about starting the feedback process. She is also beginning a process of negotiating a contract that did not take place previously. In the third intervention, the leader tunes in to the feelings of inadequacy about a social action campaign that she senses in the members. This approach can also lead to further clarification of the group's purposes and negotiation of the group's contract. With some expression of feelings on the table and a chance to look at the project, the group might be more ready to engage in action, but something appropriate to their level of experience and available time.

CONCLUSION

The group problems and interventions we have illustrated in this chapter are only a few of the many typical and atypical problems and challenges that task groups encounter. As should be apparent, although task groups are about decision making, group behavior and feelings sometimes interfere with the best laid plans and require a leader to facilitate the group process. In this chapter, we have advocated a systematic approach to problem solving that is transferable to all kinds of group practice situations you may encounter. We have also suggested that a self-critical approach to practice is highly desirable. Whether as members, leaders, chairs, organizers, or staff members, social workers invariably participate in task groups and, just as in other aspects of professional practice, they need to be able to use themselves consciously to enable a group to achieve its goals.

Discussion Exercises

1. The director of the state's foster care review board has appointed you to chair an interagency foster care review team of eight members. You are preparing for the first meeting. The team reviews cases of children placed in foster care by the city child protective services agency to be sure that the placements are appropriate.
    (a) Identify your process and task goals for the meeting.
    (b) Write out an agenda for the meeting.
    (c) Identify the tasks you will attend to before the group convenes.
    (d) Explain how you would start the meeting and how you would end it.

2. The foster care review team is having its fifth meeting. In a carryover discussion from the previous month's meeting, the group has gotten bogged down in figuring out how to handle the large volume of cases most efficiently. Two main proposals have been identified: adding extra meetings and dividing up the cases between two subcommittees. At this point, one of the committee members, Connie Williams, who missed the previous meeting, introduces a third alternative: adding more members to the committee. Mae Harris supports this new proposal. The other members get upset.
    (a) Explain what may be going on, in terms of your knowledge of group development.
    (b) Indicate what you would do in this situation.

3. This is the first meeting of a group of seven representatives from local public and private agencies who are trying to develop a citywide referral system. The staff person from the department of social services has worked hard in preparing group contacts and discussions to help develop an acceptable agenda and get the group going. She is chairing the meeting. About halfway through the meeting, a respected agency director asserts loudly, "This meeting isn't getting anywhere and I have to leave. I sure hope the next meeting is more productive!" And with that, he packs up and walks out. The members look a bit stunned and turn to you for the next move.
    (a) How would you explain what is going on?
    (b) What would you do?

4. Near the end of the first meeting of the above group, someone suggests that the group appoint a chair to conduct the meetings. The idea is received enthusiastically. When you ask for nominations, no one responds.
    (a) How would you explain what is going on?
    (b) What would you do?

5. It is the fourth meeting of a planning committee in an agency. One staff person comes in 15 minutes late. Although she has done this before, no one says anything about it, including the chairperson of the group. The late arrival is also the highest-status member of the group, representing a large department in the agency.
    (a) How would you explain what is going on?
    (b) What would you do?

6. The fifth meeting of the above agency planning committee begins with silence. Although the agenda has been prepared and members received it in advance, no one says anything. It is beginning to seem that the silence might continue for some time.
    (a) How would you explain what is going on?
    (b) What would you do?

Notes

1. "We trained hard . . . but it seemed that every time we were beginning to form up into teams we would be reorganized. . . . I was to learn later in life that we tend to meet any new situation by reorganizing; and a wonderful method it can be for creating the illusion of progress while producing confusion, inefficiency, and demoralization" (attributed to Petronius Arbiter, 210 B.C.).

2. See Chapter 1. SMARRT objectives are specific, measurable, acceptable, realistic, results oriented, and time specific.

References

Bandler, S., & Roman, C. P. (1999). *Group work: Skills and strategies for effective intervention* (2nd ed.). Binghamton, NY: Haworth Press.

Bisman, C. D. (1994). *Social work practices: Cases and principles.* Pacific Grove, CA: Brooks/Cole.

Gersick, C. G. (1988). Time and transition in work teams: Toward a new model of group development. *Academy of Management Journal, 31,* 9–41.

Hanson, P. G. (1972). What to look for in groups. In J. W. Pfeiffer & J. J. Jones (Eds.), *The 1972 annual handbook for group facilitators* (pp. 21–24). La Jolla, CA: University Associates.

Heap, K. (1977). *Group theory for social workers: An introduction.* New York: Pergamon Press.

Johnson, A. K. (1994). Teaching students the task force approach: A policy-practice course. *Journal of Social Work Education, 30*(3), 336–347.

Kirst-Ashman, K. K., & Hull, G. H., Jr. (2001). *Generalist practice with organizations and communities* (2nd ed.). Belmont, CA: Brooks/Cole.

Payne, M. (2000). *Teamwork in multiprofessional care.* Chicago: Lyceum Books, Inc.

Sampson, E. E., & Marthas, M. (1981). *Group process for the health professions* (2nd ed.). New York: Wiley.

Toseland, R., & Rivas, R. B. (1995). *An introduction to group work practice* (2nd ed.). Boston, Allyn & Bacon.

Tropman, J. E. (1980). *Effective meetings: Improving group decision-making.* Beverly Hills, CA: Sage.

Tuckman, B. W. (1965). Developmental sequence in small groups. *Psychological Bulletin, 63,* 384–399.

Tuckman, B. W., & Jensen, M. A. C. (1977). Stages of small group development revisited. *Group and Organizational Studies, 2*(1), 419–427.

Warren, M. (2001). *Dry bones rattling.* Princeton, NJ: Princeton University Press.

Zastrow, C. (1997). *Social work with groups* (4th ed.). Chicago: Nelson-Hall.

11

Using Networks and Networking

WHAT IS A NETWORK? WHAT IS NETWORKING?

Clients with multiple problems and needs are increasing. An abusive mother may require income assistance, job training, day care, psychosocial therapy, parenting education and skills, and other social supports to change her behavior. If the father is present, family therapy may be needed. If not, she may need assistance in obtaining absent parent financial and social supports. Rarely are all needed services available from a single agency; usually they must be obtained from many autonomous organizations. The social worker and the client will need to construct and manage a service network. Whittaker, Garbarino, and associates (1983) and others (Payne, 2000; Travillion, 1999) hold that assessing, developing, and managing social networks and assisting clients in their assessment, development, and management of social networks is the crux of social work practice. Client needs generally do not coincide with a single agency's service packets. The sheer number of agencies with varying service arrangements and regulations and a client's informal social supports generates management complexity for the individual client and social worker and demands commensurate network management skills. Networks are equally important to macro community practice, which largely consists of building and managing social networks. Social workers network when they refer clients to other agencies, help clients develop social supports, and work with social action coalitions.

Castelloe and Prokopy (2001) describe a networking use in community development. In recruiting, a 60-year-old Native American had the edge because of her informal community networks:

> All of the staff recognized that Ms. Helen was so successful because she had spent her entire life in the community . . . , because she had spent the previous decade (following her retirement . . .), volunteering intensely . . . Through this volunteering, Ms. Helen had become what she called a "community mom." Everyone in the community knew her, and her successful recruiting was largely the result of her reputation and her ability to draw upon the network of relationships that she had developed over the course of her life. . . . The staff viewed knowing people, being tied into local social networks, as more important than sharing the ethnicity and culture of the community. (p. 34)

Networks and networking are inherent in social work's emphasis on the client's social ecology, service coordination, and the holism of social work's person-in-environment (P-I-E) perspective. The more critical form of networking for clients and community residents is with their primary and secondary social supports. Family, friends, and neighborhood organizations provide more help than tertiary or formal social agencies (Lincoln, 2000; Payne, 2000; Phillips, Bernard, Phillipson, & Ogg, 2000; Streeter & Franklin, 1992; Whittaker et al., 1983). Networking occurs when people seek others who can or may be able to help them or whom they may be able to help. Networking involves building and maintaining social relationships with others. Networks are support systems when they provide a structure for social exchanges. This chapter will review social network theory and its underlying social theories, the dimensions of social networks, client social supports as networks, and the application of networking to social work practice.

Social networks are social arrangements of peoples, groups, organizations, or other social units that interact and engage in exchanges to achieve their purposes. A social action coalition of neighborhood organizations is an example of a social network common in community work. While systems have shared objectives or purposes (Anderson & Carter, 1984, pp. 1–23; Churchman, 1965, pp. 29–33; Hearn, 1969; Leighninger, 1978; Martin & O'Connor, 1989), a social network's units can have different objectives or purposes. What the units share is a belief that their individual objectives or needs will be bettered by the network relationship (Whittaker et al., 1983, p. 4). Nohria and Eccles (1992) maintain that social networks are not the same as electronic and mechanical networks. Social networks require social and human interaction for bonding and cohesion. McIntyre (1986) argues that networks and support systems exist in any situation involving an exchange of resources. Resources exchanged can be tangible, such as money and clients, or intangible, such as information, emotional support, or legitimization. Networks can be personal, professional and organizational, and networking can be interpersonal between individuals and interorganization between organizations and agencies. Not all network units need be in direct contact with all other network units. MacKay (1997, pp. 8–9) calling forth the Broadway show and movie, *Six Degrees of Separation*. McKay (1997, p.6) proposes that a network is an organized collection of contacts and the contacts' contacts. Client referral systems between agencies and service coordination agreements between two or more agencies are examples of interorganizational networks.

Networking is the assessment, development, and maintenance of network. It involves the actual exchanges. It is the creation of conditions for and the actual exchanges of material and instrumental and affective resources. The building of the social action organization or the negotiations of the service coordination agreements between two or more agencies referred to above are examples of networking. Mackay (1997, p. 61) defines interpersonal networking, although applicable to other forms of social networking, as "finding fast whom you need to get what you need in any given situation and helping others to do the same." Inherent in networking is sustaining reciprocity and interdependency, not dependency. *Interorganizational networking* exists when people in a network bring organizational resources and commitments beyond their personal resources to a network.

WHY NETWORKS AND NETWORKING?

Network involvement for an agency or an individual means a potential loss of autonomy and a necessity to invest some resources in developing and maintaining the network. Agencies and people are involved in networks because they expect to make gains over their expenditures of resources sufficient to compensate for their loss of autonomy. Research (Galaskiewicz & Wasserman, 1990; Woodard & Doreion, 1994) indicates that networks are developed and maintained under the following conditions:

- Network units need other units for the resources to fulfill their functions and achieve their goals. The network provides a structure, that is, a marketplace, for exchanging resources.

- The units need other units to respond to an external problem, cope with stress, opportunity, or mandate because the resources necessary to respond are available only through networking. The network provides a structure for aggregating resources and for coordinating domains politically and functionally.

- Network units that compete for domains need to regulate competition and conflict. The network provides a structure and mechanism for politically regulating competition, negotiating domain consensus, and legitimating the domains of competing network members.

SOCIAL EXCHANGES AND NETWORKS

Networks are established and maintained by social exchanges. Social exchange theory is the basic theory underlying networking. *Social exchanges* are involved when network units recognize the domains of other participating units in a network. The units *trade* or *exchange* domain recognitions. Exchanges are present when governments exchanges resources for commitments and programs compatible with the government's prevailing ideology. For reviews of ideological exchanges between the government and various constituencies on the social and political left and right, see Moynihan (1969), Murray (1984), and Pivan and Cloward (1971).

The potential exchange partners for a network usually are not limited to a single partner for a bilateral exchange between two participants. Instead, there is an *exchange set* delineated as the number of potential partners in the task environment or community. There is a field of potential exchange partners in the task environment. The number of potential partners in the exchange set determines the prevailing value of each participant's resources in likely exchanges. *Value* is the reward or gratification to the recipients of the resources or products received. The more potential exchange partners with the desired resource there are in the exchange set, the more easily realized and less costly are the exchanges for the party seeking the resource. *Costs* are the rewards, products, and resources traded and foregone in the exchange or the punishments incurred in order to obtain the desired resource. Each participant in the exchange relationship defines the value of the products received and compares this value to the cost of the products traded in the exchange.

NETWORK DIMENSIONS

Networks differ on several related dimensions critical to social work practice. It is important to understand the terminology, concepts, principles, theories, and research of networks to successfully practice social work. Nohria and Eccles (1992, pp. 4–7) contend that the actions, attitudes, and behaviors of people can be best explained in terms of their positions in networks. Networks constrain and shape actions of people in their interdependency and reciprocity. We will consider 12 basic network dimensions ranging from domain recognition and agreement of network members to the locus of authority of networks for their members (Woodard & Doreion, 1994; Mizruchi & Galaskiewicz, 1993).

Domain Consensus

Recognition and some degree of domain consensus is necessary for interpersonal and interorganization relations and networking.

Domain consensus is the recognition of and agreement by network members or units and potential network partners of a person, agency, or unit's domain claim on the task environment. Recognition of domains by network partners is required if exchanges are to occur. Domain recognition is prerequisite to domain consensus. The degree of domain consensus can vary on all or some of the domain variables, but the higher the agreement on a wider range of variables, the more likely it is that a network unit or agency will find network partners for resource exchanges.

Size

Networks can consist of as few as only two units or involve an almost infinite number of units, such as in a telephone network or the World Wide Web. The size of a network, even a social support or mutual aid network, is not geographically limited to a specific community now with the contemporary communication and transportation technology. The parlor game six degrees of separation speculates that no more than six people separate everyone from anyone else in the world. Milgram (1967) tested this assumption in a field experiment and found it convincing. The average number of links was five, not six. Of course, the challenging practice task is to identify and connect (or network) the relevant five or six people in the chain, convince them to pass back and forth relatively unchanged the exchanges between you and your target, and eventually shorten the chain of separation between you and your target to reduce your dependency on the chain.

Larger networks potentially have greater resources and more exchange partners than do smaller networks. Larger networks, however, generally are more inefficient, with resource redundancy. They require more management to regulate exchanges depending on network construction and can suffer from lower cohesion (Burt, 1992; Nohria & Eccles, 1992, pp. 288–308). Implications and relevance of size will be discussed under the dimensions of power, influence, and dependency; density; coordination and control (management); and cohesion.

Reciprocity and Exchanges

Networks are exchange mechanisms. Reciprocity is inherent in exchanges. It is both the act and obligation of returning value for value received. Individuals or network units who supply rewarding services to another obligate the receiving unit. To discharge the obligation the receiving must furnish benefit to the first. Balanced reciprocity (fairer exchanges) enhances network cohesion, stability, and use (Blau, 1964). If exchanges are viewed as unfair, then it is more likely that other exchange partners and networks will be sought and used. Research with social support networks has found this to be true (Beeman, 1997). Reciprocity in social support is associated with greater psychological well-being than when an individual unit is largely either a giver or only a recipient (Dalton, Elias, & Wandersman, 2001, p. 240).

Power, Influence, and Dependency

Power, as we have discussed it elsewhere in this text, is an ability to act and get one's way. Power is generally on a continuum, and one's power is rarely absolute. Power in networks is an ability to get resources, influence, and get things done in the network (Bragg, 1996; Willer, Lovaglia, & Markovsky, 1999, p. 231). Influence (less than absolute power) affects the behavior of others regardless of intent. Influence is rooted in the ability of a network member to alter the behavior of another network member by providing or withholding resources. Dependency is reliance upon others or another for support and desired resources. Dependent units in a network are usually subordinate to, highly influenced by, and have less power than units providing support.

Power, influence, and dependency of network units are functions of resources distributions in a network. Box 11.1 lays out the Power Equation described here. If one unit is the sole or primary possessor of a resource highly desired by a number of other potential network trading partners, the demand for the resource is likely to be high and the gains, power, and influence of the valued resource holder should be great. The holder of a highly desired and limited resource will gain

influence over other network units dependent on it for resources. The strength and vulnerability, the ability to influence and be influenced, of a network member results from the potential number of exchange partners for its resources and its competitors for a desired resource. The more the likely exchange partners or options a network member has within a network or accessible in its task environment for future networking, the less dependent it is on a single or few trading partner. A network member with a scarce resource, a resource in great demand such as leadership ability, with limited options for this resource to a network and other network-units but the resource holder has many options to exchange the resource puts the holder in a position of strength, influence, and relative power in network exchanges. The network is asymmetrical. Many potential exchange partners in a network reduce vulnerability and dependency for members of the network but can increase potential obligations and network maintenance costs. These costs are mitigated, according to Knoke (1993), by keeping networks flexible, informal, and decentralized.

Balanced exchange relationships, with all sides dependent on the other and having mutual and reciprocal influence, create countervailing power relationships. This is *interdependency*. Interdependency, with its balance, enhances stability and a sense of fair exchange to a network. A goal of network management for social work practitioners is balanced interdependency and countervailing power relationships by empowering clients.

Network units can engage in exchanges directly or through other units in a network. Indeed, intermediate units create networks beyond a dyad. Exchanges and networks can be regulated by a third party with a capacity to mandate and monitor exchanges between network participants. Mandated referrals and exchanges of resources occur when a third party requires two network units to interact. This is often the case when a superordinate agency requires re-

---

BOX 11.1	POWER EQUATION

Influence of Unit A over Unit B is a function of B's dependency on A for a resource or resources and the number of Bs competing for A's limited available resource:

$$(IA/B[FREQ](DB_n/A) + (\sigma BDA)$$

A will have influence on all Network Bs that are dependent on A for the resource.

Symbols: I = influence; n = number; / over or on; D = dependency

ferrals or particular types of exchanges among subordinate units. Health maintenance organizations and managed care direct and mandate exchanges between other health care network units consisting of health care providers and patients. The managed care agency is the superordinate network unit. It maintains its superordinate position and the responsiveness of health network units by controlling scarce fiscal resources.

The amount and desirability of a network unit's resources are important in network's exchanges and the unit's network influence. But resources alone do not determine network influence. According to research by Mizruchi and Galaskiewicz (1993), resource control and dependency's importance as a critical variable in determining influence likely are nested in variables such as social class and the networking skills of network actors. A network unit's influence or dependency on its network partners is explained as much by the network unit's bargaining skills in the use of its resources in exchanges as it is by the amount of resources. This is important for social work practice, as workers and clients will often have to compensate for a dearth of resources, with networking skills.

Cohesion

Cohesion is the internal bonding strength of a network. It helps the network remain a network. Cohesiveness is operationally defined as anything that attracts people to join, participate in, and remain in a dyad, group, organization, or network. Fair exchanges and reciprocity encourage cohesion, and network cohesion encourages more subsequent exchanges among network participants. Cohesion is also more likely to be higher in networks with primary and secondary group characteristics with more face-to-face interaction than with tertiary, limited-interest networks (Nohria & Eccles, 1992; Travillion, 1999, pp. 22–25). Practitioners seeking cohesive networks need to create opportunities for fair exchanges, broad interest among participants in each other, and face-to-face, more personalized interactions.

Network cohesion is affected by the network's symmetry and interdependence. Peter M. Blau's (1964) *superordinate-subordinate power relationship principle*, introduced with our network power discussion elaborates this network relationship. Superordinate and subordinate refer to the distribution of power and resources in a social exchange. If a relationship is too imbalanced, net-

work cohesion is adversely affected. The theory and principle holds that

- the more exchange relations between super and subordinate become imbalanced, the greater is the probability of opposition to those with power.
- the more the norms of reciprocity are violated by the superordinate, the less fair the exchanges, the greater is the imbalance.
- if networks are composed of many subordinates and few superordinates, the more subordinates experience collectively relations of imbalance with superordinates, the greater is the sense of deprivation, and the greater is the probability of opposition by the subordinates to the superordinates.

In short, dependency breeds resentment, opposition, and instability. Interdependence and fair exchanges foster network cohesion and solidarity.

The *superordinate-subordinate power relationship principle* underlies social action in community and labor organizing. Activist-organizers often help community groups, action systems, and client systems recognize and understand the imbalance of power and their subordinate positions. Lee's (1994) empowerment social work practice uses this principle in discussing the importance of helping clients assume a holistic approach in their problem analysis. They should assume a critical perspective and recognize social oppression rooted in class and ethnicity in the deconstruction of their problems. Similarly, in the construction of interventions and solutions, social oppression based on class and ethnicity must be recognized. We will discuss the political nature of client problems more fully in our chapter on community social casework practice.

Symmetry

Each network unit has some resources to exchange. This is the reason for networking. However, the resource distribution among network units is not necessarily symmetrical. Not all units have equal resources, power, and make equivalent gains and losses in exchanges. Network symmetry is the degree to which resources are evenly distributed and exchanges balanced; it is a function of the availability and distribution of network resources and the network units' skill in bargaining. If resources are aggregated and bargaining skills held by only a few of the network's units, the network's exchanges will be asymmetrical. Woodard and Doreion's (1994) study of community service networks found that less than half of the exchanges were symmetrical.

Symmetry enhances network stability and cohesion. Symmetry is promoted by and promotes fair exchanges and reciprocity cohesion. Socially marginalized clients are unlikely to have symmetrical networks. Individual clients generally have limited social resources. They have little symmetry in their network relations with community agencies and other tertiary social organizations. This lack of symmetry and its impact on power, dependency, and interdependency highlights a need for collective, countervailing mediating organizations and coalitions for clients in their networking with a largely vertical *tertiary* service system.[1]

Density and Structural Complexity

Network structures can be simple, with few units and relationships, or dense, with complex structures. Density is the number of actual relationships in the network, as compared with the possible number of relationships (Dalton, Elias, & Wandersman, 2001, p. 252–255; Specht, 1986). Potential density increases exponentially with each new network member. The addition of a single new unit to a six-unit network increases the potential number of relationships by six rather than one. In simple structures, all network units relate to each other. Simple structures are potentially dense.

Large networks can have high or low density, depending on their structure. A network with 100 units has a potential density of 4,950 relations. With increased size of a network, density and potential cohesion of the network become more difficult to manage, given the number of possible relationships between units. Each member has 99 separate relations. But if the density doesn't reach the potential density, cohesion is reduced as certain units are marginalized and do not interact with the network:

$$PD = NU(NU - 1)/2$$

where PD = potential density, and NU = number of network units.

The network management task is to reduce potential density without marginalizing members. A complex structure can reduce density by reducing the number of relationships. It essentially breaks the network into smaller subnetwork networks or departments. This allows for easier management. Organizational models with channels of communication, chains of command, and decentralized structures of subnetworks reflect this design. Subnetworks or network segments are network patterns within a network where interaction and density is greater within the segments than across segments. The subnetworks are linked into an overall network rather than a linking of individual people into one network. Segments creating smaller networks and networks of networks deal with the challenges of size and density (Dalton, Elias, & Wandersman, 2001, p. 252–255). We will examine structure more fully under the network dimensions of *centrality* and *coordination and control*.

Centrality and Reachability

Centrality and *reachability* are two critical variables contributing to network power and influence. They are also critical in leadership of community interventions. *Centrality* is present when other network positions have to go through a network position and unit in order to communicate and reach others in the network. Centrality provides a thermostatic function. The central unit can regulate the network, and alter exchanges as they pass through the it. Centrality is inherently, positively, and significantly related to power in networks (Bass & Burkhardt, 1992, p. 210). Reachability is necessary for a network position to have centrality. *Reachability* refers to a network unit's accessibility to other network units (Woodard & Doreion, 1994). A participant's power in a network is enhanced with centrality and linkage to the other network units (Knoke, 1993).

In Figure 11.1, a chain network of five positions, Position 3 (other things being equal) is in a position of greater influence than other network units because interactions must always go through it to reach the other end. The centrality of Positions 2 and 4, while not as great as 3's, is greater than that of 1 and 5. The capacity for influence is enhanced by centrality as exchanges must pass through the more central positions.

The chain network also has low density. In effect it has four segments composed of positions $1 \leftrightarrow 2, 2 \leftrightarrow 3, 3 \leftrightarrow 4$, and $4 \leftrightarrow 5$. With its low density, there is less likelihood for cohesion and stability and greater for marginalization of 1 and 5. Positions 1 and 5 are isolated and have no direct

$$1 \longleftrightarrow 2 \longleftrightarrow 3 \longleftrightarrow 4 \longleftrightarrow 5$$

Figure 11.1   Chain network.

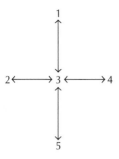

Figure 11.2   Star network.

interaction with 75% of the remaining network units. Units 2 and 4 are critical to maintaining 1 and 5 in the network.

In Figures 11.1, The Stars and 11.2, The Group, Position 3 has greater reachability by more network participants than do the other network positions. In Figure 11.2, a star network, all participants must go through 3 to reach an exchange partner. Position 3 is the star. Position 3's network influence should be the greatest, as all exchanges between any network positions must go through it. This network has low density and has four segments: 1 ↔ 3, 2 ↔ 3, 4 ↔ 3, and 5 ↔ 3. With centrality potentially comes greater network management and maintenance capacity and responsibilities. The stability of a star network depends on the star.

Position 3's centrality and influence based on network position is reduced in the third type of network, which is a group network (see Figure 11.3). In the group network, all units are equally central. This network is dense, with all network participants having direct access to all other network participants. If the density is maintained, it can be a more stable network than the other two. There is no central, more reachable, and dominant position of power or influence based on network structure. Networks with density may become unstable or require structural

centrality and segmentation as network size increases.

Coordination and Control

A network's need for coordination and control is a function of size, density, segmentation, frequency and types of exchanges, and its need for stability. The capacity for coordination and control inherently resides in network positions with centrality and reachability. *Loosely coupled networks* (Aldrich, 1971; Weick, 1976) are composed of loosely connected units with a capacity to act independently on most matters but still capable of exchanges and joint actions when needed. Loosely coupled networks often reconcile the strains between autonomy and interdependence for their members.

Network coordination in loosely coupled networks is informal between participants, with any dominance resting with the coordinators who serve as the linchpins, as Figures 11.1 and 11.2 illustrate, or, in the case of Figure 11.3, through group mechanisms. Group mechanisms lend themselves to more equality but suffer from the expense of maintaining multiple interactions and duplication.

As networks become larger and if stability is needed, they become more formal, with set protocols, rules, and procedures to coordinate and control, the management tasks, the interaction density. Individual discretion and variation is reduced and the formal protocols and structured positions govern the interaction. Individuals lose autonomy corresponding to the network's size and need to control and coordinate density. Without management and maintenance, *entropy* (a characteristic of systems) begins (Hage, 1980; Van de Ven, Delbecq, & Koenig, 1976). Figure 11.4 represents a segmented network with a management position, Position 5, to control interaction between the segments.

Practitioners in constructing and managing networks should be aware of the importance of structural positioning in the network and its influence on the flow of information and the management of exchanges. When tighter control is necessary, network design should have a posi-

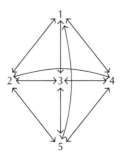

Figure 11.3   Group network.

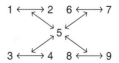

Figure 11.4   Segmented network.

tion with centrality. Practitioners needing network influence should seek to hold central positions.

Network Unit's Social Status

People and other social units come to social networks with different social statuses. Agency's networks and networking vary by the individual participants' hierarchical level within the agency and social status in the community. Agency administrators network on the policy and programmatic levels. The management-level networking is concerned with exchanges of population and problem information, fiscal and material resources exchanges, and management and domain information exchanges (Woodard & Doreion, 1994). Line-level staff can network as part of formal agency service agreements or more informally with personal networks. Line-service staff engage more often in exchanges involving client referrals, services coordination, and information exchanges for specific clients. Line-service staff often are ignorant of the management networks exchanges (Woodard & Doreion, 1994). Woodard and Doreion's (1994) research found that line-level staff networks were not always symmetrical but were more symmetrical with frequently used network partners when exchanges were viewed as fair. Generally, line-level networks were more symmetrical than were management interagency network exchanges. Healy's (1991) research on line-staff services coordination found that they preferred service coordination through informal rather than formal networks. Informal networks may develop as a response to the difficulty of participating in the large, complex and formal networks. Informal networks can indicate either a beginning for formalization or an entropy of formal networks.

The social status a participant brings to a network affects network status. Participants who bring high social status to the network tend to have high status and influence in the network (Bragg, 1999; Willer, 1999, p. 2).

Locus of Authority

Networks also can vary by the locus of authority. The locus of authority is where the authority for creating, defining, and maintaining the network's objectives and tasks resides. The locus of authority can be within or outside the network. The locus of authority is the foundation of and where the organization derives its authority. Both networks and the units can have internal or external loci of authority. If the local administrator of an agency in a network reports to or must obtain permission from a decisional authority outside the local agency, the networked unit has an external locus of authority. It is important to determine network and network partners' loci of authority because these are the centers of influence. The viability of domain and network agreements rest with the loci of authority. Decentralized structures of large complex organizations are often part of extracommunity organizations called vertical structures. The decentralization is an attempt to reduce many of the negative attributes of the behemoth organization and to assume more locally responsive structure and relationships. However, the primary criteria of the decentralized structure 's ability to engage in community networking is the capacity of local decision makers in the decentralized unit to commit the decentralized unit's resources to local community interests.

Networks composed of voluntary participants have internal loci of authority for the network, although the unit may have an external locus of authority, while mandated networks have external network loci of authority. The managed care network described earlier, and interagency coordinating groups required by funding sources such as the federal government or United Way, are examples of networks with external loci of authority. The objectives, goals, structure, and rules of exchange within the network are determined not by network members but by a superordinate external authority.

The locus of authority's effects on network performance is unclear. Schopler, (1994) after a review of the research literature, speculated on the types of tasks for which each loci might be best suited. Mandated networks with their externally proscribed rules should be best suited for clearly defined, standardized, and limited tasks, as the external mandating authority usually has reasons for creating a network. Voluntary networks with internal loci of authority should respond better to tasks requiring innovation and creativity, although they may be less efficient in operation. Morale is often higher and cohesion stronger in networks with internal loci of authority. Unlike the mandated members, no external authority holds the network together.

Horizontal and Vertical Network Relationships

Network units sharing the same geographic domains, having the same task environments, existing within the same community and with similar locus of decision making, have *horizontal* network relationships. Horizontal networks (networks primarily comprised of units with horizontal relations) are more likely to be decentralized, informal, fluid, and—at times— competitive and marketlike.

If a network unit's geographic domain and service or market area encompasses several communities and its locus of authority rests outside another network unit's community, the relationship to that unit is *vertical*. Vertically related structures are generally superordinate and have less network interdependence. The vertical or superordinate unit's interests, responsibilities, and accountability extend beyond the local community. The superordinate unit's perception of its best interests may be different from the community's good. Local concerns simply are not a priority in the superordinate unit's decision equations. As mutual support, social welfare, and health provisions become part of national and global corporations, and providers adopt proprietary models and behaviors, the relationships to local communities become vertical. As these agencies follow the profit-driven decisions and emulate other vertically controlled and economically driven organizations, the local community's well-being is not paramount to the extracommunity megastructures. Federal and state agencies are vertical to local community organizations, even if the community is the geographic and civic community of Washington, D.C. National organizations, even when physically headquartered in specific communities, are vertical in their relationships to local community organizations. And while national organizations are horizontal to other national organizations, they tend to respond in their interorganizational relations in a formal fashion. For an extensive review of the growing importance and impact of vertically related organizations and their decisions on local communities, see Barlett and Steele (1992).

Vertical and *horizontal*, as used here, describe the relationship between the network units, the network linkages, in the network and the community (Alter, n.d.). They don't describe the internal structure of a unit. The vantage point is the community. It is important for social workers in assessing agencies, organizations, and network units to determine if the relationships are vertical or horizontal. This will affect the bargaining and negotiation, influence and interdependency, the exchange agreements, the authority of local administrators and agents to make decisions responsive to community needs,

and the capacity of the organization to respond to local community change. Vertical units inherently have less community commitment than do horizontal units. Community social work practitioners develop network relationships with a more horizontal character of power equivalency and interdependence with the vertical agencies in the network through organizing the horizontal entities into a countervailing power network relationship.

ESTABLISHING AND MAINTAINING DOMAINS AND NETWORKS: THE PRACTICE CHALLENGES AND TASKS

Network units generally seek domain consensus to reduce domain conflicts and competition. Domain consensus maximizes resources and reduces the amount of energy and resources expended in bargaining to obtain resources, to protect domains, and to engage in and manage competition and conflict. Domain consensus promotes stability and predictability. Domain conflicts and competition occur whenever a social entity attempts to establish itself in or to obtain all or part of another entity's domain. The conflict and competition can be for any of the domain's tangible or intangible resources (Chetkow-Yanoov, 1997; Coser, 1964). Establishing domain consensus, developing and coordinating networks, and managing networks depend on the resources available in the task environment, the dimensions listed earlier, and the skills of the participants. Social agencies have missions and objectives related to the environment, whether the objective is to increase the economic self-sufficiency of Temporary Assistance to Needy Families (TANF) mothers, to improve social functioning of mental patients, or to reduce child abuse and neglect. Each agency seeks domains and resources and generally must network with other agencies and organizations to achieve their objectives and fulfill their mission. Agencies seek to maximize autonomy and resources. This is also the charge to social workers in client empowerment and self-determination—to maximize client autonomy. However, neither agencies nor clients operate in social isolation. Maximizing autonomy and resources require interaction with the social environment or the task environment. The task in both establishing and maintaining networks is to facilitate interdependency rather than dependency. Box 11.2 lists the basic steps for determining needed network limits.

BOX 11.2	PROTOCOLS FOR DETERMINING NEEDED NETWORK UNITS

1. Determine the total scope of the technology, tasks, and resources required to accomplish the objectives.

2. Determine the agency's (or client's) current domain of technology, tasks, and resources.

3. Compare the agency's (or client's) existing domain with the total scope of technology, tasks, and resources required to accomplish the objectives. If a gap exists, the agency (or client) will need to expand either its domain or network with resource providers: fiscal, nonfiscal, client, legitimizers, technology holders, and other complementary agencies (or social supports), to achieve its objectives.

4. Assess the community, the task environment, for the domains, the holders, of the needed resources and their exchange preferences.

5. Negotiate exchanges with the resource providers based on resource exchanges required by the resource holder (or social support). In the negotiation and networking, the importance of size, complexity, dependency, cohesion, centrality, reciprocity expectations, competition, and the other dimensions of networks should be recognized.

Competition

Competition is controlled conflict when the parties in the competition recognize that they are seeking the same domain or resource. Without recognition of the competition, conflict does not occur. Competition, as with most conflict, has the rules of the game between the competing parties (Deutsch, 1973; Kriesberg, 1982; Lauer, 1982). Governments have devoted much time and energy to developing and managing the rules for national and international marketplaces, such as the North American Free Trade Agreement (NAFTA). Electoral campaigns with their campaign rules represent rules of conflict for changes of government in a democracy. But the rules of the game are followed in conflict, competition, and change only if the competitors see the rules as fair, if others are seen as playing fairly by the rules, and if competitors believe that violating rules produces costs exceeding any potential gains.

Network participants are vulnerable to competition and conflict when other network participants think they are not fulfilling their network responsibilities and hence not allowing other network units to maintain their domain obligations. Ideological differences between network units often lead to conflict as different ideologies shape different perceptions of reality, domain responsibilities, and what constitutes a fair exchange (Chetkow-Yanoov, 1997, p. 47; Lauer, 1982, p. 182).

Conflict and competition can have value for a network. Network conflict with out-groups (nonnetwork units) increases internal cohesion and collective network identity. This "us against them" situation is useful in developing team spirit and patriotism. It can generate energy and a sense of purpose. Conflict with out-groups, and sometimes even with the network, can release emotional steam and reduce tension. Networks that survive internal conflict often are stronger, as the conflict served to clarify values and commitments (Coser, 1964; Kirst-Ashman & Hull, 1997, pp. 71–72; Kriesberg, 1982, pp. 69–108). Conflict often is critically necessary for the socially marginalized in changing the status quo.

Conflict Resolution Strategies

Coser (1964) has asserted that, as the world becomes more interdependent and closer, there will be greater need for rules of conflict and for conflict resolution. Without rules, society will disintegrate. Tannen (1998/1999, p. 48) argues that conflict is a function of our market ideology. Society is increasingly argumentative and adversarial in spirit, law, and politics. By casting everything in *either/or* dichotomies, win/lose terms, we lose nuances, middle ground, and the possibility that there can be a range and variety of viable positions. *Everything becomes a market model of competition and clash of ideas, with necessary winners and losers.* The winner/loser ideology is reflected in the pop-culture reflected reality television shows, such as *Big Brother*, *Survivors*, and the quiz show, *The Weakest Link*. Survival in this environment of any particular social entity, whether client groups, agencies, or social workers, will depend on that entity's skills in using the rules and its participation in making fair rules to be used.

Conflict requires that one or both sides recognize the conflicting areas of means or outcomes, that one or both sides are dissatisfied with the status quo, and that one or both sides have a belief that it is not the "natural order of things" and believe that conflict will change and improve conditions. Much of social action is directed toward increasing the action system's dissatisfaction with the status quo and helping the action system accept that conditions can be changed by social action. Creating a collective identity is critical for conflict strategies based on a sense of grievance and deprivation. Conflict is more likely when the social environment is neutral. If the social environment or significant parts of it is aligned with one or the other side, the momentum necessary for conflict is unlikely, as there is little environment support for the minority side. Such momentum is more likely if one or both sides believe they will get support from the social environment that will enable them to inflict and sustain punishment (Coser, 1964).

Conflict can have several outcomes as indicated by Table 11.1. One outcome is the maintenance of the status quo where neither party gains or loses resources other than those expended in the conflict. If the conflict is on fundamental issues, maintenance of the status quo is only a temporary resolution of the conflict. Maintenance of the status quo, however, is an unacceptable conflict outcome for most social work *change* efforts.

The second set of outcomes is a zero-sum solution. A zero-sum solution (a win-lose solution) exists when the gains of one side are offset with equivalent losses by the other side. The distribution of total domains and resources between contestants is changed, but the total amount of domains and resources is unchanged. This resolution generally involves the use of the various forms of social power. The side with the greater social power or the most skilled in applying its social power usually wins.

Strategies in conflict resolution include the following (Coser, 1964; Kirst-Ashman & Hull, 1997, pp. 73–80; Strom-Gottfried, 1998):

- *Retreat* is an outcome that occurs when one party leaves the conflict and the opponent wins by default. Retreat is acceptable only as a short-term strategy to preserve resources for later conflict reengagement. Otherwise, retreat is defeat.

- *Accommodation* is a variant of retreat and consists of one party's giving in and letting the other party win, to preserve the peace. It may be acceptable as a short-term solution if one side of the conflict judges that it can not carry the contest.

- *Bargaining* is the compromise strategy and involves give-and-take: winning some and loosing some. Bargaining and negotiation is the most frequently used strategy unless one side has sufficient social power to essentially ignore the other side. We will discuss bargaining in greater detail below, as it is the practice skill most useful for our conflict situations. Bargaining skills can overcome, to some degree, deficits in other forms of social power. Conflict and social action tactics such as embarrassment, loss of community support, and financial loss (such as with strikes and boycotts) and the disruption tactics of picketing and sit-ins are often used to bring the opponent to the bargaining table. Bargaining (Hardina, 2000) often tries to reframe the conflict as a non-zero-sum game involving positive exchanges with both sides winning. A *win-win* strategy involves using *collaboration* and *cooperation*, where focusing on similar contestant needs and sharing of resources becomes a means of conflict resolution. A positive exchange relationship in which both sides make gains is a non-zero-sum game. Assessing the task environment for new resources and other new domain possibilities as yet unclaimed can lead to a non-zero sum game or

TABLE 11.1 Conflict Outcomes

Conflict Resolution	Unit A Change	Unit B Change
Status quo	No change	No change
Zero-sum A gain	+	−
Zero-sum B gain	−	+
Win-win non-zero-sum	+	+
Lose-lose non-zero-sum	−	−

allying with other domain holders to add to the domains of the previously competing parties from domains not claimed by network units. The trades and gains do not have to be in the same type of resource.

- *Subjugation* is a strategy that calls for tactics to force an opponent to accommodate or retreat from the conflict. Subjugation defeats an opponent and generally involves causing the opponent to expend the resources that are the sources of the opponent's power and then isolating from additional resources and resource.

BARGAINING

Bargaining and negotiation skills are crucial to social work advocacy and practice. Bargaining is a "process whereby two or more parties attempt to settle what each shall give and take, or perform and receive, in transactions between them" (Rubin & Brown, 1975, p. 2). The conflicting parties, at least temporarily, join together in an exchange relationship, a bargaining relationship, regardless of any prior or future relationships. Bargaining concerns (a) the division or exchange of one or more specific resources or (b) the resolution of one or more intangible issues among the parties or among those whom the parties represent, or (c) both. Bargaining usually involves the presentation of demands or proposals by one party, evaluation by the other party, followed by concessions or counterproposals or both. The activity is thus sequential rather than simultaneous (Rubin & Brown, 1975, pp. 6–18). It requires clarity of communication between the parties, a willingness to compromise and seek areas of agreement and middle ground, and a mutual recognition of legitimacy of the parties to bargain. Bargaining typically is a process with several components (Deutsch, 1973; Kirst-Ashman & Hull, 1997, pp. 73–80; Rubin & Rubin, 2001, pp. 328–335; Rubin & Brown, 1975, pp. 6–18; Strom-Gottfried, 1998; Tannen, 1998/1999):

- Prior to directly bargaining, establish a BATANA (best alternative to a—or to any—negotiated agreement; (Fisher, Ury, & Patton, 1981; Strom-Gottfried, 1998). A BATANA is the best alternative available and that appears possible without negotiation. The BATANA provides a basis for comparison of any negotiated gains or losses to what might be obtained without bargaining. This provides a basis on which to determine whether negotiations should be done at all.

- Partialize or break down your position in its parts and place in priority order your areas of concern and your positions. Positions should reflect interests and areas of concern and not be too rigid and narrow to allow flexibility in the give-and-take of negotiation. You may have to leave out some low-priority issues to prevent overwhelming the process. Fragmentation of issues is always possible and doesn't preclude future negotiation on the omitted issues. Inclusion of some *throwaway* issues may help in the bargaining. A throwaway issue is an issue that you are willing to give up rather easily, as a sign of concession. It is used to persuade the other party to make similar, but (it is hoped) real, concessions.

- Attend to the *rules of engagement* before substantial bargaining. Future gains and losses in bargaining are affected by the *rules of engagement*. These rules govern where the bargaining will occur; the length and nature of the sessions; the format, agenda, and procedures; whose position will be presented first; and even the shape of the bargaining table. The rules of the game or engagement determine fairness. Biased criteria used to evaluate the fairness of proposals, positions, and solutions will bias the outcomes. In establishing procedures and protocols, avoid adversarial win-lose procedures, as they harden the opposition's position. It is important to have the criteria and rules of engagement in place, agreed upon, *and agreeable, prior* to proposal presentation and consideration of solutions.

- Encourage your opponent to present his or her position first. This will allow tailoring of your responses and prevent your prematurely conceding too much. If there are areas of agreement or near-agreement with your opponent, work on these areas first and be willing to make apparent concessions that don't fundamentally jeopardize your position. In establishing common ground, co-opt part of your opponent's position that doesn't fundamentally conflict with yours and treat it as your own. Your opponent then must bargain against the original position or accept it. If the opponent accepts it, the tactic helps to establish empathy and your image of flexibility. You also can use it as a throwaway issue.

- Seek mutually accommodating agreements that allow both sides to satisfy fundamental principles if possible. Try not to challenge your opponent's deepest moral convictions, but negotiate from your convictions. Don't give them up in the desire to reach accommodation.

Communicate your empathy with your opponent's perspective, that you can understand it but not necessarily accept it.

- Avoid rigid premature positional bargaining and try to keep your opponent from doing the same. Move from interests rather than rigid positions. Talk less of rights, which are non-negotiable, than of needs, wants, and interests that are negotiable. Separate your feelings, likes, and dislikes for the opponent from the problem. Do not demonize your opponent in the bargaining stage, because eventually you will have to join in agreement. The bargaining is on interests and issues and not on interpersonal relationships. The line from the *Godfather* movie saga is applicable: "It's not personal; it's only business."

- Don't rush to premature solutions, conclusions, and closure without seeking areas of mutual gain. This critical to a win-win approach and vital if future bargaining, cooperation, and collaboration are to be maintained. However, do not be so reasonable and conciliatory that you lose touch with your core beliefs, passions, and needs that compelled the bargaining originally. Be clear on the areas of agreement and continuing areas of disagreement.

- If the bargaining has not produced resolutions favorable to your position, keep bargaining. Again, don't rush to premature conclusions, and don't accept them. Keep the communication and bargaining process going until it can be more satisfactorily concluded.

- Prepare for future negotiation regardless of the outcome of the current bargaining. If satisfactory, the task is to maintain the gains. If unsatisfactory, the challenge is to reopen negotiations to arrive at more favorable conclusions. Emphasize and maintain communication if you wish to change your relationship with your opponent from that of a competitor to that of a network partner.

MEDIATION AND ARBITRATION

Sometimes direct bargaining is unable to arrive at mutually agreeable accommodations. Then third parties as *observers* or as *mediators* or *arbitrators* are used. Nonpartisan observers often keep the process moving, and if one side is capricious, they help to build public support for the other side. Rubin and Brown (1975) claim that observers make the process more trustworthy: "The mere presence of an audience (including the psychological presence) motivates the bar-

gainers to seek positive, and avoid negative, evaluations—especially when the audience is salient to the bargainers" (p. 44). Observation can also make the bargainers more cautious and conservative, as tentative positions are often prematurely frozen.

Mediation is a process that uses a third party (a neutral party to the conflict) called the *mediator* to clarify communicate between the parties the positions. A mediator's effectiveness rests on whether the mediator is seen as fair by all parties in the dispute. Mediation helps to reduce irrationality, nonrationality, provides opportunities for face saving, facilitates communication by lowering its tone or tension, and can regulate costs regarding third-party interests and information and evaluations of alternative solutions. Mediators and mediation can be formal or informal. Mediation helps the parties comply with the bargaining processes and protocols. The mediation and mediator's goal is accountability to a process of bargaining rather than decisions on bargaining outcomes. Mediators in addition to formal mediators can be clients, representatives of the public or other constituencies.

If mediation is unsuccessful, arbitration is another option before coercive action. A side to a dispute generally seeks arbitration only if (a) it appears to be losing, or (b) its position is most likely to be adopted by the arbitrator, or (c) both. Arbitration is the use of a superordinate third party, superordinate to the conflicting parties for purposes of the conflict resolution, to find and dictate a solution. Arbitrators generally hear both positions and apply the rules of the game to the dispute to arrive at a solution. The rules of the game can be public law when applied by the courts as arbitrators or may be privately agreed-upon rules used by major league baseball arbitrators. Arbitrators can be agencies such as the United Way with its superordinate funding position over member agencies, or they may be agencies such as the courts or other third parties with authority over all sides to the dispute. Arbitration does present dangers to all parties in the conflict, because they all surrender autonomy to the arbiter, which becomes a superordinate authority for purposes of dispute resolution.

ESTABLISHING AND MAINTAINING DOMAINS

A final task in domain conflict resolution is to establish domain boundary maintenance and protection mechanisms to reduce the expenditures of resources necessary to wage future domain conflicts. Establishing new domains is facilitated by the resource richness and dispersion in the task environment and the instability or weakness of existing domain agreements and networks. If there is consensus and stability among network units, units seeking to establish or expand domains will have to engage in conflict and competition to create instability and turbulence. This will allow them to claim domains and resources by breaking down existing networks. Conversely, once a unit has an established domain, it will seek to secure its domain by working toward stability and placidness in the task environment. However, the richer the resources of the task environment, the more all domains and networks can be sustained.

The 1960s and 1970s—with an abundance of federal funding for social agencies, a condition of resource richness—saw many new social agencies and service networks created. In the 1990s and in the twenty-first century, with growing fiscal resource stinginess, social turbulence, and social service agencies paralleling the proprietary sector, new social work skills were and are needed (Menefee, 1994). The current task environment for social agencies list the resource richness indicated by Table 11.2 as most beneficial to establishing and maintaining domains. The importance and usefulness of the rules of the game, and the techniques, mechanisms, and structures for competition and exchanges, have become more critical for social work and its clients in this era of resource scarcity. The skills of networking and bargaining in a turbulent and competitive world are essential.

CLIENTS AND SOCIAL NETWORKS

Clients exist in a web of social relations and a potential range of networks other than formal social agencies. Research and scholars have linked client empowerment to participation in natural social support networks and social networks as well as self-help groups (Anderson & Shaw, 1994; Beeman, 1997; Blau & Alba, 1982; Cochran, 1990; Dalton, Elias, & Wandersman, 2001; Gestan & Jason, 1987; Heller, 1990; Lee, 1988; Levine, 1988; Lewis & Ford, 1990; Lincoln,

2000; McCarthy & Nelson, 1991; O'Connell, 1978; Schwartz, 1986; & Whittaker, 1986, among others). Client empowerment means increasing a client's capacity to take control of his or her life to improve it. Empowerment, like power, is in the ability to act (Lee, 1994). Empowerment is the cornerstone of social work practice and social work's value of client self-determination. Empowerment requires action and is not done in isolation. It needs collective and individual actions. Empowerment requires social networks and social support networks.

Social support networks are social networks with some special qualities. Whittaker, Garbarino & Associates (1983) specify the special qualities as "the relational structure through which people request support and make demands. . . . a series of communication links. . . . a set of interconnected relationships among a group of people that provides enduring patterns of nurturance (in any or all forms) and provides contingent reinforcement for efforts to cope with life on a day-to-day basis" (pp. 4–5).

Social networks can either support or detract from the individual's social functioning; social support networks are limited to social networks that provide supports. The community psychologists Dalton, Elias, and Wandersman (2001, pp. 234–235) state that social support is not a simple, unitary concept. It represents a collection of social, emotional, cognitive, and behavioral processes occurring in social relationships that provide help and promote adaptive coping. Social support can take the following forms:

1. *Generalized social support*—Ongoing support involving a general sense of belongingness, acceptance, and being cared for. Generalized social support promotes social integration and emotional support. Social integration provides a sense of belongingness to social groupings, communities, friendships, and workplace relations. Emotional support gives comfort and caring within personal relationships, often as a result of social integration.

TABLE 11.2 Task Environment Conditions to Establish and Maintain Domains

	Establishes Domains	Maintain Domains
When Task environment is:	Unstable, turbulent, heterogeneous	Stable, placid, homogeneous
When Task environment resources are	Dispersed, rich	Concentrated, rich

2. *Specific social support*—More limited and direct problem-focused support for coping with specific stressors, often in a particular setting. Specific social support can be any of the following:

(a) *Esteem support* or encouragement—Support bolstering a sense of personal competency for dealing with specific challenges. It is task focused rather than deep, enduring emotional support and can come from a range of people. It is often more empowering when it comes from superordinates.

(b) *Informational support*—Cognitive advice and guidance, usually tailored to specific situations rather than generalized emotional support.

(c) *Tangible support*—Concrete assistance, material aid, and things.

Streeter and Franklin (1992) and Shumaker and Brownell (1984) provide similar social support categories in their review of social support network research, used six social support categories:

1. Material supports in physical things.

2. Behavioral assistance with tasks.

3. Intimate interaction such as listening, caring, expressing understanding for self-esteem in home and emotional gratification.

4. Guidance by giving specific advice, information, and instruction.

5. Feedback that provide reaction to and assessment of thoughts, behaviors, and feelings for identity enhancement.

6. Positive social interaction for fun and relaxation that aid identity and esteem. (Streeter & Franklin, 1992, p. 83)

The types of social support are not mutually exclusive, and a particular network can provide more than a single social support. A boss can provide encouragement and praise on current performance, with advice and guidance on future career opportunities (informational) as a mentor, and can provide tangible rewards with a raise. What makes something a social support, according to Streeter and Franklin (1992, p. 82) is that it is social support embedded in actual connections and a sense of belonging that people have with significant others: family, friends, colleagues, and others in their environment, as opposed to isolation and alienation from that environment. To have and use social supports, peo-

ple must perceive them as social supports. This requires that others in the network provide the actual behaviors of support and assistance.

Social support networks vary in size and density. While research indicates mixed findings, a mid-range size is typically most supportive. The effects of density, the number of possible relationships, and the amount of cohesion depend on type and amount of support needed. Less dense networks are more conducive to emotional supports.

Social support networks differ by gender traits as well (Lin & Westcott, 1991). Patterson, Germain, Brennan, and Memmott (1988) found that female natural helpers in support networks were more depend on bonding, more expressive, and more effective with friends and family than they were with neighbors and less-close contacts. Male natural helpers were more effective instrumentally, with neighbors, and less so on personal and emotional or expressive concerns.

Access to social support networks differs across societies, communities, and individuals (Walker, Wasserman, & Wellman, 1993, p. 75). As with the social agency networks, proximity and the ability to make contact (reachability) are important for individual social support networks. Though proximity correlates with reachability, the telephone, the Internet, and other modern transportation and communication technologies reduce the need for physical proximity for contact and connectedness. Proximity is important for the social support of companionship but is less critical than reachability for some of the other types of social and emotional supports.

Social Support Network Benefits

Social support networks are conceptually beneficial; this appears to be uniformly supported in the research. Social support networks provide mutual support and help with living and coping, especially during times of crisis. Members learn skills to help themselves as they are receiving help or helping others. The clinical and therapeutic effects of social support networks are positive, with benefits literally ranging across the spectrum. They reduce the need for institutional and social agency help (Balgopal, 1988). Before we review some of the specific research, we need to keep Specht's (1986) cautions in mind. Specht concluded, after his review of the research in 1986 (and his conclusion appears valid after our more recent review), that the concepts of social support and social support networks are often vaguely and broadly used. Often the labels have been used for different phenomenon. The directions of the relationships between the social support networks and the behavior or comparison variable are imprecise. The research is cross sectional and inconclusive, with the relationships being more association than causation. The alternative questions, as to whether social support networks promote well-being or if well-being allows greater social support network involvement, are not resolved.

The cohesive and integrating effects of social support networks act to reduce social isolation and alienation, especially when networks serve as mediating structures. Zimmerman and Rappaport (1988), in a cross-sectional study of community participation, concluded that greater involvement was positively associated with individual psychological empowerment and inversely associated with alienation. Psychological empowerment was described as the "connection between a sense of personal competence, a desire for, and a willingness to take action in the public domain" (Zimmerman & Rappaport, p. 746). Schore and Atkin (1993) reported on 1960s U.S. Department of Labor data that the incidence of depression declined to 12% among workers in workplaces with high levels of social support, from almost 27% in workplaces with low social supports. Social supports are positively associated with mental health and mental health gains (Dufort, Dallaire, & Lavoie, 1997; Lin, Ye, & Ensel, 1999), stable marriages and child rearing (Volling, Notaro, & Larsen, 1998), school performance (Rosenfeld, Richman, & Bowen, 2000), and reduced rates of homelessness (Letiecq, Anderson, & Koblinsky, 1998).

Social Networks and Globalization

Social networks and social support networks, always critical in representative and participatory democracy, are especially important in the vertically dominated communities of the global economy (Wessels, 1997). People and communities in a global economy need a variety and multiple levels of organizations to mediate between them and the global megacorporations (van Deth, 1997, pp. 1–25). Market competition, in the classic sense of no vendor or purchaser having the capacity to highly influence or control the market, is archaic. Individuals as consumers have no influence. A single, multinational and multifunctional corporation can have great influence on the political economy and control markets. Social fragmentation accompanies in-

dustrial and global society with its separation of work from home and often community, a functional extension of the community's physical-geographic boundaries to a global scale, movement to contract society from organic society, and a predominance of secondary and more often tertiary social interactions. An individual voter has little political influence in the act of voting, although an individual with great economic and social resources may have influence in other ways. Just as a voter can have shared political influence through mediating organizations, an individual consumer can have shared influence in mediating consumer organizations. However, one of the most urgent problems facing Western democracies is that of citizen social exclusion. Social exclusion from group life means that a person lacks the social capital derived from participation in a network of civic engagement. Interaction with others can, according to the theory of social capital (Moyser & Barry, 1997; Putnam, 2000), be expected not merely to promote personal interests and collective benefits, but also to generate a significant side benefit of social trust that can be self-reinforcing. In turn, social capital may be convertible into the political capital of collective efficacy and political trust (Parry & Moyser, 1992, pp. 44–62).

A remedy against social exclusion and the social disintegration characteristic of mass societies is, of course, the active membership of individuals in all kinds of voluntary social networks (Dekker, Koopmans, & van den Broek, 1997). Voluntary social networks provide the opportunity to meet and network with new people, develop social supports, develop civic and social engagement skills and contacts, learn interpersonal skills, and develop reciprocity and the cohesion that integrates society and reduces the impact of mass society. These networks act as a buffer between the individual and the ongoing modernization of industrial society. Participation in civic and voluntary associations is inversely correlated with economic and social inequality (Wessels, 1997). Participation in voluntary associations, especially mass political associations, part of global industrialization and serves to mediate the negative impact of the globalization. Communication technology can facilitate community and social action organizing (pp. 198–201). The core and necessary trait is primary and secondary participation, social networking, rather than just checkbook membership.

Politically and as the vehicle for civic participation, associations serve as interest groups in the social mix to determine social policy. Without the associations and participation on the microlevel of the association, the individual is limited in macroparticipation. The associations also provide the individual with a network of contacts. Associations (the networks) are political whether or not the associations are overtly political (Almond & Verba, 1963; Dekker, Koopmans, & van den Broek, 1997). They are political because they develop social skills and interlink social networks.

Membership in associations, whether or not politically motivated, leads to a politically more competent citizenry. Van Deth (1997), after a review of the literature on social participation, concluded that social participation and political involvement are correlated. "Voting behavior (turnout), a clear and direct relationship with social participation is found in most analyses, even when socioeconomic status or political orientation are taken into account" (p. 13). Joining organizations and political participation in politics reinforce one another. A similar correlation was found for other conventional modes of political behavior and social participation. Groups are not only cooperative endeavors toward mutual ends but also a means to a shared life, a civic life, and this makes for political capital.

Large-scale membership subscription or checkbook organizations as tertiary networks reduce some of the civic benefits and skills of direct participation (Maloney & Jordan, 1997, pp. 107–124). Decision making in these large-scale organizations is *anticipatory democracy* rather than *participatory democracy*. One anticipates the nature of the decisions by virtue of joining rather than by participating in the decisional processes of the network. The networks are *anticipatory* oligarchies with decisions made by a few at the top. The participation is financial in membership fees, especially for the broad base of members, rather than broad-based participation. This allows the oligarchies to function and pursue the anticipated actions. Full benefits and virtues of direct participation and networking are not realized or are marginal. The influence is less mutual and more from the mass organization to the individual.

These tertiary organizations are called new social movements (NSM). They (e.g., AARP, NRA, Greenpeace, etc.) have replaced the political party structure as a mechanism for more direct participants in the political process, and indirect as they are. Political party sizes decline as the NSMs increase. The managerial-dominated NSMs have to spend a great deal of effort and resources on raising membership, as membership is a revolving door with members constantly dropping out after a year or so. Amnesty International, for example, has a dropout rate of 40% annually, and the average membership life is 4 years.

Reciprocity

Social support networks require interdependency and reciprocity rather than dependency if they are to endure. Informal, voluntary, and primary groups need internal interdependency. Their maintenance depends on their member satisfaction. Metaresearch by Walker et al. (1993), also supported by Maton (1988), concluded that unilateral support is a myth. Social support is not one-dimensional or unidirectional. If there is true reciprocity, there must be a balancing of provider and recipient roles. Reciprocity or mutual obligation is inherent in social supports network as "providing support to someone in the same network increases the probability that one's own needs will be met in the future" (Shumaker & Brownell, 1984, p. 29). Reciprocity, as expected from the propositions of exchange theory, tends to match the recipient's view of the value of the resources supports received. When reciprocity is absent, the social support network entropies and cohesion is lost (Shumaker & Brownell, 1984, pp. 24–29; Walker et al., 1993). Reciprocity in self-help groups and social support networks enhances members' sense of well-being. The sense of well-being is higher when members give as well as receive (Dalton, Elias, & Wandersman, 2001, p. 240; Maton, 1988). Additionally, activities beyond the self-help group, where members have other networks, are a key component of self-help group efficacy. The extra group involvements may lower demands on the self-help group. Kelly and Kelly's (1985) research on natural helping, a form of social support, found that social support networks may be focused and that helpers tend to be respondent and network specific. They are not generalized helpers serving a wide number of respondents. The helpers often became helpers as payback or reciprocity for help that they received from the current respondent or others.

Costs of Social Networks

Social workers, in assisting clients with social support networks, should be aware that social support networks can have detrimental effects. Not all self-help and support networks are socially helpful to a client or community, although the client may receive some generalized or specific benefit. Not only can social support networks be simultaneously beneficial and detrimental, but different kinds of relationships can also provide different kinds of supports in emotional aid, material aid, information, and companionship. The exchanges between social support network participants are not always rational or intentional, with the actual effects sometimes differing from the intended effects. Parties may differ on perception and evaluation of benefits and helpfulness, with the differences in evaluations reducing cohesion (Shumaker & Brownell, 1984, p. 21). Social supports can have harmful effects, even when the intents are beneficial. The short- and long-term coping effects can differ, with beneficial effects in the short term and negative effects in the long term especially if the social supports lead to long-term dependency, future obligations, and reciprocal claims for future resources. The Ku Klux Klan and other ethnic supremacist groups, regardless of the ethnicity espoused as superior, can provide esteem and tangible support but the group does not assist a member in socially developing or contributing to the community's well-being. Antisocial youth gangs may be a social support to their members by providing affinitive support, protection, and often material rewards for participating in the gang activities. However, the reciprocity requirements, current and future reciprocity obligations, and situational compliance requirements to engage in violent, antisocial and self-harming behavior are demands that will inhibit the youth's positive current and future social functioning. The interceptive tasks require developing alternative sources of social supports for the youth.

Heller's (1990) review of social support network research concluded that while social networks are generally conducive to strengthening members' coping capacity to deal with personal, interpersonal, and environmental stressors, the social networks themselves can be a source of stress because of the reciprocal demands. Shinn, Lehman, and Wong's (1984) exploration of social support networks discovered that the reciprocity demands (the current and future demands for resources by the provider of current resources) on the recipient can be pernicious. If the recipient fails to reciprocate because the obligations exceed the recipient's resources and capacity, this failure creates stresses on both the provider and recipient. The provider may come to view the recipient as a free rider. The recipient has the stresses of unmet obligation and a sense of dependency and loss of autonomy, especially if the recipient is constantly a recipient and never a helper. The situational and compliant requirements to receive continuing unilateral supports are harmful to the recipient's sense of self-efficacy.

Similar to interagency networks, personal social support networks including those used by clients demand maintenance and can consume resources of time, energy, and even finances. A too-tightly integrated, dense, and cohesive network can be socially isolating and limiting. Barth and Schinke's (1984) examination of social supports for teenage mothers found that tight family networks can cut the mother off from other potential social supports. Nonetheless, network participation usually is associated with enhanced social, interpersonal, and parenting skills.

Primary, Secondary, and Tertiary Social Support Networks

Social support networks, like most organizations, can be primary, secondary, or tertiary. These concepts refer to the nature of the relationships between units in the network. *Primary* networks or networks with primary relationships have members with broad interests in each other's lives. Most typical primary networks are composed of family and close friends. *Secondary* networks have a more narrow interest in their members than do primary networks but have broader interests than do tertiary networks. Secondary networks and relationships are typically neighborhood organizations, social clubs, or membership benefit organizations such as labor unions, churches, and support groups. Members of these organizations can have primary relationships. *Tertiary* network relationships are generally more formal, with a specific and limited interest in their members' lives.

All social support networks might reasonably be conceptualized as falling somewhere along the primary, secondary, or tertiary continuum. The primary social supports are those ascribed to or into which the individual is born, such as the family, kinship, and primary groups associated with family. Secondary support groups are those with broad interest in and meaning to the individual such as informal friendship groups and more formal groupings, still with broad interest in the individual, such as church and religious groups, fraternal groups, unions and other similar associations.

Tertiary groups have more focused and circumscribed interest in the individual than the other two types. Tertiary supports include the range of therapy and formally constructed support groups as well as special interest associations such as the Sierra Club. The common feature of all of these groups is their more limited interest in the individual. As Putnam (1995) says, their ties are to common ideas or issues shared by the membership but not a commitment to the people that comprise the membership. Although more secondary relationships may grow out of the tertiary associations, as in some members' becoming close friends, the individual member does not turn to the formal association or expect it to provide a wide range of social supports. The tertiary support groups provide a forum for individuals to focus on themselves, generally only certain parts of their biography or life space such as alcoholism or sexual abuse, in the presence of others but does not concentrate on the others. Bonding between members as individuals is not required. Any group of like others is sufficient. The bonding is to the group as an whole and to the idea. It is often relatively unimportant who the others are in the audience; the audience can be transient, as long as there is an audience. This is similar to the checkbook and membership-only organizations and their memberships. The bonding is not between the members as people but between the members to the collective and the idea. They tend to be tertiary, vertical to the community, but often can serve as countervailing forces to other vertical structures. The criticism of tertiary groups is not so much on what they do, but what they don't do and their lessening that individuals will turn to more encompassing primary and secondary associations (Bellah, Madsen, Sullivan, Swidler, & Tipton, 1985, 1991; Putnam, 1995). In their packaging and limiting of relationships, tertiary groups may drive out the time, energy, and effort required for the bonding and reciprocity of more primary and secondary associations and hence reduce social supports and a general sense of community not falling within their purview.

Research findings repeatedly show that people who have primary social supports—spouses, family members and friends—who provide psychological and material support have better physical and mental health than do people who have fewer social supports (Lincoln, 2000). Most people receive most of their help through primary social relationships (Streeter & Franklin, 1992; Whittaker et al., 1983). This appears to be especially true for lower income and working-class people. A British study—reported on by Phillips et al. (2000)—of working-class Bangladeshi and white elderly demonstrated a feeling of being relatively marginal to the welfare state and its resources. Middle-income elderly had more connections to and success in obtaining and using the formal services for the elderly offered by the welfare state. Generally, most care to the working class and elderly was given by primary (family, kin) and secondary (neighbors, neighborhood groups and organizations) rather than by tertiary or formal agencies. Primary social networks also can have *negative* consequences and drain resources from the individual and support aberrant behaviors.

Practitioners need to know the client's actual and potential primary supports and possible secondary supports. Social workers, in assessing client social support networks, should not assume uniformity across clients. The client's functional social supports will vary across clients by culture, integration into the community and isolation from a primary community, and the richness of the client's task environment. Primary and secondary social support networks should be explored before turning to the often more accessible tertiary supports.

The development and strengthening of primary networks is akin to primary prevention. Primary prevention is intervention given to a population not yet at risk with the intent of reducing potential harmful circumstances. When primary supports are strengthened, this leads to weakening of tertiary relations and a dependency on tertiary prevention. We also argue that a strengthening and overreliance on the tertiary leads to a weakening of the primary. The tertiary is better suited for instrumental resources in networks. Networks resource rich with both expressive and instrumental resources are more optimal for social supports.

Agencies and Primary and Secondary Social Support Networks

The experience of Auslander and Auslander (1988) and Manzall (1986) has led them to conclude that self-help groups and volunteer networks are beneficial to agencies as well as to clients. Self-help groups and volunteers can add efficiency if they enable agencies to serve a greater number of clients, increase visibility in the client community, and link agencies with community groupings and networks. Volunteers legitimize an agency and can be effective in media relations. It is unlikely that a single social support network, especially a tertiary network, will provide all the needed supports. Volunteers and natural social support networks can link agency, clients, resources, and reduce the isolation of clients (as well as the agency) from the community and help integrate both into a social support system. Clients need to be linked with appropriate volunteers and social supports, and social agencies need to be a part of the community with active support constituencies. Social workers also need to assess a social network for positive and negative implications. Social work practice requires skills in assessing and establishing or reestablishing primary and secondary social support networks, as most help will come from these types of networks.

Social Work Practice in Networks

Social work practice can be characterized as network practice (Payne, 2000; Travillion, 1999; Whittaker et al., 1983). We have argued that development and use of primary and secondary social support networks is preferable and more conducive to client empowerment than an overreliance on tertiary social supports and social agencies. Stated plainly, we believe that social workers should work first with clients to establish or reestablish primary support systems and work with clients and communities to create and use community-based secondary social support systems. Clients should develop and use their strengths and the strengths of their families and communities for empowerment. While we don't deny the obligations of the larger community, the state and the nation to provide social supports, but the tenuous nature of their tertiary social supports in this era of welfare state devolution compels empowerment to be client and community centered.

Protocols and techniques for developing and managing client social support networks will be discussed more fully in Chapter 13's exploration of community-based practice. Developing and helping clients manage social support networks require client and community assessment skills. Community assessment techniques, discussed in greater detail in Chapter 7, include key informants, community forums, social indicators and demographics for cultural indicators, and field surveys. The techniques tend to be more effective when used in combination (Davenport & Davenport, 1982; Humm-Delgado & Delgado, 1986). We will focus here on assessing the community for client social networking.

Social mapping techniques are commonly used to assess social support networks. Social maps are also called *ecomaps* when used with individual clients. They collect and organize information into a social map of a client's community indicating potential and actual social supports, social structures, and linkages. The map provides the actual and potential ecological relationships between the client and other primary, secondary, and tertiary groups and organizations. These groups may either positively or negatively affect the client. The client's current or actual social network can be analyzed and compared to the networks needed to attain the case objectives. Social mapping starts with the case assessment (Bisman, 1994; Lukus, 1993). The assessment's intent is to understand the case's reality and meaning to the case. The first steps in community assessment involve determining with the case the critical factors in the case's community, ecology, and task environment. What is it we need to know in order to achieve the case's objectives? This requires information on the client's current social networks, a formulation of the needed network, and knowledge of the primary, secondary, tertiary groups and organizations in the community and the linkage and reciprocity requirement. The groups and organizations are analyzed and categorized by functions. Assumptions underlying ecomapping are set forth in Box 11.3.

Social work practitioners require skills in assessing and establishing or reestablishing primary and secondary social support networks, as most help will come from these types of networks. Practitioners need to know the client's primary supports, the secondary supports within a neighborhood area, and the formal services in a particular catchment area (Phillips et al., 2000, p. 851). Community assessment is critical in direct service practice. Community assessment skills are required, as different communities have different patterns. Box 11.4 specifies the basic questions to be answered with community assessment.

Community assessment in direct service practice requires an ethnographic approach. Ethnography and an ethnographic approach are "associated with some distinctive methodological ideas, such as the importance of understanding the perspectives of the people under study, and of observing their activities in everyday life, rather than relying solely on their accounts of this behavior or experimental simulations of it" (Hammersley & Atkinson, 1983, p. ix), Ethnography and other case study approaches (Yin, 1984) are concerned with understanding the case from the case's viewpoint. Meaning or a client's cognitive appraisal is critical to the understanding of a client. *Cognitive appraisal* is the meaning

BOX 11.3   ECOMAPPING ASSUMPTIONS

- Clients are not social isolates, but rather social networks that support, weaken, substitute for, or supplement the helping efforts of professionals surround them. These networks compose the client's ecosystem and can be assessed, mapped, and managed.
- A comprehensive ecosystem assessment and mapping requires that data be collected on all components of the ecosystem—family, home, community—that influence behavior. Information includes the number of components or units and their dimensions.
- Data should be collected from a range of sources including the client, significant others,

the worker's direct observations and interactions with the ecology, and available data and history.
- Assessment should gather data on all critical variables that describe the person in situation and person in environment.
- The data should be integrated into a comprehensive and coherent case theory that explains the person in situation.
- The ecosystem assessment and resultant case theory direct the repertoire of intervention strategies. Practitioners must have at their disposal interventions that are both person- and environment-changing.

---

of a person-environment (P-E) relationship and a person's emotional response to it (Folkman et al., 1991).

A variety of social support assessment measurement tools are available to assist in the assessment. Streeter and Franklin (1992) provide descriptions of a number of the social support network assessment and measurement instruments (pp. 86–95.) Actually, these tools are data-organizing tools, as either the social worker or the client does the measurement. Caution is advised when using these tools, as they were most often developed for research rather than practice. They need to be reliable, valid, and practical and usable in the practice situation. While validity generally means that an instrument measures what it is designed to measure, for practice the question is how well the instrument measures what is wanted to be measured in practice (Bisman & Hardcastle, 1998, pp. 96–

102). Triangulation or the use of multiple measurement approaches is encouraged to enhance validity.

Social Support Network Assessment

Ecomapping and ecomatrices can be done for any social unit or case. Ecomapping and ecomatrices consider three sets of relationships involved in a change effort: (a) the supportive social relationships, (b) the additional social supports required, and (c) the social relationships that hinder change.

The mapping and matrices organize information gathered from the assessment on the following questions:

1. What are the compositions of the case's networks? How do the units relate to the case?

BOX 11.4   COMMUNITY ASSESSMENT AND DIRECT PRACTICE

1. What are the case's community, ecology and the task environment's boundaries? Can the boundaries be expanded to include more opportunities?
2. What factors in the case's social environment influences the case's behavior and opportunities? What are the case's behavior and interaction patterns with the community? What are the community's communication and interaction patterns?

3. What are the factors in the social environment that will influence objective achievement and constrain it?
4. What resources are available to the case from primary, secondary, and tertiary sources? Are they adequate for objective achievement, or must the ecology be expanded? How can the case obtain the resources?

What new units can potentially be networked?

2. What are the existing networks' strengths, capacities, and limitations? How might the network be altered to reduce limitations?

3. What are the current network exchanges? Are the exchanges balanced? What new resources are needed that require exchanges? Can the exchanges be made? If not, can the case or network obtain the resources needed for exchanges? What are the obstacles to obtaining the resources and how can they be removed or reduced?

Ecomapping starts with a client or case's perspective. Streeter and Franklin (1992, p. 82) offer three dimensions to capture this perspective: social embeddedness, perceived support, and enacted social supports. *Social embeddedness* is the actual connections people have to significant others in their environment and the direct and indirect linkages that tie people with family, friends, and peers. It is a sense of belonging as opposed to isolation and alienation. *Perceived support* is a person's cognitive appraisal of the connections with others. In order to use social supports, a person must perceive social supporters as supporters. *Enacted social supports* are the specific behaviors of the supporters as they support a person by listening, expressing concern, lending money, or provide other supports. It is what the supporters actually do for the recipient. Box 11.5 provides an ecomapping protocol.

BOX 11.5   ECOMAPPING

Eco-Mapping and Matrices: Requires determining the (a) Existing primary social supports, (b) potential primary social supports potentially available but not currently used by the client, (c) barriers to use, and (d) theory as to how barriers can be overcame. The process should be completed for primary, secondary, and tertiary social supports and for for networks that are harmful or not supportive of the client. Steps (c) and (d) for harmful relationships concern how to create barriers to interaction and a theory as to how client can disengage from these networks.

1. Data Sources for mapping; remember to triangulate:
   a. client
   b. significant others and key informants knowledgeable about the client, community, or both.
   c. available data such as family records,
   d. worker observations including wind shield and shoe leather surveys,
   e. community assessment tools as directories, agency directories, and community surveys.

2. Ecosystem units to assess client's existing networks and community:
   a. Primary units such as family and friends
   b. Secondary units such as neighbors, neighborhood and other organizations and groups, churches, labor unions, and other membership benefit organizations.
   c. Tertiary or formal organizations such as schools, employers, voluntary and public agencies, and relevant proprietary organizations.

Dimensions of Mapping Social Support Networks: Assess the Following

1. Network size—The number of units in the client's social support networks.

2. Network unit lists and description of units—The name of each network unit and describe whether the network relationship is primary, secondary, or tertiary; unit type such as an individual, a group, a formal or informal organization and its auspices, and other salient characteristics of the network unit.

3. Multidimensionality of network units—The number of resources provided, number of exchanges, and number of roles fulfilled by each network unit with, to, or for the client. Primary social supports are more likely to be multidimensional.

4. Network segments—The sub-network patterns within a network where interaction is more in the segments than across the segments.

5. Density—The network ties between all network members. Density is ratio of the ac-

BOX 11.5   (CONTINUED)

tual number of network ties to the possible number of network ties. Note that size can reduce density, which is one of the reasons for segmenting.

6. Network map—Graphically lays out the relationships and connectedness or density of all network unit.

7. Perceived availability of resources from each unit—Assess by:

1. Type of resource.

   a. Material and concrete resources.

   b. Behavioral assistance.

   c. Intimate interaction, feedback and emotional support.

   d. Guidance, informational and advice giving.

   Assess whether the resource is available always, almost always, rarely, and never.

2. Criticalness of the resource—Whether the resource is very critical, somewhat critical, or only marginally needed.

7. Closeness—The proximity and availability of the network unit to the client.

8. Reciprocity—The expectation of resource reciprocity and what is expected by the network unit in exchange for its resource and when is it expected.

9. Directionality—The primary direction of the support is from client to network unit, to client from network unit, or symmetrical and bi-lateral between the client and network unit.

10. Stability—The length of time that the network relationship has existed between the client and the network unit.

11. Frequency—How often the exchanges and contacts between the client and the network unit occur.

Ecomatrix (Resources)

Network Unit Name	Type* and Social Area**	Concrete Support:	Emotional Supports:	Information/Advice:
		Always, almost always, rarely, Never	Always, almost always, rarely, never	Always, almost always, rarely, never
1. First unit				
2. Last unit				
Unit Name	Type* and Social Area**	Guidance	Resource Criticalness	Closeness
		Always, almost always, rarely, never	Very, Somewhat, marginal	Proximity of the unit of the client or case
			Proportion of resource the *very* Category unit provides.	
1. First unit				
2. Last unit				
Unit Name:	Type* and Social Area**	Reciprocity Requirements:		Directionality:
				What is the primary direction of the support between the units and the case?
		Resources reciprocity expectations		

BOX 11.5	(CONTINUED)

		High, Moderate, Low	From case to unit, to case from unit, bilateral
		Immediate, extended	
1. First unit			
2. Last unit			
Unit Name	Type* and Social Area**	Stability of Relationship:	Frequency:
			Record frequency of contacts and exchanges between the case and unit.
		Record time length.	
1. First unit			
2. Last unit			

* Indicates whether primary, secondary, or tertiary ** Description of unit type such as individual, group, organization, whether formal or informal, auspices, and other salient characteristics of functional areas.

Discussion Questions

1. Develop the network of six people between you and the president of the United States. Now do it for a client.

2. Take a client from your caseload and list what the client has to offer in exchange in a social support network.

3. What is your primary social support network? Compare the units in your social support network to those in a client's network. Use the Ecomatrix.

Note

1. Social workers have a similar need for countervailing power organizations, because they deal with the same organizations.

References

Aldrich, H. E. (1971). Organizational boundaries and interorganizational conflict. *Human Relations, 24*, 279–281.

Almond, G. A., & Verba, S. (1963). *The civic culture: Political attitudes and democracy in five nations.* Princeton, NJ: Princeton University Press.

Alter, C. F. (n.d.). *Casebook in social service administration* (2nd ed.). Iowa City: University of Iowa School of Social Work.

Anderson, D. B., & Shaw, S. L. (1994). Starting a support group for families and partners of people with HIV/AIDS in a rural setting. *Social Work, 39*, 135–138.

Anderson, R. E., & Carter, I. (1984). *Human behavior in the social environment: A social systems approach* (3rd ed.). New York: Aldine.

Auslander, A., & Auslander, G. K. (1988). Self-help groups and the family service agency. *Social Casework, 69*, 74–80.

Balgopal, P. R. (1988). Social work and Asian Indian families. In C. Jacobs & D. D. Bowles

(Eds.), *Ethnicity and race: Critical concepts in social work* (pp. 18–33). Silver Spring, MD: National Association of Social Workers.

Barlett, D., & Steele, J. B. (1992). *America: What went wrong?* Kansas City, MO: Andrews & McMeel.

Barth, R. P., & Schinke, S. P. (1984). Enhancing the social supports of teenage mothers. *Social Casework, 65*, 523–531.

Bass, D. J., & Burkhardt, M. E. (1992).Centrality and power in organizations. In N. Nohria & R. G. Eccles (Eds.). *Networks and organizations: Structure, form, and action* (pp. 191–215), Boston: Harvard Business School Press.

Beeman, S. (1997). Reconceptualizing social support and its relationship to child neglect. *Social Service Review, 71*(3), pp. 421–440.

Bellah, R. N., Madsen, R., Sullivan, W. M., Swidler, A., & Tipton, S. M. (1985). *Habits of the heart: Individualism and commitment in American life.* New York: Harper & Row.

Bellah, R. N., Madsen, R., Sullivan, W. M., Swidler, A., & Tipton, S. M. (1991). *The good society.* New York: Harper & Row.

Bisman, C. D. (1994). *Social work practice: Cases and principles.* Pacific Grove, CA: Brooks/Cole.

Bisman, C. D., & Hardcastle, D. A. (1999). *Integrating research into practice: A model for effective social work.* Brooks/Cole–Wadsworth.

Blau, J. P., & Alba, R. D. (1982). Empowering nets of participation. *Administrative Science Quarterly, 27*, 363–379.

Blau, P. M. (1964). *Exchange and power in social life.* New York: Wiley.

Bragg, M. (1996). *Reinventing influence: How to get things done in a world without authority.* Washington, DC: Pitman.

Burt, R. S. (1992). The social structure of competition, In N. Nohria & R. G. Eccles (Eds.), *Networks and organizations: Structure, form, and action* (pp. 57–91), Boston: Harvard Business School Press.

Castelloe, P., & Prokopy, J. (2001). Recruiting participants for community practice interventions: Merging community practice theory and social movement theory. *Journal of Community Practice,* 9(2), 31–48.

Churchman, C. W. (1965). *The general systems approach.* New York: Dell.

Chetkow-Yanoov, B. (1997). *Social work approaches to conflict resolution: Making fighting absolute.* New York: Haworth.

Cochran, M. (1990). Personal social networks as a focus of support. *Prevention in Human Services, 9*, 45–67.

Coser, L. A. (1964). *The functions of social conflict.* New York: Free Press.

Dalton, J. H., Elias, M. J., & Wandersman, A. (2001). *Community psychology: Linking individuals and communities.* Belmont, CA: Wadsworth.

Davenport, J., & Davenport, J., III. (1982). Utilizing the social networks in rural communities. *Social Casework, 63*, 106–113.

Dekker, P., Koopmans, R., & van den Broek, A. (1997). Voluntary associations, social movements and individual political behavior in Western Europe. In J. W. van Deth (Ed.). *Private groups and public life: Social participation, voluntary associations, and political involvement in representative democracies* (pp. 220–239). London: Routledge

Deutsch, M. (1973). *The resolution of conflict: Constructive and destructive processes.* New Haven, CT: Yale University Press.

Dufort, F., Dallaire, L., & Lavoie, F. (1997). Factors contributing to the perceived quality of life of people with mental disorders. *Social Work and Social Science Review, 7*(2), pp. 89–100.

Fisher, R., Ury, W., & Patton, B. (1981). *Getting to Yes: Negotiating agreements without giving in.* Boston, MA: Houghton Mifflin.

Folkman, S., Chesney, M., McKusick, L., Cronson, G., Johnson, D. S., & Coates, T. J. (1991). Translating coping theory into an intervention. In J. Eckenrode (Ed.). *The social context of coping* (pp. 239–260). New York: Plenum.

Galaskiewicz, J., & Wasserman, S. (1993). Social network analysis: Concepts, methodology and directions for the 1990s. *Sociological Methods and Research, 22*, 3–22.

Gestan, E. I., & Jason, L. A. (1987). Social and community interventions. *Annual Review of Psychology, 38*, 127–160.

Hage, J. (1980). *Theories of organizations.* New York: Urly-Interscience.

Hammersley, M., & Atkinson, P. (1983). *Ethnography: Principles in practice.* New York: Tavistock.

Hardina, D. (2000). Models and tactics taught in community organization courses: Findings from a survey of practice instructors. *Journal of Community practice, 7*(1), pp. 5–18

Healy, J. (1991). Linking local services: Coordination in community centres. *Australian Social Work, 14*, 5–13.

Hearn, G. (Ed.). (1969). *The general systems approach: Contributions toward an holistic conception of social work.* New York: Council on Social Work Education.

Heller, K. (1990). Social and community intervention. *Annual Review of Psychology, 41*, 141–168.

Humm-Delgado, D., & Delgado, M. (1986). Gaining community entree to assess service needs of Hispanics. *Social Casework, 67*, 80–89.

Kelly, P., & Kelly, V. R. (1985). Supporting natural helpers: A cross-cultural study. *Social Casework, 66*, 358–386.

Kirst-Ashman, K. K. & Hull, G. H., Jr. (1997). *Generalist practice with organizations and communities.* Chicago: Nelson-Hall.

Knoke, D. (1993). Networks of elite structures and decision making. *Sociological Methods and Research, 22,* 23–45.

Kriesberg, L. (1982). *Social conflict* (2nd ed.). Englewood Cliffs, NJ: Prentice Hall.

Lauer, R. H. (1982). *Perspectives on social change* (3rd ed.). Boston: Allyn & Bacon.

Lauffer, A. (1982). *Assessment tools for practitioners, managers, and trainees.* Newbury Park, CA: Sage.

Lee, J. A. B. (1988). Group work with the poor and oppressed. *Social Work with Groups, 11,* 5–9.

Lee, J. A. B. (1994). *The empowerment approach to social work practice.* New York: Columbia University Press.

Letiecq, B. L., Anderson, E. A., & Koblinsky, S. A. (1998). Social support of homeless and housed mothers: A comparison of temporary and permanent housing arrangements. *Family Relations, 47*(4), pp. 415–421.

Leighninger, R. B., Jr. (1978). Systems theory. *Journal of Social Work and Social Welfare, 5,* 446–466.

Levine, M. (1988). An analysis of mutual assistance. *American Journal of Community Psychology, 16,* 167–188.

Lewis, E. A., & Ford, B. (1990). The network utilization project: Incorporating traditional strengths of African American families into group work practice. *Social Work With Groups, 13* 7–22.

Lin, N., & Westcott, J. (1991). Marital engagement/disengagement, social networks and mental health. In J. Eckenrode (Ed.), *The social context of coping* (pp. 213–237). New York: Plenum.

Lin, N., Ye, X., & Ensel, W. M. (1999). Social support and depressed mood: A structural analysis. *Journal of Health and Social Behavior, 40*(4), 344–359.

Lincoln, K. D. (2000). Social support, negative social interactions, and psychological well-being. *Social Service Review, 74*(2), 230–2542.

Lukus, S. (1993), *When to start and what to ask: An assessment handbook.* New York: W. W. Norton.

MacKay, H. (1997). Dig your well before you're thirsty. New York: Currency Book

Maloney, W. A., & Jordan, G. (1997). The rise of the protest business in Britain. In J. W. van Deth (Ed.), *Private groups and public life: Social participation, voluntary associations, and political involvement in representative democracies* (pp. 107–124). London: Routledge.

Manzall, M. (1986). Utilizing volunteers to enhance informal social networks. *Social Casework, 67,* 290–298.

Martin, Y. M., & O'Connor, G. G. (1989). *The social environment: Open systems application.* New York: Longman.

Maton, K. I. (1988). Social support, organizational characteristics, psychological well-being and group appraisal in three self-help group populations. *American Journal of Community Psychology, 16,* 53–77.

McCarthy, J., & Nelson, G. (1991). An evaluation of supportive housing for current and former psychiatric patients. *Hospital and Community Psychiatry, 42,* 1254–1256.

McIntyre, E. L. G. (1986). Social networks: Potential for practice. *Social Work, 31,* 421–426.

Menefee, D. (1994). *Entrepreneurial leadership in the human services: Trends, implications, and strategies for executive success in turbulent times.* Unpublished manuscript. University of Maryland at Baltimore, School of Social Work.

Milgram, S. (1967). The small world problem, *Psychology Today, 1,* 60–67.

Mizruchi, M., & Galaskiewicz, J. (1993). Networks of interorganizational relations. *Sociological Methods and Research, 22,* 46–70.

Moynihan, D. P. (1969). *Maximum feasible misunderstanding: Community action in the war on poverty.* New York: Free Press.

Moyser, G. & Parry, G. (1997). Voluntary associations and democratic participation in Britain. In J. W. van Deth (Ed.), *Private groups and public life: Social participation, voluntary associations, and political involvement in representative democracies* (pp. 24–46). London: Routledge.

Murray, C. (1984). *Losing ground: American social policy 1950–1980.* New York: Basic Books.

Nohria, N., & Eccles, R. (1992). Face to face: Making network organizations work. In N. Nohria & R. G. Eccles (Eds.). *Networks and organizations: Structure, form, and action* (pp. 288–308). Boston: Harvard Business School Press.

O'Connell, B. (1978). From services to advocacy to empowerment. *Social Casework, 59,* 195–202.

Parry, G., & Moyser, G. (1992). More participation—more democracy. In D. Beetham (Ed.). *Defining and measuring democracy* (Sage Modern Political Series, No. 36, pp. 44–62). London: Sage.

Patterson, S., Germain, C. B., Brennan, E. M., & Memmott, J. (1988). Effectiveness of rural natural helpers. *Social Casework, 69,* 272–279.

Payne, M. (2000). *Teamwork in multiprofessional care.* Chicago: Lyceum.

Phillips, J., Bernard, M., Phillipson, C., & Ogg, J. (2000, December). Social support in later life: A study of three areas. *British Journal of Social Work, 30*(6), 837–859.

Pivan, F. F., & Cloward, R. A. (1971). *Regulating the poor: The functions of social welfare.* New York: Pantheon Books.

Putnam, R. D. (1995). Bowling alone. *The Re-*

sponsive Community: Rights and Responsibilities, 5(2), 18–33.

Putnam, R. D. (2000). *Bowling alone: The collapse and revival of American community.* New York: Simon & Schuster.

Rosenfeld, L. B., Richman, J. M., & Bowen, G. L. (2000). Social support networks and school outcomes: The centrality of the teacher. *Child and Adolescent Social Work Journal, 17*(3), 205–226.

Rubin, H. J., & Rubin, I. S. (2001). *Community organizing and development* (3rd ed.). Boston: Allyn & Bacon.

Rubin, J. Z., & Brown, B. R. (1975). *The social psychology of bargaining and negotiation.* New York: Academic Press.

Schopler, J. H. (1994). Interorganizational groups in human services: Environmental and interpersonal relationships. *Journal of Community Practice, 1*(1), 7–27.

Schore, L., & Atkin, J. (1993). Stress in the workplace: A response from union member assistance programs. In P. A. Kurzman & S. Akabas (Eds.), *Work and well-being: The occupational social work advantage* (pp. 316–331). Washington, DC: National Association of Social Workers.

Schwartz, B. (1986). Decide to network: A path to personal and professional empowerment. *American Mental Health Counselors Association Journal, 8*, 12–17.

Shinn, M., Lehmann, S., & Wong, N. W. (1984). Social interaction and social support. In A. Brownell & S. A. Shumaker (Eds.), *Social support: New perspectives in theory, research, and intervention* (pp. 55–76). New York: Plenum.

Shumaker, S. A., & Brownell, A. (1984). Toward a theory of social support: Closing a conceptual gap. In A. Brownell & S. A. Shoemaker (Eds.), *Social support: New perspectives in theory, research, and intervention* (pp. 11–36). New York: Plenum.

Specht, H. (1986). Social support, networks, social exchange and social work practice. *Social Service Review, 60* (2), 218–240.

Streeter, L. L., & Franklin, C. (1992). Defining and measuring social supports: Guidelines for social work practitioners. *Research on social work practice, 2*(1), 81–98.

Strom-Gottfried, K. (1998). Applying a conflict resolution framework to disputes in managed care. *Social Work, 43*(5), 393–401.

Tannen, D. (1998/1999). The rules of engagement and the argument culture. *The Responsive Community, 9*(1), 48–51.

Travillion, S. (1999). *Networking and community partnership* (2nd ed.). Aldershot, Hants, UK: Ashgate Arena.

van Deth, J. W. (1997). Introduction: Social involvement and democratic politics. In J. W. van Deth (Ed.), *Private groups and public life: Social participation, voluntary associations, and political involvement in representative democracies* (pp. 1–23), London: Routledge.

Van de Ven, A., Delbecq, A. L., & Koenig, R. (1976). Determinants of coordination modes with organizations. *American Sociological Review, 41*, 322–338.

Volling, B. L., Notaro, P. C., & Larsen, J. J. (1998). Adult attachment styles: Relations with emotional well-being, marriage, and parenting. *Family Relations, 47*(4), 355–367.

Walker, M. E., Wasserman, S., & Wellman, B. (1993). Statistical models for social support networks. *Sociological Methods and Research, 22*, 71–98.

Weick, K. (1976). Educational organizations as loosely coupled systems. *Administrative Science Quarterly, 21*, 1–19.

Wernet, S. P. (1994). A case study of adaptation in a nonprofit human service organization. *Journal of Community Practice, 1*, 93–112.

Wessels, B. (1997). Organizing capacity of societies and modernity. In J. W. van Deth (Ed.). *Private groups and public life: Social participation, voluntary associations, and political involvement in representative democracies* (pp. 198–219). London: Routledge.

Whittaker, J. K. (1986). Formal and informal helping in child welfare services: Implications for management and practice. *Child Welfare, 65,* 17–25.

Whittaker, J. K., Garbarino, J., & Associates (Eds.). (1983). *Social support networks: Informal helping in the human services.* New York: Aldine.

Weller, D. Ed. (1999). *Network Exchange Theory.* Westport, CN: Praegor

Willer, D., Lovaglia, M. J., & Markovsky, B. (1999). Power and influence: A theoretical bridge. In D. Willer (Ed.), *Network exchange theory* (pp. 229–247). Westport, CT: Praeger.

Woodard, K. L., & Doreion, P. (1994). Utilizing and understanding community service provision networks: A report of three case studies having 583 participants. *Journal of Social Service Research, 18*, 15–16.

Yin, R. K. (1984). *Case study research: Design and method.* Beverly Hills, CA: Sage.

Zimmerman, M. A., & Rappaport, J. (1988). Citizen participation, perceived control, and psychological empowerment. *American Journal of Community Psychology, 16*, 725–250.

12

Using Social Marketing

- A full-page ad appeared in the *New York Times* (August 21, 2000, p. A11) displaying a young African American male's picture with a bold heading proclaiming, "Jared Has the Grades and the Determination. Now He Has the Tuition Too." Another full-page advertisement asked, "Why Do So Many People Celebrate the Birthday of a First-Century Rabbi?" (*The New York Times*, December 9, 1997) and proceeded to answer the question with Biblical references. A third featured a photograph of a woman literally being squeezed by a giant hand and a bold heading "Please Don't Squeeze the Actors!" (*The New York Times*, September 12, 2000, p. A25B).

- A family services center, after a drop-off in clients, decides to keep its office open in the evenings to better serve potential clients who work during the day.

- A private social work practitioner does pro bono work in an abuse shelter with physicians and other community professionals. In casual discussions with them, the social worker describes the scope and focus of her practice.

- A social agency establishes an advisory group of clients to advise the agency on ways to improve service delivery.

- A mental health agency manager regularly appears on radio talk shows as an expert on school violence and mental health approaches to school violence prevention.

The full-page advertisements were not promoting specific tangible products or immediate services. The advertisements were promoting social ideas to influence people's perceptions, values, and attitudes. Their intent was to alter people's social constructions and behaviors to become favorable to the ad's sponsors. These were examples of social marketing. The first advertisement explained how Jared's educational opportunities were enhanced by the Philip Morris Companies' contributions to the Thurgood Marshall Fund. (In fact, Philip Morris has been the largest contributor to the African American educational fund for the past 13 years.) The ad is not promoting cigarettes or macaroni and cheese. The promotion is for the idea that the Philip Morris Companies are good community citizens (Drayfuss, 2000). It is encouraging an image as a precursor to promoting tangible products.

The second broadside also promoted an ideology more than a tangible product. It offered a free book asserting that as Jesus was a Jew and Jews can accept Jesus as the Messiah and still remain observant Jews. It wanted the ad's Jewish readers to eventually alter basic religious beliefs. Sponsorship was attributed to the ambiguously named *Friends of the Chosen People Ministries*.

The third advertisement, borrowing an image from a once-popular ad campaign for toilet tissue, contained the names of a long list in the words of the ad, of "well-known to the unknown"(The New York Times, September 12, 2000, p. 25B) actors and performers as champions for its message. Its sponsors were labor unions (the Screen Actors Guild and The American Federation of television and Radio Artists) for a rather unique group of laborers: television, radio, and film actors and performers. The ad ran during a strike by these unions against the American Association of Advertisers, who wanted to reduce the compensation for actors in television commercials. The ad's intent was to change the public's image of television commercial actors as highly paid superstars. It claimed that over 80% of the memberships of the two unions, the unknown actors, earned less than $5,000 annually as actors.

Agencies and social workers are engaged in marketing as they make themselves more usable to their clients and communities. They are adapting their service provision to reach new users, making their services known, doing market research, and staging social problems in ways that they can address.

This chapter presents an overview of and introduction to strategic marketing of social services, social marketing and staging of social issues, and applications of essential concepts, theories, and methodologies of marketing to the social and human services. The chapter also analyzes some of the characteristics of nonprofit agencies, whether voluntary or public, and the social work profession that present particular challenges to the strategic marketing of social and human services.

MARKETS AND MARKETING

A *market* is a set of people who have an actual or potential interest in the exchange of goods, products, services, and satisfactions with the others in the set and the ability to complete the exchange (Enis, 1974; Fine & Fine, 1986; Kotler & Andreasen, 1987). Markets are composed of people who have some need, desire, or preference and are willing to exchange something in order to have that need, desire, or preference met (see Table 12.1). A *target market* is that part of the public with whom the marketer wants to make an exchange. A target market has tangible or intangible resources sought by the marketer as necessary or useful to achieving the marketer's objectives.

A *preference* is a need or, more accurately, a desire of the target market or a target market segment (TMS). Target market preferences are not decided by the marketer but by a TMS: buyers, users, clients, exchange partners. *Preferences* and *needs* mean the same thing in this chapter. Needs beyond a survival level are difficult to define and distinguish from preferences. Needs are shaped by culture, and the individual decisions in defining needs are shaped by individual and cultural preferences. In market exchanges, the concern is with social preferences and effective demand to use an economic conception. An *effective demand* occurs when people express a need or preference and are prepared to back that expression with resources and behavior (Bradshaw, 1977). Exchanges represent behavior and effective demand. The people may be called *buyers* and *sellers*, *customers* and *vendors*, *consumers* and *producers*, *service providers* such as social workers and *clients*, or *doctors* and *patients*, or *fund seekers* and *fund providers*. However, in order to form a market, the people must be real, reachable by others, and interested in an exchange.

Marketing, formally defined, is the analysis, planning, implementation, and control of carefully formulated programs designed to bring about the voluntary exchange of values by one part of the market with another part of the market (the target market or markets), for the purpose of achieving the objectives on the part of

TABLE 12.1 A Market

Potential Exchange Partners	Resources Needed	Available Resources for Exchanges
Mental health center	Fiscal resources; mentally impaired clients in need of improved social functioning	Services to improve the social functioning of mentally impaired clients
County government	Improved social functioning for mentally impaired citizens	Fiscal resources; mentally impaired citizens in need of improved social functioning

the market seeking the exchange. It is the active processes of the market (Kotler & Andreasen, 1987, p. 61). Kotler (1971) defines marketing as "the set of human activities directed at facilitating and consummating exchanges" (p. 12). Enis (1974) provides an even more encompassing definition of human behavior in his conception of marketing. "Marketing is a fundamental human activity. . . . *Marketing* encompasses exchange activities conducted by individuals and organizations for the purpose of satisfying human wants" (p. 21).

Social marketing is the subset of marketing most necessary for social welfare. Andreasen (1995, p. 3) defines social marketing as "the application of marketing technologies developed in the commercial sector to the solution of social problems where the bottom line is behavior change." Its intent is to influence the voluntary behavior of target audiences or people in the community to improve their personal welfare and the community's. Success or failure is judged first and foremost by what the TMSs actually do.

Marketing, including social marketing, is more than a set of techniques and technologies to promote exchanges. It is a philosophical perspective to look for what can be done to provide value for others in order to get your needs met. Marketing is the exchange of value: what others value that you may have or can produce for what they have that you value or need. Both sides are better off, in their own estimation, after the exchange.

MARKETING CHALLENGES FOR THE SOCIAL SERVICES AND THE SOCIAL WORK PROFESSION

Markets and marketing as social exchanges and meeting needs are intrinsic to human behavior, to human services, and to social work practice. While historical marketing has not been generally accepted nor practiced by social workers, its knowledge and skills are essential for today's social workers in our currently turbulent, resource competitive, and overly commercialized world. Services to promote human and social well-being are treated as commodities offered by a growing number of competitive nonprofit and proprietary vendors. To successfully engage in marketing, social workers and not-for-profit agencies (including public agencies) must meet several challenges often not faced to the same degree by their proprietary competitors.

Product Orientation

Perhaps the greatest challenge is that many nonprofit agencies and social workers have a product orientation rather than a consumer and market orientation (Andreasen, 1984; Cooper & McIlvain, 1983; Kotler & Andreasen, 1987; Lovelock & Weinberg, 1984). A *product orientation*, according to Kotler and Andreasen (1984), "holds that the major task of an organization is to put out products that it thinks would be good for the public" (p. 38). A product orientation is an inward-looking orientation and a belief by the agency and professional that they know best, that they know what is good for clients, and that their products and services are intrinsically good.

A product orientation propagates a tendency to view markets as having homogeneous preferences, with one or a few products determined by the producer as best satisfying consumers' preferences. The diversity of consumers and their preferences is ignored. To paraphrase a quote attributed to Henry Ford with the introduction of the mass-produced automobile: The public can have any color car it wants as long as it's black.

Organizational Orientation

A product orientation is similar to an organizational and bureaucratic orientation, a condition suffered by many social service agencies. An organizational and bureaucratic orientation is a preoccupation with rules, norms, and policies of the agency and a belief that it is unique. Andreasen (1995, pp. 42–48) calls this orientation an *organization-centered mind-set*. This orientation views the agency's mission as inherently good. This orientation leads to a passion for the agency and its particular products and service rather than a fervor to be of service to clients and community. If the agency, its services and products are not valued by a community or client, this orientation holds, it is because of client and community ignorance, lack of motivation, or insensitivity. Clients are problems rather than resources. Marketing is limited largely to promotion, public relations, advertising, and getting the agency's story out. There is an aversion to discovering what client and user prefer. Clients are seen and treated as a homogeneous mass and not as individuals with different preferences and needs. Often agencies and people with this orientation make a fatal mistake or ignoring the competition. Competition is ignored because the agency or professional sees itself as unique. This view limits competitors to agency clones. Since professionals in the agency see themselves as unique, there can be no clones or competitors. Eventually, competitors replace the myopic holders of this orientation.

Professional Orientation

Professionals, including social work professionals, are socialized to assume a stance of professional expertise. Professions are rightly concerned with professional autonomy and authority. However, when that mind-set produces a rigidity to changing a professional service because the professional knows best and also produces a belief that a particular service, a particular therapy, or a particular theory serves all clients, that professional has the blinders of a professional orientation (Rothman, Teresa, Kay, & Morningstar, 1983, pp. 62–78).

Assumption of Consumer Ignorance

Consumer ignorance assumption is a necessary companion assumption to product, organizational, and overdeveloped professional orientations (Andreasen, 1984, p. 133). This assumption holds that clients do not really know what they need, what is good for them, and the services required to meet their needs. The professional, by virtue of education, training, expertise, and experience, or the agency drawing upon a variety of professions and professional wisdom and experience, is in a better position to determine the client, community, or market's true needs and service requirements. After all, it is on the basis of the profession's and agency's knowledge and skills that the public's sanction has been given to deal with these needs.

Social workers and agencies need to discard this assumption and develop client, community, and market orientations with the preferences of clients and markets determining service designs and delivery if they expect to survive in this turbulent era. Even clients required to receive a service, such as parents accused of child abuse referred to Child Protective Services, have preferences as to time, location, and format of services. The parents might deliver their product or behavior—nonabusive parenting behavior— more readily if their preferences are considered within the constraints of the mandated services.

Marketing Is Selling

For agencies and professionals with a product orientation, and for those who view consumers or clients as ignorant, the rational and logical approach to marketing is production and selling (Andreasen, 1984; Kotler & Andreasen, 1987, p. 39). If the product is good, the public and the clients will be better off with more of it. If the public will be better off with more of the product, the agency should produce more of it. If the agency produces more of it, the marketing task is to convince an ignorant consumer or public to use it. A *selling orientation* occurs when marketing is seen as convincing ignorant consumers that they need the agency's products. There will be an overemphasis on promotion and packaging. Communication will flow one way, from the agency and professional to the client, rather than both ways, between agency or professional and client. Marketing is narrowly viewed as selling, public relations, advertising, and persuading.

Professional Antipathy to Entrepreneurial Approaches

Professions and nonprofit human service agencies often have an antipathy to the idea of competition among professional and social agencies and an aversion to entrepreneurial approaches to meet the demands of competition (Kotler & Andreasen, 1987; Reichert, 1982; Rosenberg & Weissman, 1981; Shapiro, 1977). Their conception of competitors is limited to clones or agencies that fairly exactly replicate them. Marketing is viewed as unprofessional and inhumane. Adherents to this position are repelled by the apparently self-interested nature of market transactions, the ideas of a buyer and a seller, of marketers and markets, in what should be a social welfare or altruistic activity. This may be due, as Kotler (1977) indicates, to a low level of consciousness and ignorance regarding marketing.

Declining Prestige of Social Services Agencies

Secular and public not-for-profit social service agencies suffer in public prestige compared to their proprietary or faith-based competitors. Privatization is a shibboleth. If done by the private sector, it is assumed to be done better and more efficiently than if done by government. And the pinnacle of the private sector is the proprietary auspice rather than not-for-profit agencies. The projections are for more privatization, commodification, and proprietarization of social services. Privatization and proprietarization are basic tenets of faith in the United States.

Another tenet of faith in the United States is the growing political perception that faith-based charities should be a major vehicle for publicly financed social services delivery. This political conviction was made public social policy by the charitable choice provision of the inelegantly and murkily titled *Personal Responsibility and Work Opportunity Reconciliation Act of 1996*, (PL 104–193) more commonly called *welfare reform*. The charitable choice provision encourages states to contract with faith-based organizations to deliver social services and maintain their religious character in the design and delivery of the services, although not in client selection. The White House Office on Faith-Based and Community Initiatives was established by the Bush administration to encourage growth of faith-based agencies through public-sector funding. Contrary to the rhetoric, according to Professor Byron R. Johnson of the University of Pennsylvania's Center for Research on Religion and Urban Society, there is little reliable evidence indicating the effectiveness of the faith-based programs and how they measure up to secular programs (Goodstein, April 24, 2001, p. A12). Our intent here is not to analyze the veracity of the claims for faith-based agencies in comparison with secular agencies, but to point out the political acceptance of their greater efficacy over secular nonprofit and public social services, even though no reliable evidence exists to support the assertion. The decline in the prestige of the secular nonprofit agency in comparison with the prestige of the faith-based or proprietary agency is a marketing challenge for pubic and secular nonprofit agencies.

Government Regulations

Although politicians use marketing to develop and promote their products and ideology, local, state, and federal governments often restrict social agencies to certain marketing activities. The complexities of the 23 different categories under the Internal Revenue Code's Section 501, the section of the tax code that confers tax-exempt status, limit the ability of nonprofits to use certain promotional strategies and engage in some political and entrepreneurial activities available to proprietary, for-profit agencies (Bryce, 1987, pp. 28–48; Cooper & McIlvain, 1983; Kotler & Andreasen, 1987, pp. 7–8, 12–17, 19–20; Lovelock & Weinberg, 1984). Many nonprofits avoid other legitimate marketing activities out of fear that they may lose their tax-exempt status (Kotler & Andreasen, 1987, p. 13). The constraint of government regulations on nonprofits should not be overdrawn as a difference between nonprofits and proprietary agencies. The public sector has intruded into the proprietary sector with environmental, health, safety, employment, and product regulations, even though the regulations and regulators have met with political disfavor.

Social Regulation

Nonprofits face significant social regulations beyond those generally faced by proprietary enterprises and often beyond any formal governmental regulations (Cooper & McIlvain, 1983; Lovelock & Weinberg, 1984). Much of the activity of nonprofits that deals with clients concerns significant and controversial behaviors and with confusion regarding the products of the agencies. Sometimes the products appear counterintuitive. Services oriented toward birth control and safe sex for adolescents, for example, are often assumed by certain segments of the public to promote promiscuity.

Using funds donated for services and charitable purposes is seen by critics as an improper use when such funds are spent on certain marketing activities, such as product advertising and promotion or market research (Kotler & Andreasen, 1987, p. 21). This position assumes a product orientation and believes that marketing is unnecessary if the services and other products are really needed. Like the product orientation, this position assumes that spending money for market research reduces the money that could be spent for services, is a waste, and should not be necessary. If the agency and the professionals are competent, they should know, probably intuitively, what their clients need. If they do not know or if their services are not used, then they are not needed. They should not try to develop new products or services to meet new needs. After all, aren't nonprofit human service agencies and professional social workers trying to work themselves out of a job? Of course, none of these arguments are applied to proprietary enterprises that are entering the human services marketplace. The arguments are losing ground with the expansion of propriety agencies into the human services, as both types of agencies struggle for resources.

Another reason that the public feels more at ease in regulating nonprofits is that nonprofit agencies operate as public trusts. There are no owners who bear the risk, nor are revenues always dependent on satisfying the preferences of consumers. Boards of directors act not for owners or even for users of the agency's services. They are stewards acting for the public and for the public's good (Anthony & Young, 1988, pp. 59–60). Public sector agencies are viewed as belonging to the public. And if nonprofit and public sector agencies are owned by everyone, everyone sees himself or herself as having a say in the operations.

Difficulty in Measuring Success

Proprietary enterprises generally have two clear criteria that are useful in measuring success: profit or return on the investment and share of the market. Nonprofits differ from for-profit agencies in that nonprofits do not have clear measurements, such as profit and market share as benchmarks of success. There is no direct imposed market discipline, that is, survival does not depend on product demand and the ability to satisfy that demand as well as or better than competitors (Bryce, 1987, pp. 92–114; Cooper & McIlvain, 1983; Kotler & Andreasen, 1987, pp. 13–24; Lovelock & Weinberg, 1984).

Profit and market share are both goals and measurements for the profit organizations. Proprietary firms seek to improve life for their customers and markets through their services. The ultimate measurements of how well the profit agency has done this are market share and profits. The users of the products and the exchange partners in an economically competitive market determine if the products improve their quality of life by exchanging their resources (money) with the profit organization, the seller. The more the buyers judge the products of a particular producer superior in meeting their needs and preferences over alternative products available to them in the marketplace, the more the buyers will turn to that producer's products. As demand increases, the producer will attempt to make more of the products for the potential buyers, both to meet the demand and to charge more for the product to balance that demand. The higher prices for the preferred products result in higher profits for the producers. When certain products meet consumer preferences, more consumers want them. If the producer can produce more of these products, the producer will gain a bigger share of the market, raise prices, or both.

This way, market share and profit represent measurements of success in meeting consumers' preferences in a consumer-driven market.

The nonprofit agency is more limited in its ability to use market measures to judge success. First, as discussed earlier in this text, coordination and market restrictions to prevent service duplication are valued more than are competitive markets by public and nonprofit agencies. Without competition and recognition of competition, market share is inconsequential as an indicator of meeting client preferences. An agency's market share demonstrates its success compared with alternative choices available to consumers or clients. Profit is inherently not a benchmark for not-for-profit agency success, nor should fund balancing beyond those prudent for survival be a mark of good performance and sensible management even in our entrepreneurial era of proprietary emulation. However, the social agency is not without a *bottom-line* measurement of performance. The bottom line for most social service agencies is behavioral change by clients or community (Andreasen, 1995), and public use of their services when choices are available.

Multiple Goals

A challenge to nonprofit agencies expressed by some authorities (Lovelock & Weinberg, 1984; Shapiro, 1977) is the nature of their products. Nonprofit agencies generally produce services and intangible products rather than physical commodities. The quality and even the quantity of services and other intangible products are generally harder to measure than the quantity and quality of tangible physical products. With services, the measurements tend to assess the characteristics of the service providers, their education and credentials, or the effects of the services on the users. The actual services dispensed and the interactions between service providers and recipients often are hidden from observation and measurement. Judgments of quality generally rely on the effects of the services on the recipients, the average amount of time spent with the recipients, and the staff-to-recipient ratios. The number of service hours provided, the number of clients, or similar measurements are most often used to quantify service units. Meaningful measurement and fiduciary responsibility require a substantial commitment to the bottom-line criterion of behavioral change.

Public welfare agencies, typical of most nonprofit agencies, generally have multiple and often conflicting goals. Is the public assistance agency successful if the recipient rolls are reduced, if the recurring pregnancy rates of mothers receiving Temporary Assistance to Needy Families (TANF) are down, if the average length of time recipients are on assistance is reduced, if the families raise socially productive children, if the poverty of children is ameliorated, or if public spending for public assistance is reduced? Is the agency successful if it meets some goals but not others? And does meeting some of the goals preclude meeting other goals? Reduce poverty of children may be counterindicative to reducing the public assistance rolls and the average length of time on welfare. Welfare rolls can be reduced by restricting eligibility to five or fewer years for mothers and their children. Public dependency is reduced but not poverty. The public's representatives—the federal and state legislative and executive branches—are clarifying the goal of the public assistance system as reducing welfare rolls by decreasing the length of time a mother and her family are eligible, generally emphasizing work, raising the age required to be an eligible mother, and generally curtailing services (Anderson, 1995; Gillespie & Schellhas, 1994; Gingrich, Armey, & the House Republicans, 1994).

The distinction between nonprofit agencies providing intangible products and proprietary and for-profit agencies producing tangible commodities is becoming more hazy and was never that clear. With increased government contracting for services from the proprietary sector (called *privatization*) for everything from transportation services to education and corrections, and with the growth of the proprietary sector in publicly funded health and mental health, the distinction is archaic. Governments are fulfilling more of their responsibilities through contracts with the private sector. For-profit and proprietary enterprises, medical doctors in private practice, and doctors in practice within health care corporations have long been the major providers of health care services. The proprietaries and the profit sector provide services, often intangible, ranging from mental health services to recreation and entertainment to financial and personal advice and management. Many nonprofit agencies are beginning to sell tangible products to support their nonprofit service activities. Distinctions between the for-profit and nonprofit sectors appear to reside more in ownership, mission, accountability, and views on competition than in any significant differences in the products produced.

Multiple Publics

Nonprofit agencies have multiple publics or TMSs (Andreasen, 1984; Lovelock & Weinberg, 1984). There is generally a separation of clients and service recipients from the sources of revenue for the agency. The nonprofit agency's product-revenue relationship is often indirect. Consumers or users of the services usually are not the agency's major sources of revenue. TANF recipients do not provide the revenue for public assistance or the services offered by the public assistance agency.

Multiple publics for nonprofit agencies go beyond the clients and funding sources to include a range of constituencies and publics in the task environment relevant and critical to the agency, such as professional associations, public and professional regulators, licensing and accrediting bodies, legislatures, employee associations and groupings, collaborating and complementary agencies serving as sources or recipients of client referrals, and volunteers, to name only a few (Holmes & Riecken, 1980).

The reality of multiple publics also is becoming more characteristic of proprietary businesses with the growth of government regulations and regulators, consumer advocate groups, environmental advocates, employee unions and associations, and so forth. However, proprietary businesses do not have as many segments as do nonprofit agencies.

Lack of Market Data

The challenges, especially the product orientation and the assumption of consumer ignorance, have often resulted in nonprofits suffering from a lack of sophisticated data on the market's preferences, wants, and needs and from a lack of the social characteristics required to facilitate product development and exchanges to thrive in today's turbulent task environment. Agencies with product, organization, and professional orientations believe that their products are inherently good, that they are unique, and that they know best—such agencies will assume it is unnecessary to develop information on the preferences of clients. Similarly, the agency will not develop information on resource providers' preferences if the agency's choice of services or products is ideologically driven. An agency with these orientations will view market research as a waste of resources that can better be used to generate more of its products.

> **Client empowerment** and **self-determination** require providing a client with the maximum information on product, prices, and benefits so the client can make an informed decision and give truly **informed consent**.

A MARKET ORIENTATION FOR THE PROFESSION

Social workers and nonprofit agencies need to develop a market and consumer orientation. Market and consumer orientations are compatible with professional functioning and values. Although nonprofits face greater challenges in marketing than do proprietary agencies, marketing and its techniques are compatible with social work, nonprofit agencies, and social services. A market orientation, or Andreasen's marketing mind-set (1995, p. 37), requires that all decisions emanate from a regard for target clients and target systems. Social work and the human services industry should be equipped by training to adopt a marketing orientation and constructively practice marketing to the benefit of their public and themselves. Marketing requires knowledge of the behavioral and social sciences to assess, understand, reach, and engage people. The basic means of achieving improved social welfare is through influencing behavior. The ultimate objectives of the behavior change are benefits to the client systems, the community, or society and not to the marketer. A market orientation has several essential components.

Client or Consumer Orientation

At a market orientation's core is consideration of clients' views of their needs, satisfactions, and preferences and an accounting for these preferences in program design and service delivery. A consumer orientation, or in social work's case a client orientation, lies at the opposite end of a true continuum from product and agency orientations. Product and agency orientations assume that a marketer is the best judge of client needs

and then design and deliver products in ways that the marketer decides will best meet client needs. No effort is made to study clients as a market or to design products and deliver products in ways that meet the market preferences as defined by the market.

A client orientation assumes that clients as a market are experts on their needs and preferences. Consequently, it compels market assessment to gather client information to design and deliver products in ways that meet the preferences of the market as defined by the market. A client orientation goes beyond being *client focused* and *having a concern about clients* to the involvement individually and collectively of clients in the decision processes on service design and delivery. The client is seen as someone with unique perspectives, perceptions, needs, and wants. Assessment and market research is vital. The marketer gathering knowledge about clients individually and collectively through client and community assessment. The bottom line of a client orientation is client behavior change by meeting needs and wants.

Pure product or pure consumer orientations rarely exists empirically. Most professional service providers fall someplace between the purity of the polar opposites but can be depicted by their predominant product or consumer orientation.

Behavioral Change as the Bottom Line

The marketing orientation for human services recognizes that the bottom line is behavior change on the part of target systems in order to improve community and client welfare. This is true whether the targets are clients in family therapy or the community power structure in social action. Intervention efforts or adherence to an intervention model are important only if they produce behavioral change. Advertising, persuading people to use or fund a service, public education, and public relations are marketing tactics to produce behavioral change. The people with behavior to be changed are resources because the bottom line can't be reached without them. They are resources to social workers or agencies in reaching their missions and achieving objectives. The reduction or elimina-

Product   Consumer
Orientation   Orientation

Figure 12.1   Product orientation/consumer orientation.

tion of child abuse requires change in abusive behavior. This requires access to child abusers. The abusers are resources, because changes in their behaviors are necessary for an agency to achieve its objective of eliminating or reducing child abuse. Detection, investigation, treatment, or full caseloads are relevant only if they lead to behavioral change.

Competition

Every choice, every action by the target system and client involves giving up some other choice or action. The alternative choices and actions perceived by the target are the competitors. Competitors are not clones of the service provider or change agent, or even limited to other service providers. There is always competition for the client's and target market's resources even when a social agency has a monopoly on a particular service to a particular segment of a community. In social services, including gratis services, clients have alternative uses of their time, energy, and effort. The TMS, including clients and potential clients, determines the alternatives and makes the decision on the alternative uses of the resources. As Andreasen states (1995), "Consumers [i.e., clients] always have choices—if only to continue their existing behavior. This can be very compelling competition" (p. 80). He further observes that "competition is always there, and it is typically always changing" (p. 54). Inertia and past behavior, the comfortable and familiar, are competitors to change. A social worker "trying to persuade a teenage drug user to . . . give up drugs must explicitly recognize that the drugs and lifestyle that goes with them are vigorous competitors for the new alternative. The present use of drugs undoubtedly meets all sorts of personal and social needs of the target audience members" (p. 153).

Social workers must develop market and consumer orientations and understand all forms of competition. They need to assess what they provide to the target.

There is no question that social workers, the human services, and the nonprofit sector are marketing. Markets exist. Social workers and human services are marketing whenever they try to facilitate exchanges with their task environments with formal and informal information and referral networks, fund-raising and solicitation networks, outreach efforts, needs and satisfaction studies, advisory groups, public information efforts, and adapting office hours to meet clients' preferences. The appropriate query is not "Should we market?" or "Are we marketing?" but rather "How can we market more effectively in an increasingly competitive and turbulent world?"

MARKETING AND COMMUNITY PRACTICE

A market, as discussed earlier in this chapter, is a set of people who have an actual or a potential interest in the exchange of tangible or intangible goods, products, services, and satisfactions with others, and the ability to complete the exchange. The determining feature of a market is that the sets of people must be actually or potentially in an exchange relationship. This requires that the people be real, interested in making exchanges, and capable of making exchanges with potential trading partners.

Marketing is a continuing, planned process. The American Marketing Association emphasizes the deliberate process of marketing in its definition: "the process of planning and executing the conception, pricing, promotion and distribution of ideas, goods, and services to create exchanges that satisfy individual and organizational objectives" (Fine, 1992, p. 47). Marketing is the "development and management of exchange relationships through purposeful benefit configuration, communication, facilitation, and evaluation processes. . . . As such, marketing is compatible with basic ideologies and methods of social action" (p. 47). Marketing is concerned with transactions or exchanges between people in the market. It involves how transactions are created, stimulated, facilitated, valued, and completed (Kotler, 1977, pp. 22–25). Marketing is appropriate for all organizations that have publics, not just consumers, with whom they make exchanges.

Marketing is voluntary rather than coercive. The capacity of one party to impose or force its will on the other party, according to Fine (1992, pp. 23–24), is not marketing but coercion. Good marketing rests on the ability of potential trading partners to choose whether or not to engage in the exchange.

Marketing is advocacy. It is not merely the advocacy, or promotion, of particular products but rather the commitment that the TMS (the particular clients, customers, and other exchange partners) will get their preferences met.

Last, and most important, marketing is change. In social marketing and social services marketing, the ultimate objective is behavioral change to benefit clients, the community, and society.

Exchange Theory and Marketing's Propositions

Exchange theory (Blau, 1964, pp. 88–114; Homan, 1958; Specht, 1986; Turner, 1982, pp. 242–273) is basic to community and interorganizational practice. It is the explicit theory underlying marketing. To review briefly, exchange theory's central proposition is that people act in their self-interest as they define it, whether that self-interest is economic, social, or psychological. Exchange is the act and process of obtaining a desired product from someone by offering in return something valued by the other party. The products can be tangible or intangible (such as social behavior), and the exchanges do not have to consist of the same types of products. Exchanges can include counseling and community organization services for money, adoration and praise for compliant behavior, information for status, political influence for PAC donations or for votes, and so forth. Whether an exchange actually take place depends on whether the two parties can arrive at the terms of exchange that will leave each of them better off or at least not worse off, in their own estimation, after the exchange compared with alternative exchanges possible and available to them.

An example of a social exchange occurs when a securely middle-class donor contributes to a homeless shelter. The donor makes a monetary donation to receive intangible products rather than shelter. The donor does not expect to use the shelter either now or in the future but expects to receive good feelings of doing a generous deed and perhaps the rewards of a more humane social environment. The marketer (that is, the homeless shelter) competes with all other alternative uses by the donor of the money that might provide the donor with good feelings, and a more humane social environment, or any other satisfaction.

Several conditions are necessary for markets to exist and exchanges to occur in addition to those found in other social network exchanges (Kotler, 1977):

1. At least one of the social units wants a specific response from one or more of the other social units. The social unit seeking the response is the marketer and the social unit from whom a response is sought is the market. The response sought from the market is acceptance in the short or long run by the market of the market's product, service, organization, person, place, ideology, and/or social idea. The marketer wants the market to respond with the resources and behaviors sought by the marketer.

2. Each social unit perceives the other social unit and is perceived of by the other social unit as being capable of delivering the benefits in return for the benefits received. Each social unit communicates the capacity and willingness to deliver its benefits to the other social unit in return for desired benefits received.

3. Each social unit can accept or reject the benefits of the other social unit in the exchange, although if the social unit withdraws from the exchange relationship, it forgoes the benefits and may pay an opportunity cost. Marketing exchanges are voluntary.

4. Marketing's indispensable activity is the marketer's creation and offering of value to the market as the market defines value. Effective marketing is the marketer's choice of actions that are calculated to produce the desired response from the market in behaviors and resources desired by the marketer.

5. Both social units gain and pay in an exchange. The value of the exchange above its cost, or profit, is determined by the value of benefit received less the cost of the resource exchange for the benefit (Profit = Benefit received − Cost of resource exchanged or lost). Each social unit in an exchange relationship estimates the cost of the resources given and the value of the resources or benefits received.

6. Marketing assumes that the marketer can alter the market's response. Marketing is a process by which the marketer alters the market's responses. The marketer wants to produce a desired, voluntary response by creating and offering desired products with value to the market.

The indispensable activity is the marketer's creation and offering of value as defined by the market. Effective marketing consists of actions that are calculated to produce the desired response from the market.

Let us illustrate these axioms with a case example. A community mental health agency (the marketer) is trying to develop and implement a counseling service for adults who were abused as children and who are suffering from anxiety as a result. These adults constitute potential clients (the market). The agency has examined the research on various forms of therapy and the findings of a small focus group from the market to determine the most effective service. The projected service (product) is a combination of individual counseling, offered in 30 sessions of 50 minutes once a week in a given calendar year, and social support groups and networks. The sessions will be offered in the evenings and on weekends, because most of the adults are employed. The number of sessions is limited by the requirements of the third-party payers. The agency has to respond to two sets of actors in the community: the potential clients and the third-party payers.

The agency is seeking specific responses from potential clients and third-party payers. It wants potential clients to become actual clients, for clients to reduce and effectively manage their anxiety, a value to clients and agency, and for third-party payers to pay for the service.

Potential clients' responses are not fixed; they may or may not become clients. The agency (the marketer) wants them to become clients and tries to achieve this by offering the therapy at convenient times. The likelihood that the potential clients will become actual clients can be altered by the agency's actions in terms of outreach, public information, recruitment, and referral networking; by ensuring that the design, location, and timing of the service meet the potential clients' preferences; and by ensuring that the service is effective. However, service effectiveness—the ability of counseling and support to reduce the anxiety of these persons—is relevant only if the potential clients use the service.

Using continuous marketing, the agency will try to design its products to meet the needs and preferences and give value to potential clients, and demonstrate to them how the products will help and give value to them. The responses of the potential clients (the market) are voluntary; they are neither obliged nor coerced to become clients. They will engage in exchange with the agency, that is, become clients, because the agency's services meet their needs better than other options available to them.

Social Marketing

Social marketing is a specialized form of marketing with the marketer offering social ideas to obtain a behavioral response from the market. Fox and Kotler (1987) define social marketing as social cause–oriented marketing. It is "the design, implementation, and control of programs calculated to influence the acceptability of social ideas" (p. 15). In Andreasen's conception of social marketing given earlier, it is clear that its *sine qua non* is the target's behavior change in ways desired by the marketer. Social marketing is the application of marketing concepts, theory, and techniques to promoting social ideas rather than physical commodities and services. Although the label has been used for almost any marketing activity by nonprofit organizations, social marketing is different from much nonprofit marketing. Andreasen's (1995, p. 7) conception of social marketing emphasizes the marketer's motives rather than technology as paramount in establish whether a marketing effort is social marketing. It is used, however, in fund-raising, lobbying, and campaigning for political candidates with an intent to promote social ideas. This conception of social marketing is similar to our concept of staging discussed later.

Social marketing has the following defining traits:

1. Its ultimate objective is to benefit target individuals or society and not the marketer.

2. The basic means of achieving improved social welfare is through influencing and, in most cases, bringing about behavior changes.

3. The target audience—the target market or target system—is the core determinant of marketing strategies and processes.

See the examples at the start of this chapter and the "Save the Bay" advertisement (Box 12.1) for illustrations of social ideas promoted and behavioral changes sought by social marketing. The "Save the Bay" ad, which has appeared in several publications over the past decade, illustrates social marketing by promoting the Chesapeake Bay Foundation with the social idea of saving the Chesapeake Bay.

BOX 12.1	SAVE THE BAY

That's been our cry since the beginning. Won't you help?
The Chesapeake Bay is in serious trouble. . . .

You can help by becoming a member of the Chesapeake Bay Foundation.

Staging

Staging is fundamental to social marketing. Staging is crucial to any social acceptance of a social problem conception and the perception of social realty. It is part of the *claims-making* process discussed in Chapter 3 of this text. Staging presents to the community and target decision makers the marketer's construction of social realty as presumed realty, the social condition as a challenge to the public's welfare, and generally proposes interventions, behaviors, and services contributing to the public good. Successful staging captures the broad range of the community standards, interests, and ideology. Staging's goal is acceptance by the relevant publics of the marketer's social constructions, rather than just informing them. It builds on as well as shapes the public's values and ideologies. Staging is not limited to nonprofit organizations. It pertains to the promotion of a social idea and not to the marketer's auspice or motives. Staging is and has been used by a range of political and proprietary for-profit organizations in the promotion of social ideas when the social ideas are congenial with political or profit-oriented concerns. We are all familiar, in our media-driven culture, with the marketing tactics of political campaigns. Newman and Sheth (1987) discuss the penetration of marketing into political campaigns when potential voters are treated as consumers rather than as participants in the political processes. Campaigning is marketing to a *voter market*, using marketing tools of assessment and research through polls and focus groups, differentiation and positioning a candidate as product design, and using a range of promotion techniques to sell the candidate. Staging's analytical market approach can be used for a range of social ideas, products, and policies.

Staging often is more important in the public's acceptance of social constructions than are valid data and scientifically technical theory. The sociologist Herbert Blumer (1969) indicated that the social definitions and not the objective makeup of any given social condition determine the way a condition exists as presumed social reality. Themba (1999) states it more emphatically:

There is only so much that information can do to improve social conditions because, contrary to conventional wisdom, information is not power. Power is having the resources to make changes and promote choices; to be heard; and to define, control, defend and promote one's interests. Many of the problems facing communities stem from the lack of power—not the lack of information. . . .

Therefore, it is not giving people information that's the key to motivating them to act, but validating their perceptions and conveying a sense that the change they dare to imagine in their private spaces is achievable and desired by a great many others. (pp. 21–24)

Economic enterprise and the political right (Lewin, 2001, p. 20) have long understood the importance of staging. Health insurance companies during the 1994 national health coverage debates with their "Harry and Louise" television ads opposed the Clintons' effort to develop national health insurance legislation. The companies claimed their opposition was rooted in the American value of freedom of choice rather than profits. The Health Insurance Association of America (HIAA) representing small- and medium-sized insurance companies had a staging success with the "Harry and Louise" television ad campaign that cost $14 million. In September 1993, 67% of respondents to a *Washington Post*/ABC News poll indicated approval of the Clinton health care plan. By February 1994, the same organizations using the same questions and panel found that the approval rate had declined from 67% to 44%. The "Harry and Louise "ads are given credit for creating public doubt in the proposal (West & Francis, 1996, pp. 25–26).

The tobacco companies in the 1990s equated governmental limitations on their ability to promote smoking and the use of tobacco products as an infringement on the consumer's freedom of choice and the basic freedom of all U.S. citizens from unwarranted government intrusion. "The smell of cigarette smoke annoys me. But not nearly as much as the government telling me what to do," extols a purported nonsmoker in

Our position, word by word . . .
Courtesy

At Philip Morris, we believe that common courtesy and mutual respect are still the best ways for people to resolve their differences.

By respecting each other's rights and preferences, both groups can easily work things out.

Source: The *New York Times*, November 1, 1994, p. A9.

an R. J. Reynolds Tobacco Company full-page advertisement in the July 26, 1994, *New York Times* (p. A11). And if the government is allowed to regulate tobacco, admonishes ever-vigilant R. J. Reynolds Company in another message, next perhaps alcohol, caffeine, and even high-fat-content foods next will be taken from us by a intrusive government (*New York Times*, June 24, 1994, p. A11). The tobacco companies have elevated respect for a smoker's right to smoke to a level similar to respecting other forms of social diversity.

The staging of social ideas is a prelude to or accompanies the promotion of more tangible products and target behaviors. Freedom of choice, the freedom to choose whether to smoke or not, is essential to a tobacco company's ability to sell tobacco products. Nonprofits might promote the social ideas of conservation with membership in particular organizations as the Nature Conservancy or Sierra Club, of children's rights or mental health as preludes to more tangible services such as parenting training and mental health counseling.

Staging can also help a marketer's image and social position with potential exchange partners. The sponsorship of collegiate academic All-Americans by GTE, an electronics firm, helps with the positive acceptance of the firm's other products. A social worker visibly promoting the social idea of gender equality, women's rights, might help obtain women clients.

In the 2000 presidential election, the Republican Party successfully staged the idea that conservatism is compassionate and caring. The art and technology of selling conservatism as compassion, caring, and fair ideology is taught at the Leadership Institute, a conservative training school for the young at Arlington, VA. The training school is to teach how to present conservative ideas to be palatable and to network and place young conservatives in political, governmental, and media jobs. The strategies taught here seem to have real-life Republicans echoes, as when President Bush poses in Florida's Everglades or among California's giant sequoias while advocating an energy policy based on drilling for oil and building power plants (Harden, 2001, p. A8).

In staging, the creation and use of *Potemkin* and *false-front* interest groups and organizations is helpful (Pollack, 2000; Rubin, 1997). Potemkin organizations are hollow organizations that give an impression of representing a broad community or the public interests. A dozen or so people can create several organizations with the same overlapping memberships. False-front organizations are organizations with names that disguise their real interests, indicate broad membership, and convey a positive public interest. Such organizations include the Coalition for Health Insurance Choices (CHIC), which sponsors the "Harry and Louise "commercials against the Clinton health care proposals. The Health Insurance Association of America solely sponsored the CHIC. Other examples are the Alliance for Energy Security established by the lobbying association for natural gas producers, The Natural Gas Suppliers Association, and Citizens for Better Medicare, another health insurance organization established during the 2000 campaign. The aim of Potemkin and false-front organizations are to mould the public's perception of a narrow self-interest position to perceiving it as a broad public interest and good position. Selling cigarettes or protecting insurance or energy company profits is not the stated goal, but the preservation of choice, freedom, and security. The selection of a name should capture a target's view of the public interest. A social worker coalition advocating the extension of third-party vendor payments to only cover clinical social workers might use the name, Coalition for Patients' Right to Choose. The name disguises a coalition almost exclusively composed of social workers. The patients' right to choose is expanded by one profession by adding only social workers to the eligible vendors list. The coalition's name indicates a broad concern for patients' rights and choice—a public good—but the intended change is rather narrow.

Staging and social marketing's products are the social ideas and the value received by the market as satisfaction in upholding the social ideas, such as respect for the environment, concern for future generations and money savings in energy conservation, and the preferred behaviors and satisfaction the social ideas allow the market to pursue and receive (Fox & Kotler, 1987, p. 17). While other incentives may be added to manipulate the market's response and increase satisfaction, such as the giving away of coffee mugs and tote bags in fund-raising by national public radio and public television stations, the social idea is the basic product. In public radio, for example, the programs essentially are free goods to the individual listener; that is, the programs can be listened to regardless of the listener's contributions to the radio station. The programs are free to the individual listener. The fund appeals generally address listeners' values in the social ideas promoted by public radio and television; the specific commercial-free programs; and the provision of more tangible products such as records, tote bags, and coffee mugs to encourage the marginally committed listener to donate. The tangible items also have value in conveying the user's public image of concern and providing free publicity to the marketer, especially if they have appropriate logos, as well as any user utility of the record, tote bag, or cup.

STRATEGIC MARKETING AND MARKET MANAGEMENT

Successful marketing requires developing and implementing a market strategy. Lauffer (1986) defines *strategic marketing* as "a comprehensive and systematic way of developing the resources you need to provide the services that others need. By responding to the needs of the consumers, providers [of resources], and suppliers, it becomes possible to minimize some of the disruptions in supply and demand that otherwise play havoc with agency programs" (Lauffer, p. 31).

Effective strategic marketing involves an outside-inside marketing approach. This marketing strategy begins with the consumer's or target market's needs and preferences (the outside), not with the organization's product (the inside). The product is developed to meet the preferences of the consumers, clients, and targets of the proposed exchange.

Stoner (1986) asserts that strategic marketing is a planning strategy that involves developing answers to the questions Where are we? Where do we want to be? and How do we get there? Strategic planning and implementation of the plan answers these questions. Strategic planning is a social planning model similar to social work's generic problem-solving model, reviewed in Chapter 1. The essential tasks are to determine the primary markets, those central to the agency's core functions and achievement of its mission, and the secondary markets, those important but not essential to the agency's mission. The primary and secondary markets include all the social entities in the task environment: the individuals, groups, and organizations from which resources and exchanges are sought. Target markets for social agencies, in addition to clients, include client referral sources, fiscal resource providers, nonfiscal resource providers, and sources of legitimation.

Determining and locating primary and secondary markets is market positioning. *Market positioning* consists of the processes by which an agency selects its markets. It involves determining the market's location, assessing its prefer-

ences, estimating the competition for the market, and appraising the potential for exchanges (Lauffer, 1986, p. 37). The processes of determining primary and secondary markets and market positioning are discussed later in the chapter under "Purchasers," addressing the development of target market segmentations and exchange partners.

The marketing literature (Fine, 1992; Kotler & Andreasen, 1987; Winston, 1986) presents the components of a strategic marketing plan with varying precision by a series of related Ps. Although the number and conceptualization of the Ps vary with the authority, we will use the following six:

1. *Probing:* the market research to determine the preferences and needs of relevant publics (clients, donors, etc.) or market segments.

2. *Purchasers:* the TMS, the relevant publics or the exchange partner sought.

3. *Products:* the goods and services offered to the purchasers and market segment.

4. *Price:* the cost of the products to the purchasers and market segment.

5. *Place:* the locations for exchanges with the purchasers and market segments and the paths by which the segments get to the places for exchange.

6. *Promotion:* the communication of the anticipated values and prices of the products and places for exchange to the purchaser and market segment.

Fine (1992, pp. 4–5) uses an additional P for *producer*, for the source of promotional message and products. Winston (1986, p. 15) uses *people*, for all people involved in the organization, including volunteers, if they affect the exchange. Fine's producer and Winston's people are marketers. Moore (1993) separates *path* from *place*, with path being the processes potential exchange partners (purchasers, clients, or customers) use to get to the place of the exchange.

Probing

Probing is the generic P for market research. *Market research* consists of the formal and informal processes and methods used to determine the TMSs, the potential and actual exchange partners, their preferences, and how these preferences can be met. The market segment's needs and preferences are the outside of strategic marketing, and developing products to meet these

Market studies include surveys of clients' and potential clients' needs and preferences; community assessments to determine community needs and resources; focus groups to determine potential clients' needs or preferences; case and client studies and analysis; follow-up studies; and client satisfaction studies, with the intent of answering questions on resources available, targeting market preferences, and gaining knowledge of conditions conducive to or inhibiting exchanges with the target market segments.

preferences is the inside. Community assessment, discussed earlier, can be seen as a market research methodology. Market research task is to segment primary markets and any additional secondary markets. Functional segmentation of the market are discussed later in the chapter under "Purchasers."

In market research, the purpose of the outside-inside approach, and of determining and segmenting primary and secondary markets, is to establish the desired competitive market position with the resource providers (the purchasers) based on their preferences (Lauffer, 1986). At the conclusion of market research, the marketer should have answers to the key questions listed below (Winston, 1986, pp. 9–12). Direct service practitioners, whether independent or agency-based, can use the same set of questions to study their markets by substituting themselves for the organization. Clients often are used here as the illustrative exchange partner or TMS. However, as is discussed a little later, a TMS is any part of the task environment, any potential partner, with whom an exchange is sought. Other potential exchange partners and TMS include potential funding sources, client referral sources, and volunteers.

There are several questions that a social services marketer should answer in the process of market segmentation.

1. What is our organization's or practice's mission and purpose? What do we want to achieve with what parts of our task environment?

2. Who has the resources needed or desired to achieve our goals and objectives and fulfill our mission? Where are the resource holders located? Are they accessible? What are their social,

behavioral, and demographic characteristics that can or will affect the exchanges? Market studies and community assessments are done to determine the location of target markets, their preferences, and how those preferences will affect product design and delivery, how the target markets communicate, and whether the target markets requires additional segmentation.

3. Are the needed resources general or specific? Are resources generally distributed evenly across the target market or clustered around specific traits of the TMS? Is the target market's capacity uniform in ability to pay the price for our products and meet our expectations? Resources that are clustered indicate additional target market segmentation to expedite exchanges. If the capacity to provide the exchange is not essentially equivalent across the market, then additional segmentation is indicated.

4. What are the most effective and efficient ways to obtain the resources? Is one approach sufficient or are multiple stratagems necessary? Will different product designs, delivery systems, and pricing strategies enhance exchanges? If multiple approaches (different approaches to different parts of the target market) facilitate exchanges, then greater market segmentation is indicated.

5. How does the target market get its information? Is it uniform across the market, or are there different patterns of communication and information getting? What are the optimal marketing approaches to communicate and facilitate exchanges with the TMSs? How can the value and price of the products compared with those of competitors in meeting TMS's preferences and the place for exchanges be best communicated to the TMS? What things interfere with effective communication? Greater segmentation is indicated when communication patterns differ.

6. How does each TMS define its preferences and needs? How does it determine value? Are the presences, products desired, and values uniform or different across the market? A family services agency offers family therapy to families suffering from discord. Family therapy is the agency's product. The segment's preference, however, is a reduction of family discord and not the therapy. The family might be happier to avoid therapy if their stress can be reduced in other ways. The therapy is a means to achieve the family's preference. Value is rooted in how well the product meets preferences.

7. What product prices and places for exchanges most encourage exchanges by the TMSs? How can price be kept lower than the value to the TMSs but above our costs?

8. Who are the competitors? What other organizations and entities are trying to meet the TMS's preferences? What are the alternative ways the TMS can use its resources? Remember, a competitor is any alternative way a TMS can use its resources that we are seeking, including the resource of its behavior.

9. What are our strengths and competencies? Have we it built from or can we build from our strengths and competencies in designing new products to meet potential TMS preferences?

10. What are our weaknesses that require attention? Can the weaknesses be corrected? Weaknesses requiring attention are deficiencies that interfere with exchanges and place the organization at a competitive disadvantage in the TMS's assessment for its resources use.

Market Study and Market Audit Methodologies

Market research's methodologies and techniques are similar to those of community assessment discussed earlier in the text. The first step is defining the market segmentation, discussed under *Purchasers*. The market research and audit should be completed before the marketing plans are developed. Some of the methodologies of market research are as follows:

1. *Case studies* (Lovelock & Weinberg, 1984; Yin, 1986) of similar marketing efforts by the agency or other agencies. Case studies look at how successful marketers design, develop, and deliver services that meet the preferences of the TMS or similar market segments, with the intent of replicating the successful efforts. Unsuccessful cases also should be scrutinized to avoid their failures.

2. *Surveys* of particular TMSs for their needs, preferences, and capacity and willingness to make the exchanges—pay the price—and preferences for the location of exchanges can be done by client exit interviews or other opinionaires and evaluations; surveys of TMSs such as consumer and client satisfaction surveys; or surveys of potential donors. Political polls are surveys. Surveying the TMSs reveals why the segment uses or would use the agency, makes a donation, becomes a volunteer, accepts the social idea, and so forth.

Surveys (Rubin & Babbie, 2001), while a potentially powerful assessment tool, have several limitations. Not the least are the costs of developing, pretesting, distributing, and administering them and analyzing the results. Meaningful surveys of the TMS require a representative sam-ple, that is, a sample containing all the important traits and characteristics related to the market segment's preferences for products, prices, and places. If the people who respond to the survey do not represent the TMS, the survey's results will not reveal the true preferences of the TMS and will not be helpful in the design and delivery of the products.

3. *Focus groups* are a less costly approach to market research that are now widely used. A focus group (Bernard, 1994; Greenbaum, 1987; Kreuger, 1988; Morgan, 1988) is a relatively homogeneous group that addresses, or focuses on, providing information about what appeals and does not appeal to them about messages, ideas, and products. A carefully constructed focus group representing a specific TMS can provide much information on the segment's preferences. The group should have from 6 to 12 members, with 8 being the most popular size, and should be reasonably homogeneous. The crucial issues are whether the focus group truly represents the TMS, whether the members of the group believe they can reveal their true preferences in the group situation, and the agency's willingness to be open and candid with the focus group about its plans. If the members do not know each other in other roles and are socially similar, communication is enhanced. Diversity of group members, which may represent different TMSs, may inhibit communication. For different TMSs, different focus groups should be used. The focus group leader should be a skilled group leader with the ability to lead but not direct the group, to prevent one or two members from dominating, and to keep the group focused on the question or concern without being judgmental about the group's response.

4. *Advisory boards* and *panels* can provide information similar to that of focus groups by sharing their opinions on product design, service delivery, and similar agency concerns. However, advisory groups differ from focus groups in that they often represent diverse constituencies or TMSs, include members who have social relations outside of the group, and have internal structures that allow the domination of one or a few members.

5. *Mall surveys*, using quota and purposive sampling techniques, are frequently used in market research. The mall survey takes its name from the market researcher's practice of going to a shopping mall and asking shoppers what they look for in products and places to shop. The data are analyzed according to a predetermined profile of consumer characteristics. The social service agency or practitioner can use similar tech-

niques in other areas, where samples of its target market are located. If an agency is interested in developing a program for hard-to-reach adolescents, it can locate and send someone to the places where they congregate. In this example, it may indeed be the mall. The mall survey is relatively inexpensive and easy to conduct. Its weaknesses are the weaknesses of all surveys, especially those conducted with samples of convenience: whether the participants are representative of the target population, their willingness to participate in the survey, and the truthfulness of their responses. As with the focus group, participants in a mall survey are not truly anonymous, although their responses may be kept confidential, and this may inhibit their responses.

6. The *market audit* is the most complete and powerful approach to market research. This technique incorporates most of the above methodologies. Market audits address the questions presented in the previous section and collect information on the agency's task environment, including competitors for resources, the agency itself, and the *P*s of the purchasers (TMSs), product, price, place, and promotion. The audit should help the marketer learn its weaknesses and deficiencies, its strengths, and where it is dominant and deals most effectively with its competition. The audit report should contain recommendations and proposals to improve the organization's market access and share. A sample audit guide is included at the end of the chapter.

7. A *market matrix* is a simple approach to market research and analysis. In filling the cells, the market researcher has to specify for relevant TMSs the product, price, place, and promotion. The market matrix addresses the *P*s of purchasers (TMS), product, price, place, and promotion (see Table 12.2). The sixth *P*, probing, is

the research and analysis necessary to complete the matrix's cells. Of course, each TMS indicated above will require greater segmentation. Rarely are clients, funders, political influencers, legitimizers, or volunteers internally homogeneous groupings.

Purchasers

Purchasers and donors or resource suppliers are the most important TMSs. Purchasers are those parts of the task environment that control or represent resources necessary for the agency to achieve its objectives. Purchasers include all of the types of resource suppliers indicated above. Market segmentation, which determines and establishes the TMSs, is essential to effective product development and exchanges.

Market Segmentation

Market segmentation is to obtain the precision necessary to facilitate exchanges by allowing specificity in product, price, place, and promotion strategies for each segment. For-profit businesses have different market segments for different product lines. A cereal company may produce a variety of breakfast cereals to meet fairly specific preferences of different TMSs. An automobile manufacturer develops and sells several models to meet specific target market preferences. Nonprofit agencies have different TMSs with different preferences. They should not attempt to have one product line for all. The mental health agency that has only one form of therapy, formatted in the same way, offered during the same hours in the same places to all potential clients, regardless of demographics or other conditions, probably is not meeting the

TABLE 12.2 Market Matrix

Target Market Segments, or Purchasers (Describe each target market segment, such as those listed below.)	Product (What is the product desired by and for the segment?)	Price (What is the price of each the product for the segment?)	Place (What is the place of exchange with each segment?)	Promotion (What promotion is needed exchange segment?)
Client segments				
Fiscal resource suppliers				
Political influencers				
Volunteers				
Providers of legitimacy				
Other segments				

TABLE 12.3 Market Segmentation and Social Work Values

. . . starting where the client is. Who are the clients? Where are the clients? What do they prefer? Market segmentation makes exchanges easier by permitting the marketer to more precisely design products with benefits, places of exchange, and prices to meet the preferences of specific types of people.

Target markets	That part of the task environment or community with the necessary resources sought by the marketer to achieve objectives and with whom the marketer seeks exchanges.
Target market segments	Those parts of a particular target market sharing specific traits of behavior, values, and preferences that influence the exchange. Segments share some traits with the total target market but differ on some traits with other parts of the target market. A particular target market generally has more than a single segment.
When to segment?	Segment when traits of a potential target market are diverse and the diversity will affect the exchange and product design and delivery. The target market is segmented to achieve greater homogeneity in each segment.
How to segment?	Cluster the target market's traits that affect the exchange: for example, education, preferences, values, capacities, motivation, or other traits that will influence exchanges in the target market.
How much segmentation?	Additional segmentation is indicated if exchanges with the target market are low: The agency is not obtaining resources and behavior changes from the target market.

preferences of all potential market segments. The agency may therefore lose clients. Market segmentation as demonstrated by Table 12.3 is compatable with social work's administration to "start where the client is."

A TMS is a smaller portion, a subset, of the target market, sharing some the traits with the general target market but also possessing some unique characteristics and traits that set it apart and will affect the exchange. Segmentation is desirable unless the marketer can reasonably assume that all people in the target market have the same preferences that can be responded to in the same ways. Appropriate segmentation requires knowledge of the traits, characteristics, and preferences of a target market and any subgrouping's clustering of traits and preferences. Probing or market research and community assessment is a necessary prerequisite for viable segmentation. Box 12.2 lays out the segmenting protocol.

A product line can mean different things to different constituencies (clients, funding sources and so forth) and therefore, in effect, represents different products. The nonprofit agency's perception of its products delivered may differ from the perceptions of these products by different constituencies. Nonprofit agencies need to recognize how the products, even in the same product line, are perceived by different market seg-

ments. These perceptions may be very different from those of the agency.

The degree of market segmentation is based on (a) the specificity of resource exchanges that the marketer wants from the task environment (i.e., whether the resource desired is homogeneous and general or diverse and specific), (b) the nature of the potential trading partners (homogeneous or diverse), (c) the distribution of the resources sought (concentrated in a few trading partners or widely distributed in the task environment), and (d) the products desired by the potential trading partners (uniform or diverse).

As a guideline, the variables can be summed using the numbers 1 or 2 preceding the subvariables. The higher the sum, the greater the need for market segmentation. If the resource desired is homogeneous (I.1), there are many potential trading partners who have the resource (II.1), the potential trading partners are similar on important traits (III.1), and their product preferences are uniform (IV.1), the summed score is 4 and little segmentation appears necessary. By contrast, if the resources desired are specific and diverse (I.2), held by a few potential trading partners (II.2), who have diverse characteristics (III.2) and desire diverse products in exchange for their resources (IV.2), the summed score of 8 represents a complex market and the need for greater segmentation to facilitate exchanges.

BOX 12.2	SEGMENTING PROTOCOL

1. Marketer determines resources and behaviors necessary to achieve objectives.
2. Marketer assesses task environment (community assessment) to determine who has the resources and behaviors and where they are located.
3. Marketer assesses the target market's preferences.
4. Marketer assesses whether the resource holders' product and benefit preferences are homogeneous or heterogeneous across the target market.
5. If resources, behaviors, and preferences are homogeneous, then segmentation is now complete; if they are heterogeneous, then additional segmentation is needed until the resource, behavior, or product preferences holders are clustered into reasonably homogeneous segments.
6. Marketer assesses where the exchanges can occur and where the preferences will be met.
7. If a single place for exchange exists, then no additional segmentation is needed; if a single place for exchange does not exist, then additional segmentation is needed until sufficient places exist.

In market segmentation, physical, psychological, attitude, demographic, economic, and other social diversity; use patterns; cost efficiencies of segmenting; neglected segments; and preference differences should be considered. Each segment should have relatively homogeneous traits in terms of its product response. If part of the segment responds differently to the product, it probably represents another TMS. The final target market segmentation represents a balance of the market's diversity and the economy or the affordability of more finite segmentation. Segments should be large enough to be served with a product economically and specific enough to

---

Guidelines for Target Market Segmentation

I. Resource desired from the task environment
  1. Homogeneous and general, or
  2. Diverse and specific
II. Number of potential trading partners
  1. Many
  2. Few
III. Nature of potential trading partners
  1. Homogeneous
  2. Diverse
IV. Products desired by potential trading partners
  1. Uniform
  2. Varied

---

allow the product to be differentiated and individualized.

Product

Products are tangible goods such as food, services such as counseling, and ideas such as nondiscrimination or conservation, developed by the agency or the professional (the marketer) and offered in exchange for the resources needed from the TMS (Fine, 1992). Product development presumes product mutability rather than immutability. Product *mutability* means that products can be designed and adjusted to accommodate the preferences of specific TMSs. The TMS is not forced to fit the product, but rather the reverse. This is marketing's outside-inside philosophy, discussed earlier.

The product, as discussed earlier, may be an intangible, such as an opportunity for the TMS to fulfill a certain ideology or value. The aim of the promoter of the idea, such as conservation or good parenting behavior, is the adoption not only of the idea but also of the behaviors resulting from it. The product for the target market is the end results of the behaviors flowing from the idea—a better environment or safer, healthier children (Kotler & Roberto, 1989, p. 140). Even more tangible products, such as counseling services, training, or case management, are designed to produce behaviors from the TMS. However, as has been constantly emphasized, the primary consideration of product design is the product's capacity to provide value to a TMS, as judged by that segment.

PRODUCT MANAGEMENT

After market segmentation, the agency or professional must engage in *product management.* This entails selecting the criteria by which target segments and consumers will be selected, designing the products, positioning the products in the market, and providing an appropriate mix of products for different segments.

The product design component should consider and balance the following criteria (Fine, 1992, pp. 40–41):

Specificity: Products are designed to meet the needs and preferences of a specific TMS. The use of generic product labels such as *counseling* or *psychotherapy* may be too broad, and such use assumes little differentiation in the target market segment's needs and preferences.

Flexibility: Products should be designed to be adaptable to changing markets and TMSs' preferences.

Attainability: Products should be designed within the limits of the agency's or professional's capacity, resources, and competencies and should be built on the strengths of the agency or professional.

Competitive advantage: Products should be built on the strengths of the agency or professional and should emphasize qualities of the marketer that are not possessed by the competitors.

Care must be exercised in product development to avoid the product orientation discussed earlier. If we become enamored of our products at the expense of consumers' preferences, we may not gain the resources desired from the TMS. A product orientation leads marketers to ignore and be ignorant of generic competition, concentrates on the products delivered, and blinds them to the actual values received by the TMS. A product orientation does not consider ways that the preferences of the client or consumer may be met by competitors. A consumer orientation and awareness of what consumers prefer and are actually receiving facilitates marketing. What an agency believes it is delivering may differ from the products it really produces and delivers. An example is an agency dealing with unruly behavior of students. The agency may believe that the product is counseling and therapy to provide the student with insight into the unruly behavior. However, the product received by the student is rooted in the student's satisfaction with it and its value to the student. If the student neither seeks nor receives insight, the product received by the student is different from the one the agency seeks to deliver. The product received by the student may be an hour spent with the counselor out of the classroom or playground. The student will appraise this hour compared to alternative uses and costs of the time.

Another agency may claim to deliver job skills training to TANF recipients. But if some people do not want a job or the job skills, don't believe they will have the required job skills for employment at the end of the training, or believe they will have jobs at the end of the training, the products they receive are different from those the agency's personnel assume they are delivering. The products received by the clients may be entertainment, structure to life by getting out of the house and doing something during the day, a way to stay eligible for TANF benefits, an opportunity to socialize with others in the training program, and a way to maintain or reciprocate for the cash benefits (Reid, 1972). The agency's training program is competing with other products that can provide the client with entertainment, structure, and socialization preferences. Client participation in the training may be motivated only by the need to maintain eligibility and reciprocate for cash benefits. Participation, commitment, and expenditure of energy and time will be curtailed to a level consistent with a client's view of a fair exchange. If a client does not perceive that participation is necessary to remain eligible for cash benefits or has no need to reciprocate, the client will not participate. If coerced to participate in the training program, the client will perceive the product received as punishment for being on TANF. Motivation, energy, and effort only will be at a minimal level.

The product delivered relates to the views of the providers; the product received relates to the preferences of, use of, and value to the recipient. In the case of mandatory therapy for spouse abusers, the court, the agency, and the professional therapist may view the product delivered as therapy to help abusers alter their behavior. However, the abusers may view the product received, especially if they do not want to alter their behavior, as a way to avoid imprisonment and meet any requirements set by the court to continue a relationship with their spouses. These spouse abusers will expend only enough resources to achieve their preferences. Exchanges are more likely to occur, as Box 12.3 indicates, when both sides get their preferences met.

PRODUCT POSITIONING

Product positioning is the location, or position, the marketer seeks for its products in terms

BOX 12.3	EXCHANGES BETWEEN MARKETER AND TARGET MARKET SEGMENT ARE PROMOTED WHEN

| resources and behaviors wanted by marketer from the target market segment (TMS) | match the resources of and behaviors within the capacity of TMS, with | Benefits sought and value preferences of TMS | matching the marketer's product benefit as evaluated by TMS better than do the competitors'. |

EXCHANGES BETWEEN MARKETER AND TARGET MARKET SEGMENT ARE IMPEDED WHEN

| resources and behaviors wanted by marketer from TMS | don't match the resources of and behaviors within the capacity of TMS, or | Benefits sought and value preferences of TMS | don't match marketer's product benefit as evaluated by TMS better than do the competitors'. |

of the TMSs: intended consumers, clients, or users. The market position is the niche the product occupies in satisfying some segment of the range of potential TMSs. The community mental health agency, discussed earlier, that is trying to develop and implement a therapeutic service to adults who were abused as children and are now suffering from anxiety as a result, is positioning itself in the market. It is pursuing a particular TMS and has designed a particular service to meet the preferences of this segment. The design of its services and the hours offered will not meet the preferences of all adults or even of all adults who want mental health services, but these should meet the preferences of the particular TMS.

The TMS's image of the product and the marketer (the producer), then, is an important ingredient in market position. *Image* is the way the product is viewed by the TMS in meeting its preferences. A marketer may view the product as meeting certain needs, but if the segment does not share that image, there will be no exchanges. An agency's personnel may believe its counseling is helpful and nonstigmatizing, but what is critical image is whether the TMS (potential clients) view it similarly. Their view, or product image, will determine the exchange (Stern, 1990; see Table 12.4).

Market Mix

The *marketing mix* is the number and kinds of products matched to the number and kinds of TMSs and to the prices charged the TMSs. Wein-

berg (1984) describes the marketing mix for nonprofit agencies as the "maximization of the amount of products or services which are consumed or utilized, subject to the amount of revenues and donations being at least equal to the cost of providing the service" (p. 269). The marketing mix results from determining the product preferences of the selected TMSs, designing the products, and pricing them appropriately.

Price

Price is a significant factor in product management. *Price* is the total contribution and cost required by the TMS in money, time, energy, effort, psychic costs, social costs, and lifestyle changes exchanged for the product and its benefits. The price needs to be competitive with the prices of alternative products and benefits available to the TMS. Although the marketer determines to a degree the components of the price, the TMS, not the marketer, decides the value received. *Value received*, the satisfaction received relative to price and to alternative commodities and their value and price, will guide the TMS in its product selection. The marketer must, in the long run, keep the monetary price equal to or above the costs of producing, promoting, and distributing the products and the value above the price to the TMS in comparison to alternative uses of the price by the TMS. Its the value the TMS receives that ultimately will regulate product exchange and use. A TMS's willingness to *pay a price* is a function of capacity to pay and

TABLE 12.4 Product Image and Position

Questions for the Target Market Segment	Agency Image	Product Image
1. How would you like each image to be seen by the target market segment?		
2. How is each image seen by the target market segment?		
3. How is the image held by the target market segment determined?		
4. How satisfied are you with the image held by the target market segment?		
5. How does the image held by the target market segment promote exchanges?		
6. What factors help or hinder changes in the image held by the target market segment?		
7. What are the strategies for changing the image held by the target market segment?		

the price compared to benefits. It is this subjective meaning of price that is important and will determine completion of the exchange.

$$Value = Benefits - Price$$

An exercise video has a fiscal price, but it also has a social and personal price if its benefits are obtained. The monetary price may be a few dollars, or it may be borrowed from a library or from a friend, but the benefits are dependent on paying the social and personal price of devoting time, effort, and energy and altering a lifestyle to the exercises. There is a psychic price of admitting that one needs to exercise and the risk to self-image of not exercising after recognizing the need. A healthy diet has fiscal price, often lower than the price of an unhealthy diet, but the social and personal price may often preclude its benefits. The enjoyment and benefits of a healthy lifestyle and a healthy diet are evaluated by the potential consumer in comparison with the prices of giving up the fatty foods with their stronger, more satisfying tastes and ease of preparation. Similar costs-to-benefits comparisons can be made with mental health counseling (see Table 12.5).

A marketer needs to appraise prices and meanings to potential users and look for ways to reduce price or improve benefits. Again, market studies are critical here. Remember, value is a function of price as well as benefits. Increasing benefits or lowering price or both can further value to the TMS and produce exchanges. The mental health counseling marketer needs to ensure delivery of counseling's benefits, not just the counseling, and devote attention to lowering the costs in order to increase value for the user.

Pricing is a critical component of regulating demand. For example, a long waiting list may indicate underpricing for the agency's services, while idle time for the service providers may indicate overpricing. Once a pricing policy is es-

TABLE 12.5 Mental Health Counseling

Benefits	Costs
• Healthier self-concept • Improved social functioning • Potentially greater longevity • Possible improved status depending on view of therapy • Attention of a concerned, caring person • Possibly pleasant activity	• Monetary cost of therapy process • Time expended in preparation for and going to therapy and in any processes of behavioral change • Energy and effort of going to and participating in the therapy and of processes of behavioral change • Lifestyle changes of any effects of therapy • Possible stigma associated with therapy

tablished, it is generally easier to lower the price than to raise it, especially in a competitive market. Fine (1992) states, "The key to pricing is to build in value into the product and price it accordingly" (p. 42).

Nonprofit social agencies and their staffs often view their products (services) as "free goods" to their clients if the clients do not pay a monetary price. Donors or the government rather than clients customarily pay the monetary costs of the agency's services. However, the clients pay a social price. A *social price* is the nonmonetary price paid by the purchasers (the clients). Social prices are common in the use of social agency and professional services and products even when there are no direct monetary costs, and the marketer should consider them in developing a pricing policy. There are four common types of social price: time, energy or effort, lifestyle, and psyche (Fine, 1992).

TYPES OF SOCIAL PRICES

Time prices. These include the time the user spends in receiving, using, and obtaining the benefits from the product. It is the time the purchaser devotes to making the exchange and receiving the product's value. There are four elements of time price:

1. *Direct time price*, or the time spent going to and from the place of the exchange and the time spent there waiting to make the exchange. Examples of direct time price in a counseling situation include the time spent in the counseling, getting to the counselor's office and, once there, waiting for the counselor.

2. Beyond the direct times price, such as the time spent in counseling or training, there is the *performance time*, the time required to learn and carry out the desired social behavior. This might include stress reduction exercises or other behaviors that are part of the intervention.

3. Another element of time price is the *flexibility/fixity of time*, or whether the exchange and the behavior can be carried out when the client prefers or must be done on a fixed schedule. Other aspects of flexibility/fixity relate to frequency (how often the social behavior must be performed to be effective), the regularity of the social behavior required, and how long it must be performed.

4. The last factor is *disruption/simultaneity*, or to what extent the social behavior requires the TMS to rearrange its current time preferences. Can it be done at the same time as other behaviors or in conjunction with other behaviors? How much will it disrupt other behaviors?

Services and products that have little time flexibility and high time demand compared with alternative uses of time and alternative products carry a higher price and may not be used by clients. This is especially true if the clients, such as those in a particular form of therapy, perceive that little value is received from the time investment compared with alternative uses of time in meeting their preferences. The time price of therapy to a client includes the time spent in therapy sessions, the time required to get to and from the therapist's office, the time used in waiting there, the rigidity of the therapy hours, how convenient the sessions are for the client's schedule, and the time demanded outside the therapy to receive its benefits. The client's evaluation of benefits compared with price will include the time price. We make other exchange decisions, such as the selection of our bank or grocery store, based partially on time price. It is reasonable to assume that clients consider time in their evaluation of social work interventions.

Effort and energy prices. These prices include the effort, both physical and emotional, required by the TMS to obtain benefits from the products compared with alternative available products, including doing nothing. For a client in therapy, the investment includes the effort and energy spent in the therapy, getting to and from the therapist's office, and energy demands outside the therapy to receive its benefits. The client's evaluation of benefits compared with price will include the energy price.

For those of us in poor physical shape, our physical condition generally is not a result of ignorance of how to get into shape or its potential physical and emotional benefits. It is not a function of money. It depends on our willingness to devote time and energy to getting into shape and making certain lifestyle changes. We remain flaccid and lethargic because it is less expensive, at least in the short run; it has a lower price in time, effort, and energy.

If the TMS or the individual exchange partner can obtain the same results, the same or equivalent value as they perceive it, with little energy expenditure, exchange theory indicates that the more energy-saving alternative will be used. If a TANF recipient believes he or she will remain unemployed after conclusion of a training program or perceives no greater benefits from employment than from unemployment, the client probably will not pay the price of time and energy to succeed in the training program unless coerced. The expected value (no job) is similar for the client whether the client participates with a high or low expenditure of time and energy. Rationality urges the client to save the time and energy.

Lifestyle prices. These prices are the changes the TMS must make in lifestyle to use and receive value from the products. Lifestyle price recognizes that in the exchange, the TMS is required to give up certain aspects of life that are rewarding in order to use the product and produce the desired effects. Willingness to pay the lifestyle price is related to the value placed on the gains received by using the product or engaging in the service and the belief that the product or services will produce these gains. Older persons returning to college for a graduate social work degree must alter their lives when they reenter school. They must give up time with family and friends for classes and study and often must lower their standard of living as they cut back on work to allow class and study time and to pay for tuition and books. Their willingness to do so is predicated on the belief that this is the price they must pay to receive the future benefits of a master's degree in social work. Clients often must make lifestyle changes that may represent costs to them in order to receive benefits from the intervention. Their willingness to pay the price is a function of their valuation of the current or future benefits received from the lifestyle change.

Psyche price. This is the emotional cost in self-esteem and self-image the TMS pays in using the products. The older social work graduate student is now back in a student role after perhaps having been a competent professional, perhaps a supervisor or administrator, a parent, and a mature, responsible adult. This return to the student role may impose psyche costs. To take another example, if a client believes that mental illness is a weakness and a stigma, and that mental health treatment is a public recognition or assignment of the stigma, the use of treatment carries a psyche price and will be considered in the client's valuation of the treatment. It is the client's valuation that determines the psyche price, not the agency's or the public's. If the client perceives no greater stigma with treatment than she or he currently suffers, there is no increase in psyche price.

Agency marketers that wishes to increase product demand can look for ways to reduce the social prices. Conversely, an increase in social prices will reduce demand and clients' use of a service. This is occurring in federal and state efforts to increase the stigma of being a TANF recipient.

The concept of social price needs to be distinguished from social cost and public price. The *social cost* is the cost imposed on the community by the product and the exchange. It is the externalities of the exchange beyond the costs and benefits to the marketer and the exchange partner. A homeless shelter or drug treatment center may be perceived by the surrounding neighborhood as having a social cost that the neighborhood rather than the center, its staff, and clients, pay. The *public price* is the price paid by the public for the product.

A Market Segmentation Approach to Social Pricing

A market segmentation approach to social pricing consists of the following steps:

1. Identifying relevant publics or TMSs, such as clients, funders, and legitimizers. This involves community assessment market research and probing.

2. Identifying social exchange approaches and mechanisms to bring about social exchanges and social change (the products) for the TMS.

3. Assessing the perceived prices, including the social prices of time, energy, lifestyle, and psyche, paid by the TMS using market research.

4. Constructing a segmentation matrix of product, price, place, and promotion for the TMS.

5. Ranking the TMS on its acceptance of the price using market research.

6. Examining possible ways to reduce the perceived price and increase the value of the product to the TMS by altering the product to meet the segment's preferences, reduce time demands, increase time flexibility, and reduce effort, lifestyle, and psyche costs.

7. Determining specific pricing programs and strategies to encourage the TMS to replace its present behavior or products with the agency's products.

Place

A successful market strategy requires the development of viable mechanisms and places for exchanges to occur. *Place* includes the social characteristics of the physical location where the exchanges occur, along with the associated social prices, convenience, credibility, and legitimacy of the place to the TMS (Shapiro, 1977, p. 110). The physical facilities, immediate environment, and, as Moore (1993) indicates, the paths and routes consumers and exchange partners take to get to the products, access services, and make exchanges are factors associated with place. Winston (1986) states, "The place component . . . consists of the characteristics of service distribution, modes of delivery, location, transportation, availability, hours and days opened, appointment (requirements), parking, waiting time, and other access considerations" (p. 15).

Place is intimately related to price, especially social price, and to promotion. The marketer (agency or professional) should try to facilitate exchanges by making the place for exchange— the physical facility and its environment, its ease of access, and its comfort level—compatible to the exchange partner's preferences. Does it add to the TMS's financial, time, effort, lifestyle, or psyche prices or to the sense of benefits received? Can the prices associated with place be reduced? A central location can make exchange easier; a more remote one can effect client flow.

Place has a series of prices or costs to the marketer: The facility has a price such as rent, taxes, equity costs, utilities and maintenance. There is a cost of delivering services to the client in their location. Place also has a range of prices to the TMS in fiscal and social prices: location, treatment by staff, dignity of service, safety of the social and physical environment, confidentiality.

Benefits of place to TMS −

Prices of place to TMS =

Value of place to TMS

The conception of place, however, in the social services' exchanges goes beyond a narrow conception of place as an office or service facility. With social products and social goals and objectives—goals beyond a fiscal profit—the conception and meaning of place expands. The purpose of the social work exchange is (a) for the marketer to obtain resources from the TMS, (b) for the marketer to achieve behavioral objectives other than profit, and (c) for the TMS to obtain benefits beyond the tangible or intangible services received in an office is more complex than just the office or physical facility. The concept of place includes where the bottom-line behaviors occur. For a TMS, place is both where the segment exchanges its resources for the product's benefits and values and where the segment re-

> **Benefits and Place**
>
> If the benefits, value, and outcome of drug treatment are to enable the client to live a drug-free life, the treatment must consider where the client's life occurs. Is the place conducive to realizing the intervention's benefits? Or must changing place be part of the intervention?

ceives any benefits and value. The marketer's evaluation of place and its impact on product consideration of place should appraise whether the product's benefits can be received in a particular TMS's social environment.

If the place where the client is to demonstrate the bottom-line behaviors is harmful to the behaviors or requires too high a price in the client's estimation, the likelihood of achieving this objectives is low. Drug treatment in high drug use environments is notoriously unsuccessful. The practitioner-marketer needs to alter place to be conducive to achieving the behavioral objectives.

The marketer can influence the value of place to a TMS and individuals constituting a TMS by (a) determining the price and benefits of the place as perceived by a TMS and (b) working to lower price and improving benefits as perceived by a TMS. This will increase the TMS's estimation of value.

Place, when possible, should add to rather than distract from the product's value. The place also communicates to the potential exchange partner the marketer's evaluation of the partner. Dingy waiting rooms where clients' confidentiality is not respected and where clients are kept waiting for hours add to the product's price. The value of the product has to be increased to compensate for the price of place.

Promotion

Promotion, marketing's last P task, is the agency's or professional's communication of information to the appropriate TMSs. The information deals with (a) the product, (b) how the product will meet the market segment's preferences, (c) its price, (d) the place or places, and (e) the processes of exchange. Promotion is often equated with advertising, but, as implied above, promotion goes far beyond advertising. Promotion also includes *all* messages the agency and the professional communicate to the TMS regarding their views of the TMS, the value and benefits of the TMS to the agency and professional.

Effective promotion motivates its target "to take specific action and promises a desirable benefit if they do" (Stern, 1990, p. 74). An agency's or professional's office and waiting room, behavior toward and respect for clients, and the demeanor of all those in contact with clients all communicate the value the agency or professional assigns to clients, the agency's products, and the products' capacity to meet clients' preferences.

Communication involves language and its meaning, symbols and their meaning, the medium of communication, and all the formal and informal ways of receiving and sending information used by clients and potential clients. Effective promotion requires demassification of U.S. culture in formal and informal communication and a use of symbols (Halter, 2000). The targets of promotion need to understand the meaning of the message. This, in turn, necessitates that the marketer understands what defines and determines meaning to a target market, both in content and context of messages. Context shapes the meaning of content. The same message in its words, construction, and syntax, heard over the radio while commuting home from work or from a telemarketer interrupting dinner, is received differently and probably has different meaning.

Different TMSs require different communications and venues shaped to carry the desired message to each market segment. Rothman and his colleagues (Rothman, 1980; Rothman et al., 1983) consider the need for differences in communication and promotion in their discussion of the diffusion of the results of social research and development (social R & D). Diffusion, in Rothman's social R & D model, is basically promotion and dissemination of the products—the findings of the social R & D—such as new knowledge or skills in ways that the Social R&D consumer can evaluate and use the findings. Social R & D itself is an outside-inside marketing strategy, because it starts with a client's problem or need.

Promotion can be mass promotion with low or high intensity. An example of low-intensity diffusion and promotion is advertising to a general, unsegmented target market. High-intensity promotion is targeted, individualized, personalized, and often with direct contact with the recipients of the communication.

Communication strategies and techniques used to reach potential clients include feeding information into client networks and support systems, providing key informants with information and using other word-of-mouth techniques, and holding community forums and special events for target client groups. Once clients or other TMSs begin the exchange process, communication is generally high intensity.

PROMOTION AND CLIENT EMPOWERMENT

Client empowerment and *self-determination* require providing the client with the maximum information on product, prices, and potential benefits and risks to enable the client to make a truly informed decision. This is the essence of good promotion: communicating with the client and potential clients and other potential stakeholders so they can make informed decisions. It is a requisite for genuine informed consent (see Box 12.4).

PUBLIC RELATIONS AND PUBLIC INFORMATION

Any time the agency or professional (the marketer) deals with any actual or potential TMSs, it is engaging in public relations. The publics can be clients, prospective staff, donors, potential or current supporters of the agency, legitimation sources, and potential volunteers. Kotler and Andreasen (1987) define public relations as the image-building function that evaluates the attitudes of important publics, identifies the policies and procedures of an individual or organization with the public interest, and executes a program

---

BOX 12.4	QUESTIONS FOR TRUE INFORMED CONSENT IN PROMOTION

1. How should content and context affect messages to different cultural, ethic, and socioeconomic target market segments?
2. Does informed consent require communication of benefits, all prices (including all social prices), and risks?

3. Should social and psychological interventions require the same warning labels on risks and side effects as do physical and pharmacological interventions?

of activities to earn understanding and acceptance by these publics. Sometimes a short definition is given, which says that PR stands for *performance* plus *recognition* (pp. 576–577).

While recognizing the overlap between the concepts, Brawley (1983) distinguishes public relations from public education. Public relations are "efforts intended to interpret the characteristics, functions, and activities of human service workers to the general public or particular segments of it" (p. 12). Public education, as Brawley uses the concept, has less precise targets and is more akin to staging, general image building, and educating on general social condition: "Public education is . . . the provision of information to the general public or a given audience about social issues, social problems, categories of people with special needs, appropriate and inappropriate collective or individual responses to particular problems or needs, the functions of specific human service programs, and needs for new or changed social policies or programs" (p. 12).

Developing and Assessing Communication

In developing and assessing a public relations, information, and promotion program, the following questions should be answered:

1. What is the specific public or TMS with which the agency or professional wants to develop an exchange relationship? Are there any special circumstances and traits—location, demographic characteristics, boundaries, other factors—that affect communication?

2. What is the exchange—the benefits offered to and responses sought from the TMS? What specific actions or responses are sought from the TMS?

3. How does the TMS obtain its information? What sources of information and venues for the information—specific print media, television (specific programs and times), word of mouth, information and opinion leaders, networks—are used by the TMS? What level of information is sought or required in order to make an exchange?

4. What type of information is needed by the TMS to make a decision? What specific information is needed by the TMS to perform the desired behavior and engage in the exchange? What are the specific benefits to the TMS? What is the price to the TMS?

5. How will the agency or professional know that an exchange has occurred, that is, that the

TMS has received the desired product and the agency has received the desired behavior and resources in return? What are the feedback mechanisms?

Public relations and education are exercises in communication. As with all communication, the tasks for the message sender are to determine whether (a) the message reached the intended target (b) in the manner intended, (c) in a way that the target can understand and respond (d) in the way the sender intended, (e) to produce the outcome behavior desired by the sender, and (e) in a way that will allow the sender to know that the desired outcome behavior by the target has occurred. The communication management task is to have the message reach the target in a timely fashion in the manner intended with the content intended.

Good formal communication as part of promotion has the following characteristics: (a) brevity—it is only as long as needed, (b) appeal—it focuses on the possible positive outcome in the exchange, and (c) honesty—it provides honest information about the product, price, and place. Messages and communication, to reemphasize the earlier discussion, go beyond advertisements and formal communication to include all the interactions between the TMS and the agency or marketer.

Readability

A challenge in developing written and verbal messages is assessing the educational level required to understand the message. Assessing educational appropriateness is important if a message is to convey meaning. There are several ways to do this. Perhaps the best way is to field test the message with a representative sample or focus group of the target audience. These methods suffer from the expense of developing the inventory of the target population, constructing the sample or focus group, field testing the message, and repeating the process until the appropriate message level is developed.

There are many computer software programs that will test the readability level of written messages. This is done by entering the message into the software, which will then assess the message for the readability grade level necessary to comprehend it.

A less expensive and quick (though with suspect validity) method is the SMOG Readability Formula (Office of Cancer Communication, 1992, p. 77). It is used to calculate the reading grade level necessary to comprehend the written material. SMOG's application steps are as follows:

1. Take the beginning, approximate middle, and last 10 sentences of the message, for a total of 30 sentences, and count the number of polysyllabic words. A sentence occurs when the phrase ends in a period, question mark, or exclamation mark, even though it may not be a complete sentence. A polysyllabic word is a word with three or more syllables. The intent is to obtain a representation of the total message. Random sampling to obtain the 30 sentences from all of the sentences could be done, although this is probably spurious precision.

2. Consider that numbers, whether written or numeric, abbreviations such as *etc.*, and hyphenated words to have the number of syllables that they have when spoken. For example, *192* has five syllables and *etc.* has four syllables. Hyphenated words are counted as one word.

3. Compute the square root of the number of polysyllabic words in the 30 sentences to the nearest whole square root. For example, the square root of 193 is 13.89 and the nearest whole square root is 14. The square root and nearest whole square root of 9 is 3. The square root of 10 is 3.16, and the nearest whole square root is 3.

4. Add a constant of 3 to the square root, and the sum is the minimum educational level, within 1.5 grade levels, necessary to understand the message. The .1.5 grade levels is the possible error range.

For example, if a 30 sentence message contains 60 polysyllabic words, the computation of the readability level is as shown in Box 12.5.

The message being evaluated via the calculations shown in Box 12.5 should be appropriate for someone with an 11th-grade reading level, although the error range indicates that it might be readable by someone with as low as a 9.5 grade reading level or would perhaps require a reading level of 12.5 years (that is, graduation from high school and some college). With a TMS that has a general reading level of 10.0, given the error range, the marketer probably should lower the readability level. This can be done by lowering the number and ratio of polysyllabic words per sentence.

Messages with fewer than 30 sentences can be converted into a format appropriate to SMOG by using an adjustment process. The adjustment process is to divide the total number of polysyllabic words by the total number of sentences in the message and multiply the results by 30. This will provide the adjusted number of polysyllabic words. The adjusted product is then entered into Step 1 of the calculations and the remaining steps are completed. For example, if a communication has 15 polysyllabic words in eight sentences, the following calculation converts the data into a format appropriate for evaluation via SMOG:

$$\text{Total number of polysyllabic words to be used} = 15/8 = 1.875 \times 30 = 56.25$$
$$\text{adjusted polysyllabic words}$$

The adjusted total number of polysyllabic words is entered into the computation procedures as shown in Box 12.6, with a resulting estimated readability level of 9.5 to 11.5.

SMOG only provides a rough approximation of readability level. It uses the same methodology employed by the readability software programs. Complexity and readability are judged by the complexity of words, with polysyllabic words assumed to be more complex and sentence structure. SMOG assumes that a message with long, complex sentences is likely to contain more polysyllabic words than are ten short declarative sentences. These messages generally require more education to understand them. If a message yields a score above the minimum education level targeted, it probably is a good idea to rework the communication to use shorter de-

BOX 12.5	READABILITY TEST CALCULATION STEPS
Total number of polysyllabic words	60
Square root	7.75
Nearest whole square root	8
Addition of constant	3
Approximate minimum grade level	11
Approximate appropriate grade level range (+ or − 1.5 grade levels)	9.5 to 12.5

BOX 12.6	READABILITY TEST CALCULATION STEPS FOR LESS THAN 30 SENTENCES

Total number of polysyllabic words	56
Square root	7.5
Nearest whole square root	8
Addition of constant	3
Approximate minimum grade level	11
Approximate appropriate grade level range (+ or − 1.5 grade levels)	9.5 to 12.5

clarative sentences and avoid polysyllabic words where possible.

SMOG's advantage is that it requires little time and expense when compared with alternative methods. No representative panels of the TMS are required. The time and expense of field testing are eliminated. No computers, software, or computer expertise are required. The costs for this assessment method are the costs of a calculator to compute the square roots (less than $10) and the time needed to count the sentences and polysyllabic words. SMOG's disadvantage is that it provides only a crude approximation of the readability grade level.

THE USE OF MEDIA

TMSs are often reached through the media, although the particular venue and media may be different for each segment. When the media are used, they become exchange partners, and their needs, preferences, and operating procedures must be considered. As with all exchanges, the marketer needs to increase the value and decrease the price for the exchange partner. The media respond to promotional efforts when they see gains.

The previously discussed general communication issues apply to the use of media. Communication is focused, brief, and honest. Information is presented in a manner to present the least work and cost to the venue. The marketer should be available to the venue for any follow-up questions for a fuller story and other stories that the venue may be seeking. The journalistic criteria of the five *W*s (who, what, when, where, and why) and sometimes the *H* (how) are reflected in the message and media releases (Rose, 1995):

1. *Who* are you; *who* is interested in the information (a TMS)?

2. *What* is the newsworthy event or occurrence of interest? *What* will be expected of a TMS? *What* will be the TMS's benefits?

3. *When* will or has the event occurred?

4. *Where* will or did the event occur?

5. *Why* is the event important to a TMS?

6. *How* did the event come about?

Articles should be written in a manner that involves the least work and cost to the venue. Venues should be surveyed and relationships developed with the appropriate editors and reporters to discover the preferred length, timing, style, and format. The marketer should be available to the venue to answer follow-up questions for a fuller story, as well as for additional follow-up and other stories that the venue may be seeking.

The social agency or social work marketer can expedite the use of the media with a media information file (Rose, 1994). This file, computerized or manual in a file box or Rolodex, should contain the following information:

1. Names, addresses, and telephone numbers, including fax numbers and e-mail addresses, of the main media outlets and contacts in each outlet. If contacts are personalized, exchanges are helped.

2. Names, addresses, and telephone numbers, including fax numbers and e-mail addresses, if any, of the media outlets' decision makers, such as the editors and producers. Again, contacts in each outlet should be personalized.

3. Specific information about each outlet's news, information, and entertainment interests; special features; when published, circulated, or broadcast; target audiences, and which of the marketer's TMSs this medium reaches, as well as the geographic audience radius.

4. Deadlines for media and for venues within the media as news stories, feature stories, and columns in the print media and differing program types in radio and television.

5. A brief analysis of the successes and failures for each contact and venue.

Information on the media can be obtained from the white pages and yellow pages of the telephone directory and media directories. Many outlets provide media kits to promote their use. Rose, the *NASW News* columnist on marketing, emphasizes the use of smaller media outlets, "such as local weekly papers or community radio or television stations or programs. These are usually in need of material and may use just about anything you send them. They reach a smaller audience, but the coverage is free . . . this way is gravy" (1994, p. 5). It is also often beneficial to hold media events such as press conferences, if there is significant timely news, and media receptions. However, the success of media use is measured not by the amount of coverage but if the coverage communicates the intended message to the intended target audience.

MEDIA OUTLETS

The following five media outlets are most useful:

1. *Print media:* Op-ed pieces, press releases, letters to the editor, feature stories, and information contacts with reporters and columnists are ways to use the print-media as outlets. Human interest and case studies that grab readers' attention and tell a compelling story are often preferred over statistics, although statistics may supplement the story. Magazines are often useful outlets for feature stories. Multiple letters to the editor by different writers stressing the same subject and message have a better chance of being published than a single letter. They generate media interest. Most newspapers and magazines publish only a small fraction of the letters they receive. *The New York Times,* for instance, publishes less than 5% of the letters it receives (Zane, 1995).

2. *Television:* Talk and interview shows, tabloid shows, cable and public access TV, news shows with visuals and sound bites, and public service announcements provide opportunities for communication through television.

3. *Radio:* Using call-in and talk shows, public service announcements, interview shows, buying radio time or having a regular time-slot show on a problem area (all it takes is a sponsor), news shows, and crafting sound bites are tactics for radio use. Multiple calls and callers will probably be required for the call-in and talk shows. Generally the talk shows screen calls and limit repeat callers within a given time period. The producers also screen calls to be supportive of the host or sometimes serve as a convenient foil.

4. *Electronic bulletin boards and networks:* These emerging venues are gaining wider use as communication approaches. They are useful in reaching particular target audiences.

5. *Volunteers:* Volunteers, in addition to providing personnel resources, are a promotional and linking mechanism. They link the agency to a range of networks. Sources of volunteers include business firms, service clubs, "helping hand" programs in schools, and student internship programs in college departments such as business, journalism, and communications, and social work. These volunteers carry into and talk about positive and negative experiences in other aspects and networks of their lives. A popular Baltimore radio columnist and commentator on business investments and financial matters regularly volunteers at a homeless meals center. He often talks about his volunteer experiences on his radio show. After his radio talks, donations and volunteers to the center increase for a short time. This is valuable free promotion for the center.

Reliance solely on journalists and the media to get the information out, for staging, and for public education is risky. Reporters are professional skeptics and can't be counted on to convey a particular message in the way intended by the marketer. However, media advocacy has impact on policy-makers and the public (see Box 12.7). There are also considerations of timeliness when the schedules of the media and the marketer are

---

BOX 12.7   MEDIA ADVOCACY IN STAGING

Media reporting and advocacy → Influence on policymakers → Media reporting policymakers' response → Public opinion shaped by response → Policymakers respond to public opinion → Media report policymakers' response → Public opinion shaped → Policymakers respond with social policy

different. Many social marketers supplement media efforts with advertisements and purchased media space and time. This increases the marketer's control, although it doesn't have a news article's or TV spot's credibility (West & Francis, 1996).

MARKETING: A SUMMARY

Marketing is a philosophy and strategy of service development and delivery and an approach to expediting exchanges. Marketing starts and ends with the TMSs and attempts to promote exchanges by meeting the preferences of these segments. Marketing is compatible with the social work ethics and values of client self-determination, starting where the client is, and client advocacy. Marketing can be used with any exchange partner or TMS. The steps of the marketing philosophy and strategy can be summarized in the following questions:

1. What resources are necessary to complete the mission and achieve the objectives?
2. From whom are the resources sought (the TMS)?
3. What are the benefits (products) to be offered to the TMS for its resources?
4. What is the value of the benefits to the TMS? How will the resources meet TMS preferences? How was this determined?
5. What is the price to the TMS? What are the social price components? How does the price compare with the value as determined by the TMS?
6. What are the places and processes of exchange with the TMS? Does the place contribute to the value or price of the benefits to the TMS?
7. What are the best methods of communicating to the TMS the product's capacity to provide benefits and meet preferences, as well as its price and place of exchange?

THE MARKETING AUDIT GUIDE[1]

1. Mission Review

Does the organization have a written mission statement or bylaws that detail the mission? What are the mission and objectives? Are objectives stated as outcome terms? If no written mission statement and objectives exist, how does the agency convey its mission and objectives to staff and other relevant publics? How does the organization determine success?

2. Task Environment

Has the agency determined the resources it needs from its task environment to achieve its mission and objectives? What are the TMSs that have the necessary resources (publics, groups, organizations, agencies, and others)?

3. New Markets

Are new TMSs needed for the agency to achieve or expand its mission? What are they? How can the agency locate and assess these TMSs for resources and preferences? Have other communitywide surveys been conducted by either the agency or some other group that can be used to assess the market?

4. Communication

How does the agency communicate with each TMS? List the publics or markets that have known barriers to effective communication. What are the barriers? How are the needs and preferences of each TMS assessed? What is the agency's image with each TMS? Is the image the one desired by the agency?

5. Referral Sources

List all organizations or individuals that refer patients/clients to the agency, starting with those that refer most often. Is the agency satisfied with its communication and with the results of the referral network? How does the agency provide feedback to referral sources? Are they satisfied with the feedback? What is the annual turnover, if any, of referral sources? Are the reasons for this turnover known? What changes or shifts in clients/patients have affected referrals?

6. Clients[2]

What are the products for each client TMS? What are the services, broken down into the smallest complete components? What is their value to the TMS? What client preferences do they meet? What is the price to the TMS? What do clients exchange for the products? How does the agency obtain information on the TMS? What does the agency do with the information it receives from clients or patients? Is the agency satisfied with its communication with clients and potential clients? What is the agency's image with clients? Is the image different from the agency's intended image?

Which current services and products bring the agency the most income and other resources? The least? How do the resources exchanged by the client TMS help the agency meet its objectives?

7. Competition

List all known and potential competitors of the agency by resources sought, include size of staff, ownership, services, service area, fees, caseload, size, and annual growth rate. Describe the one agency or group that is thought to be the chief competitor. How can this competition be met? Compare the agency's fees and other social prices with those of similar organizations; are they comparable and competitive, higher or lower?

8. Market Management

Does the agency have a spokesperson? If yes, who is that person and what is the position's title? Is there an agency public relations director or a person responsible for public relations? Is there an agency marketing director or a person responsible for overall marketing direction? Do all agency staff members understand their functions as agency representatives, spokespeople, and marketers? Is there a board public relations committee and a marketing committee? Do all board members understand their functions as agency representatives, spokespeople, and marketers? If the agency has not had marketing research or planning, how have user needs been determined in order to expand existing services or add new ones?

9. Promotional and Public Information Strategies

Does the agency have a written press relation's policy? Where is it located and how is it used? Do all agency members understand it? How has the policy benefited the organization in the last 2 years? How were benefits determined? Does the agency have a brochure or other written information for distribution that explains the agency's mission, objectives, and services? When was the material last revised? Which TMSs get the material? Is it adapted to meet the needs, interests, and preferences of the specific TMSs that get the brochure? Does the agency have an internal newsletter or publication, an external newsletter or publication, direct-mail operations for fund-raising and information distribution, a regular news release program, a newspaper clipping service, a radio or television news recording service, radio and television public service announcements (PSAs)? Which benefits and products are covered in the radio and television PSAs? To which publics are the radio and TV PSAs directed? Are representatives of any TMSs consulted in preparing the public information program? Which TMSs are consulted and why?

Does the agency have policies and protocols for press releases? Which of the following do press releases address: new personnel (particularly managers or department heads), new services, new equipment, revised policies, procedures, special events, recruitment of employees and volunteers, financial and statistical data, and feature and human interest stories promoting the successes of the agency and its clients? How does the agency determine how well its purposes, objectives, problems mission, and new distribution policy are understood by the news media?

Are annual reports published? If not, how does the agency direct the flow of information that normally is found in an annual report?

Does the agency have a speaker's bureau? Which publics are addressed in activities or promotion of the bureau? Which main messages are the agency's speakers conveying to audiences? What and who determines the subject matter of speeches? Does the agency hold community seminars, symposia, or lectures? Are volunteers, board members, and other auxiliary personnel used in community relations? How does the agency benefited from their activities?

Does the agency use print, radio, and television advertising? To which TMSs are these messages addressed? Do the ads bring the agency new clients or patients or other new markets? How is this determined?

Are all staff members involved in or have the opportunity to participate in promotion and make suggestions for improvement? Does management consider the suggestions?

10. Locating New Markets

How does the agency find new TMSs—clients, fiscal and nonfiscal resource providers, other resources? Who is (are) designated to find new clients, referral sources, employees, and sources of funding? Is case finding an agency practice? Do auxiliary members or volunteers perform community relations, resource location, and case-finding functions for the agency? Does the organization attract or encourage walk-in users? If yes, how do such users discover the organization?

11. Agency Fees

Does the agency have a fee structure? How do clients characterize the fee structure (acceptable, unacceptable, no opinion)? How is this determined? How is the fee structure communicated to current and potential clients? Does the agency convey an image that it can provide more free or reduced-fee care than it actually can deliver? How is this determined? What questions about fees do referral network representatives ask? How does the agency communicate the main points of its fees to its key TMSs? How often in the last 2 years has the agency raised its fees? How was this received by key TMSs? Was increased value perceived by the segments?

Notes

1. See Rubright & MacDonald, 1981, for a more complete market audit form, questions, and discussion.

2. This section and subsequent sections can be modified for the other significant TMSs: referral sources, financial providers, complementary agencies, volunteers and nonfinancial providers, and providers of legitimation and sanction.

References

In addition to the marketing references indicated below, readers may want to review the burgeoning literature in social services, human services, and professional marketing. Some additional references include the *Journal of Health Care Marketing, Health Care Marketing Quarterly, Journal of Marketing for Mental Health, Praeger Series in Public and Nonprofit Sector Marketing,* and the *Journal of Professional Marketing,* to name only a few.

Anderson, E. (1995). Welfare by waiver: A response. *Public Welfare, 53*(2), 44–49, 50–51.

Andreasen, A. R. (1984). Nonprofits: Check your attention to customers. In C. H. Lovelock & C. B. Weinberg (Eds.), *Public and nonprofit marketing: Cases and readings* (pp. 131–135). Palo Alto, CA: Scientific Press.

Andreasen, A. R. (1995). *Marketing social change: Changing behavior to promote health, social development, and the environment.* San Francisco, CA: Jossey-Bass.

Anthony, R. N., & Young, D. W. (1988). *Management control in nonprofit organizations* (4th ed.). Homewood, IL: Richard D. Irwin.

Bernard, H. R. (1994). *Research methods in anthropology: Qualitative and quantitative approaches* (2nd ed.). Thousand Oaks, CA: Sage.

Blau, P. M. (1964). *Exchange and power in social life.* New York: Wiley.

Blumer, H. (1969). *Symbolic interactionism: Perspective and method.* Englewood Cliffs, NJ: Prentice Hall.

Bradshaw, J. (1977). The concept of social need. In N. Gilbert & H. Specht (Eds.), *Planning for social welfare* (pp. 290–296). Englewood Cliffs, NJ: Prentice Hall.

Brawley, E. A. (1983). *Mass media and human services: Getting the message across.* Beverly Hills, CA: Sage.

Bryce, H. J., Jr. (1987). *Financial management for nonprofit organizations.* Englewood Cliffs, NJ: Prentice Hall.

Cooper, P., & McIlvain, G. E. (1983). Factors influencing marketing's ability to assist nonprofit organizations. In P. Kotler, O. C. Ferrell, & C. W. Lamb (Eds.), *Cases and readings for marketing for nonprofit organizations* (pp. 10–18). Englewood Cliffs, NJ: Prentice Hall.

Dreyfuss, R. (2000, March 27–April 10), Philip Morris money. *The American Prospect,* pp. 20–22.

Enis, B. M. (1974). *Marketing principles: The management process.* Pacific Palisades, CA: Goodyear.

Fine, S. H. (1992). *Marketing the public sector: Promoting the causes of public and nonprofit agencies.* New Brunswick, NJ: Transaction.

Fine, S. H., & Fine, A. P. (1986). Distribution channels in marketing social work. *Social Casework, 67,* 227–233.

Fox, K. A., & Kotler, P., (1987). The marketing of

social causes: The first ten years. In P. Kotler, O. C. Ferrell, & C. W. Lamb (Eds.), *Strategic marketing for nonprofit organizations: Cases and readings* (3rd ed., pp. 14–29). Englewood Cliffs, NJ: Prentice Hall.

Gillespie, E., & Schellhas, B. (Eds.). (1994). *Contract with America: The bold plan by Representative Newt Gingrich, Representative Dick Armey, and the House Republicans to change the nation.* New York: Time Books.

Gingrich, N., Armey, D., & the House Republicans. (1994). *Contract with America.* New York: Time Books/Random House.

Goodstein, L. (2001, April 24). Church-based projects lack data on results. *The New York Times,* p. A12.

Greenbaum, T. L. (1987). *The practical handbook and guide to focus group research.* Lexington, MA: D. C. Heath.

Halter, M. (2000). *Shopping for identity: The marketing of ethnicity.* New York: Schocken Books.

Harden, B. (2001, June 12). In Virginia, young conservatives learn how to develop and use their political voices. *The New York Times,* p. A8.

Holmes, J., & Riecken, G. (1980). Using business marketing concepts to view the private, non-profit social service agency. *Administration in Social Work, 4,* 43–53.

Homan, G. C. (1958). Social behavior as exchange. *American Journal of Sociology, 63,* 597–606.

Kotler, P. (1971). *Marketing management* (2nd ed.). Englewood Cliffs, NJ: Prentice Hall.

Kotler, P. (1977). A generic concept of marketing. In R. M. Gaedeke (Ed.), *Marketing in private and public nonprofit organizations: Perspectives and illustrations* (pp. 18–33). Santa Maria, CA: Goodyear.

Kotler, P., & Andreasen, A. R. (1987). *Strategic marketing for nonprofit organizations* (3rd ed.). Englewood Cliffs, NJ: Prentice Hall.

Kotler, P., & Roberto, E. L. (Eds.). (1989). *Social marketing: Strategies for changing public behavior.* New York: Free Press.

Kreuger, R. A. (1988). *Focus groups: A practical guide for applied research.* Newbury Park, CA: Sage.

Lauffer, A. (1986). To market, to market: A nuts and bolts approach to strategic planning in human service organizations. *Administration in Social Work, 10,* 31–39.

Lewin, T. (2001, May 20). 3 conservative foundations are in throes of change. *The New York Times,* p. 20.

Lovelock, C. H., & Weinberg, C. B. (1984). Public and nonprofit marketing comes of age. In C. H. Lovelock & C. B. Weinberg (Eds.), *Public and nonprofit marketing: Cases and readings* (pp. 33–42). Palo Alto, CA: Scientific Press.

Moore, S. T. (1993). Goal-directed change in service utilization. *Social Work, 38,* 221–226.

Morgan, D. L. (1988). *Successful focus groups.* Newbury Park, CA: Sage.

Newman, B I., & Sheth, J. N. (1987). *A theory of political choice behavior.* New York: Praeger.

Office of Cancer Communication, National Cancer Institute. (1992). *Making health communication programs work: A planner's guide.* (NIH Publication No. 92–1493). Washington, DC: U.S. Government Printing Office. Retrieved June 13, 2003, from http://cancer.gov/pinkbook

P.L. 104–193, Personal Responsibility and Work Opportunity Reconsideration Act of 1996 (August 31, 1996). Retrieved July 18, 2003 from http://www.lexisnexis.com/congcomp

Pollack, A. (2000, November 4). Protecting a favorable image: Biotechnology concerns in Quandary over drug giants. *The New York Times,* p. B1.

Reichert, K. (1982). Human services and the market system. *Health and Social Work, 7,* 173–182.

Reid, W. J. (Ed.). (1972). *Decision-making in the Work Incentive Program.* Final report submitted to the Office of Research and Development, Manpower Administration, U.S. Department of Labor, Report Nos. DLMA 51-15-69-08, DLMA 51-37-6911, DLMA 51-24-6910. Chicago: University of Chicago, School of Social Service Administration.

Rose, R. (1994, October). Marketing: To build clientele, build a media file. *NASW News, 39,* 5.

Rose, R. (1995, February). Marketing: Hook editors with a pro-caliber release. *NASW News, 40,* 5.

Rosenberg, G., & Weissman, A. (1981). Marketing social services in health care facilities. *Health and Social Work, 6,* 13–20.

Rothman, J. (1980). *Social R & D: Research and development in the human services.* Englewood Cliffs, NJ: Prentice Hall.

Rothman, J., Teresa, J. C., Kay, T. L., & Morningstar, G. C. (1983). *Marketing human service innovations.* Beverly Hills, CA: Sage.

Rubin, A., & Babbie, E. (2001). *Research methods for social work* (4th ed.). Pacific Grove, CA: Brooks/Cole.

Rubin, B. R. (1997). *A citizen's guide to politics in America: How the system works & how to work the system.* Armonk, NY: M. E. Sharpe.

Rubright, R., & MacDonald, D. (1981). *Marketing health and human services.* Rockville, MD: Aspens Systems Corp.

Shapiro, B. P. (1977). Marketing for nonprofit organizations. In R. M. Gaedeke (Ed.), *Marketing in private and public nonprofit organizations: Perspectives and illustrations* (pp. 103–115). Santa Maria, CA: Goodyear.

Specht, H. (1986). Social support, social networks,

social exchange and social work practice. *Social Service Review, 60,* 218–240.

Stern, G. J. (1990). *Marketing workbook for nonprofit organizations.* St. Paul, MN: Amherst H. Wilder Foundation.

Stoner, M. R. (1986). Marketing of social services gains prominence in practice. *Administration in Social Work, 10,* 41–52.

Themba, M. N. (1999). *Making policy, making change: How communities are taking law into their own hands.* Oakland, CA: Chardon Press.

Turner, J. H. (1982). *The structure of sociological theory* (3rd ed.). Homewood, IL: Dorsey Press.

Weinberg, C. B. (1984). Marketing mix decisions for nonprofit organizations: An analytical approach. In C. H. Lovelock & C. B. Weinberg (Eds.), *Public and nonprofit marketing: Cases and readings* (pp. 261–269). Palo Alto, CA: Scientific Press.

West, D. M., & Francis, R. (1996, March). Electronic advocacy: Interest groups and public policy making. *PS: Political Science & Politics,* pp. 25–29.

Winston, W. J. (1986). Basic marketing principles for mental health professionals. *Journal of Marketing for Mental Health, 1,* 9–20.

Yin, R. K. (1986). *Case study research: Design and method.* Beverly Hills, CA: Sage.

Zane, J. P. (1995, June 19). A rivalry in rabble-rousing as letter writers keep count. *The New York Times,* p. D5.

13

Using the Advocacy Spectrum

Economic goods are not the only kind of goods that are subject to considerations of justice; a minimal amount of a wide variety of social and psychological goods is also owed to each member of society as a matter of justice.

J. C. Wakefield (1994, p. 48)

Change *never* ever, ever comes from the top down.

B. A. Mikulski (1982, p. 22)

MAKING CHANGE HAPPEN

As agents for change, we need to explore where we want to go and how to get there—ends and means. Therefore, this chapter will cover different types of advocacy available to practitioners. Advocacy and action have been conceptualized here in a variety of ways to illustrate the far-reaching nature and flexibility of these practice tools. Empowerment is a secondary focus. Another purpose of the chapter is to facilitate better communication between micro- and macro-practitioners by spotlighting language and leaders of importance to change agents.

Values

The four cornerstones of social work, according to Saleebey (1990, p. 37), are *indignation, in-quiry, compassion and caring,* and *social justice.*

Social workers whose indignation as well as compassion quotients run high are primed for professional advocacy. Hearing about situations like this, we want to do something!

> Overcrowding . . . is a constant feature of schools that serve the poorest. . . . 11 classes in one school don't even have the luxury of class-rooms. They share an auditorium in which they occupy adjacent sections of the stage and back-stage areas. . . . "I'm housed in a coat room," says a reading teacher at another school. . . . "I teach," says a music teacher, "in a storage room. . . . " The crowding of children into insufficient, often squalid spaces seems . . . inexplicable. . . . Images of spaciousness . . . fill our . . . music . . . [children] sing of "good" and "brotherhood from sea to shining sea." It is a betrayal of the things that we value when poor children are obliged to sing these songs in storerooms and coat closets. (Kozol, 1991, pp. 158–160)

Our values lead us to want to alleviate or transform acute, chronic, and seemingly unfixable misery (Kleinman, Das, & Lock, 1997; Mayadas & Elliott, 1997; Swenson, 1998; Von Bretzel, 1997; Witkin, 1998). There are numerous ways in which inequities of this type can be addressed by caring social workers, especially those dedicated to justice.

Process

Social and political critics highlight "present inanities" (Ivins & Dubose, 2000) and urge penetrating change. Within individuals and society, there is a desire for continuity as well as change, but we want to avoid getting stuck. In 1970, pioneering change agent Paulo Freire addressed how social workers figure into larger change. " 'The social worker,' Freire wrote, 'has a moment of decision. Either he picks the side of change . . . or else he is left in the position of favoring stagnation' " (Kozol, 1990, p. 137). Social change goals can embrace better circumstances for service users, amelioration of particular oppression, or a more egalitarian society. These are progressive in that they aim to improve the lot of the disadvantaged and are carried out in a manner consistent with democratic values (Bombyk, 1995). When we set out to make changes, that process is known as *directed*, *purposive*, or *intentional* change. Change *strategies* vary widely and can include "nonviolent direct action, advocacy, political action, and conscientization [raising of consciousness]" (Reeser & Leighninger, 1990, p. 75; see also Abramovitz, 1993; Mandell, 1992; VeneKlasen, 2002). Checkoway (1995) describes six strategies—each with its own "practice pattern"—in connection with community change: mass mobilization, social action, citizen participation, public advocacy, popular education, and local services development (p. 2).

Advocacy and *social action* are strategies or means to an end. Such strategies are employed by progressive professionals and by a wide variety of concerned citizens (Lewis, 1998) and organizations that vigorously oppose the status quo. These concepts are similar. The list in Box 13.1, based on Panitch (1974), suggests the variety of techniques used by social workers engaged in advocacy and reform. In addition, there are new technologies (Hick & McNutt, 2002). Differences in advocacy and action include size variations in the societal unit normally worked with (task group versus a larger population), adherence to norms, and typical interventions. Let us consider them.

What Is Advocacy?

Definitions and Characteristics

Advocacy, whether individual or systemic, case or class, means championing or speaking for the interest of clients or citizens. Social work managers, for example, often promote causes involving service users with officials and decision makers (Menefee & Thompson, 1994, p. 18). Advocacy has a role in transforming private troubles into public issues or personal problems into social issues. It has a role in challenging inhumane conditions at a micro- or macrolevel. Social workers also advocate within our field for a particular mission, program, or course of action. In direct service work, advocacy is often part of client support and representation and, if possible, involves client self-advocacy. *Case advocacy* emphasizes ensuring service delivery in one's field of practice and securing resources and services for particular clients in one's caseload (Grosser, 1976; Hardina, 1995; Jackson, 1991;

BOX 13.1	TECHNIQUES OF ADVOCACY AND SOCIAL ACTION

1. Conferring with other agencies
2. Appealing to review boards
3. Initiating legal action
4. Forming interagency committees
5. Providing expert testimony
6. Gathering information through studies and surveys
7. Educating relevant segments of the community

8. Contacting public officials and legislators
9. Forming agency coalitions
10. Organizing client groups
11. Developing petitions
12. Making persistent demands

Source: From *Direct Social Work Practice* (pp. 506–507), by D. H. Hepworth and J. A. Larsen, 1993, Pacific Grove, CA: Brooks/Cole.

Johnson, 1995). *Cause advocacy* involves groups, institutions, and modification of social conditions (Johnson, 1995); Schneider and Lester (2001) define it as "promoting changes in policies and practices affecting all persons in a certain group or class" (p. 196).

History. The advocacy tradition evolved from the legal field out of attempts to implement the Bill of Rights and humanitarian reform. Early *cause advocates* called the attention of those in office or high places to the predicament of certain exploited or ignored sectors of society. Examples include Dorothea Dix, who inspected and reported on prisons and insane asylums (Gollaher, 1995), and Reginald Heber Smith, who implored attorneys to provide legal aid for the poor. Today, advocates use Web sites as advocacy tools to interact with the larger public (Shultz, 2002, p. 205; see also McNutt & Boland, 1999). Social work literature separates advocacy from social movements but sometimes views cause or class advocacy as the same as social action. The primary distinction is that most forms of advocacy stay within established employer guidelines and procedures and traditional political processes.

What Is Social Action?

DEFINITIONS AND CHARACTERISTICS

Social action is a collective endeavor to promote a cause or make a progressive change in the face of opposition. It often involves bringing together aggrieved persons, who begin to take direct action. If necessary, agitation or disruption may be used (Specht, 1969). It builds on the self-advocacy of the affected part of the population by mobilizing them (J. Gamson, 1991). Wallerstein views community empowerment as a social action process that "promotes participation of people, who are in positions of perceived and actual powerlessness, towards goals of increased individual and group decision-making and control, equity of resources, and improved quality of life" (1993, p. 219).

Scope. Compared with advocacy, the goal of social action is broader. In direct service work, social action often means tackling "cumulative problem situations and issues" (Staub-Bernasconi, 1991, p. 36). Romanyshyn (1971) defined social action as "efforts at systemic intervention designed to prevent problems, expand opportunities, and enhance the quality of life" and believed that such efforts "may be seen as a quest for community and a better polity [body politic]" (p. 153). Activities can entail changing the agency from within, working with mobilized

populations, or conducting community-controlled participatory action research (Alvarez & Gutierrez, 2001; Kling & Posner, 1990; Thursz, 1971; Wagner, 1991).

A distinguishing feature of social action is its emphasis on internal change through consciousness raising and changing. Certain thought patterns discourage our involvement— for example, believing critics who say we are going too fast or too far. In contrast, William Gamson has analyzed what facilitates involvement. He describes three collective action frames—injustice, agency, and identity—used by the mind to justify action. The *injustice* component is the moral indignation that can be summoned as part of political consciousness. The *agency* component refers to the sense that we can do something— "alter conditions or policies through collective action" (W. A. Gamson, 1992, p. 7). The *identity* component creates a mental adversary, a "they"—human agents who can be affected or turned around (1992, p. 7).

History. Concerned with power holders and challenging groups, social action comes out of insurgency, movement, reform, and third-party traditions against the so-called evils of life. It often involves "the collective struggle of oppressed people acting in their own behalf to improve conditions affecting their lives" (Burghardt, 1987, p. 298). For a model of collective struggle, numerous organizers have drawn from the philosophy and tactics of Saul Alinsky. In the same tradition, Ernesto Cortes, Jr., was awarded the MacArthur "genius" award for his lifelong work in community organizing in San Antonio and other places. Today, social action manifests itself in media events, in ambitious citywide and statewide campaigns for all manner of reforms, in the years of organizing on both sides of the abortion issue, and in "issue networks" (Burghardt, 1987, p. 292) that begin with information sharing and swell into action coalitions. Social action is used internationally—a demonstration held in Florence, Italy, in autumn, 2002, drew a half-million people to protest the proposed U.S. attack on Iraq and globalization-corporatization issues.

Which Change Modalities Are Relevant to Direct Service?

Advocacy and action have been successfully melded in three contemporary forms of change:

- Ensuring individual rights: pursuing actual delivery of what it is assumed everyone should have

- Public interest advocacy: participating in society's decisions and sharing benefits, power, and responsibilities

- Transformation: perceiving the possibility of a better, and profoundly different, society and moving to bring it about

All three manifestations of change make invisible groups more visible, address social misery and disenfranchisement, link individuals, and presuppose the advocate's optimism or hope.

ENSURING INDIVIDUAL RIGHTS

Fairness may require the continuous creation of new rights for designated groups and for those eligible for certain entitlements. Adherents of getting one's rights aim to ensure delivery of rights and services that society has pledged to everyone. They believe that individuals and groups who fight for their own rights contribute to other members of society by creating a level playing field. For instance, citizens have used the courts to obtain equal protection under the law when an immutable trait (such as gender or race) has kept them from receiving what they should have had all along—fair access to jobs, apartments, and voting. Advocates are also needed. For example, right-to-shelter battles are fought on behalf of diverse individuals (in burdensome circumstances such as homelessness) and large families (fair housing). The Innocence Project and the Center on Wrongful Conviction use journalists, private investigators, and attorneys to find evidence to free wrongly convicted death row inmates. Their record of successful exonerations led the governor of Illinois to halt all executions.

This mode of change influences our practice in many ways. Social workers sometimes help secure or create new rights—such as the right to treatment or to die—and often help implement or enforce such rights. We also mediate when there are competing claims—for example, between family members. We can be criticized when our agency is perceived as interfering with the rights of those in a category, such as adoptees or adopters; clashing with a particular group, such as recipients; or ignoring a group, such as those caught up in the court system (Lynch & Mitchell, 1995).

The rights under discussion fall into three categories: (a) due process (a concept of fairness) or procedural rights, (b) substantive rights, and (c) basic human rights. The first two flow from the Bill of Rights (the first 10 amendments to the Constitution of the United States) and other provisions of the Constitution, legislative directives,

or court orders. Due process rights can involve such issues as the right to a fair hearing before being removed from school or public housing or the right to receive timely and specific notice (Handler, 1979, p. 36). Substantive rights can inure or accrue to everyone (free speech), to those in a category (the right to Medicare benefits if criteria are met), or to a particular group (e.g., due to past discrimination). Some are remedial; nursing home residents now can enjoy the same things as the general public, such as the right to open their own mail (Horn & Griesel, 1977). Some are meant to prevent abuse; families of residents are lobbying to be allowed to install "grannycams" (video cameras) in their loved ones' rooms. Basic human rights such as those promoted by the United Nations include freedom from arbitrary government restrictions and the right to food. Immigrants lacking citizenship rights have humanitarian appeals made on their behalf. To this, our profession would add client rights such as self-determination (Tower, 1994) and participation (O'Donnell, 1993).

Rights may be won at a societal level on behalf of a *class*, such as Temporary Assistance to Needy Families recipients, but "can be enjoyed only on an individual level," where advocates can help implement them (Grosser, 1976, p. 276). Social work practitioners aid *individuals* by informing them of their rights and monitoring to see whether those rights are respected in the course of receiving services. Simon (1994) warns that it "would be a grave error to assume, without inquiring, that one's client has good knowledge of his or her rights as a citizen and as a consumer of services," since few of us know our own "rights and entitlements" (p. 20). Those who seek process rights, such as adequate representation at trial, also care about ultimate outcomes, such as the disproportionate number of African Americans on death row.

PUBLIC INTEREST ADVOCACY

The second mode of change involves societal responsibility and a determination to "get a place at the table," to participate in decisions. Citizen civic action and democratic policymaking are associated with public interest advocacy. This approach uses

- social/legal reform to promote pluralism and entrée to government by strengthening outsider groups (Handler, 1978, p. 4),

- access and investigative methods to force accountability in the private and public sectors (Powers, 1977), and

- community education to develop life skills and civic skills in the populace (Boyte, 1980; Isaac, 1992; Mondros & Wilson, 1994).

While the rights approach often focuses on government wrongs and remedies, the public interest approach challenges corporate abuse as well. A Harris poll conducted for *Business Week*, before the Enron, Worldcom and Anderson corporation scandals, revealed that 73% of the public considered the pay packages of chief executives to be excessive, 74% thought business had too much power over them, and only 47% believed that what is good for big business is good for most Americans (Bernstein, 2000). This advocacy—for classes of citizens who can rarely defend their own interests—relies on citizen evaluation, expertise, awareness of pressure points, freedom of information statutes, and media.[1]

Giving voice to the voiceless entails representation of *general* and *dispersed*, often disorganized, *interests* (in contrast to concentrated special interests) and of *underrepresented views*. Those with an interest in keeping public schools strong are dispersed, compared with parents of children in private schools who argue collectively for vouchers. Middle-class taxpayers seeking tax relief are dispersed, in contrast to the organized business community that secures tax loopholes. Low-income people, who have particular interests but lack resources to push claims on their own behalf, are counted among the underrepresented. Promoting pro bono (for the public good) work and legal access for indigents is thus important, along with test-case law reform. Public interest advocacy tries to "strengthen the position of weak, poorly organized, or unarticulated interests in society" (Handler, 1978, p. 4).

Unlike the rights approach, in which an individual may be part of an *observable* protected class (such as classes based on gender, race, and so on), many who benefit from public advocacy are *indistinguishable* (such as renters). These might be actual or potential consumers. For example, a critique regarding what community mental health centers might have been was once written on behalf of those who *potentially* could have benefited from innovative services and meaningful community involvement. It has been said that an advocate of this type is "the champion we never knew we needed against an enemy we never suspected was there" (Frost, 1994, quoting *Life* magazine). Thus, efforts to protect the environment epitomize public interest advocacy (Rogge, 1993). Policy reform beneficiaries are numerous but faceless (Powers, 1984).

Lack of knowledge disadvantages people. Respected journalist Paul Williams (1978) says,

"Given the complexities of life today, finding out how things work is a full-time job" (p. 9). In this change mode, investigative reporters, public interest lawyers, librarians, and social workers can join to assist citizens who feel that everything is out of their control due to little-understood forces or legalities (Lynch & Mitchell, 1995). Through exposé and explanation, we can show "how to deal with these forces . . . and how power is exercised" (Williams, 1978, p. 5). Public interest advocacy says to social work: "We have to be public citizens and wherever there is a need we must work to meet it" (Mikulski, 1982, p. 18). The need, for instance, may be protection from predatory lending rather than traditional social services.

TRANSFORMATION

Structural change is more fundamental in terms of ends and more concerned with vision than the first two change modalities (Ackerman & Alstott, 1999; Fabricant & Burghardt, 1992; Wagner, 1990). It is supported by sundry groups, including faith-oriented networks that work to change the structural causes of poverty and injustice (Nepstad, 1997). Those who would transform themselves and their environment must be able to perceive how society really is and could be (Henley, 1999). There must be what some feminists colloquially call a "click" experience, as well as a willingness to color outside the lines. A well-known example of the latter occurred when Youth Commissioner Jerome Miller, D.S.W., shut down Massachusetts's isolated, custodial-oriented institutions for delinquents to force communities to develop local alternatives. Transformation is proceeded by visions of a different world, a world with fewer cars or one without rape or one with abundant health care in every nation in Africa.

Transformative change results in profound alteration or revitalization of society, although overthrow of an existing government or economy is not required. For example, think of the rise of desperately poor indigenous people in Chiapas. Their leader is Subcomandante Marcos, a former social worker. After a fierce 7-year struggle, he and others in the Zapatista Army of National Liberation were invited to negotiate with the new president of Mexico about the rights and future of Indian Mexicans. Alinsky (1972) says, "History is a relay of revolutions; the torch of idealism is carried by the revolutionary group until this group becomes an establishment, and then quietly the torch is put down to wait until a new revolutionary group picks it up for the next leg" (p. 22). Such change in social welfare spotlights contesting ideologies of service and justice (L. V. Davis, Hagen, & Early, 1994; A. Lawson & Rhode, 1993; Van Soest, 1994).

There are numerous examples, such as consciousness raising (Wood & Middleman, 1991), of how those on the service front lines can play a role. Hyde (1994) believes clinical and social action approaches can be blended since the "caseworker is in an ideal position to help a client begin to consider new life goals. As part of that exploration, the possibility of participation in a macro change effort should be included" (p. 61). Walz and Groze (1991) call for a new breed of *clinical activists* who might also serve as advocacy researchers; such clinicians would gather data, analyze connections between individual situations and social forces, and measure their success through "multiples" who had been helped (p. 503). Moreau (1990) singles out "unmasking power relations" (p. 56) as pertinent to direct practice, that is, being open with clients about power relationships (Hartman, 1993; Sherman & Wenocur, 1983). The worker will promote individual awareness and a belief in human agency or instrumentality. Workers and clients, as "co-investigators," can explore reality, critical thinking, and liberating action (Freire, 1971, p. 97). This Freire style of dialogue involves "reducing unnecessary social distance between worker and client . . . sharing information and demystifying techniques and skills used to

help," according to Moreau; it means that clients can see their files and that no "case conferences concerning them are held without their presence" (Moreau, 1990, pp. 56–57). Many believe that numerous individual transformations contribute to a collective metamorphosis.

PRACTICE IMPLICATIONS

At the macrolevel, social justice often results when all three modes of change are combined. Think of the many change modes being utilized to overcome homophobia. Social workers take social change from an ideological to a programmatic level (Lord & Kennedy, 1992). At the microlevel, the practitioner's orientation toward change will influence interactions with clients. Box 13.2 presents a simplified example of how social workers might respond to a question from a service user in accordance with all three philosophies of change.

ADVOCACY SPECTRUM: SPANNING PEOPLE AND POLICY

Along the spectrum

Advocacy aims to bring about change in order to benefit people in many circumstances. Advocacy work ranges from helping oneself or another individual to helping a group or class of

---

BOX 13.2	OPTIONAL RESPONSES

Client: Why aren't benefits higher? Our income is way below the poverty level.

Conventional responses:

It'd be nice if they were higher. Can we make a list of your expenses to see if I might have any suggestions to help you make ends meet with the check you receive?

I wish I could get you more money, but we have to work with what we've got—given the cutbacks and today's politics.
(Goal: to avoid being personally blamed, and to express empathy)

Rights-oriented response:

Perhaps you aren't receiving all you are entitled to. Want me to review your finances with you? Maybe we can appeal.
(Goal: to secure rights collaboratively)

Public interest advocacy response:

A coalition is trying to influence the governor to supplement the amount the feds provide. Do you want some information about this fight to raise benefits?
(Goal: to involve the client, increase civic skills, and secure the client as a witness or letter writer)

Transformation or critical consciousness responses:

What do *you* think the reason is?
If a family with more money traded places with yours for a week, what would they learn?
Does it ever make you angry?
Who, in your opinion, decides who gets government benefits?
(Goal: to start a dialogue and raise consciousness about income and power distribution, sociopolitical and economic forces)

people change an institution in very basic ways. It can be carried out *directly* with a client or *indirectly* on behalf of a client or group or for the public good. One advocate can operate at different points along the advocacy spectrum, or problems can be addressed simultaneously by people working in different areas of the same field.

As professionals, we have no reason to limit our intervention to the domain where we receive it. "The way the problem is defined is of major importance in determining what type of advocacy, if any, is to be attempted and what the target system will be," says Grosser (1976, p. 270). If a young child playing with a cigarette lighter starts a fire that destroys a house and kills his brother, this situation is likely to be received in the individual sphere, where a social worker might help the family by advocating for material help. Some service agencies might also treat the death as a family counseling matter. Yet, the fire is not simply an individual matter. Poorly designed lighters caused enough fires and deaths that federal regulations had to be written to require childproof lighters. In a service only or family therapy intervention, a "bad" child is left with guilt; whereas, in moving to political intervention, this "normal, curious" child provides evidence of the need for product redesign, regulation, and enforcement.

Since the level of intervention influences the methods and skills of intervention (individual to institutional), the spectrum of advocacy possibilities combines level and modality variables. The different points on the spectrum are as follows:

1. *Self-advocacy:* A practitioner who wants to start a client group must convince the boss of the project's worth.

2. *Individual advocacy:* A practitioner helps a client take steps to collect unpaid child support.

3. *Group advocacy:* A practitioner speaks on behalf of clients at a hearing on monitoring home health aides (or personal care attendants).

4. *Community advocacy:* A practitioner helps neighbors get the police commissioner to introduce a new community policing program.

5. *Political or policy advocacy:* A practitioner is asked to serve on a panel that is recommending human service reforms at a hearing.

6. *Advocacy for systems change:* A practitioner convinces a school system to commit resources to cut the dropout rate in half.

The actions taken usually will be determined by the involved organizations' standard mode of operation (although advocates sometimes get organizations to change standard practices), by the worker's skills, and by strategic decisions concerning the most effective and efficient interventions.

Advocates may need to consider multiple strategies for addressing an individual or social problem. To return to our early example of the crowded schools, we can think of *many types of advocacy with which to address the problem*. The parents could advocate for themselves as taxpayers on behalf of their children. A social worker could write a letter to the board of education or lobby an influential alumnus to call for improvements. A worker could take the concerns of parents from several schools to the media and help the parents conduct interviews. A worker could organize a campaign to get local firms to forego their annual holiday parties one year in order to buy textbooks, or could organize parents and neighborhood churches to boycott school until demands for improvement are met. A worker could drive a group of parents to meet with their legislator regarding equity in education. A worker could build a coalition to overturn property tax–based school funding.

With an ongoing and complex issue, it is common—though not always necessary—to begin with individual advocacy and progress to institutional change. Consider an addictions worker who counsels individuals and then becomes involved with Mothers Against Drunk Driving (MADD). Initially, the worker helps support the members' personal feelings and provides community education, and later engages in joint efforts with the organization to secure tough yet humane sentencing. This advocacy finally leads the worker to oppose the advertising of alcohol. Activities along the spectrum can be conducted consecutively or simultaneously. *Parts of the spectrum interrelate and the process, even for a single advocate, is dynamic.* These examples presuppose that the worker is comfortable considering an advocacy approach on any scale and supports the advocacy endeavors of others.

LEVELS AND FORMS OF ADVOCACY

Self-Advocacy

As social workers, we must learn to advocate on our own behalf as well as for our clients (Braverman, 1986). Much of the advocacy exercised on behalf of clients and oppressed groups, however, is undertaken by clients and group members who decide to make changes in their lives or to demand redress (Miller, 1986, p. 118; Murase, 1992; Pantoja, 2002).

Maggie Kuhn's story exemplifies this process. Until recently, men retired at age 65 with gold watches; some women, including Kuhn, were given sewing machines. Today, forced or mandatory retirement is usually illegal, but in 1970, Kuhn (1991)had no recourse:

> In the first month after I was ordered to retire, I felt dazed and suspended. I was hurt and then, as time passed, outraged. . . . Something clicked in my mind and I saw that my problem was not mine alone. Instead of sinking into despair, I did what came most naturally to me: I telephoned some friends and called a meeting. Six of us, all professional women associated with nonprofit social and religious groups, met for lunch. . . . My office at work was next to a Xerox machine, so it was easy to slip over there and whip out copies of a notice for a [large] meeting. . . . We agreed we should all band together to form a new social action organization. (pp. 130–131)

Kuhn headed the Gray Panthers for 25 years, until her death. Her story epitomizes Gutierrez's point: "Empowerment can transform stressful life events through increasing self-efficacy, developing a critical consciousness, developing skills, and involvement with similar others" (1994, pp. 204–205).

Self-advocacy in social work includes self-help and helping others to help themselves (Mackelprang & Salsgiver, 1996). Workers can provide the knowledge and encouragement that clients need to act personally and collectively on their own behalf. When citizens are on the move, we can facilitate their personal and organizational development. This can be done through *administrative* and *technical assistance*, such as clerical and volunteer help and providing meeting rooms. We help by *encouragement and acknowledgment* of the worth of the endeavor, that is, by giving it legitimacy. Another vital support is to provide *information sharing* for people concerned with the same issue. (Regarding mutual assistance and "horizontal supports," see S. M. Rose, 1990, p. 50.)

This expanding self-advocacy also occurs in low-income groups. Box 13.3 features a person who started a soup kitchen in her house and began feeding thousands of people each Thanksgiving. Her first step, however, was advocacy for her own family. We can learn from self-advocates with organizational skills. We want to be on the lookout not only for indigenous leaders, but for clients who make progress in self-advocacy in a less public way.

Challenges arise in working with clients who have circumstances that restrain their desire or ability to act (N. A. Brooks, 1991), but these can be met. For instance, a Client Support and Representation program for people coping with psychiatric problems stresses self-determination and client control. "Advocacy in this context becomes a form of personal self-assistance, based on self-identified needs, that unfolds within the context of a very supportive interpersonal relationship with an advocate" (Moxley & Freddolino, 1994, p. 96). Although clients receive knowledge, assertiveness, and problem-solving skills from advocates in the roles of "mentor,

---

BOX 13.3	THE START OF A COMMUNITY RESOURCE

I said, "There's three stores here. Let's go to each store . . . and see if they will give us some food." Everybody stood in their doorways. They laughed at me. . . . I was scared, but I said, "I'm going 'cause . . . I need food for me and my children to eat. . . ." I went to my church and asked the pastor would he loan me the big garbage can on wheels. I got up the courage. I went to this store and said, "Mister, would you please give me food you're going to throw away tonight, so we can eat it tomorrow?" He said, "What did you say?" And I repeated it. 'Cause, you know you can't run out of the store. You're not going to back out of the store, you're just going to say it again. So I said it. And he said, "Yes I will." He filled up that garbage can in his store. [After visiting the other two stores, she ended up with three garbage cans of food and a long line at her door.] And I said, "Ain't no stopping now! . . . what I'm gonna do is open up an emergency center." 'Cause I've asked God to show me how to feed me and my children first and then I will help others.

Source: Bea Gaddy, who for decades fed the inner-city poor (Powers, 1994).[2]

coach, supporter, and representative" and assistance with environmental challenges, they must take action, for example, to express a disagreement and ask for a hearing to resolve it (pp. 96-98).

An exciting example of self-advocacy is the growth of the mental health consumer movement. It was started 30 years ago, according to *U.S. News and World Report,* by groups such as Network Against Psychiatric Assault, Mad Pride, and the Insane Liberation Front. "Although it began with a marginalized collection of former mental patients demanding the closure of state hospitals, today it's a national, mainstream movement, representing the entire array of psychiatric diagnoses and challenging psychiatrists and other 'helping professionals'" (Szegedy-Maszak, 2002, p. 55). Thus, individual desires for self-determination led to a collective effort. Today, some formerly homeless, brain-disordered people are employed by or in charge of mental health associations. For instance, self-advocate Joseph Rogers, who used to protest at American Psychiatric Association meetings, now manages a $12.1 million agency budget to help his peers (Szegedy-Maszak, p. 55). Haitian people have become self-advocates in Florida as they fight an immigration system that rewards Cubans who make it to U.S. shores with citizenship and political power but immediately deports Haitians who boat, swim, and crawl ashore seeking refuge.

Individual Advocacy

Those knowledgeable about dealing with the system, whether BSWs or community workers, often guide beneficiaries through housing assistance and other governmental mazes. The situation may get complicated before an attorney or an MSW gets involved. Even lay advocates—a family friend or someone from church—sometimes help with the initial steps. This may not matter, though, since many of those requiring advocacy (e.g., low-power groups, the unsophisticated or institutionalized) need a tenacious advocate more than a highly credentialed one (Shapiro, 1993).

For a social worker, starting an advocacy relationship is not too different from starting a therapeutic relationship. The presenting problem itself may call for advocacy, or we may engage in conventional direct service activities out of which a need for advocacy arises. The client directs us as much as possible. In turn, we try to demystify aspects of society about which we are knowledgeable.

Advocacy as an Influence Process Involving Action

Individual and family-level advocacy often involves attempting to influence organizational or institutional decisions or policies on behalf of a third party. Once we agree to serve as advocates, we cannot countenance or condone having our clients demeaned, whether or not they are in our presence. While this principle seems basic, it is not easy to follow because so many clients interact with an array of officials who make a practice of belittling them or treating them as objects.

Working With Instead of For

In cases where clients are jailed or ill and unable to act for themselves, such as the one illustrated by Box 13.4, the advocate honors their expressed wishes and acts on their behalf. Even people who are healthy and at liberty are not always able to advocate for themselves or to par-

BOX 13.4	GET ME OUT OF HERE!

A mother declared her teenage daughter incorrigible and in need of protection by juvenile services. Since the emergency shelter was full, Theresa was placed at a holding facility in a room where unfortunate youngsters stayed until foster homes were available. The matron soon had Theresa babysitting for 10 young children housed at the facility. When the teenager rebelled after a week and refused to babysit, she was locked up behind bars. Her worker was stunned when she came to visit, for there had been no hearing, nor had she or Theresa's family been contacted. The worker was so indignant that she told her supervisor she wanted to write a letter to the judge in charge of Theresa's case. The supervisor expressed doubt that anything would be done but agreed to humor his young supervisee. The worker wrote a letter to the judge requesting Theresa's release. The teenager was released from her cell the day the judge received it.

ticipate jointly. In most cases, though, advocates must guard against taking a "benefactor" or "liberator" role (Simon, 1994, p. 7). We want to create situations in which individuals can develop into their own heroes rather than being dependent on a human service worker. Self-advocacy is preferred.

Advocacy for an individual arises naturally out of a trusting relationship. A request may seem trivial, yet the stakes can be high; minor incidents can turn into violent episodes. For instance, a 17-year-old Latino boy has trouble in school and needs someone to believe him. Since his mother is afraid to call the school and demand to know what was happening, the boy turns to a youth worker, who accompanies him to a meeting with the head of the school. In our earlier example, although the advocate gets her client out of jail, the system is not magically reformed. Neither is this school. Nevertheless, one benefit of advocacy is that individuals, families, or groups who are usually undervalued experience being supported and feeling worthy of attention.

Box 13.5 illustrates this surrogate strength. A woman of modest means tries to find out what has happened to her brother-in-law's welfare check. Mentally ill, Barney was hospitalized for 13 years before coming to live with June and her husband. A neighbor relates the incident. Were the narrator to continue in this role or go to the office without June, he could obtain a signed form authorizing him to be her representative. Still, even this informal partnership with June highlights three goals of individual advocacy: influence the decision of the power person, support the individual, and teach—leading to self-advocacy.

Group Advocacy

Group advocacy often arises with a particular reform and may not be part of an ongoing community organization and development process or a social movement. A group can clearly advocate for itself and "regain a sense of control" (Toseland, 1990, p. 167). For instance, parents of children who are both physically and mentally challenged and thus cannot use existing group homes might band together to get facilities modified or built to meet their children's needs. They could make demands of an individual worker or of a county or state agency. In our classification scheme, this would be an instance of self-advocacy. However, when the advocate is not a member of a particular victimized group (such as Latino high school students)—even if the advocate shares characteristics with the larger group (e.g., is Latino himself)—and is acting on the group's behalf, we consider this a case of group advocacy.

Jaime Escalante, a teacher-advocate, is one well-known example; his story was told in the film *Stand and Deliver* (Menendez & Musca, 1988). An East Los Angeles math instructor, Escalante was finally able to overcome low expectations in his high school to prove that students who resided in low-income neighborhoods could learn calculus. From the school system he secured the support his class needed to pass national calculus achievement examinations. When the students performed much better than expected of Chicanos, Escalante had to defend them against a charge of cheating. In brief, internal advocacy (in the school) and external advocacy (in the community) were required to provide students with the same higher education

---

BOX 13.5   AN ADVOCATE BY REQUEST

Barney's welfare check failed to arrive; and when June called to find out why, a social worker told her Barney was no longer eligible. . . . After June received the same response on two more calls to the social services bureau, I suggested she go down to the welfare agency herself and volunteered to go with her. . . . [W]e finally got to see a social worker, who informed us that since Barney Moseby's file was missing, the social services department had assumed he was no longer eligible for public assistance. When we explained that his situation was the same as before, the worker apologetically agreed to have him reinstated, admitting that it was not the first time a file had been lost. June was convinced that had I not been along, dressed in my respectable gray suit and carrying an empty brief case, nothing would have happened. "It was because somebody was there who looked like somebody, that's why they treated us like people," she said. "If you come in looking stupid like you don't know anything, then they don't pay you no mind." The next month Barney's check came on time.

Source: Howell, pp. 180-181

opportunities afforded to students living in wealthier areas.

In discovering the group nature of a problem, we may start with individuals and end up advocating for a group. A social worker might be troubled that classmates are teasing a boy in speech therapy about his stuttering and might talk to his teacher. This same concern, writ large, might lead that advocate to write to a television show that pokes fun at a character who stutters. A worker who has a mentally ill client in jail, as a result not of a crime but of his symptoms, should tend to that person's needs but can also note other inmates who are clearly ill. The worker can then try to find out what is happening and how to aid such prisoners. Sometimes we work on behalf of people who are scattered and are never seen by each other or the worker. This can happen because workers regularly move beyond an individual's particular plight (Wood & Middleman, 1989, p. 22). In the example in Box 13.6, the social worker is moving from individual to political advocacy with the purpose of helping an invisible group; her primary role remains direct service.

Part of an advocate's role is to ensure that maximum benefits are delivered to the greatest number of clients—not at the expense of the original client's position but in furtherance of it. Bringing together many persons who have been harmed in the same way or who seek the same remedy to a common problem helps define the parameters of a problem. Having more people involved increases the availability of information and provides documentation of a pattern of abuse. Evidence that 10 apartment building tenants are without heat and hot water is more credible than a similar complaint on behalf of one resident.

The group may already exist, such as a tenant's organization, or may form after the advocate starts with one individual and finds others.

In either case, the advocate must get to know each member of the group, understand the group dynamics as the process unfolds, and be accountable to the group, which is equally true in the next situation. Practitioners often work with members of a group who cannot communicate their concerns easily. Therefore, the advocate has to work through ethical issues and authority issues in this regard. When representing inarticulate, perhaps bedridden or confined clients, all the various subinterests within the group must be considered; otherwise, only members who are present and articulate will prevail. In addition, interpersonal conflicts and positive allegiances will also affect group cohesion and the ultimate agenda for action. When members want to organize for self-government or to fight discrimination or hardship, the advocate must inform the group of potential risks but should follow the group's lead.

Community Advocacy and Action

Community advocacy has many facets. For instance, Ezell (2001) sees community *education* as the best strategy to challenge the status quo and to "alter attitudes and beliefs that support particular policies and practices" (p. 121). Here, though, we discuss the skill of representation and the make-it-happen dimension of community advocacy.

JANE ADDAMS AS ROLE MODEL

Community advocacy often arises from situations that dishearten, disadvantage, aggravate, or harm a segment of a community. A classic social work example of advocacy started in 1889 on behalf of a neighborhood in West Side Chicago (see Box 13.7). Jane Addams settled into a tenement area to "reduce the distance between the social classes" (Brieland, 1990, p. 134). To-

---

BOX 13.6	CONCERN ABOUT A SET OF PERSONS AT RISK

Consuella conducts home visits to frail elderly people living alone. Several women were burned recently in cooking accidents because their bathrobe sleeves caught fire. She attempts to locate safer nightwear for them, but there is nothing on the market for adults. Curious, she explores the issue of manufacturers' obligations regarding flammable fabrics and is directed to a federal agency. Personnel there are interested in Consuella's local cases, and she, in turn, learns more about regulations. Although she simply wanted to prevent more injury, in the process of repeating her story she engaged in advocacy and navigated corporate and governmental systems. She used her direct-service knowledge to help similarly situated individuals.

| BOX 13.7 | ALLEY CONDITIONS IMPROVED BY ADVOCACY |

We began a systematic investigation of the city system of garbage collection . . . and its possible connection with the death rate in the various wards of the city. . . . Twelve [Woman's Club members] undertook in connection with the residents, to carefully investigate the condition of the alleys. During August and September the substantiated reports of violations of the law sent in from Hull-House to the health department were one thousand and thirty-seven. . . . In sheer desperation, the following spring when the city contracts were awarded for the removal of garbage, with the backing of two well-known business men, I put in a bid for the garbage removal of the nineteenth ward. My paper was thrown out on a technicality but the incident induced the mayor to appoint me the garbage inspector of the ward. . . . Perhaps our greatest achievement was the discovery of a pavement eighteen inches under the surface of a narrow street [after the removal of eight inches of garbage]. . . .

Many of the foreign-born women of the ward were much shocked by this abrupt departure into the ways of men, and it took a great deal of explanation to convey the idea even remotely that if it were a womanly task to go about in tenement houses in order to nurse the sick, it might be quite as womanly to go through the same district in order to prevent the breeding of so-called "filth diseases." . . .

The careful inspection, combined with other causes, brought about a great improvement in the cleanliness and comfort of the neighborhood and one happy day, when the death rate of our ward was found to have dropped from third to seventh in the list of city-wards and was so reported to our Woman's Club, the applause which followed recorded the genuine sense of participation in the result, and a public spirit which had "made good."

Source: Addams (1910) pp. 200-205

gether, she and her neighbors changed conditions and social policies by tackling a wide array of tasks (S. J. Rose, 1999). To initiate reform, they conducted investigations of "factory conditions, housing conditions, truancy, sanitation, typhoid fever, tuberculosis, cocaine distribution" (Brieland, 1990, p. 136; Spain, 2001). They represented their community before decision makers.

DEFINITIONS AND ROLES

Residents can advocate on their own, or nonresidential advocates can advocate for the community. Certainly, social workers have an obligation to raise a professional voice on behalf of the unorganized, subgroups, and pressing issues unique to a community. Collective advocacy is covered in other chapters. Our emphasis here is on what an individual can do to advocate for and with residents of a given community. Ezell (2001) suggests that this may involve undertaking an advocacy needs assessment and delineating the decision system (see Chapter 8). Take the case of LaPlata, Maryland, which had 8 minutes' warning before a powerful tornado hit. Despite four previous tornadoes, the town had no sirens or other early warning system to alert residents. Moreover, no money had materialized to put special weather radios in schools, even though

13 children had been killed in a schoolhouse in a tornado some decades earlier. In a communitywide situation, while many focus on their private interests, the advocate focuses on prevention and other public interest concerns.

This section depicts rural and urban community advocacy activities (Rankin, 2000). Consider Brookburg (a composite of three actual towns), a country town of 500 in a county of 12,000 residents. While communitywide advocacy may be needed anywhere, what could be accomplished in a village with a post office; a cemetery; one gas station; three parks; one combination fire, police, and government hall; two churches; and two restaurants? Well, first, the advocate might organize events that *enhance or sustain the quality of the community*. Even small towns surrounded by farms or ranches have street festivals or fairs that draw people from neighboring areas. Money raised can pay for street lights and upkeep of parks. Yearly events such as a Halloween parade may draw in rural families. Second, advocacy often involves efforts to *maintain the status quo of a community*. Hence, in some areas, there is advocacy for zoning ordinances, restrictions on development or for establishing a bypass around the town to keep traffic from destroying the quality of life. If the Brookburg post office were under threat of relocation, an advocate could try to keep a place where people may see each other and connect. If the Brookburg cemetery were endangered by development, an advocate would explore how to protect the place (Perlman, 2000).

Third, advocates may demand *public access to resources*. The village of Brookburg is 10 miles from grocery stores and medical clinics and 50 miles from the nearest city. Some neighborly volunteer projects can help, but transportation needs might require a service plan and appeals to the state government (Warner-Smith & Brown, 2002). Fourth, advocates want *local officials to be accountable*. Let's say residents are increasingly afraid because officials have ignored several unusual incidents. After the beautification association put up new welcome signs, someone destroyed the signs but was never caught. A number of mutilated animals have been found in empty lots and the parks. Yet, when townspeople call Brookburg's part-time officials, they feel as if they are starting from scratch each time—that no cumulative record is being kept. In this case, the advocate could document the incidents, go to see officials, establish a reward fund for information, call a town meeting, and consider whether to ask for assistance from outside Brookburg. Fifth, advocates may *initiate social inclusion campaigns* that provide citizens with justice and dignity.

Urban advocates work on these same five community advocacy concerns and, in the tradition of Jane Addams, on housing and neighborhood improvement, as they holistically address needs of low-income persons. (Some of these advocates work for today's settlement houses, under the umbrella of the United Neighborhood Center Association.) Successful nonprofit activities are one avenue for change. Advocates pull together citizens to accomplish something they have long desired but could not convince officialdom to do. For example, community advocates have used the Community Reinvestment Act to save neighborhoods that were dying because banks would not loan money to those hoping to buy houses there. In fact, advocates are responsible for creating that law and monitoring its enforcement, until today thousands of moderate- and low-income families have obtained reasonably priced mortgages.

Frontline public-sector advocates can be another force for community change. Of course, only practitioners who truly do their jobs and are fearless about repercussions are embraced by citizens as their advocates—as people who place the community before governmental and business interests. Building inspector Jim Delgado, for example, sees himself as having a warrior spirit. He has become the "go-to" man, aggressively using building and zoning codes as part of a community policing program to get government to work in poor people's interest. One of 10 children of Puerto Rican immigrants, Delgado experienced dreadful housing firsthand and has a personal as well as a political commitment to cutting through bureaucratic roadblocks. He earns $51,000 annually but has spent as much as $3,000 per year out of his own pocket on expenses such as photography and for items such as cell phones that help enforcement but are not in the department budget (Perl, 1999, pp. 26-27). Such determination creates local heroes.

Even municipal legislators (S. J. Rose, 1999) and managers can serve as community advocates so long as they have "an absolute impatience for change" (Loeb, 2000). Michael DiBerardinis, a community organizer who was appointed Philadelphia's Commissioner for the Department of Recreation, is described that way in social work literature. His background meant that he brought uncommon commitment to community development and enhanced citizen participation (Perlmutter & Cnaan, 1999). Here is another exemplar. In the 5 years after he was appointed the receiver of a troubled system, David Gilmore transformed public housing in the District of Columbia by being accountable to tenants. "Besides a deep commitment to poor people and a fierce desire for reform, he brought to Washington the experience of a lifetime spent in the field of public housing, specializing in dramatic turnarounds" (Loeb, 2000, p. 4). Among other things, Gilmore convinced gang members to become staff members. While community advocacy can achieve intangible benefits, credibility usually comes from discernible gains such as the vacancy rate of public housing units going from 17% down to 2%. Bottom-line results that improve depleted lives are the ones that count.

RELEVANCE TO DIRECT PRACTICE

Practitioners can use their skills to link people and assist them in making connections through friendships and shared tasks. They can similarly encourage participation in the process when a need arises to engage in community intervention. Mondros and Wilson (1994) make explicit the tie between organizing techniques and direct practice tasks, stating that a "clinician who works with a group of homeless mothers used these techniques to help them organize for repairs and police protection in a park where they frequently took their children. She saw this work as a natural extension of her clinical work with her group" (p. xvii). Burghardt (1982) has illustrated how intertwined the skills are in clinical and macropractice. Bringing various parties together for a case conference is similar to bringing block leaders together for an issue strategy session. Like a counseling relationship, a community project has a beginning, a middle, and an end.

Practitioners can bring people together in numerous ways—block parties, day camps, health fairs, holiday parties for a disadvantaged group, recycling, and single-issue support groups. Participants in community education/support group meetings (with topics such as "incontinence" or "giving up the secret of adult children with AIDS") will benefit from the privacy of a living-room setting. Convenience and privacy for participants are obviously reasons to meet in a home, but practitioners can also learn something new—for example, about the conditions that families must contend with in their home environment and how these conditions can be modified. This same home meeting format can be used in other settings, such as shelters, union halls, women's circles, social agency lunchrooms, and with many issues.

Advocacy that happens at the community level can have the beneficial effect of bringing different groups together around common values. This happened in Washington, D.C., when Gallaudet students successfully advocated against appointment of yet another hearing president for the university. They wanted a leader who shared their personal experience. In the United States, we like to see people stand up for themselves. Different income and ethnic groups bonded, savoring the victory and resulting pride of the Deaf community. We should encourage and celebrate such linkage.

Political and Policy Advocacy

DEFINITIONS AND ROLES
The public policy or political advocate sounds a ringing call for a system change and reiterates it in the face of predictable opposition. Paul Wellstone, the late U.S. Senator from Minnesota who championed many social work issues, illustrates this point. He voted his principles about poverty or peace and was willing to be a lone dissenter even if the vote was 99 to 1. Prairie populist Wellstone started out as a tireless, tenacious advocate for rural residents, ordinary people, and "little fellers" and fought for causes as a political science professor. Just before he died in a plane crash in 2002, Wellstone risked his re-

election to vote against a resolution authorizing force against Iraq. In this way, Wellstone was like Jeanette Rankin (1880–1973) of Montana, the first woman elected to the U.S. Congress, who voted against entry into both world wars. "Wellstone's passion for underdogs and life's most helpless people was shaped by visits to his brother in a mental hospital. . . . He became one of the Senate's leading advocates for expanding federal health-care benefits for mental problems and chemical dependency" (Smith & Lopez, 2002).

At any level of government, someone who seeks change through electoral and political party processes is a *political advocate*. For instance, numerous advocates have been active in the campaigns of, among others, Representative John Lewis of Georgia, Senator Barbara Mikulski of Maryland, and Senator Ron Wyden of Oregon, because the advocates had worked with them on issues before the elected official ran for office. Most policy and political advocates, however, are not elected officials but citizen advocates. Increasingly, such advocates not only run field operations for campaigns but also lobby and create databases that can produce vital information at key moments. Salcido and Manalo (2002) involved social work students in state electoral campaigns in California through "a voter registration drive, an absentee ballot drive, a student rally/forum, and a 'get-out-the-vote' drive" (p. 55). In addition, initiative campaigns and campaigns for third-party candidates afford great opportunities to gain political advocacy experience.

At any level of government, someone who designs, enacts, defeats, or changes ordinances, acts, regulations, and other policies is a *policy advocate*. Policy advocacy may be undertaken by an individual such as Michigan nursing home reformer Cathie Wallace of ACTION who made many long drives to her state capitol to meet, in one legislative session, with 124 (of 148) legislators. It can also be undertaken by a group such as United Senior Action, which pushed successfully for more advocate representation on the Indiana licensing board and convinced the attorney general to file actions against 92 nursing home administrators. Those who excel at policy formulation, legislative drafting, policy briefs and educating the population in key districts have been called policy "entrepreneurs" (Mintrom & Vergari, 1996; Sundet & Kelly, 2002). In fact, advocates have been so effective at getting members or constituents to send e-mails (117 million e-mails in 2001) that, currently, congressional representatives seldom read such messages (Congress Online Project, 2002, press release, para 3). Policy advocates can prevail despite unfavorable political odds. For example, under a Republican administration, policy advocates were successful in convincing Congress to restore funding to community medical centers. Social work advocates can still draw on idealism and emotionalism in decision makers. Policy successes are common; in fact, research on the congressional agenda reveals that liberalism is thriving there, if not at the ballot box (Berry, 1999).

These policy advocacy and political advocacy roles can overlap and can involve pressure tactics, as in the case of a social work professor, students, and other advocates who forced a governor to reverse an action he had taken that harmed people with disabilities (Soifer & Singer, 1999). The Irish say, "You can accomplish more with a kind word and a shillelagh, than you can with just a kind word." Policy and political advocates influence decision makers through their constituents and persuasion tactics (e.g., advocacy advertising, field trips to see conditions), knowing that politicians and civil servants may be as concerned with their personal images as with issues.

Political/policy advocacy in the legislative, regulatory, administrative, and judicial arenas to achieve social and political welfare can take many forms. For instance, as noted in Box 13.6, Consuella's search led her to a federal regulatory agency. Like Consuella, direct service practitioners sometimes drift into political action; infrequently, they enter electoral politics. We often represent our agencies in coalitions and may be asked to bring a busload of supporters to a rally in the state capital. We may also be asked to find individuals or families in a certain category who are willing to appear at governmental hearings, as both the media and decision makers often seek an individual, family, or situation that epitomizes the problem or the solution (Ross, 1993). Social workers work in many governmental jobs that involve full-time advocacy, including county commissions, state staff positions, or even as legislative directors in the U.S. Senate. Some participate in media and political campaigns that involve field organizing.[3] Social workers can enter the policymaking process part-time and succeed (Avner, 2002; Dear & Patti, 1981; Soifer, 1998). Richan (1996) and Brueggemann (2002, Chapter 13) provide guidance for beginners in social policy advocacy.

LEGISLATIVE ADVOCACY

Legislative advocacy usually involves proposing or stopping a particular piece of legislation (Pertschuk, 1986). The lobbying part of that activity means asking decision makers to help in the effort or to make some commitment, usually in exchange for votes or other support. "Multifaceted activity is needed to pass a law that might rectify a political ill," says McFarland (1984, p. 108) about Common Cause. This citizen organization uses publicity (including publicity on legislators' positions), research, litigation, campaigns for public commitments, and a field organization that helps generate mail, arrange meetings between members and elected officials, and network with friends of elected officials (1984, Chapter 6). Lappé and Du Bois (1994) remind us that it is "one thing to get policy passed and quite another to see it happen" (p. 181). In their view, citizen lobbying means "citizens learning how to influence decision making and hold others accountable" (p. 179). Despite many complexities in the political process, there are victories like the one described in Box 13.8. For additional examples and terminology, see Haynes and Mickelson (2002) and web sites: *www.moveon.org* and *www.fcnl.org*.

BOX 13.8	POLICY CHANGES THROUGH POLITICAL ADVOCACY

Today, lobbying efforts may involve e-mails, faxes, manufactured letters, and postcards (Schneider & Lester, 2001). As the *Congressional Quarterly Weekly* points out, the Internet "enables people with limited physical mobility to mount a fast, agile lobbying campaign." A few years ago, such advocates helped expand health care for disabled workers. They contributed to a successful lobbying effort, in part, by utilizing e-mail to mobilize their allies. The advocates had been blocked from adding their health plan to a bill. Yet, Majority Leader Trent Lott slipped a provision to extend duck hunting season in Mississippi into that same bill. Livid, the advocates started a ducks versus disability protest and soon Republican lawmakers were flooded with faxes and telephone messages. "Over and over, people quacked into the receiver in a coordinated chorus of duck calls" (Kirchhoff, 1999, p. 2762).

BUILDING CREDIBILITY

We cannot assume credibility because we are professionals, but our expertise is welcomed. For instance, one day "DeAnn" was on the telephone with a colleague critiquing a draft of a proposed state bill on end-of-life directives. By the next day, she had been invited to join a lobbying coalition that was ultimately successful in re-drafting the bill.

Local political activists stress that familiarity breeds respect. One social worker described his early activist days this way: "I recall going down to the election board trying to get some voter information and being treated [like] 'who do you think you are?'" He gained experience in political work, making presentations at hearings and sharing information with elected officials. He found that decision makers want help in thinking things through: "You can come in and sound off . . . but if you never get beyond that, then people tune you out. It's the business of bringing information to the people who make decisions. . . . I can recall while I was there in Omaha, going into City Council sessions, not even asking to be on the agenda and having the president look up and say, Mr. Evans, do you have anything you want to say on this? By that time I had been there enough and spoken enough, he felt I probably had something to say."[4]

USING CLIENTS AS WITNESSES

Of all the actors in the political arena, it is the direct service practitioner who is most likely to provide examples of suffering that has been or will be caused by cutbacks or policy decisions or to find examples of overcoming or successfully "coping with barriers" (Chapin, 1995, p. 511). Finding clear-cut examples quickly can be surprisingly hard to do. Few of us can describe our personal situations in a concise and intriguing manner, and those we serve are no exception. Many might be nontelegenic or unconvincing at hearings. Being able to identify an appropriate *problem exemplar* and to prepare him or her to address the media or a decision-making body is a vital task for caseworkers and frontline practitioners. Advocates at the national and state levels make many calls to local offices to obtain anecdotes that make the news, appear in speeches, and humanize funding appeals. If someone's privacy is protected with a pseudonym during the initial publicity, advocates must be able to prove the person exists, has the problem in question, and actually will be affected positively or negatively. Reporters check out such stories.

PROTECTING CLIENTS AND CITIZENS

It is unethical and unwise to thrust already vulnerable individuals into public view without first having their trust and permission, because they are likely to say anything under stress. We must advise clients of the risks inherent in *any* type of advocacy, including testifying; such risks could include retaliation, reduction of benefits, or the anger of family members. Social workers can also protect witnesses by accompanying them and handling the technical aspects of testifying allowing them to simply tell their stories, without intimidation or exaggeration. Both expert and human-interest testimony are often prepared for the same hearing. Witnesses should dictate or write their own statements, letting the advocate type and smooth out the final manuscript. The facts must be within the grasp of the witness for easy oral recitation.

Systems Advocacy and Change

Institutional change implies "widespread and basic alteration" despite strong resistance (Brager, 1967, p. 61). Think of the long fight to overcome tobacco interests. *Many systems affect our clients and society in general, and we want to be able to influence them.* Individual, state, and national economic investment is one example of an effective tool. For instance, socially responsible (domestic) investments can help develop grassroots, community-oriented, and self-help organizations. Their power as a source of leverage was shown in the campaign of the 1980s spearheaded by Randall Robinson to end apartheid by withholding U.S. investment from South Africa. As part of the advocacy spectrum, we have already discussed the political system. But the average American is also affected by the insurance system, the medical system, and the media as an institution (Gitlin, 1980). Failed public and private systems generate fights for institutional change.

Many challenges have been made to various societal systems, even overarching systems such as capitalism and patriarchy, and challenges continue to be made nationally and internationally (Fisher & Shragge, 2000; Goldberg, 1991). While a given community or neighborhood might be organized in a year or two, major challenges to the social order play out over decades. Many recent studies of large-scale movements employ a resource mobilization framework (McCarthy & Zald, 1987) that emphasizes social movement organizations rather than individuals. However, individual actions count, along with group and collective action. Some examples: Elizabeth Cady Stanton and Susan B. Anthony toiled to abolish slavery, restrict liquor, and obtain property, marriage, and voting rights for women; "Granny D." Haddock walked 3,200 miles at age 90 to crusade for clean money campaign reform; Mother Jones started organizing coal miners at age 47 and continued for 40 years (Gilbert, 1993; Jones, 1980). George Wiley gave up a career as a celebrated chemistry professor at age 33 to fight for the down-and-out in civil rights and welfare rights struggles (Kotz & Kotz, 1977). James Chaney, Andrew Goodman, and Michael Schwerner gave their lives in the Mississippi Freedom Summer of 1964. The first social workers, and early ones such as Harry Hopkins and Frances Perkins, were involved in many progressive battles for change, such as workers' rights, honest government, and Social Security. These leaders united others.

Most people never achieve national recognition, but they still derive benefit from participation in actions to express their values. Kansas's farmers and other ordinary citizens tried to change banking, monetary, and trade institutions 100 years ago. Writing about these populists, Goodwyn (1978) captures what is important about social movements and change endeavors to the rural or urban people who are part of them (Box 13.9). These words describe the aims of many of today's movements and embryo political parties. Today's protestors resist the latest version of a giant industrial engine. The International Monetary Fund and the World Bank, debtors and donors, have been brought to public attention. Globalization and extreme poverty have become part of our public discourse because of the insistence of advocates for systems change.

Large-scale social change endeavors often have tendrils reaching into community advocacy, political advocacy, and systems change. The civil rights and women's movements are good examples (Hahn, 1994, 114; B. Ryan, 1992). After working for years to achieve political change through suffrage and the Equal Rights Amendment (a failed constitutional amendment), women turned back to their communities and outward to larger systems, seeking other types of equality—in jobs, in education, in insurance rates, and even public sanction regarding the sharing of domestic chores. After winning important gains in the judicial and legislative areas for years, African Americans have experienced community setbacks tied to street crime and institutional setbacks tied to standardized testing. In short, progress can be undercut in insidious ways or occur in unexpected ways; both the attack and the defense interweave multiple advocacy approaches. Yet victories continue. The South has elected numerous African Americans to public office. Such progressive victories are not unique to the U.S. For instance, France has changed its political representation system, requiring females to receive half of the candidacy slots, a reform that should dramatically increase the number of female elected officials.

Relevance to Direct Practice

The interconnections between various types of advocacy are clear. Past struggles influence much about our lives today—our work, our legacy. Our professional work frequently pertains to rights and programs that were won earlier through systems reform, which indicates that there truly is *give* in the system. In response to events such as elections, we often feel under

---

BOX 13.9	THE HOPE OF CONCERTED ACTION

[Populism] was, first and most centrally, a cooperative movement that imparted a sense of self-worth to individual people and provided them with the instruments of self-education about the world they lived in. The movement gave them hope—a shared hope—that they were not impersonal victims of a gigantic industrial engine ruled by others but that they were, instead, people who could perform specific political acts of self-determination. . . . the men and women of the agrarian movement [were] encouraged and enhanced by the sheer drama and power of their massive parades, their huge summer encampments, their far-flung lecturing system. . . . Populism was, at bottom, a movement of ordinary Americans to gain control over their own lives and futures, a massive democratic effort to gain that most central component of human freedom—dignity.

Source: Goodwyn (1978), pp. 196-197

siege from those opposed to what we value. Perhaps, though, reading history, we can more appropriately say to ourselves, "Let us celebrate" because so much has been won by and for social work. If there is ever any question as to whether we have allies or as to the existence of a flourishing spectrum in action, all we need do is find a national list of advocacy groups (Walls, 1993).

CLIENT ADVOCATE AND OTHER PRACTICE ROLES

Advocacy and Action Roles

To accomplish the important work of service user advocacy, the professional's work extends from supportive personal advocacy to showdowns to help clients. Box 13.10 reminds us that client and community advocacy can transpire in ways other than heated controversy. For example, as advocates attempt to persuade powerful people whose decisions affect clients, Schneider & Lester (2001) recommend that they use these practice principles:

1. Identify issues and set goals

2. Get the facts

3. Plan strategies and tactics

4. Supply leadership

5. Get to know decision makers and their staff

6. Broaden base of support

7. Be persistent

8. Evaluate advocacy effort (Chapter 5).

This section seeks to clarify the terminology and challenges surrounding client advocacy. It discusses advocacy obligations, nuances involved, and (often overlapping) roles. What Henderson and Thomas (1987) say about neighborhood work is true as well for client advocacy: "The worker often has to handle [varied] situations within a short space of time, and he or she is therefore always working with different audiences and constituencies from varied role positions" (p. 19).

Community social caseworker, clinician, home visitor, therapist, job coach, life coach, and group worker are some of the roles in micropractice. Roles in macropractice are, if anything, even more wide-ranging—including paid roles such as community liaison, program planner, community educator, issue director, community organizer, and unpaid roles such as communitywide advisory group member. Macropractice roles may include such work as identifying, training, and utilizing indigenous grassroots leadership; developing and coordinating a program to reintegrate clients into the community following hospitalization; and fund-raising. Those who advocate as part of their work soon realize that the advocacy realm is complex and requires cognizance of the possibilities and pitfalls (Gibelman & Kraft, 1996).

Job Descriptions and Advocacy Postures

Some workers who undertake an advocacy task are hired for that purpose as client advocates, lobbyists, or change agents, while others have job descriptions that emphasize service provision or counseling. In a clinical position, however, the need or the desire for advocacy may still crop up. As one social worker commented on a computer bulletin board, while dis-

BOX 13.10	NOT A RANCOROUS ROLE

Basic tenets of effective advocacy are sensitivity, caring and a commitment to other persons who, either out of incapacity or inexperience, cannot resolve a problem without assistance from others. . . . Advocacy involves confronting opposition, but seldom should result in hostility. An effective advocate uses an honest, constructive and steadfast approach. An opponent may be intensely challenged or displeased by an advocate but ultimately should be able to recognize, and perhaps acknowledge the advocate's thoughtfulness and fairness. This is important because the objective of advocacy is to end with favorable, beneficial changes (behavioral, environmental, program or policy changes and problem solutions) which can be understood and upheld.

Source: From "Advocacy for Nursing Home Reform" (p. 28), by Elma Holder, in G. L. Maddox (Ed.), *Encyclopedia of Aging* (2nd ed.), 1995, New York: Springer Publishing Company. Copyright 1995 Springer Publishing Inc. Used with permission.

cussing a mistreated patient, "I was developing a pretty strong hankering to do some serious advocacy work here, even though it is not my job as a clinician." Hybrid jobs that combine service and advocacy, advocacy and complaint handling, advocacy and organizing, or administration and lobbying are common. As social workers, we need not always act as advocates ourselves if we can steer the person to an effective complaint handler, such as a fraud department or media outlet specializing in solving complaints.

Advocate and Ombudsperson

Definitions. The advocacy role and the ombudsperson role are frequently confused. An *advocate* pushes a point of view or states a political philosophy. An *ombudsperson*[5] often serves as a go-between, an interpreter, and a problem solver, untangling various points of view. However, an ombudsperson is not a conventional mediator or alternative dispute resolution player but rather an effective criticizer who tries to "set right" the government system that is "out of gear" (K. C. Davis, 1975, p. 286). An advocate often works outside government, while an ombudsperson frequently works as a grievance handler and red-tape cutter for government agencies. Some states, universities, and newspapers have hired ombudspersons who, although on their payrolls, work for citizens/consumers, not management. Tower (1994) argues that client-centered social service agencies should similarly "establish ombudsmen or other client assistance programs to resolve conflicts between the agency and its consumers" (p. 196).

The ombudsperson's powers are "to investigate, criticize, recommend, and publicize" (K. C. Davis, 1975, p. 286). Such ombudspersons often have license to constructively critique their employers, even publicly, although they usually function quietly, providing information, referral, and complaint resolution. Advocates vary in their license to criticize.

There is a 50-state system of paid long-term-care ombudspersons and volunteer assistants; state units are usually located in departments of aging. To ensure independence, none are employed by the institutions they monitor. As would be expected, the ombudspersons act as *intermediaries* and resolve disputes between facilities and residents. Their activities include reporting violations. They help the facilities too—for example, to get paid when a resident's finances are in disarray. Social workers and these ombudspersons are resources for each other (Netting, Huber, Paton, & Kautz, 1995, p. 355).

Others in human services, such as patient advocates in hospitals, also creatively combine the seemingly incompatible roles of ombudsperson and advocate. The important thing is to have adequate authority, since the job involves questioning professionals about their actions or inactions and ruffling feathers.

Internal and External Advocates

Definitions. Advocacy can ensue inside or outside the agency. An *internal advocate* makes changes for the client through vigilance and intervention inside the agency, using decision-making channels, where possible, and informal influence systems. Schneider and Lester (2001) believe, "Internal advocates can be very effective in carrying out their role of representing the needs of those who cannot speak out or who do not have natural advocates within a service delivery system" (p. 307). One advocate says:

> We can do things systemically to help an individual or group of clients. I've done this on the clinical and administrative levels—bringing about equity that impacts a particular client. . . . I've worked in instances where it's my own *system* that's decided to interpret a regulation or policy in a rigid manner that constricts the client's ability to have an opportunity for change or growth . . . you have to begin with your own . . . system. The success from that frequently gives us data, information, and even self-confidence to move outside of an organization.[6]

Mounting a major change effort in a system that serves as one's employer is obviously a challenge. Usually one can rely on some colleagues to help, but it may require "keeping community groups informed of agency developments that go against their community interests (Galper, 1975, p. 205).

Internal advocacy is pertinent for those who work for large city, county, or state agencies. One state child welfare administrator sees internal advocacy and working the system effectively as synonymous.

"Make the system work for you. At this level of administration, which is the macro level, you're not doing anything different in terms of skills. The same insight you needed to understand a family system, you need to understand this system. In the same way you want to make changes in that family, well, I want to make changes in this system. So I need to look at it and understand how it works, so I can make the change that I want to happen."[7] Such systems have to work for the advocate and for those being served. Otherwise, workers in a system such as foster care will soon be targets of advocacy by workers outside it (Spolar, 1991).

Ezell (2001) explains that *external advocacy* occurs when change is sought in agencies other than one's agency of employment" (p. 26). An external advocate, either a volunteer or someone paid by an outside source, tries to hold an agency accountable by using different tactics than an internal advocate would use. How might a social worker become an external advocate? The parent of a learning-disabled child assigned to a special education class might come to a child welfare worker, employed outside the school system, desiring a due process hearing. A food stamp recipient wanting to appeal a reduction in aid might ask an advocate employed not in the public benefits office but in the community for assistance. Public schools and the food stamp programs have rules that advocates can use to (a) help individuals and (b) hold the agencies responsible for these programs accountable. Agencies must comply with their own regulations and rules, as well as with rulings on court cases that guarantee certain rights.

Complexities. We are, with a few exceptions, expected to direct our advocacy attention to situations outside the agency. A social worker trying to obtain health care for the homeless is expected to do external battle on behalf of the homeless with various health bureaucracies. Similarly, the professional working with a battered woman's shelter is expected to be an external advocate with the police concerning protective orders. Even so, some problems may also be internal, especially in key government agencies. In any instrumental organization, we will be asked to intervene in-house on behalf of those working elsewhere.

Organizational culture. Within the first weeks on a job, it is important to figure out who is likely to support or resist action taken internally or externally. A supervisor who encourages pulling out all the stops externally may not want employees to rock the boat on internal issues. In contrast, a supervisor may encourage testing and prodding the internal bureaucracy but may be wary and cautious about dealing with the media, city hall, or any other external institution. A hospital discharge planner who is positioned to spot problems in places where patients are being sent may want to report these problems to a

licensing agency, only to be told to keep quiet and not risk losing a placement.

Advocacy involves sizing up situations. We need to determine if our supervisor views service and advocacy as compatible (Hardina, 1995). We want to know what language is most acceptable—is *representation* or *negotiation* preferred over *advocacy*? Since managers also act as advocates, social workers new to an agency might observe their style as they go about their work—"representing the agency, expressing management's viewpoint to staff and vice versa, lobbying at the local, state, and national level, testifying, and establishing contact with legislators and government administrators" (Menefee & Thompson, 1994, p. 18). This may reveal agency traditions or norms regarding internal and external advocacy.

More than supervisors' temperaments, the organizational culture may dictate constraints. Tower (1994) urges administrators who care about the clientele to "support and enhance the advocacy efforts of their frontline workers. After all, they are the ones most acutely aware of the client's unmet needs. It is likely that the main reason that more practitioners are not currently involved in consumer movements is fear of repercussion, primarily from their employers" (p. 196).

Realistically, certain positions constrain needed advocacy. Even though a particular employee assistance program may be improving employee productivity and thus is on good terms with employers, a consultant may hesitate to advocate with them about the causes of job stress problems (Ramanathan, 1992). Examples can also be found in correction systems, where social workers must advocate for inmates and staff but where complete allegiance to either inmates or the institution may be naive (Severson, 1994). We must think about our auspices and weigh the pluses and minuses of our particular slot or job requirements for success in advocacy.

Views of Empowerment and Advocacy

EMPOWERMENT AS A JOINT PROCESS WITH SERVICE CONSUMERS

Definitions. Employed early on by social workers such as Solomon (1976), the term *empowerment* is used to describe both the process of getting stronger and the result. As Lee (1994) says, "Empowerment is both the journey and the destination" (p. 207). One robust definition of empowerment, provided by Simon (1990), views it "as a series of attacks on subordination of every description—psychic, physical, cultural, sexual, legal, political, economic, and technological" (p. 28). Critical here is the notion of people developing and using skills to get needed resources or to influence decisions affecting their lives (Gutierrez, 1990). Empowerment should bring about mutual responsibility, but this will not happen without genuine listening and openness on the part of the social worker (S. M. Rose, 2000; Weaver, 2000).

Many interventive tools are used to enhance client empowerment. Vehicles differ as we work with clients in various social categories and in each case. Lee (1994) gives an example of a mother with AIDS who empowered herself by writing a journal (at the worker's suggestion) that she could share with her children and leave as a legacy (p. 206).

Ackerson, Burson, Harrison, and Martin (1995) studied the meanings of empowerment to clinicians and found that they usually thought of it in conjunction with enablement and self-determination—useful on a personal level when clients "feel they are not in control of their lives" (p. 10). This is consistent with the previous example of the mother with AIDS. However, several of the social workers interviewed had not found it easy to engage in empowerment as a joint process with clients due to perceived client limitations, setting or program constraints, and control (even liability) issues (p. 8). Those with mentally ill clients were most conflicted. A number of the social workers interviewed did not associate empowerment with groups, social systems, and larger processes, but some were conscious of tensions surrounding empowerment and paternalism (p. 11).

Yet, empowerment is equally relevant at the community level. There, many people must come to envision what could be. The catalyst may be a grassroots group, agency, church, school, or government program (Itzhaky & York, 2002; Krajewski & Matkin, 1996). We are just beginning to analyze which characteristics of community settings are empowering (Maton & Salem, 1995).

EMPOWERMENT AS A JOINT PROCESS WITH ADVOCACY

As Messinger (1982), a social worker and city official, describes the ways in which she provides constituent services, she pinpoints individual advocacy, then empowerment, then community advocacy:

> Many people . . . [contact a] politician because they need something done. . . . I or my staff . . . give them an address, make a phone call, track down a check, do whatever is necessary, but we try, always, to notify the people we assist about whom we are calling, what the most useful telephone number is, how they might do the same thing for themselves, and what to do if they do not get help.
>
> Sometimes, too, it is necessary for my staff to intervene to rescue individuals from becoming victims of the system. We recognize that it takes a mass effort by many people to make systems work better, but we do not . . . turn every problem with the bureaucracy into a cause. Nevertheless, we look for patterns in this work with constituents and for areas in which it is of mutual advantage to organize a lobbying and advocacy force rather than just to give help. (p. 216)

Advocacy is appropriate in some situations, empowerment in others.[8] Wood and Middleman (1989) make an interesting point in regard to obtaining benefits for an entitled client: "We value the positive experience which people can have as they work together and take action in their own behalf, even if they do not succeed. . . . But when [rights] are at stake, we do not value the psychological experience above task accomplishment. . . . we believe that the positive feelings associated with accordance of one's rights are more real and more lasting, irrespective of the extent to which one has obtained it through one's own efforts" (p. 145). Pressing needs may not wait for empowerment, and the social worker will have to make this judgment call. For instance, one could still do advocacy on behalf of involuntary clients who resist mutuality and empowerment measures. Not every client can be empowered; clients include babies and brain-damaged or comatose patients. Nor can every client be empowered by every experience. Within an advocacy framework, there are many roles still to be played. Lawyers argue on behalf of the families of people killed or people unable to speak for themselves due to accidents.

Support groups may be empowered by advocating for one of their own. Box 13.11 relates the success of a worldwide online mental illness discussion group whose members became advocates for a delusional woman, whom they did not even know personally, who had attempted to pay for coffee with a quarter and a packet of cocoa. Few people participating in support groups have training in advocacy. However, experience teaches support group members, who are willing to go public, to carefully formulate

BOX 13.11	ADVOCACY AND EMPOWERMENT VIA INTERNET

The schizophrenia discussion group (SCHIZOPH) is an open, unmoderated group composed of approximately 250 individuals at any given point in time. They come from all over the world and their main interest is in discussing about issues related to severe mental illnesses, in particular schizophrenia. The members of this forum are consumers, parents, and professionals from various disciplines . . .

It all started with a simple posting by one member of the group to the listserv.

Are you familiar with the 44-year-old woman with schizophrenia who has broken into David Letterman's house on more than one occasion, and had delusions that she was his wife?

Well, it seems this same woman had a cup of coffee in a diner in Fon Du Lac, Wisconsin yesterday. She tried to pay her 79-cent bill with a quarter and a package of instant hot cocoa mix. The diner called the police, and they arrested her.

She refused to have her mug shot taken and fingerprints taken because she believes that the government can eliminate her from the human race if they are allowed to take these things from her. She is being held in the city jail until she consents to the photographs and fingerprints.

Pretty big deal over a cup of coffee. I'd say.

This posting generated many responses from the group.

What's the name of the restaurant? I'll send them their money with a (nice) letter attached.

I certainly would write a letter and send the rest of the bill. How much was it?

Hi. Thanks for your words of support and encouragement. The bill was only 79 cents, but

I figure if everyone sends the money and a letter, it would make quite a statement, don't you?

Yes, I think we should send letters and $.79 to the restaurant and a copy of the letters to the police.

If you call the TV station, you may be able to find out the name of the restaurant. However, it might have a greater impact to send the 79 cents plus letters to the TV station rather than the restaurant, anyway!!!

I SECOND THAT MOTION!!!!!

On Thursday, 20th of March 1997, less than a week after the first posting of the incident, the group got the news that someone was listening to their voice.

That evening the WBAY news carried the whole story explaining what had occurred and had interviews with psychiatrists and others involved. The group felt that they had made their point and affected the community.

The arrest of a woman in North Fond Du Lac last week touched a nerve nationwide . . . Action 2 News has since received numerous letters containing 79 cents—the cost of the coffee—as well as e-mail.

. . . All expressed dismay that someone with a mental illness was arrested for not paying for a cup of coffee. (WBAY News)

The judge in the case decided that the 17 days the person served in jail was adequate punishment and ordered her release. The members of SCHIZOPH were euphoric about the success of their campaign.

Source: From "The 79-Cent Campaign: The Use of On-Line Mailing Lists for Electronic Advocacy" (pp. 75–79), by G. M. Menon, 2000, *Journal of Community Practice, 8*(3), Copyright 2000 by *Journal of Community Practice.* Used with permission.

their thoughts. Here is one illustration. A member of a support group learns to say to outsiders: "This [cruel depiction, promising reform, etc.] affects my [friend, family, etc.] this way [adds to distress, gives us hope for our other child, etc.]." To use our example in Box 13.11, an appropriate statement might be "This victory on behalf of a mentally ill person who was jailed after not paying properly for a cup of coffee affects all of us with this disease by showing that we can act to help each other and challenge the rigidities of society."

BEST INTERESTS VERSUS STATED WISHES OF CLIENT

Professional interpretations. Lawyers and social workers agree that advocacy requires being in tune with the desires of those requesting advocacy. Differences between professionals arise when the lawyer seizes on the currently stated wishes of the client, while the social worker believes that the government has an obligation to protect the young, helpless, or incompetent. Consider the case of a 10-year-old boy (an involuntary client) who was physically abused by his parents and removed from their custody. Decisions are being made about his future. The boy says he definitely wants to go home. Lawyers for the child (or his family) will do all they can to get the judge to honor his request. Social workers (from the agency acting as his guardian) might wonder if he realizes that other options may be preferable, even though their unfamiliarity makes them a frightening choice.

Compared with a lawyer, a social worker working in programs such as family preservation, may find it less clear whether the client is the child or the family and whether ultimate allegiance is to the child, the agency, or society as a whole. Attorneys find this discomforting. Those who urge self-advocacy by clients or work with people who have disabilities sometimes warn against the "best interests" approach (Moxley & Freddolino, 1994, p. 99). To ascertain children's wishes and desires, guardian ad litem programs and court-appointed special advocates (CASA) programs provide the child with a personal advocate and friend (Courter, 1995).

The case of the senior citizen who wants to be left alone may sharpen these issues. Suppose neighbors report that a 75-year-old recluse is feeding herself and 11 dogs on a meager income and that several rooms of her house are filled with waste. The health department and social services start to intervene when the woman asks for help to stay in her home with her pets. The lawyer will insist that she meet all city and humane society regulations but will defend her right to live as she chooses and will fight institutionalization. The social worker will think about resources such as homemaker service, SSI, and possible guardianship. Coordination between the two professions would result in the best advocacy in such situations.

CONCILIATORY VERSUS ADVERSARIAL STRATEGIES

A second issue involves how long to cooperate, coerce, or compromise before becoming adversarial. Wood and Middleman (1989) warn against escalating too soon on behalf of powerless clients, who, unlike the worker, will suffer the consequences if the action fails. They insist that the roles of broker and mediator must be tried first (p. 142; see also Kolb, 1994; Parsons, 1991). On the other hand, Patti and Resnick (1972) urge workers who want to change their *agencies* to consider both collaborative and adversarial strategies, depending on circumstances. One consideration should be whether or not the target of change is "rational, open to new ideas, and acting in good faith" (Patti & Resnick, p. 224). We must strategize with colleagues to decide whether a combative or a facilitative stance will be most productive for each situation.

The Legitimation of Advocacy

Advocacy for various population groups has been institutionalized by government through a number of acts—Older Americans, Rehabilitation, Americans with Disabilities, and so on. The advocacy agenda for such groups includes representation but also protection of citizen and human rights, public awareness, and public policy endeavors. This valuable work is carried out by institutions or offices such as the Legal Services Corporation (federal) and the Office of the Public Advocate (New Jersey), as well as through programs or advocacy systems such as the Protection and Advocacy Systems (P&As) for the Developmentally Disabled, the Client Assistance Project (CAPs) in vocational rehabilitation, and Protection and Advocacy for Individuals with Mental Illness (PAIMI) These are congressionally mandated, legally based agencies. For more information on this important representation, access, and assistance resource, see the Web site of the National Association of Protection and Advocacy Systems, Inc. (http://www.protection andadvocacy.com).

We are a federally funded program. If you have a psychiatric disability and feel you are being abused, neglected or denied your legal rights, we can help you secure the rights and services to which you are entitled . . . We are not psychiatrists, psychologists or social workers. We are not a government agency. We are advocates and lawyers who can work for you . . . Just call us on the phone and let us know if you, or someone you know, have been prevented from getting appropriate services, benefits, or treatment because of fear, discrimination, abuse, neglect, or lack of information about individual rights. (Protection and Advocacy for Individuals with Mental Illness, n.d.)

Employees in such systems are advocates for a class of people who seek full community membership, not traditional client advocates who counsel or see clients on a regular basis. Besides helping with their information clearinghouse function, these advocates may focus on revised research about the population, organizational interventions, or work with nonprofit organizations statewide and client organizations such as the National Alliance for the Mentally Ill (Rapp, Shera, & Kisthardt, 1993, p. 728). Such workers may think of themselves as programmatic advocates, government or systems advocates, political advocates, or issue-oriented advocates. In bringing about reforms leading to "greater consumer involvement in other spheres of systems change," for example, they may take action such as getting the mentally disabled on planning boards and councils that oversee their own programs (Segal, Silverman, & Temkin, 1993, p. 710).

KEY ADVOCACY SKILLS

This final section highlights four skills used in advocacy processes and summarizes practice wisdom that should be useful to those interested in improving their performance as advocates.

Basic Skills

PERSUASION

The process of social influence has been studied in many fields interested in human behavior (Cialdini, 2001; Simons, 1995). Persuasion is a key interpersonal skill used in both micro and macro interchanges. It involves promoting, marketing, working for favorable interpretations for a client or a cause, and changing minds (Mondros & Wilson, 1994). Persuasion is part of many practice situations, as for example, during program development, case conferences, discharge planning, and many others. It is a pivotal skill in policy situations, which require knowing the pressure points and how to use them (Flynn, 1985). Persuasion can take many forms; an advocate may win a public argument by using a dramatic story that can "unify and energize community and reinforce values and inspire collective action" (Felkins, 2002, p. 50).

As Ezell (2001) states, "Many times the success of advocacy is reduced to one's ability to persuade another person in a certain way [using] logic, emotion, or values" (p. 184). In addition, having personal persuasiveness (Burghardt, 1982) and projecting "personal authoritative-

ness" (Jansson, 1990, p. 201) with a solid command of the facts can be compelling.

Rules of thumb for persuading others are as follows:

Know what you want.
Know the facts and have them available.
Understand your source of power.
Rehearse.
Dress conventionally and comfortably.
Use clear, simple, graphic images.
Appeal to emotions *and* logic.
Make eye contact (or be similarly effective in written or e-advocacy).

REPRESENTATION

As societal transactions grow increasingly complex, it becomes more difficult for individuals to have the knowledge and capacity to conduct all of their affairs on their own behalf. Consequently, most of us need an experienced person to lead us through certain areas. Just as we turn to instructors to teach us first aid or how to drive a car, others request our help to obtain public housing, credit counseling, or job protection during pregnancy. When one's house, insurance, or public benefits are involved, individuals and families can be downright panicky about their circumstances. Mr. Ayala, an 83-year-old Hispanic man, responded this way to a letter from Social Security accusing him of cashing a check he was not due, "It embarrasses me that they think I have done this. It will embarrass me greatly if they tell the grocery store about this. Sometimes I cannot sleep wondering how I am going to resolve this. They asked me to come to the agency and they told me they would send an investigator to check everything in my house. What will they do with me? Not having anyone to defend me or listen to me I feel defenseless before the government and educated people" (Anzaldua, Reed-Sanders, Wrinkle, & Gibson, 1988, p. 109).

Representation begins when one person asks another, the second person agrees to become a spokesperson, and the two of them define the nature of their relationship. To represent someone is to take that person's view (or to work out a meeting of the minds together) while being forthright about chances, prospects, and when nothing can be done. Adeptness is required in communication, finding out the client's real wants and needs—not our picture of them—and educating and motivating the client to assist in the process.

Rules of thumb for representation include the following:

Establish whether someone besides the affected party needs to be involved.
Share what you know with the client.
Discover and check out what your client wants.
Lay out options and let client decide which ones are desirable and their order of importance.
Investigate the particular situation.
Determine the level of formality of the process.
Coordinate with each other.
Guard against divide-and-conquer tactics.
Allow the client to hire and fire you.

Representation often involves a forum such as a meeting or session or assembly (Schenider & Lester, 2001, p. 96) where the advocate and person seeking help together make a case. Nonlawyers can act as authorized representatives, if requested, by an eligible person or recipient for federal programs including Social Security, Medicare, SSI, veterans, and public housing. Lurie, Pinsky, Rock, and Tuzman (1989) explain the training needed to be effective in such a role. Here is an example of the type of representation form that is used by some agencies to formalize the relationship. It could be used by Mr. Ayala to deal with Social Security.

AUTHORIZATION AND WAVER OF CONFIDENTIALITY

To _____ [agency]:
This is to notify you that I, _____ [client's name], residing at _____ [client's address], hereby authorize _____ [representative's name] of _____ [advocate's agency] to act as my representative regarding _____ [program]. You are authorized to release any and all records and information relating to me and/or my case, including confidential information, as my representative may request.
_____ [client's signature]

Interacting with Authority Figures[9]

There is an entire representation–persuasion–advocacy–bargaining–negotiation continuum with concomitant skills. Yet, developing one particular ability usually makes an advocate effective. An advocate must know *how to contend,*

how to insist. This means defending and protecting an individual, getting those who hold power to change their minds or behavior, and holding one's ground with intimidating people. The skill is knowing what to do and doing it in the face of opposition. In most cases, advocates confront sources of resistance.

THOSE IN KEY POSITIONS

Authority is the power to influence or command thought, opinion, or behavior, and an authority figure is a person in command who has legitimate power to make decisions. Social workers have different views than clients, citizens, and service users on who is an authority figure. Therefore, let us think of an *authority figure* as a person who holds or is perceived to hold power and influence in the situation at hand. The need to dispute or correct such a person is difficult for novices, yet any professional who wants to help others or make changes in a community must deal with authority figures. The way such persons are dealt with can be a major determinant of the results. We must learn what rules and policies a given authority figure is subject to or must abide by, as well as those that she or he controls.

To students, field supervisors are authority figures. To service users, the person who collects a deposit before a telephone can be installed is in a position to help or hurt them and is thus in a position of authority. There may be nothing sinister or malevolent about authority figures, but they can exercise discretion and may be intimidating in their bearing, demeanor, or tone of voice. Social workers may be perceived as authority figures, based on knowledge or status, on their control over a client's family, and on formal and informal determinations they make, such as whether to report certain behavior to a court.

Advocates constantly bump up against people with different positions, people who dislike clients singly or en mass, and people who can change a client's present situation or future. Years ago, Grosser (1965) argued that advocacy was necessary because arbitrariness and discretion can create an uneven playing field:

Often the institutions with which local residents must deal are not even neutral, much less positively motivated, toward handling the issues brought to them by community groups. In fact, they are frequently overtly negative and hostile, often concealing or distorting information about rules, procedures, and office hours. By their own partisanship . . . they create an atmosphere that demands advocacy on behalf of the poor. . . . If the community worker is to facilitate productive interaction between residents and institutions, it is necessary . . . to provide leadership and resources directed toward eliciting information, arguing the correctness of a position, and challenging the stance of the institution. (p. 18)

These words are equally relevant today, yet confrontation is not inevitable. Many situations are resolved amicably. It is important for advocates to be aware that those in key positions view their reputations or jobs as being on the line, much as we feel about our clients and our jobs. We should respond to antagonism with firmness (see Chapter 8).

Social conflict can be uncomfortable. Examples of situations where we may experience difficulty or discomfort when we must—as an ethical or professional obligation—challenge an authority could include the following:

- Informing an employer of his or her responsibilities on behalf of your client population (whether day laborers, teenagers, displaced homemakers, or persons who have seizures)
- Arguing the merits of a group or halfway house before a hostile zoning board
- Contradicting an elected official who has wrongfully maligned your program in the press

"The impulse to obey authority and the reluctance to confront it are deeply ingrained in the human psyche" (Bell, 1994, p. 136). Transactional analysts might say that many of us overadapt. We may become passive-aggressive. Workers and clients are likely to react similarly to those who have the power to influence outcomes—with awe, avoidance, and anger. As professionals, those who make themselves interact anyway go on to become effective advocates.

PREREQUISITES FOR FACING AUTHORITY FIGURES

There are certain hints for approaching and, if necessary, challenging a person who is in a position to grant or deny a request or to control someone's future. Rules of thumb for dealing with authority include the following:

Know the system you are up against.
Know your facts.
Be ready to demonstrate that you have done your part.
Know what you want (but also what you will take).

Consider all options about the time, place, and manner of engagement.
Have materials organized in serviceable fashion for use under pressure.
Speak in an even tone.
Listen carefully and take notes.
Look for a clear decision.

ILLUSTRATING INTERACTION WITH AUTHORITIES

A common example of a task-oriented encounter involves the probable utility shutoff for a household unless negotiations with a utility company representative are successful. See Box 13.12. Utility payments can be difficult for low-income households; think of California in recent years where electricity costs quadrupled overnight. One of the first decisions an advocate must make regarding a meeting with a corporation representative is whether someone representing the household should be present. This decision will depend on deciding how that individual might fare during the encounter and whether she or he wants to participate. If the utility customer is present, the advocate must show respect for that person (e.g., not talking over her or him) and must make sure that the authority figure shows respect; Simon (1994) entreats us to "interrupt contempt" (p. 189). However, the advocate must anticipate a variety of responses from the authority figures involved because each company representative has a different personality.

Advocates must know the chain of command in any situation. In bureaucracies "the power of the advocate is the potential power to escalate the problem, to raise it to higher levels in the hierarchy" (Wood & Middleman, 1989, p. 142). The situation presented in Box 13.12 illustrates this. It also highlights how frequently language that is unfamiliar to the lay person is used, whether in a utility or a psychiatric case. Note these other points. We must not let others shift the burden of responsibility on every point to us. We cannot assume that a person who has the authority to make a certain decision can decide or order anything we want. We notice the directness with which an advocate converses with a decision maker. No time and effort is wasted in making pleasant small talk, trying to appease, ingratiate or bully, or overexplaining or excusing the client's situation.

Negotiation

Community practitioners negotiate informally and formally on behalf of neighborhoods, pro-

BOX 13.12	ADVOCATES CONFRONT MYRIAD PROBLEMS WITH CLIENTS

Setting: Office of customer relations representative

Advocate: I am a community service worker with the Neighborhood Center. Our office provides assistance in housing and utility issues. This is Mrs. Edna Gardner. We requested an appointment because she received a telephone call stating that her service would be terminated today due to nonpayment of bills.

U. Rep: Yes, I am aware of Mrs. Gardner's bill. (To client) Mrs. Gardner, you are two months in arrears, plus the current bill for June is due. We have received no payment. You did not contact us to say when we could expect payment, so we have no alternative but to discontinue your service.

Client: Look, I have three children at home. There has to be another way. Don't turn off the gas.

U. Rep: There is another way. Pay your bills on time like any other good citizen.

Advocate: That is exactly why we are here today. To work out an arrangement so Mrs. Gardner can pay her bill. Mrs. Gardner and I have discussed the situation and feel a deferred payment plan might be a solution.

U. Rep: In some situations deferred payment is a solution. When we feel there is a strong likelihood that individuals will live up to their obligations to make installment payments, we agree to such a plan. Quite frankly, Mrs. Gardner, you don't appear to fit into that category.

Client: (Angry) What do you mean? I have tried very hard to pay all my bills and it's not easy. Have you ever tried coping as a single parent?

Advocate: (To client) Just a minute, Mrs. Gardner. (To utility rep) Let me explain that Mrs. Gardner moved in March, so she did not receive a bill in April. Therefore, her bill in May was over $175. She did try to explain her inability to pay to your office, but unfortunately a payment agreement was not proposed at that time. Also, Mrs. Gardner had not received written notification that her service was to be terminated and did not realize how serious the situation was until today. Mrs. Gardner is prepared to make an initial payment on her bill right now.

U. Rep: Well, we require at least half of the amount in arrears, which would be approximately $85 to $90.

Advocate: We are prepared to pay $60 today.

U. Rep: I just told you we need at least half of the amount in arrears.

Advocate: I've worked with your office before, and the policy has been to accept initial payments as low as one-third of that amount.

U. Rep: $80.

Advocate: Let me check with Mrs. Gardner (talks to her quietly, then to the utility rep). $70 is the most we can pay today, but we'll assure you of three installment payments of approximately $35 to pay the rest.

U. Rep: How do you expect to make the payments if you can't even come up with $80?

Advocate: We will manage that aspect of our agreement. What we need to do now is put the terms of this agreement in writing, in Mrs. Gardner's file, and issue the stop order on the turnoff.

U. Rep: You'll pay $70 today and $35 for 3 months?

Client: Yes.

U. Rep: However, since Mrs. Gardner's service was scheduled to be turned off today, the service men are probably at the house now.

Advocate: We just mutually agreed to a plan.

U. Rep: Well, it's all right by me, and if we had entered into the plan yesterday or before the truck started on its rounds. . . . Now, once the reconnect charge is paid, our arrangement will go into effect.

Advocate: Your company policy has been not to terminate service once a payment plan has been set up. There can't be a reconnect charge either under the circumstances. You must be able to stop the shutoff.

U. Rep: You came too late. There is no way I can reach the men now.

Advocate: Someone must have contact with the service truck.

U. Rep: I don't.

Advocate: Then let me speak to your supervisor.

U. Rep: You'd like to speak with my supervisor?

Advocate: Yes, we would.

Source: National Public Law Training Center script in Advocacy Spectrum manual.

grams, and projects and during issue campaigns. Kahn (1991) uses this definition: "Negotiations occur when the two sides (or three or four) sit down together and try to come up with a resolution that is acceptable, if not completely satisfactory, to all parties concerned" (p. 175). Lappé and Du Bois (1994) believe that the negotiation process maintains the dignity of all parties, makes resolution of problems more possible, and makes it more likely that agreements will be upheld (p. 262). It is important to learn quickly whether the negotiator has decision-making authority. The major approaches to negotiation are bargaining and problem-solving.

BARGAINING OR PROBLEM-SOLVING

The negotiation literature on agreement-building compares bargaining and problem-solving approaches. Those who emphasize *bargaining* (Halpern, 1999; Kolb & Williams, 2000) are more likely to stress control and tactics. Bargainers ponder where to sit at the table, timing, reading the opposition, and so forth. In order to know how to bargain during the actual negotiation, negotiators engage intensively with those they represent. The worksheet shown as Table 13.1 illustrates bargaining preparation and various positions to plan together. The gas utility case described in Box 13.12 provides our facts.

In contrast, the parties can view themselves as problem solvers, working toward a collaborative solution which concludes in a workable agreement. Ideally, each party leaves the negotiation feeling that they have attained something that they wanted. Those who emphasize *problem solving* (Gibelman & Demone, 1990; Sebenius, 2001) are more likely to stress the big picture, understanding, and what-if questions.

Let us use interest-based negotiation, an outgrowth of the Harvard Negotiation Project, as an illustration of the problem-solving approach. One key to success is vigorous brainstorming about options—possibly a dozen—which can be put on the table because what could make the other side happy may not be apparent. Perks, predictability, or evidence of respect may be as important as money or compliance. Take, for example, a social worker negotiating with the

school system on behalf of a slow learner. Knowing the family has been hurt by unfeeling educators, the social worker may believe that a demonstration of concern by the school's negotiator about the child's humiliations may be as significant as the kind and amount of services being offered.

Interest-based negotiation stresses the following elements of a successful, principled negotiation (Field, 2000):

1. *Interests* (parties' needs, desires, concerns and fears)
2. *Options* (potential solutions parties can take together)
3. *Alternatives* (each party's independent choices)
4. *Criteria* (established standards for legitimacy, fairness)
5. *Communication* (organized thinking; addressing misunderstandings, questioning, listening)
6. *Relationships* (establishing trust, working relationship)
7. *Commitment* (forming clear, feasible agreements)

This style of negotiation has been detailed in *Getting to Yes* by Fisher, Ury, and Patton (1981). These authors coined the phrase "best alternative to a negotiated agreement" (BATNA) to remind negotiators of possible results they can secure without negotiating. To use our previous example, the parents can remove the slow learner from the school or sue the school. However, parties must be realistic about their options.

SKILLS AND RULES OF THUMB

Reaching a successful negotiated agreement is not easy but the good news is that negotiation is a learnable skill. There is a procedural and psychological process to negotiation—of give and take. Author Jack Kaine (1993) believes that one controls a negotiation by questioning not arguing. Kaine gives invaluable advice on how to

TABLE 13.1 NEGOTIATING TACTICS: UTILITIES EXAMPLE

Issue	Initial Position →	Subsequent →	Fallback →	Bottom Line
Prevent shutoff	$60 payment today	$70 payment	$70 today + three $35 monthly payments	Unknown
Reconnect fee	Demand no fee	Etc.		

steer negotiations, be clear, and make the other side more receptive: "For example, before making a point, the expert negotiator says, 'I would like to make a point.' He then makes his point. He says, 'May I ask a question?' and then asks a question. If he has a concern, he will say, 'I have a concern,' and then states it. . . . Good negotiators do not label their disagreements. They do not say 'I disagree with you because . . .' [They might say] 'I have this point I would like to discuss with you. It is . . . , and as a result, I disagree'" (p. 40).

In their book on making deals, Gottlieb and Healy (1990, Chapter 3) give the following advice. They say that negotiators should prepare to deal effectively with an adversary by taking an inventory of their party's assets and liabilities; make thorough preparations by knowing the needs of the other party and their end goal; not underestimate the amount of strength they possess in this process; project a belief that the deal they are offering is the best available; rely on their expertise as a problem solver; remember they can decide to walk away; exercise patience and control because many concessions take place late, close to a deadline. To engage successfully in negotiation, Gottlieb and Healey (pp. 38-44) also say to

- Explore your possible options and alternatives and closely examine areas of conflict to help establish a creative, problem-solving climate where people collaborate rather than compromise.

- Utilize trading off, which is the process of sorting, evaluating, and deciding which options would work most effectively for your party and the other side. Be sure and analyze how a trade-off affects the other variables in your equation and what you are getting for it from the other party.

- Seek to control the pace of communication. Do not allow yourself to be rushed into agreement. Continually assert that issues are open until agreed upon, because they are interrelated and changes in one will affect the others.

- Maximize your impact as a negotiator, by personalizing yourself and the situation.

ILLUSTRATIVE EXERCISE: AN ACTUAL NEGOTIATION

Officials finally cracked down on slum landlords. They condemned an apartment building that had hundreds of housing code violations and announced the owner would receive criminal penalties as well as fines. But the city insisted that the building had to be emptied for repairs. Community advocates argued the plan was unfair to the tenants who, after living in lousy conditions for years, now would be forced to find scarce affordable housing. The advocates entered into negotiations with city officials, the owner-landlord, and the owner's lawyer. A compromise was achieved. The building was sold to the tenants for one dollar. Social workers and tenant leaders coordinated the cleanup and rehab of the building. The property owner paid for extensive repairs to the building. He was not jailed but was prohibited from owning any more residential property in the city.

Explain how this example illustrates a win-win negotiation. What leverage was used to achieve this result? Were the advocates negotiating with one, two, or three parties?

PUTTING ONESELF TO THE TEST

The following scenario will allow you to practice negotiation skills. Decide if you will take a bargaining or a problem-solving approach.

As director of your county mental health program, you have been handed a hot potato assignment. Bordering your headquarters is a parcel of land and a boarded-up county mental hospital, relic of an earlier era. The county has decided to sell the land and building with half of the proceeds going to your program's group homes and transitional housing program. Zoning regulations permit the property to be used for a variety of purposes. However, concerns about appropriate uses have been debated for months in the press. The worth of the property has also been the subject of intense speculation. County Council Head Beverly Basey once asserted the land is worth at least $3 million.

Today, you receive a copy of a fax addressed to the Council from a prospective buyer, Douglas Younger, the head of the Ballet and Modern Dance Academy. Their organization has unexpectedly received a huge bequest that will enable them to purchase the land and make massive renovations to the building. On behalf of the Academy, Younger offers a total purchase price of $4 million to be paid in two segments three years apart, plus an annual payment of $75,000 for 20 years in lieu of property taxes. Since he wishes to immediately launch a capital campaign, Younger concludes:

"I request an immediate meeting with you, Madame Chair, or your authorized designee to negotiate a mutually acceptable purchase agreement, in order that this important project may see fruition."

You get a follow-up e-mail from Chairperson Basey asking you to represent the county in negotiations and to quickly respond to Younger. County lawyers will be involved after you have resolved any initial sticking points.

What should your primary consideration be in preparing to handle the County Council's directive? Are there creative ways to negotiate benefits for your client group?[9]

Discussion Exercises

1.   Read the works of Pertschuk, Shapiro, Tower, or Courter included in the reference list below and discuss the attributes of an individual advocate.

2. George Wiley was admired by social workers who worked with him in the welfare and civil rights movements. His belief was that he should use himself fully. His biographers (Kotz & Kotz, 1977) describe him as

- well organized, energetic, and uninhibited;
- committed to obtaining information and data;
- able to present information clearly and powerfully;
- able to link diverse, strong-minded allies; and
- able to get others involved.

Wiley's biographers portray him as someone who

- believed he could convince others—even foes,
- juggled myriad tasks but kept his eye on the target,
- applied heady ideas in practical ways,
- made and kept lists (e.g., resources, contacts),
- listened well,
- sought out mentors and fund-raising help, and
- wanted to achieve concrete gains.

Pick someone you know who is successful at community practice. What traits and skills does she or he have?

3.   Read Bombyk's (1995) *Encyclopedia of Social Work* article on progressive social work. Bombyk challenges us to name a social worker with a national reputation for championing the interests of underdogs: "Is there a Ralph Nader of social work?"

4.   Read T. R. Lawson's (1995) *Encyclopedia of Social Work* article on music and social work. What songs have you incorporated into practice? Do newer causes (disability, gay rights) use music the way the civil rights, labor, and peace movements did?

5.   As a research project, trace the legislative and advocacy history of the Mental Health Parity Bill (S. 1028, the Domenici-Wellstone coverage option, 1996) and the Mental Health Parity Bill (discrimination) considered by a conference committee in 2002. Continue to trace bills S 486, S 1832, and HR 953 in the 108th Congress. Find out the names of the key individual lobbyists (social workers and others) who advocated for the mentally ill. Who was most effective and why? For specific suggestions on conducting an advocacy campaign, see the Kansas Community Toolbox Web site at http://ctb.ukans.edu/tools/advocateforchange/outline.jsp

Notes

1. In this approach, corporations (and Republicans) are presumed to control the government apparatus and most forms of media. However, inroads are possible, in part because of the self-interest of these entities. For publicity and media advocacy tips, see Brawley (1985/1986, 1997), C. Ryan (1991), and Wallack, Dorfman, Jernigan, and Themba (1993).

2. The late Bea Gaddy of East Baltimore, a recipient of a national Caring award. Interview by Jennifer Nelson in Powers (1994).

3. Many famous organizers (e.g., Wade Rathke) and training centers operate outside social work. Some associated with those groups have master's degrees in social work, like Arnie Graf, who has worked with the Industrial Areas Foundation for 30 years. After social work, the ministry is the profession that engages most in organizing, while political campaigns are where people from other fields get organizing experience.

4. Jim Evans, active in NASW, the Urban League, and welfare rights, in an interview by Brenda Kunkel in Powers (1994).

5. The United States borrowed the ombudsperson concept. Sweden has had an ombudsperson since 1809, Finland since 1919, and Denmark since 1955.

6. Rosalind Griffin, D.S.W., manager (drug dependency, mental health, cross racial-ethnic counseling expert), in an interview by Rachel Schwartz in Powers (1994).

7. Linda Heisner (clinical social worker turned children-and-family-services government leader), interviewed by Cathy Raab in Powers (1994).

8. For more interweaving of advocacy and empowerment, see "Case Complaint System" in F. Brooks (2001, pp. 79-81). For an interesting look at specific ways that social workers react to and interact with homeless people, see Marvasti (2002).

9. Some of the material on authority figures is taken from a videotape and manuals by the National Public Law Training Center (NPLTC), a former advocacy training organization. Robert Hoffman and Pat Powers produced the video. George Hacker, William Fry, Barry Greever, Cathy Howell, and Pat Powers, among others, contributed to NPLTC's Advocacy Spectrum training manual.

10. Scenario inspired by American Arbitration Association materials that were used for teaching purposes by Thomas Saltonstall and William Lincoln.

References

Abramovitz, M. (1993). Should all social work students be educated for social change? [PRO, in Point/Counterpoint]. *Journal of Social Work Education, 29*(1), 6–11.

Ackerman, B., & Alstott, A. (1999). *The stakeholder society.* New Haven, CT: Yale University Press.

Ackerson, B., Burson, I., Harrison, W. D., & Martin, A. (1995, March). *The paradoxical meanings of empowerment to clinicians: Results of a constant-comparative study.* Paper presented at Council on Social Work Education meeting, San Diego, CA.

Addams, J. (1910). *Twenty years at Hull House.* New York: Macmillan.

Advocacy Spectrum (n.d.). Manual developed by the National Public Law Training Center, a nonprofit organization. Washington, D.C.

Alinsky, S. D. (1972). *Rules for radicals: A pragmatic primer for realistic radicals.* New York: Vintage Books.

Alvarez, A. R., & Gutierrez, L. M. (2001). Choosing to do participatory research: An example and issues of fit to consider. *Journal of Community Practice, 9*(1), 1–20.

Anzaldua, H., Reed-Sanders, D., Wrinkle, R. D., & Gibson, G. (1988). *Hispanic elderly: A cultural signature.* Edinburg, TX: Pan American University Press.

Avner, M. (2002). *The lobbying and advocacy handbook for nonprofit organizations: Shaping public policy at the state and local levels.* Saint Paul, MN: Amherst H. Wilder Foundation.

Bell, D. A. (1994). *Confronting authority: Reflections of an ardent protester.* Boston: Beacon Press.

Bernstein, A. (2000, September 11). Too much corporate power? *Business Week,* 144–158.

Berry, J. M. (1999). *The new liberalism: The rising power of citizen groups.* Washington, DC: Brookings Institution.

Bombyk, M. (1995). Progressive social work. In R. L. Edwards (Ed.-in-Chief), *Encyclopedia of social work* (19th ed., pp. 1933–1942). Washington, DC: National Association of Social Workers.

Boyte, H. C. (1980). *The backyard revolution: Understanding the new citizen movement.* Philadelphia: Temple University Press.

Brager, G. (1967). Institutional change: Parameters of the possible. *Social Work, 12*(1), 59–69.

Braverman, L. (1986). Social casework and strategic therapy. *Social Casework, 67*(4), 234–239.

Brawley, E. (1985/1986, Winter). The mass media: A vital adjunct to the new community and administrative practice. *Administration in Social Work, 9,* 63–73.

Brawley, E. A. (1997). Teaching social work students to use advocacy skills through the mass media. *Journal of Social Work Education, 33*(3), 445–460.

Brieland, D. (1990). The Hull House tradition and the contemporary social worker: Was Jane Addams really a social worker? *Social Work, 35*(2), 134–138.

Brooks, F. (2001). Innovative organizing practices: ACORN's campaign in Los Angeles organizing workfare workers. *Journal of Community Practice, 9*(4), 68–85.

Brooks, N. A. (1991). Self-empowerment among adults with severe physical disability: A case study. *Journal of Sociology and Social Welfare, 18*(1), 105–120.

Brueggemann, W. G. (2002). *The practice of macro social work* (2nd ed.). Belmont, CA: Wadsworth (Brooks/Cole).

Burghardt, S. (1982). *The other side of organizing.* Cambridge, MA: Schenkman.

Burghardt, S. (1987). Community-based social action. In A. Menahan (Ed.-in-Chief), *The encyclopedia of social work* (18th ed., pp. 292–299). Silver Spring, MD: National Association of Social Workers.

Chapin, R. K. (1995). Social policy development: The strengths perspective. *Social Work 40*(4), 506–514.

Checkoway, B. (1995). Six strategies of community change. *Community Development Journal, 30*(1), 2–20.

Cialdini, R. B. (2001). The science of persuasion. *Scientific American, 284*(2), 76–81.

Congress Online Project (2002). Press release, August 2002. Congress making progress in taming "email monster." Retrieved on July 29, 2003 from http://www.congressonlineproject.org/080702pr.html

Courter, G. (1995). *True stories of a child advocate: I speak for this child.* New York: Crown.

Davis, K. C. (1975). *Administrative law and government.* St. Paul, MN: West.

Davis, L. V., Hagen, J. L., & Early, T. J. (1994). Social services for battered women: Are they adequate, accessible, and appropriate? *Social Work, 39*(6), 695–704.

Dear, R. B., & Patti, R. J. (1981). Legislative advocacy: Seven effective tactics. *Social Work, 26*(4), 289–96.

Ezell, M. (2001). *Advocacy in the human services.* Belmont, CA: Brooks/Cole.

Fabricant, M., & Burghardt, S. (1992). *Welfare state crisis and the transformation of social service work.* Armonk, NY: M. E. Sharpe.

Felkins, P. K. (2002). *Community work: Creating and celebrating community in organizational life.* Cresskill, NJ: Hampton Press, Inc.

Field, C. G. (2000, December). *Description of principled negotiations.* Handout at workshop on Interest-based negotiation held in Baltimore, MD.

Fisher, R., & Shragge, E. (2000). Challenging community organizing: Facing the 21st century. *Journal of Community Practice, 8*(3), 1–19.

Fisher, R., Ury, W., & Patton, B. (1981). *Getting to yes: Negotiating agreement without giving in.* Boston: Houghton Mifflin.

Flynn, J. P. (1985). *Social agency policy: Analysis and presentation for community practice.* Chicago: Nelson-Hall.

Freire, P. (1971). *Pedagogy of the oppressed.* New York: Herder & Herder.

Frost, D. (1994). October 21). "The David Frost Special" Interview with Ralph Nader. Washington, DC: PBS Journal Graphics Aired on public television.

Galper, J. H. (1975). *The politics of social services.* Englewood Cliffs, NJ: Prentice Hall.

Gamson, J. (1991). Silence, death and the invisible enemy: AIDS activism and social movement "newness." In M. Burawoy et al. (Eds.), *Ethnography unbound* (pp. 35–57). Berkeley, CA: University of California Press.

Gamson, W. A. (1992). *Talking politics.* New York: Cambridge University Press.

Gibelman, M., & Demone, H. W., Jr. (1990). Negotiating: A tool for inter-organizational coordination. *Administration in Social Work, 14*(4), 29–42.

Gibelman, M., & Kraft, S. (1996). Advocacy as a core agency program: Planning considerations for voluntary human services agencies. *Administration in Social Work, 20*(4), 43–59.

Gilbert, R. (1993). *Ronnie Gilbert on Mother Jones: Face to face with the most dangerous woman in America.* Berkeley, CA: Conari.

Gitlin, T. (1980). *The whole world is watching: The making and unmaking of the new Left.* Berkeley: University of California Press.

Goldberg, R. A. (1991). *Grassroots resistance: Social movements in twentieth century America.* Belmont, CA: Wadsworth.

Gollaher, D. (1995). *Voice for the mad: The life of Dorothea Dix.* New York: Free Press.

Goodwyn, L. (1978). *Democratic promise: The populist movement.* New York: Oxford University Press.

Gottlieb, M. R., & Healy, W. J. (1990). *Making deals: The business of negotiation.* New York: New York Institute of Finance.

Grosser, C. F. (1965). Community development programs serving the urban poor. *Social Work, 10*(3), 15–21.

Grosser, C. F. (1976). *New directions in community organization: From enabling to advocacy* (2nd ed.). New York: Praeger.

Gutierrez, L. M. (1990). Working with women of color: An empowerment perspective. *Social Work, 35*(2), 149–152.

Gutierrez, L. M. (1994, June). Beyond coping: An empowerment perspective on stressful life events. *Journal of Sociology and Social Welfare, 21*(3), 201–219.

Hahn, A. J. (1994). *The politics of caring: Human services at the local level.* Boulder, CO: Westview.

Halpern, R. G. (1999). Opening a new door to negotiation strategy. *Trial, 35*(6), 22–29.

Handler, J. F. (1978). *Social movements and the legal system: A theory of law reform and social change.* New York: Academic Press.

Handler, J. F. (1979). *Protecting the social service client: Legal and structural controls on official discretion.* New York: Academic Press.

Hardina, D. (1995). Do Canadian social workers practice advocacy? *Journal of Community Practice, 2*(3), 97–121.

Hartman, A. (1993). The professional is political. *Social Work, 38*(4), 365–366.

Haynes, K., & Mickelson, J. (2002). *Affecting change: Social workers in the political arena* (5th ed.). New York: Longman.

Henderson, P., & Thomas, D. N. (1987). *Skills in neighbourhood work.* London: Allen & Unwin.

Henley, P. (1999). *Hummingbird house.* Denver, CO: MacMurray & Beck.

Hepworth, D. H., & Larsen. J. A. (1993). *Direct social work practice.* Pacific Grove, CA: Brooks/Cole.

Hick, S., & McNutt, J. G. (Eds.). (2002). *Advocacy, activism, and the Internet: Community organization and social policy.* Chicago: Lyceum Books.

Holder, E. (1995). Advocacy for nursing home reform. In G. L. Maddox (Ed.), *Encyclopedia of aging* (2nd ed., pp. 28–29). New York: Springer.

Horn, L., & Griesel, E. (1977). *Nursing homes: A citizens' action guide.* Boston: Beacon.

Howell, J. T. (1973). *Hard living on Clay Street: Portraits of blue collar families.* Garden City, NY: Anchor.

Hyde, C. (1994). Commitment to social change: Voices from the feminist movement. *Journal of Community Practice, 1*(2), 45–64.

Isaac, K. (1992). *Civics for democracy: A journey for teachers and students.* Washington, DC: Essential Books.

Itzhaky, H., & York, A. S. (2002). Showing results in community organization. *Social Work, 47*(2), 125–131.

Ivins, M., & Dubose, L. (2000). *Shrub: The short but happy political life of George W. Bush.* New York: Random House.

Jackson, J. F. (1991). The use of psychoeducational evaluations in the clinical process: Therapists as sympathetic advocates. *Child and Adolescent Social Work Journal, 8*(6), 473–487.

Jansson, B. S. (1990). *Social welfare policy: From theory to practice.* Belmont, CA: Wadsworth.

Johnson, L. C. (1995). *Social work practice: A generalist approach* (5th ed.). Boston: Allyn & Bacon.

Jones, M. H. (1980). *The autobiography of Mother Jones.* Chicago: Charles H. Kerr.

Kahn, S. (1991). *Organizing: A guide for grassroots leaders.* Silver Spring, MD: National Association of Social Workers.

Kaine, J. W. (1993). Don't fight—Negotiate. *Association Management, 45*(9), 38–43.

Kirchhoff, S. (1999, November 20). Disability bill's advocates rewrite the book on lobbying, *Congressional Quarterly Weekly,* 2762–2766.

Kleinman, A., Das, V., & Lock, M. (Eds.). (1997). *Social suffering.* Berkeley, CA: University of California Press.

Kling, J. M., & Posner, P. S. (1990). *Dilemmas of activism: Class, community and the politics of mobilization.* Philadelphia: Temple University Press.

Kolb, D. (1994). *When talk works: Profiles of mediators.* San Francisco: Jossey-Bass.

Kolb, D. M., & Williams, J. (2000). *The shadow negotiation: How women can master the hidden agendas that determine bargaining success.* New York: Simon & Schuster.

Kotz, N., & Kotz, M. L. (1977). *A passion for equality: George Wiley and the movement.* New York: W. W. Norton.

Kozol, J. (1990). *The night is dark and I am far from home* (Rev. ed.). New York: Simon & Schuster.

Kozol, J. (1991). *Savage inequalities.* New York: HarperCollins.

Krajewski, B., & Matkin, M. (1996). Community empowerment: Building a shared vision. *Principal, 76*(2), 5–7.

Kuhn, M. (with Long, C., & Quinn, L.). (1991). *No stone unturned: The life and times of Maggie Kuhn.* New York: Ballantine.

Lappé, F. M., & Du Bois, P. M. (1994). *The quickening of America: Rebuilding our nation, remaking our lives.* San Francisco: Jossey-Bass.

Lawson, A., & Rhode, D. L. (Eds.). (1993). *The politics of pregnancy: Adolescent sexuality and public policy.* New Haven, CT: Yale University Press.

Lawson, T. R. (1995). Music and social work. In R. L. Edwards (Ed.-in-Chief), *Encyclopedia of social work* (19th ed., pp. 1736–1741). Washington, DC: National Association of Social Workers.

Lee, J. A. B. (1994). *The empowerment approach to social work practice.* New York: Columbia University Press.

Lewis, B. A. (1998). *The kid's guide to social action* (2nd ed.). Minneapolis, MN: Free Spirit.

Loeb, V. (2000, July 30). How one man's receivership turned D.C. public housing around. *The Washington Post,* pp. B1, B4.

Lord, S. A., & Kennedy, E. T. (1992). Transforming a charity organization into a social justice community center. *Journal of Progressive Human Services, 3*(1), 21–37.

Lurie, A., Pinsky, S., Rock, B., & Tuzman, L. (1989). The training and supervision of social work students for effective advocacy practice. *The Clinical Supervisor, 7*(2/3), 149–158.

Lynch, R. S., & Mitchell, J. (1995). Justice system advocacy: A must for NASW and the social work community. *Social Work, 40*(1), 9–12.

Mackelprang, R. W., & Salsgiver, R. O. (1996). People with disabilities and social work: Historical and contemporary issues. *Social Work, 41*(1), 7–14.

Mandell, B. R. (1992). Firing-up students for social change: Some teaching tactics for the 1990s. *Journal of Progressive Human Services, 3*(1), 53–69.

Marvasti, A. B. (2002). Constructing the service-worthy homeless through narrative editing. *Journal of Contemporary Ethnography, 31*(5), 615–651.

Maton, K. I., & Salem, D. A. (1995). Organizational characteristics of empowering community settings: A multiple case study approach. *American Journal of Community Psychology, 23*(5), 631–656.

Mayadas, N. S., & Elliott, D. (1997). Lessons from international social work: Policies and practice. In M. Reisch & E. Gambrill (Eds.), *Social work in the 21st century* (pp. 175–185). Thousand Oaks, CA: Pine Forge Press.

McCarthy, J. D., & Zald, M. N. (Eds.). (1987). *Social movements in organizational society: Collected essays.* New Brunswick, NJ: Transaction.

McFarland, A. S. (1984). *Common Cause: Lobbying in the public interest.* Chatham, NJ: Chatham House.

McNutt, J. G., & Boland, K. M. (1999). Electronic advocacy by nonprofit organizations in social welfare policy. *Nonprofit and Voluntary Section Quarterly, 28*(4), 432–451.

Menefee, D. T., & Thompson, J. J. (1994). Identifying and comparing competencies for social work management: A practice driven approach. *Administration in Social Work, 18*(3), 1–25.

Menendez, R. (Writer/Director), & Musca, T. (Writer/Producer). (1988). *Stand and deliver*. [Motion picture]. United States: Warner Bros.

Menon, G. M. (2000). The 79-cent campaign: The use of on-line mailing lists for electronic advocacy. *Journal of Community Practice, 8*(3), 73–81.

Messinger, R. W. (1982). Empowerment: A social worker's politics. In M. Mahaffey & J. Hanks (Eds.), *Practical politics: Social work and political responsibility* (pp. 212–223). Silver Spring, MD: National Association of Social Workers.

Mikulski, B. A. (1982). Community empowerment and self-help strategies. In *Social Welfare Forum, 1981* (pp. 11–23). New York: Columbia University Press.

Miller, J. B. (1986). *Toward a new psychology of women*. Boston: Beacon Press.

Mintrom, M., & Vergari, S. (1996). Advocacy coalitions, policy entrepreneurs, and policy change. *Policy Studies Journal, 24*(3), 420–34.

Mondros, J. B., & Wilson, S. M. (1994). *Organizing for power and empowerment*. New York: Columbia University Press.

Moreau, M. J. (1990, June). Empowerment through advocacy and consciousness-raising: Implications of a structural approach to social work. *Journal of Sociology and Social Welfare, 17*(2), 53–67.

Moxley, D. P., & Freddolino, P. P. (1994). Client-driven advocacy and psychiatric disability: A model for social work practice. *Journal of Sociology and Social Welfare, 21*(2), 91–108.

Murase, K. (1992). Organizing in the Japanese-American community. In F. G. Rivera & J. L. Erlich (Eds.), *Community organizing in a diverse society* (pp. 159–180). Boston: Allyn & Bacon.

Nepstad, S. (1997). The process of cognitive liberation: Cultural synapses, links, and frame contradictions in the U.S.–Central America peace movement. *Sociological Inquiry, 67*(4), 470–487.

Netting, F. E., Huber, R., Paton, R. N., & Kautz, J. R., III. (1995). Elder rights and the long-term care ombudsman program. *Social Work, 40*(3), 351–357.

Netting, F. E., Kettner, P. M., & McMurtry, S. L. (1993). *Social work macro practice*. White Plains, NY: Longman.

O'Donnell, S. (1993). Involving clients in welfare policy making. *Social Work, 38*(5), 629–635.

Panitch, A. (1974). Advocacy in practice. *Social Work, 19*, 326–332.

Pantoja, A. (2002). *Memoir of a visionary*. Houston, TX: Arte Publico Press.

Parsons, R. J. (1991). The mediator role in social work practice. *Social Work, 36*(6), 483–487.

Patti, R. J., & Resnick, H. (1972). Changing the agency from within. *Social Work, 17*(4), 48–57.

Perl, P. (1999, June 27). Building inspector with a bulletproof vest. *The Washington Post Magazine*, pp. 1–8, 25–30.

Perlman, E. (2000). Rest in place: Development is endangering many rural cemeteries. *Governing, 14*(2), 18

Perlmutter, F. D., & Cnaan, R. A. (1999). Community development as a public sector agenda. *Journal of Community Practice, 6*(4), 57–77.

Pertschuk, M. (1986). *Giant killers*. New York: W. W. Norton.

Powers, P. (1977). Social change: Nader style. *Journal of Education for Social Work, 13*(3), 63–69.

Powers, P. R. (1984). *Focused energy: A study of public interest advocates*. Unpublished doctoral dissertation, University of Maryland, College Park.

Powers, P. (Ed.) (1994). *Challenging: Interview with Advocates and Activists Monograph*. Baltimore: University of Maryland at Baltimore, School of Social Work.

Protection and Advocacy for Individuals with Mental Illness (n.d.) Retrieved on July 22, 2002 from http://members.sockets.net/~mopasjc/paimi.htm

Ramanathan, C. S. (1992). EAP's response to personal stress and productivity: Implications for occupational social work. *Social Work, 37*(3), 234–239.

Rankin, T. (Ed.). (2000). *Local heroes: Changing America*. New York: W. W. Norton and the Center for Documentary Studies.

Rapp, C. A., Shera, W., & Kisthardt, W. (1993). Research strategies for consumer empowerment of people with severe mental illness. *Social Work, 38*(6), 727–735.

Reeser, L. C., & Leighninger, L. (1990). Back to our roots: Towards a specialization in social justice. *Journal of Sociology and Social Welfare, 17*(2), 69–87.

Richan, W. C. (1996). *Lobbying for social change*, 2nd ed. Binghamton, NY: Haworth.

Rogge, M. E. (1993). Social work, disenfranchised communities, and the natural environment: Field education opportunities. *Journal of Social Work Education, 29*(1), 111–120.

Romanyshyn, J. M. (1971). *Social welfare: Charity to justice*. New York: Random House.

Rose, S. J. (1999). Social workers as municipal legislators: Potholes, garbage and social activism, *Journal of Community Practice, 6*(4), 1–15.

Rose, S. M. (1990). Advocacy/empowerment: An approach to clinical practice for social work. *Journal of Sociology and Social Welfare, 17*(2), 41–51.

Rose, S. M. (2000). Reflections on empowerment-based practice. *Social Work, 45*(5), 403–412.

Ross, J. W. (1993). Media messages, empathy, and social work. *Health and Social Work, 18*(3), 163–164.

Ryan, B. (1992). *Feminism and the women's movement: Dynamics of change in social movement ideology and activism.* New York: Routledge.

Ryan, C. (1991). *Prime time activism: Media strategies for grassroots organizing.* Boston: South End.

Salcido, R., & Manalo, V. (2002). Planning electoral activities for social work students: A policy practice approach. *Arete, 26*(1), 55–60.

Saleebey, D. (1990). Philosophical disputes in social work: Social justice denied. *Journal of Sociology and Social Welfare, 17*(2), 29–40.

Schneider, R. L., & Lester, L. (2001). *Social work advocacy: A new framework for action.* Belmont, CA: Brooks/Cole.

Sebenius, J. K. (2001). Six habits of merely effective negotiators. *Harvard Business Review, 79*(4), 87–95.

Segal, S. P., Silverman, C., & Temkin, T. (1993). Empowerment and self-help agency practice for people with mental disabilities. *Social Work, 38*(6), 705–712.

Severson, M. M. (1994). Adapting social work values to the corrections environment. *Social Work, 39*(4), 451–456.

Shapiro, J. P. (1993). Believing in a friend: Advocating for community life. In A. N. Amado (Ed.), *Friendships and community connections with and without developmental disabilities* (pp. 181–196). Baltimore: Paul H. Brookes.

Sherman, W., & Wenocur, S. (1983). Empowering public welfare workers through mutual support. *Social Work, 28*(5), 375–379.

Shultz, J. (2002). *The democracy owners' manual: A practical guide to changing the world.* New Brunswick, NJ: Rutgers University Press.

Simon, B. L. (1990). Rethinking empowerment. *Journal of Progressive Human Services, 1*(1), 27–39.

Simon, B. L. (1994). *The empowerment tradition in American social work: A history.* New York: Columbia University Press.

Simons, R. L. (1995). Generic social work skills in social administration: The example of persuasion. In J. Rothman, J. L. Erlich, & J. E. Tropman (Eds.), *Strategies of community intervention* (5th ed., pp 163–172). Itasca, IL: F. E. Peacock.

Smith, D., & Lopez, P. (2002, October 26). A voice for the "little fellers." *Minneapolis Star Tribune.*

Soifer, S. (1998). Mobile home park lot "rent control": A successful rural legislative campaign. *Journal of Community Practice, 5*(4), 25–37.

Soifer, S., & Singer, J. (1999). The campaign to restore the Disability Assistance and Loan Program in the state of Maryland. *Journal of Community Practice, 6*(2), 1–10.

Solomon, B. B. (1976). *Black empowerment: Social work in oppressed communities.* New York: Columbia University Press.

Spain, D. (2001). *How women saved the city.* Minneapolis: University of Minnesota Press.

Specht, H. (1969). Disruptive tactics. *Social Work, 14*(2), 5–15.

Spolar, C. (1991, April 19). Two who dared to take the stand: D.C. foster care workers told of crying children, broken promises. *The Washington Post,* p. A10.

Staub-Bernasconi, S. (1991). Social action, empowerment and social work: An integrative and theoretical framework for social work and social work with groups. *Social Work With Groups, 14*(3/4), 35–51.

Sundet, P. A., & Kelly, M. J. (2002). Legislative policy briefs: Practical methodology in teaching policy practice. *Journal of Teaching in Social Work, 22*(1/2), 49–60.

Swenson, C. R. (1998). Clinical social work's contribution to a social justice perspective. *Social Work, 43*(6), 527–537.

Szegedy-Maszak, M. (2002, June 3). Consuming passion: The mentally ill are taking charge of their own recovery. *U.S. News & World Report, 132*(19), pp 55–57.

Thursz, D. (1971). The arsenal of social action strategies: Options for social workers. *Social Work, 16*(1), 27–34.

Toseland, R. W. (1990). *Group work with older adults.* New York: New York University Press.

Tower, K. D. (1994). Consumer-centered social work practice: Restoring client self-determination. *Social Work, 39*(2), 191–196.

Van Soest, D. (1994). Strange bedfellows: A call for reordering national priorities from three social justice perspectives. *Social Work, 39*(6), 710–717.

VeneKlasen, L. (with Miller, V.). (2002). *A new weave of power, people & politics: The action guide for advocacy and citizen participation.* Oklahoma City, OK: World Neighbors.

Von Bretzel, N. C. (1997). Social work practice with marginalized populations. In M. Reisch & E. Gambrill (Eds.), *Social work in the 21st century* (pp. 239–248). Thousand Oaks, CA: Pine Forge Press.

Wagner, D. (1990). *The quest for a radical profession: Social service careers and political ideology.* Lanham, MD: University Press of America.

Wakefield, J. C. (1994, September). Debate with author of "Social Work and Social Control: A Reply to Austin." *Social Service Review, 68*(3), 48.

Wallack, L., Dorfman, L., Jernigan, D., & Themba, M. (1993). *Media advocacy and public health.* Thousand Oaks, CA: Sage.

Wallerstein, N. (1993). Empowerment and health: The theory and practice of community change. *Community Development Journal, 28*(3), 218–227.

Walls, D. (1993). *The activist's almanac: The concerned citizen's guide to the leading advocacy organizations in America.* New York: Simon & Schuster.

Walz, T., & Groze, V. (1991). The mission of social work revisited: An agenda for the 1990s. *Social Work, 36*(6), 500–504.

Warner-Smith, P., & Brown, P. (2002). "The town dictates what I do": The leisure, health and well-being of women in a small Australian country town. *Leisure Studies, 21*(1), 39–56.

Weaver, H. N. (2000). Activism and American Indian issues: Opportunities and roles for social workers. *Journal of Progressive Human Services, 11*(1), 3–22.

Williams, P. N. (1978). *Investigative reporting and editing.* Englewood Cliffs, NJ: Prentice Hall.

Witkin, S. L. (1998). Chronicity and invisibility. *Social Work, 43*(4), 293–94.

Wood, G. G., & Middleman, R. R. (1989). *The structural approach to direct practice in social work.* New York: Columbia University Press.

Wood, G. G., & Middleman, R. R. (1991). Advocacy and social action: Key elements in the structural approach to direct practice in social work. *Social Work With Groups, 14*(3/4), 53–63.

14

Using Organizing:
Acting in Concert

El pueblo, unido, jamás será vencido! (A people, united,
will never be defeated!)

DIRECT ACTION CHANT

How can we bring together a community to change the status quo? Think struggle. Think engagement. Think stories. Those who seek to strengthen the power of people, social connections, and community capacity[1] frequently operate from one of three distinct (though often overlapping) traditions: (a) organization and mobilization, (b) coordination and participation, and (c) innovation, narration, and liberation.[2] It is not suggested that there are only three. Changing society is never easy, but this chapter will describe ways to mobilize community within each tradition, whether the focus is on a problem, place, or program. The idea is to provide pictures of what is happening at the level of the street.

VALUES-DRIVEN COMMUNITY INTERVENTION: AN EXAMPLE

Before explicating three traditional ways that community members are being connected with each other, we provide an account of abuse, neglect and depersonalization in a group home.

This story illustrates why social workers must know how to act in concert with others to protect service users.

The Community Calls to Us to Stop Human Hurt

In the social service world, those concerned about fairness and accountability play the role of *caring critics*, often intervening when others have not served the community well. Communal responsibility must substitute for individual responsibility in those cases, such as group homes for teenagers or the physically and mentally challenged, where abuse and death can occur (Levy, 2002a, 2002b, 2000c; Schwartz, 1992, Chapter 5). Professionals who monitor such homes must research the government oversight structure and the private contractor network to determine who is making, or deferring, decisions and how to best access and influence them. In Box 14.1, a newspaper reporter[3] documents what can happen when a service delivery system and a vulnerable group exist in isolation.

BOX 14.1	INVISIBLE DEATHS: DELAYED TREATMENT

More than 1,000 people under city care are scattered among 150 homelike facilities run by private contractors. . . . The services the retarded receive—in their group homes, and in therapy, skills training or work programs they attend daily outside the home—cost as much, per person, per year, as four years at Harvard. . . . The ideal of compassionate care and municipal accountability has yielded to a reality of profiteering and fraud, facilitated by city agencies that have for years demanded little accountability and little human decency in return for a vast outlay of public money. For corporate wrongdoers, the consequences for cruelty and neglect have been negligible. For the city's retarded men and women—men and women who are politically, and sometimes literally, voiceless—the consequences have been swift, direct and sometimes fatal.

A review of tens of thousands of documents from four city agencies and the federal courts revealed more than 350 incidents of abuse, neglect and robbery of retarded residents in the '90s. . . . Yet none of these and other documented reports of abuse led to fines or criminal penalties against the offending group home operators. . . . And then there are the dead. Fifty-three group home residents have died in the last three years. . . . only three [deaths] have received even cursory inquiry from the city.

A WORLD WITHOUT WORDS

. . . There is a particular tragedy in being born with very little and losing some or all of that. In being 22-year-old, retarded, paraplegic Robert, who has legs the length of rulers, feet short some toes, chronically sopping Huggies—and a mind uncannily able to recall every song in the hymnal.

Given up by his birth mother, then a foster one, he now has been sent by the city to his first group home. [His] smile says, Stay and talk. . . . "Where do you live?" Robert asks a rare visitor, fingering his bib. "Do you love me?" He allows that he has learned his address and his ABCs. But his attempts at dinner-table conversations are interrupted. His profoundly retarded housemates have forsaken their chicken noodle soup to hurl themselves against the living room walls.

There are benevolent laws on the books. There is money in the budget. There is magic in this lonely, miniature man. But officials have placed him in a world without words . . .

O beautiful, for spacious skies
For amber waves of grain.

Urgently, exquisitely, Robert tries to do what his city hasn't done for him. He comforts himself. He sings until the heads hitting drywall overwhelm.

Source: Quoted excerpts from Boo (1999, p. A1)c. 2001. *The Washington Post.* Reprinted with permission.

We Respond to the Community

BRINGING OURSELVES INTO READINESS

How would you address a case of human degradation and government indifference such as that described in Box 14.1? To spark an outcry that will lead to change, you must develop many action plans. As a student, you could start with student organizations or citizen groups engaged in advocacy for the mentally disabled. Here is one way to start: First, pull together the deans or directors of the social work, sociology, and psychology programs in the area. (Make your first call to the dean deemed to be most reform oriented.) Elicit their ideas, but make it clear that you expect them to put their values into action. Before the meeting, draft a letter to the investigative reporter, requesting a briefing so you can follow up intelligently on what she

found. Ask the deans to sign the letter and to meet with the reporter, because investigative reporters, social workers, and policy makers can coalesce and build policy agendas. Second, invite your elected representatives to visit the site and let them meet—in person—those in need. Put together a list of contacts in legal aid and organizations for the developmentally disabled with the help of each representative's staff. Ask the representatives to call their contacts in the mayor's office. Third, involve any group home residents in the area who can participate in action, fund-raising, and publicity efforts.

Put solutions on the table; think how to prevent recurrences; measure results (Itzhaky & York, 2002). After the exposé (see Box 14.1), chagrined city officials created an independently governed $29 million monitoring foundation to assure compliance with a plan agreed to by advocates. Finally, be kind: Find Robert a suitable home.

Throughout, let your outrage strengthen your effectiveness: "The root layer of organizing is about passion, compassion, the firing line. Techniques and skills can be built on top of this layer of caring. They can be taught or transferred. . . . I'm not sure gut level caring can. Organizing without the caring becomes a profession of day planner totin' technocrats" (Barry Greever, personal communication, June 20, 2001).

DRAWING ON COMMUNITY STRENGTHS

Pulling in the community at large can aid people who are living in grim institutions. In a parallel situation, nursing home reform groups have mobilized the public and influenced decision makers in various ways. Some organizers have joined forces with frontline employees to improve the pay and working conditions of staff as a way to improve residents' lives. Some groups train community volunteers to visit homes as objective observers. An Illinois group resolves individual grievances from many facilities, files complaints, holds inspectors accountable, and sends information on facility violations to local news outlets.

It is easy to blame all social ills and individual pain on the political party in power or on huge social forces. Group homes, nursing homes, and the spread of AIDS are "blindingly obvious" (Mallaby, 2002) situations in the public sphere where our profession should instigate change, drawing upon community strengths in the process.

CONVINCING OUR PEERS TO ACT

The social worker can operate at a personal level to address social injustice or draw attention to an issue. Here are ways to engage sympathetic people and those in your social circle:

- Become knowledgeable about a subject so that others trust your expertise and recommendations. Share provocative newspaper articles and editorials.

- Ask people to do tasks and get engaged in projects, events, and actions. Figure out a concrete way for peers to participate in 4-hour stints.

- Provide everything needed for a project: leaflets, poster paper, addresses, reports or documents, computers.

- Convey your appreciation to people—at an event and afterward. Send copies of newspaper coverage to all participants. If there is television coverage, alert participants to the time and station.

- Telephone people who planned to attend, but did not, to ask about complications such as transportation or child care (no guilt tripping).

- Urge people to arrive early for activities to go over talking points or last-minute concerns and to stay afterward to discuss what happened.

THE ORGANIZATION AND MOBILIZATION TRADITION

Organizing has a proud history. Victories won by organized people have improved multiple facets of each of our lives.

Background

According to social work professors Robert Fisher and Eric Shragge (2000, p. 6), organizing involves "building community *and* engaging in a wider struggle for social and economic justice." Traditionally, organizing emphasizes "mobilizing community residents to form their own identities, renew their interest in public life, and fight for their rights across a broad range of issues" (Kingsley, McNeely, & Gibson, 1997, p. 27). Organizing also entails economic and social analysis. Success comes from "strong people skills to bring people together and keep them inspired and working well; capable organization to assure that the work involved actually gets done; and strategic savvy in order to pick the right objectives and the right public actions to win them" (Shultz, 2002, p. 97).

The Discount Foundation, which has supported community organizing, uses five criteria to examine an organization's strengths, limitations, and potential. These exemplify the goals of many organizing projects:

1. Winning concrete improvements and policy changes through collective action

2. Permanently altering the relations of power at the local, state, or national level

3. Developing citizen leaders in poor, urban communities of color

4. Increasing civic participation at local, state, and national levels

5. Building stable and viable organizations, accountable to the communities in which they

are located (Neighborhood Funders Group, 2001a, The Discount Foundation approach)

Broad Orientations

Fisher and Shragge (2000) compare and contrast two approaches to organizing—social action versus community building and development. The latter approach was covered in Chapter 5. These approaches are sometimes labeled conflict versus consensus organizing. They define social action as "an engagement in the struggle for social change through organizing people to pressure government or private bodies" and say that "the use of conflict strategies and tactics" is central, although not the only approach (pp. 1–2). Here are two national examples that fit their definition:

1. A sophisticated Web and mailing campaign by the Social Investment Forum Foundation and Co-op America, two nonprofit organizations, generated approximately 6,000 individualized emails and postcard protests to Citigroup in the 5-month period prior to the U.S. banking giant's decision to cease the abusive lending practice known as *upfront premium credit insurance* (personal communication July 22, 2003 with Fran Teplitz).

2. The Aids Coalition to Unleash Power known as ACT UP and other groups have organized hundreds of civil disobedience actions across the country, focusing not only on AIDS but on the increasing climate of homophobia and attacks on lesbians and gay men. On October 13, 1987, the Supreme Court was the site of the first national lesbian and gay disobedience action, where nearly 600 people were arrested protesting the decision in Hardwick vs. Bowers, which upheld sodomy laws (Act Up, n.d.)

WORKING WITH CONFLICT

Authentic community initiatives are interactive by nature. As community members ask for changes, eventually making demands, and seek more control of their lives, conflicts with the target are inevitable.[4] "Change means movement. Movement means friction," explained organizing virtuoso Saul Alinsky (1972, p. 21). See Box 14.2.

Some organizers plan for friction and use it to train and develop leadership. They want oppressed people to get their ire up when privileged people make statements of the let-them-eat-cake variety. Alinsky proved that even though have-nots lack power and money, their numbers allow them to start and stop many things. Putting one's body on the line to face police dogs is one example, but leaders speak more of justice, education, pressure, and action than of outright physical confrontation with targets. Simply moving one's body to the right place at the right time and bringing along 10 friends is also people power; rallies can draw thousands of people. Nationally, more than 50 mass-based and church-based organizations hold or stage "accountability sessions" with officials to guarantee public input (Bobo, Kendall, & Max, 2001, Chapter 8), often filling huge halls and ensuring plenty of news coverage.

For individual change leaders, the courage to deal with conflict requires a willingness to be bold and to "push" against foes. Former U.S. Congressman Parren Mitchell tells a story about his days of traveling around as head of Maryland's Human Relations Commission.

> I was young and foolish. We had been on the Eastern Shore and I was friendly with this young white reporter. He said, "Do you want to go to a Klan meeting?" and I said "Sure;" so I went. The Klan met in a yellow school bus. We got on. Nobody spoke to us and we said "How you doin?" They acted all befuddled. I asked the guy sitting there, "Can I sit next to you?" and he said "no" and I said, "Oh, come on." I sat down. The guy who was heading the meeting stood up in front with the driver. They kept conferring, and finally said, "There'll be no meeting tonight, the meeting is canceled."[5]

Having a witness, the element of surprise, and a casual demeanor protected Mitchell as he employed the tactics of disruption and calling someone's bluff.

WORKING WITH CONSENSUS

Social work leader Terry Mizrahi (2002) suggests that we "assume the principle of least contest," (p. 6) escalating or antagonizing only to the degree needed. Some organizers today talk of reciprocal or shared power and choose to work closely with decision makers in the private sector. For example, the Consensus Organizing Institute in San Diego (http://www.rohan.sdsu.edu/~consensu/) recommends bringing cross-sectoral leaders together to find common ground as they work on an issue. Michael Eichler (1995), a proponent of the collaborative approach, describes consensus organizing as "a yearning for partnerships—a desire by all the parties to succeed and a sense that everyone has to pull to-

BOX 14.2   SAUL ALINSKY AND GRASSROOTS ORGANIZING

Saul Alinsky (1909–1972) was the son of a Russian tailor; his parents were Orthodox Jews. After studying sociology at the University of Chicago, Alinsky married a social worker. He started as a street worker concerned about the social milieu of delinquents and eventually inspired thousands of organizing projects. Alinsky, who hated to see fellow humans pushed around, demonstrated that (a) mass-based organizing can be accomplished with unsophisticated people and (b) organizing skills can be taught.

His time-honored book *Rules for Radicals* (1972) details conflict tactics involving simple props—gum, baked beans, shopping carts, rats—and shows how he deliberately provoked average Joes in order to observe their reactions and take their measure as potential leaders: "Do you live over in that slummy building?" "What the hell do you live there for?" "Did you ever try to get that landlord to do anything about it?" (Alinsky, 1972, p. 103).

Alinsky's approach was to work with talented individuals and to build a huge coalition for years until local leaders gained enough recognition that dominant employers such as Eastman Kodak would negotiate with them. In the 1940s, Alinsky organized the Back of the (Stock) Yards, a working class Polish area in Chicago, in part by uniting labor and Catholics—groups that historically had been at odds. He convinced people that it was in their self-interest to form a federation. His forte was strategic thinking, spontaneous tactics, and getting in with influential people. Marshall Field, III, heir to a department store fortune; Bishop Bernard Shiel; and Kathryn Lewis (daughter of labor leader John L. Lewis) helped establish the Industrial Areas Foundation (IAF) to support Alinsky's work in furthering democracy. Gordon Sherman used Midas Muffler money to help Alinsky launch a training institute. Long after his death, Alinsky is remembered as a fighter for the disenfranchised and someone who put democracy into action. For a detailed interview with Alinsky, see Norden (1972); for a biography, see Horwitt (1989).

---

gether in order to succeed" (p. 257). Once the target comes to the table, there is a presumption of consensus between the action system and the target. For groups that make decisions mainly in consensus mode (e.g., Native Americans, Quakers), that could be the best way to mobilize them into action. (For additional background on consensus organizing, see http://www.cpn.org/tools/dictionary/organizing.html at the CPN website.)

Consensus and conflict orientations are not diametrically opposed. Eichler concedes that consensus building does not work when key partners refuse to participate and will not be brought to the table. Beck and Eichler (2000) believe "organizers and community practitioners should learn both techniques so that the issue can guide the strategy" (p. 98). Organizer Bob Moses reminds us that even conflict organizing involves an underlying *consensus among the nonelite*, that is, consensus within the action system: "Part of what happened in Mississippi was . . . tapping into a consensus. People agreed that if they could get the vote it would be a good thing and they would be better off" (Moses & Cobb, 2001, p. 111). Activists inevitably reach moments when they have to decide whether to include or pressure those who are dominant in the community. It is important to (a) be aware of both options and (b) be willing to vigorously use either of them.

OTHER CONSIDERATIONS

Is it more essential to win power and respect by building on commonalties or by assisting those labeled as different by society? Some scholars link this debate to "new" social movements that do not focus on class or economic issues, such as gay rights or antinuclear movements (Cox, 2001); others discuss it in terms of pragmatism versus challenging existing frameworks (Calpotura & Fellner, 1996). Progressives who argue for a commonality focus believe that building on what unites is more strategic and lasting. Those who support identity politics remind us to start where people are, and add that an initial spotlight on uniqueness and differences—with the attendant discrimination and alienation—may lead people later to broader social concerns (Guinier & Torres, 2002).

Some organizers focus on one issue such as shutting down the U.S. Army training school formerly called the School of the Americas (http://www.soaw.org/new/) to stop human rights abuses, promoting the separation of church and state, or challenging privatization of hospitals and prisons. Other organizers seek to build community capacity to face a multitude of challenges. A single issue may be easier to win, but a broad base is needed to challenge institutional power. Debates over campaign breadth tend to quiet down as accomplishments grow more visible. An example is the Idaho Community Action Network, which "won expanded in-home care services for more than 1,200 people with disabilities" and propelled "the restructuring of Idaho's medical indigence program, resulting in $6 million in new Medicaid services" (Neighborhood Funders Group, 2001, "Health," para. 3).

Although the above distinctions are useful, there are more commonalties among organizers than differences. Our position is that social workers need to engage in far more organizing and social action, using whatever *mode* works best for those they serve (see Chapter 2, this volume).

Organizing Skills

BUILDING RELATIONSHIPS

A born organizer, the late Senator Paul Wellstone was "famous for talking not just to the customers of the cafes he loved to frequent, but for going into the kitchen, talking up the dishwashers and fry cooks, urging them not only to vote

for him but also to demand more for themselves. He befriended U.S. Capitol security guards and brought them home to dinner" (Smith & Lopez, 2002, p. 1). Such behavior brought 20,000 people to a memorial service and celebration of his life. Having an affinity and respect for people is crucial; skills can be built on such values.

Building relationships is a necessary first step in "belief bonding" with the constituency, that is, in creating a belief that, together, the organizer and the group can effect a change. Earlier, we listed some ways to engage peers and mobilize those who already trust us. Organizers must also gain the trust of *strangers* and create a climate where people want to mobilize themselves (see Box 14.3).

Besides attending community events, organizers spend as much informal time in conversation with friendly residents as they can. They patiently gather information in easygoing ways: "How's work?" "What have you done since I saw you last?" They schedule as many planning meetings as possible in living rooms. When the group wishes to reach out, the organizer may suggest "house meetings," events held in homes for base-building purposes, usually involving around eight people. Organizers try to talk to new people every day.

Organizers frequently use food and beverages (a potluck or even a cocktail party) to create a relaxed environment and to advance one-on-one recruitment to the cause. Cesar Chavez went to the homes of migrant workers at mealtime and

BOX 14.3	THE RECRUITMENT OF A FAMOUS ORGANIZER

An anecdote about two well-known organizers embodies the topics in this section. Legendary organizer Fred Ross (who was being funded by Alinsky) went to the Chavez home in San Jose, California, three nights in a row to ask the couple to sponsor a meeting in their home. He first won the trust of Helen Chavez. At the meeting—over the babble of babies and children—soft-spoken Ross had to capture the attention of Cesar Chavez (then a 25-year-old laborer), his *pachucos* (tough-guy friends), and his neighbors, as they sat on old couches that "sagged audibly under the weight of too many people" (Ferriss & Sandoval, 1997, pp. 37–39). Ross described neighborhood problems but also his organization's success in the firing and jailing of Los Angeles police officers who had nearly killed seven

young Chicanos. Thinking back, Chavez recalls, "I knew about the Bloody Christmas case, and so did everyone else in that room. . . . Fred did such a good job of explaining how poor people could build power that I could taste it. I could really *feel* it. I thought, Gee, it's like digging a hole; there was nothing complicated about it" (p. 43). Ross got Chavez to attend another organizing meeting with him that very night. Within months, Chavez was recruiting strangers himself through house meetings and canvassing and then a mass meeting. This made him "nervous to the point of illness, afraid no one would come", but since he had organized well, a slow trickle eventually swelled to a crowd of over four hundred (p. 51). The man—with an eighth grade education—was a success.

let them feed him as a means of bonding. The organizers who created the Solidarity Sponsoring Campaign, an association for low-wage workers in Baltimore, were keenly aware of the need to establish trust. On cold nights, social worker Kerry Miciotto set up a stand on the street and served hot tea to janitors and other workers as they came and went from office buildings. A member of the Association of Community Organizations for Reform Now (ACORN) takes the discussion beyond trust: "When you set up a meeting for poor people, make sure to provide transportation and food. The hungriest people are who you want at an action" (Brooks, 2001, p. 73).

Techniques. Gestures that say "we are listening to you" build relationships. Chavez successfully recruited farmworkers with a simple procedure: After passing around self-addressed three-by-five cards with space on the back for the worker's name and address, Chavez asked a question that each person could answer on the card: "What do you consider to be a just hourly wage?" His method of surveying farm workers was an instant hit—because these workers were being consulted for the first time. As one worker said, "It's like letting us vote . . . on what we think" (Levy, 1975, p. xxi). Likewise, ACORN organizers visited 500 workfare sites in Los Angeles and asked workers about their concerns (Brooks, 2001, p. 72). Local leader Gustavo Torres made a considerable effort with Maryland day laborers to learn and provide what they wanted: a sign-up system, a work-pickup site, and legal backup. In turn, the emergent leaders began to control crowds that were gathering at intersections and upsetting the neighbors (Ly, 2001).

Clearly, successful organizing involves *analysis* of relationships, not just "banners, literature, and personalities" (Robinson & Hanna, 1994, p. 80). Kerry Miciotto interviewed many workers and potential allies by "taking a meeting." Here is how Robinson and Hanna (1994) describe the careful listening and probing that occur in such meetings: "The focus is on discovering the core motivational drives: Why did the person do what they did; why does the person feel this way; why is the person concerned about this issue? Childhood experiences, pivotal life events, and watershed personal decisions often figure in. The answers to these questions will reveal the person's value system" (p. 85).

Making each person count. Groups and actions work best when the strengths of each participant can be tapped. Organizers make it their business to know who plays the piano, who likes taking minutes, who is happiest without assigned responsibilities but so she "choose" to set up or clean up. The organizer furthers relationships between members, too. In building bonds and developing leadership, organizers find ways to give strokes to members—in front of other members—to bolster the self-confidence that leads to leadership. Pointing out skills and competencies of individuals to their peers in an even-handed manner eases interactions later, during situations when people have to rely on each other's strengths. Organizers also need to assess—and be realistic about—who will be good leaders and work well in trying circumstances and who will not. It averts later headaches to find meaningful roles for those constituents who are incompatible with others.

REFLECTING THE COMMUNITY

The issues you choose to focus on must be of interest to the community. Bob Moses (2001) recalls how, as civil rights organizers framed the community's everyday issues, they had to slowly and deliberately "search out where [consensus] was lodged beneath layer after layer of other concerns" (p. 85). Leaders should also reflect the community. Though more and more indigenous leaders are being hired, the average organizer may not match the neighborhood culturally or demographically. Bob Moses himself, who is acclaimed for his work with uneducated people young and old, had a master's degree from Harvard when he started working in the backwaters of Mississippi. Thus, although there was a racial match, there was not an education match. Moses succeeded because he was determined to reflect the community's wishes. More recently, a Lutheran church in Milwaukee, Wisconsin, solved its diversity challenge by recruiting "peer ministers," volunteers from the neighborhood whose presence made the institution more inviting and trustworthy (Staral, 2000, p. 90). Community people often expressed their true sentiments to them. Finally, direct action tactics must be matched to the norms of community participants (Alinsky, 1971).

USING COMMUNITY TALENT

Practice wisdom suggests that you follow these steps:

1. Recruit people to serve in specialized ways—a lawyer to keep your group out of trouble; a writer to keep your message clear; someone

to call local, regional, and national radio talk shows.

2. Meet key political figures at the local and state level. Get letters of endorsement from esteemed people for your cause.

3. Use people in your group to recruit friends, neighbors, and relatives.

4. Convince a liberal group to move beyond talk in a particular sphere or limited way. Even if only a few members step forward, you can carry out an action such as picketing or testing for discrimination.

5. Expect the best from everyone. Do not tolerate sloppy, inaccurate, or late work from volunteers or members. Expect leaders to practice before they speak in public or to the media. The group's credibility and reputation are at stake.

WIDENING THE CIRCLE OF PARTICIPATION

Building internal relationships and a support network is not enough. Members should be encouraged to bring others to important meetings and events. One way to promote this is to have members make lists of the people they pledge to bring. These lists are submitted in advance to help the organization prepare for the expected turnout. At the event, guests and newcomers who show up are compared with the lists to see which members met or exceeded their goals and can be counted on in the future. In some organizations, members tell the entire assembly whether they reached their pledge. Public accountability brings results but ought to be handled in a fashion that avoids humiliation or blame. Members need to feel involved and valued before they can turn difficulty into determination. Here, as in many contexts, it is prudent to learn what members want from an experience and to be there for them. The bottom line is that organizers try to expand the number of supporters and allies who will support the cause.[6]

WIDENING THE CIRCLE OF RESPONSIBILITY

"To fulfill its promise, democracy must meet the challenges of equity, accountability and responsiveness," says Marshall Ganz (2003, intro, para. 1) who teaches at the Kennedy School of Government. The importance of his words is highlighted by an incident in California where a young woman was murdered after leaving public transportation. The media played the story as a drama: Public safety was mentioned only in the form of warnings and advice about *individual* behavior such as the suggestion to carry your

keys in your hands. Lawrence Wallack (2002) points out that such messages "place almost total responsibility for safety on the rider," and asks what would be required to "make the environment safe, regardless of what various individual passengers do? The stories did not focus on environmental factors such as lighting in the station area, cutbacks in station security personnel, or the much larger issue of violence against women" (p. 349). Immediate direct action such as vigils to raise consciousness are a start, but organizers ultimately must hold the right parties accountable. The goal is to increase the number of targets, that is, individuals and institutions who can fairly be held *accountable*. Ultimately, organizers will focus on those targets who can accomplish **X** [in this case, change for women, *equity*] and will enlist targets who want to be *responsive* to the larger public. (See Appendix A regarding widening responsibility.)

To make the most of scarce resources, organizing requires what Ganz (2003) calls strategic capacity, as well as basic strategies to:

- concentrate resources at the point they will do the most good;
- act at the moment when the group's chances of success are greatest; and
- undertake activities consistent with the group's capacities (Devising strategies and tactics, para. 1).

Formulating strategies involves a process and an ability that are important to professionals in many fields who must function with little power and little money. (For David versus Goliath strategies, see Ganz, 2003; Rosin, 2003.)

Formulating Strategies: Key Elements

"Today the five hundred richest people on the planet control more wealth than the bottom three billion, half of the human population" (Loeb, 1999, p. 3). The kind of people who are drawn to social action naturally yearn to be able to immediately remedy that situation by any means possible, including revolution. It is exceedingly difficult to focus on ambitious but more obtainable goals such as "improving the lives of half of those in poverty in the United States through the work of community organizations." (Remember this goal because it will be mentioned again at the conclusion of the discussion of this tradition.)

Once activists formulate obtainable goals, they still need to formulate winning strategies and action plans or roadmaps (Shultz, 2002). Here are key elements and practical points they can consider.

GOALS

The goals of organizers and the community are most likely to coincide when everyone understands and agrees on the larger purposes. Ordinarily, organizers focus on a hot issue and later articulate underlining principles, but for action strategy purposes, the vision and resultant goals must be made explicit.

For instance, suppose our organizer's vision is to HELP LITTLE GUYS AROUND THE WORLD. Hundreds of goals could flow from this aim, but our organizer settles on the *long-term* goal of *preventing unnecessary deaths and injuries*. On further reflection, our organizer focuses on an *intermediate* goal of *banning landmines*. From here on the goals must be more measurable; our organizer chooses as a *nearer-term* goal *getting the United States to join the landmine ban treaty*. The next step is a specific *short-term* goal such as *win over an influential* person (e.g., *convince the Children's Defense Fund to add this goal to its issue agenda*). Finally, our organizer selects a strategic *objective* such as *get an appointment with Marian Wright Edelman*. The goals element makes us ask if we truly know what we are about and if we can identify doable steps to further our ends.

ORGANIZATIONAL CONSIDERATIONS

Once organizers and residents have decided what should be done, they must think realistically about numbers of members or allies, budget, time lines, reputation and history of the organization, and other resources, such as office space or van transportation. Key questions include the following (Speeter, 1978, p. 68): What internal resources (from the group) do we need in order to get where we want to go? What external resources? Who might support us? Given time pressures on members and allies, MacNair (1996) recommends conducting an "energy assessment" to examine sources of individual energy and to ensure project energy will not be dissipated (pp. 193–194). This element makes us ask if we are truly prepared and equipped to act effectively or to finesse our weaknesses.

CONSTITUENTS, ALLIES, AND OPPONENTS

Constituents need not belong to your organization; they can be all those who identify with your cause and who may benefit if you attain your goals. Your organization's primary loyalty is with them and vice versa. Opponents can usually be identified through newspapers, broadcast news shows, and trade papers. If necessary, you can track down your opposition's officers and directors by examining the organization's incorporation papers on file at the courthouse. Here are questions to consider about allies:

- Who are your major allies? How strong are the links between you?
- Who are your necessary or potential allies? What is your plan for enlisting their support?
- Are you aware of the wider circle of supportive people you could call on?
- Who is in your network of consultants?
- What is the common ground between your group and your potential allies? What larger perspective unites you? (Shields, 1994, p. 88)

When strategizing, it is a good idea to make lists of who on key issues is already with, possibly with, or probably against your group. If time permits, have small groups make the lists independently and compare their different perspectives. For instance, a parent organization dedicated to increasing and enforcing gun control might come up with this list of players:

Potential constituents: Mothers (parallel to MADD), siblings, and other students (parallel to SADD), peace churches and organizations, local chapters of Million Moms March, handgun control groups

Potential allies: Emergency room personnel, community leaders in high-crime areas, socially concerned faith-based organizations, police

Potential opponents: National Rifle Association chapters, gun dealers, pawnshop owners, hunters, farmers, gun-owning county council members

A role should be found for any interested person or task group, even if training is necessary for some constituents to be effective. Recognize that certain allies would be particularly valuable—in this case, doctors and nurses from emergency rooms overburdened by gun victims. This element makes us ask who can be enlisted to act or form a coalition and whether we can outwit our opposition.

TARGETS

Selecting appropriate targets often combines investigation, research, and organizing skills (see the illustration at the beginning of this chapter). A case from Paul Speer and Joseph Hughey reveals how targets are pinpointed. A community organization discovers that a service agency is paying absentee landlords to house its immigrant clients in buildings unfit for tenants and deleterious to nearby homeowners. When the agency refuses to demand that the landlords bring the housing up to code, organization leaders track down the agency's funding sources and then gather 500 area residents. At the event, they ask for a show of hands from those willing to send letters to the agency's funders asking them to terminate funding if the agency does not pressure its landlords to improve the properties. "The collective power of a hall full of raised hands in the presence of the media and many public and private officials produced the agency's capitulation on the spot" (Speer & Hughey, 1995, p. 743). *This is traditional organizing in which opponents are made to feel the heat so that they will see the light.* Smart organizers will not call for a vote until they know they have a clear majority.

Organizer Makani Themba (1999) recommends asking the following key questions in choosing a target:

- Who or what institutions have the power to solve the problem and grant your demands?

- Whom must you get to before you can influence those with the real power?

- What are the strengths and weaknesses of each potential target? How are they vulnerable?

- Which targets are appointed? Elected?

- How do you have power or influence with them (as voters, consumers, taxpayers, investors, shaming, etc.)?

- What is their self-interest in this issue?

- Who would have jurisdiction if you redefined the issue (e.g., turned a tobacco advertising issue into a fair business practice issue)? Does this help you? (p. 95)[7]

This element makes us ask if we know whom to hold accountable and how, and whether we can cogently explain the connection to the public.

TACTICS

Sometimes when a new group or organization is eager for a victory, the organizer considers a "fixed fight"—a sure winner—to build confidence. To accomplish this requires tactical thinking. Perhaps the target is almost certain to say yes because public information is involved. Perhaps the organizer has inside information about a decision that is soon to be announced. Perhaps the request is noncontroversial. (In the earlier group home example, the deans will agree to sign a letter asking the reporter to meet with them.) A quick victory gives people a sense that they are potent members of society.

Involving organization members or townspeople in designing tactics is important. Tactics range from holding candlelight vigils to catching someone on camera; the Organizer's Collective, which is particularly interested in electronic organizing, is compiling a database of 1,000 social change tactics. (Also see Shaw, 2001; Box 14.4, which has a checklist from the Midwest Academy; and Appendix A, for organizing tactics.)

The group will enjoy coming up with imaginative tactics and the media will relish them. Alinsky said, "People hunger for drama and adventure, for a breath of life in a dreary, drab ex-

---

BOX 14.4   CHECKLIST FOR PLANNING AN ACTION

- Will your action be both fun and based on real power?

- Is everyone in your group comfortable with the plan?

- Will the plan be outside the experience of the target? Are you going outside the "official channels"?

- Are your demands clear and simple? Do you have fallback demands?

- Has the group decided who will present information at the action [and] who will be its spokesperson?

- Have you held a dress rehearsal?

- Do you have a good turnout plan, including last-minute reminder phone calls?

- If you want the media, have they been notified and given a reminder?

- Do you know who will debrief the action with participants and where?

Source: Bobo, Kendall, & Max (2001, P. 79) Copyright 2001 by Seven Locks Press. Used with permission.

istence" (1972, pp. 120–121). Hands-on exercises are preparatory, creative, and mobilizing. Organizers help blend tactics so the group can do an action "on" decision makers (Bobo et al., 2001, p. 70). Organizing is a serious and yet fun-loving tradition. Experience has shown that participants must enjoy or be challenged by tactics; however, concrete wins are important, not just symbolic exercises (Rathke, 2001).

Debriefing sessions after an action encourage not only participant responsibility but creativity, and they help cultivate leadership. (The U.S. Army calls debriefs of direct experience "after-action reviews".) In describing the aftermath of an accountability session with elected officials, one social worker explained, "Part of the teaching includes the next step, where do we go from here, what happened during the action, laying out the political players, why did this happen, evaluating the press, how did our leaders do up front, how did the mayor react or respond, and what follow-up do we need to do now?"[8] This element makes us ask whether our plan will be effective and will influence decision makers.

Using a Strategy Chart

Given the complexity of large-scale change, breaking problems into small, manageable steps makes sense. A strategy chart is a macrolevel assessment tool whose simplicity and versatility make it a helpful planning process for seeing the terrain and for mapping out a route to change. It can be used not only in community projects but also in organizational settings. See Box 14.5 for one example. Strategy analysis that can lead to coalition building is a central part of the organizing training conducted by the Midwest Academy in Chicago (Felkins, 2002, pp. 380–389). The prototype of a strategy chart described here was designed by the esteemed organizer and trainer Heather Booth and has been used to educate thousands of organizers in workshops, training sessions, classrooms, and in the field. Strategists can be creative as they fill in the chart to fit their situation, formulating multiple strategies to raise their odds of success.

Let us use the goal of achieving "potty parity" to illustrate the ease of developing an action plan through informal strategizing. A strategy can be written in shorthand like this:

Situation: In a building used primarily by females, restrooms are divided equally between men and women, resulting in lines at break and lunchtime
Vision: Obtaining equality for women

Goal: Converting some of the men's restrooms into women's restrooms
Objective: Raising awareness and getting access to decision maker
Organizational considerations: No one who wants to get fired or to be in trouble, no money, no organized constituents, no existing action group to lead the bathroom brigade
Constituents, allies: Female staff, visitors to the building (analyze by gender), managers oriented to productivity (possible allies); for leadership, female staffers with medical problems or female visitors with children who have been inconvenienced
Targets: Company head and official who makes decisions about the building/plant
Tactics: Consciousness raising, warning flyers in restrooms, then placement of "Women" sign over the "Men" sign on the restroom most want to convert, with females beginning to use it

Infrastructure and Contributions

Resources developed over the years are an underlying strength of the organization and mobilization tradition. There are networks of community organizations run by such groups as the Pacific Institute for Community Organizations (PICO) and the Gamaliel Foundation. In addition, a growing national infrastructure supports community change work of many varieties (Brooks, 2001). There are traditional organizations, such as the United Neighborhood Centers Association and the Association for the Advancement of Social Work With Groups, and there are new resources, such as the Neighborhood Funders Group and the National Organizers Alliance (http://noacentral.org/). The community-based service system is sprawling, but the organizing network is tighter. In fact, over the years, diverse organizers have shared trainers, funders, or both (see Box 14.6).

For example, building infrastructure among organizers and state and regional issue collaborations is one of the Charles Stewart Mott Foundation's stated goals. The foundation gives grants to "enhance the variety, geographic spread, power and effectiveness of the community organizing field . . . by increasing resources to institutions, organizations, technical assistance providers and networks that produce, nurture or expand community-based organizations."

Some of the same organizations or foundations have given money to diverse organizing

BOX 14.5   STRATEGY CHART

Midwest Academy Strategy Chart

After choosing your issue, fill in this chart as a guide to developing strategy. Be specific. List all the possibilities.

Goals	Organizational Considerations	Constituents, Allies, and Opponents	Targets	Tactics
1. List the long-term objectives of your campaign	1. List the resources that your organization brings to the campaign. Include money, number of staff, facilities, reputation, canvass, etc. What is the budget, including in-kind contributions, for this campaign?	1. Who cares about this issue enough to join in or help the organization? • Whose problem is it? • What do they gain if they win? • What risks are they taking? • What power do they have over the target?	1. Primary Targets A target is always a person. It is never an institution or elected body. • Who has the power to give you what you want? • What power do you have over them?	For each target, list the tactics that each constituent group can best use to make its power felt. Tactics must be • In context. • Flexible and creative. • Directed at a specific target.
2. State the intermediate goals for this issue campaign. What constitutes victory? *How will the campaign* • Win concrete improvement in people's lives? • Give people a sense of their own power? • Alter the relations of power?	2. List the specific ways in which you want your organization to be strengthened by this campaign. Fill in numbers for each: • Expand leadership group • Increase experience of existing leadership • Build membership base • Expand into new constituencies • Raise more money	• Into what groups are they organized? 2. Who are your opponents? • What will your victory cost them? • What will they do/spend to oppose you? • How strong are they?	2. Secondary Targets • Who has power over the people with the power to give you what you want? • What power do you have over them?	• Make sense to the membership. • Be backed up by a specific form of power. Tactics include • Media events • Actions for information and demands • Public hearings • Strikes • Voter registration and voter education • Lawsuits • Accountability sessions • Elections • Negotiations
3. What short-term or partial victories can you win as steps toward your long-term goal?	3. List internal problems that have to be considered if the campaign is to succeed.			

Source: Bobo, Kendall, & Max (2001, p. 33), *Organizing for Change,* Copyright 2001 by Seven Locks Press. Used with permission.

| BOX 14.6 | COMMUNITY CHANGING AND ORGANIZING |

Along with some schools of social work, there are long-established organizations that initiate and sponsor community changes.

A SAMPLE OF WELL-KNOWN ORGANIZERS AND TRAINERS

Acorn (Association of Community Organizations for Reform Now): http://acorn.org/
Center for Community Change: http://communitychange.org/
Center for Third World Organizing (C2): http://ctwo.org/
Highlander Research and Education Center: http://hrec.org/
Industrial Areas Foundation: http://www.iafnw.com/
Midwest Academy: http://midwestacademy.com/
National Training and Information Center, National People's Action: http://ntic-us.org/

A SAMPLE OF SUPPORTIVE PHILANTHROPIC ORGANIZATIONS

Annie E. Casey Foundation	Edna McConnell Clark Foundation
Ford Foundation	Funding Exchange
Robert Wood Johnson Foundation	Kellogg Foundation
John D. and Catherine T. MacArthur Foundation	Charles Stewart Mott Foundation
Ms. Foundation for Women	Needmor Fund
Pew Charitable Trust	Rockefeller Foundation

networks and local organizations. Over a 30–year period, the Catholic Campaign for Human Development "provided nearly $300 million to more than 3,500 projects." For example, the campaign has given $375,000 to the Colonias Development Council in New Mexico, one of our nation's poorest states. According to an evaluation study, the work of the diverse groups funded by the Catholic Campaign "benefited an estimated 38.5 million people, of whom 18.2 million were poor. This represents half of the U.S. poverty population in 1994. . . . The groups changed laws and policies and generated billions of dollars for low-income communities and their residents. Even the least successful groups had some victories" (Neighborhood Funders Group, 2001b, How the Catholic Campaign for Human Development approaches evaluation, para 3).

In the earlier section on formulating strategy goals, we pointed out that affecting half of the U.S. poverty population through organizing was an ambitious but realizable goal. Moving those 18.2 million people out of poverty would be much better, of course. However, organizing deals with the art of the possible. Moreover, organizers believe in celebrating accomplishments as they are achieved, and the Catholic Campaign statistics represent extraordinary outreach. In conclusion, organizing and mobilizing are part of a cosmic battle, and yet techniques developed within this tradition can be used locally to further the interests of constituents or any downtrodden—or feisty—group.

Illustrative Exercises

1. What could make a prospective leader feel like hot stuff? Put your ideas here: _____

   Hint: Think opportunities or assignments. Let the person achieve something—this is not about building self-esteem through compliments.

2. Research the organization and mobilization accomplishments of Dolores Huerta (farmworkers), Ella Baker (civil rights), and Jody Williams (landmines).

3. Find comprehensive organizing ideas and exercises online in The Citizen's Handbook (http://www.vcn.bc.ca/citizens-handbook). (An enlarged and revised print edition of the handbook, entitled *The Troublemaker's Teaparty: A manual for effective citizen action*, by Charles Dobson is available from New Society publisher). For action steps on world debt, see the Jubilee USA Network website (http://

www.j2000usa.org/debt/edpac/organiz.ht m). (Organizational information is available at http://www.jubileeusa.org/start.htm).

THE COORDINATION AND PARTICIPATION TRADITION

Community Coordination

Being aware of and pulling together the pieces is part of the social worker's responsibility (Ross, 1958). Our profession stresses forms of participatory democracy: partnerships for human empowerment, consumer involvement, client and community-led collaboration, co-inquiry, and participatory research. In some rural areas, the few social workers must capitalize on local resources and create a community infrastructure (Martinez-Brawley, 2000, p. 250). Where there are many agencies, the challenge is to work together harmoniously, creatively, and in interdisciplinary fashion. Things will progress best and benefit constituents most when each social worker gives the best to the joint effort that he or she has to give. We will describe interventions and complications in accomplishing these objectives.

We see linkage as a vehicle for creating systems where residents can use and shape community services, experience dignity and empathy, and receive redress when coordination and participation break down (Neiman, 1999). A professional approach to enhancing community capacity often involves improving community and social services and reaching the underserved. For example, the State of Washington Department of Health received a federal community-organizing grant to ensure the integration of oral health with maternal, infant, and child health services through local coalition building. An organizer was hired to facilitate the process of networking and to figure out how to get dentists to take Medicaid-eligible patients.[9]

Coordination means assembling resources, synchronizing activities, providing order, and encouraging teamwork to connect and engage far-flung or disparate elements of a potential system. Logical action outgrowths are block clubs, neighborhood crime watch organizations, and lobby coalitions (Bobo et al., 2001; Kahn, 1991).

Types of Coordination Options and Strategies

To illustrate the challenges, we turn to Burton Cohen's (1980) metaphor about coordination in the complex realm of social concerns:

Suppose we imagine a game being played by human players on a field covered with numerous patches of dense fog. Due to the fog, the players cannot make out the boundaries of the field or even see the ground around their feet very well. In fact, they do not even know what type of field it is or what game is being played. Nor are they sure of the rules under which they are playing or of what constitutes "winning," or even of who is on which team. Often, the players become frustrated because just when they think they have the game figured out, something will happen to offset any momentary gains they thought they had made. For example, someone whom they thought was on their team all of a sudden behaves as if he were not.

Now, the story that has just been told is really a story about coordination, or the lack of it, and can be transposed to the context of delivering services to . . . whatever service system we are interested in. (pp. 83–84)

Fortunately, inventive thinking can come to the rescue. Cohen's entertaining metaphor addresses coordination strategies and attempts to overcome obstacles.[10]

CONTINUE ON

Continuing to play in the fog has a downside; players can waste time or do more harm than good. (Think of ongoing communication and turf problems in U.S. intelligence agencies that surfaced after 9-11.) Often the strategy is to muddle through, hoping the fog will lift, and do something in the clear patches. In an example of continuing to work in the current health system "game" but seizing opportunities to be creative, Miyong Kim of Johns Hopkins School of Nursing created a favorably received community program for non-English-speaking older Koreans who previously had no linguistic access to health care (Carlson, 2001). A first-generation Korean American herself, Kim coordinates care for 50 in a weekly clinic held at a senior center.

GO UP IN A BLIMP

Cohen (1980) uses a Goodyear blimp image to suggest the distance strategy, so the player "can look down and see the whole thing, or at least a larger portion than can be seen from the midst of it" (p. 85). For instance, Bruner and Parachini (2000) "looked down" and noticed three teams playing separately on the field of community betterment. A synthesis of service systems reform, community organizing, and economic development made more sense than duplicating or disrespecting each other's efforts. This strategy enabled them to think big.

APPOINT A REFEREE

The film *Traffic* (2000) depicts the dire consequences of a fog game. Each new presidential administration appoints a czar to coordinate prevention, treatment, enforcement, and interdiction aspects of illegal drug activity. Appointing a heavy, who, through the weight of his position, is supposed to straighten it all out, often turns out to be a way of handing off authority up the line or laterally. The risks are in creating false confidence and more layers to coordinate. The plus is that one person or place truly becomes the focal point. Locally, court receiverships play this role when human service, housing, or justice systems fail. A receiver or a judge becomes the referee who can make decisions about interactions among players, enforce rules, and ultimately decide who wins the game (Cohen, 1980, p. 85).

EXCHANGE PLAYS

Players in the game will be less lost, Cohen (1980) suggests, if they talk to each other to share observations, personal insights, and theories, and form liaisons so "each member will have a better understanding of what the others are doing" (p. 86). Think of partnerships, collaboratives, cluster committees, alliances for service integration, and lobbying coalitions (Butler & Seguino, 2000; Mizrahi, 1999). Trust is central to such interconnection; in rural areas especially, getting to know the other person is more important than any details of the game (McNellie, 2001). Coordination can prevent turf wars, eliminate duplication, and encourage cross-sectoral cooperation. In one city, after feuding among key racial and cultural groups diminished their clout with city authorities, seven multicultural leaders formed an executive council that regularly holds town hall meetings to make decisions collectively. "They have slowly increased their ranks, becoming a powerful force in that city" (Institute for Democratic Renewal, 2000).

SWITCH PLAYERS

Scrutinize team composition. Who is most affected by the issue? Do any players *have* the problem? Is everyone a professional? What about paraprofessional staff and client group participation (Arches, 1997)? Who has a vested interest (e.g., providers)? In short, maybe the wrong players are on the field. Bring in the hot-dog and peanut sellers or the fans, who may see patterns more clearly than the players do. Who

ought to be connected? With whom are you coordinating? Other agencies? Families? Expansion of faith-based (Koch & Johnson, 1997) and military programs may require coordination with new players, and there is always a need to involve the greater community to end domination from "parochial interests" (Masilela & Meyer, 1998, p. 4).

CREATE A NEW GAME

Cohen (1980) asks what happens if the fog does not lift and we cannot find out from others what is going on. He is most interested in a strategy where, after a rare moment of startling realization, the players can come together on the field and create "their own game" (p. 86). One historic example is the Christmas Truce of 1914, when thousands of British and German soldiers met between their trenches for an informal holiday from World War I. Currently, a campaign is being waged through the Children's Health Insurance Program (CHIP) to aid the near poor, and yet the same effort could have gone into creating a Canadian type of universal system (no uninsured or underinsured). The point is not whether that would have been wiser but that it would have been a new game.

Coordination Description

See Box 14.7 for a positive example of community coordination. The facilitator role is critical because people are vague on how to involve others and to sustain involvement once the beginning phases of the project are completed.

COORDINATION THROUGH INFORMATION

Townspeople can be connected by myriad means: ballot initiatives, service credits, fundraisers, citizen monitoring teams. While lots of coordination is face-to-face, it also involves clearinghouse and dissemination functions, as when messages from one newsletter or website are picked up and promoted by other newsletters or websites—spreading central ideas. Certainly, communities are as likely to have information gaps as service gaps. *Community education* can be thought of as targeted coordination of experts and outreach to (a) diverse lay audiences that are able to respond to alerts and advice and (b) opinion leaders who help diffuse information.

SELF-ASSESSMENT

Before tackling major information or service gaps through mutual cooperation, agency staff

BOX 14.7	MISSOULA COORDINATES, CONNECTS

In a remarkable social experiment, a town and county of 90,000 has come together to help people have a positive dying experience. Back in 1996, family practice doctor Ira Byock and gerontologist Barbara Spring wanted to open a public dialogue. Byock remembers, "We had this small group of people interested in hospice care and we framed the challenge: 'How can we integrate dying into the ongoing life of our community?' Barbara and I said, 'Let's call a meeting and see.' We took a small conference room at the Aging Services office and it was packed, people out in the hall. We got a bigger hall for the next meeting and again there wasn't enough space for the turnout. And then, frankly the enthusiasm became infectious." Early on, a survey examined townspeople's attitudes and experiences about the end of life. Meanwhile, a tiny staff and 100 volunteers created a structure and office and raised funds. Among the task forces developed and coordinated by volunteers are advance-care planning and linkage to faith communities, schools, workplaces, neighborhoods, and the arts. Care circles are being created to help spouses practically and emotionally during the dying process. Efforts grow out of stated needs, desires, and fears. One project printed hundreds of copies of a 1-to-10 pain rating scale on small cards carried by professionals and patient alike. The scale enables patients to make their degree of pain known.

Note: Edited excerpts from Atcheson (2000, pp. 60–62) Reprinted with permission from Modern Maturity. Copyright (2002) AARP.

should ask themselves: Do we understand current service delivery problems? How well do we use our own network to engage and empower citizens or to develop programs of social association? Do we understand what is required in building a meaningful partnership? Up to now, have we ever established or led a local coalition? Do we understand the implications of federation or consortium building? Have we thought out collaborative agreements? Have the coalitions to which we belong evaluated themselves in terms of their stage of development and effectiveness (Goldstein, 1997)?

Community Participation: Putting Service Users at the Center

Social workers agree with many others that a small group of decision makers ought not to run towns or cities; instead, governments and large local companies such as Hershey Chocolate are better off including community members in planning from the "get-go." This tradition stresses democracy, public participation in decision making, multistakeholder accountability, and maximum feasible participation by the poor (Gamble & Weil, 1995; Kramer, 1969; New Economics Foundation, 1998; Potapchuk, 1996, p. 54). *The goal of community participation is broad involvement of citizens in all phases of the improvement process until residents "own" it and it is sustainable.* This usually requires benefits to flow from engagement: tangible, such as a job, and intangible, such as inclusion or self-determination.

In homecare and other direct services, increased attention is being given to consumer direction, consumer-guided services, stakeholder control, and service user empowerment (self-determination). People with problems may want to proceed their own way. For instance, family members in Marietta, Georgia, decided to organize the Suicide Prevention Advocacy Network (http://www.spanusa.org/). Eleven survivor support groups already existed in the state, and these people with suicide losses wanted to engage in a national advocacy effort. Similarly, community residents want to influence their environments—not carry out someone else's ideas—and think of "partnership arrangements as a way of giving local people a major say over what happens in the area" (McArthur, 1995, p. 66). If not control—in planning, service creation, governance or evaluation—beneficiaries should at the minimum have peer representation (Masilela & Meyer, 1998). There should be larger numbers and more types of consumers in any collaborative or consortium.

Participation Programs and Precepts

Mutual engagement with service users and the citizenry is more than a goal; it is our professional obligation to do what is necessary to involve a diversity of community members (Daley

& Marsiglia, 2000, p. 83). We mostly know our own professional fields, our own circles, our group's opinions. Rounding up "the usual suspects" for projects (Norris & Lampe, 1994, p. 6) or "the old reliables, all of whom hold essentially the same point of view" (Ross, 1958, p. 8) for intergroup committees will not create the shared ownership that leads to successful engagement.

According to Miley, O'Melia, and DuBois (1998), three factors that increase the likelihood of consumers' successful participation are

1. a clear mandate for their participation
2. a power base from which to assert their rights to participate, and
3. recognition of their legitimacy as spokespersons. (pp. 379–380)

In contrast, a community can be set up for failure when residents are expected to (a) understand jargon and talk like the middle class, (b) donate considerable time as unpaid volunteers, and (c) keep things going after professionals complete their project and more or less set them adrift (Lewis, Lewis, & Rachelefsky, 1996).

Box 14.8 suggests ways to avoid being paternalistic. After the marginalized are included, the bottom line still remains: Do their views count?

Involving people in task forces or coalitions and sustaining their participation in oversight or community betterment efforts is not an easy task (Bennett, 1995). Some speak of a continuum of participation but things are more complicated than that phrase implies. Think of isolated rural areas where there are few local resources to coordinate, where reaching out means coordinating across distances, where there may not even be telephones (McNellie, 2001). Moreover, service users may have little or no family support. Add to this the fact that there are joiners and nonjoiners in society. It is important to get participation from all parts of the community, not just those associated with the Rotary Club, 4-H, or the volunteer fire company or rescue squad. If we coordinate solely with joiners and meeting-goers, we disregard most stakeholders. It is equally inappropriate to work only with those who agree with us, who have pleasant personalities, or who can meet at times and places convenient for us. Ironically, after outreach, we still should be prepared for disinterest or ambivalence, lack of trust in the practitioner, and personalized rather than communal outlooks.

Applications

Forming a representative group and enlarging the sphere of participation are worthwhile challenges, as the following examples illustrate.

A SYSTEM

Desiring participation from parents, students, and residents, the Denver Public Schools created *collaborative decision-making committees* (CDMs) to

---

BOX 14.8	**GUIDELINES FOR WORKERS URGING COMMUNITY INVOLVEMENT**

- Identify your own values, agendas, interests, and goals and those of the people you are working with and distinguish between the two.
- Own your own role and power; recognize the skills and information you have and never assume that others share it.
- Recognize that enabling people's involvement is an essential community work task in itself and not something that can be taken for granted in pursuit of other goals.
- Build on the skills and experience that people have.
- Give people the opportunity to work out their own forms and objectives for involvement and be aware of the danger of unintentionally imposing your own.

- Make realistic assessments with people of what is actually achievable in any given situation; what the possible outcomes are and what the costs may be so that people can make an informed decision about what they want to do.
- Be sensitive to the fears and uncertainties people have.
- Appreciate and respond to people's need for self-confidence and assertiveness in working with you.

Source: Croft and Beresford (1988, pp. 278–279). Copyright *Community Development Journal.* Used with permission of Oxford University Press and the authors.

provide opportunity for systematic involvement in local schools, including hiring and budget decisions (Kreck, 2001). The CDMs are composed of the following members:

1. The school principal
2. Four teachers chosen by faculty vote
3. Four parents or guardians nominated by the school's PTSA or other parent/community organizations, or self-nominated and elected by the majority of parents who have children in the school
4. One classified employee (not a principal or teacher) chosen by a vote of classified employees at the school
5. One business/employer or community representative from the local community nominated by a member of the CDM committee and approved by other CDM members
6. In middle and high schools, two student representatives selected by the student council. In middle schools, student representatives will serve in an ex officio capacity (Kreck, 2001, p. 25A).

But when issues get hot, things bubble up directly from neighborhoods and people become impatient. According to Kreck, several incidents have occurred:

• In Montbello, frustrated residents bypassed the formal process, found the principal they wanted to lead the school out of troubled times, and successfully lobbied to get him the job.
• Padres Unidos [a group of Latino, African American, and Anglo parents] bypassed the school's CDM in its efforts to bring reform to Cole Middle School. . . . They knocked on more than 400 doors in the neighborhood to talk about conditions at Cole. . . . Padres visited schools in New York City that did a particularly good job with low-income students of color. They came back enthusiastic, armed with ideas for reform (2001, p. 25A).

Padres Unidos is organizing and connecting in the coordination-participation tradition. Such organizations pose a dilemma for Denver's school superintendent: how to balance feedback-demands from the established decision-making committees (who may be out of step with the community) with feedback-demands from grassroots groups (who may be only narrowly representative). Yet how much better to be faced with this dilemma than with apathy.

A SUMMONS

Since several Canadian provinces are working to make the citizen the ultimate voice in health planning, they encouraged communities to cut a wide swath in forming health-planning groups. The experiment, analyzed by Joan Wharf Higgins (1999), found that certain Canadians were heard from less than others, if at all: people with mental illness, persons with disabilities, single parents, street youth, teenagers in general, and First Nation bands (tribes) on and off the reserve (p. 288). Professional people, often white and middle class, usually have the wherewithal to work the system. Higgins found that Canadians who participated in the planning "possessed the discretionary financial and personal resources necessary to attend evening meetings and weekend forums, and to devote a large amount of time and effort to the process" (p. 293). Such participants felt more connected to their locality before they even started, so empowered people became more empowered (p. 295). Higgins conducted focus groups with the unintentionally excluded and found that "male, female, Caucasian and aboriginal nonparticipants alike echoed a desire to be valued as citizens" (p. 296). Higgins criticizes a "reliance on a shallow repertoire of participation techniques" that reach only the middle class, but adds that the burdens, alienation and sense of inadequacy of the excluded cannot be easily overcome even with a bigger or more flexible participation menu (p. 301). If agencies want more participation in community development from traditionally underrepresented citizens, their staff must reach out to them and become involved in their lives (p. 302). Finally, the socially marginalized need the ability to act—tactics and means. Otherwise, "participation" is a social therapy activity.

Including the Often Ignored

Practitioners ceaselessly experiment with ways, such as holding community dinners, to involve the public. This means that community workers strive to be flexible in routine situations where representatives of the public are involved. To give one example, members with precarious health can be encouraged to send proxies to planning meetings to ensure that their views get heard (Cornelius, Battle, Kryder-Coe, & Hu, 1999). It means that community workers strive to create partnerships of many types. Social workers often work with marginalized people, with people who are unwanted in community activities because they are disabled, ugly or do not look "put together," have contagious medical conditions, or are labeled, for instance, as mentally retarded. John McKnight (1995), who has sought ways to incorporate ignored or excluded people into community life, has observed good results when community leaders and informed individuals serve as "community guides" for such left-out people. Guides can spot the capacities of a left-out person and use an interest as a *link*, for example, hooking that person up with a church choir (pp. 119–121). Or the community worker can tap interests and values of community guides who are willing not only to connect personally with socially ostracized or excluded persons but to take them along to their own ongoing activities (see Chapter 2 in Schwartz, 1992).

Ensuring True Representation

When Great-Society, war-on-poverty, model-cities, or empowerment-zone programs expand and look for indigenous leadership, certain people often push themselves forward. Social worker Nat Branson puts it this way, "When you have social programs coming into areas, there is a tendency for the more upwardly mobile elite to take charge and to profit at the expense of the poor."[11] This is a participation challenge. While hustlers and the upwardly mobile may not be the most representative people, at least they are from the neighborhood. Much worse, as organizer Si Kahn (1970) reminds us, the power structure historically cultivated leaders: "Your leaders, the poor community was in effect told, must be people you can be proud of: well-dressed, well-housed, educated, articulate. By implication, a poor man, a man who wore overalls and work shoes, who stumbled in his speech and used 'ain't' instead of 'isn't,' who lived in a shack instead of a brick house, who walked instead of riding in a Chrysler, who worked in a field or mill instead of an office or classroom, had no business representing himself in the centers of power" (pp. 40–41). Actually, a leader is someone whom others follow. Young Minnesotans who voted in large numbers and affected the outcome chose television wrestler and radio talk-show host Jesse Ventura to be their governor despite, or because of, the establishment's view of him.

Saul Alinsky talked about the difference between self-determination and phony participation. Citizens understand "the difference between participation and control" (Ewalt, 1998, p. 4).[12] A savvy practitioner will consider these points:

1. Have you consulted with members of communities about whom they want appointed?
2. Have you asked current consumer representatives whom they look to for advice and help with decisions?
3. Have you identified those who are widely admired by their peers? or those who epitomize a segment of the community?
4. Are you conversing with grassroots critics of your program, agency, or organization about who should be added to the team? Conversely, are you considering only those individuals who are acceptable to agencies and political offices?
5. Have you checked around in the community to see if the prospective representatives are viewed as feet kissers or Uncle Toms?
6. Once a name is suggested, ask, Would this person bring a new perspective or speak for an underrepresented aggregate? How many followers could this nominee turn out for an event? What might this person need in order to serve (transportation, child care)?

In summary, the authors of this text agree with Stukas and Dunlap (2002), who call for "greater attention to be paid to all of the constituent groups in the community involvement spectrum and the necessarily respectful and equitable relationships that must be forged among them" (p. 411). This means that ultimately neighbors must allow other neighbors to belong, join, and lead, regardless of religion, race, gender and other characteristics (Horwitt, 1989).

Illustrative Exercises

The purpose is to involve all stakeholders in community building, especially the powerless.

1. Maternal and Child Health is offering Community Integrated Service System organizing grants. You are pulling together street youth and their advocates to improve services and obtain a clean-needle program. Plan how to approach (a) provider agencies, (b) youth networks, and (c) different groups within the addict population. Select an example from each and prioritize. The form below may be of help in this exercise or in your agency work.

Whom would you involve? (be specific)	Why would you involve that entity?	How and when?

2. Your community foundation awards grants to augment ongoing *linkage* projects. As a staff member of the foundation, you will be asking each organization for references. Who could give you the best information and why? Put the ideal reference here:

_____

3. Your task is to establish an advisory board composed of former and current clients. In the past, several service users said that the agency needed a more suitable way to handle gripes. The director has given you a telephone number for one client who had a gripe in the past. Put below what you will do (action steps) and in what order.

a. _____

b. _____

c. _____

THE INNOVATION, NARRATION, AND LIBERATION TRADITION

Background

The third connecting tradition is grounded in creativity and positive group consciousness (Delgado, 2000; Walz & Uematsu, 1997). In contrast to the mass-based tradition where folks speak of putting their bodies on the line, this approach asks people to put their minds on the line. It draws more upon cultural action and communications work, discourse, and dialogue than on the organizing-mobilizing principles, tactics, and methods covered earlier.

Professionals in this tradition leave the trodden trail to explore alternative paths. Culture workers seek fresh ways to connect with denizens of the city or country and to connect them with each other and society. Much of the population of Rochester, New York, for instance, read and talked about the same book (Ernest J. Gaines's *A Lesson Before Dying*), as a way to con-

nect people to issues, literature, and each other (National Public Radio, 2001); other cities also are trying this experiment. Vehicles as diverse as community gardens and algebra/math-literacy projects have been used to pull people together and to help them stand up to uncaring authorities. The Community Development Institute, a program of the Social Planning and Research Council of British Columbia, has offered these workshops: "Storytelling Ways: Exploring the Narrative Form," "Creating Political Street Theatre: A Crash Course," "Building Community Through Song," "Drumming: the Heartbeat of Life," and "The Medicine Wheel—Creating Sacred Space." In short, community workers operating out of this tradition creatively use what is at hand. Innovation can stave off burnout and release the energies of both grassroots activists and professionals.

Box 14.9 summarizes the types of programs being undertaken across the country at the community level, as tracked by progressive fundraisers.

If any of the above sounds far out, it may be reassuring to community change funders and administrators to hear that Robert Putnam (2000), an influential academic, concludes his book *Bowling Alone* with this agenda-for-change item:

> To build bridging social capital requires that we transcend our social and political and professional identities to connect with people unlike ourselves. This is why team sports provide good venues for social-capital formation. Equally important and less exploited in this connection are the arts and cultural activities. Singing together (like bowling together) does not require shared ideology or shared social or ethnic provenance. . . . Let us find ways to ensure that by 2010 significantly more Americans will participate in (not merely consume or "appreciate") cultural activities from group dancing to songfests to community theater to rap fes-

BOX 14.9	WHAT'S GOING ON OUT THERE

Arts and cultural work	Constituency organizing
Coalition building	Film, video, and radio productions
Direct action	Legal action
Economic strategies	Electoral work
Grassroots organizing	Long-range planning
Mass mobilization	Infrastructure
Labor organizing	Leadership development
Popular education	Public education

[The italicized items fit our innovation, liberation, and narration tradition.]

Source: From Chapter 3 of *Robin Hood Was Right: A Guide to Giving Your Money for Social Change*, by Chuck Collins and Pam Rogers (with Joan P. Garner), 2000, New York: W. W. Norton. Copyright 2000 by Haymarket People's Fund. Used with permission of W. W. Norton & Company, Inc.

tivals. Let us discover new ways to use the arts as a vehicle for convening diverse groups of fellow citizens. (p. 411)

Young people already are leading the way in these experiments (e.g., rap festivals), and we can learn from them.

Different Types of Change in the Innovation Tradition

Certain approaches to change ask us to step outside our comfort zones and be with others. Cultural activism, multicultural organizing, feminist organizing, and the Freirean approach are "interflowing" (Bradshaw, Soifer, & Gutierrez, 1994, p. 32) *mainsprings of this tradition*. These approaches share common elements: (a) a strong oral tradition, (b) self- and group realization, (c) cognitive liberation, and (d) the resilience and expressive power of people. A word about items c and d: *Cognitive liberation* (Ash, 1972; McAdam, 1982) is freedom from prevailing dogma and openness to new possibilities—that other species can be treated unjustly, for instance, or that God is feminine. *Resilience* embodies the human capacity for laughter and for festivals or carnival (Irving & Young, 2002, p. 25; also see Felkins, 2002, p. 55). Self-expression can serve the purpose of liberation and rebellion, as when Koreans sang coded folk songs during the Japanese occupation.

CULTURAL ACTIVISM

Scottish patriot Andrew Fletcher once wrote, "If one were permitted to make all the ballads, one need not care who should make the laws of a nation" (Cultural Environment Movement, 1999). Thus, cultural activism can arise from any population; for example, francophones who want to preserve French culture in Canada, or singing revolutionaries in South Africa. Artists and other *culture workers* use cultural symbols in their organizing.

Cultural activism is a means to dramatize and expose injustice and strengthen those who struggle by connecting them to their history, according to Richard Hofrichter (1993) who has coordinated a network of environmental justice groups. As a social change strategy, cultural activism also seeks the rewriting of political consciousness and political unity. Organizers consider how to challenge the dominant view and to connect disregarded people in vision and action, as director Spike Lee did in *Do the Right Thing* (1989). Tactics vary: guerilla theater, rap and slam contests, documentary film (for a good resource, see Appalshop.org); for decades, Bread and Puppet from Vermont created gigantic figures to augment parades and marches. Here is one action. The 64 Beds Project involved artists who made beds to use in an all-night street performance, community people who slept or thought in them, and homeless representatives who spoke at the event. Activist Sally Jacques took this participatory project to many cities (Hofrichter, 1993, p. 93).[13]

Cultural activism creates opposition to pervasive but invisible consciousness shaping. The activist does this by asking questions: Why is there a business but not a labor section in the newspaper? (Hofrichter, 1993, p. 88). Knowing that people are ill equipped to resist corporate culture, the change agent helps people analyze links between communication, power, and politics. "I watch soap operas," said Paulo Freire, "and I learn a lot by criticizing them. . . I fight with [television], if you can understand. A commercial rarely catches me unawares" (as cited in Gadotti, 1994, p. 78).

To create concrete applications, we must become attuned to others' experiential realities. Si Kahn (1997) urges social workers to reach people through "cultural work," which he defines as "the conscious and strategic use of culture, craft and art to achieve political goals . . . The power of culture can also be an antidote to people's racialized and gendered inertia, to their inability to see beyond their own eyes. . . . Cultural work can transform consciousness, can perform the acts of political education that, combined with community organizing, make social change transformational" (p. 128).

Like Woody Guthrie and Pete Seeger before him, Kahn has inspired many through his own music. (See Berger, 2000, for a thoughtful look at the role of protest music in organizing and social movements.) Kahn is urging far more than entertainment by folk or mariachi players at the end of a program or rally. Given the opportunity, we all have the capacity to express ourselves, to make rather than consume culture. Still, the issue is who gets heard and who gets ignored, "which stories are legitimated and by whom?" (Rappaport, 1995, p. 805).

MULTICULTURAL ORGANIZING

"Disenfranchised, abandoned, and underserved communities of color need organizers . . . [to help] these communities establish and reestablish dignity and opportunity," Rivera and Erlich declare (1998, p. 256). Other subjugated groups in liberation struggles also need new ways to engage, inspire, and unleash the imagination. Since transformation can be visceral and emotional, old organizing approaches may not work. Intellectual education methods "aren't always adequate to deal with a transformative process, particularly one which challenges racism, sexism, homophobia, anti-Semitism, and other barriers that divide people from each other," asserts Kahn (1997, p. 128). Glugoski, Reisch, and Rivera (1994) recommend that we "identify similarities as well as differences shared by all groups" (p. 85) and "adopt the role of an active listener interested in discovering the people's world through dialogue" (p. 90). To do so requires in-depth exploring of least one facet of another's world.

Beyond identity politics, Salcido (1993) urges culturally appropriate interactions, such as the interactions that occur when Anglos reach out to Latinos. Yet, when the culture and community are unfamiliar (Daley & Wong, 1994), this is hard to do. How much, for instance, does a native-born African American social worker know about West Indians and foreign-born blacks, let alone Bosnian or Afghan immigrants? To give another example, there are challenges—and satisfactions—for most social workers in working with newcomers from Southeast Asia:

> Monks in orange robes dashed through a muddy field . . . passing out pamphlets printed in Laotian, Burmese, Tibetan, and Vietnamese . . . [at] an all-day Buddhist festival celebrated yesterday by an estimated 2,000 people at the Fauquier County Buddhist temple. . . . Wearing a suit with a yellow flower pinned to his lapel was Souk Sayasithsena, an organizer of the festival that celebrates the birth, enlightenment, and passing of the Lord Buddha. All he could do was feel proud. "When I first came to the Washington area, there was one Buddhist center," said Sayasithsena, who came here from Laos in the late 1960s. "Now there are 53 centers." (Wax, 2001, p. C4)

News stories such as this one can provide us with (a) the names of indigenous organizers or leaders and (b) times and places to introduce ourselves to them.[14] Rubin and Rubin (1995) suggest that, to begin, we "elicit illustrative stories, narratives, and examples and infer the taken-for-granted rules" (p. 175); also see Liese (2003).

The better acquainted we become with *religious* customs other than our own, the more commonalties we see. Unfortunately, many references from outsiders are discounting or negative. Before and after the 2000 presidential election, pundits and Republicans continually made sarcastic references to the *Buddhist temple* as a shorthand for questionable fund-raising. "It's weird and unsettling for Buddhists to see that this is the only reference to Buddhism, in a context subject to ridicule" (Kraft, 2000, p. 23). We have to be in communication to even learn about such hurts. After the terrorist attacks in 2001, a number of religious groups reached out to local Muslims. Friendships developed during joint activities—ice skating, light suppers, visits by young people to the other group's religious education classes. Such activity promotes "intergroup solidarity" (Gutierrez, Alvarez, Nemon, & Lewis, 1996) like that promoted by old and new settlement houses (Koerin, 2002).

In multicultural organizing, we are learners and, surely, in the area of religious diversity, there is much to learn about each other's religions (Magida & Matlins, 1999). Who was Joseph Smith? Why do Sikhs take the name Singh? Should we write "Koran" or "Qur'an"? Which faith communities will join in political coalitions?

FEMINIST ORGANIZING

Women often focus on different social change goals and concerns, for example, quality day care, and prevention of the hundreds of thousands of rapes and sexual assaults every year. *Goals* such as "taking back the night," defending abortion clinics, and guaranteeing fairness to prospective lesbian and gay adoptive parents are feminist. Yet, feminist organizing *tactics*—from community education to field organizing to use of the Internet—may not be that different from those of organizing people in general. So what is feminist organizing? Certainly, some organizing by and for women is simply standard good organizing: think of securing increased funding for breast cancer research. However, many feminist organizers emphasize emancipatory or discourse change and other unique features (Hyde, 1986; Peterson & Lieberman, 2001; Weil, 1986).

A list of feminist methods and techniques for liberating practice developed by Bricker-Jenkins suggests that we (a) use dreams, fantasies, and stories to surface strengths and perceptions of power; (b) use symbols, myths, and rituals grounded in actual and desired realities; (c) encourage woman-affirming reading in professional and popular literature; (d) use client journals, creative writing, art, dance, play, and theatre;[15] and (e) make women's strengths and culture visible in the environment (Bricker-Jenkins & Lockett, 1995, p. 2934). These points tie to Gutierrez and Lewis's (1994) philosophy about feminist organizing: "Organizing involves both the rational and nonrational elements of human experiences, with emotions, spirituality, and artistic expression used as tactics for unifying women and expressing issues. Involvement in social change is considered organic, not an adjunct, to women's lives" (p. 31). To illustrate, zany performance artist Pat Oleszko creates elaborate costumes, in fact inflatable sculptures, which have been displayed in the National Museum for Women in the Arts. In one video, she appears in a black dress covered with white gloves and starts a rhythmic chant that lasts minutes: "Git yer hands off her, git yer hands off her." Oleszko's sometimes silly, sometimes shocking videos can trigger an impassioned response about pornography, harassment, and violence against women. After a fervent interchange about identity, sexuality and power, a feminist group often unites in a way that leads to political action.

From early youth on, boys hear that they are meaner (more mischievous, violent, and selfish) than girls. Once in a while an alternative narrative puts aside stereotyped views of gender, considers the human ability to bond, and fortifies other traits of caring, thoughtfulness, and friendship. For example, a *Responsive Community* piece detailed the following: "When sixth-grader Ian began losing his hair because of cancer treatment, 13 of his San Marcos, California, classmates went to the barber and shaved their own heads 'because we didn't want Ian to feel left out.' It started when Ian's friend Taylor Herber visited him in the hospital after an operation for non–Hodgkin's lymphoma: 'I thought it would be less traumatizing for Ian.' The other boys joined Taylor and laughingly called themselves the Bald Eagles. 'What my friends did made me feel stronger,' says Ian. 'It helped me get through all of this. I was really amazed that they would do something like this for me'" (Communitarian Skinheads, 1994, p. 79). Feminist organizers can reprint such anecdotes to show that the practice of caring about others is not inherently female; both genders exhibit it when encouraged and socialized to do so.[16]

FREIREAN APPROACH

Indigent and indigenous communities are the focus of this approach. To get a sense of the political world as Paulo Freire saw it, imagine the Southern Hemisphere with a giant mouth—forced open—into which the North pours its culture. Then imagine the poor and illiterate, prohibited from resisting, while the dominant in their own country demand passivity and the educated force-feed knowledge down their throats.

By contrast, Freire thought that everything was political and that humans had critical curiosity ready to be triggered in a situation of learning among equals. Consider this scenario: A child or adult is eager to read. Such a skill is a ticket to voting, economic survival, liberation. Freire directed literacy teachers to spend time learning the idiom, the phrases, the potent words and themes of the area. The teacher or alphabetizer had to figure out approximately two dozen words that not only taught the vowels but were relevant enough to stimulate reading. (See Box 14.10.) Drawings were often used.

Freire (1994) viewed popular education as nonformal interchange with people who dis-

BOX 14.10	PAULO FREIRE AND LIBERATION

Born in 1921 in Recife, Brazil, Paulo Freire (in Portuguese, pronounced Pall-ou FRAY ree) studied law, but became a teacher. His philosophy was to relate education to a social context and to avoid "banking"—where students are empty vessels into which teachers pour their accumulated knowledge and maintain external authority. Interested in illiterates, who would benefit from social transformation, Freire started working in cultural circles, exploring liberating themes and words (hunger rather than food) that related to problems lived by the group.

What a track record he had. In northeast Brazil, he taught 300 adults to read and write in 45 days. At Con Edison in New York, he used an inner-city vocabulary to teach functional illiterates to read at a sixth- to seventh-grade level

in 13 weeks. Paulo Freire wrote books such as *Pedagogy of the Oppressed* that still sell worldwide. Exiled from his own country for 15 years, the good-natured Freire made common cause with others, including social workers who admired his bottom-up change model. During his career, he held government positions in education and worked for diverse institutions—the Institute of Cultural Action in Geneva, Harvard University, and the World Council of Churches.

With a goal of political transformation, Freire modeled quiet ways to liberate the oppressed. An optimist, he experimented his entire life with ways to enable people to break out of passivity and silent subjugation.

Sources: Based on Associated Press (1997), Cashmore & Rojek (1999), and Gadotti (1994).

cover that they are capable of knowing (pp. 46–47). Such education, he believed, could trigger reflection and action (praxis) and social transformation. For empowerment education or program development, Wallerstein (1993) says, "Freire offers a three-stage method. The first step is listening for the key issues and emotional concerns of community people. . . . The second step is promoting participatory dialogue about these concerns. The third step is taking action about the concerns that are discussed" (p. 222).

As a person who was able to politicize as he taught literacy, Freire grew in influence as organizers looked for role models that not only respected oppressed and discounted peoples but also immersed themselves in their world. Among the U.S. models were Dorothy Day, who established Catholic Worker hospitality houses, and Myles Horton of the Highlander Center in Tennessee (Horton & Freire, 1990).

Social Work Connection

Community practitioners are experimenting with many ideas from Freire's philosophy. These include (a) *basing nonformal education on everyday experience* (Castelloe & Watson, 1999, pp. 73–76; Gadotti, 1994, pp. 18–19); (b) *giving up the superiority of being more learned* (Carroll & Minkler, 2000, p. 28; Freire, 1994, pp. 46–47); (c) *becoming humble to empower someone else* (Blackburn, 2000, p. 13; Freire, 1994, pp. 22–27; Glugoski, Reisch & Rivera, p. 90) (d) *facing and overcoming limit situ-*

ations, i.e., concrete realities (Freire, 1994, pp. 205–207; Sachs & Newdom, 1999, p. 98); and (e) *bringing forth social, political, critical consciousness* (Gadotti, 1994, pp. 147–149; Reisch, Wenocur & Sherman, 1981). The last two points are illustrated in Box 14.11, which shows Freire confronting fatalism.

Using Narration

While Freire's work has challenged social workers for decades, narration is now coming to the fore as a tangible way to recognize and support strengths and to create a public conversation. A narrative can tell us something about people, their worldview, and their needs. Narration is a dimension and a tool of cultural activism, multicultural organizing, feminist organizing, and Freirean popular education.

DEFINITION AND TYPES

Narrative deals with meaning, myth, metaphor, dialogue, and culture transmittal. A narrative can lament or celebrate an individual, a group, a community, a tribe, a quest. It can exemplify shared experience or convey respect for roots. It can crystallize professional values and highlight whether we do what we say we value, practice what we preach (Walz, 1991). A narrative can be in the form of stories, rap, or conversation and its message may be overt or covert, such as resistance to oppression (Themba, 1999, pp. 22–23). Julian Rappaport describes three

| BOX 14.11 | DIALOGUE: A "SPACE OF POSSIBILITY" |

Members of popular (populist) groups and other illiterate people looked up to Paulo Freire for having studied. In the following excerpt from his book, *Pedagogy of Hope* (1994), Freire recalls the dialogue that occurred at one of his meetings:

[Freire] *"And why couldn't your parents send you to school?"*

[Audience member] *"Because they were peasants like us."*

"And what is 'being a peasant'?"

"It's not having an education . . . not owning anything . . . working from sun to sun . . . having no rights . . . having no hope."

"And why doesn't a peasant have any of this?"

"The will of God."

"And who is God?"

"The Father of us all."

"And who is a father here this evening?"

Almost all raised their hands, and said they were. [Freire] *picked out one of them and asked him,* "How many children do you have?"

"Three."

"Would you be willing to sacrifice two of them, and make them suffer so that the other one could go to school and have a good life, in Recife? . . ."

"No!"

"Well, if you, . . . a person of flesh and bones, could not commit an injustice like that—how could God commit it?" . . .

A silence . . . Then: *"No! God isn't the cause of all this. It's the boss!" . . .*

[Freire concluded:] *From that point of departure, we could have gotten to an understanding of the role of the "boss," in the context of a certain socioeconomic, political system.*

Source: Freire (1994), p. 48. Used with permission.

types of narratives: dominant societal-cultural narratives, community narratives, and personal stories (Salzer, 1998, p. 570). Joseph Davis (2002) contrasts self-narratives that are personal with movement-narratives that are oppositional and subversive, that is, war stories that help form collective recognition and identities (pp. 22–26).

Background and Roles

Liberation. Professionals can elicit, hear, and steer narratives to encourage empowerment and liberation. Clinicians may use narrative therapy, which holds that "people can continually and actively re-author their lives" (Freedman & Combs, 1996, pp. 15–16). Community practitioners can shape or direct narrative to help people come together, achieve something, overcome a difficulty or change, or regain self-respect. Oral histories, a form of narrative, can reveal journeys from accommodation to self-determination and effective resistance. To wit, in interviews he conducted, Couto (1993) found "common elements in the stories such as a member of the community looking at a dominant person in the eye and the art of challenging a dominant person without incurring retaliation" (p. 70). If the conventions of daily life in society so dominate us that we are unable to challenge, as some theorists believe, then narratives may provide a means to stumble into, arise into, or discover means of liberation from conventionality and passivity

(Loeb, 1999, p. 212). Thus, narratives offer "new possibilities for staging a resistance to the damaging effects of social, cultural, and political dominant narratives and for *inviting subjects to write for themselves more empowering, less subjugated narratives* [italics added]" (Wyile & Paré, 2001, p. 171).

Inclusion, expression. A desire to bring out and give respect underlies ethnographic writing, which can be defined as accounts of the cultural-social world frequently rendered in the form of tales (Van Maanen, 1988). Kearney reminds us that "any story represents other stories unheard, untold, and unknown; we need to bring out those stories also, especially for groups of people whose stories have not been heard" (as cited in Soska, 2001, p. 17). Hence, we want to listen to the oldest narratives of our land from the Inuit and other First American tribes, stories that can trigger profound insights (Storm, 1972). In any town or city about which we care, we want to listen to large and small aggregates through "community telling."

Transformation. It is possible, communications professor Norman Denzin (1997) proposes, to integrate narration with community change through a feminist, communitarian, and ethical form of ethnography: "It seeks to produce narratives that ennoble human experience while facilitating civic transformations in the public (and private) spheres. This ethic promotes universal human solidarity. . . . The ethnographer discovers the multiple 'truths' that operate in the social world—the stories people tell one another about the things that matter. . . . These stories move people to action" (pp. xiv–xv). Denzin also suggests merging ethnography with applied action research and the new public journalism (see Chapter 3, this volume). In his view, caring professionals could take on new roles. These would include acting as a scribe or "cultural critic" (p. 225) and as a "watchdog" for the local community, one who tells "moving accounts that join private troubles with public issues" (p. 282).

Consciousness Raising and Activism with Flair

Significantly, narratives are told and heard by inactive as well as politically active members of society. The average person rarely tunes out stories as quickly as manifestos, which is why most U.S. citizens know about the Trail of Tears or Japanese internment camps. Here we mean alternatives to the imposed narratives that often flow from partisan politics. Wyile and Paré (2001) speak of unhorsing privileged narratives and letting common people "seize the reins of meaning" (p. 156).

An amazing variety of *influencers* emerge from this tradition, both uncelebrated citizens and famous performers. To use a dramatic example, who or what did more to expose and change public feeling about lynching: prominent lawmakers or anonymous news photographers? Lofty sermons or Billie Holiday's song "Strange Fruit"? Such change agents can be at risk just like political dissidents. Some years ago the worst happened in a Chilean stadium. The political right publicly killed beloved singer Victor Jara. A variety of *spokespersons* for the wretched of the earth have emerged, including the lead singer for the Irish rock group U2. Bono (BAWN-oh) has been more than a concert fundraiser (Live Aid); he once brought the United Nations a petition signed by 21.2 million people. "It's hard to imagine, but Bono is a serious player on Third World debt, one of those vital but arcane issues" (Memmott, 2001, p. 1A). Bono explains, "Unless these types of issues become *pop*, they don't become *political*. . . . As a performer I understand it takes a picture of me with the Pope or a president to get debt cancellation onto the front pages. Otherwise it's just too obscure a melody line" (Memmott, 2001, p. 2A). While the orga-

nizer maintains a low profile and supports grassroots leaders, the storyteller who connects people and problems can be famous or unknown. Social workers can look for dedicated community stars that can help an issue "become pop"; or, to get the story heard, can themselves adopt the earmarks of Bono's leadership: confidence, commitment, knowledgeability, and flair. The key is reaching audiences. This chapter opened with a group home news article that illustrates how compelling the story can be (also see Kotlowitz, 1997).

The Purposeful Use of Narrative

Narratives have potency at the macro level. Persuasive arguments embedded in a story form can be an effective springboard for internal transformation of an organization, says Stephen Denning (2001), and for gaining support from external constituencies, according to Pursey Heugens (2002). Change agents use narratives to achieve a practical outcome, to help people make a leap in understanding, to encourage groups to bridge across differences, to create confederations, and to forward causes. One sociologist argues that social movements consist of "bundles of narratives" (Fine, 2002). Joseph Davis (2002) explains, "Through stories, participants, actual and potential, are called . . . to identify and empathize with real protagonists, to be repelled by antagonists, to enter into and feel morally involved in configurations of events that specify injustice and prefigure change. . . . [Key] events—be they sit-ins, nuclear accidents, or court decisions—are interpreted and made the basis for action through stories. . . . [Storytelling] specifies valued endpoints and stimulates creative participation" (pp. 24–27).

The purposeful use of narrative has other functions too. *At a practical level, narrative allows us to reach those who cannot read.* Song stories have often served this purpose. Mexican revolutionary leader subcomandante Marcos (2001) has composed free verse about values, which is more easily memorized than most expository political statements. "Zapatismo poses the question[s]: 'What is it that has excluded me?' [and]'What is it that has isolated me?' " (p. 440). Marcos writes parables and updates old stories that can be related and discussed around a bonfire, part of normal social practices. Some poke fun at the weaknesses of the establishment ("The Parrot's Victory"), while others encourage acceptance of differences such as sexual orientation ("The Tale of the Little Seamstress"). Zapatistas use the Internet to spread their message, so they reach computer literate sympathizers around the globe as well as illiterate indigenous people. Thus, the narration method can include broad use of simplified stories to liberate and to combat oppression, to provide information, mental images, and coordinated messages (Themba, 1999, pp. 140–141).

At a psychological level, narratives allow the powerless to reframe their lives. Just as many individuals spend time in therapy ridding themselves of limiting personal scripts inculcated in them by others, so people in certain aggregates cope with social typing that limits them. Narratives can also disempower (Rappaport, 1995, p. 805). Those who live in public housing deal with "pathological narratives" from outsiders. In response, residents tell *defending* stories and *group enhancement* stories (Salzer, 1998, pp. 578–579). Despite people's reluctance to forgo their defending stories, there are transforming possibilities in their group enhancement stories. People like to hear about "imminent possibility and triumph grounded in real circumstances," notes Saleebey (1994, p. 354). He continues eloquently:

Tales of the quest for respect, relief, or redemption or the creation and reviving of symbols that unite hopes with action have moved people and have encouraged them to alter or defy their circumstances. . . . So stories and myths and narratives can be the instruments of empowerment—individual and collective (p. 354).

As the growing literature on narration stresses, ultimately the storyteller should come to view himself or herself as a story *maker*.

Telling or Hearing Stories Establishes Connections

It is worth noting that the Midwest Academy, which trains social activists and community organizers, now includes a session on storytelling as an organizing tool. The focus of the session is on the need to know people's life stories as a necessary step in developing leadership and framing issues (also see Ganz, 2001). In the same vein, author and lecturer Paul Loeb (1999) believes that social involvement takes us into new worlds where we will "take on new priorities, gain new skills, meet new people, hear and heed new stories" (p. 214).

Some organizations use stories to connect people who are physically apart (Ball-Rokeach, Kim, & Matei, 2001). The Digital Clubhouse in Sunnyvale, California, draws stories from 10 ethnic groups and a variety of human situations. There are narratives by and about a Tuskegee World War II airman, a 25-year-old succumbing to muscular dystrophy, and a teenage girl living in a homeless shelter—"all members of a silently separated community," (p. 1). As Abdulezer (2001) summarizes, "The Clubhouse has become a testbed for connecting communities around a digital hearth" (p. 1).

Stories can be powerful in unexpected ways. Much of society operates by fiat: Here is how it is! But stories are more unpredictable and cannot be controlled by the authorities. For instance, before the change in governments in Czechoslovakia, political leader and playwright Vaclav Havel used the country's black light theater tradition and the underground press to send political messages. These messages contributed to a "velvet revolution," where millions marched up the main street and took over leadership without a shot fired.

Conversely, listening to stories can also be powerful in unexpected ways. Shields describes a situation in which scores of Australian men reacted with name-calling and near violence to the fact that some Australian women had decided to demonstrate, alone, against the U.S. military. Several male peace activists decided to listen to the angry, intoxicated men: "With a few chairs and a simple sign, 'Men Willing to Listen,' they set themselves up near the self-proclaimed 'Men Against Dykes (M.A.D.)' camp. . . . Anger and fear dominated their talk—that they, as men, were excluded, not needed, rejected. As they were allowed to talk out this anger and fear, a more pressing fear was able to surface: that this [near riot] situation, which they had created, was getting out of control and lives could be in danger. . . . With a sense of urgency [those who had been listened to] left to have a 'pow-wow' which led to the M.A.D. camp breaking up" (Shields, 1994, pp. 47–48).

To recap, this change approach has been used in myriad ways to link disparate people and unify communities, build revolutions, or stop conflict between human groups. Bringing it back home, direct service practitioners can elicit client narratives and highlight them as they stage public issues. Through client narratives they can find common patterns of collective identity and a common sense of grievance and community discontent. Similarly, rural and urban practitioners can help get narratives disseminated, draw linkages with community problems and assets, and note commonalties between narratives that allow disparate groups to find common ground. Social workers can create awareness in change groups of dominant community and societal-cultural narratives so such narratives can be challenged and transformed.

Illustrative Exercises[17]

1. Narrative is not just speaking, signing, and writing; stories are told through videos, puppets, cartoons, and so on. This exercise is derived from Augusto Boal, who developed the Theatre of the Oppressed, and Douglas Paterson (1995) of the University of Nebraska-Omaha, who extended it:

   Write a short scene about someone (protagonist) dealing with oppression and failing because of obstacles (antagonists). Present it before your class. The exercise facilitator then tells the audience that the scene will be presented again and when you would behave differently from the protagonist, stand up and yell. At that point the 'actor' sits down and the audience member joins the troupe to show his solution (to audience applause). The facilitator has the class discuss the proposed solution and offer more alternatives.

2. Research the innovation-narration-liberation accomplishments of Muhammad Yunus (banker), Judy Chicago (artist), and Jacob Riis (photographer and author). How would you distinguish between innovative and trendy? Look up Dr. Patch Adams (humor in medicine) and Dr. Madan Kataria (laughing clubs). Discuss the pros and cons of ego in a change agent. Watch the movie *Bowling for Columbine* by effective liberal communicator Michael Moore (2002), and discuss his use of self as the narrator.

THE THEME OF CONNECTING

It is clear that community practitioners can play the role of connector. We complete our discussion with some worthwhile advice from a cultural historian (p. 335, p. 336). Gene Wise (1979) urged the necessity for a "connecting imagination . . . since few critical problems ever get understood, let alone resolved by attacking the problem alone. Contemporary cultural problems require understanding in their full interacting context. . . . [We need] a different quality of mind, a 'connecting mind' which can probe beyond the immediacy of the situation to search for everything which rays out from it" (pp. 335–336).

APPENDIX A: SKILLS VIGNETTE

A TRUE STORY ABOUT PUBLIC PRESSURE

We're in our building's auditorium. On stage, six liberal and conservative mayoral candidates—having given their individual pitches—are answering questions in phlegmatic fashion. Scattered throughout the hall are folks waiting for the right moment to bring up our issue, our solution, and our demand. Ah, here we go.

A person in our group stands up to declare his dismay with conditions at board-and-care homes. Politicians are accustomed to hearing about people's self-interest and seem surprised to be asked an altruistic question. One candidate asks how a 20-year-old became interested, and he explains. I smile across the room at our young fellow after he sits down. Someone else in the audience asks about taxes and another about roads. Then at the back of the room a young woman from our group holds up her hand and talks about how worried she is about her nana who resides in a big, understaffed facility.

A different politician asks her name and the name of the facility and commiserates about loved ones getting old. A few more questions come from others in the audience about trash and bus routes. Then a man too nervous to stand speaks from his seat. He says the newspaper reported people had died from neglect in two board-and-care homes.

One after another of the now alert mayoral candidates proclaims that they will be looking into the board-and-care situation (obviously a hot topic for this audience). The moderator seizes on the motif and asks if anyone in the audience has *positive* suggestions about how to improve the facilities. As planned, a woman who is widely known in local politics states that, as a nurse, she worries about many of the facilities she has to send the frail and elderly to from the hospital. Standing in the middle of the auditorium and speaking so all can hear, she states her eagerness to help *if* the city will support citizen involvement. A long discussion ensues among the candidates on the stage about what oversight exists now and how the city could legally or administratively get involved.

At a critical point, I rise to point out that the mayor signs the fire licenses for board-and-care facilities, which could be a handle. I offer as a social worker to pull together a citizen monitoring team to check up on the facilities and offer help, if the new administration will endorse it. There is sudden note-taking by reporters electrified to have news from a routine candidate forum. There are big smiles from the moderator and the candidates, who are relieved at having a solution for a problem they had not even thought about before. To our amazement but great satisfaction, all six candidates promise—if elected—to vigorously support a citizen monitoring team to oversee and improve board-and-care homes. The meet-the-candidates event ends and reporters interview several of those who spoke for us.

Four months later, we celebrate on behalf of poor, institutionalized, oppressed elderly persons when the real victory happens. After the election, the social workers, nurses, and citizens on our team are deputized by the mayor to coordinate, have access, write reports, and provide assistance. Immediately, we begin visiting facilities. Eventually, a coalition forms around the project, and a year later a Senate committee commends our monitoring team project.

PRACTICE WISDOM ON ADVANCING THE CAUSE

Why did the plan work? It was easily grasped and did not cost the city anything. The spokespersons knew the problems, solutions, regulations, and licensing requirements and gave succinct personal examples. With a huge contingent, sitting in a block is effective; with fewer activists, being scattered conveyed broad support. Politicians grasp what troubles the public, maneuver to avoid scenes, and take the path of least resistance. The issue was new so candidates had no established position. Board and care operators were not big campaign donors, but every voter has elderly relatives. Scandals and deaths capture the attention of politicians, who do not want to be held accountable. Usually they hear, "You do something," not "We want to do something." The *Organizing for Social Change* manual (Bobo et al., 2001) includes this statement: "The principle of this tactic is deceptively simple and direct. You ask for something, and more often than not, you get it. It's like magic and you say, 'Why didn't we do this months ago?' The answer is that it probably wouldn't have worked months ago because you hadn't built up your organized strength, nor had you made the necessary strategic calculations" (p. 71). You cannot get what you do not ask for: Grab the moment.

Discussion Questions

1. Using the Skills Vignette, discuss how things could have gone wrong or fallen apart. What would get the effort back on track?

2. Some change agents are interested in public service; others want public transformation. Where does the coordination and participation tradition fit? What does it mean to let people define their own issues?

3. Given discrimination, coming out about one's sexuality is an act of defiance (Stockdill, 2001). Debate this question: Is coming out, by itself, a gesture that epitomizes the social action tradition or the innovation-narration-liberation tradition?

4. Interpret the following adage: "When you're pushing the wagon, don't forget to sing."

5. Using the Internet, look up "study circles," a popular new phenomenon, on the Study Circles Resource Center website (http://www.studycircles.org). These may involve people in a town; Red Deer, Alberta, Canada has a study circle. These may involve a common interest; Middlebury College in Vermont has an Arabic study circle. In which tradition of connecting people does the study circle best fit?

6. *A challenge:* Reread Norman Denzin's (1997) suggestions for new roles. Review earlier chapters to clarify terminology. Are you able to explain his rather complicated ideas in your own words?

7. *Role-play:* You tell your governing board that you plan to involve interested indigenous leaders, service users, and service providers. Board members ask (a) how you will identify interested and indigenous stakeholders, and (b) why you want to line up those already interested rather than those who never participate but should be interested? Respond.

Notes

1. For background on community capacity, see Bowen, Martin, Mancini, & Nelson (2000); Chaskin, Brown, Venkatesh, & Vidal (2001).

2. The organization-mobilization tradition is similar to Rothman's social action mode and to Jeffries's direct action and social campaign modes (see Chapter 2, this text). The coordination-participation tradition is similar to Rothman's social planning and Jeffries's partnership promotion mode. The innovation-narration-liberation tradition can be likened to Rothman's locality development mode and Jeffries's capacity and awareness promotion mode but is a more encompassing and experimental practice model. For more on community organizing practice models, see Hardina (2002, Chapter 4).

3. In 2002, journalist Katherine Boo received a MacArthur "genius award" for her writing about the less fortunate; earlier, the Pulitzer Prize public service committee singled out her work.

4. Experienced organizers know that connecting through action, for example, in a political campaign or a social movement, usually brings an increase in power (see Chapter 4, this text) and that standing up for social justice may trigger red-baiting and name-calling ("anti-American"); see Horwitt (1989, Chapter 16). Yet, as the old labor song "Joe Hill" tells us, it takes more than names, elections, or even guns to kill the organizing spirit.

5. Parren Mitchell was interviewed by Michael Oppenheim for Powers, P. (Ed.). (1994). *Challenging: Interviews with Advocates and Activists* [Monograph]. Baltimore: University of Maryland at Baltimore, School of Social Work.

6. For more on recruiting members, see Bobo et al. (2001) and Kahn (1970, 1991). For 20 strategies used to reclaim a park by involving more and more people, see Steve Coleman's article, "Organizing and Programming Across Cultural Boundaries" (*Urban Parks Online*, 2002) at the Project for Public Spaces Web site (http://www.pps.org/topics/parkuse/coleman2).

7. Copyright 1999, by Makani N. Themba. Reprinted by permission of Chardon Press and John Wiley & Sons, Inc.

8. Kerry Miciotto, formerly of Solidarity Sponsoring Committee (SSC) and IAF, interviewed by Karen Sokolow and Sharronda Jackson. Janice Fine (n.d.) calls Miciotto "a talented organizer who interned with Solidarity as part of her MSW training and subsequently joined the staff" (p. 14).

9. The example in the text is a project funded by Community Integrated Service Systems (CISS). CISS seeks ways to assist communities to better meet *consumer identified* needs, fill gaps in service, coordinate systems building efforts, and support community organization activities. CISS is part of the U.S. Maternal and Child Health Bureau.

10. Copyright is held by the *Administration in Social Work* journal. Excerpts from Cohen are used with permission from Haworth Press.

11. Nathaniel Branson, University of Maryland at Baltimore, interviewed by Maria Luisa Tyree (March 27, 2001). In Horwitt's biography of Alinsky (1989), a powerful contrast is made between the roles taken by upwardly mobile Robert J. Dunham and Dan Carpenter versus true community member James R. Norris.

12. Community engagement and public consultation materials can be found on-line at the websites Principles of Community Engagement (http://www.cdc.gov/phppo/pce) and Association for Community Organization and Social Administration (www.acasa.org). For more on identifying leaders, see Kahn (1991) and Bobo et al. (2001); on identifying stakeholder groups, see Chrislip (1995); on stakeholder management, see Huegens (2002).

13. For advice on planning cultural actions, see *Incite! Women of Color Against Violence* (available through P. O. Box 6861, Minneapolis, MN).

14. Keep an eye and ear out for resource people. For example, a radio show on ethnic media had four guests concerned about various immigrant groups: Andrew Lam (Vietnamese), Pilar Marrero (Latino), Ibrahim Nidal (Arab) and Mei Ling Sze (Chinese). Expand your contact list by culling names from media outlets.

15. Think of the *Vagina Monologues* play. See Halperin (2001) for group work and theatre.

16. At a practical level, rape victim and author Anne Marie Aikins of AMA Communications has written "Authentic Boys/Safer Girls: A Teacher's Guide to Helping Boys Break Free of Gender Stereotyping" (133 Morse St., Toronto, ON Canada M4M2P9) to bust the negative "boy code" that distorts the boys' real selves. At a theoretical level, while our example exemplifies sincerity, not performance or farce, identifying the artificiality of gender distinctions and moving toward a deconstruction of traits would fit with feminist theorist Judith Butler's idea of gender as a form of "drag" with no core (Klages, 1997).

17. Here is an *online* experiment with nontraditional change. For an introduction to issues about the Nike corporation, see the home page of Professor David Boja at New Mexico State University (http://cbae.nmsu.edu/~dboje/) and click on the link "Nike Studies".

References

Abdulezer, S. (2000). A community of stories. *Converge, 3*(1), p. 62.

Act Up (n.d.). History of nonviolence. Retrieved on July 20, 2003 from http://www.actupny.org/documents/CDdocuments/HistoryNV.html

Alinsky, S. D. (1971). *Rules for radicals: A pragmatic primer for realistic radicals.* New York: Vintage.

Arches, J. L. (1997). Connecting to communities: Transformational leadership from Africentric feminist perspectives. *Journal of Sociology and Social Welfare, 24*(4), 113–124.

Ash, R. (1972). *Social movements in America.* Chicago: Marham.

Associated Press. (1997, May 4). Paulo Freire dies at 75; Brazilian literacy expert. *The Washington Post,* p. B8.

Atcheson, R. (2000). The Missoula experiment: How a small town in Montana learned to make dying a part of life. *Modern Maturity, 43W*(5), 60–62, 88.

Ball-Rokeach, S. J., Kim, Y-C., & Matei, S. (2001). Storytelling neighborhood: Paths to belonging in diverse urban environments. *Communication Research, 28*(4), 392–428.

Beck, E. L., & Eichler, M. (2000). Consensus organizing: A practice model for community building. *Journal of Community Practice, 8*(1), 87–102.

Bennett, S. (1995). Community organizations and crime. *Annals of the American Academy of Political and Social Science, 539,* 72–84.

Berger, L. M. (2000). The emotional and intellectual aspects of protest music: Implications for community organizing education. *Journal of Teaching in Social Work, 20*(1/2), 57–76.

Blackburn, J. (2000). Understanding Paulo Freire: Reflections on the origins, concepts, and possible pitfalls of his educational approach. *Community Development Journal, 35*(1), 3–15.

Bobo, K., Kendall, J., & Max, S. (2001). *Organizing for social change* (3rd ed.). Santa Ana, CA: Seven Locks Press.

Boo, K. (1999, March 15). Residents languish; profiteers flourish. *The Washington Post,* p. A1.

Bowen, G. L., Martin, J. A., Mancini, J. A., & Nelson, J. P. (2000). Community capacity: Antecedents and consequences. *Journal of Community Practice, 8*(2), 1–21.

Bradshaw, C., Soifer, S., & Gutierrez, L. (1994). Toward a hybrid model for effective organizing in communities of color. *Journal of Community Practice, 1*(1), 25–41.

Bricker-Jenkins, M., & Lockett, P. W. (1995). Women: Direct practice. In R. Edwards (Ed.-in-Chief), *Encyclopedia of social work* (19th ed., pp. 2529–2539). Washington, DC: National Association of Social Workers.

Brooks, F. (2001). Innovative organizing practices: ACORN's campaign in Los Angeles organizing workfare workers. *Journal of Community Practice, 9*(4), 68–85.

Bruner, C., & Parachini, L. (2000). *Building community: Exploring new relationships among service systems reform, community organizing, and community economic development.* Washington, DC: Together We Can.

Butler, S. S., & Seguino, S. (2000). Working in coalition: Advocates and academics join forces to promote progressive welfare policies. *Journal of Community Practice, 7*(4), 1–20.

Calpotura, F., & Fellner, K. (1996). *The square pegs find their groove: Reshaping the organizing circle.* Retrieved June 13, 2003, from http://comm-org.utoledo.edu/papers96/square.html

Carlson, E. (2001). In the neighborhood. *John Hopkins Magazine, 53*(2), 36–40.

Carroll, J., & Minkler, M. (2000). Freire's message for social workers: Looking back, looking ahead. *Journal of Community Practice, 8*(1), 21–36.

Cashmore, E., & Rojek, C. (1999). *Dictionary of cultural theorists.* New York: Oxford University Press.

Castelloe, P., & Watson, T. (1999). Participatory education as a community practice method: A case example from a comprehensive Head Start program. *Journal of Community Practice, 6*(1), 71–89.

Charles Stewart Mott Foundation (2003). Grant programs: Pathways out of poverty: Guidelines. Retrieved July 16, 2003 from http://www.mott.org/programs/p-guidelines.asp#boc

Chaskin, R. J., Brown, R. J., Venkatesh, S., & Vidal, A. (2001). *Building community capacity.* New York: Aldine de Gruyter.

Chrislip, D. D. (1995). Pulling together: Creating a constituency for change. *National Civic Review, 84*(1), 21–29.

Cohen, B. (1980). Coordination strategies in complex service delivery systems. *Administration in Social Work, 4*(3), 83–87.

Collins, C., & Rogers, P. (with J. P. Garner). (2000). *Robin Hood Was Right: A Guide to Giving Your Money for Social Change.* New York: W. W. Norton & Company.

Communitarian skinheads (1994, Fall). From The Community at Large Section, *Responsive Community, 4* (4), 79

Cornelius, L. J., Battle, M., Kryder-Coe, J. H., & Hu, D. (1999). Interventions to developing community partnerships for HIV prevention planning: Successful macro applications of social work principles. *Journal of Community Practice, 6*(1), 15–32.

Couto, R. A. (1993). Narrative, free space, and political leadership in social movements. *Journal of Politics, 55*(1), 57–79.

Cox, E. O. (2001). Community practice issues in the 21st century: Questions and challenges for empowerment-oriented practitioners. *Journal of Community Practice, 9*(1), 37–55.

Croft, S., & Beresford, P. (1988). Being on the receiving end: Lessons for community development and user involvement. *Community Development Journal, 23*(4), 273–279.

Cultural Environment Movement. (1999). Who's telling these stories? [Brochure]. Philadelphia, PA: Author.

Daley, J. M., & Marsiglia, F. F. (2000). Community participation: Old wine in new bottles? *Journal of Community Practice, 8*(1), 61–86.

Daley, J. M., & Wong, P. (1994). Community development with emerging ethnic communities. *Journal of Community Practice, 1*(1), 9–24.

Davis, J. E. (Ed.). (2002). *Stories of change: Narrative and social movements.* Albany: State University of New York Press.

Delgado, M. (2000). *Community social work practice in an urban context: The potential of a capacity-enhancement perspective.* New York: Oxford University Press.

Denning, Stephen (2001). *The springboard: How storytelling ignites action in knowledge-era organizations.* Boston, MA: Butterworth-Heinemann.

Denzin, N. K. (1997). *Interpretive ethnography: Enthnographic practices for the 21st century.* Thousand Oaks, CA: Sage.

Eichler, M. (1995). Consensus organizing: Sharing power to gain power. *National Civic Review, 84*(3), 256–261.

Ewalt, P. L. (1998). The revitalization of impoverished communities. In P. Ewalt, E. M. Freeman, & D. L. Poole (Eds.), *Community building* (pp. 3–5). Washington, DC: National Association of Social Workers.

Felkins, P. K. (2002). *Community at work: Creating and celebrating community in organizational life.* Cresskill, NJ: Hampton.

Ferriss, S., & Sandoval, R. (1997). *The fight in the fields: Cesar Chavez and the farmworkers movement.* New York: Harcourt Brace.

Fine, G. A. (2002). The storied group: Social movements as "bundles of narratives." In J. E. Davis (Ed.), *Stories of change: Narrative and social movements.* Albany: State University of New York Press.

Fine, J. (n.d.). Moving innovation from the margins to the center for a new American labor movement. Retrieved July 16, 2003 from http://www.mit.edu/~ipc/Fine.pdf

Fisher, R., & Shragge, E. (2000). Challenging community organizing: Facing the 21st century. *Journal of Community Practice, 8*(3), 1–19.

Freedman, J., & Combs, G. (1996). *Narrative therapy: The social construction of preferred realities.* New York: W. W. Norton.

Freire, P. (1994). *Pedagogy of hope* (with notes by A. M. A. Freire; R. R. Barr, Trans.). New York: Continuum Publishing Company.

Gadotti, M. (1994). *Reading Paulo Freire: His life and work.* Albany: State University of New York Press.

Gamble, D. N., & Weil, M. O. (1995). Citizen participation. In R. Edwards (Ed.-in-Chief), *Encyclopedia of social work* (19th ed., pp. 483–494). Washington, DC: National Association of Social Workers.

Ganz, M. (2001, August). *The power of story in social movements.* Paper presented at the annual meeting of the American Sociological Association, Anaheim, CA.

Ganz, M. (2003, January). *Course Syllabi: Graduate Organizing: People, Power and Change.* Kennedy School of Government, Harvard University. Retrieved on July 15, 2003 from http://www.cpn.org/tools/syllabi/ganz.html.

Ganz, M. (2003). Why David sometimes Wins: Strategic capacity in social movements. In J. Goodwin and J. Jasper (Eds.) *Rethinking social movements: structure, meaning, and emotion (people, passion, and power).* Lanham, MD: Rowman & Littlefield.

Glugoski, G., Reisch, M., & Rivera, F. G. (1994). A wholistic ethno-cultural paradigm: A new model for community organization teaching and practice. *Journal of Community Practice, 1*(1), 81–98.

Goldstein, S. M. (1997). Community coalitions: A self-assessment tool. *American Journal of Health Promotion, 11*(6), 430–435.

Guinier, L., & Torres, G. (2002). *The miner's canary: Enlisting race, resisting power, transforming democracy.* Cambridge, MA: Harvard University Press.

Gutierrez, L., Alvarez, A. R., Nemon, H., & Lewis, E. A. (1996). Multicultural community organizing: A strategy for change. *Social Work, 41*(5), 501–508.

Gutierrez, L. M., & Lewis, E. A. (1994). Community organizing with women of color: A feminist approach. *Journal of Community Practice, 1*(2), 23–44.

Halperin, D. (2001). The play's the thing: How social group work and theatre transformed a group into a community. *Social Work With Groups, 24*(2), 27–46.

Hardina, D. (2002). *Analytical skills for community organization practice.* New York: Columbia University Press.

Heugens, P. P. M. A. R. (2002). Managing public affairs through storytelling. *Journal of Public Affairs* (Henry Stewart Publications), *2*(2), 57–70.

Higgins, J. W. (1999). Citizenship and empowerment: A remedy for citizen participation in health reform. *Community Development Journal, 34*(4), 287–307.

Hofrichter, R. (1993). *Toxic struggles: The theory*

and practice of environmental justice. Philadelphia: New Society.

Horton, M., & Freire, P. (with Bell, B., Gaventa, J., & Peters, J.). (1990). *We make the world by walking: Conversations on education and social change*. Philadelphia: Temple University Press.

Horwitt, S. D. (1989). *Let them call me rebel: Saul Alinsky—his life and legacy*. New York: Vintage Books.

Hyde, C. (2001). Experiences of women activists: Implications for community organizing theory and practice. In J. E. Tropman, J. L. Erlich, & J. Rothman (Eds.), *Tactics and techniques of community intervention* (4th ed., pp. 75–84). Itasca, IL: F. E. Peacock.

Institute for Democratic Renewal. (2000). *A community builder's tool kit*. Claremont, CA: Author.

Irving, A., & Young, T. (2002). Paradigm for pluralism: Mikhail Bakhtin and social work practice. *Social Work, 47*(1), 19–29.

Itzhaky, H., & York, A. S. (2002). Showing results in community organization. *Social Work, 47*(2), 125–131.

Kahn, S. (1970). *How people get power: Organizing oppressed communities for action*. New York: McGraw-Hill.

Kahn, S. (1991). *Organizing: A guide for grassroots leaders*. Washington, DC: National Association of Social Workers Press.

Kahn, S. (1997). Leadership: Realizing concepts through creative process. *Journal of Community Practice, 4*(1), 109–136.

Klages, M. (1997). Gender trouble: Judith Butler. Retrieved on July 22, 2003 from http://www.colorado.edu/English/ENGL2012Klages/butler.html

Kingsley, G. T., McNeely, J. B., & Gibson, J. O. (1997). *Community building: Coming of age*. Washington, DC: Development Training Institute, Inc., and the Urban Institute.

Koch, J. R., & Johnson, D. P. (1997). The ecumenical outreach coalition: A case study of converging interests and network formation for church and community cooperation. *Nonprofit and Voluntary Sector Quarterly, 26*(3), 343–358.

Koerin, B. (2002). *Community building and the Settlement House tradition: A thing of the past?* Paper presented at Council of Social Work Education meeting, Nashville, TN.

Kotlowitz, A. (1997). Where was the village? In S. R. Shreve and P. Shreve (Eds.), *Outside the law: Narratives on justice in America* (pp. 106–110). Boston: Beacon Press.

Kraft, K. (2000). Engaged Buddhism: Modern Buddhism addresses politics and social action. *Interfaith Insights, 1*(2), 20–25. Washington, DC: Interfaith Alliance Foundation.

Kramer, R. M. (1969). *Participation of the poor: Comparative community case studies in the war on poverty*. Englewood Cliffs, NJ: Prentice Hall.

Kreck, C. (2001, July 15). Parents demand more school clout. *Denver Post,* p. A25.

Lee, S. (Producer, Director, and Writer). (1989). Do the right thing [Motion picture]. United States: Universal Pictures/Forty Acres and a Mule Filmworks.

Levy, C. J. (2002a, April 28). For mentally ill, death and misery. *New York Times,* p. 1, pp. 34–37.

Levy, C. J. (2002b, April 29). Here life is squalor and chaos. *New York Times,* p. A1, pp. A26–27.

Levy, C. J. (2002c, April 30). Voiceless, defenseless and a source of cash. *New York Times,* p. A1, pp. A28–29.

Levy, J. (1975). *Cesar Chavez: Autobiography of la causa*. New York: W. W. Norton.

Lewis, M. A., Lewis, C. E., & Rachelefsky, G. (1996). Organizing the community to target poor Latino children with asthma. *Journal of Asthma, 33*(5), 289–297.

Liese, H. (2003). Documentaries: Powerful tools for community building and social change. *The ACOSA Update, 17*(3), p. 7, p. 13.

Loeb, P. R. (1999). *Soul of a citizen: Living with conviction in a cynical time*. New York: St. Martin's Press

Ly, P. (2001, December 13). Leader gives Latinos strong voice in area. *The Washington Post,* Montgomery section, pp. 12–13.

MacNair, R. H. (1996). Theory for community practice in social work: The example of ecological community practice. *Journal of Community Practice, 3*(3/4), 181–202.

Magida, A. J., & Matlins, S. (1999). *How to be a perfect stranger: A guide to etiquette in other people's religious ceremonies*. Woodstock, VT: Skylight Paths.

Mallaby, S. (2002, October 14). An optional catastrophe. *The Washington Post,* p. A29.

Marcos, S. (2001). *Our word is our weapon*. New York: Seven Stories.

Martinez-Brawley, E. E. (2000). *Close to home: Human services and the small community*. Washington, DC: National Association of Social Workers Press.

Masilela, C. O., & Meyer, W. A., III. (1998). The role of citizen participation in comprehensive planning: A personal view of the experience in Morgantown, West Virginia. *Small Town, 29*(3), 4–15.

McAdam, D. (1982). *Political process and the development of Black insurgency, 1930–1970*. Chicago: University of Chicago Press.

McArthur, A. (1995). The active involvement of local residents in strategic community partnerships. *Policy and Politics, 23*(1), 61–71.

McKnight, J. (1995). *The careless society: Community and its counterfeits*. New York: Basic Books.

McNellie, R. B. (2001). The advanced rural generalist. *The New Social Worker, 8*(1), 16–18.

Memmott, M. (2001, June 15–17). Rockin' the debt: Bono leads Third World crusade. *USA Today*, pp. 1A-2A.

Miley, K. K., O'Melia, M., & DuBois, B. L. (1998). *Generalist social work practice: An empowering approach* (2nd ed.). Needham Heights, MA: Allyn & Bacon.

Mizrahi, T. (1999). Strategies for effective collaboration in the human services. *Social Policy, 29*(4), 5–20.

Mizrahi, T. (2002). Basic principles for organizing: Perspectives from practice. Retrieved July 15, 2003 from http://www.hunter.cuny.edu/socwork/ecco.bpfo.htm

Moses, R., & Cobb, C. E., Jr. (2001). *Radical equations: Math literacy and civil rights.* Boston, MA: Beacon Press.

National Public Radio. (2001, March 15). Morning Edition: *Rochester reads 'A Lesson Before Dying.'*

Neighborhood Funders Group. (2001a). *The community organizing toolbox: CO accomplishments.* Retrieved June 9, 2003, from http://www.nfg.org/cotb/17coaccomplishments.htm

Neighborhood Funders Group (2001b). The community organizing toolbox: Measuring results: How to evaluate co initiatives. Retrieved July 15, 2003 from http://www.nfg.org/cotb/33measuring.htm

Neiman, T. (1999). Creating community by implementing holistic approaches to solving clients' problems. *Journal of Poverty Law, 33*(1/2), 19–24.

New Economics Foundation. (1998). Participation works! 21 techniques of community participation for the 21st century.

Norden, E. (1972). Saul Alinsky, A candid conversation with the feisty radical organizer. *Playboy, 19*: 3; retrieved in weekly installments from May to August 2003 from The Progress Report at http://www.progress.org/2003/alinsky (no longer available online).

Norris, T., & Lampe, D. (1994, Summer/Fall). Healthy communities, healthy people. *National Civic Review, 280*–289.

Paterson, D.L. (1995). Theatre of the Oppressed workshops: Forum Theatre. Retrieved on July 21, 2003 from http://www.wwcd.org/action/Boal.html

Peterson, K. J., & Lieberman, A. A. (2001). *Building on women's strengths: A social work agenda for the twenty-first century* (2nd ed.). Binghamton, NY: Haworth Press.

Potapcheck, W. R. (1996). Building sustainable community politics: Synergizing participatory, institutional, and representative democracy. *National Civic Review, 85*(3), 54–59.

Putnam, R. D. (2000). *Bowling alone: The collapse and revival of American community.* New York: Simon & Schuster.

Rappaport, J. (1995). Empowerment meets narrative: Listening to stories and creating settings. *American Journal of Community Psychology, 23*(5), 795–807.

Rathke, W. (2001, Summer). Tactical tension. *Social Policy, 31,* 13–18.

Reisch, M., Wenocur, S., & Sherman, W. (1981). Empowerment, conscientization, and animation as core social work skills. *Social Development Issues, 5*(2/3), 62–67.

Rivera, F. G., & Erlich, J. L. (1998). *Community organizing in a diverse society* (3rd ed.). Boston, MA: Allyn & Bacon.

Robinson, B., & Hanna, M. G. (1994). Lessons for academics from grassroots community organizing: A case study—The Industrial Areas Foundation. *Journal of Community Practice, 1*(4), 63–94.

Rosin, H. (2003, December 9). People-powered: In New Hampshire, Howard Dean's campaign has energized voters. *The Washington Post,* pp. C1–2.

Ross, M. G. (1958). *Case histories in community organization.* New York: Harper & Row.

Rubin, H., & Rubin, I. S. (1995). *The qualitative interview: The art of hearing data.* Thousand Oaks, CA: Sage Publishers.

Sachs, J., & Newdom, F. (1999). *Clinical work and social action: An integrative approach.* New York: Haworth Press.

Salcido, R. M. (1993, March). *A cross-cultural approach to understanding Latino barrio needs: A macro practice model.* Paper presented at Council of Social Work Education meeting, New York.

Salzer, M. S. (1998). Narrative approach to assessing interactions between society, community, and person. *Journal of Community Psychology, 26*(6), 569–580.

Saleebey, D. (1994). Culture, theory, and narrative: The intersection of meanings in practice. *Social Work, 39*(4), 351–359.

Schwartz, D. B. (1992). *Crossing the river: Creating a conceptual revolution in community and disability.* Newton Upper Falls, MA: Brookline Books.

Shaw, R. (2001). *The activist's handbook: A primer.* Berkeley: University of California Press.

Shields, K. (1994). *In the tiger's mouth: An empowerment guide for social action.* Gabriola Island, BC: New Society Publishers.

Shultz, J. (2002). *The democracy owners' manual: A practical guide to changing the world.* New Brunswick, NJ: Rutgers University Press.

Smith, D., & Lopez, P. (2002, October 26). A voice for the "little fellers." *Minneapolis Star Tribune.*

Speer, P. W., & Hughey, J. (1995). Community organizing: An ecological route to empowerment and power. *American Journal of Community Psychology, 23*(5), 729–747.

Soska, T. M. (2001). Building a transatlantic dialogue on community development and social inclusion. *ACOSA Update, 15*(1), 12–19.

Speeter, G. (1978). *Power: A repossession manual.* Amherst, MA: Citizen Involvement Training Project.

Staral, J. (2000). Building on mutual goals: The intersection of community practice and church-based organizing. *Journal of Community Practice, 7*(3), 85–95.

Stockdill, B. C. (2001). Forging a multidimensional oppositional consciousness: Lessons from community-based AIDS activism. In J. Mansbridge & A. Morris (Eds.), *Oppositional consciousness: The subjective roots of social protest.* Chicago: University of Chicago Press.

Storm, H. (1972). *Seven arrows.* New York: Harper & Row.

Stukas, A., & Dunlap, M. (2002). Community involvement: Theoretical approaches and educational initiatives. *Journal of Social Issues, 58*(3), 411–427.

Themba, M. N. (1999). *Making policy, making change: How communities are taking the law into their own hands.* Berkeley, CA: Chardon Press.

Van Maanen, J. (1988). *Tales of the field: On writing ethnography.* Chicago: University of Chicago Press.

Wallack, L. (2002). Media advocacy: A strategy for empowering people and communities. In M. Minkler (Ed.), *Community organizing and community building for health* (pp. 339–352).

Wallerstein, N. (1993). Empowerment and health: The theory and practice of community change. *Community Development Journal, 28*(3), 218–227.

Walz, T. (1991). *The unlikely celebrity: Bill Sackter's triumph over disability.* Carbondale: Southern Illinois University Press.

Walz, T., & Uematsu, M. (1997). Creativity in social work practice: A pedagogy. *Journal of Teaching in Social Work, 15* (1/2), 17–31.

Wax, E. (2001, May 27). Buddhists feel at home, celebrate in Fauquier. *The Washington Post,* p. C4.

Weil, M. (2001). Women, community, and organizing. In J. E. Tropman, J. L. Erlich, & J. Rothman (Eds.), *Tactics and techniques of community intervention* (4th ed., pp. 204–220). Itasca, IL: F. E. Peacock.

Wise, G. (1979). "Paradigm dramas" in American studies. *American Quarterly, XXXI*(3), 293–337.

Wyile, H., & Paré, D. (2001). Whose story is it, anyway? An interdisciplinary approach to postmodernism, narrative, and therapy. *Mosaic, 34*(1), 153–172.

15

Community Social Casework

Mrs. J., a 30-year-old white female, was referred to a family services agency (FSA) for help. Her husband chronically physically and emotionally abuses her. Mrs. J. quit high school in her sophomore year because of pregnancy with her first child. She didn't return to school or obtain a high school equivalency certificate. The child, John, is now 14 years old. Mrs. J.'s current husband is not John's father. This is a source of conflict in the family. John and Mr. J. do not get along. Mr. J. is repeatedly physically and emotionally abusive to the boy. John is habitually absent from school, insolent, and a member of a loose-knit gang of antisocial white youth who call themselves skinheads. He often is out of Mrs. J.'s control.

Mrs. J.'s second child, Susan, is 10, She is Mr. J.'s daughter, and he adores her. Susan worships John, and Mrs. J. is worried that Susan is picking up John's wild ways.

The family moved to the community about 6 months ago from another state. They moved so that Mr. J. could find employment. He obtained work as an auto mechanic (his occupation) and has been working consistently since their move. He financially supports the family. John's biological father provides neither financial nor emotional support. He doesn't have any contact with John.

Mrs. J. has not worked outside the home for the decade of her marriage. Prior to her marriage, she worked for about 3 years as a waitress. Her mother babysat John. Mrs. J. met Mr. J. at her waitress job. She has no other paid employment experience. She now wants to find a job so that she and John will be less financially dependent on Mr. J. Her desire for a job is a source of friction between her and her husband. He believes that supporting the family is his responsibility, and that Mrs. J. is responsible for the children's upbringing. He tells her she is not doing a good job raising the children. They are "going bad." How does she expect to both work outside the home and properly bring up the children when she can't bring up the children now? She should, her husband believes, devote her energy to being a homemaker and supervising the children. He does want John to get a job, because John is not passing or attending school regularly. Their discussions on these matters generally result in violent arguments.

Mrs. J. has neither close friends nor relatives in the new community and rarely gets out of the home except for household duties. She does not have a primary social support system. She feels socially isolated and marginalized, in addition to her marital and family problems.

Mrs. J. came to the FSA on a referral from an emergency room doctor treatment for an injury apparently caused by her husband's abuse. Mrs. J. told the emergency room doctor that she fell, although the indications were that the injuries were from abuse. The physician made no police referral, because Mrs. J. was adamant that it wasn't abuse. The doctor urged her to go to FSA in any case. Mrs. J. did tell the FSA intake social worker about her violent arguments with Mr. J. and that she would like to figure out a way to either end Mr. J.'s abusive behavior toward John and her or to find a job and leave the home with her children. John has told her that he will leave home and live with his skinhead friends if the abuse continues. Mrs. J. is afraid that John's violent friends may seek revenge on Mr. J. For now, Mrs. J. is at a loss to do anything, because she has no close friends or family supports in this community, no place to go, no money of her own, no source of income other than Mr. J., and no idea where to turn for help.

WHAT IS COMMUNITY SOCIAL CASEWORK?

Mrs. J., like many clients, is caught in a web of social conditions requiring myriad community resources and social supports and her own capacity and strengths to improve her life. Unfortunately, if community resources exist, they usually are not organized in ways conducive to easy access and use by clients. Often, clients like Mrs. J. (and the social workers they turn to) are ignorant of the social reasons for their problems and the community resources available to address them. They are also often naive of the importance of primary and secondary resources. The social worker retreats to a biopsychological problem construction and intervention leading to a mental illness diagnosis out of fear of venturing into the community. For successful integration of a client into the community, the client and social worker have the tasks of community assessment to locate and then use community skills to network with primary, secondary, and tertiary resources and social supports. The social worker needs to be a community social caseworker.

Community social casework draws from a rich heritage and antecedents of prepsychotherapeutic social casework (Richmond, 1917, 1922). The International Association of Schools of Social Work (IASSW) and the International Federation of Social Workers (IFSW) drew from this heritage in their joint definition of social work intervention. "Social work intervenes at the point where people interact with their environments. . . . Social work in its various forms addresses the multiple, complex transactions between people and their environments ("IASSW, IFSW Announce Joint Definition," 2001, p. 31).

Community social casework recognizes that most social supports are provided by a community's primary and secondary groups rather than by formal tertiary social agencies and social services providers (Adams & Nelson, 1995; Barber, 1991; Gordon & Donald, 1993; Henderson, Jones, & Thomas, 1980; Karabanow, 1995; Payne, 2000; Phillips, Bernard, Phillipson, & Ogg, 2000; Quinn, 1995; Smale, 1995; Whittaker, Garbarino, et al., 1983; Whittaker & Tracey, 1989). Community social casework views the community as (a) a source of resources for addressing and resolving concerns and (b) the locus of problem-perpetuating interaction. Social workers should work with and within the community and the family and other secondary groups rather than attempting to substitute for them. Community social casework accepts that professionals are not at the center of helping systems. Others do most of the caring and managing: families, kin, neighborhood networks, informal groups, and formal organizations such as churches and schools. Effectiveness depends on how well the professional caregiver interacts with the whole complex of formal and informal elements to strengthen a community's capacity to care for its members and address shared needs and concerns (Adams & Nelson, 1995, p. 6).

Community social casework draws heavily from the British models of casework with their community and network analysis and *patch* approach (Adams & Krauth, 1995; Gordon & Donald, 1993; Payne, 2000). The patch approach focuses on neighborhood-sized geographic catchment areas or *patches* where the resources of informal networks of kin and neighbors are used and built upon to address individual and community problems (Adams & Krauth, 1995, p. 89; Adams & Nelson, 1995). The patch is generally the neighborhood, but it can be a geographic area with a population as large as 20,000, to allow for a sufficient resource base of assets (see Chapter 5, this text). The patch approach localizes and integrates services at a neighborhood level without overly *clientizing* the client. *Clientizing* means making the client dependent on the caseworker—or therapist—and social agencies. Community social casework is inherent in good patch work. It calls for a unitary practice approach recognizing the integrality of social supports, social problems, and client problems. It acknowledges a need for client involvement in neighborhood and community's formal, informal, and political organizations and processes. This is vital to solving both client and community problems. Community social caseworkers use a patch approach to weave clients into primary social supports, a neighborhood's secondary social supports, and a community's more formal tertiary social supports (Adams & Nelson, 1995, p. 8–9; Adams & Krauth, 1995; Barber, 1991; Smale, 1995).

Community social casework stresses what Sheppard (1991) calls indirect helping as "activities that the worker undertakes *on behalf* [italics added] of the client to further mutually agreed upon goals" (p. 3). Indirect helping is work with others designed to influence a client's behavior and/or circumstances. Sheppard's British conception of indirect practice differs from the more typical U.S. conception of indirect helping put forth by Taylor and Roberts (1985, p. 18), which equates indirect helping or practice with community organization and administration using a *direct-indirect practice dichotomy* along a *micro-macro* continuum. This model of indirect practice is client focused. Community social casework views community practice as indispensable in casework. Casework requires understanding, modifying, and using the community to mold and pursue case objectives. It assesses, modifies, and uses a client's social and cultural context. Community social casework is radical because it goes back to the profession's roots.

Community social caseworker continues the development of the comprehensive case management model discussed in the previous edition of this text. We have discarded the case management label as antiquated in this text. Case management has been co-opted by agencies and has lost its original community flavor.[1] Walker (2001) asserts that the language and modeling of management and protection of the enterprise have become more dominant. Case management as a social work practice model has been co-opted from its social work roots by the agency. The social work mission has become confused with its organizational and institutional contexts. Management controls the worker's relationship with clients to the detriment of both workers, as professionals, and service users.

Management language with its rhetoric of *clients as customer* and *evidence-based practice* defines the helping process rather than the profession's language.

We discussed in the first edition of the text several unifying themes for social work. These underlie community social case work:

- All people have the capacity to improve.
- Individual lives are entwined with the social environment.
- Social networks and organizational infrastructure affect professional practice.
- Strengthening community can solve individual and community problems.
- Community is cardinal in current views of personhood and nationhood.
- Knowledge of the larger world is empowering.
- Collective, as well as individual, activity is of value.
- At every system level, there are myriad ways to exert influence.

Our model of community social casework understands, as do Swartz (1995), Raheim (1995), Smale (1995), and Lee (1994), that all social work is political and must be directed toward client empowerment. It is political because it is concerned with the power distribution in communities. Change in an ecological model must involve community as well as individual. The client must be community involved. Although using social marking skills and market analysis, this model rejects the commercial rhetoric and constructions of practice as products and clients as consumers and customers. Client community involvement is an *instrumental* action toward *efficiency and effectiveness* in addressing client problems. It is a *normative* action because it is *right*, as well as a client right and community citizen responsibility. Interventions either preserve or change the status quo for clients. Everything in treatment, intervention, and social services programs can be presented in a way that promotes client consciousness, change, and empowerment. There is no objectivity or professionalism in maintaining a socially marginalized client's status quo. A social worker has a responsibility to demystify and help clients understand (a) the processes of services, (b) their regulatory functions, and (c) how both services and a client role promote the status quo. The scarcity of social welfare resources and extreme concentration of resources in the upper strata of society pits various client and community needs, client groups, community constituents, and service providers against each other. This is heightened by the elite's current infatuation with globalization, the market model, and the privatization and commercialization of education, health, and social welfare services. It is a professional responsibility and part of empowerment to radicalize clients and communities and help them understand the political nature of social welfare. Hidden injuries of class and caste should be revealed. The social worker needs to take sides when people are wronged, if the professional value of social justice is to be meaningful.

Community social work, by its many labels, recognizes clients as partners and necessarily active participants in any change processes, and not as passive recipients of services. Community social casework is a *unitary and holistic practice approach*. The *change partnership* of client and professional with community civic structures allows and provides the client with opportunities to reciprocate the community for service, recognizes client strengths, enables clients to contribute to building community strength and cohesion, and promotes both client and community empowerment.

COMMUNITY SOCIAL CASE WORK KNOWLEDGE, SKILL, AND TASKS

Case Management Skills

Individual clients like Mrs. J. face a resource management and coordination challenge. Essential resources are integrated into a total system for goal accomplishment (Wolk, Sullivan, & Hartman, 1994, p. 154). The community social caseworker and client's tasks include case management tasks. The disparate and unorganized, but potentially available community resources and primary groups support groups as well as the client's personal resources, need to be accessed, organized into a system, and managed (Travillion, 1999, p. 53). Community social casework approaches social intervention with the logic of management by objectives. It is a client-centered, client-level, service-coordinated, goal-oriented approach to service integration (Chazdon, 1991). Fundamental management skills of community social casework include (a) planning; (b) organizing and managing the services system; (c) directing and controlling; (d) advocacy, negotiation, brokerage, and contracting with other service providers; (e) reporting; and

(f) evaluating the service system's effectiveness (Dinerman, 1992; Morrow-Howell, 1992; Rubin, 1987; Washington, 1974; Wolk, Sullivan, & Hartmann, 1994).

Social Casework Skills

Community social casework incorporates the range of direct service knowledge and skills characteristic of and necessary to a social casework and clinical social work practice case plan: client assessment, developing case theory, establishing case and intervention SMARRT objectives, contracting with the client on SMARRT objectives, implementing and monitoring interventions, teaching and modeling of intervention skills for a client and others in the action system to use, and the evaluation with the client and other significant stakeholders of objectives' success. Modeling and teaching are essential casework intervention tasks. The intent of teaching the knowledge and demonstrating and modeling the skills to clients is to enable clients to do their own assessment, development, and management. Clients better able to develop and manage their own social support systems will be able to better manage their lives. Modeling and teaching improves client self-efficacy and promotes client empowerment (Pecukonis & Wenocur, 1994). Clients will need the skills to manage their lives long after the social caseworker is gone. These skills ought to be common to all direct service practice.

Community Practice Skills

Community social casework recognizes the social component and context of the client's condition and problems and uses formal and informal community resources in the intervention. The community social work approach emphasizes primary and secondary networks as much as tertiary resources. A good understanding of the local community, including the client's personal community, is fundamental. Different communities have different patterns of behavior, power, and resources. This requires community assessment skills.

Patch Analysis

Community practice skills of community social casework are set forth in Box 15.1. Most have been discussed extensively elsewhere in this text. The foundation for all community practice is *community and network analysis, ecomapping, and patch analysis*. The first sets of skills have

BOX 15.1	COMMUNITY SOCIAL CASEWORK TASKS

- Interpersonal communication (verbal, written, nonverbal), self-awareness, and oral and visual physical presentation of self
- Outreach to reach potential clients and potential primary social supports
- Client assessment, SMARRT objective setting, and case theory building
- Ethnography
- Community, patch, and network assessment
- Network development, management, and consultation

- Client advocacy, brokering, negotiation, and contracting
- Direct casework
- Teaching and modeling
- Reassessment and evaluation
- Problem staging, public education, social advocacy, and social marketing
- Monitoring quality

been extensively discussed elsewhere in this text, so we will not review them at length here. *Patch analysis* is a specific form of community analysis. It is an intensive form of microcommunity assessment that is neighborhood and client centered. It inventories a neighborhood's primary, secondary, and tertiary resources and the networking requirements that are potentially most available to a client population. It enables the localization and integration of neighborhood level services and social supports assessable to clients. It is client focused and intimate. True patch work involves both worker and clients in the community (Adams & Krauth, 1995; Dalton, Elias, & Wandersman, 2001; Dutton & Kohli, 1996; Payne, 2000).

ETHNOGRAPHY

Patch analysis and the patch approach require ethnographic skills with the worker functioning as participant observer. A community social caseworker's research expertise must go beyond quantitative and survey research skills to proficiency in ethnography. Ethnography is "associated with some distinctive methodological ideas, . . . the importance of understanding the perspectives of the people under study, . . . observing their activities in everyday life, rather than relying solely on their accounts of this behavior or experimental simulations of it" (Hammersley & Atkinson, 1983, p. ix).

Ethnography draws on a range of philosophical and sociological ideas: symbolic interactionism, phenomenology, hermeneutics, naturalism, and linguistic philosophy, to mention but a few. Its field methodology is participant observation. A community social caseworker both observes and participates with a client in the client's community. Ethnography's is concerned with events, relationships, and, most significantly, the meaning of these to their participants. People *interpret* stimuli and events, and these interpretations, continually under revision as events unfold, shape their actions. The same physical stimulus and events can mean different things to different people and to the same person at different times (Blumer, 1969; Hammersley & Atkinson, 1983, p. 7). The community social caseworker needs to appreciate these meanings.

Community, patch, network analysis, and *ecomapping* are not ends but only means to developing client supports, achieving community integration, and reaching case objectives. These skills will need to be accompanied by the skills necessary to create, access, and integrate clients into primary social supports and a community's secondary and tertiary social support systems. Negotiating, brokering, bargaining, and client advocacy skills enable networking, exchange, and social support to occur. Advocacy, as Payne (2000, p. 323) asserts, goes beyond arguing and includes social action on behalf of and with the client. Advocacy promotes client community empowerment and humanizing the client into full citizenship status.

Community social casework skills are client centered but are not limited to a single client. Community problem staging and advocacy for resources development are used to translate clients' private troubles into public concerns. Social marketing and social activism for services and community change are part of a complete community social caseworker's repertoire. Again, these are done with and not just for clients.

COMMUNITY SOCIAL CASEWORK PROTOCOL

1. Preliminary Community Assessment and Patch Analysis

A requisite step in any community social casework protocol is a preliminary community and patch analysis. The analysis is get the basic lay of community: resources and requirements, values and norms, and behavior patterns. The assessment is baseline and preliminary and must be refined for each client and client grouping.

2. Assessment, Refinement of Community and Patch Analysis, and Establishing SMARRT Objectives

Client assessment, refinement of a community assessment and patch analysis, and establishing SMARRT objectives are interdependent components. SMARRT objectives are *specific, measurable, acceptable, realistic, results oriented,* and *time specific* (see Chapter 1 of this text for the SMARRT format). SMARRT objectives are stated in behavioral and measurable language. Their viability is dependent on the available resources and a client's strengths. Resources necessary to assist a client to achieve SMARRT objectives are contingent on the specific SMARRT objectives selected. Conversely, availability of resources will expand or constrain the capacity to realize specific SMARRT objectives. The SMARRT formatted objectives guide the social worker and client in their resource assessment, development, coordination, and management.

A community social casework process uses marketing's outside-inside philosophy, beginning with an assessment of the client's conception and meaning of the problems and objectives rather than a preconceived agency boiler plate diagnosis. Assessment calls on the caseworker's ethnographic skills. It is mutual, a task performed conjointly with a client, and involves understanding a client's construction and meanings of problems and social ecology, a client's strengths and resources, establishing SMARRT objectives, and refining the community and patch analysis to be client focused and to assess its resources relative to the SMARRT objectives (Bisman, 1994, pp. 111–176). It must be recognized that a client's situation usually is both unique and multifaceted. Overly reductionist views of cause and effect should be avoided. The causes of any problems lie in a range of complex social phenomena. Solutions will probably also require an array of personal, primary, and community resources appropriately coordinated and managed.

Assessment results in a theory of the case. The case theory explains a client's situation and organizes case information to provide a map, a plan, of intervention to accomplish the SMARRT objectives (Bisman, 1994, pp. 111–121, Bisman & Hardcastle, 1999, pp. 44–62, 151–162). At the end of the first assessment phase, there must be mutual understanding and agreement between caseworker and client leading to a shared construction and understanding of problems and SMARRT objectives. Joint agreement by casework and client on an assessment and a case plan is critical to its success if a plan requires the caseworker and client to work together to achieve a plan's SMARRT objectives. As yet, we know of no social work methodologies that can achieve SMARRT objectives without client participation.

Application of SMARRT Criteria to Mrs. J.'s Case

Mrs. J. can have a series of related goals such as the following: (a) to establish and maintain a physically and emotionally safe home for herself and her family; (b) to financially support herself and her children at her current income level and be financially independent of her husband; (c) for John and Susan to achieve grade-level school performance, graduate from high school, and not engage in antisocial activities; (d) for the family to become socially integrated into the community and develop social support networks.

Each of these objectives can be stated in a SMARRT format. In establishing the objectives, Mrs. J. and her caseworker need to complete a community assessment and patch analysis to establish her potential social support resources, develop information for networking and community integration, and locate and assess secondary and tertiary resources potentially available and their requirements for networking and exchange. Potential interventions necessary to achieve each essential objective and any requisite sequencing and requirements of the change agent system are elaborated in the case theory. Mrs. J. and her family are components of the change agent system. If the resources and interventions are not available, objectives will be modified to fall within the constraints of potentially available resources.

The first objective, to establish and maintain a physically and emotionally safe home for herself and her family, *can be operationalized and evaluated by the SMARRT criteria:*

1. *Specific:* Establiching a physically and emotionally safe home, one absent of physically and emotionally traumatic behavior in interactions between family members, is a specific criterion. It is an *outside-inside* approach focusing on the client's concept of needs and not on a specific intervention or product offered by the caseworker. *Physically and emotionally safe* and *traumatic behavior* will have to be conceptualized and operationally defined in language meaningful to Mrs. J., her husband, and the children, with a shared understanding if not acceptance of the meanings. Interventions can range from a combination of family therapies, from expansion of the family's social support networks to relieve and alter internal dynamics, to the extreme of Mrs. J. and the children's leaving the home. The objective doesn't dictate a specific intervention but guides along with the case theory in selecting interventions most likely to achieve the objective. It's the objective, not the intervention, that is critical.

2. *Measurable:* Physical and emotional trauma and their absence can be measured by observations and the judgment of Mrs. J., the children, and the caseworker, as well as by medical measurements. Care needs to be taken to avoid spurious precision and incoherent meaning for the J. family. The phenomena of concern are the physically and emotionally abusive interactions experienced by Mrs. J., John, Susan, and perhaps even Mr. J. The critical feature of any measurement process is its truthfulness and meaning to the family's experiences.

3. *Acceptable:* The objective needs to be acceptable to Mrs. J., the J family, and anyone voluntarily providing resources and cooperation in the change effort. Mr. J. will need to accept the objective and its measurement if he remains a part of the household. Acceptance by all participants is critical, unless the caseworker has the ability to coerce compliance with an objective and to compel the provision of resources and behavior.

4. *Realistic:* The caseworker and Mrs. J. need to assess the potential of any intervention and resources available to establish and maintain a physically and emotionally safe home. If it is projected that Mr. J. will leave the home, then an alternative physical and safe living arrangement will have to be established or a way for the family to remain in the house without Mr. J. The criterion that objectives must be *realistic* assesses the probability, given the potential resources and strengths of the interventions, that the objectives will be accomplished. If Mrs. J. and the caseworker project that none of the options are accomplishable, unfortunately this objective will need to be recast.

5. *Results oriented:* The objective is changes in Mrs. J.'s and Mr. J.'s behaviors, lifestyles, and social interactions rather than a process of treatments and interventions. Interventions and networks are used because of their theoretical potential to achieve the objectives. The objectives are outcomes, not the means used to produce outcomes. The value of the casework and networks are determined by how well they achieve an absence of physically and emotionally traumatic behavior in interactions between family members. Their value doesn't rest on adherence to a model of a process or techniques used.

6. *Time specific:* The caseworker and Mrs. J. will need to arrive at a specific projected time for a safe home to be established. The projected time is based on their assessment of the potential resources, including the J. family's strengths and the power of the available intervention technologies. As Mrs. J. is new to the community, without many social supports in the community and with low economic skills, the time needed to achieve the specific target will be longer than if these social supports were more available immediately or if Mrs. J. had a greater and more recent employment history. The time frame can be modified with unfolding circumstances, but a realistic time-specific target is needed to guide the intervention and provide a basis for reassessment. Without a time-specific objective, Mrs. J. might indefinitely remain in an abusive situation and be involved in an ineffective intervention.

The other case objectives need similar SMARRT formatting.

Assessments and theory construction rest on basic and abstract assumptions of the nature of client behavior and the importance of the client's community and social ecology.

The Nature of Client Behavior

The *biopsychomedical reductionist models* of behavior generally hold that dysfunctional client behavior results from biological and emotional pathologies, whether due to genetic content or faulty early socialization. Psychological theories such as psychoanalytic psychology fall within this set of models. Treatment involves altering the client's emotional content separately from the social context. Interventions applied to intrapsychic content frequently are called psychotherapies. Community social casework rejects these models as overly reductionist, limited in explanatory ability, and naive. The biopsychomedical reductionist models make community social casework a largely irrelevant intervention. Intervention is centered on the client's disease, pathology and physiology, and psychological deficits and aberrations. The models emphasizing therapy and treatments rather than social resources development and management don't hold community social casework's assumptions central or necessary to successful client treatment. Treatment compliance, biopsychological condition management, and providing services to compensate for client deficiencies are the major features of any social intervention. If a biopsychomedical model is used by Mrs. J.'s caseworker, social and community influences, constraints, and primary, secondary, and tertiary social supports and resources are unlikely to be pursued. Intervention will focus on pathology in the family.

Educational models see problems in client behavior and in management of social relations and the social environment as learned inappropriate behavior. If learned behavior, it can be unlearned and functionally appropriate behavior learned. Interventions address unlearning inappropriate behavior and learning and substituting socially appropriate behaviors. Operant and behavioral theories reflect these models. The educational models require, in treatment based on social learning theory, that the caseworker demonstrate or teach (generally by operant conditioning, cognition, or a combination of the two) the functional behaviors. Community social casework also rejects these models again as being an overly reductionist and simplistic view of human behavior that ignores the fundamental and multiple impact of different social variables on behavior.

Psychosocial models posit that client behavior and management of the environment are a function of an individual's psychological content in interaction with a social context. Interventions confront the psychological content in its social context and the social context's impact on the psychological content and behavior. These models emphasize social variables and conditions that are useful to community social casework.

Biopsychosocial models of human behavior promote a more complex view of client behavior as a function of the client's biological and psychological content in a social context. Behavior is the result of a complex interaction of biological, psychological, and social factors and forces. Behavior has social elements. Poverty and limited social environments, social marginalization and isolation, abuse, and limited interpersonal and social skills all affect behavior. All components need considering in the case theory and intervention. As with the psychosocial models, intervention must address the context as well as the content of behavior. It can include providing education and improving management skills as well as altering a client's environment. This model is the most comprehensive and adaptable to community social casework.

Obviously this classification schema of the models of human behavior, like biopsychomedical reductionist models, suffers from oversimplification. Empirically, the models rarely exist or are applied in some kind of pure form. However, a social worker's selection of a model of human behavior has implications for case theory and implementing an intervention plan. Community social casework is more compatible with the social models with their strong social content and context.

The Conception of the Community, the Social Resources, and the Task Environment

We have emphasized in this text the importance of community as a major force in shaping and limiting behavior and the lives of people. Community social casework holds to this *systems approach* to community and the individual. A system's elements must be coordinated and share some common purposes (Churchman, 1965, p. 29; von Bertalanffy, 1967; Leighninger, Jr., 1978; Martin & O'Connor, 1989). A client's physical and social environment can be a cornucopia of potential social supports and resources, but the resources don't exist as a system until they are coordinated and integrated. Each potential resource may have no or limited interest in a specific client's life. An employment agency's interest is limited to employment. A landlord's concern for a client may be limited to the client's ability to rent space without damaging it. Each service vendor and resource provider can achieve its limited objective without much interaction, coordination, compatibility, or meeting a client's objectives. An individual client may need a support system in this turbulent and complex environment; it is not equally crucial for any unit in the set's survival or functioning to support an individual client. A community social caseworker's and the client's tasks are to create and manage a client-centered support system from a set of sometimes indifferent and often competing resource suppliers.

> *The model of behavior used by the community social caseworker and Mrs. J. will guide the assessment and provide a basis for constructing its case theory. A limited biopsychomedical model or educational model will direct information gathering and assessment to focus on family members as individuals and their interaction. Explanations of causation and projections of interventions and solutions will center on these same units. If more expansive models are used, although family members and their interactions are still assessed, the impact, limitations, and opportunities provided by the social environment are basic to developing a case theory and plan.*

3. Determine Resources Necessary and Required to Achieve Goals and Objectives

Once the objectives have tentatively been established and SMARRT formatted, the necessary resources to achieve the objectives need to be determined, located, and acquired. The community assessment and patch analysis is made specific to this case.

A. ASSESS THE CLIENT STRENGTHS, THE CLIENT'S PRIMARY SUPPORT SYSTEMS, AND THE COMMUNITY SOCIAL CASEWORKER'S RESOURCES RELATIVE TO THE RESOURCES REQUIRED TO ACHIEVE THE SMARRT OBJECTIVES

The first potential source of resources and the first with responsibility to help achieve the case plan's SMARRT objectives, are the client and the client's primary systems. The sociologist and communitarian Amatai Etzioni (1993) contends, *"First, people have a moral responsibility to help themselves as best they can"* (p. 144, italics original). All people have an obligation, no matter how disadvantaged or handicapped, to be responsible for themselves as best they can and to the maximum extent of their capacity. This is the fundamental basis of empowerment, self-efficacy, and self-determination. Etzioni continues, *"The second line of responsibility lies with those closest to the person,* including kin, friends, neighborhood, and other community members" (p. 144, italics original).

Self-responsibility comes first and is linked directly with autonomy, empowerment, self-efficacy, and self-determination. To not consider the client as a primary source of strength and responsibility promotes powerlessness and dependency. Primary group responsibility comes second. Primary support groups provide the most help. This is where reciprocity and interdependence, rather than dependency, are most balanced and the client is least vulnerable. Mutual support is best given and received under conditions of mutual obligation and responsibility. Community and network cohesion, as well as primary group efficacy, are enhanced, trust is facilitated, and interdependence is promoted with primary group reciprocity. The client and community social caseworker should seek, whenever possible, to strengthen primary structures and build or rebuild primary support networks. These networks help the client reintegrate into the community, reduce the social and emotional isolation, and provide some buffering from the stresses of larger social institutions. A client's primary system includes immediate family and other personal support networks that can be called on to support and assist a client in fulfilling the case plan. As the protections, the safety nets, of the welfare state are eliminated or reduced with the devolution and reformulation of the welfare state and the social environment becomes more competitive and demanding, primary support systems are more vital to clients.

Community, patch, and network assessment are used to determine, locate, and appraise actual and potential primary and secondary social support networks and systems. The social supports are largely unique to each client, and a case plan should be individualized accordingly. These should be explored and developed prior to referral to tertiary systems.

The community social caseworker recognizes and helps Mrs. J. understand her own and her family's strengths. Strengths include recognizing a problematic situation for herself and her family, wanting to change the situation, and wanting to reduce her dependency on Mr. J. Although she has not worked outside the home for several years, she has worked. She wants to preserve the family and strengthen her relationship with Mr. J. by altering the nature of the relationship. Leaving Mr. J. is the option of choice only if the abuse and the nature of their relationship are unchanged. Even without a more thorough assessment of Mrs. J.'s current and potential intellectual and social capacities, it is clear there are many strengths. By recognizing and acting on these strengths, Mrs. J. will increase her sense of self-efficacy.

Mr. J.'s strengths are also considered in developing the case theory. Although he has abused Mrs. J. and John, he has been a consistent provider and feels strongly about his responsibilities as the breadwinner. He wants the children to be responsible citizens. He doesn't want a family breakup. Like Mrs. J., he wants change, although they do not agree on the specific change needed. These are strengths to use in beginning the case theory and plan.

B. ASSESS THE DIFFERENCES BETWEEN THE CLIENT, COMMUNITY SOCIAL CASEWORKER AND AGENCY RESOURCES AVAILABLE, AND THE RESOURCES REQUIRED TO ACHIEVE THE CASE PLAN'S GOALS AND OBJECTIVES

Community, patch, and network assessment will need to locate potential social supports for the family to achieve their objectives and the requirements of the supports for networking. The community resources including secondary and tertiary resources needed from the set of social agencies is determined by any deficit of client resources and strengths and community social caseworker's and host agency's resources compared to the resources required to achieve the case plan's SMARRT objectives. If the community social caseworker and the client possess all the required resources, or if the client has the necessary network assessment and management skills, there is no need for additional resource development and networking by the community social caseworker. However, the basic biopsychosocial model assumes behavior is a function of social factors. It is unlikely that all resources will be contained within the family unit. These resource deficits determine the required secondary and tertiary resources and guide social support network construction. The client and community social caseworker should look to resources from the larger community only when the client, the client's primary groups, and the community social caseworker and the host agency do not possess them. The client participates in the assessments, development, and management of the networks to the maximum extent of the client's capacity.

If Mrs. J. and her family have either the resources or the knowledge and skills to assess employment resources, to manage John's and Susan's socialization and education, to establish any needed social support system, and to manage their relationship, there is little need for the caseworker to do it. However, it appears that supportive primary and formal tertiary services in addition to family resources are needed.

Members of the J. family, especially Mrs. J., are socially isolated and marginalized. She is also becoming more marginal within the family. Social supports are needed for a range of intervention efforts to achieve the SMARRT objectives.

4. Assess the Community to Locate Needed Resources and Their Exchange Requirements

Etzioni (1993) holds that the third imperative for support beyond the client and primary groups is the community. "As a rule every community ought to be expected to take care of its own. . . . Last but not least, *societies (which are nothing but communities of communities) must help those communities whose ability to help their members is severely limited*" (p. 146, italics original).

The community and the society or state imperatives of responsibility come into operation after the client and the primary support systems. Responsibility works outward, with personal, primary, neighborhood, and community responsibility explored before state responsibility. The community social caseworker recognizes that public education, social marketing, and staging of social problems often are necessary to help the community and state recognize their responsibilities.

After the client and the community social caseworker have assessed the resources they and the primary groups possess relative to the case plan's goals and objectives, the location, the domains, and reciprocity requirements of the additional required resources indicated by the community and patch analysis are reviewed. The basic questions of this protocol's phase are (a) What are the additional resources needed? (b) Where are the resources located? and (c) How can the resources be secured? The assessment using community, patch assessment, networking, and market research methodologies discussed elsewhere appraises the agencies and community structures with the resources, the social prices of the resources, and the networking and reciprocity requirements.

The community social caseworker and Mrs. J. assess the community resources needed to achieve the case SMARRT objectives. These resources will allow Mrs. J. and her family to create a new social environment and community of interaction. The ability of Mrs. J. to access the resources of agencies and organizations providing family counseling, education, and job training and placement is critical. Client advocacy and preparing the family for the exchanges is required. Before embarking on intervention, the community social caseworker determines how legal aid and a possible safe haven can be established for Mrs. J. and the children, if needed.

Mrs. J. will need to explore social supports (the more primary groups and also the secondary organizations such as churches, neighborhood associations, and PTAs) to reduce her social marginalization and emotional isolation. She will also need to develop an understanding of how her husband's conception—and her prior conception—of a *woman's* role is a political construction contributing to her marginalization. Although Mrs. J. is new to the community, she shares her social isolation and a lack of appropriate primary and secondary social support networks with many clients. John need tutorial assistance and an alternative secondary social support group to replace the skinhead gang he is now using.

5. Evaluate the Case Plan's Goals and Objectives Relative to the Total Resources Available From the Client, the Client's Social Support Networks and Potential Networks, the Community Social Caseworker, and the Community

If the currently and potentially available resources do not appear appropriate and adequate to meet the case plan's SMARRT objectives, they will need to be modified to fit within available resources. This, however, should be an incremental modification, not a wholesale discarding of the original objectives. The client and community social caseworker may want to pursue the original goals and objectives with a subsequent case plans after some more preliminary objectives have been achieved, or the client can independently pursue the objectives after developing greater self-case-management skills.

Community social caseworkers should not assume that resources are unavailable simple because the community social caseworker doesn't have contacts with the domain (the holder) of the desired resource. The task, as discussed in Chapter 11 (networking), is to assess and establish the linkage or chain of contacts between the client and the desired resource. When resources are not available or not even potentially available, the task is a community development and staging task to establish a community-shared perception of need for and develop the essential resources.

6. Negotiate Exchanges and Link the Client With the Resource Domains

After the potential resources have been identified, located, and their exchange preferences determined, the next task is to make the exchanges and obtain the resources for the client. This establishes a client-centered network. This protocol entails marketing the client or community social caseworker's resources as a resource to a trading partner or resource holder meeting their objectives or needs. It requires brokering, negotiating, linking the client to social supports, and the community social caseworker's use of power (Dinerman, 1992; Hagen, 1994); Levine & Fleming, 1985).

Community social caseworkers need to understand and be able to use power in their networking. Power has been discussed here in the theories of community practice. *The crucial consideration in power is the willingness to use it.* A source of power inherent in a case plan is the power derived from the client as a potential resource to another service provider (Dinerman, 1992, pp. 5–6). The client may bring with him or her resources such as vouchers and third-party payments. The client and the community social caseworker, or both, can help the trading partners achieve their goals. Both exchange and learning theory, discussed earlier, tell us that a trading partner, the holder of the resources needed by the client, is more likely to engage in exchanges when its needs are met and the exchanges are perceived as fair.

The community social caseworker also should possess and use the power derived from the expertise and skill in assessment, system development and management, and bargaining and client advocacy discussed earlier. Negotiation and bargaining is advocacy for the client or case. Advocacy can cause strains in network relationships, but the strains can be minimized if the negotiations are cast in a win-win or non-zero-sum construction and are viewed as fair by all participants. Advocacy calls for professional judgment in when to engage in it, and skill in how to use client advocacy without ending the collaborative relations with other network professionals.

The community social caseworker negotiates for needed resources and prepares Mrs. J. to be a resource in exchanges and her own advocate. She affects the quality of services received by what she contributes to the resource provider in exchanges. Mrs. J. and other family members are resources to the other units in the network if they can help the other network units achieve their objectives. Mrs. J. will need to demonstrate that she is indeed a resource by reciprocating appropriately. For example, for training agencies to be successful, they need trainable clients who can and will be employed. As Mrs. J. learns what she can bring to the exchange (how she can reciprocate), her self-efficacy and sense of power increase.

7. Monitor the Network and the Exchanges for Fair Exchanges

Networks as systems do not automatically maintain themselves (Churchman, 1965, p. 33). They require managing, monitoring and intelligence, and maintenance to ensure that the negotiated fair exchanges occur and all parties in the exchange network fulfill the bargains. Without attention, a network as a system will undergo entropy. *Entropy*, an enduring property of systems according to systems theorists (Anderson & Carter, 1984, pp. 3–36; Hearn, 1969, p. 66; Martin & O'Connor, 1989, pp. 38–109), is a tendency of systems to deteriorate, becoming disorganized and random. Entropy in a client-centered system or network occurs when network units, often including the client, no longer engage in the agreed-upon resource exchanges necessary to achieve the objectives.

Monitoring and evaluating by Mrs. J. and the community social caseworker address the contributions of network service and resource providers and Mrs. J.'s participation in the exchanges. For exchanges to be fair, all parties in a network have to uphold their part of a contract. Mrs. J. needs to reciprocate appropriately.

8. Teach and Model the Networking Protocols to the Client So the Client Can Assess, Construct, and Manage His or Her Social Support and Resources Networks (Client Empowerment)

Client empowerment is both an ethical obligation and practice objective. A practice task is to teach and model the knowledge, skills and behaviors so that clients can assess, develop, access, and manage their social support systems and mediating structures. Client empowerment is enhanced as their capacity to control their own lives is increased.

Social learning theory (Bandura, 1977; Bushell & Burgess, 1969; Kunkel, 1975; Minhauyard & Burgess, 1969; Thyer & Hudson, 1986/1987) states that personal and environmental influences are bidirectional, interactional, and interdependent. Over time they can become self-reinforcing, with less need for external stimuli and reinforcements. Client involvement in developing and implementing a case plan allows the client to learn and a community social case-worker to teach and model (Kunkel, 1975, pp. 51–76; Pecukonis & Wenocur, 1994; Weiser & Silver, 1981;). As clients learn and use appropriate community practice skills—community assessment, bargaining, negotiation and self-advocacy, construction of client-centered networks and systems, systems management and monitoring—their sense of efficacy should increase and dependency on the community social caseworker should decrease.

Mrs. J. is empowered when she recognizes what she has to exchange and learns how to access and negotiate with social and community resources. The resources can be job training, educational and social supports for her children, or financial and emotional supports from the children's fathers. As Mrs. J.'s skills in assessment, bargaining, negotiation, advocacy, and management increase, Mrs. J.'s dependency on the community social caseworker deceases. Equally critical is Mrs. J.'s need to increase her necessary knowledge and skills to access, negotiate, manage, and reciprocate with the range of social supports required in any healthy, functional life. The community social caseworker recognizes that an integral part of community social casework is modeling and teaching skills to Mrs. J.

EFFECTIVENESS OF COMMUNITY SOCIAL CASEWORK

As yet there have been few studies of community social casework's effectiveness in this country. Research in the United Kingdom, where the concept of community social casework is more advanced, is promising (Bond, McGrew, & Fekete, 1995; Dutton & Kohli, 1996; Gordon & Donald, 1993; Karabanow, 1999; Payne, 2000; Phillips et al., 2000). The literature assessing the effectiveness and efficacy of case management, a subset of community social casework, generally presents a positive picture, although the literature is not methodically rigorous. The case management models generally have not been fully developed or tested (Cheung, Stevenson, & Leung, 1991; Fiene & Taylor, 1991; Kantor, 1991; Korrs & Cloninger, 1981; Polinsky, Fred, & Ganz, 1991; Rapp & Chamberlain, 1985; Rife, First, Greenlee, Miller, & Feichter, 1991; Rothman, 1991; Rubin, 1992; Sonsel, Paradise, & Stroup, 1988; Wright, Sklebar, & Heiman, 1987; Zimmerman, 1987).

Washington and his colleagues (Washington, 1974: Washington, Karman, & Friedlob, 1974) concluded, as a result of their seminal and most extensive case management social research and development work, that the model of case management used can achieve outcomes beyond client satisfaction. The models of choice moved toward a community social casework model. Effectiveness was related to the manager's assessment, negotiation, and broker skills; it was also associated with available funds to purchase needed services. With cutbacks in government and private financial resources, this ability will continue to be reduced.

Case management was not particularly effective in overcoming the limitations of a resource-starved task environment. Community social casework will have the same difficulties in this era of devolution and declining public support for social services. However, with its emphasis on primary and secondary social supports, it may be more promising.

SUMMARY: A COMMUNITY SOCIAL CASEWORK MODEL

Community social casework requires the knowledge and skills explicated in this text. It rests on several assumptions regarding the client and the community.

1. The community is the context of an individual's behavior, provides both opportunities and limits, and behavior can only be understood in this context.
   (a) People live in communities and often are beset by a range of living and environmental management problems or social isolation.
   (b) Human behavior is not solely the province of an individual's biopsychological capacity and content.
   (c) Regardless of the model of human behavior used, social coping needs are real and require addressing if a person is to function more effectively in the community and be empowered.
   (d) Human problems and coping needs are usually embedded in their social marginality to and isolation from community supports.
2. Community social casework's *objectives* are to improve a client's social context and assist the client in managing the social context to improve social functioning.
   (a) The community is the situs of a client's life, not the service center, social agency, or therapist's office. Intervention should occur in the community.
   (b) While clients vary in their individual capacity to cope with and manage their social context, all clients have strengths to be used.

(c) All communities potentially have strengths, with primary and secondary supports, if not tertiary supports.

If the client and community propositions are valid, a reasonable case model can be described as follows:

1. Case objectives are behavioral and measurable and in a SMARRT format.
2. Case objectives, the dependent variable, are client behavior and social functioning, and the independent and intervening variables are the client's community and support systems, including the community social caseworker and the service system.
3. A case plan's strength is in its emphasis on specified objectives stated in behavioral and measurable terms and a shared clarity of objectives with client, community social caseworker, and other critical resource providers in the service delivery and social support networks. A fundamental generic goal of community social casework is to integrate clients into a supportive social environment.
4. Community social casework's strength is in its flexibility that allows the community social caseworker and client to use an array of possible primary, secondary, and tertiary supports to achieve objectives and integrate clients into the community rather than limiting interventions to specific agency services.
5. Community social casework's service protocol flow requires that the community social caseworker understand a client's construction of reality, the client's community or social context, and an ability to help a client perceive and define realistic objectives in a given social context.
6. The community social caseworker's network management for a client depends on the client's capacity, knowledge and skills to function in the social context.
7. A fundamental goal of all intervention is client empowerment. Empowerment occurs in a social context. Therefore, community social caseworkers need knowledge and skill in client, community, patch, and organizational assessment; negotiating, bargaining, contracting, advocacy; and social support networks development and management, as well as the capacity to model and teach a client these skills. Self-management as self-control is the essence of empowerment.

Note

1. To review the community base of comprehensive case management, see the 1997 edition of this text.

References

Adams, P., & Krauth, K. (1995). Working with families and communities: The patch approach. In P. Adams & K. Nelson (Eds.), *Reinventing human services: Community and family-centered practice* (pp. 87–108), New York: Aldine de Gruyter.

Adams, P., & Nelson, K. (Eds.). (1995). *Reinventing human services: Community and family-centered practice.* New York: Aldine de Gruyter.

Anderson, R. E., & Carter, I. (1984). *Human behavior in the social environment: A social systems approach* (3rd ed.). New York: Aldine.

Bandura, A. (1977). *Social learning theory.* Englewood Cliffs, NJ: Prentice Hall.

Barber, J. G. (1991). *Beyond casework.* Basingstoke, UK: Macmillan.

Bisman, C. (1994). *Social work practice: Cases and principles.* Pacific Grove, CA: Brooks/Cole.

Bisman, C., & Hardcastle, D. (1999). *Integrating research into practice: A model for effective social work.* Pacific Grove, CA: Brooks/Cole, Wadsworth.

Blumer, H. (1969). *Symbolic interactionism.* Englewood Cliffs, NJ: Prentice Hall.

Bond, G. R., McGrew, J. H., & Fekete, D. M. (1995). Assertive outreach for frequent users of psychiatric hospitals: A meta-analysis. *Journal of Mental Health Administration, 22*(1), 4–16.

Bushell, D., Jr., & Burgess, R. (Eds.). (1969). *Behavioral sociology: The experimental analysis of social process.* New York: Columbia University Press.

Chazdon, S. (1991). *Responding to human needs: Community-based social services.* Denver, CO: National Conference of State Legislatures.

Cheung, K-F. M., Stevenson, K. M., & Leung, P. (1991). Competency-based evaluation of case management skills in child sexual abuse intervention. *Child Welfare, 70,* 425–435.

Churchman, C. W. (1965). *The systems approach.* New York: Dell.

Dalton, J. H., Elias, M. J., & Wandersman, A. (2001). *Community psychology: Linking individuals and communities.* Belmont, CA: Wadsworth.

Dinerman, M. (1992). Managing the mazes: Case management and service delivery. *Administration in Social Work, 16,* 1–9.

Dutton, J., & Kohli, R. (1996). The core skills of social work. In A. A. Voss (Ed.), *Social work competencies: Core knowledge, values, and skills* (pp. 62–82). London, UK: Sage.

Etzioni, A. (1993). *The spirit of community: Rights, responsibilities and the communitarian agenda.* New York: Crown.

Fiene, J. I., & Taylor, P. A. (1991). Serving rural families of development ally disabled children: A case management model. *Social Work, 36,* 323–327.

Gordon, D. S., & Donald, S. (1993). *Community social work: Older people and informal care, a romantic illusion.* Aldershot Hants, UK: Ashgate.

Hagen, J. L. (1994). JOBS and case management: Developments in 10 states. *Social Work, 39,* 197–205.

Hammersley, M., & Atkinson, P. (1983). *Ethnography: Principles in practice.* New York: Tavistock Publication.

Hearn, G. (Ed.). (1969). *The general systems approach: Contributions toward an holistic conception of social work.* New York: Council on Social Work Education.

Henderson, P., Jones, D., & Thomas, D. N. (1980). *The boundaries of change in community work.* London, UK: Allen & Unwin.

IASSW, IFSW announce joint definition of social work. (2001, Fall). *Social Work Education Reporter, 49*(3), 31,37.

Kantor, J. S. (1991). Integrating case management and psychiatric hospitalization. *Health and Social Work, 16,* 34–42.

Karabanow, J. (1999). Creating community: A case study of a Montreal street kid agency, *Community Development Journal, 3*(4). 318–327.

Korrs, W. S., & Cloninger, L. (1981). Assessing models of case management: An empirical approach. *Journal of Social Service Research, 14,* 129–146.

Kunkel, J. H. (1975). *Behavior, social problems, and change: A social learning approach.* Englewood Cliffs, NJ: Prentice Hall.

Lee, J. A. B. (1994). *The empowerment approach to social work practice.* New York: Columbia University Press.

Leighninger, R. B., Jr. (1978). Systems theory. *Journal of Sociology and Social Welfare, 5,* 446–466.

Levine, I. S., & Fleming, M. (1985). *Human resources development: Issues in case manage-*

ment. Baltimore: Maryland Mental Health Administration, Center for Rehabilitation and Manpower Services, Community Support Project.

Martin, P. Y., & O'Connor, G. G. (1989). *The social environment: Open systems application.* New York: Longman.

Minhauyard, D. E., & Burgess, R. L. (1969). The effects of different reinforcement contingencies in the development of social cooperation. In D. Bushell, Jr., & R. L. Burgess (Eds.), B*ehavioral sociology: The experimental analysis of social process* (pp. 81–108). New York: Columbia University Press.

Morrow-Howell, N. (1992). Clinical case management: The hallmark of gerontological social work. *Journal of Gerontological Social Work, 18,* 119–131.

Payne, M.(2000). *Teamwork in multiprofessional care.* Chicago: Lyceum.

Pecukonis, E. V., & Wenocur, S. (1994). Perceptions of self and collective efficacy in community organization theory and practice, *Journal of Community Practice, 1,* 5–21.

Phillips, J., Bernard, M., Phillipson, C., & Ogg, J. (2000, December). Social support in later life: A study of three areas. *British Journal of Social Work, 30*(60), 837–859.

Polinsky, M. L., Fred, C., & Ganz, P. A. (1991). Quantitative and qualitative assessment of a case management program for cancer patients. *Health and Social Work, 16,* 176–183.

Quinn, W. H. (1995). Expanding the focus of intervention: The importance of family/community relations. In P. Adams & K. Nelson (Eds.), *Reinventing human services: Community and family-centered practice* (pp. 245–259), New York: Aldine de Gruyter.

Raheim, S. (1995). Self-employment training and family development: An integrated strategy for family empowerment. In P. Adams & K. Nelson (Eds.), *Reinventing human services: Community and family-centered practice* (pp. 127–143), New York: Aldine de Gruyter.

Rapp, C. A., & Chamberlain, R. (1985). Case management services for the chronically mentally ill. *Social Work, 30,* 417–422.

Richmond, M. E. (1917). *Social diagnosis.* New York: Russell Sage Foundation.

Richmond, M. E. (1922). *What is social casework? An introductory description.* New York: Russell Sage Foundation.

Rife, J. C., First, R. J., Greenlee, R. W., Miller, L. D., & Feichter, M. A. (1991). Case management with homeless mentally ill people. *Health and Social Work, 16,* 58–66.

Rothman, J. (1991). A model for case management: Toward empirical based practice. *Social Work, 36,* 520–528.

Rubin, A. (1987). Case management. In A. Minahan (Ed.), *Encyclopedia of social work* (Vol. I, 18th ed., pp. 212–222). Silver Spring, MD: National Association of Social Workers.

Rubin, A. (1992). Is case management effective for people with serious mental illness? A re-

search review. *Health and Social Work, 17,* 138–150.

Sheppard, M. (1991). *Mental health work in the community: Theory and practice in social work and community psychiatric nursing.* London, UK: Falmer.

Smale, G. G. (1995). Integrating community and individual practice: A new paradigm for practice. In P. Adams & K. Nelson (Eds.), *Reinventing human services: Community and family-centered practice* (pp. 59–80), New York: Aldine de Gruyter.

Sonsel, G. E., Paradise, F., & Stroup, S. (1988). Case management practice in an AIDS service organization. *Social Casework, 69,* 388–397.

Swartz, S. (1995). Community and risk in social service work. *Journal of Progressive Human Services, 61*(1), 73–92.

Taylor, S. H., & Roberts, R. W. (Eds.). (1985). *Theory and practice of community social work.* New York: Columbia University Press.

Thyer, B. A., & Hudson, W. W. (1986/1987). Progress in behavioral social work: An introduction. *Journal of Social Service Research, 10,* 1–6.

Travillion, S. (1999). *Networking and community partnership* (2nd ed.). Aldershot Hants, UK: Ashgate.

Von Bertalanffy, L. (1967). *Robots, men and mind.* New York: Braziller.

Walker, S. (2001). Tracing the contours of postmodern social work. *British Journal of Social Work, 31*(1), 29–39.

Washington, R. O. (Ed.). (1974). *A strategy for service integration: Case management.* East Cleveland, OH: East Cleveland Community Human Service Center.

Washington, R. O., Karman, M., & Friedlob, F. (1974). *Second year evaluation: Report of the East Cleveland community human service center.* Cleveland, OH: Case Western Reserve University, School of Applied Social Sciences, Human Services Design Laboratory.

Weiser, S., & Silver, M. (1981). Community work and social learning theory. *Social Work, 26,* 146–150.

Whittaker, J. K., Garbarino, J., & Associates (Eds.). (1983). *Social support networks: Informal helping in the human services.* New York: Aldine.

Whittaker, J. K., & Tracy, E. M. (1989). *Social treatment: An introduction to interpersonal helping in social work practice.* New York: Aldine de Gruyter.

Wolk, J. L., Sullivan, W. P., & Hartmann, D. J. (1994). The managerial nature of case management. *Social Work, 39,* 154–159.

Wright, R. G., Sklebar, H. T., & Heiman, J. (1987). Patterns of case management activity in an intensive community support program: The first year. *Community Mental Health Journal, 23,* 53–59.

Zimmerman, J. H. (1987). Negotiating the system: Clients make a case for case management. *Public Welfare, 45,* 23–27.

Subject Index

Name Index